Understanding Health Information Systems

FOR THE HEALTH PROFESSIONS

Jean A. Balgrosky, PhD, MPH, RHIA - Lecturer and Dean's
Board of Advisors Member, Fielding School of Public Health,
University of California at Los Angeles, Los Angeles, California.
Founder, Bootstrap Incubation, LLC, Solana Beach, California,
Chief Information Officer, MD Revolution, La Jolla, California

JONES & BARTLETT
LEARNING

World Headquarters
Jones & Bartlett Learning
5 Wall Street
Burlington, MA 01803
978-443-5000
info@jblearning.com
www.jblearning.com

Jones & Bartlett Learning books and products are available through most bookstores and online booksellers. To contact Jones & Bartlett Learning directly, call 800-832-0034, fax 978-443-8000, or visit our website, www.jblearning.com.

Substantial discounts on bulk quantities of Jones & Bartlett Learning publications are available to corporations, professional associations, and other qualified organizations. For details and specific discount information, contact the special sales department at Jones & Bartlett Learning via the above contact information or send an email to specialsales@jblearning.com.

14962-3

Production Credits
VP, Product Management: Amanda Martin
Director of Product Management: Cathy Esperti
Product Manager: Danielle Bessette
Product Assistant: Tess Sackmann
Director, Project Management: Jenny Corriveau
Digital Products Manager: Jordan McKenzie
Senior Marketing Manager: Susanne Walker
Manufacturing and Inventory Control Supervisor: Amy Bacus
Composition: codeMantra U.S. LLC
Project Management: codeMantra U.S. LLC
Cover Design: Michael O'Donnell
Rights & Media Manager: Shannon Sheehan
Rights Specialist: John Rusk
Cover Image (Title Page, Part Opener, Chapter Opener):
   © Kheng Guan Toh/ShutterStock, Inc.
Printing and Binding: McNaughton & Gunn
Cover Printing: McNaughton & Gunn

Library of Congress Cataloging-in-Publication Data
Names: Balgrosky, Jean A., author.
Title: Understanding health information systems for the health professions / Jean A Balgrosky.
Description: Burlington, MA: Jones & Bartlett Learning, [2020] | Includes bibliographical references and index.
Identifiers: LCCN 2019003113 | ISBN 9781284148626 (paperback)
Subjects: LCSH: Medical informatics. | Information storage and retrieval
   systems—Medical care. | BISAC: BUSINESS & ECONOMICS / Human Resources & Personnel Management.
Classification: LCC R858 .B354 2020 | DDC 610.285—dc23
LC record available at https://lccn.loc.gov/2019003113

6048

Printed in the United States of America
23 22 21 20 19   10 9 8 7 6 5 4 3 2 1

Dedication

This book is dedicated to the patients whose health and comfort is our priority, and for whom we strive as health professionals.

This book is also dedicated to my parents, Steven A. Balgrosky and Evelyn Margaret Cook Balgrosky, whom I love and miss every day.

Jean Balgrosky

Contents

SECTION III　Managing Health Information Systems　141

SECTION IV　Harvesting the Fruits of Your Labors　261

Preface

To improve the state of health care in this country, we must have better experienced, and more powerful and effective health information systems (HIS). To have better HIS, we must invest in the educations of future leaders, providers, and innovators in the field of health care. *Understanding Health Information Systems for the Health Professions* is meant to further those goals.

As a chief information officer (CIO), educator, and bootstrap entrepreneur doing and managing information systems and technology in health care for my entire career, sharing what I have learned over the years has always been a goal of mine. Currently, this goal feels particularly urgent, given recent massive investments in information technology in health care, the unmet promise of those efforts and investments, the need to adapt the U.S. health system from fee-for-service to value-based care, and the ineffective status of health care in the U.S., which spends about twice as much of its GDP on health care than other countries and results in worse outcomes in almost every category.[1] Additionally, serious issues exist in the user interface and user experience in use of EHR systems by physicians and other clinicians, to the point that many are considering leaving their practices.[2]

These problems are not for the faint of heart, nor are they superficial, but with the right preparation and approach, they are solvable. HIS touches every one of these issues and holds a key to engaging patients and helping providers deliver more effective care. A core part of the solution to these problems is education about a systemic, deep-rooted problem: only the IT staff, vendors, and consultants know what goes on in the "black box" of IT and HIS, keeping all other parties at a distance, many of whom are the "beneficiaries" of and participants in these efforts. With a wide range of results, these contributors are often left with little feeling of true involvement other than following instructions and procedures. Successful HIS adoption involves *all* disciplines touched by an implementation in meaningful ways, as well as those responsible for managing core functions of the organization, for everything is affected by a major implementation; the ripples are felt from corner to corner of the organization.

In my experience as a CIO, the greatest challenge has been doing this work in organizations full of intelligent, hard-working, committed, compassionate, highly trained healthcare professionals, from clinicians, to the board of trustees, to registration personnel, when precious few of them have had access to any training or education in HIS or IT at all. The motivation for this book is to provide accessible, comprehensive understanding of HIS to those preparing for a health profession such as medicine, nursing, management, and public health, in addition to those working in IT, law, computer science, or other disciplines applied to health care. A lack of this HIS training and education makes the hard work of HIS

---

1 https://www.oecd.org/unitedstates/Health-at-a-Glance-2017-Key-Findings-UNITED-STATES.pdf.
2 http://med.stanford.edu/content/dam/sm/ehr/documents/SM-EHR-White-Papers_v12.pdf.

implementation and adoption even harder. And certainly, this overhead of frustration and unhappiness contributes to current problems in quality and the high cost of health care in the U.S. These results could be so much better and must improve for the health and well-being of our society. While better training is helpful, the answer to these user experience problems is embedded deep within the design of these systems and must be ferreted out. The answer is not to bring in more consultants or provide scribes to follow around physicians to do data entry work. No. The answer is to break out of this trap *through education*. Providing a comprehensive, foundational HIS education to *all* health professionals is where we break the back of this monster of a dilemma, and fight our way back to solutions that help, protect, delight, and heal. It is all possible.

This book is my humble contribution to that cause, and I hope every student of medicine, nursing, health law, software engineering, management, public health, and analytics has access to some class based on this type of book if not this one, and enters their career armed with confidence in HIS information, skills, and perspective so that they may be active participants in the planning, design, implementation, enhancement and use of HIS, rather than passive recipients of whatever IT and the vendors deliver.

Understanding Health Information Systems for the Health Professions is a broad, introductory book that covers the totality of modern HIS: systems and management, data and analytics; people and processes; and global health, research, and policy. It provides in-depth coverage of the principles and techniques of HIS planning and management to help organizations achieve cost-effective and quality health care, while emphasizing population health management, innovation, patient engagement, and prevention. Written to the audience of graduate and upper-level undergrad students taking classes such as Health

Information Systems, Health Informatics, or Health Information Technology, it is written to those studying to be health managers and administrators, physicians, nurses, other clinicians, engineers, attorneys, analysts, researchers, and policymakers—and all those learning to be responsible in some way for planning, implementing, and managing systems in healthcare settings. The contents are organized into five sections.

I.   HIS Basics: Definitions, Contexts, and Scope
II. HIS Strategy, Planning, and Governance
III. HIS Systems and Their Management
IV. Harvesting the Fruits of Your Labors
V.   A Changing HIS World

Let me outline the chapters of the book in each section.

▶ Section 1: HIS Basics: Definition, Contexts, and Scope

Chapter 1: HIS Fundamentals

This chapter introduces the basics of HIS, including HIS fundamentals and key concepts; provides the HIS Model, a graphic that helps students conceptualize the total scope of HIS, which is then described step-by-step in the text. Basic HIS terminology and definitions are presented to give students a solid grasp of common terminology used when speaking the language of HIS. This chapter provides descriptions of key concepts in the working relationship between vendors and providers and gives a brief history of HIS, so students can be aware of deep-rooted issues and lessons learned.

Chapter 2: The Scope, Definition, and Conceptual Model of HIS

In this chapter, the student learns about systems and their management in the context of the HIS Model, providing a comprehensive understanding of all layers of the totality of HIS. This model provides the student with a conceptual framework for learning key elements of HIS as an organizing construct for the subsequent chapters of the textbook. In addition to describing the total view of HIS, this chapter describes varieties of uses of HIS in organizational and community settings.

Chapter 3: Aligning HIS in the Dynamic Healthcare Environment

In Chapter 3, the student learns about alignment between HIS and the dynamics and challenges of health care today. Understanding how this relates to the types of core systems needed strategically, current types of HIS initiatives, as well the relationship between HIS and population health management gives perspective to uses of HIS and challenges of health professionals in their use in the dynamic healthcare environment.

▶ Section II: HIS Strategy, Planning, and Governance

Chapter 4: HIS Strategic Planning

This chapter provides the student with an understandable approach to HIS strategic planning, taking the mystery out of which types of systems belong in a healthcare organization HIS portfolio. This is done through the application of a straightforward HIS Planning Framework that can be used to define essentials systems for any type of healthcare organization.

Chapter 5: HIS Planning Tactics

In this chapter, the student learns HIS planning tools and techniques for carrying out HIS planning activities, such as how to construct an HIS business plan including the use of a five-year cost estimate spreadsheet, as well as other planning techniques, readily applicable to hands-on HIS planning work. Lessons learned also prepare the student to be an active and confident participant in these important activities.

▶ Section III: HIS Systems and Their Management

Chapter 6: Application Systems and Technology

Chapter 6 describes the wide variety of HIS software systems and familiarizes the student with applications and uses of each of these types of software. The basics of technologies and networks used to support and enable the software systems are also covered in this chapter.

Chapter 7: HIS Management and Technology Services

Chapter 7 describes the methods, roles, and processes used to manage and deliver HIS technology services in organizations. Students will understand the foundation of a well-run IT department from the materials in this chapter.

Chapter 8: HIS Implementation and Managing Change

Chapter 8 provides students with knowledge and perspective of the all-important implementation of HIS and managing change associated with those projects. This chapter also covers project management including techniques to be applied in managing change and the role of a project manager. Also presented are insights into EHR system implementations, along with lessons learned to inform students of reasons for successes and failures in implementations.

▶ Section IV: Harvesting the Fruits of Your Labors

Chapter 9: Adopting New Technologies

This chapter presents the theory of diffusion of innovation in adopting new technologies as well as real life lessons of implementations, history of HIS innovation, unintended consequences of HIS uses, effects of new technologies on existing HIS, and the importance of including new technologies in the training and education of healthcare providers.

Chapter 10: Data

Chapter 10 introduces the student to the world of data, including the current status of the data explosion in our modern world, the discipline of managing data, concepts and principles of data ownership, stewardship, security, requirements for data for regulations such as MACRA, and data challenges and best practices. To understand HIS, one must understand data.

Chapter 11: Analytics, Business Intelligence and Clinical Intelligence

Chapter 11 presents the exciting topic of analytics and BI/CI, including the history of BI/CI, data and architectural models, challenges, artificial intelligence (AI), and the future these capabilities.

▶ Section V: A Changing HIS World

Chapter 12: HIS and Digital Health

Chapter 12 discusses evolving digital health technologies, capabilities, and uses. The importance of informatics in digital health is emphasized along with human-centered design, and techniques for involving insights and expertise of subject matter experts, in this case, health professionals, in the determination of ways to use new technologies in digital health.

Chapter 13: HIS Around the Globe

This chapter shifts gears, immersing the student in insights about what can be learned from HIS uses in countries around the globe, comparing HIS adoption according to different countries' health system structures, policies, expenditures, and health outcomes. Each country faces its own challenges, with themes and trends providing perspective to HIS initiatives everywhere. Observations provide insights into U.S. as well as global HIS challenges, giving students food for thought into how some of those problems might be solved.

Chapter 14: Key Issues in HIS and Future HIS

This chapter describes key topics that speak to future HIS such as the development of digital health capabilities and their role in the changing healthcare landscape. Issues in HIS adoption include disparities in access to these technologies, unintended consequences such as physician dissatisfaction with EHR user interface and user experience, and widespread dependency on scribes due to poor EHR design.

Additional topics describe future HIS directions and possibilities for students of the health professions, who must each understand HIS and apply their subject knowledge to forward progress in health care, with the help of HIS.

I hope that students of the health professions and their instructors find this text a useful resource for learning about HIS in ways that can be applied in real practice, to help them have satisfying, productive careers, to improve their patients' and their own experiences and health, and by extension, our health overall.

Jean A. Balgrosky, PhD, MPH, RHIA

Prologue

"I am "excited about this book! The topics are very appropriate for what the industry expects to see from graduates.""

"I believe students will be glad to see where IT is going in their industry"

"Includes topic across the spectrum, from health information technology to health informatics"

These are the types of comments that reviewers have provided for *Understanding Health Information Systems for the Health Professions*. They didn't just happen; they reflect the extensive Health IT experience, the diverse teaching experience, and the successful textbook experience that Dr. Jean Balgrosky brings to her newest Jones and Bartlett Learning textbook.

Dr. Balgrosky brings to health information systems (HIS) her extensive experience implementing HIS at Scripps Health and Holy Cross Health System (now Trinity Health) and her ongoing experience supporting digital health start-up companies as founder of Bootstrap Incubation and as CIO of MD Revolution, as well as studying and teaching HIS at the University of California Los Angeles. Her experience places her in a unique position to understand and teach both the theory and the practice of HIS.

Understanding Health Information Systems for the Health Professions is designed for a broad range of health professions from advanced undergraduate and graduate students to health managers, administrators, clinicians, and policymakers. It is structured as a textbook with learning objectives, case examples, numerous graphics, and a range of ancillary materials to help instructors engage students in the excitement of HIS.

The textbook takes a broad introductory approach that covers the totality of modern HIS. It covers the principles of HIS planning and management to help organizations achieve cost-effectiveness, quality improvement, efficiency, population health management, innovation, patient engagement, and prevention. Students will discover how these goals are enabled by technology, data, and analytics. These skills are increasingly needed for institutional survival in a continuously changing healthcare landscape.

The world of HIS is an exciting one which holds the promise for making health care safer, more accessible, more effective, and more efficient. New systems do not happen by magic or by pressing a button. They require the skills of a wide range of professionals who understand both the art and the science of HIS. As Dr. Balgrosky writes "A well-architected and orchestrated HIS system is a thing of beauty…"

The future of HIS is unfolding, limited only by our imaginations. *Understanding Health Information Systems for the Health Professions* will guide your way into this emerging world and help you cope and contribute.

Richard Riegelman, MD, MPH, PhD
Professor and Founding Dean, Milken Institute School of Public Health, The George Washington University

Acknowledgments

I have had the privilege and pleasure of teaching this subject for the past 10 years to the outstanding graduate and extension students at the University of California Los Angeles Fielding School of Public Health. These excellent students have provided valuable feedback and input regarding ways to introduce key HIS concepts and subject matter. My colleagues through the years, including those at Scripps Health, Holy Cross Health System (Trinity Health), Peat Marwick, MDRevolution, and UCLA, have been instrumental in shaping the approach I have taken in my work as a CIO and thus explaining the essential elements of this complicated topic, any one of which could be a book in itself. These professionals include physicians, nurses, and other clinicians, information technology specialists, attorneys specializing in software law, fellow CIOs, healthcare business people, and many more. I am grateful for these many experiences and interactions, just as I am for the encouraging words from my students, colleagues, and mentors who recognize the need for a comprehensive textbook on this topic.

I owe my passion for connecting the worlds of health care, public health, and information technology to my education and training at UCLA's Fielding School of Public Health, where I earned my bachelor of science degree in Health Services with a specialization in Medical Records Science, Masters of Public Health in Health Services with a concentration in Health Information Systems, and PhD in Health Services with a cognate in Health Information Systems and Technology. I must thank several people along that journey in particular. In my early days as an undergraduate,

Ms. Olive Johnson, RHIA, and Dr. Ray Goodman guided my academic path in meaningful ways. Ms. Johnson was a woman ahead of her time, teaching not only the science of managing medical records for clinical, legal, and business purposes, but how to harvest data from the treasure trove of these records for research, analytics, and quality applications. I would also like to thank Dr. Jonathan Fielding, my long-time mentor, who has been an advocate for my academics and work in public health and HIS, and pursuit of my career as CIO, entrepreneur, and innovator. Also since my undergraduate days, Dr. Paul Torrens has provided me with enthusiastic support in my studies and work in health information systems and technology, including serving on my PhD dissertation committee. Dr. Jack Needleman has served as my PhD advisor and chairperson of my PhD committee, providing guidance through the dissertation research process. Dr. Diana Hilberman has been a mentor in teaching and provided important opportunities for me to integrate the discipline of health information systems and technology into graduate programs in health policy and management at UCLA. Much of the success of my early career is owed to a lucky break from Sister Geraldine M. Hoyler, C.S.C., who hired me into my first CIO role at Holy Cross Health System where I served for over 11 years. Jay McCutcheon and Bart Neuman, early leaders in the HIS field and inventors of the HIS planning model that I use to this day, provided me mentorship and early guidance as a consultant.

I'd like to thank my Bootstrap Incubation and Venture Partner as well as MD Revolution colleagues who have picked up the slack and patiently waited as I went through the spurts and marathon of writing and revising. Thank you for helping me stay current and involved in new directions in health care, as every day we strive to create innovations enabled by health information technology. I am ever so grateful for a team inspired in the pursuit of digital health, population health management, care management, empowered patients, and better experiences for providers.

I owe special thanks to my author comrades and contributors, Jim Brady (Chapters 6 and 7) and Ric Speaker (Chapters 10 and 11). They threw their hats willingly into the ring to help get this text written, tackling incredibly vital and challenging chapters. Bravo to their contributions and commitment to the text, among all their other responsibilities. I am lucky and so grateful to have loyal friends and brilliant collaborators such as you.

Dr. Richard Riegelman, editor of the *Essentials of Public Health* series and champion and advocate of *Understanding Health Information Systems for the Health Professions*, has provided me with the extraordinary combination of opportunity, guidance, constructive feedback, support, and enthusiasm for this volume. He has contributed so much to the advancement of health care and public health, and we all are beneficiaries of his understanding of the relevance of health information systems to that quest.

At Jones & Bartlett Learning, my publisher, I'd like to thank Mike Brown, recently retired as Publisher, for accepting my proposal for this book, providing strategic guidance of the process to get it adopted by the publisher, and supporting this work. Danielle Bessette has filled his shoes expertly and without a

hitch, and I appreciate her support, guidance, and encouragement in the daunting challenge of authoring this comprehensive textbook on a complex topic. Thank you also to Tess Sackman of J&B Learning, who has handled the daily back-and-forth with me to get this book through the gauntlet and delivered in full to the publisher.

Deepest thanks to my editor, Jessie Chatigny, talented writer, and story wrangler, who has provided constructive virtual teamwork and timely pep talks through the heavy lifting of organizing and writing the 14 meaty chapters of this book, for both me and to my contributors, Jim Brady and Ric Speaker. Jessie, I couldn't have done this project without you.

Last and most importantly, to my family— nothing in life is possible without you. To my dear husband Parker, thank you for your support and encouragement and for understanding how cathartic it has been for me to do this textbook, a way to distill 30 years of CIO'ing out of my brain and onto the pages of this book. To my children, Jessica, Wyatt, CJ, Steven, Melissa, Seth, and Sarah, thank you for being you and for being our children and giving us grandchildren—you and your families are my inspiration for all things. I also want to express my love and gratitude to my parents, who, although no longer with us, instilled in me the value of education and the importance of books; thank you for your love, encouragement, and motivation to strive to do something good with my life. And to my sister Wendy, brother Steve, and niece Robyn, thank you for your constant love and support, which has always provided such great comfort and joy. To each and every member of my family—I cannot imagine my life without you and every day, I am profoundly grateful we have each other.

About the Author

Jean Balgrosky, PhD, MPH, RHIA, teaches Health Information Systems and Technology at UCLA Fielding School of Public Health, where she also received her PhD in Health Services with a cognate in health information systems and technology, her MPH in Health Services, majoring in health information systems management, and BS in health services with a specialization in medical record science. In 2015, she published her first textbook, *Essentials of Health Information Systems and Technology*. Balgrosky's career in health information systems and technology has included the role of chief information officer (CIO) in large, complex healthcare organizations for more than 30 years, consulting and teaching this topic at the graduate level. More recently, she has become an entrepreneur, mentor, and board member for start-up companies in life sciences, digital health, software-as-a-service, and healthcare analytics arenas. She is currently also CIO of a digital health company.

Understanding Health Information Systems for Health Professionals is Balgrosky's second book, for which she draws largely from her long career as a CIO, consultant, and entrepreneur. She has authored numerous papers and articles, is a frequent speaker, moderator, and panelist at health information technology conferences, and plans to publish the results of her dissertation research regarding physician adoption of electronic health records in small versus large practices.

Balgrosky has provided leadership throughout her career to the evolving health information systems and technology industry, maintaining her accreditation as a Registered Health Information Administrator as the foundation of her knowledge of medical record management and electronic health records. Her goal in writing this and subsequent books is to develop courses and resource materials for health information systems curricula, as well as to infuse necessary information technology topics into other courses taught in schools of public health and health management. Examples of courses that now require information technology components include financial and human resources management, quality, organizational behavior, strategic planning, marketing, and medical and nursing educational programs.

Dr. Balgrosky lives in Del Mar, California, with her husband of 34 years, Parker. They have seven children and, at current count, nine grandchildren. Their family brings them the greatest joy and meaning every single day.

Contributors

James Brady, PhD, CHCIO, FHIMSS

Chapters 6 and 7

Dr. Brady is the recipient of the Becker's Hospital Review 2018 and 2017 List of Hospital and Health System CIOs to Know, the Los Angeles Business Journal 2015 CIO of the Year Award, the HIMSS 2015 Distinguished Fellows Service Award, and the HIMSS SoCal 2015 Chapter of Year and President Level Advocacy Awards. He has three decades of experience leading technology and security initiatives in complex academic medical center and multihospital healthcare settings. His expertise in ITIL standards for IT service management and delivery, and ISO/IEC 27001 for information security compliance bring unique insight into Chapters 6 and 7. Brady is CIO for Los Angeles Department of Health Services, Past President of HIMSS, and adjunct faculty at National University. He most recently served as Area CIO for Kaiser Permanente Orange County 2013–2018. During his PhD studies, Dr. Brady wrote his dissertation on information technology security in health care.

Ric Speaker

Chapters 10 and 11

Mr. Speaker has 40 years of executive business experience, consulting, and lecturing in the field of healthcare technology. As a successful serial entrepreneur and expert in health BI/CI, Speaker guides his clients—largely healthcare providers, services, and technology companies—to harvest meaningful, actionable information from HIS; govern data; and enact effective security protocols. His expertise makes Chapters 10 and 11 excellent resources for readers. He is a Managing Partner of Commonwealth Health Advisors, Board Member and Charter Member of the Healthcare Summit at Jackson Hole, Chairman of the Board at the Sursumcorda Resource Group, Industry Advisor at LRVHealth Venture Capital, and Chief Visionary Officer at Bear Creek Works.

HIS Basics: Definitions, Context, and Scope

CHAPTER 1

Health Information Systems Fundamentals

LEARNING OBJECTIVES

By the end of this chapter, the student will be able to:

- Describe the importance of fundamentals in the Health Information Systems (HIS) discipline and why fundamentals exist.
- Understand key HIS concepts and why they are important.
- Describe the HIS Model and its use in understanding HIS.
- Define key HIS terminology and how that term fits with others in the HIS construct.
- Explain the various categories and types of systems used in HIS.
- Describe players in HIS, including a variety of HIS end users, customers, participants, and professionals involved in HIS.
- Illuminate the roles and responsibilities of HIS professionals.
- Describe the basics of HIS history to assist in comprehending the unique development pathways that have brought us to today's state of HIS in the U.S.

▶ Introduction

The topic of HIS is a vast, complex story involving technology, data, people, and processes. A well-architected and orchestrated HIS is a thing of beauty, helpful to those who use it to do their work more effectively and capable of inspiring with new capabilities to pull us forward into better ways of doing things and improved outcomes. To even begin to tell this story, a common lexicon and consistency in principles, terminology, and methods are required. Often, professionals well versed in their respective disciplines, such as clinical care, financial management, or research, who are well-meaning in intent and committed to collaboration, fail to understand one another as they discuss and attempt to tackle HIS goals, issues, and projects. This struggle plagues many HIS projects and initiatives, and the primary reason why the dialogue gets off on the wrong foot is due to an inability to truly communicate, since core principles and ideas are not shared and agreed upon. Thus, this chapter is devoted to **fundamentals**—those ideas, methods, practices, and principles that are so basic to HIS that more advanced, elegant, and complex HIS initiatives and capabilities cannot be imagined or discussed, let alone achieved, without complete agreement on these basic building blocks from the beginning.

An analogy that makes this point well is the game of baseball. Key skills of throwing, catching, and hitting the baseball with a bat are the first things a beginner is taught before trying to learn the rules of the game, the various positions on a team, and certainly before attempting to compete against other teams or manage a team and a game, with winning and losing at stake. These fundamental skills are not just taught to new learners of the game, but they are also relentlessly and forever practiced for the entire career of any player, whether that career ends after Little League or after a 20-year professional baseball career. Those skills—throwing, catching, and hitting—are excellent examples of fundamentals, the essential building blocks of playing the game of baseball. Why are they called the fundamentals? There are numerous reasons, but here are a few. Can you imagine a baseball team in which every player threw, caught, and hit the ball differently, using different methods and random styles? I doubt the team would be very good. Also, mistakes happen—in baseball, these are called errors. When an otherwise talented player makes an error, the team fails to get the out, make the base, or score the run. Or that player's team fails to defend and the other team scores, steals a base, wins. So, errors are to be avoided at all cost. When this talented player makes an error, another thing happens—the otherwise successful player is stunned and loses confidence, and the entire team can be thrown off kilter. For one error. How important it is to remember that none of us is perfect, and life is not perfect. We all must accept the fact that errors, mistakes, or random

occurrences will happen when we are not expecting them. So, what do we do? Go back to fundamentals. Fundamentals are important because when an error occurs, and everyone makes errors from time to time, the way the player gets back on track, stems the problem for the team, and regains their confidence is by going back to the fundamentals—the specific proven ways, best practices, standards, and time-honored, honed, and most basic skills according to their training. Then, they can move forward again with confidence.

In HIS, fundamentals are just as important. Key skills, training, methods, standards, and principles must guide the planning, design, testing, implementation, maintenance, and enhancement of HIS and their architectures for healthcare organizations, whether used for clinical, business, or analytical purposes. Let's get started with the fundamentals that all professionals involved in HIS activities and initiatives must share.

▶ HIS Fundamentals

This text is designed to walk through HIS principles and time-honored methods that yield predictable results. These areas of knowledge cover HIS strategic planning, governance, and policies; managing HIS including system selection and change; implementing HIS; harvesting the yield from HIS including data management, business and clinical intelligence (BI/CI), analytics, and creating new knowledge; HIS regulatory compliance and risk management; and HIS standards, governance, and policy. Let's take these one at a time.

HIS Strategic Planning

The business plan of a healthcare organization aligns the future state of the healthcare organization to its market and external environment, and adapts the organization to the complex changing needs of the population it services and the providers who work within it. The **HIS Strategic Plan** thus aligns the HIS and technologies to these strategic business directions and initiatives of the organization, not only to support, but in many cases also to enable the strategies to be accomplished. A good HIS strategy insists upon the definition of a desired future state of an organization, 5, 10, 15, 20 years hence. This future template and the roadmap that leads the organization along the way to it contain the ingredients for defining and organizing the HIS strategies and initiatives needed to motivate and propel the organization from where it is to that desired future state as an organization. The HIS Strategic Plan produces an actionable, balanced portfolio of systems that support and enable the clinical, business and administrative, and connectivity needs and activities of the organization as it engages with its community of patients and providers.

Trying to select software systems in the absence of a HIS Strategic Plan is akin to shopping without a list—you tend to buy things that might satisfy an impulse or a perceived need but may not be affordable or meet your requirements once you get them home. Buying HIS to fulfill a balanced HIS portfolio of systems for your organization without an HIS Strategic Plan grounded in the organization's strategic business plan would be akin to attempting to build a house without a plan, budget, or blueprint. Before *any* activity regarding HIS takes place, the HIS Strategic Plan must be developed for any type of healthcare organization—this principle applies not just to hospitals or health systems but also to provider practices of all types and sizes, to home health organizations, hospice, community health centers, free clinics, imaging centers, and outpatient surgery centers. To do otherwise is a recipe for disappointment, if not disaster for the organization. Concepts, Principles, and Methods for HIS strategic planning are covered in detail in subsequent chapters (Chapters 2–4).

Governance

Governance in healthcare organizations includes the use of consistent management methods, policies, decision rights, and processes across all units and departments. For HIS, governance often translates to structural methods including steering committees, standards, auditability, and consistent policies and processes for decision making and accountabilities for expenditures. While these structural and oft-times top-down methods are part of good governance, enlightened approaches also include a culture of ethics, integrity, and personal accountability, controls within which those purchasing, using, and accessing technology do so within understood methods that allow for greater accessibility to systems, technology, data, and information (Meyer, 2005). Good HIS governance assures sound guidance, interdisciplinary communication and collaboration, oversight, accountability, and reinforcement of organizational HIS policies and procedures. This includes detailing the rules and practices regarding HIS strategic planning, decision making, management, setting priorities, resource allocation, budgeting, key performance indicator definition, dialogue, and other processes intended to fairly and properly steward HIS resources in the context of the overarching needs and capacity of the organization. Good governance requires regular, face-to-face interaction, grounded in the general policies and practices of the organization and consistent with the organization's overarching governance philosophy, starting with the Board of Trustees on down. Many organizations tend to avoid or isolate HIS policies, standards, and decision making: this is a mistake. HIS must be mainstreamed with the organization's activities and oversight overall; in other words, HIS governance should be integrated with organizational governance. In 2013, HIS expenditures comprised 3.06 percent of overall expenditures for healthcare organizations (leading up to that, expenditures in 2012 had responded to the HITECH

Meaningful Use program, yielding an average of 2.74 percent of the total operating expenses spent on information technology (IT) in 2012, up from 2.39 percent in 2011 and 2.40 percent in 2010) (Becker's Hospital Review, 2014b).

In 2018, HIS expenditures rose to 3 percent of the gross revenues of a healthcare organization, an increase of 8.8 percent in 2018 over 2017, compared to increases of about 6 percent in IT expenditures in all industries in the U.S. during the same time period (Kass & Bazzoli, 2017). So the stakes are high for making sure these mission-critical expenditures are properly handled. Governance of anything that is substantial or strategic is everyone's business in the organization, not just the concern of the IT department or an isolated set of processes and policies. Governed and managed well, HIS is essential to the organization successfully navigating its future successes and challenges. This paves the way for a bright and predictable future as the healthcare organization adapts to market conditions over time, delivers consistently high-quality care, and meets its business and fiduciary responsibilities to its constituents. Good governance involves the give-and-take of feedback and accountability, which requires the efforts, education, awareness, and energies of all stakeholders including professionals and patients. HIS governance establishes and oversees the HIS Steering Committee for the organization, establishing plans, priorities, policies, procedures, and key metrics for measuring HIS activities and performance. Details and methods for HIS governance are covered in Chapter 12.

Managing HIS

Managing HIS involves the techniques and activities deployed to achieve HIS goals and objectives in a healthcare organization. These HIS management methods include generally accepted methods and standards for planning, implementing, supporting, and managing core HIS (the foundational center of the HIS Model). These activities involve an organization's IT department (e.g., information services, information resources, technology, and information systems) responsible for planning and managing HIS and infrastructure, data, analytics, people, operational support and customer service, implementation of systems and managing change, training technology staff and end users of systems, and myriad other activities involved in providing excellent HIS for an organization. Managing HIS is one of the essential functional areas of a healthcare organization, along with clinical operations, finance, human resources, strategic planning, marketing, and overall leadership of the organization. HIS expenditures comprise a significant portion of the organization's capital and operating budgets and provide the support systems and infrastructure necessary for the organization to function efficiently and effectively. This warrants attention from the highest levels of the organization. Managing HIS includes key HIS activities such as planning and budgeting, system selection, system implementation, managing change, and managing vendors.

HIS Planning and Budgeting

Using the organization's strategic business plan as a guide, HIS planning and budgeting should reflect exactly the forward movement and enablement of the organization toward its business and clinical strategies, and not stray one iota from efforts and expenditures in those directions. From the 5- to 10- to 15-year view of the HIS Strategic Plans, annual or near-term plans and budgets must be established to fuel progress year by year. Annual HIS plans often reflect a set of one- to five-year strategic HIS initiatives, as significant HIS projects usually take more than one year. HIS annual plans describe in detail the activities the HIS function is accountable for accomplishing each year, and these annual plans drive the annual HIS capital and operating budgets. HIS plans and budgets must include everything needed and feasible to accomplish in the coming fiscal year to meet the needs of the organization as well as to live within the means of the organization. The result is an HIS agenda for each year that is planned in concert with the strategic and operational needs of the organization, working with the percentage of capital and operating funds agreed collectively to allocate to HIS. Annual HIS plans and budgets must also stay in exact tune with the HIS Strategic Plan, which is a direct reflection and interpretation of the organization's strategic business plan into HIS initiatives and terminology. Deviations from the HIS Strategic Plan are dangerous, rendering the HIS strategies impotent and diminishing their impact in moving the organization toward its strategic future.

HIS Selection

System selection is the process by which decisions are made about which new software systems to bring into the organization. Methodologies for HIS selection are widely known, repeatable processes consistent with and essentially standardized throughout well-run organizations. Methodologies for system selection include project description and requirements definition, budgetary requirements estimation (both capital and operating expenditures over five years), documentation of how this new system will fit into the HIS Strategic Plan and overall portfolio of applications, justification of the new system (an analysis of why a *new* system is proposed vs. not using something that already exists in the organization's HIS portfolio), as well as draft implementation plan and timetable, staffing and other resource requirements, technical underpinnings and specifications of the new system, interface and integration requirements, data management plans, reporting requirements and key performance indicators produced through the use of the new system, system selection decision timing and process, key contract guidelines and performance criteria for the winning vendor, and other components, all documented in a comprehensive HIS business plan. The HIS Steering Committee is responsible for overseeing the process, and the rules of engagement are published at the outset so that expectations are clear and adhered to throughout the selection process.

Implementing HIS

Implementing HIS is the set of activities that results in a software system going from a business plan to a fully utilized HIS, usually replacing a previous or legacy system that has limited functionality and capabilities. The art and science of implementing new systems challenge even the most sophisticated and well-resourced organizations. Like system selection, successful system implementations follow a disciplined methodology that drives a carefully executed and highly detailed project plan. Implementation includes not only activating new software that runs on new hardware, operating systems, programming languages, storage, and other infrastructure, but also a carefully designed and timed training program for preparing end users to use the new system, then activating the new system in a stable, predictable manner, transitioning all processes, systems, and end users away from the old system to the new. HIS implementation also includes testing and evaluating the new system once it is implemented to make sure it is functioning as designed. Any issues are prioritized and worked on until they are resolved, and the vendor is held accountable for doing their part to make sure the new HIS works as promised in the contract. The new HIS must meet the requirements and definition as outlined in the business plan. Successful system implementation is challenging, harrowing, and rewarding work. The organization benefits greatly from a well-managed implementation that supports the full cooperation and efforts of all disciplines involved.

Managing Change

Managing change is the earthy reality of what happens when new HIS are brought into use in the organization, from ideas expressed in the HIS Strategic Plan all the way to changes in clinician or administrative workflow. Even post-implementation issue resolution may bring enhancements and additional functionality into a successfully implemented HIS. Managing change emphasizes communication, preparing the organization by satisfying participants' need for involvement, orientation, and confidence in what's about to happen. This happens by involving interdisciplinary teams actively in the design, requirements definition, training, testing, activation, and use of the new system. Equally important is staying in close collaboration with end users, management, clinical staff, and others throughout the processes of planning, system selection, system build, implementation, and post-implementation evaluation and enhancement. Also, those in the organization who may not be as involved in the actual process must be kept in the communication loop so that they are aware and understand the changes that are to occur. All members of the organization should know how a change in work for those directly connected to the system connects to the work of those not directly using the new system. They are connected to it through use of data or process touch points throughout the organization.

Managing Vendors

This is one of the most important areas in which to become proficient when managing and implementing new HIS, since organizations rely heavily on external companies (vendors) whose business model is to produce, deliver, and support HIS software, hardware, and services. It is essential to keep this in mind and remember why these companies are called vendors. They are in business to create value for their shareholders (if they are publicly traded companies) or returns for their owners and investors (if they are privately held companies) by creating and selling HIS software, technology, and services to customers, usually healthcare organizations of various types. They are

for-profit corporations that answer to their boards of directors and shareholders on a quarterly basis about whether they have hit their sales and financial earnings targets. Although these companies are full of good people, most of whom care deeply about health care and technology, they are measured not by the well-being of their client organizations but by hitting their numbers. In Chapters 5 and 7, we will discuss successful practices for managing vendors.

Harvesting the Yield from HIS

HIS implemented to support the work of clinicians, business people, and support staff within the organization have another equally important role of creating and capturing data valuable to improving patient care, organizational procedures, policy and oversight, and best practices. Yet, with the massive undertaking of creating and implementing an HIS Strategic Plan, the sheer magnitude of the work often prevents an organization from taking full advantage of the data and information resources it is creating. By carefully stewarding these data resources produced and captured as a result of core system efforts, precious information resources become available to the organization for creation of new knowledge, through analytics, business intelligence and clinical intelligence (BI/CI), and research. This brings additional value and returns on the investment in the core HIS. This is especially important to emphasize, since many, if not most, of today's healthcare executives and managers were trained before these types of analytical and intelligence systems were available or used to actually manage an institution (Bresnick, 2017). This means the value garnered from HIS is widely underachieved. These types of analytics systems and activities are described as BI/CI, outcomes analysis, data warehousing, and data management, and knowledge management. Chapters 10 and 11 are devoted to the areas of data and analytics, with descriptions of these types of systems and data activities as follows.

Data Management and Stewardship

Perpetually growing troves of data are created and captured in the core clinical and business workflow/transaction systems. In order to gain further yield and value from these data, they must be carefully and continuously tended. What does it mean to steward these data resources? To steward means to manage, oversee, and take care of a resource, such as property, finances, or other assets. When we think of this in the context of data as an asset, stewardship of data means to make sure the definition of each data element is accurate and consistent in its use by those interacting with it, take responsibility for ensuring it is managed according to the goals of the organization, and take care of it by regularly checking on consistency, accuracy, accessibility, and safety of data. Data stewardship accompanies an overall data management program, inserting into the fabric of the organization the necessary leadership, roles, responsibilities, and education as part of the organization's data resource management.

Business, Clinical, and Artificial Intelligence

BI/CI and artificial intelligence (AI) systems provide analytical systems, resources, data management, and personnel capabilities to support gaining insights, knowledge, and their application to improving business and clinical processes and outcomes. Chapter 11 is devoted to these topics.

Creating New Knowledge

Health care is a function of information and knowledge workers coming together to help patients, healthcare organizations, patient populations, and communities overall. The learning organization creates and manages information in ways that enable it to learn from experiences through data analysis and evidence, information and data-driven processes. The needs of patients evolve over time and healthcare organizations must continuously adapt to these changing needs. The ability to be data driven and put new knowledge into practice relies on an organizational culture that embraces this adaptation and thirst for new knowledge, as well as implementing it into clinical and administrative processes.

HIS Regulatory Compliance and Risk Management

Each of the areas described requires significant know-how, attention, organizational commitment, and expertise—but those alone are not enough. Actions, systems, policies, and management techniques used to accomplish these initiatives must be done in compliance with regulations that govern health care and systems. These regulations include the Health Information Portability and Accountability Act (HIPAA), Medicare Access and CHIP Reauthorization Act (MACRA) of 2015, the Center for Medicare and Medicaid Services (CMS) Quality Payment Program including Merit-based Incentive Payment System (MIPS) and Advanced Alternative Payment Models (APMs), Department of Health Services (DHS) regulations, the quasi-regulatory program of the Joint Commission on Accreditation of Healthcare Organizations (Joint Commission), and other regulatory programs and requirements (Centers for Medicare & Medicaid Services, n.d.; Quality Payment Program, n.d.). Health care is highly regulated for several reasons. Health care is paid for by government and third-party insurance programs; fraud comprises about 10 percent of the total cost of health care in the U.S.; and patient safety, data, and privacy must be protected. Clinical care, regulatory compliance, and policy enforcement require the full attention of management at technical, business, and clinical leadership levels (Schulte, 2017).

HIS Security

The security of HIS, data, and protected health information (PHI) has always been a primary goal in health care, but threats and damage to security are increasing, as hackers, black market, and ransomware experts are unfortunately succeeding in threatening HIS. Preventing hacking and ransoming healthcare data, system shutdowns, and general havoc on health data systems are amongst the highest priorities on any HIS agenda (Yaraghi, 2016).

HIS Standards

To communicate across providers, insurers, and users of health care, HIS technical and data standards must be in place. The importance of common protocols and terminology cannot be overstated. These standards are critical for goals of interoperability, quality, and cost-effective care, to name a few. If HIS at the radiology facility in Utah where one's leg was broken doesn't communicate to the physical therapist's HIS in New Jersey, technology is no better than paper.

However, health care has been reluctant and slow to develop and adopt standards in technical and data management arenas. For many years, vendors have developed proprietary software systems to strategically withhold opportunity and flexibility for healthcare organizations to blend and access multiple software products from different vendor products simultaneously. Some progress is being made in the development of technical, data, and reporting standards, but the road ahead in this effort is long. Clearly this is an area that needs improvement, to facilitate interoperability as well as analytics across multiple data sources.

This text emphasizes key concepts as well as specific information about HIS, data, and technology. The ability to conceptualize something in HIS is essential to becoming proficient in this discipline, superseding knowledge or expertise in any particular type of technology. Technologies are constantly advancing and changing, and will continue to do so for as long as any of us can imagine (Dovey, 2018). How those various technologies are used, however, in concert with people and process, tells the real story. Think about the number of different vendors that supply software for **electronic health record (EHR)** systems, enterprise resource planning (ERP) systems, analytical databases, network infrastructure, and other HIS. Every one of those software systems provided by competing vendors that do the same types of things, differently, have shining successes and abysmal failures. There are successful, mediocre, and failed implementations of every one of the leading EHR system vendors in healthcare organizations (Green, 2017).

🔍 CASE EXAMPLE: COMMON FUNDAMENTAL FAILURES

Often, the same software, implemented and managed differently, yields very different results. Common mistakes in HIS are usually connected to a lack of access to or a dismissal of HIS fundamentals. Examples of these include the following:

- New HIS introduced into the organization without the new system being rooted in the strategic plan of the organization
- Inadequate funding of an HIS initiative or project
- Poorly or randomly designed HIS without input and regular collaboration with key stakeholders and subject matter experts (SMEs) who understand necessary workflows

- HIS built by programmers who are neither cohesively managed nor following an overall development plan according to good methodology, including thorough testing
- HIS implemented without adequate communication, relevant training, and support for all end users
- HIS not consistently maintained and kept up-to-date with new releases, versions, and enhancements from the software or technology vendor
- Lack of efficient support for end users from a well-trained, customer service-oriented technology department

Success depends upon fundamentals. Sometimes people think that because fundamentals are basic, they are elementary, simple, and boring. But the fact is that for something as complex as HIS planning, development, and implementation in diverse settings called healthcare organizations—with their many layers, specialties, and nuances—fundamentals are the tools that help us through the maze of complexity inherent in HIS.

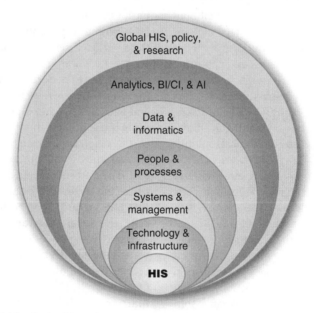

FIGURE 1.1 HIS Model for the health professions.

▶ HIS Model

The HIS Model provides a visual representation of the overall scope of HIS and the gradual layers that build upon one another to create a comprehensive HIS arena. This visual model will be referenced throughout the text to help readers contextualize and connect the subject matter (**FIGURE 1.1**).

▶ HIS Terminology

This text relies on consistent terminology to convey the ideas and instruction contained within. For purposes of this text, the following definitions and terminology will be used.

Health Information Systems (HIS): **HIS** comprise an organized combination of system components, including infrastructure, hardware, middleware, application software, devices, and other technologies intended to support an organization or key processes in health care.

Technology Infrastructure: Elements of **infrastructure** include technology and network components such as fiber optics, routers, and switches; bandwidth connectivity; middleware; intranet; Internet; and extranet capabilities.

Hardware: **Hardware** comprises the backbone of computing environments, whether in an organization's data center or provided by a vendor for cloud-based services, providing the technology upon which software operates, accessed by end users. Hardware also consists of the physical computing equipment and devices such as personal computers, laptops, tablets, and other components used by those accessing and using the software supporting their work.

Software: HIS requires computer programs written to support knowledge workers, patients, and providers in health care. **Software** applications can be clinical, administrative, analytic, or business-oriented in functionality. Types of core software programs in the clinical arena include EHR systems, the scope of which includes patient access systems such as registration, admissions, emergency medicine, orders management, results reporting, clinical documentation, laboratory, radiology/imaging, pharmacy management and other clinical processes, functions, reporting, and departments. Key administrative software programs include ERP systems, including general ledger, accounts payable, fixed assets management, supply chain management, human resources and payroll, reporting, and other business functions. (See Chapter 6 for in-depth software information.)

Middleware: **Middleware** is software that connects software applications to the data and technology supporting the application. As a transaction layer, it enables communications and data management for multiple or distributed software applications.

Networks: In HIS, as in other computerized industries, computers linked together exchange data with each other using technical and data connections, forming a **network** via linkages, which are enabled through fiber optics, cables, wires, routers, switches, Wi-Fi, and other technologies; these enable data communications and resource sharing among a wide variety of users.

End Users: Variety abounds among **users** of HIS, or **end users**: they include clinical professionals, business people, and analysts using systems and information to meet their professional goals and obligations. These knowledge workers and professionals are experts performing work in areas of clinical, business, informatics/analytics, and patients, both within organizations and at external third parties. Users of HIS are those who rely on its capabilities, reporting capabilities, and connectivity to perform the work of the organization. Users drive workflow, processes, and data creation and capture as a byproduct of their use of HIS—they are the human part of the computer-human interface, connecting workflows and processes with technology. Their workflow and information needs drive the types of features and functions that HIS are programmed to perform. Typically, the **"user interface" (UI)** is activated through typing on a keypad, speaking into a voice-activated device, or by other means of connecting the user to the HIS or computer. Quantitatively, there are myriad features and functions in HIS that users interact with to do their work. Qualitatively, the "user-experience," or UX, is the ease or difficulty with which the user is able to use the HIS. An easy, delightful, energizing UX is the goal and sets one HIS apart from others in not only *what* features and functions exist in the system but also *how* those features and functions operate in relation to the end user.

Roles: **Roles** in HIS cover a wide array of responsibilities in planning, governance, management, design, development, activation/implementation, and ongoing maintenance of HIS products and services. In fact, this text is designed to provide the fundamental understanding of these roles for health professionals so that they are prepared to participate in HIS activities such as HIS planning and governance. **HIS planning** directly ties the investment in and prioritization of HIS resources and systems to the strategic plan of the organization. Professionals participating in this work have training and education in IT, management, planning, and health care. **HIS governance** is the proper, interdisciplinary oversight, policy-setting, fiduciary and regulatory assurance, and strategic alignment of the HIS function and portfolio of systems. Individuals performing HIS governance comprise leaders from all key disciplines and stakeholders in the organization, who hopefully have a combination of subject matter expertise in their clinical or business discipline, as well as a foundation of fundamentals of health IT, data, analytics, and other essential HIS-related elements. Proper **HIS management** includes day-to-day oversight, controls, and quality assurance of systems planning, people, process, and technology. HIS professionals with years of experience of increasing complexity and scope are capable of leading HIS professionals, with excellent verbal and written communication skills, healthcare knowledge, and multidisciplinary HIS acumen in order to plan, manage, and oversee the activities of technology professionals. HIS design connects the content and framework of systems to the workflow of the organization's knowledge workers. HIS design also takes the human-computer interface into account, achieving qualitative as well as quantitative aspects of workflows, features, and functions of each software system. We've all experienced the difference between a well-designed car, appliance, or process with those that do essentially the same things but are poorly designed. Design is essential to the quality of architecture, engineering, art, and computer systems, among many other endeavors. HIS professionals involved in

systems design are the most experienced, talented software planners, engineers, and technical experts the organization can acquire, with skills specific to the type and purpose of system being developed. **HIS development** includes user and system/workflow planning, design, building or programming the system, testing, documentation, deployment, and maintenance according to the steps of the process called software/systems development life cycle (SDLC), discussed in Chapter 6. Development is the creation by software engineers and other technical staff of programs and interfaces needed to construct a software system. The professionals doing the development work include programmers, analysts, and those managing and overseeing their work. **Activation/implementation** includes putting the new software system into use to do real work of the organization or putting the system "into production." Types of professionals involved in activation/implementation are a multidisciplinary, technology-proficient team including HIS management, project managers, training professionals who provide training curricula, a comprehensive training plan including train-the-trainers, and ongoing training for the organization; a variety of software engineers who support the software programs and technology that comprise the system; technical support staff for devices and printers and other access points; and superusers who are both SMEs and HIS proficient, often including informaticists in their particular arena, such as nursing, medical, and business informaticists. **Ongoing maintenance** includes training, updates and fixes to programs and equipment that break, answering end-user questions, updates and upgrades to the system software, hardware, and access points, and providing these services on a measured, timely basis usually through a help desk system. The roles and processes employed to plan, design, build, test, implement, evaluate, and support systems on an ongoing basis are many. Successful systems initiatives are dependent upon interdisciplinary cooperation and collaboration, with a wide variety of experts in clinical, business, technology, and management domains. Thus begins the life and journey of a software system, a life that contains continuous effort—you are never finished.

Communication: The importance of **communication** (including active listening skills) cannot be overemphasized. It is key to sincere, relevant participation of all parties, bringing to bear the needed interaction and dialogue to foster collaboration, and eventual acceptance of change associated with the introduction of new HIS that enable new ways of doing work.

▶ Vendor and Provider Relations

HIS development began in the 1960s in the U.S. HIS beginnings were local, humble, and generally rooted in the data processing departments of hospitals. Technology was in such a different place than it is now. It is difficult to imagine computerizing these processes so much more simply than they are configured today, since we are so accustomed to today's massive and complex enterprise systems. The early systems did not have the advantage of the use of the Internet to connect capabilities inside and outside organizations, nor did they have ubiquitous availability of infrastructure in the form of smartphones, wireless, high-speed networks, and cloud computing. This now-huge market brings along with it numerous unintended consequences compared to the straightforward, ground-breaking, purposeful efforts of early HIS development pioneers. Some of the long list of unintended consequences include the collision of business interests of wealthy publicly traded or private vendor corporations vs. health provider, community and patient interests: a David vs. Goliath situation. Examples of these issues include ethical problems regarding use of data for monetary gain vs. patient health;

protection of vendor problems and failings vs. transparency on behalf of patients and providers; undercutting and overwhelming the efforts of those who work in not-for-profit community, safety net, religious, and research organization as well as teaching hospitals and health systems. The literature abounds with stories referencing hospitals suffering financial hardship, even going bankrupt trying to implement expensive vendor systems such as Epic EHR (Becker's Hospital Review, 2013; Jayanthi & Ellison, 2016; Moukheiber, 2012). When community hospitals are going bankrupt due to software implementations, it is urgent for those working in HIS and HIS-adjacent fields to strengthen our understanding of the dynamic vendor marketplace and business aspects of HIS in order to protect the mission and vision of healthcare provider organizations and the professionals who practice within them. The topic of untoward effects on the very institutions intended to be "helped" with HIS will be covered in detail in Chapter 8.

The contrast between the early days of HIS and today's massive, ubiquitous HIS capabilities couldn't be greater. Typically, those early projects focused on automation of the accounting functions, with a few rare clinical specialty or research niche initiatives as exceptions. HIS got its start with the health-minded professionals who wanted to improve the care and business processes of the places they worked—hospitals, clinics, and physician practices. The following section describes the history of HIS in the U.S.

▶ History of HIS

The Early Days

Amid the sense of urgency and recent major legislative and regulatory thrusts to stimulate the adoption of HIS and technology in the U.S., one might think this was a brand-new idea, an innovation just emerging from the laboratories of Silicon Valley technology firms and Cambridge software development start-ups. The early beginnings of HIS and technology of the 1960s closely followed the advent of computerization of U.S. society in general. The few hospitals that were able to afford expensive mainframe hardware and programmers to write software developed the first health-care computer application software systems. These mainframe computers were so large and generated so much heat that they had to be cooled by water, which required a significant investment in this infrastructure and the data centers that housed them. Early software applications focused primarily on accounting and financial applications, with rare instances of specialty clinical research applications being developed by these hospitals' data processing departments. Clinical applications were few and far between, predominantly isolated in single research departments or siloed specialty areas.

Early HIS began largely as support for hospital finance and accounting departments because finance departments controlled budgets and accounting information, and their processes followed Generally Accepted Accounting Principles (GAAP) rules. Plus, the "data" of finance and accounting involved dollars and cents, data elements long standardized and universally understood. Thus, these departments and processes adhered to well-known accounting standards, which made computerization easier: accounting functions represented repeatable, consistent functions and tasks that lent themselves to being programmed into computer systems.

In the 1970s, with the advent of air-cooled minicomputers, things began to change. Companies that distributed and supported hospital financial software applications emerged. These were the early HIS and technology vendors. One example of such a vendor was Shared Medical Systems (SMS), an early version of today's application services provider or software as a service (e.g., "the cloud") provisioning method. SMS, which was acquired by the German company, Siemens, in the late 1990s, and then acquired by Cerner in 2015, remains a very viable competitor in the financial and patient accounting HIS software market, supporting many hospital systems remotely from its data centers in Malvern, Pennsylvania (Becker's Hospital Review, 2014a). Financial patient accounting systems have always been the roots and mainstay products of SMS, throughout its journey through Siemens and now subsumed within Cerner.

In the meantime, the hospitals that made the early decision to independently invest in hardware, programmers, and data centers developed much of their own software for financial, patient accounting, and order communications systems. This early HIS work gave rise to the first HIS professional organizations: Hospital Information Systems Sharing Group (HISSG) and Electronic Computing Hospital Organization (ECHO). Each of these professional organizations consisted of hospital members who developed software and collaborated on the further development of software for use in their hospitals. In addition to sharing ideas and functionality definitions for these software systems, the members actually "shared" or exchanged software programs and applications with one another. For example, if one hospital had developed (programmed) a successful patient accounting software system and another had developed a successful software system for laboratory, personnel from the two hospitals could meet one another and establish a collaborative relationship through which they would exchange copies of the software programs for use in their respective institutions. ECHO was the organization for the hospitals using IBM hardware, and HISSG served the same purpose for the hospitals using non-IBM hardware. In those days, it was all about which type of "iron" (hardware) was used in the data center of the hospital: "Big Blue" (IBM) mainframes or non-IBM minicomputers (e.g., Digital Equipment Corporation and eventually Hewlett-Packard).

The first HIS were really extensions of charge-capture systems for patient billing system purposes. The first comprehensive medical information system (akin to today's EHR systems) was designed and built through a federal grant to Lockheed Martin; it was eventually commercialized and named Technicon, and initially implemented at El Camino Hospital in Mountain View, California, in 1971. The people who developed this software came out of the aerospace industry and worked with those who understood hospitals and health care. Also, in the 1970s, Science Applications International Corporation (SAIC)—a large, successful employee-owned company with expertise in information systems work for the defense industry and federal government—developed an early clinical information system for VA hospitals. (This system was replaced in 1982 with a newer version system called Veterans Health Information Systems and Technology Architecture [VistA], an integrated EHR that is currently in use in more than 1,400 VA hospitals and ambulatory clinics across the U.S. (World VistA, n.d.).)

The 1980s ushered in the era of the minicomputer, which offered fierce competition to the expensive, water-cooled mainframes of the 1960s and 1970s; the "minis" were smaller, generated less heat than the big mainframes, and were more affordable and easier to support because they could be cooled with less expensive air conditioning rather than water systems. Hewlett-Packard, Digital Equipment Corporation, and eventually even IBM developed highly competitive air-cooled minicomputers. Not only were these minicomputers more efficient and less expensive to buy and operate, but fewer and less expensive personnel were also needed to operate the computers and keep them up and running compared to the systems engineers and other highly technical professionals required for mainframe support. This trend made automation more affordable for hospitals, large clinics, and even large physician practices, which in turn stimulated the development of clinical applications as well as more widespread adoption of the typical financial accounting systems.

Vendors of software packages also started to emerge from entrepreneurial communities in great numbers in the 1980s. This trend occurred in part because a huge market was budding: the improved affordability of systems for more hospitals and some large, multispecialty physician practices (think Mayo or Scripps Clinics). Because valuable software had been developed by hospitals for their own use in the 1970s, vendor companies could be formed to commercialize these software developments as "software packages." During the 1980s, many hospitals and a number of larger physician practices began to buy and implement computer systems to support their financial systems, and increasingly ancillary clinical (e.g., laboratory, radiology, and pharmacy) and practice management (e.g., registration, scheduling, and billing) systems. Numerous entrepreneurs sought to acquire software from hospitals that had developed such programs in-house; these entrepreneurs then relicensed the software to other hospitals—and the hospital information system software industry was born. Occasionally, these entrepreneurs would develop software from scratch within their companies' development teams as well but did so less frequently than commercializing the already-developed software that had been built within healthcare organizations. As a result, the roots of very few vendor software systems today were actually developed by vendor companies; rather, many of the early software systems sold by vendors were originally developed in hospital data processing departments for the sponsoring hospital organization. Notable exceptions to this model exist, including the HIS vendors Technicon, Cerner, Meditech, and Epic, although each of these companies needed a brave hospital or clinic to be willing to step forward for the "alpha" implementation project to get started and establish a toehold in the emerging HIS industry.

Evolution of Clinical Systems and the EHR

The first-generation HIS clinical order entry systems were really extensions of charge-capture systems for patient billing system purposes, rather than systems with functionality truly grounded in clinical care processes. The ethos of the financial underpinnings and motivations of hospital information systems were reflected in the early clinical systems built and implemented primarily to capture charges to feed billing and claims processes. As noted earlier, Technicon developed the first comprehensive medical information system—a system focused on clinical care—in the mid-1970s. The requirements document for this system reads very much like the requirements documentation for one of today's modern EHR systems. This was truly an innovation that disrupted the healthcare industry. The VistA system, also described earlier, was another early HIS that—in a continually more advanced version—is still in use today in VA hospitals across the U.S. Specialized, niche ancillary clinical systems began to emerge especially in the 1980s, seeking to provide automation of profitable hospital departments such as laboratory, radiology, and pharmacy management. These niche systems often competed to be recognized as "best-of-breed" systems. Also blossoming were physician practice management systems for large medical practices.

At this point, hospitals still developed much of their own software in-house and used their IT staff to interface a growing number of vendor-supplied systems with their in-house developed systems. To do so, they would build a data center, buy hardware, hire programmers and systems analysts, contract with SMEs who are knowledgeable about the processes being automated, and create data processing departments to work with clinicians and administrators to design and develop systems internally. Universities developed some software, usually oriented to specialized clinical departments or siloed functions. Initial clinical information systems included "order entry" systems, early versions of computerized provider order entry (CPOE), one of the core capabilities of EHR systems. For some functions, these software applications were modeled after hotel software; think about the similarities in workflow between checking in and out of a hotel and being admitted, transferred, and discharged from a hospital. In the outpatient arena, only very large medical practices could afford computer systems and data processing departments during this time period.

From then through the 1990s, the number and types of healthcare organizations implementing computer systems expanded vigorously. The advent of the Internet transformed healthcare computing, just as it transformed computing and telecommunications in all industries. In lockstep with this disruptive innovation, the federal government enacted HIPAA to protect the security and privacy of citizens' data in anticipation of the significant increase in use of the Internet along with an increasing scope of electronic systems and technology in healthcare processes (U.S. Department of Health and Human Services, n.d.). While HIPAA was intended to ensure the security and privacy of PHI, as that information was transferred from one insurance plan to another (thus the "insurance portability and accountability" language in the title of the legislation), this legislation has had sweeping effects regarding the privacy and security of *all* PHI: (1) for patient care purposes as data are created and captured in EHR systems that share data across multiple organizational settings involved in a patient's care and (2) as information is created via secondary uses of those data for analytics and data sharing among providers. Since 1999 and 2001, when the Health and Medicine Division (HMD) of the National Academies of Sciences, Engineering, and Medicine published its watershed reports *To Err Is Human: Building a Safer Health Care System* and *Crossing the Quality Chasm*, respectively, healthcare organizations have been building comprehensive HIS and technology architectures in earnest, with the intent of improving quality and efficiency of care as summarized in the Six Aims of *Crossing the Quality Chasm* (described in Chapter 3).

The implications of these HMD reports—and the outright shock at their revelations about the preventable problems occurring in healthcare quality in U.S. hospitals—have driven the HIS and technology and regulatory agenda for the decade of the 2000s, as a potential means of improving the dire statistics published by the HMD.

The Current Climate

As we proceed through the decade of the 2010s, in the aftermath of the HMD reports and the recent update of the *To Err Is Human* study, as well as in the face of unsustainably high levels of healthcare expenditures, we are compelled to improve the quality and efficiency of health care in the U.S.—and HIS and technology are essential tools in that process. Significant governmental federal legislation on this front has included the American Recovery and Reinvestment Act (Public Law 111-5) that includes the HITECH Act of 2009. Under Title XIII of this $787 billion economic stimulus bill, the U.S. Department of Health and Human Services has invested $36 billion since 2009, providing incentives and technical support for the adoption of EHRs among hospitals and physician practices; in addition, it hopes to generate savings of about $10 billion through the application of Meaningful Use criteria as part of that incentive program, through adoption of technical and data standards to facilitate the secure sharing of data between clinicians through system interoperability (athenahealth, Inc., 2009). HITECH funding also provides training grants to colleges and universities to prepare the estimated 57,000 health IT workers needed to accomplish widespread EHR adoption. These criteria

and standards are being designed to improve patient safety, reduce instances of repeated diagnostic tests and other medical processes, increase timeliness of care by speeding transmission of information to clinicians, and bring greater overall efficiency to the U.S. healthcare system.

As hospitals and physician practices persevere through the challenges of implementing EHR systems and meeting Meaningful Use criteria, the shape and texture of healthcare delivery are changing on a widespread basis. Will this massive effort and investment in HIS and technology bridge the chasm between early systems and later adopters? Between regulators and vendors? Between vendors and patients? These questions are the agenda of today's HIS efforts in healthcare organizations. The answers are up to all of us to figure out from here.

Summary

In summary, as health professionals who are involved in HIS development every step of the way, the task at hand is to provide the education and support to create the kinds of systems we need in today's challenging and rapidly changing healthcare environment. Also, each and every health profession now uses HIS in order to perform its work. So clinical, business, and technology health professions now can *only* be done proficiently with HIS knowledge, ability, and activity. The U.S. health system and healthcare organizations have perhaps some of the greatest challenges to overcome due to historical reliance on the fee-for-service reimbursement methodology now attempting to evolve to a value-based reimbursement system. Reliance by healthcare organizations on the vendor marketplace as the source of solutions complicates and increases the cost of automation of health care. Added to this challenge is the fact that acute care can no longer be the complete focus of hospitals and health systems—prevention, wellness, chronic care management, and care coordination now dominate the scene, all of which happen outside institutions while current structures and systems and professionals are set for an acute, medical, sickness-based, institutional scenario.

Key Terms

Activation/implementation
Communication
Electronic health record (EHR)
End users
Hardware
Health Information Systems (HIS)

HIS design
HIS development
HIS fundamentals
HIS governance
HIS management
HIS planning
HIS Strategic Plan
Infrastructure

Middleware
Network
Ongoing maintenance
Roles
Software
Users
User interface (UI)

Discussion Questions

1. Describe why a basic understanding of the fundamentals of HIS is important for any healthcare provider, support staff, or leader.
2. How might the work of launching an implementation differ from that of HIS ongoing maintenance?
3. What kind of new knowledge does HIS help create?
4. Name one organization or governmental department that oversees HIS-related regulation.
5. Describe the beginnings of HIS. What functions did the first HIS support?

References

athenahealth, Inc. (2009). A summary of the HITECH Act: Whitepaper. Retrieved from http://athenaheath .com/_doc/pdf/HITECH_Fact_Sheet_Whitepaper .pdf

Becker's Hospital Review. (2013, December 19). St. Francis bankruptcy partially due to IT upgrade. *Becker's Hospital Review.* Retrieved from https://www .beckershospitalreview.com/healthcare-information -technology/st-francis-bankruptcy-partially-due-to -it-upgrade.html

Becker's Hospital Review. (2014a, August). 10 things to know about Cerner's acquisition of Siemens Health Services. *Becker's Hospital Review.* Retrieved from https://www.beckershospitalreview.com/healthcare -information-technology/10-things-to-know-about -cerner-s-acquisition-of-siemens-health-services.html

Becker's Hospital Review. (2014b, August). 25 things to know about hospitals, health systems' investments in IT. *Becker's Hospital Review.* Retrieved from https://www.beckershospitalreview.com/healthcare -information-technology/25-things-to-know-about -hospitals-health-systems-investments-in-it.html

Bresnick, J. (2017, November 20). 47% of IT professionals say their executives are big data illiterate. *HealthIT Analytics.* Retrieved from https://healthitanalytics. com/news/47-of-it-pros-say-their-executives-are-big -data-illiterate

Centers for Medicare & Medicaid Services. (n.d.). MACRA. Retrieved from https://www.cms.gov /Medicare/Quality-Initiatives-Patient-Assessment -Instruments/Value-Based-Programs/MACRA -MIPS-and-APMs/MACRA-MIPS-and-APMs.html

Dovey, D. (2018, February 15). The future of technology is uncertain as Moore's Law comes to an end. *Newsweek.* Retrieved from https://www.newsweek.com/future -technology-uncertain-moores-law-comes-end -807546

Green, J. (2017, October 31). 10 EHR failure statistics: Why you need to get it right first time. *EHR in Practice.* Retrieved from https://www.ehrinpractice.com/ehr -failure-statistics.html

Jayanthi, A., & Ellison, A. (2016, May 23). 8 hospitals' finances hurt by EHR costs. *Becker's Hospital Review.* Retrieved from https://www.beckershospitalreview

.com/finance/8-hospitals-finances-hurt-by-ehr-costs.
html

Kass, E. M., & Bazzoli, F. (2017, December 27). 2018 tech
budgets to rise about 8.8% for healthcare organizations.
Health Data Management. Retrieved from https://
www.healthdatamanagement.com/news/2018-tech
-budgets-to-rise-about-88-for-healthcare-organizations

Meyer, N. D. (2005, February 28). What is governance
and what should IT leaders be doing about it? *CIO
from IDG*. Retrieved from https://www.cio.com
/article/2448788/governance/governance-what-does
-governance-mean.html

Moukheiber, Z. (2012, June 18). The staggering cost of an
Epic electronic health record might not be worth it.
Forbes. Retrieved from https://www.forbes.com/sites
/zinamoukheiber/2012/06/18/the-staggering-cost
-of-an-epic-electronic-health-record-might-not-be
-worth-it/#602fa01146d3

Quality Payment Program. (n.d.). MIPS overview.
Retrieved from https://qpp.cms.gov/mips/overview

Schulte, F. (2017, July 19). Fraud and billing mistakes cost
Medicare—And taxpayers—Tens of billions last year.
The Center for Public Integrity. Retrieved from https://
www.publicintegrity.org/2017/07/19/21011/fraud
-and-billing-mistakes-cost-medicare-and-taxpayers
-tens-billions-last-year

U.S. Department of Health and Human Services. (n.d.).
Health information privacy. Retrieved from http://
www.hhs.gove/ocr/privacy/

World VistA. (n.d.). VistA history. Retrieved from http://
worldvista.sourceforge.net/vista/history/

Yaraghi, N. (2016, April 1). A health hack wake-up call.
U.S. News and World Report. Retrieved from https://
www.usnews.com/opinion/blogs/policy-dose
/articles/2016-04-01/ransomware-hacks-are-a
-hospital-health-it-wake-up-call

CHAPTER 2

The Scope, Definition, and Conceptual Model of HIS

By the end of this chapter, the student will be able to:

- Describe the definition, purpose, and scope of health information systems (HIS) using the conceptual model.
- Define the components of HIS according to the conceptual model, including technology and infrastructure; systems and management; people and processes; data and informatics; analytics; and global HIS, policy, and research.
- Explain the progression and maturation of HIS.
- Describe the organizational and community settings in which HIS and informatics can be used.

▶ Introduction

Before delving into the depths of HIS, it is important to lock in some key concepts regarding the scope of HIS. Reviewing the overall structure of how systems and their uses fit together takes the mystery out of computer systems. The conceptual model adopted in this text provides a tool for understanding—not just the "systems" of HIS but also the art and science of making use of systems and information (informatics), the data created and captured in these systems, and the variety purposed for the data, such as research, policy, and public health. Each of these uses of data depends on the foundational HIS that create and capture data through clinical and administrative work in healthcare organizations of all types, shapes, and sizes. This chapter describes and builds the layers that comprise the scope of HIS Model.

In this text, we will define the scope of HIS as including all computer systems (e.g., hardware, software, operating systems, and end-user devices connecting people to the systems), networks (the electronic connectivity between systems, people, and organizations), and the data those systems create and capture through the use of software. Each key layer of this progression through the totality of HIS relies on the foundation of core systems and requires professionals who specialize in that layer's work. Next, we look at the various layers of HIS one at a time: systems; health informatics; data and analytics; and research, policy, and public health.

▶ Systems and Their Management

Well-architected, properly managed computer systems form the foundation of the ability to create, transmit, and use information. With the availability of the Internet, development of cool new devices, and advertisements everywhere from vendors touting the ease of "cloud computing," it is sometimes tempting to think that access to high-quality, useful systems and information is as easy as 1-2-3—all that is necessary is to "plug into" one of these devices or some other easily accessible computing modality. The hard truth is that the myth of "plug-and-play" simply delays the realization that meaningful health information and data—whether available via the Internet, over a secure internal network, or through the use of an iPad or new innovative device—are only as good as the HIS platform and technical foundation that serves as the data source. In other words, the access devices and networks do not actually create data; instead, **data** are created and captured in painstakingly and properly implemented HIS that provide features and functions to support the **workflows** (sequences of common tasks) and **processes** (end-to-end methods) of healthcare providers and organizations, patients, and public health professionals.

HIS that create and capture data (which can then be coalesced into meaningful information and used for multiple purposes) serve as the *foundation* upon which all other information- and data-related capabilities depend. It might seem old-fashioned, but the source systems and devices that support the

work of providers and healthcare organizations remain the essential building blocks of all other advanced uses of data and information, and computerized workflow support modalities such as health informatics, data analytics and outcomes analysis, research and public health data surveillance, and predictive modeling techniques (Restuccia, Cohen, Horwitt, & Shwartz, 2012). We will talk more about these source systems and their management in Chapters 5–7.

The HIS Model in **FIGURE 2.1** depicts this relationship: HIS and their management form the footing for health informatics; data and analytics; and research, policy, and public health uses of HIS. These components of the total scope of HIS, in turn, rely on the fundamental HIS for the capabilities and data that HIS provide so that these components can exist. For example, without the foundational HIS, informatics would have no systems capabilities, features, nor functions to work with in redesigning workflows and calculating rules and alerts, or clinical decision support (CDS) and artificial intelligence (AI) aids to help in the advancement of the practice of medical, nursing, or other health-related professions.

Likewise, without well-managed HIS used to support key work processes such as the many clinical care (within and among clinical settings) and administrative functions (e.g., billing and payroll), data would not be created and captured for use. Data to be used for informatics, analysis, research, policy analysis, and public health surveillance need to come from somewhere—they need to be *real* data values, emanating from *real* healthcare processes and patients, which are then made available for these secondary purposes on any large scale (Kern et al., 2011).

Health Informatics

Informatics is the use of information systems and technology to redesign, improve, and

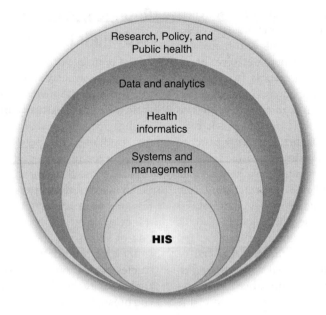

FIGURE 2.1 Scope of HIS Model for the Health Professions.

recreate the way work is done in disciplines such as medicine, nursing, medical imaging, and public health. In most cases, informatics focuses on certain quality- or process-improvement objectives, but this varies based on the setting in which the informatics activities take place. Informatics comprises the "use" of the computer capabilities that HIS provide to end users. In health care, this includes the activities of physicians, nurses, and other clinicians in the various settings in which they do their work, as well as professionals working in public health in its various environs, such as community settings, public health clinics, and other public health organizations. Through informatics, HIS are expected to enable improvements in the efficient delivery of health care, quality of services provided, and health outcomes across the U.S. population.

Data

Much of the value of systems goes beyond their support of clinical and administrative workflows and processes and is locked up in their data. Creating this resource can yield additional value, the rewards of which are reaped at an exponential scale through secondary uses of these data. While primary uses of data involve the transactions that support day-to-day activities of professionals and organizations, the only way to create *information* is through the **aggregation** and compilation of these data to create something greater than the single units of data. In other words, data aggregation creates meaningful information that is relevant to people of health care. Thus, the creation of information and ability to conduct analysis and gain knowledge are completely dependent upon the creation and capture of the individual data elements in the first place.

If someone attempts to create information out of proxied, extrapolated, or estimated data even for a very specific purpose, the only fruits of those data will be educated guesses. Or if data are not readily accessible from bona fide data systems such as those used in the real world to document clinical care, researchers and analysts must perform primary data collection, which is time-consuming, arduous, and limited as a practical matter. It involves hand-abstracting of medical records (with proper permission, of course) or personal information. For example, if a researcher wishes to study the quality of care in a diagnostic category such as heart failure, it is vastly easier to do so with the availability of real-life HIS data sources than by attempting to gather that data piece by piece. With real data, emanating from real activities conducted in real organizations through real processes, high-quality analysis and research drawing meaningful inferences, associations, outcomes, and evidence can be accomplished. Data created and captured in systems represent a treasure trove to be carefully stewarded and valued every step of the way. Everything else in the conceptual model displaying the progression of information from HIS rely on these data.

The importance assigned to data is not unique to the healthcare field. "**Business intelligence" (BI)** is a popular term for the value realized by flexibly analyzing comprehensive stores of data representing the totality of an organization or the provider's scope of activity. In other words, data from various systems that support clinical and financial transactions can be combined to enable analysis and insights into the entirety of the activities within the scope of that entity. In health care, this concept leads to the notion of "**clinical intelligence" (CI)**.

Research, Policy, and Public Health

At the pinnacle, data created and captured in HIS become available for research. These data fuel the work of university researchers—with their inherent expertise, curiosity, and desire for insight—and enable analysts to measure the health of patient populations and provide evidence for improving efficiency and effectiveness of healthcare processes and outcomes. Policy makers rely on research that predicts the long-term implications of steps taken in the delivery of health care and implementation of healthcare laws and regulations; that is, they rely on researchers' findings, such as studies carried out in university settings, or analyses performed by governmental agencies and organizations dedicated to health care and public health (Davis, Doty, Shea, & Stremikis, 2008; Fryer, Doty, & Audet for the Commonwealth Fund, 2011; O'Malley, Grossman, Cohen, Kemper, & Pham, 2009). The simple data captured, one patient at a time, in **electronic health record (EHR)** systems at separate organizations are ultimately aggregated into databases that can be made available to researchers and analysts. These aggregated data for research and analysis—the proverbial acorn—ultimately guide the work of policy makers and public health professionals responsible for governmental, political, and legal decisions about healthcare directions, policies, programs, and investments—the mighty oak tree (**FIGURE 2.2**).

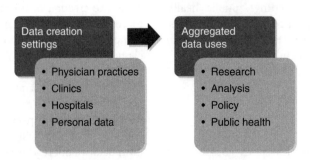

FIGURE 2.2 Data creation/data aggregation.

Public health officials are in a position to harvest the bounty of the entire HIS data chain, as the scope of their work expands from the purview of a person, an organization, or a group of patients, to the entire country, ultimately reflecting an international scope. As data are aggregated from systems that support clinical care or business activities across organizations and geographies, they can be analyzed according to several dimensions, such as demographic characteristics (e.g., female versus male, age groups, or race or ethnicity), pathogen (e.g., tuberculosis or anthrax), disease (e.g., cancer, heart disease, or acute illnesses), providers (e.g., hospitals, primary care physicians, or specialists), payment mechanisms (e.g., fee-for-service, health maintenance organization [HMO], preferred provider organization [PPO], Medicare, Medicaid, or uninsured), or other characteristics to better understand trends across an entire population. Such analysis of population-wide characteristics and activities is not confined to the boundaries of an organization (e.g., a hospital) or a segment of the population (e.g., patients insured by a certain carrier or analyses pre- and post-healthcare reform). Rather, inquiries and reports of interest to public health officials reflect the full expanse of their responsibility or perspective, such as a county, region, nation, or the world, as opposed to a subset consisting of those persons who are covered by insurance, are cared for at a particular institution, or live in certain geographies that may be over-represented by the available data. The options or variations available for a particular scope are completely determined by the data available for such analyses and the generalizability of those data to an appropriate population. In this text, we also consider the types and sources of data that can be used for these analyses.

Progression and Maturation of HIS Through the HIS Conceptual Model

We can outline the steps in the progression of the use of HIS and HIS data according to the HIS conceptual model.

1. Foundation (HIS). The progression begins with a strong foundation of technology and infrastructure and core HIS and their effective and proper management. None of the subsequent layers of HIS can exist without the foundational, infrastructure, and core systems.

2. Use (People, Process, Data, and Informatics). HIS software system capabilities support clinical and business transactions and the knowledge-workers who use them, enable key supporting processes, and facilitate redesign and improvement of these workflows and processes, a discipline referred to as health informatics. A key concept in HIS is that success is not just a function of technology and systems but is also an outcome of the balanced involvement of people-process-technology. People in this case are the clinical and administrative health professionals, who, through their involvement in the definition of requirements for HIS, think of new, better ways to work and care for patients (processes) using HIS that the systems then enable (technology). The support of healthcare activities—and use of HIS by the professions of medicine, nursing, and public health to develop more effective workflows in the care of patients—is the unique discipline of informatics. All these systems create and capture data that can then be analyzed to improve outcomes and assess the effectiveness of processes. The term "informaticist" has emerged as our world has become automated. This role is found at the intersection of computers and the work of professionals using those systems, such as physicians, nurses, and public health experts, and the work of IT professionals designing, building, and implementing those systems, such as computer systems engineers, systems analysts, programmers, trainers, and testers.

3. Learning/Knowledge (Analytics: BI/CI/AI). The use of data for learning and gaining new knowledge begins when transactional data are created and captured in HIS through the use

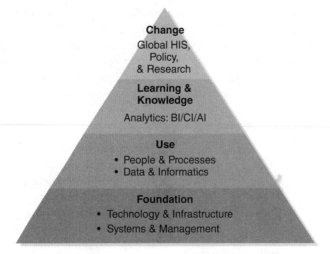

FIGURE 2.3 HIS progression and maturation.

of HIS software and then coalesced into databases and **analytics** platforms. Subsequently, these data are used for analysis and creation of information, including CDS, BI, and CI, ultimately leading to enhanced knowledge about health care and public health (**FIGURE 2.3**). AI employs newer technological capabilities, such as machine learning and natural language processing, that change the interaction between people and technology, releasing them from the more menial key-stroke navigation of an already programmed workflow, to tapping more into their creativity and power of thought due to the precision and speed of these analyses. Newly gained knowledge through these analytical capabilities represents secondary uses of data, which can reveal ways to improve healthcare processes, health outcomes, population health, and overall efficiency and effectiveness in health care (Committee on Data Standards for Patient Safety, 2003).

4. Change (Global HIS, Policy, and Research). Eventually the progression and maturation of the use of HIS and the data they produce and our exploitation of these data will improve our ability to conduct research, create effective policy, and improve the public's health through change. The path to change for the better is illuminated by evidence produced through use of systems, analytics, and research using data created and captured in HIS.

▶ HIS Uses in Organizational and Community Settings

With so many different types of organizations and players using health data, the answer to the question "What does this organization or entity use HIS for?" will differ for each type of organization or entity. Likewise, the mission, vision, and goals of each organization will drive the types of systems that are "core" to its purpose. In each instance, one must answer the question "What is the fundamental reason for using HIS?" This requires thinking through the types of systems and access to data that different kinds of providers will need to deliver care to their patients and measure outcomes of that care, as well as the types of HIS needed by different types of payers, patients/consumers, public health agencies, or research organizations.

Inpatient, Outpatient, and Ambulatory Healthcare Provider Organizations

Provider organizations comprise the settings in which healthcare services are delivered, including hospitals such as free-standing community hospitals, academic medical centers, specialty hospitals, rural hospitals, and multihospital systems, integrated delivery networks, physician offices, physician groups and multispecialty practices, home health agencies, and outpatient clinics of all types, such as surgical centers, community clinics, imaging centers, and urgent care centers. Anywhere care is delivered, HIS and the data they house are playing an increasingly essential role. The Internet was a game-changer in the spread of HIS across all these settings, spearheaded by the work of a few pioneering organizations such as Kaiser Permanente, Intermountain Health care (IHC), the Veterans' Administration (VA), and many others.

The current norm in U.S. health care is for processes in all areas of financial, administrative, and clinical activity to be automated. The HIS and technology products and services supporting the highly diverse collection of healthcare providers are the basis of what has grown into a multibillion-dollar HIS industry.

The market for commercial HIS products for all areas of the HIS Planning Framework, along with consulting services to help an increasing number of hospitals, clinics, and physician practices implementing them, has fueled the steady growth of HIS in healthcare organizations for the past 50 years. Coverage of the healthcare landscape is progressively broadened from the original hospital-centric model to clinics, provider offices, hospice facilities, home health groups, and other clinical delivery settings. Of course, these HIS also connect to external partners such as retail pharmacies, reference laboratories, medical equipment stores, clinics for employees in businesses and for students in schools, and now the retail world of minute clinics in grocery stores and other commercial environments. From the early HIS origins in hospitals and large clinics, systems have spread to all types of healthcare delivery organizations as well extended out from those organizations to patients and consumers where they work and live.

Patients'/Consumers' Homes

Consistent with the spread of mobile computing and use of the Internet throughout our society and world, patients can increasingly access their patient records and providers wherever they chose to do so, as well as monitor their personalized health data. Additionally, vast sources of health-related information are accessible through the Internet for consumers interested in learning about various health or medical conditions, services, and products. The age of patient engagement is upon us. Increasingly, members of the C-suites of healthcare institutions have realized that they can achieve the best outcomes in organizational performance and clinical care by enlisting patients in the process. Likewise, many people now expect to be part of their own healthcare process, consistent with how they drive participation in other types of commerce and consumption of goods and services.

While this sounds quite logical, it is a far stretch from the not-too-distant era of the "passive patient," a time in which physicians were seen as almost god-like figures and providers were reluctant to share the contents of a patient's medical information with the patient or family. In fact, part of the author's education in medical records science in the 1970s consisted of learning how to carefully manage the situation in which patients asked to see the contents of their medical records. Legally, patients have always had a right to that information, but providers actively avoided showing them the information for fear they would not understand it or could not handle knowing what was going on inside their own bodies. The language and values of health care reflect this traditional expectation of the obedient patient as being either "compliant" or "not compliant" with the instructions or prescriptions of the expert, superior clinician. Patients who do not "follow doctor's orders" are seen as deviant or irrational and are blamed for poor outcomes (Euromed Info, n.d.). In fact, the term "patient" is linguistically derived from the passive voice in the English language and implies the entity receiving something, in an inferior position, from someone or something (in this case, the clinician or physician who prescribes a regimen of treatment and therapy) from a superior, dominant position (Wanner, 2009).

Modern-day consumers are playing an increasing role in their health care by taking advantage of the connectivity and empowerment of access to information—a role inherent to the information age. Just as we use computers to research and obtain services and products in retail, food, and entertainment, we now *expect* to be able to access our personal health information from providers and interact electronically in the care process from our homes or places of work. A growing body of evidence is now emerging in the literature showing that clinical outcomes, patient satisfaction, and cost performance improve when patients are engaged and activated in the processes of their care. HIS is a powerful facilitator of such engagement (Courneya, Palattao, & Gallagher, 2013; Hibbard & Greene, 2013). Plus, as the tipping point is within our collective sight vis-à-vis the adoption of EHRs in most hospitals and physician practices, innovators are enthusiastically embracing new means of personal connectivity and engagement in the healthcare arena using IT tools widely applied in other industries (Lohr, 2009; Office of the National Coordinator for Health IT, 2013).

Payers, Insurance Companies, and Government Programs and Agencies

The mechanism by which hospitals, physicians, clinics, and all other healthcare providers are paid for the healthcare services provided to their patients involves insurance companies or payers of one type or another. Several types of payers are found in the U.S.: private insurance companies, government programs, and, of course, self-pay. Private payers or health insurance companies include companies such as United Health, Aetna, Blue Cross/Blue Shield, Cigna, and others. Government-funded health coverage programs include Medicare (health insurance for people aged 65 or older or with certain illnesses such as permanent kidney failure and those with certain disabilities), Medicaid/MediCal (state-specific health insurance for people and families with low incomes), State Children's Health Insurance Plan (SCHIP, state-administered programs using federal money for uninsured children younger than 19 years of age from low-income families), TriCare (health insurance for active and retired members of the military and their families), and Department of Veterans Affairs (government-sponsored programs for military veterans, covering the care they receive from doctors, hospitals, emergency rooms, and immunizations) (Brigham Young University, n.d.; Healthcare.gov., n.d.). Self-pay is becoming a larger piece of the healthcare pie now with an increased proportion of plans including high deductibles. Many people choose to forgo health insurance altogether due to the high cost and lack of accessibility because of denials and other barriers.

Public Health Organizations

Public health organizations exist to monitor, protect, and improve the public's health. Among other roles, they serve as a "safety net" by providing health care for patients who are uninsured or underinsured (e.g., through public health county hospitals and community clinics). In addition, public health services include preventive programs operated by municipal or county Departments of Public Health, such as free clinics, school-based immunizations, health-related and nutrition educational programs, birth control education, distribution of condoms, inspection and safety

🔍 *CASE EXAMPLE: VISTA'S FUTURE: EXCHANGING INNOVATION FOR COMMERCIALIZATION?*

In the 1980s and 1990s, some of the pioneering work that led to the development of EHRs was done in military healthcare settings. The Veterans Health Information Systems and Technology Architecture, commonly referred to as the VistA system, provided an early and shining example of the benefit and power of a comprehensive, integrated EHR. The VistA system was enormously important to the development of EHRs because it supports not only care delivered in inpatient hospital settings, but care for ambulatory patients as well.

A group of adventurous, committed programmers used the tools at hand including the availability of the MUMPS (Massachusetts General Hospital Utility Multi-Programming System) programming language, like many clinical HIS still in use today, some inexpensive equipment, and bootstrapped the development of a computer system pretty much below the radar of the senior management and mainstream "mainframers" of the day, eventually emerging with what became the VistA system. Not only was great progress made in the evolution of HIS through these efforts, but also over the years the thousands of VA hospitals and clinics have served as training grounds in which numerous medical students and clinicians learned to care for patients using computers to support the care and administrative processes. In fact, this system is so widespread that nearly 70 percent of all physicians practicing medicine in the U.S. today have used it as part of their medical training.

Given the Harvard Kennedy School Innovations in American Government Award in 2005, the VistA system has served the healthcare needs of veterans and those caring for them for the past 35 years. Its early story is worth telling as it is an example of what is now referred to as the agile development methodology. The VistA system:

- supports in-patient and ambulatory care,
- has analytical and research support capabilities,
- is integrated,
- is distributed but standardized, with data from all VA hospitals and clinics available for analytics and benchmarking purposes, and
- is interoperable.

And they say it can't be done.

Contrary to commercial EHR vendors, VistA does not withhold functionality in order to maximize profit. Rather, it was built with taxpayer dollars and therefore is in the public domain. So, the software is available for the cost of the media for delivering it. It is open source, meaning the code underpinning the system is freely available and may be redistributed. VistA is interoperable, built using standard programs, and built collaboratively with physicians who guided the functionality on behalf of clinical care. Contrast this with commercial HIS products currently available:

VistA Characteristics	Commercial HIS Characteristics
End-users collaborated in requirements	Built by company team for commercial use
Clinically oriented	Billing oriented
Standardized programming using MUMPS	Applications interfaced

(continues)

🔍 CASE EXAMPLE: VISTA'S FUTURE: EXCHANGING INNOVATION FOR COMMERCIALIZATION? *(continued)*

VistA Characteristics	Commercial HIS Characteristics
Decentralized	Centralized
Grassroots innovation, mission oriented	Commercial goals
Longitudinal data	Episodic data
Built for veterans, altruistic	Built to sell commercially, profit motivation
Open source programmers	Billionaires

The VistA story is a massive, unequaled success. At last count, 167 hospitals nationwide, on the same system, integrated and interoperable, with analytics on a massive longitudinal data set to evaluate clinical effectiveness and develop clinical guidelines. And, of course, a few well-publicized problems along the way. Let's look at the themes identified throughout this book that encourage successful HIS projects and outcomes. The VistA system involved the key end-users, the physicians, in the definition and development process. The project failed politically, ultimately, but succeeded in its intent. *Currently, the U.S. is on the brink of retiring VistA and deploying a commercial system.* Why is the VistA system seemingly at the end of its life cycle now? Politics and leadership problems. Ironically, this was a missed opportunity for all citizens, since VistA was not allowed to participate in the healthcare.gov initiative.

So, now, what do we do? These mavericks, who probably didn't view themselves that way when they started, but eventually adopted that identity, developed a system that has done more than any other HIS in the U.S. It has served its constituents very well, not perfectly, but very well. Software decisions are difficult and often, as in this case, highly politicized. We must ask the tough questions and ensure that we don't exchange innovation for commercial gain.

Data from Allen, A. A 40-year 'Conspiracy' at the VA. (2017). Politico. Retrieved from https://www.politico.com/agenda/story/2017/03/vista-computer-history-va-conspiracy-000367; WorldVistA. (2004). Retrieved from http://worldvista.sourceforge.net/vista/history/

ratings of restaurants, violence prevention programs, environmental health alerts, and a host of other services aimed at maintaining and preserving the health of a population of people within a certain region, state, or locale. Put simply, the role of these public health organizations and initiatives is to attend to the "public's health." In other words, public health organizations always think in terms of the populations whom they serve; they are *not* invested in the for-profit or medical care business of health care. Such organizations are typically funded by government programs at the federal, state, county, or local level, and they exist to keep the entire community of people in their jurisdiction or community protected from environmental risks and able to maintain their health to the degree feasible. A public health organization measures its target population's health by collecting and examining statistics such as infant mortality; mortality and morbidity rates; biological surveillance; immunization rates; rates of communicable diseases such as tuberculosis, HIV/AIDS, and meningitis;

deaths and injuries due to violence; air quality; and a variety of other metrics that tell public health officials about the status of and threats to a population's health (World Health Organization, n.d.).

Public health organizations whose primary goal is to measure, monitor, and report key public health statistics nationally are another type of entity whose mission it is to maintain, monitor, and improve the public's health. These organizations depend on a variety of data sources to create such public health information:

- Data from hospitals, clinics, and physician practices gathered through the claims administration processes for Medicare, Medicaid, SCHIP, and other

government-sponsored health insurance programs.

- Data from laboratories across the nation set up specifically for bio-surveillance and homeland security.
- Data voluntarily provided to federal or research organizations that are committed to the study and evaluation of healthcare quality and cost issues.
- Data from their own healthcare provider settings for caring for their patients and monitoring health issues and risks to the communities they serve.

Examples of national organizations of this type include the following (Medical College of Wisconsin, MPH Program, n.d.) (**TABLE 2.1**):

TABLE 2.1 Organizations Participating in Various Layers of the HIS Model

Layers of HIS Model	Organizational Setting				
	Primary Care (Physician Practices, Clinics)	Community Hospitals	Academic Medical Centers, Health Systems	Public Health Organizations	Policy, Research, and Quality/Cost Third Party Reporting Organizations
HIS Tech and Infrastructure	X	X	X	X	
Systems and Management	X	X	X	X	
Data and Informatics	X	X	X	X	X
People and Processes	X	X	X	X	X
Analytics, BI/CI/AI			X	X	X
Global HIS, Policy, and Research			X	X	X

- Centers for Disease Control and Prevention (CDC): Provides online resources for dependable health information.
- Public Health Institute: Promotes health, well-being, and quality of life for people across the nation and around the world.
- Rural Assistance Center: Provides health services-related information for rural America.

Each of these institutions rely on their version of HIS, to study the effects of risks to populations, to monitor the occurrence and etiology of disease, to intervene in outbreaks affecting the public's health, to communicate with populations and other agencies, and to care for patients. Both primary and secondary uses of data are extensive in public health organizations and initiatives.

Health Information Exchanges and Regional Health Information Organizations

Since the early 2000s, provider organizations in some regions have been entering into collaborative arrangements of varying scopes and business models with the goal of sharing patient-related health information, securely, between providers organized into not-for-profit, collaborative "data sharing" organizations in that region. Examples of regional organizations that might participate in these consortia include hospitals and hospital systems, clinics, physician practices, emergency responders such as paramedics, tumor registries, imaging centers, community clinics, public health institutions, and others. The idea is that these providers seek to make patient data that they have in their own systems available to other providers if needed to support care for the same patient. The aim is to improve the timeliness of data availability, support clinicians in emergency situations when patients need care at an organization where they typically do not receive care, make existing data available in an emergency to help speed diagnosis and treatment, reduce the need to repeat tests that have been performed at another clinical setting for which the results are stored and readily available within that organization's EHR, save the patient the discomfort and inconvenience of repeated care and testing, facilitate cross-continuum care models such as **accountable care organizations (ACOs)** and **medical homes**, and reduce costs and waste when possible.

These pioneering cooperative, collaborative efforts have met with mixed success, but have sprouted (such as the Rhode Island statewide information network) and in some cases taken root (such as the Michiana Health Information Network) across the U.S. Many of these initiatives have struggled mightily and then failed due to lack of a sustainable business model, unworkable technical models, lack of cooperation on the part of member organizations, difficulties extracting data from member organizations' systems, or lack of cooperation between competitor providers and vendors. Despite these challenges to forerunners in **health information exchange (HIE)**, progress continues and is beginning to show signs of sustainability. However, questions exist as to the best way to share data, and **interoperability** has entered the scene as the method of choice for the government through the **Health Information Technology for Economic and Clinical Health (HITECH) Act** and **Meaningful Use (MU)**, although not without great controversy as to method and vendor compliance. As EHRs have become more commonplace, integrative technologies that enable extraction and sharing of data securely have also become more robust, but the question remains: will EHR vendors honestly enhance their products' capabilities and provide the technology and software capabilities necessary to share patient data securely as a standard part of their software? Each of these factors may facilitate sharing this information among regional providers.

In addition to today's rapid advancement of ubiquitous technological capabilities in the private sector, a federal mandate related to

HIE, included as part of the American Recovery and Reinvestment Act (ARRA) of 2009, is contained in the HITECH Act. This act has allocated funding of $27 billion in incentives for hospital and physician providers to adopt EHRs and achieve MU criteria (Figure 2.1), including, among many types of EHR capabilities, electronic HIE (Blumenthal & Tavenner, 2010). Thus, organizations designed to accomplish HIE—sometimes called **regional health information organizations (RHIOs)**—have gained momentum as a result of the HITECH Act; HIEs enable participating provider organizations to securely exchange patient care-related data and achieve MU criteria in their quest to reap the rewards of HITECH's financial incentives. By sharing patient data securely according to the requirements set out by HITECH and MU criteria (**FIGURE 2.4**), HIEs and other forms of HIE move us slowly but surely closer to a more integrated, less wasteful U.S. health system. Examples of successful HIEs include Rhode Island Health Network, Michiana Regional Health Information Network, Delaware Health Information Network, and others. Examples of failed RHIOs include Santa Barbara RHIO, early iterations of California Health Information Network, and others. Thus far, smaller regions have achieved the best early results. Owing to their more cohesive, less competitive provider environment and smaller scale, these less complex regions have improved the chances of connecting a more manageable scope of organizations, data, and patients for whom data are exchanged (Adler-Milstein, Bates, & Jha, 2009, 2011). Providers participating in these HIEs and taking advantage of their interoperability capabilities vary widely, and widespread use of such capabilities will likely take many years to realize (**EXHIBIT 2.1**).

Of course, all this work in MU initiated through the HITECH Act is now being built upon by Medicare Access and CHIP Reauthorization Act of 2015 (MACRA). MACRA combines quality and process improvement activities into one program, the new Merit Based Incentive Payments System (MIPS) and the Quality Payment Program (QPP), discussed in more detail in Chapter 9. To summarize the relationship of MACRA and the QPP including MIPS on MU, MIPS consolidates several programs, including Medicare EHR Incentive Program for Eligible Clinicians, Physician Quality Reporting System (PQRS), and the Value-Based Payment Modifier (VBM), into one program. So, MU requirements and incentives for eligible clinicians have given way now to MIPS requirements and incentives. MIPS emphasizes progress and reporting in

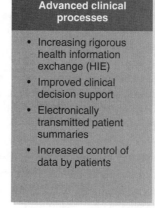

Stage 1 Data capture and sharing	Stage 2 Advanced clinical processes	Stage 3 Improved outcomes
• Capture health information in a standardized format • Track key clinical conditions • Support care coordination • Report clinical quality measures and public health information • Engage patients and families	• Increasing rigorous health information exchange (HIE) • Improved clinical decision support • Electronically transmitted patient summaries • Increased control of data by patients	• Improving quality, safety, and efficiency • Decision support for high-priority conditions • Self-management tools for patients • Comprehensive data through HIEs • Improving population health

FIGURE 2.4 Summary of Meaningful Use Criteria Stages 1, 2, and 3.

EXHIBIT 2.1 MU Stage 2 and Health Information Exchange Highlights

The MU Stage 1 and Stage 2 define a common data set for all summary of care records, including an impressive array of structured and coded data to be formatted uniformly and sent securely during transitions of care and, upon discharge, to be shared with the patient themselves. These include the following:

- Patient name and demographic information
- Vital signs
- Diagnosis
- Procedures
- Medications and allergies
- Laboratory test results
- Immunizations
- Functional status, including activities of daily living and cognitive and disability status
- Care plan field, including goals and instructions
- Care team, including primary care provider of record
- Reason for referral
- Discharge instructions

Data from The Office of the National Coordinator for Health Information Technology (ONC). EHR incentives & certification: How to attain meaningful use. Retrieved from http://www.healthit.gov/providers-professionals/how-attain-meaningful-use

four areas: Quality, Promoting Interoperability (PI), Improvement Activities in the areas of care processes and patient engagement in and access to care, and Cost. Provider incentive payments are now being replaced through MIPS (Quality Payment Program, n.d.).

External Regulatory, Reporting, Research, and Public Health Organizations

Each type of healthcare provider is accountable to its community and board constituents as well as to regulatory oversight bodies, and each collaborates with myriad third-party organizations ("third party" means an organization or agency that is not part of the provider organization). Some third-party organizations set standards (metrics) for healthcare providers to use when measuring the quality and cost of the services they provide. The third-party organizations then collect the reported measures from participating health providers and create statistical benchmarks from the aggregate data for those providers to use when evaluating

their performance against the performance of other like organizations and implementing quality-improvement and cost-control initiatives. Examples of such third-party or external organizations include The Leapfrog Group, whose mission is to promote improvements in the safety of health care by giving consumers data to make more informed hospital choices, and state organizations such as the California Health Care Foundation's report cards on hospitals and long-term care facilities, among others. These external organizations may also be state or federal regulatory agencies that are given the responsibility of monitoring the safety and compliance of provider organizations serving certain constituents (e.g., state or county populations, cardiology patients, children, or aged patients); their responsibilities are typically outlined by governmental regulations that are often funded by a governmental agency.

A third-party external reporting agency may also monitor key metrics regarding quality of care for a particular state or the country as a whole. For instance, the Department of Health Services (DHS) and Office of Statewide Health

Planning and Development (OSHPOD) of the California Health and Human Services Agency are state-based agencies charged with ensuring safety in hospitals and other healthcare settings. Provider organizations are required to report data to those state agencies on a regular basis about all services provided to their patients and communities, as well as any untoward events, such as wrong-site surgeries or hospital-acquired infections, that occur to patients. Chapter 11 discusses external reporting organizations in more detail.

Other examples of external organizations to which healthcare providers submit vast amounts of data and reports reflecting services provided, safety practices, costs, and outcomes of care include **The Joint Commission**, a quasi-regulatory organization that inspects and accredits hospitals based on their ability to meet a rigorous set of scored criteria, and the Cardiac Reporting Organization, which was established to monitor cardiac mortality rates nationally (Shahian et al., 2011; The Joint Commission, n.d.). Regulatory requirements are mandatory and failure to provide required data and reports—or submission of data reflecting poor performance that could harm patients—may result in the hospital or provider being reprimanded and monitored, fined, subjected to a temporarily suspended or revoked license, or closed. Other third-party reporting relationships may have to do with a provider organization voluntarily providing data and reports to an external reporting group so that it can be compared to similar organizations regionally or nationally in an effort to continually improve participants' cost performance, clinical quality of care, and transparency to their communities. Examples of these types of relationships include the Institute for Health Care Improvement (IHI), The Advisory Board, The Leapfrog Group, and the Cal Hospital Compare (formerly known as California Hospital Assessment and Reporting Taskforce [CHART]) (Agency for Healthcare Research and Quality, n.d.; California Hospital Assessment and Reporting Taskforce,

n.d.; Leapfrog Group, n.d.). CHART for example, is a voluntary program in which 86 percent of California hospitals are participating; it provides scores for clinical quality, patient experience, and patient safety for California hospitals, is searchable by zip code, rates hospitals on a five-level scale of superior to poor, and provides a web capability to report issues (Cal Hospital Compare, n.d.) (**EXHIBIT 2.2**).

To support this kind of reporting, the third-party organization's reporting databases must be populated with and reporting capabilities able to create a compilation of clinical and cost-related data from hospitals, clinics, and physician practices, that is, data originating in these providers' own smaller-scale HIS that support their clinical and business processes and activities. Data submitted to the third-party organizations come directly from the multiple HIS supporting patient care and reporting capabilities at the provider organizations; none of these external organizations is the original source of the data. Rather, these external entities review, report, aggregate, and consolidate data from many provider organizations; then benchmarks or report cards on the provider organizations' performance can be compared to the benchmarks or report cards for all other organizations that submit data and reports to that same third-party reporting organization. Whether such reporting is voluntary or mandatory, it is the job of all provider organizations to responsibly, promptly, and transparently report the numbers, types, mishaps, costs, and quality associated with the services they provide to interested parties, such as quality monitoring groups, payers, government, communities, and patient populations. Such reporting relationships represent **secondary uses of data**, data originally created and captured in the clinical and administrative transaction systems of health provider organizations. In contrast, the original patient care and administrative transactions represent the **primary uses of data** created and housed in these providers' HIS. **FIGURE 2.5** is an overview of

EXHIBIT 2.2 Sentinel Events Most Frequently Reported to The Joint Commission

Top 10 most frequently reported sentinel events for 2017	
Unintended retention of a foreign body	116
Fall	114
Wrong-patient, wrong-site, wrong-procedure	95
Suicide	89
Delay in treatment	66
Other unanticipated event*	60
Criminal event	37
Medication error	32
Operative/post-operative complication	19
Self-inflicted injury	18

*Includes asphyxiation, burn, choked on food, drowned, or being found unresponsive.

https://www.jointcommission.org/assets/1/18/Physician_Leader_Monthly_March_2018.pdf

Reproduced from DYK (Did You Know?). Sentinel events most frequently reported to The Joint Commission. Available at http://webmm.ahrq.gov/dykarchivecase.aspx?dykID=40. Reprinted with permission of AHRQ WebM&M.

the primary and secondary uses of HIS data and systems by providers of care and others in the healthcare ecosystem (Committee on Data Standards for Patient Safety, 2003).

Public Health Reporting Systems. Local, county, state, and national public health organizations and reporting agencies exist to monitor and protect the public's health for the citizens living within their purview. Just as healthcare provider organizations must automate their clinical and administrative processes using HIS, so public health organizations must design, implement, and use

computer systems to collect and analyze data reflecting the health of a population. This paves the way for implementing effective programs to support that population's health status and create initiatives for the management of chronic disease (O'Carroll, Yasnoff, Ward, Ripp, & Martin, 2003). Examples of such HIS reporting systems for public health purposes include systems for detection and monitoring of public health problems; analysis of public health-related data; and public health knowledge management, alerting, and response. The Public Health Information Network (PHIN) initiative of the federal government

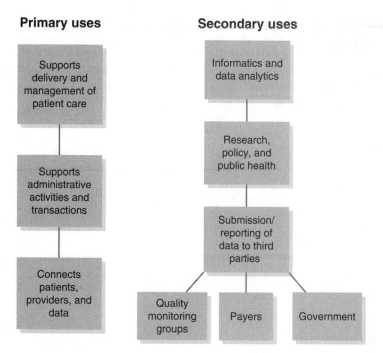

Primary uses

Supports delivery and management of patient care

Supports administrative activities and transactions

Connects patients, providers, and data

Secondary uses

Informatics and data analytics

Research, policy, and public health

Submission/ reporting of data to third parties

Quality monitoring groups

Payers

Government

FIGURE 2.5 Primary and secondary uses of HIS data.

Data from the Institute of Medicine Report *"Key Capabilities of an Electronic Health Record System: Letter Report."* Washington, DC: The National Academies Press, 2003.

works in conjunction with the National Health Information Infrastructure to establish standards (Consolidated Health Information) for automation of clinical health data for public health reporting purposes. Timely access to such clinical data and connectivity between laboratories to facilitate sharing results data will improve the opportunities for responding to public health issues such as outbreaks of disease, disaster, or terrorism (Public Health Informatics Institute, n.d.).

Summary

The scope of HIS includes a universe of data-related systems, processes, and new knowledge created from using those systems and the data derived from them. The ability to maximize the depth and breadth of HIS utility for the goals of improving outcomes and developing knowledge depends on the development and maturation of systems and their

use as reflected in the HIS conceptual model. The layers of this model provide a comprehensive view of the total scope of HIS activity:

- *HIS and Management:* Building the foundational HIS that support healthcare activities and the competent management of those systems so they support and feed the other layers of the Model.
- *Health Informatics:* Enhancing the use of those systems to improve how work is done and deriving meaning from data.
- *Business Intelligence/Clinical Intelligence:* Using data and creating information from which to learn and build knowledge, which leads to further creation of relevant information and new uses of data for analytics, including CDS, BI, and CI.
- *Research, Policy, and Public Health:* Eventually improving the health of populations through evidence-based change driven by well-informed research, policy, and public health.

HIS supporting clinical, administrative, and research/reporting activities are used extensively in a wide variety of organizational and community settings, including inpatient and outpatient healthcare provider organizations; patients' and consumers' homes and places of work or livelihood; payers, insurance companies, and government programs and agencies; public health organizations; HIEs and RHIOs; and regulatory, reporting, and research organizations.

Key Terms

Accountable care
   organizations (ACOs)
Aggregation
Analytics
Business intelligence (BI)
Clinical intelligence (CI)
Data
Electronic health record
   (EHR)

Health Information
   Technology for Economic
   and Clinical Health
   (HITECH) Act
Health information exchange
   (HIE)
Informatics
Interoperability
Meaningful Use (MU)

Medical homes
Primary uses of data
Processes
Public health
Regional health information
   organization (RHIO)
Secondary uses of data
The Joint Commission
Workflows

Discussion Questions

1. What are the key steps in the progression of HIS according to the HIS conceptual model? What is the relationship between the various layers?

2. Why is it necessary to be attentive in entering data elements that may not have a clear relationship to the work being done? How does the information use or data collection of a laboratory technician in a hospital differ from that of a public health administrator at a county agency or a specialist physician at an outpatient facility?

3. As more healthcare provider organizations adopt EHRs, what do you think will be the effect on healthcare-related research? On public health issues?

4. Why are healthcare organizations just in the beginning stages of engaging patients in their care? Do you think HIS has anything to do with this change? Do you think this will have a beneficial effect for the organizations? For the patients? Explain.

5. Insurance companies use a lot of data from provider organizations' HIS to process claims and calculate reimbursement. How important is this practice to the overall healthcare process? Given that this process involves money for the provider organizations, which is more important: HIS for patient care or HIS for gaining reimbursement for that care?

6. Military personnel and veterans often get their care from military or VA healthcare providers, but some of their care is received in non-military settings. How might clinical data from one setting be sent to another for purposes of caring for these military patients?

7. What are *primary* uses of HIS? What are *secondary* uses of HIS? Which of these can best help the U.S. healthcare system improve?

8. Public health reporting and surveillance systems have gotten much more

attention since the terrorist attacks on the U.S. on September 11, 2001. Do you think this is justified? Who do you think should be responsible for surveillance—healthcare providers like hospitals and physician offices or the government?

References

Adler-Milstein, J., Bates, D. W., & Jha, A. K. (2009, March/April). U.S. regional health information organizations: Progress and challenges. *Health Affairs, 28*(2), 483–492.

Adler-Milstein, J., Bates, D. W., & Jha, A. K. (2011, May). A survey of health information exchange organizations in the United States: Implications for meaningful use. *Annals of Internal Medicine, 154*(10), 666–671.

Agency for Healthcare Research and Quality. (n.d.). About us. Retrieved from http://www.ahrq.gov/index.html

Blumenthal, D., & Tavenner, M. (2010). The "Meaningful Use" regulation for electronic health records. *New England Journal of Medicine, 363*, 501–504. Retrieved from http://www.nejm.org/doi/full/10.1056/NEJMp1006114

Brigham Young University. (n.d.). Government-sponsored healthcare programs. Retrieved from http://personalfinance.byu.edu/?q=node/533

Cal Hospital Compare. (n.d.). Third Annual C-Section Honor Roll Hospitals Annouced. Retrieved from http://calhospitalcompare.org/

California Hospital Assessment and Reporting Taskforce. (n.d.). Retrieved from http://www.chcf.org/projects/2009/california-hospital-assessment-and-reporting-taskforce-chart

Committee on Data Standards for Patient Safety. (2003). *Key capabilities of an electronic health record system: Letter report.* Washington, DC: National Academies Press.

Courneya, P. T., Palattao, K. J., & Gallagher, J. M. (2013, February). Innovation profile: HealthPartners' online clinic for simple conditions delivers savings of $88 per episode and high patient approval. *Health Affairs, 32*, 2385–2392.

Davis, K., Doty, M. M., Shea, K., & Stremikis, K. (2008, November 25). Health information technology and physician perceptions of quality of care and satisfaction. *Health Policy, 90*(2–3), 239–246. Retrieved from http://www.ncbi.nlm.nih.gov/pubmed/19038472

Euromed Info. (n.d.). The patient as a passive recipient of care. Retrieved from http://www.euromedinfo.eu/the-patient-as-a-passive-recipient-of-care.html/

Fryer, A. K., Doty, M. M., Audet, A. M. J., & Commonwealth Fund. (2011, March). Sharing resources: Opportunities for smaller primary care practices to increase their capacity for patient care. Retrieved from https://www.commonwealthfund.org/sites/default/files/documents/___media_files_publications_issue_brief_2011_mar_1489_fryer_sharing_resources_smaller_primary_care_practices_ib_v2.pdf

Healthcare.gov. (n.d.). Health insurance basics. Retrieved from https://www.hhs.gov/healthcare/index.html

Hibbard, J. H., & Greene, J. (2013, February). What the evidence shows about patient activation: Better health outcomes and care experiences; fewer data on costs. *Health Affairs, 32*, 2207–2214.

Kern, L. M., Wilcox, A. B., Shapiro, J., Yoon-Flannery, K., Abramson, E., Barron, Y., & Kaushal, R. (2011, April). Community-based health information technology alliances: Potential predictors of early sustainability. *American Journal of Managed Care, 17*(4), 290–295.

Leapfrog Group. (n.d.). About Leapfrog. Retrieved from http://www.leapfroggroup.org/about

Lohr, S. (2009, April 5). Health care industry moves slowly onto the Internet. *New York Times.* Retrieved from http://bits.blogs.nytimes.com/2009/04/05/health-care-industry-moves-slowly-onto-the-internet/

Medical College of Wisconsin, MPH Program. (n.d.). National public health organizations. Retrieved from http://www.mcw.edu/mphprogram/Resources/PublicHealthOrganizations.html

O'Carroll, P. W., Yasnoff, W. A., Ward, M. E., Ripp, L. H., & Martin, E. L. (Eds.). (2003). *Public health informatics and information systems.* Series: Health Informatics. New York, NY: Springer-Verlag.

O'Malley, A. S., Grossman, J. M., Cohen, G. R., Kemper, N. M., & Pham, H. H. (2009, December 29). Are electronic medical records helpful for care coordination? Experiences of physician practices. *Journal of General Internal Medicine.* Retrieved from http://www.commonwealthfund.org/Publications/In-the-Literature/2009/Dec/Are-Electronic-Medical-Records-Helpful-for-Care-Coordination-Experiences-of-Physician-Practices.aspx

Office of the National Coordinator for Health IT. (2013). ONC releases data on hospital EHR adoption, meaningful use. Retrieved from https://dashboard.healthit.gov/evaluations/data-briefs/non-federal-acute-care-hospital-ehr-adoption-2008-2015.php

Public Health Informatics Institute. (n.d.). New health IT framework available for ACOs. Retrieved from http://www.phii.org/blog/new-health-it-framework-available-acos

Quality Payment Program. (n.d.). MIPS overview. Retrieved from https://qpp.cms.gov/mips/overview

Restuccia, J. D., Cohen, A. B., Horwitt, J. N., & Shwartz, M. (2012, September 27). Hospital implementation of health information technology and quality of care: Are they related? *BMC Medical Informatics and Decision Making, 12*, 109.

Shahian, D. M., Edwards, F. H., Jacobs, J. P., Prager, R. L., Normand, S. L. T., Shewan, C. M., ... Grover, F. L. (2011). Public reporting of cardiac surgery performance: Part 1—History, rationale, consequences. *Annals of Thoracic Surgery, 92*(3), S2–S11.

The Joint Commission. (n.d.). About The Joint Commission. Retrieved from http://www.jointcommission.org /about_us/about_the_joint_commission_main.aspx

Wanner, A. (2009). *Deconstructing the English passive.* Berlin/Boston, MA: De Gruyter Mouton. Retrieved from http://www.degruyter.com/view/product/40717

World Health Organization. (n.d.). Public health surveillance. Retrieved from http://www.who.int /topics/public_health_surveillance/en/

CHAPTER 3

Aligning HIS in the Dynamic Healthcare Environment

▶ Introduction

In this chapter, we will be exploring the volatile and dynamic work environment in which HIS play their part. Now, many industries can describe their work places as dynamic, but few come as close to the field of health care. Lives are at stake, over 13 million people have jobs in health care (The Henry J. Kaiser Family Foundation, 2017), and the government is very invested in the work that we do. The U.S. fee-for-service health system is reeling as it tries to transition to value-based care, challenged to cost-effectively

care for an aging, chronically ill population. About 150 million Americans have at least one chronic condition, 100 million have more than one, and 30 million live with five or more— those 30 million account for 40 percent of healthcare spending (Buttorff, Ruder, & Bauman, 2017). In a world that is rapidly changing, so is health care: technologies move forward, and yet only some HIS processes do. This chapter examines what this means to surviving and thriving in this environment of change and how HIS can help pave the way. There is special attention paid to the issues of moving from fee-for-service to value-based care, value-based reimbursement, and population health management.

Strong vision and leadership, coupled with functional HIS systems, will take us from where we are and have been to where we need to go. This chapter addresses the context of this necessary adaptation buoyed by HIS.

▶ Health Care's Current State

Health care in all its related parts is undergoing massive change and experiencing deep challenges in the process. The drivers of change and challenges include the following: (1) inadequate quality; (2) a historical focus on acute care with an increasing incidence of chronic illness; (3) an aging population (10,000 people in the U.S. turn 65 years old every day) (Pianin, 2017); (4) high degrees of variability in healthcare processes; (5) increasing cybersecurity threats to the security and privacy of personal health information and the stability of healthcare organizations (Donavan, 2018); (6) electronic health record (EHR) systems that have turned out beloved physician knowledge-workers into data entry clerks who are suffering burnout at increasing rates (Toussaint & Correia, 2018); and (7) unsustainably high cost of health care, which lowers the value of each health care dollar spent (Ellison, 2017; Verghese, 2018).

The three major issues that describe health care today in this country are also the three areas facing significant change in future. More on the future later in this chapter, but for the purposes of describing the current state of affairs in the field of health care, hold these issues in mind: programs of care designed around **fee-for-service**, untenable costs, and ineffective care. We will examine these issues as they relate to HIS implementation and use.

Fee-for-Service

HIS systems were historically designed to support the fee-for-service reimbursement methodology, in which payers such as commercial insurance companies or government programs reimburse providers for each service, such as procedures or diagnostic tests, provided. Thus, early clinical HIS systems were built to support billing systems rooted in this methodology. With value-based care upon us, our struggle to adapt is in part because billing and reimbursement for procedures is more straightforward than for value and health outcomes.

Healthcare Costs

The cost of health care in the U.S. continues to grow, a deepening problem. What is worse is that the U.S. is not just spending more than other developed countries, but its outcomes are also worse for most important health measures (Rapaport, 2018). This lack of value not only hurts the effectiveness of health care and health status in the U.S., but also degrades the entire economy. To put it in perspective, the estimated 30 percent of healthcare dollars wasted, approximately $785 billion (with a "B"), is more than what is spent for all of kindergarten through twelfth grade in the U.S. (Peter G. Pederson Foundation, 2018). Furthermore, healthcare spending per capita in the U.S. is more than two times the average of other developed countries and is a key driver in our overall economic condition. As evidence of the not only rapid, but also uncontrolled growth, in 2012, health care accounted for 17.2 percent of the U.S. gross domestic product (GDP); this is equal to $2.8 trillion, or $8,915 per person, and with an average annual projected growth rate of 6.2 percent per year for 2015–2022, health spending could comprise 19.9 percent of the GDP by 2022 (Peter G. Pederson Foundation, 2018). Multiple estimates project that health care will comprise 20 percent of the GDP by 2025 (Peter G. Pederson Foundation, 2018). In 2018, this number is expected to increase by 5.3 percent, a higher growth rate than the 4.3 percent rise in 2017 (Peter G. Pederson Foundation, 2018). The overall U.S. economic condition thus is largely influenced by health care, including the fact that health care is the largest driver of government spending increases. Of course, this can also be a reflection of other economic and systemic difficulties, such as lack of health insurance through employers and unemployment rates, so it is important to look deeper into statistics to understand the deeper reasons why they might be occurring. Healthcare spending is a function of many determinants of health and economic well-being (**FIGURES 3.1–3.3**) (Peter G. Pederson Foundation, 2018).

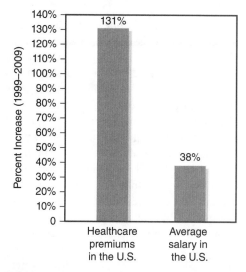

FIGURE 3.1 The rising cost of health care.

Healthcare Quality and Effectiveness

If the HMD estimates that 30 percent of healthcare dollars are wasted, ineffective, overpriced, or unnecessary services, one must look into the multiplicity of reasons behind that unacceptable result. The HMD's role in measuring and reporting evidence of high cost, medical errors, and other problems in quality has been a profound one, shining a disturbing light on health care, notwithstanding the steadfast work of millions of highly qualified health professionals.

The HMD reports are clear in pointing out that it is the failure of the system, not the individuals, in the vast majority of these negative occurrences. They spell out their suggested reasons why these problems exist, in two watershed reports that focused the industry and woke up its players to the fact that quality was not as good as people wanted to believe. These reports are *To Err Is Human* (1999) and *Crossing the Quality Chasm* (2001), which provide solid evidence of alarming quality problems and make recommendations for improvement. *To Err Is Human* describes high levels of avoidable medical errors in U.S. hospitals that result in as many as 98,000 patients dying every year—patients who should have been discharged from the hospital successfully (The Institute of Medicine, 1999). *Crossing the Quality Chasm* outlines

FIGURE 3.2 The cost of health care: how does it compare to the costs of other goods?

The cost of health care: how much is waste?

Waste:
$765 Billion
30% of 2009 total
healthcare spending

Wasted healthcare costs:

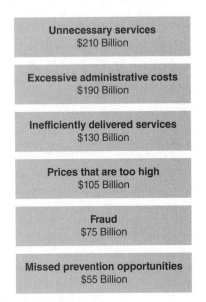

Unnecessary services
$210 Billion

Excessive administrative costs
$190 Billion

Inefficiently delivered services
$130 Billion

Prices that are too high
$105 Billion

Fraud
$75 Billion

Missed prevention opportunities
$55 Billion

FIGURE 3.3 Healthcare spending: 30 percent is waste.

Data from the National Academies of Sciences, Engineering, and Medicine: Health and Medicine Division. The Healthcare Imperative: Lowering Costs and Improving Outcomes: Workshop Series Summary. Washington, DC: The National Academies Press. https://doi.org/10.17226/12750. Retrieved from http://resources.nationalacademies.org/widgets/vsrt/healthcare-waste.html

six key aims necessary to improve the quality of care (The Institute of Medicine, 2001):

- *Safe*: Ensuring care helps and does not harm patients.
- *Effective*: Providing services based on scientific evidence to all who could benefit and refraining from providing services to those not likely to benefit.

- *Patient centered*: Providing respectful and responsive care according to patient preferences, needs, and values.
- *Timely*: Reducing delays for those who receive and those who give care.
- *Efficient*: Avoiding waste of materials and resources in patient care processes, including equipment, supplies, ideas, and energy.
- *Equitable*: Providing care that is consistent in quality regardless of a patient's characteristics, such as gender, ethnicity, geographic location, and socioeconomic status.

Unfortunately, despite significant efforts on many individuals' and organizations' parts, the U.S. health system remains inefficient and ineffective compared to the health systems of other developed nations by the majority of standard population-based outcome measures. Sadly, these numbers have not improved since the two seminal HMD reports were published more than a decade ago. An updated evidence-based analysis estimates the number of deaths due to medical errors in U.S. hospitals to be more than 400,000 per year; the same analysis cites poor incident reporting processes (only 14 percent of total adverse events) as contributing to this phenomenon and appeals for greater patient involvement in identifying errors and preventable harmful events (James, 2013).

To Err Is Human studied 33.6 million hospitalizations in the U.S. Based on the resulting data, the HMD estimated that each year an estimated 44,000–98,000 patient deaths occur during hospitalizations, not because of the patient's condition, but rather due to mistakes occurring in hospitals. This number was greater than the number of deaths per year due to motor vehicle accidents, breast cancer, and AIDS combined. This devastating statistic translates on average into 1,310 to 2,917 deaths per 1 million hospitalizations due to medication errors every year, year after year. If the business leadership paradigm Six Sigma Level of Reliability is applied, that ratio equates 114 avoidable deaths per 1 million hospitalizations due to medical errors. (Six Sigma is a quality improvement methodology that strives to eliminate errors in processes to a near-perfection level through data analysis techniques.) Challenges to the report's methodology occurred at the time, and a revised analysis suggested a lower death rate of 44,000–45,000 hospitalized patients per year who died of medical errors in U.S. hospitals. Unfortunately, if any one of those persons included in the avoidable death statistics is your family member or loved one, this is 100 percent of what matters to you. The HMD report *To Err Is Human* provides all the motivation needed to face the facts, buckle down, and improve quality, outcomes, and focus on patient safety. It sheds light on the whole U.S. healthcare system, rather than focusing on any one caregiver or provider. And although this report was published 20 years ago, it is, unfortunately, still relevant today. More recently, John James's study published in 2013 showed that avoidable deaths in U.S. hospitals average 210,000–400,000 per year (James, 2013). This study indicates that the average rate of avoidable deaths per year in U.S. hospitals has increased, according to the evidence. The bottom line is that the costs of health care continue to rise and quality problems have not only persisted but have grown. But what is the connection to HIS?

The answer lies in the HMD's second watershed report, *Crossing the Quality Chasm*. This report identified four key reasons for the significant gap in the U.S. health system between reality and ideal quality:

- *The growing complexity of science and technology, with delays between innovation and implementation.* Modern medicine is becoming increasingly multifaceted, with increasingly specialized areas of practice emerging. Also, new biomedical equipment and information technologies are being developed at an exponential rate, all of which make the access to complete and current information and the interaction between the various new technologies equally complex. This trend has been relentless for decades, as expressed more than 30 years ago by David Eddy: "The complexity of modern medicine exceeds the inherent limitations of the unaided human mind." (2001). HIS initiatives must target this gap and help close it.

- *The increase in chronic illness burden with a system centered on acute illness.* The aging demographics of the U.S. population and the increasing incidence of chronic illnesses such as obesity, cancer, diabetes, and heart disease occurring within a health system that emphasizes the "medical model" of care have resulted in a lack of effectiveness in dealing with the majority of today's illnesses. The mismatch between an epidemic of chronic illness and settings oriented toward acute care dominates the U.S. health system, resulting in a failure to successfully address these conditions (The Commonwealth Fund, 2017). By the time a person with diabetes is sick enough to come to the hospital, it is too late to treat that condition in a way that addresses the root cause of the illness. Making it increasingly difficult for millions of people to obtain the health insurance, they need to access care in the U.S. is only making the problem worse. The U.S. ranks last among 11 high-income countries in financial access to care, with barriers to care highest for those who are uninsured (The Commonwealth Fund, 2017). All that can be done in a hospital setting is address the symptoms and outcomes of a patient's condition as presented—this is not the optimum treatment for chronic illness, which requires care in less costly settings such as clinics and doctors' offices, and importantly, in patients' homes and as patients go about their everyday lives. The inpatient hospital setting is equipped to deal with the progressive outcomes of these prevalent chronic conditions only; hospitals are set up to address acute issues, not manage chronic illness continuously or prevent it in the first place.

- *The inadequate use of information technology (IT).* The HMD report *Crossing the Quality Chasm* asserts that HIS can be instrumental in preventing or catching many types of medication errors and other medical errors that cause avoidable deaths and countless injuries and near misses each year. This was certainly true when a new EHR system was implemented at a large, downtown hospital in San Diego, California. The quality assurance system and processes showed that in total the reported errors went up in the six months following the implementation. Upon closer examination of the data, only the number of class 1 and 2 errors (on the medical errors scale of 1–4) went up, showing in better reporting and detection of errors. Fortunately, these class 1 and 2 were the kind of errors that did not result in harm to the patient. What's more, the more serious errors (class 3 and 4) involving patient harm or death actually went down in the same time period, even though the *total* number of reported errors went up, showing a safer system. Many HIS capabilities contained within EHRs are designed with capabilities to prevent errors, such as drug-drug interaction alerts, allergy alerts, **computerized physician order entry (CPOE)**, and others. Also, the HMD report indicates that many of the errors responsible for avoidable patient deaths occur in "hand-offs" of patient information between caregivers, between departments of the hospital or clinics such as the laboratory and nursing, or between physicians in their offices and the hospital settings. These paper or verbal hand-offs can be eliminated or reduced through the use of computer systems such as EHRs that transmit information electronically, greatly reducing the risk of errors in the information as it is transmitted.

- *A payment system that provides conflicting incentives and does not reward quality improvement.* For decades, doctors and hospitals have not been paid based on the quality of their services or on patient outcomes. Instead, they are paid just for providing those services and properly documenting this care. Thus, there is little correlation between how well patients do and how well the provider is paid. This translates into a lack of financial incentives for quality outcomes and instead provides incentives for volume of services, regardless of the outcome for the patient. In primary care, this translates into a disincentive for preventive and early stage care and a preference for higher-impact procedures down the road. Quality improvement is not "baked into" the processes surrounding patient care, but is rather seen as an additional effort and expense to the providers (Wilensky, 2018).

The State of Health Care as It Relates to HIS

Adler-Milstein and DesRoches report that in 2015, 75 percent of hospitals reported having at least a basic EHR system, this statistic showing steady progress from the 59 percent reported in 2013 (Adler-Milstein et al., 2015). However, of those without a basic EHR system, 61 percent did not include the adoption of physician notes, a key portion of any medical record, whether electronic or paper (Adler-Milstein et al., 2015). These statistics reflect clear progress in EHR systems adoption by hospitals. By 2015, 80.5 percent of hospitals adopted at least a basic EHR system, with about half of those hospitals adopting performance improvement or patient engagement capabilities, associated with value-based care and population health (Adler-Milstein et al., 2017). For office-based provider settings, as of 2015, EHR implementation rates for office-based physicians using any EHR system was reported by the Centers for Disease Control and Prevention (CDC) at 86.9 percent, and percent of office-based physicians with a basic system is 53.9 percent (Centers for Disease Control and Prevention, 2015). A basic system includes the following functionalities, which are implemented at least partially: patient history and demographics, patient problem lists, physician clinical notes, comprehensive list of patient medications and allergies, computerized orders for prescriptions, and ability to view laboratory and imaging results electronically (Donavan, 2018). What is not known from these statistics is how fully these capabilities are implemented in each practice—how many of the providers in the practice use some or all of the functions is not discernible from these statistics. What is known is that in the survey gathering these data, enough of the functionality was adopted to justify a "yes" answer from the respondent.

Accomplishing **interoperability**, or sharing patient data between practices electronically, has proven to be far more difficult and, in many cases, less achievable than originally imagined. It remains a highly variable capability, one of the most pressing demands of systems, vendors, and providers today. Current approaches to interoperability are mostly vendor driven and the effectiveness of their approach is questioned by many. For interoperability to be helpful, it must be widespread—otherwise, spotty coverage results in unpredictable capability. For example, as of 2015, the number of physicians who had sent patient data electronically to another practice ranged from 19.4 percent in Idaho to 56.3 percent in Arizona; the number that received patient data electronically from another provider ranged from 23.6 percent in Louisiana to 65.5 percent in Wisconsin; the percentage of physicians who had electronically integrated patient health information from other providers ranged from 18.4 percent in Alaska to 49.3 percent in Delaware; the percentage of physicians who had electronically searched for patient health information ranged from 15.1 percent in the District of Columbia to 61.2 percent in Oregon (**FIGURE 3.4**) (Landi, 2016).

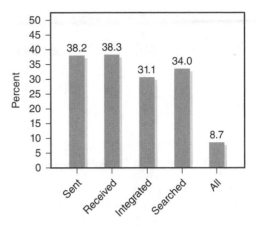

FIGURE 3.4 Percentage of office-based physicians who sent, received, integrated, or searched for patient health information electronically in the U.S.

Data from the Centers for Disease Control, National Center for Health Statistics, National Electronic Health Records Survey, 2015.

This should not be an either/or proposition: financial documentation *and* ease of use *and* opportunities for inclusion of patients in the entry of data and management of their care *and* data analytics *and* new user interface applications (e.g., portals and mobile applications) should be emphasized and valued by teams leading HIS. These types of embellishments of the foundational EHR systems add value and satisfaction to health professionals and consumers using the systems and help address the frustration they might feel over pressures to make sure all clinical actions are documented for the assistance of others, rather than for the improvement and support of clinical processes. This is the true and original vision for EHR systems. Power dynamics historically active in an organization will reveal themselves in the use of EHR systems, just like anything else going on in that institution. For example, if the financial disciplines dominate, the culture will insist that finances dominate the priorities attached to the use of HIS (a hefty investment of money, time, and energies). Helping HIS to thrive is much more like a blending of multiple perspectives into the fabric of the systems rather than the technical whizz-bang of earlier imaginings of EHR systems.

🔍 CASE EXAMPLE: INTEROPERABILITY

In health care, interoperability is the ability of different information technology systems and software applications to communicate, exchange data, and use the information that has been exchanged. The industry is diligently striving toward a state of interoperability, where patient data is securely and efficiently shared or made available as needed. Healthcare integrations help reduce duplicative services, lower costs, and improve patient satisfaction. It is important to understand distinctions between a few related terms that are sometimes used interchangeably: interoperability, integration, and interface.

Interoperability is used to describe the general state of integration and data sharing among parties in the healthcare domain. For example, The Office of the National Coordinator for Health Information Technology (ONC) (2017) published a report that is referred to as the Nationwide Interoperability Roadmap. **Integration** is used to describe the connectivity and sharing of healthcare data between separate systems within an organization or within a limited geographic area. For example, you might say, "ABC Hospital is well integrated. They have interface connections with local practices, the state's Health Information Exchange (HIE), a reference lab, and they boast high utilization of their patient portal." The most basic term used when discussing healthcare interoperability is **interface**. An interface is a single connection typically used to convey one specific type of message between two HIS systems or trading partners. For example, when a new patient receives care at a practice and their demographic and insurance information is entered into the office's practice management system, an interface from that system to the EHR system helps create the patient's record to hold their clinical information from other healthcare facilities, such as a hospital or emergency room. See the following chart for a visual representation of interoperability, integration, and interfacing.

Integration improves the efficiency of the healthcare system: at the heart of healthcare interoperability is the concept of **standardization**. Simply, the industry has (in theory, at least) agreed to a set of standards. Health Level Seven International (HL7) is one of the largest and most influential organizations "dedicated to providing a comprehensive framework and related standards for the exchange, integration, sharing, and retrieval of electronic health information that supports clinical practice and the management, delivery and evaluation of health services." (Health Level Seven International, n.d.).

Examples of healthcare interoperability follow:

- A pediatrician's office electronically sends patient immunization information to a state registry.
- A radiology report is sent from a diagnostic imaging center's Radiology Information System (RIS) to a patient's online health portal.
- A patient's clinical summary is sent via an HIE from a physician's office to a hospital emergency room across town.
- Data collected from a patient's wearable device, such as a smart watch, are then sent to a health insurance company's underwriting system.
- A bi-directional integration in which electronic orders are sent from a provider's EHR to a laboratory, which then sends back a result report once the tests are complete.

Let us discuss the lab integration example in greater detail. Interfaces with laboratories are one of the most common types of integrations in health care today. This is because blood chemistry tests are one of the most common tools used by clinicians to assess a patient's health. While some providers may have the necessary equipment "in house," it is common to refer patients to the lab of a local hospital, or perhaps a neighborhood patient service center of a national laboratory organization. The use of electronic interfaces improves the quality of the transaction, reduces the likelihood of an error, and is understood to be more efficient than printing a paper lab requisition and handing it to the patient (who often loses it or forgets to bring it to the lab appointment). When a doctor's office is integrated with a lab, they simply select the tests they want from a list, (essentially a menu of available thing to order) and click send. Seconds later the order is received in the Laboratory Information System (LIS). The phlebotomist will know exactly what to do when the patient arrives. Once the lab test is complete, the result is instantly communicated to the ordering provider for their review. Often times it is simultaneously shared with the patient via their healthcare portal.

Compare that experience to the way things used to be. For example, normal lab results might have been sent via postal mail, or perhaps they were faxed. For an urgent order or result that requires immediate attention (e.g., a child testing positive for Lyme disease) they might have called the provider's office to make sure the test results were known ASAP. (Calling to report urgent results is still commonplace today, to complement the electronically transmitted report.)

To help appreciate healthcare interoperability, and more specifically the HL7 standard, think of an envelope used to mail a letter via the U.S. Postal Service. The upper-left corner is where you should find the sender's name. The upper-right corner is reserved for the stamp. The recipient's info, right in the center, should include details such as City, State, and Zip Code.

With HL7, specific data elements are required or expected to be in a particular place inside of each message. If the data are missing or incorrect, the message will likely not reach its intended destination. Below are sample messages pertaining to a lab order and result.

Order Message (Sent the Provider's EHR)

```
MSH|^~\&||ABCPractice|||20060307110114||ORM^O01|MSGID20060307110114|P|2.3
PID|||12001||Jones^Joseph||19000101|M|||123 FakeSt.^^San Diego^CA^92122^USA||||||
PV1||O|OP^PAREG^||||2342^Doctor^Fake|||OP|||||||||2|||||||||||||||||||||||20060307110111|
ORC|NW|20060307110114
OBR|1|20060307110114||962^Basic Metabolic Panel|||20060307110114
```

It is a bit cryptic, but from this message we can see that a Basic Metabolic Panel has been ordered for patient Joseph Jones. Notice the "PID" to the far left of the patient's name. That tells us (and the computers processing these messages) that we are in the Patient Identification (PID) section of the message.

Result Message (Sent by LIS)

```
MSH|^~\&||XYZLab|LAB||20060308110514||ORU^O01|MSGID20060307|P|2.3
PID|||12001||Jones^Joe||19000101|M|||123 FakeSt.^^San Diego^CA^92122^USA||||||
PV1||O|OP^PAREG^||||2342^Doctor^Fake|||OP|||||||||2|||||||||||||||||||||||20060307110111|
OBR|1|20060307110114||962^Basic Metabolic Panel|||20060307110114
OBX|1|NM|1001^Glucose|82|MG/DL|70-110||||F
OBX|2|NM|1002^BUN|9|MG/DL|10-26||||F
```

The complete result is not shown here, because it is quite long, but hopefully you get the idea.

The OBX segments (observation/result, one of several types of HL7 message segments used to transmit patient clinical data) of the messages contain the values that correspond to each test component, along with their reference ranges. The "F" at the end signifies that that is a final test result.

Do you notice anything different about the bold fields in the result message? The patient's name is listed as "Joe" rather than "Joseph" as it was in the order. Perhaps the patient gave his nickname when he showed up at the lab. The EHR should be smart enough to know that is the same person, but in all likelihood this lab result did not make it to the patient's chart and is instead waiting for someone from the doctor's staff to work through the error log in their system and make the determination that "yes, in this instance Joe and Joseph are the same person." That user can then reconcile the seemingly erroneous lab result. From this example, for one lab test, one can begin to appreciate the complexity and detail involved in major interfaces, integrations, and interoperability

(continues)

🔍 CASE EXAMPLE: INTEROPERABILITY   (continued)

efforts accomplished by information technology professionals each and every day. This example also displays the importance of the HL7 standard to HIS capabilities.

True interoperability in health care is far from achieved, though vast improvements have been made in the last decade alone.

Layered upon the need to facilitate interoperability is the need for patient engagement as the key to unlock the door to effective care management in the value-based healthcare environment, all of which makes population health management possible. Although foundational EHR systems are implemented in the majority of healthcare provider organizations according to the important benchmarking research done every few years by Adler-Milstein, DesRoches, and Jha, what is not clear is the degree to which the providers who have not adopted the EHR systems will proceed now that the program's penalties have kicked in. The question is, "will the Meaningful Use (MU) penalties have an effect?" As of 2016, over 60 percent of U.S. office-based health providers have participated in HITECH Meaningful Use Incentive program for EHR adoption by demonstrating MU of certified EHR systems (The Office of the National Coordinator for Health Information Technology, 2016). The question remains, what will the approximately 40 percent of physicians' experience who have not participated, or who have not complied fully with the Meaningful Use (MU) thresholds as penalties kick in? What has this program created for the practice of medicine and delivery of ambulatory care as a result of trying to provide incentives to stimulate the adoption of EHR systems? (**FIGURES 3.5** and **3.6**)

Technology is not the sole source of progress in widespread EHR systems usage. Additional gain will come from addressing deeper sociotechnical issues surrounding EHR system usage, taking into consideration the interaction between people and technology in workflow and process design. At this point in the evolution of EHR systems, physicians and other clinical professionals are frustrated by the amount of time spent doing clerical work, mostly on behalf of reimbursement-related documentation requirements, or some other need for those outside the clinical care process. The time spent making sure these documentation needs are met intrudes on clinicians' face-to-face time with patients and

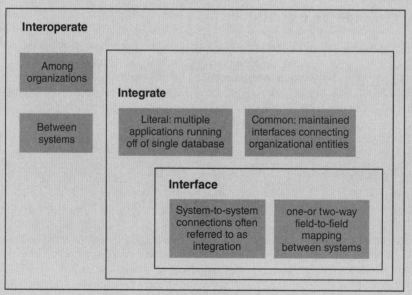

FIGURE 3.5 Hierarchy of data-sharing mechanisms.
Based on Patrick Zummo's Integration Diagram.

with the art, science, and intuitive aspects of practicing medicine, nursing, or other clinical disciplines. The financial implications and reimbursement requirements related to electronic documentation put pressure on clinicians to spend more time doing this data entry. Clinicians most satisfied with use of EHR systems are in settings where it is not just the technology advancements that are emphasized, but also the teamwork, training, workflow design, and other sociotechnical interactions that are supported (Stanford Medicine, 2018). These more subtle activities are often underemphasized, if not due to cultural priorities and perspective then due to the leadership, effort, time, expense, and expertise needed to do so. Most implementations come to life when a respected clinical leader or leaders get involved and devote significant energies to leading the organization in capitalizing not just on billing and reimbursement requirements, but also on clinical design, process, training, and outcomes. Rightly or wrongly, other powerful influencers of quality are in active play, parties that deal with business priorities and do not take clinical quality or patient safety into consideration. For example, merger and acquisition risks patient safety, as described by Masterson and warned by the medical community (Mastersen, 2018).

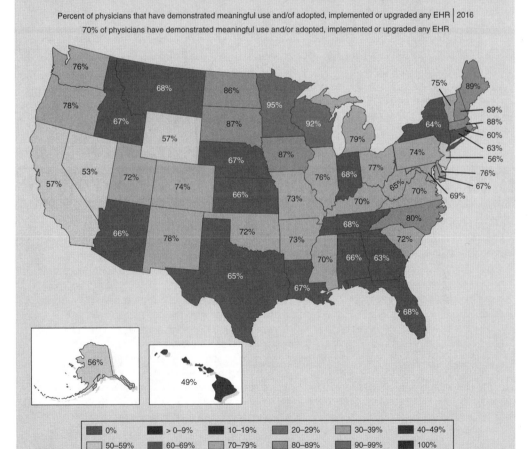

FIGURE 3.6 Percent of physicians who have demonstrated MU and/or adopted, implemented, or upgraded and EHR (2016).

Reproduced from Office of the National Coordinator for Health Information Technology. 'Office-based Health Care Professionals Participating in the CMS EHR Incentive Programs,' Health IT Quick-Stat #44. dashboard.healthit.gov/quickstats/pages/FIG-Health-Care-Professionals-EHR-Incentive-Programs.php. August 2017.

Case Example by Patrick Zummo.

🔎 CASE EXAMPLE: PUTTING CLINICAL PROCESSES FIRST

An EHR system focused on reducing points of friction for clinicians… Can it be? A company called Elation Health is gaining traction with a new approach.

The daughter and son of a Canadian general practitioner used to work in their dad's office, helping out during summers and weekends. They learned about clinical processes without the burden of charge capture, billing, claims processing, accounts receivable, and reimbursement processes, due to Canada's national health system (single payer). Fast forward 10 years and those high school students are college graduates working in Silicon Valley in tech and teaching economics at the university level. They saw what EHR systems did in U.S. primary care provider practices through the lens of their father's experience. This disjunction—and the problems it caused in the U.S.— propelled the siblings to build an EHR system mimicking the clinical workflows and processes that they experienced as kids working in their father's office in Canada.

They now have hundreds of customers and thousands of providers networked into their virtual EHR that was developed to: (1) take out all points of friction in the workflows, (2) integrate with practice management systems, and (3) work differently than a charge capture system dressed up as an EHR. Their motto is to "build tools physicians love." The system can be learned in an hour and creates a virtual team of providers based on the needs of the patient, unrestricted by the four walls of the organization that controls and "owns" the EHR system.

🔎 CASE EXAMPLE: CHANGE OF CONTROL CALAMITY

A large-scale Catholic multihospital system had just completed the selection of a new patient accounting system when the vendor offered a deep, year-end price discount for the system. What luck! The project was planned, staffed, and underway, expected to be ready to begin implementations by the end of the year. But progress was slow, and the vendor personnel weren't behaving as one would expect: rather than pushing to meet their incented project milestones and implementation dates, activity levels were sluggish, with delays and rescheduled meetings a regular occurrence. How could this be? What was going on? Well, six months into the project, *whammo*. A call from the vendor executives let the healthcare organization know that the vendor had been acquired by a non-healthcare IT company (a deal that had been in the works when the system was sold to the healthcare organization). The acquiring company was a credit card transaction company that had decided it wanted to get into the booming healthcare market, and so it bought a major patient accounting system vendor and its customers along with it. Progress on the patient accounting system implementation, slow to date, ground to a halt.

Having done its due diligence, the Catholic healthcare system had written an assignment clause in the contract, which would cover almost all types of changes of control. This would release it from the contract and hopefully help save millions of dollars and give it options if a change of control occurred during the life of the contract. However, as the acquiring company's lawyers pointed out, the transaction was a stock transfer and not a "purchase"—the assignment clause did not apply. So, the health system was stuck. To add salt to the wound, the new owner company didn't want to continue to use the software it had acquired: the executives just wanted the customer base. The company decided it would develop a new patient accounting system and all its newly acquired customers would have to transition over. Luckily, the health system had a well-supported internally developed patient accounting system that had served it excellently over many years; it was able to just continue to use this accounting system while everything else shook out. After all, it takes years to develop an industrial-strength patient accounting system, robust enough to support a complex set of clients and health systems. Alas, the years of development turned out to be harder than the new owner company could withstand. So, after about two years of struggling to develop this new system, the company made another decision to abandon the move into health care altogether. All of its clients were left hanging in the balance through this ordeal. In the case of the Catholic health system, it was able to continue to use its in-house system, eventually replacing it years later with another vendor's system. The lesson? Buyers beware. Do your due diligence, and always have a fallback plan for circumstances involving change of control, since the world of vendors and software systems can be treacherous.

Current HIS Initiatives

The most significant change that healthcare providers, payers, agencies, and vendors are grappling with is that reimbursement is changing: the industry is shifting away from fee-for-service and toward **value-based care**. Factors that play into this shift include changes in health care for disease management and population health management. HIS must adapt to this new framework and reimbursement methodology.

As described in the previous sections, numerous forces drive change. Change is upon HIS, a rapidly evolving field, essential to healthcare services as they exist today, to the advancement and improvement in health care, and to creation of new knowledge in the many disciplines comprising health, medicine, and services delivery. Technological advancements, health information technology vendor and business forces, governmental regulations, politics, public health issues, and good as well as ambitious motivations are shaping health care's future. Let us take a look at some of the larger categories of influence—the players that are shaping the transition from fee-for-service to value-based care—today.

Vendors

Vendors of software, hardware, services and analytics have commercial agendas. And no wonder. The gap between current and necessary competencies in healthcare providers stimulates activity, commerce, and profits in massive amounts—but all of this misses the mark for truly useful HIS.

Levels of technical innovations and the start-up companies attempting to bring them to market are similar to the .com period in the late 1990s when the Internet went mainstream. The results of this explosion of commercial activity will no doubt continue to be similar to the .com bust of 2000. Some make it, and most do not. Of course, this activity is juxtaposed to and intertwined with the for-profit HIS giants—Epic Systems, Cerner Corporation, Meditech, Greenway, and more—that have survived the big-fish-eat-little-fish process of consolidation over the last decade. As of 2017, 365 EHR systems comprised the ambulatory market and yet the consolidation process, which can take decades, is underway. The effects of these vendor dynamics reach far into health care. For instance, as EHR vendor consolidation occurs, those providers and organizations with each vendor product are vulnerable to their EHR system provider going out of business or being acquired by another. As vendors struggle, perhaps on their way to being acquired or going out of business, provider customers are vulnerable to the instability this causes. Disruption to continuity of support to customers is highly likely when changes of control occur for vendors (Mastersen, 2018).

One memorable example of this is the change of control of a patient accounting system at a national Catholic health system, which caused great risk to the financial health of the organization and to the critical health care it provided. If not for the in-house developed and supported patient financial and general financial systems, it certainly would have met with disaster. (See the adjacent Case Example.)

The examples in the adjacent case example provide evidence that the business models of current players in HIS, such as software vendors and consultants, have been fueled by regulatory imperative and financial reimbursement and incentives, and have grown significantly to become huge and wealthy corporations that have become accustomed to charge exorbitant prices. They make huge profits, all on the backs of healthcare organizations and providers. This includes enormous paychecks for vendor executives: Epic CEO Judy Faulkner's net worth clocks in at $2.8 billion and Cerner's former CEO and co-founder Neal Patterson earned $6,599,410, or 102 times the $65,000 median pay for employees at his company (Monegain, 2015). This is not sustainable. It may have been possibly during the big push to get EHR systems implemented as part of the HITECH Act, but most of the foundational work has been accomplished. Now, the difficult work is refining the user interface and streamlining workflows. For the vendors and consultants, the market they have helped create and now depend upon is a market that is saturated and consolidating. At this point vendors are trying to figure out how to survive and how to adapt.

Government

In the U.S., requirements of reimbursement and attendant regulations not only force change, but also shape the forms and types of healthcare services available to patients. The old saying "follow the money" applies here. The history of health services modalities

in this country and others is driven by the types of funding available, from the days of the Hill-Burton Act of 1946 for construction of hospital beds following World War II, to fee-for-service, to indemnity-type insurance driving a steep healthcare cost curve, to digital health codes intended to reach outside institutions to connect providers and patients in new ways. One has only to look at the differences between national health systems and their funding mechanisms to recognize the power of the methods of payment on the size and specifics of health services available to citizenry of various nations. The force of reimbursement methods takes numerous forms, including the types and content of HIS available to patients and providers in hospitals and clinics. Unfortunately, the complexity of U.S. regulatory and reimbursement processes also adds cost to the system and has created negative effects on quality, like the lack of reimbursement for preventive care historically that has driven the vast majority of resources to in-patient or in-institutional care and de-emphasized prevention and primary care. Current HIS are as much "charge-capture" systems as systems supporting clinical excellence, with estimates ranging from 30 to 44 percent for administrative cost and waste in the U.S. This influence on healthcare organizations, patients, and providers has shaped health care as we know it today.

HIS requirements of current regulatory changes are complex, but are trying to re-focus on the shift from fee-for-service to value-based reimbursement. Changing from one deeply rooted system to another is much harder than a fresh start and building a new system from the ground up, of course. Add to that, volatility due to politics, regulatory adjustments, government contracts such as Department of Defense (DOD) and the VA, changes or uncertainty in massive programs such as Medicare, and a change is that more difficult. HIS play an important role here, even as they are swept up in regulatory changes since the documentation of meeting those requirements must be created and captured in those systems.

Additionally, requirements such as public health priorities, including guidelines from the Centers for Disease Control (CDC), must be monitored and best efforts to prioritize and address within the delivery of health care to communities served by health systems and clinics. For example, carrying out the initiatives associated with 2017 CDC guidelines—including Zika and pregnancy, antibiotic resistance, HPV and cancer, prescription drug overdose, global health security, and rapid response to outbreaks—is hefty work for many, if not most, organizations. These types of initiatives require leadership, investment of time, effort, change, and programmatic implementation. All would require the support of agile HIS that allow for necessary capabilities including needed data collection, detection, measurement, analysis, programs, reporting and responsiveness through the variety of requirements of providing health services and appropriate medical and preventive care.

Several seminal laws and research reports have marked the U.S. government's current involvement in the evolution of HIS activities and in response to the unsustainable escalation of healthcare costs. These important elements include the following:

- The **Health Insurance Portability and Accountability Act (HIPAA)** of 1996
- The HMD reports *To Err Is Human* and *Crossing the Quality Chasm*
- The HMD report *Health IT and Patient Safety: Building Safer Systems for Better Care*
- President George W. Bush's and President Barack Obama's healthcare initiatives
- The American Recovery and Reinvestment Act (ARRA) of 2009: Title IV—Health Information Technology for Economic and Clinical Health (HITECH) Act
- The Affordable Care Act (ACA) of 2010

⌕ CASE EXAMPLE: THE ETHOS OF U.S.-BASED HIS

The implications of the fee-for-service, volume-based reimbursement methods and the need for change to value-based care goes well below the surface, all the way down to the "ethos" built into software. About 20 years ago, at the beginning of the rise of EHR systems from commercial vendors in the U.S., the chief financial executive from Great Britain's National Health Service (NHS) visited the U.S. to explore commercial EHR systems as a possibility for the U.K. During that trip, he paid a visit to speak to the chief information officer (CIO) at a national health system in the U.S. The reason for the visit was to talk about the NHS representative's research into clinical systems. The conversation centered on early EHR systems from U.S. vendors since the U.S. had commercial products that the NHS was interested in considering for implementation in Great Britain. There was a robust dialogue, enlightening both parties, as the needs and priorities of Great Britain (single payer with a small percentage of private pay) and the U.S. (fee-for-service and derivations thereof) were compared. As the conversation wound down, he leaned forward and said, "What is most striking to me and surprising, is the ethos embedded inside these U.S. systems is not clinical; it's financial." The CIO paused and wanted to protest, but realized she couldn't. He was right. We still struggle with this issue today, 20 years later. The ethos behind the programs and software capabilities in U.S. EHR systems is "charge capture" and documentation for financial reimbursement purposes. This dearly taxes the time and patience of providers and clinicians. We are well-served as we go forward to be aware of this trait of U.S. systems as we transition from volume-based to value-based care and make room for EHR systems that are truly clinical in nature, not financial.

The Health Insurance Portability and Accountability Act

Initially introduced to ensure that individuals' insurance would be portable across states and jobs, HIPAA had far greater impact through its "administrative simplification" (Title II) elements. HIPAA requirements for **electronic data interchange (EDI)** anticipated the need for data standards for electronic claims in health care, in addition to seeing that electronic records required standards for privacy and security. These standards, originally targeting the Medicare claims processes, introduced far-reaching administrative simplification attributes, including the following:

- Standards (the first mandate for electronic HIS standards for data transmission protocols)
- Requirement that Medicare providers and health plans participate
- Privacy and security of **protected health information (PHI)**
- Preempted state laws, thus reducing fragmentation across the U.S.
- Imposed penalties for noncompliance, giving these regulations and laws teeth (Centers for Medicare & Medicaid Services, n.d.)

Title II Administrative Simplification Act

The Title II Administrative Simplification Act aimed to improve the U.S. health system's efficiency by introducing standards governing the use and communication of healthcare information. The rules include protection of identifiable PHI and apply to all provider and payer organizations, called "covered entities" by the legislation. Covered entities include health plans, healthcare billing services, and healthcare providers (hospitals, clinics, and physician practices) that transmit healthcare data, submit claims, and receive reimbursement from Medicare. While the scope of these regulations refers to organizations participating in Medicare, the impact reaches far beyond Medicare to virtually all healthcare entities, because Medicare standards and practices set the benchmark standards for all payers. HIPAA's administrative simplification rules include the following:

- Privacy Rule: Regulates the use and disclosure of PHI, implemented in 2003. It mandates that a person's medical information with identifying information attached to it cannot be used, viewed, or shared by anyone in a healthcare organization other than a healthcare professional or business practitioner who has the need to look at that information for the purposes of taking care of or addressing the business needs of that person. The privacy rule applies to PHI on any medium—electronic or paper.
- Transactions and Code Sets Rule: Establishes EDI standards for healthcare claims. Claims sent to payers for reimbursement, and subsequent reimbursement to the providers, must be sent electronically in a certain technical format, standardizing electronic claims processing and thus making it more efficient.
- Security Rule: Defines administrative, physical, and technical security safeguards. This rule establishes specifics for ensuring secure transmission of data through systems and over the Internet, so that even though HIS and the Internet are used, the data traveling on these networks and in these systems are secure.
- Unique Identifiers Rule: Establishes National Provider Identifier (NPI) standards for providers. This rule establishes unique identifiers for providers, ensuring accuracy of electronic provider payments.
- Enforcement Rule: Defines civil financial penalties for HIPAA violations. If providers violate HIPAA rules, then they face significant financial and other penalties.

HIPAA rules and regulations have set the bar for government participation in defining the way forward in automating healthcare administrative and clinical processes while protecting individuals' privacy and allowing for public health issues to be addressed to prevent disease, injury, or disability. Driven initially by the need to ensure portability by establishing standards for electronic claims transactions for Medicare, HIPAA standards for electronic data transmission, privacy, and security of PHI have redefined HIS's and the U.S. healthcare system's norms and practices.

ARRA and HITECH

Responding to the findings outlined in the *To Err Is Human* and *Crossing the Quality Chasm* reports, the federal government established two waves of policies intended to encourage the implementation of HIS in the U.S. health system. With added emphasis on improving quality and cost-effectiveness in health care, the federal government identified the implementation of HIS initiatives as a priority, particularly the implementation of EHRs for all U.S. patients by 2014, first by President George W. Bush and then by President Barack Obama.

President Bush signed several initiatives into law to provide "seed grants" to fund pilot projects testing various uses of IT in healthcare settings. One of these initiatives was the Medicare Prescription Drug Improvement and Modernization Act of 2003; it included provisions for the development of standards for electronic prescribing, an initial step in the implementation of EHRs. This move precipitated the establishment of a Commission on Systemic Interoperability to plan the establishment of technical interoperability standards for e-prescribing systems (O'Sullivan, Chaikind, Tilson, Boulanger, & Morgan, 2004). Also, under executive authority of President Bush, the Office of the National Coordinator of Health Information Technology (ONC) within the Department of Health and Human Services (HHS) was established.

Next, also under the administration of President Bush, came Executive Order 13335 of April 27, 2004, titled "Incentives for the Use of Health Information Technology and Establishing the Position of the National Health Information Technology Coordinator," as well as the "President's Health Information Technology Plan," calling for a 10-year plan to get EHRs online for all Americans (Thompson & Brailer, 2004; White House Office of the Press Secretary, 2004). These national policy interventions built upon other major national initiatives, including the Consolidated Health Informatics initiative in 2003 involving HHS, the Department of Defense, and Veterans Affairs, which established the goal of uniform standards for electronic exchange of clinical health information across all federal healthcare entities.

While these national and presidential initiatives provided encouragement and incentives for hospital and physician providers to invest the money and time in the daunting task of automating their organizations and practices using HIS, the stimulus with the greatest impact has been ARRA, the legislation that includes the HITECH Act. This act greatly expanded the resources available for HITECH activities. First, it created a strategic plan for a nationwide interoperable HIS, a plan that is required by this act to be updated annually. Second, it called for a leadership structure consisting of two committees to advise the coordinator: a Health Information Policy Committee and a Health Information Standards Committee. As part of the $787 billion ARRA stimulus package, the HITECH Act requires the government to lead the development of standards that allow for nationwide electronic exchange and use of health information to improve the quality and coordination of care.

Through the HITECH Act, the government invested about $36 billion in HIT infrastructure and Medicare and Medicaid incentives to encourage doctors and hospitals to implement certified EHR systems and use HIS to electronically exchange patients' health information. The Congressional Budget Office (CBO) calculated that this investment will save the government $10 billion and will generate additional savings throughout the health sector through improvements in quality of care and care coordination, reductions in medical errors, and duplicative care. The HITECH Act also strengthens federal privacy and security laws to protect identifiable health information from misuse as the healthcare sector increases the use of HIS. The CBO (2009) estimates that as a result of this legislation, approximately 90 percent of physicians and 70 percent of hospitals will be using comprehensive EHR systems by 2020. These standards are having a seismic effect on vendor products for EHRs and other HIS software, which must now meet these standards or else face quick elimination from the marketplace because they will not qualify organizations to receive their incentives based on meeting these standards.

HITECH established "MU" criteria for EHR implementations that have had to be met for qualified hospitals and physicians (provider organizations) to receive incentive payments (for Medicare patients) since the HITECH Act of 2009, implemented starting in 2012. **Meaningful Use (MU)** criteria, the features,

functions, and capabilities of EHRs, are shown to improve care in three stages of advancing criteria. The MU criteria measure EHR system adoption of these capabilities, such as the percentage use within an organization of EHR capabilities such as CPOE, as a way of encouraging EHR adoption. Specifics laid out in the Stages 1, 2, and 3 criteria (**FIGURE 3.7**), Stage 3 then replaced by Medicare Access and CHIP Reauthorization Act of 2015 (MACRA), result in incentive payments to qualifying providers receiving increases in Medicare payments if qualifying providers and hospitals meet these criteria. Eventually, if these criteria are not met, a penalty is levied in the form of reduced Medicare reimbursement for services provided by those noncompliant hospitals and physicians. Hospitals will lose percentages of their annual updated reimbursements from Medicare under the **diagnosis related groups (DRGs)** system (which is used for calculating payments for various conditions and treatments). These increases (incentives) or reductions (penalties) in Medicare payments will significantly impact the financial well-being of these provider organizations, as Medicare patients account for a major proportion of patients and participation in Medicare is the only realistic course for the vast majority of provider organizations to remain viable.

Stage 1 Data capture and sharing	Stage 2 Advanced clinical processes	Stage 3 Improved outcomes
• Capture health information in a standardized format • Track key clinical conditions • Support care coordination • Report clinical quality measures and public health information • Engage patients and families	• Increasing rigorous health information exchange (HIE) • Improved clinical decision support • Electronically transmitted patient summaries • Increased control of data by patients	• Improving quality, safety, and efficiency • Decision support for high-priority conditions • Self-management tools for patients • Comprehensive data through HIEs • Improving population health

FIGURE 3.7 MU Stages 1, 2, and 3.

The HITECH Act paved the way for increased use of EHR system functionality, along with increased demand associated with the Affordable Care Act of 2010 (ACA), and made available major training grants to stimulate the establishment of university- and community college-based HIS training programs as a means of addressing the current shortage of approximately 60,000 HIS professionals needed to support implementation of EHR systems and other HIS activities called for in the HITECH program. All of this infusion of EHR systems and other HIS features and capabilities such as quality reporting, the beginnings of patient engagement, and interoperability into hospitals, practices, clinics, federally qualified health centers, and other clinical settings provides a foundation for what is the longer-term goal of value-based care and population health management.

Security

Other looming changes for patients as well as providers of health care stem from the security of systems and by extension, institutions and identity. This issue reaches into the realms of artificial intelligence (AI) and the monetary capitalization of data by insurance companies.

First, security of EHR systems goes far beyond around the boundaries of HIPAA, which only covers institutional personal health data. For example, AI is being used by insurance agencies to harvest scads of data on people from social media and other data sources to predict risk associated with personal habits of those people, then using that predictive information to increase their insurance rates, exclude them based on assumptions from coverage based on where they live or what their demographics are, and restrict access to care

🔍 CASE EXAMPLE: THE CRIPPLINGLY HIGH COST OF SOFTWARE

Aging technology that has been in place in many healthcare organizations for decades is expensive to maintain and even more expensive to replace. This challenges the capacity and financial means of even well-managed institutions that are good stewards of their resources. In fact, hospitals and health systems have experienced financial catastrophe due the high-prices and costs of acquiring and maintaining EHR systems and HIS technology. Examples include:

- University of Texas MD Anderson experienced a $160.5 million decrease in financial position in 2016, a 56.6 percent decrease in adjusted income over seven months, attributed by the health system to its Epic EHR system implementation;
- Partners Healthcare in Boston experienced a $200 million reduction in financial capacity over a three-year period due to expenses associated with its Epic EHR system implementation;
- Brigham and Women's Hospital in Boston experienced $27 million in unplanned expenses more than the $47 million planned for its Epic EHR system implementation;
- Sutter Health in Sacramento experienced a 31.5 percent decrease in operating income while it rolled out its Epic system, ultimately facing increases in operating expenses from $9.7 billion in 2014 to $10.7 billion in 2015; and
- During their Epic EHR system implementation, Allegheny Health System had sustained a net operating income loss $10.9 million greater than the projected loss of $9.7 million for the first quarter of the year in 2016 due to greater than expected one-time implementation costs.

Of course, many of these one-time costs have a long-term sustained cost for maintenance and on-going support, training, and operations (Jayanthi & Ellison, 2016).

based on algorithms that may or may not be correct across a population or stratum in order to reduce expenditures and increase profits of the insurer (Allen, 2018).

This type of activity puts patients and providers at a severe disadvantage in a number of ways. First, the insurance companies are not playing a fair game. They are using other data to make assumptions, often discriminating or generalizing incorrectly. Second, they are negotiating with providers to set rates based on assumptions that may or may not be true, and certainly armed with data beyond what the provider has to work with (or even *would* work with, since most community-, religious-, and not-for-profit-based health systems and providers care for patients regardless of their ability to pay).

▶ HIS: A Key for Change?

Given this background, what does HIS mean to health care? Is HIS just a collection of computers and technologies used by those practicing modern medicine and delivering healthcare services to automate their work? Or is HIS a transformative force that can radically alter and improve the work processes by which health care is delivered? The answer to both questions is "yes." HIS can both speed up existing processes and enable brand new ways of delivering health care to people. It is also important, as we delve into the complex world of HIS, to always ask the question, "What are the benefits and what are the risks of adopting any new technology?" New and computerized is not always better than how things have been done traditionally, if they have been done safely and in a well-organized fashion.

Thus, when we move to computerize health care, we must constantly ask the question, "What are we trying to accomplish and why?" We must evaluate whether we have achieved what we set out to and make necessary adjustments along the way as we make sweeping

changes throughout the U.S. health system, including computerizing our systems and processes. From the broadest perspective, the future of HIS in health care will entail the automation of processes we know and the adoption of new processes that have yet to be created. It is difficult to predict whether this transition will be truly disruptive or simply innovative, and to evaluate the difference between those two. The net effect of HIS, however, must be positive—the health of people depends on it.

It is time for HIS to evolve to the next level of cost-effectiveness, ease of use, and living up to their original promise. Due to high costs and low effectiveness of historic models of fee-for-service reimbursement, the focus of providers and government agencies is shifting to value-based reimbursement, patient engagement, and other means of improving the cost-quality ratio, also known as value. The hope is that this shift will better address prevention, primary care, and avoidance of chronic illness and behaviorally driven problems, as well as improve health care overall. The promise of HIS to make value-based care possible must now be realized; however, we have some serious work to do to bring these promises to fruition. As a baseline requirement, healthcare settings have rightly placed HIS implementation high on their priority lists. This is because patients, physicians and nurses, managers of these healthcare organizations, the government, public health organizations, policy makers, and quality improvement organizations have an extreme sense of urgency about implementing HIS due to reimbursement incentives for EHR implementation, as well as a means of improving the quality and efficiency of health care.

Alleviating Clerical Work

Assuming continued positive progress on the EHR system adoption front, when done properly, this computerization of clinical tasks relieves health professionals of many mundane manual tasks and improves efficiencies and documentation for reimbursement and analytics purposes. However, evidence is building that providers are frustrated and that physicians and patients feel the benefits of EHR systems do not outweigh the detractors (Meyerhoefer, 2018). The negative experience of physicians today is in part due to the additional two hours of documentation for one hour of patient contact. The complexity of EHR documentation today is exhausting physicians' and other clinical professionals' energy (Verghese, 2018).

▶ Population Health Management and HIS

Population health management takes a holistic view of health and care, and provides needed health services for a defined group or population of patients, along with acceptance of financial risk and clinical responsibility by a health system or group of providers, in its simplest definition. What does this mean for healthcare organizations and HIS? For organizations, population health management requires a turn from fee-for-service reimbursement and structures: organizations are no longer paid for the *volume* of services provided, but for the *value* as calculated by evolving methods of measuring quality for cost, while meeting of the health needs of the population they serve according to quality and outcome measures. Programs vary by providers, programs, and payers involved.

HIS plays a key role in enabling successful population health management. Essential strategies provide insight into types of HIS capabilities needed to identify, provide services, manage, and evaluate key program metrics, based on needs of patients belonging to that defined population. Central capabilities include: identification and definition of the population, patients, and program metrics;

data coordination and integration across sites along the continuum of care as well as outside the institutional setting; business and clinical intelligence, with analytics helping to guide decisions; care management; and patient and caregiver engagement.

Value-Based Care

What is value-based care and why has this term grabbed hold in health care? One would think, on a logical level, that of course care would be value-based, or valuable. Why would such a term be needed? The sad truth is that this terminology is needed, because many in health care have lost sight of the core of what health care is about—the interaction and relationship between patient and provider. Instead, with the fee-for-service and resulting volume-based reimbursement incentives and the many silos of activity in a complex health system, entrepreneurs and opportunists have followed the money, made fortunes, and lost sight of mission. The dollars are so great in health care, adjacent markets such as pharmaceuticals, biotech, mobile devices, consulting, computer systems, imaging modalities, home care, long-term care, and other massive components of the healthcare industry, each unto themselves a submarket, have been fueled by fee-for-service reimbursements. It isn't a stretch to see how perspective could be lost amongst those who might have an altruistic motive initially, but get swept away with the pressures and bounty of big business. Value? Value is in the eye of the beholder at a certain point.

So, providers, researchers, health economists, policy analysts, and others who study the system as they slice and dice the data point out that the cost per unit is exorbitant, no matter how you look at it, and it all adds up to an unaffordable bill for health care for people who end up with the bill, whether through taxes, health insurance premiums, out-of-pocket costs, or higher prices of goods and services from companies who pay their number one supplier (health insurance companies) for their employees' health insurance. In contrast with the fee-for-service reimbursement method, value-based means the tests and procedures and services delivered to the patient create an improved outcome, in such a way that the benefits outweigh the costs. Value equals the ratio of quality or benefit to cost. Common sense tells us that it costs far less to keep a person healthy than to cure or manage a long-term illness once a patient is sick. Improving value means spending less to achieve better outcomes, and requires measuring success by measuring outcomes, rather than by measuring numbers of volume of procedures or tests completed.

Value-based care is most relevant now because, as previously stated, the U.S. has the highest costs per capita, and lowest outcomes of the Organisation for Economic Co-operation and Development (OECD) countries (The Organisation for Economic Co-operation and Development, 2017). The problem? High cost yielding poor outcomes. Compared to other countries, such as Italy, where the cost of care for patients with uncontrolled diabetes is less than half the cost of the average across OECD countries, the cost of such care in the U.S., multiplied by the numbers of patients involved, yields a health system that either can or cannot take care of its patients affordably. Considering the high incidence of chronic illness and the need for care coordination outside the institutional setting, the U.S. health system is not only challenged, but headed in the wrong direction as it struggles to reorient itself to a different way of acting and thinking.

HMD was correct with its four reasons for avoidable medical errors in health care. These themes or reasons bear repeating in the discussion of value-based care:

1. *The growing complexity of science and technology, with delays between innovation and implementation.* A good example of this as it relates to the use of HIS is technology-enabled capabilities that speed up

access to new information and evidence from the scientific process to those caring for patients, such as through clinical decision support systems as part of EHR systems. It is estimated that it takes 17 years for clinical evidence from clinical trials to make it into actual practice in healthcare institutions (Morris, Wooding, & Grant, 2011). This bears out the HMD's finding that the traverse from "research bench to bedside" is indeed a very long one, and that for innovation borne out by proper research to take such a long time to become part of clinical practice is indeed a problem that needs to be solved. HIS and technology is one way to improve this lag time, by conveying evidence and data-driven guidance more immediately through EHR systems and other technology-enabled systems to provide the right information to the right person, in the right format, within the right medium and channel, at the right time in the workflow. This concept has appeared for many years regarding the availability of properly placed information for clinical purposes, whether the record is paper or electronic. Technology has an opportunity to systematize the achievement of these Five Rights and improve the information capabilities for clinical decision support among other areas. In this case, the right information should be evidence-based, and based on a combination of guidelines and the actual data involving the patient within their condition and context. The information should also be delivered to the person who can act upon that information. The information should also be delivered in the right format to support the intervention needed. For example, a picture archiving and communication system (PACS) can provide needed information in the form of an image to a clinician in a format that enhances their ability to make a decision and act, rather than as a dictated and transcribed report that is delivered to the patient's chart many days after the radiology study was acquired. The right medium refers to the information getting to that right person via a conduit that makes the information most accessible for the needs of the situation, such as a smartphone vs. the clinical notes section of an EHR system for a stat result for a lab test. Many of us remember the note from a triage nurse buried in the nurses' notes section of the EHR system of the Texas hospital where a patient with the Ebola virus was sent home because the physician didn't have feasible visibility to that note when examining the patient (Khazan, 2014). Already, mature HIS systems are being shown to reduce hospital mortality (Lin, Jha, & Adler-Milstein, 2018).

2. *The increase in chronic illness burden with a system centered on acute illness.* The facts bear this dilemma out. Every day 10,000 people age into Medicare age, thus managing the chronic care needs of the growing population of Medicare-age individuals is of paramount importance in addressing today's cost and quality problems.

3. *The inadequate use of information technology*, especially in the legible and accurate transmission of data and information, advanced reminders and alerts to providers, clinical decision support, access to information by individuals involved in the patient's care, and other key features of ubiquitous information availability.

4. A *payment system that provides conflicting incentives and does not reward quality improvement.* The fee-for-service reimbursement system rewards increasing volume of care, measured by those procedures and tests that are codified into standard nomenclatures such as ICD-10 and CPT methodologies, originally devised to identify and count discrete activities as measurable data elements. This ability to count episodic events perpetuated the reimbursement system that has provided strong incentives for performing more of these measurable and reimbursable events, rather than performing care that might involve non-institutional interactions, prevention, education, and other less distinct activities. HIS systems enable the recalibrating of events and interventions by predicting health risks of individuals across a population and prioritizing activities targeted at avoiding deterioration of their health status, based on their data and evidence.

Value-Based Care in Action

Value-based care *versus* fee-for-service: what is it and what does it mean for healthcare organizations and provider, and what does it mean for HIS? What do providers do differently to achieve value-based care? They need to work in ways that improve quality while reducing cost, or, stated another way, improve outcomes more efficiently than ways learned and derived from the fee-for-service reimbursement system that rewards maximized volumes of justifiable medical services with payment and encourages an emphasis on productivity around those services to produce high incomes. Value-based care means providing proactive, comprehensive medical and behavioral care managed in such a way to enhance the overall outcomes and wellness for the patient (Tse, 2018).

By being able to proactively address healthcare activities that intervene in the progression of illness, before it advances to requiring intensive, in-patient or institutionally based care, we can slow the increases in avoidable episodic and acute healthcare expenditures as means of battling chronic illness. What do we achieve by reframing the problem and reorganizing our approach to it? We are able to be proactive and cost-effective. Today's overall health system in the U.S., according to outcomes measures compared between countries with similar means but different approaches, does not produce the types of clinical or cost outcomes we hope for or expect. What do healthcare providers lose through the status quo and the perpetuation of the fee-for-service approach and its systematized incentives, workflows, and remnants? We lose the ability to control costs and improve quality, and, most importantly, we lose the health of our population. What changes does this mean for healthcare organizations? It means thinking differently, first and foremost, and orienting our thoughts and actions to focus on the care and interventions that bring improvement in health outcomes in the population served by each institution and provider, versus thinking about efficiently delivering the highest volume of care and maximizing throughput. It means being able to proactively gather data, information, and evidence about patients by involving them and their families directly in the management of their health, learning about exposures and experiences of patients when they are not in the institutional setting, but in their daily lives through social determinants of health, and thus addressing a bigger picture of the true causes and effects of health as they influence the cost of healthcare

delivery. This harkens to the lessons and goals of the public health system, as incentives and methods align between healthcare delivery organizations and public health organizations through the concept and practice of population health management.

What changes must providers make to thrive? The key for providers to successfully navigating the transition to population health will be to transition to proactive management of comprehensive health care and wellness of patients and focusing on cost-effective health outcomes. What changes for patients? Patients will be more involved in defining their goals for health and in working directly with their providers in the management of their health and care. HIS enables direct connectivity when not face-to-face to make continuous care feasible and affordable. Suppliers of systems and services must adapt their product offerings to be flexible in stretching across the continuum of care and become the open enabler of secure, ubiquitous connectivity as needed for effective care based on patient needs to be provided. Hopefully the results will improve the outcomes as well as improve the value of every dollar spent on health care in the U.S.

Emphasizing Prevention and Care Management

Mature use of HIS will help restructure processes away from focus on acute episodic care (treating illnesses in a hospital-centric fashion) to the prevention of disease and care management (including chronic care management). This important shift toward value-based care requires horizontal integration (HIS systems can do this) vs. vertical emphasis of institutional care, resulting in silos of information, which are not patient-centric, but institution- and payer-centric.

Now, to take us to the next level, the evolution of those systems must allow us to affordably and effectively push back on the tsunami of chronic illness and other non-acute problems that plague our nation. Traditional paper-based records and work processes are inadequate for addressing the complexities of medical care and the interactions between healthcare organizations involved in the care of patients in today's environment, particularly as many require a variety of care settings and services. To achieve value-based care, administrative processes and business systems in health care must evolve to anticipate risk and provide incentives and rewards to organizations achieving higher value in the cost-quality ratio, as well as engage patients in the management of their health and medical conditions. This results in an increased demand on clinical, administrative, and analytical HIS.

▶ Challenges for HIS and Health Professionals Using Them

Deep-rooted, systemic quality and cost problems in health care leave health professionals and patients alike challenged to find a productive and desirable way forward. The transition from fee-for-services to value-based reimbursement confronts those working in health care as well as creates new requirements for HIS. Issues for HIS to support quality, value-based care, interoperability, and improved experiences with EHR systems and other HIS are complex, deep, and pervasive, as they struggle to continue to grow when they are part of the unsustainable cost structure of U.S. health care. These issues include:

1. Legacy HIS systems: an industry built upon fee-for-service reimbursement methods and finances is unaffordable on a sustained basis. Additionally, support processes are being actively changed in healthcare organizations. Thus, these legacy HIS products must change in their core and in the ethos embedded within the purpose and logic contained within their functionality and capabilities (i.e., capturing charges and documentation for regulatory requirements associated with fee-for-service billing and reimbursement processes).

2. Aging technology: major EHR and HIS systems with major market share are rooted in older technologies that have lasted longer than anyone ever imagined—the programming and operating system of numerous of them is MUMPS, originally developed in the 1960s. Vendors, and the talent needed to work on these software systems, need to evolve. This will imply additional effort and expense for healthcare organizations, most of which are community resources.

3. Workflows, incentives, and organizational cultures built around the fee-for-service market: If the government and commercial insurers successfully incent the evolution of payment for healthcare services from fee-for-service to value-based reimbursement (and they have the power to do so), great disruption and fall-out will occur among the current HIS marketplace, including providers, HIS systems, vendors, talent, and methods.

4. Massive industry consolidation: continued mergers and acquisitions will result in many healthcare providers needing to replace their current EHR system with another. This places additional strain, expense, and effort on those practices and organizations upon their already significant investment in these systems (Barker, 2017). As a smaller number of vendors become increasingly prevalent and thus powerful, more data and information are

under their control. With increasing amounts of data captured in these systems, these vendors gain increasing control over the flow of information, reducing transparency through data (Powderly, 2017). Healthcare organizations are tied into contracts that do not uphold their rights to the degree that they should be. In Chapter 5, how to negotiate effectively with vendors will be presented: it is one of the most important areas for health professionals to understand and regain some semblance of control through good data management practices.

The changing context of health care and the role of HIS merges institutional care delivery, public health, and population health management, and connects with people where they live and work. New technologies are emerging, and along with them, new attitudes of how interdisciplinary teamwork among information technology and health professionals is the needed norm in order to develop streamlined workflows, value-based functionality, and improved human-computer interface. New ideals regarding HIS activities balancing activity and control between IT professionals and health professionals—as well as involving patients directly—will evolve us to a new locus of control centered on health, people, patients, and

relationships between patients and providers. As a result, new connections will be created among providers, organizations, patient data, HIS, pharmaceutical firms, research, public health, genomics, medical devices, and communities. Democratization of data will be within our reach. Improvement of health outcomes will become possible, with better outcomes supported by new solutions.

What does this mean for a person learning about HIS? What does this mean for organizations using HIS? What does this mean for providers, patients, and health care at large? What does this mean for the HIS market? Solutions and answers to these questions include involving providers more in development of solutions, adopting a holistic approach to care and prevention, and making HIS an integral part of training of all health professionals, in their own right.

Summary

The evidence against fee-for-service is mounting, and the healthcare industry is proving to be more dynamic and volatile than ever. Health care must become more affordable, higher quality, and sustainable. The shift toward value-based will depend in part on HIS that can support new processes outside the four walls of healthcare institutions and provide health professionals with the information, resources, and connectivity to support new organizational models and processes.

Key Terms

Computerized physician
   order entry (CPOE)
Crossing the Quality Chasm
Diagnosis related groups
   (DRGs)
Electronic data interchange
   (EDI)

Fee-for-service
Health Insurance Portability
   and Accountability Act
   (HIPAA)
Integration
Interface
Interoperability

Meaningful Use (MU)
Protected health
   information (PHI)
Standardization
To Err Is Human
Value-based care

Discussion Questions

1. What does the term "fee-for-service" mean regarding health care? How, in your opinion, did this form of reimbursement come to be standard practice?

2. Contrast fee-for-service with value-based care.

3. Describe the current climate among healthcare vendors. How does that climate affect the policies and decisions that healthcare organizations have ahead of them?

4. How have U.S. government agencies and administrations shaped HIS policies and law? Describe one act, law, or policy.

5. Why was the report *To Err Is Human* shocking? How did the follow up report, *Crossing the Quality Chasm*, add to that information?

6. Describe how the U.S. provides care and reimbursement as compared to other nations.

7. What is interoperability and why is it important to the practice of value-based care, cost-effectiveness, and public health?

References

Adler-Milstein, J., DesRoches, C. M., Kralovec, P., Foster, G., Worzala, C., Charles, D., … Jha, A. K. (2015, December 1). Electronic health record adoption in US hospitals: Progress continues, but challenges persist. *Health Affairs*. Retrieved from https://www.healthaffairs.org/doi/10.1377/hlthaff.2015.0992

Adler-Milstein, J., Holmgren, A. J., Kralovec, P., Worzala, C., Searcy, T., & Patel, V. (2017, November 1). Electronic health record adoption in US hospitals: The emergence of digital "advanced use" divide. *Journal of American Medical Informatics Association*. Retrieved from https://www.ncbi.nlm.nih.gov/pubmed/29016973

Allen, M. (2018, July 17). Health insurers are vacuuming up details about you—And it could raise your rates. *ProPublica*. Retrieved from https://www.propublica.org/article/health-insurers-are-vacuuming-up-details-about-you-and-it-could-raise-your-rates

Barker, E. (2017, April 20). How consolidation is reshaping health care. *Leadership+. HMFA*. Retrieved from http://www.hfma.org/Leadership/E-Bulletins/2017/April/How_Consolidation_Is_Reshaping_Health_Care/

Buttorff, C., Ruder, T., & Bauman, M. (2017). Multiple chronic conditions in the United States. *The RAND Corporation*. Retrieved from https://www.rand.org/blog/rand-review/2017/07/chronic-conditions-in-america-price-and-prevalence.html

CBO. (2009). CBO Letter estimating federal direct spending and revenues of HITECH to Honorable Charles B. Rangel, Chairman Committee on Ways and Means, U.S. House of Representatives. Retrieved from https://www.cbo.gov/sites/default/files/cbofiles/ftpdocs/99xx/doc9966/hitechrangelltr.pdf

Centers for Disease Control and Prevention. (2015). Electronic medical records/electronic health records (EMRs/EHRs). *Centers for Disease Control and Prevention*. Retrieved from https://www.cdc.gov/nchs/fastats/electronic-medical-records.htm

Centers for Medicare & Medicaid Services. (n.d.). Electronic Data Interchange System Access and Privacy. *Centers for Medicare & Medicaid Services*. Retrieved from https://www.cms.gov/Medicare/Billing/ElectronicBillingEDITrans/SystemAccess.html

Donavan, F. (2018, July 10). CHIME says healthcare cybersecurity should be innovation focus. *HealthIT Security*. Retrieved from https://healthitsecurity.com/news/chime-says-healthcare-cybersecurity-should-be-innovation-focus

Ellison, A. (2017, June 13). Why the "new normal" for healthcare cost growth isn't sustainable. *Becker's Hospital Review*. Retrieved from https://www.beckershospitalreview.com/finance/why-the-new-normal-for-healthcare-cost-growth-isn-t-sustainable.html

Health and Medicine Division of the National Academies of Sciences, Engineering, and Medicine. (1999, November). To Err Is Human: Building a safer health system. Retrieved from http://www.nationalacademies.org/hmd/~/media/Files/Report%20Files/1999/To-Err-is-Human/To%20Err%20is%20Human%201999%20%20report%20brief.pdf

Health and Medicine Division of the National Academies of Sciences, Engineering, and Medicine. (2001, March). Crossing the quality chasm: A new health system for the 21st century. Retrieved from http://www.nationalacademies.org/hmd/~/media/Files/Report%20Files/2001/Crossing-the-Quality-Chasm/Quality%20Chasm%202001%20%20report%20brief.pdf

Health Level Seven International. (n.d.). Retrieved from http://www.hl7.org/

James, J. T. (2013, September). A new, evidence-based estimate of patient harms associated with hospital care. *Journal of Patient Safety*. Retrieved from https://www.ncbi.nlm.nih.gov/pubmed/23860193

Jayanthi, A., & Ellison, A. (2016, May 23). 8 hospitals' finances hurt by EHR costs. *Becker's Hospital Review*. https://www.beckershospitalreview.com/finance/8-hospitals-finances-hurt-by-ehr-costs.html

Khazan, O. (2014, October 3). The Ebola patient was sent home because of bad software. *The Atlantic*. Retrieved from https://www.theatlantic.com/technology/archive/2014/10/the-ebola-patient-was-sent-home-because-of-an-electronic-health-record-problem/381087/

Landi, H. (2016, November 2). CDC: Only on-third of physicians electronically shared information in 2015. *Healthcare Informatics*. Retrieved from https://www.healthcare-informatics.com/news-item/ehr/cdc-data-brief-only-one-third-physicians-electronically-shared-information-2015

Lin, S. C., Jha, A. K., & Adler-Milstein, J. (2018). Electronic health records associated with lower hospital mortality after systems have time to mature. *Health Affairs*. Retrieved from https://www.ncbi.nlm.nih.gov/pubmed/29985687

Mastersen, L. (2018, April 9). M&A risks patient safety, JAMA report warns. *Healthcare Dive*. Retrieved from https://www.healthcaredive.com/news/ma-risks-patient-safety-jama-report-warns/520815/

Meyerhoefer, C. D., Sherer, S. A., Deily, M. E., Chou, S., Guo, X., Chen, J., ... Levick, D. (2018, May 16). Provider and patient satisfaction with the integration of ambulatory and hospital EHR systems. *Journal of the American Medical Informatics Association*. Retrieved from https://academic.oup.com/jamia/article-abstract/25/8/1054/4996914?redirectedFrom=fulltext

Monegain, B. (2015, August 27). See how much Cerner CEO, others, earn. *Healthcare IT News*. Retrieved from https://www.healthcareitnews.com/news/see-how-much-cerner-ceo-others-earn

Morris, Z. S., Wooding, S., & Grant, J. (2011, December). The answer is 17 years, what is the question: Understanding time lags in translational research. *Journal of the Royal Society of Medicine*. https://www.ncbi.nlm.nih.gov/pmc/articles/PMC3241518/

New 11-country study: U.S. health care system has widest gap between people with higher and lower incomes. (2017, July 13). *The Commonwealth Fund*. https://www.commonwealthfund.org/press-release/2017/new-11-country-study-us-health-care-system-has-widest-gap-between-people-higher

O'Sullivan, J., Chaikind, H., Tilson, S., Boulanger, J., & Morgan, P. (2004). *Overview of the Medicare Perscription Drug, Improvement, Modernization Act of 2003*. http://royce.house.gov/uploadedfiles/overview%20of%20medicare.pdf.

Peter G. Pederson Foundation. (2018). Infographic: U.S. healthcare spending. https://www.pgpf.org/infographic/infographic-us-health-spending?utm_source=google&utm_medium=cpc&utm_campaign=healthcareinfographic&gclid=EAIaIQobChMIkY33-6iW3AIVDdRkCh0Vjg2CEAAYASAAEgKPCPD_BwE

Pianin, E. (2017, January 2011). 10,000 boomers turn 65 every day. Can medicare and social security handle it? *The Fiscal Times*. http://www.thefiscaltimes.com/2017/05/09/10000-Boomers-Turn-65-Every-Day-Can-Medicare-and-Social-Security-Handle-It

Powderly, H. (2017, April 12) Trump effect on health IT? New vendors, EHR consolidation, big data explosion. *Heathcare IT News*. https://www.healthcareitnews.com/news/trump-effect-health-it-new-vendors-ehr-consolidation-big-data-explosion

Rapaport, L. (2018, March 13). U.S. health spending twice other countries' with worse results. *Reuters*. https://www.reuters.com/article/us-health-spending/u-s-health-spending-twice-other-countries-with-worse-results-idUSKCN1GP2YN

Symposium focuses on improving electronic health records. (2018, June 7). *Stanford Medicine*. http://med.stanford.edu/news/all-news/2018/06/symposium-tackles-electronic-health-records.html.

New 11-country study: U.S. health care system has widest gap between people with higher and lower incomes. (2017, July 13). The Commonwealth Fund. https://www.commonwealthfund.org/press-release/2017/new-11-country-study-us-health-care-system-has-widest-gap-between-people-higher

The Henry J. Kaiser Family Foundation. Total Health Care Employment. (2017, May). The Henry J. Kaiser Family Foundation. https://www.kff.org/other/state-indicator/total-health-care-employment

The Office of the National Coordinator for Health Information Technology. (2016). Office-based health care professional participation in the CMS EHR incentive programs. The Office of the National Coordinator for Health Information Technology. Retrieved from https://dashboard.healthit.gov/quickstats/pages/FIG-Health-Care-Professionals-EHR-Incentive-Programs.php

The Office of the National Coordinator for Health Information Technology. (2017). Connecting health and care for the nation: A shared nationwide interoperability roadmap. *The Office of the National Coordinator for Health Information Technology.* Retrieved from https://www.healthit.gov/sites /default/files/hie-interoperability/nationwide -interoperability-roadmap-final-version-1.0.pdf

The Organisation for Economic Co-operation and Development. (2017). Health at a glance 2017: OECD indicators. *The Organisation for Economic Co-operation and Development.* Retrieved from https://www.oecd.org/unitedstates/Health-at-a -Glance-2017-Key-Findings-UNITED-STATES.pdf

Thompson, T. G., & Brailer, D. J. (2004). The decade of health information technology: Delivering consumer-centric and information-rich health care: Framework for strategic action. Retrieved from http://healthit.hhs.gov /portal/server.pt?open=512&objID=1263&mode=2

Toussaint, J. S., & Correia, K. (2018, March 19). Why process is U.S. health care's biggest problem. *Harvard Business Review.* Retrieved from https://hbr.org/2018/03/why -process-is-u-s-health-cares-biggest-problem

Tse, A. (2018, June 8). Transitioning to value-based care: What physician groups need to know. *Becker's Hospital Review.* Retrieved from https://www .beckershospitalreview.com/hospital-physician -relationships/transitioning-to-value-based-care -what-physician-groups-need-to-know.html

Verghese, A. (2018, May 16). How tech can turn doctors into clerical workers. *The New York Times Magazine.* Retrieved from https://www.nytimes.com /interactive/2018/05/16/magazine/health-issue-what -we-lose-with-data-driven-medicine.html

White House Office of the Press Secretary. (2004). Executive order: Incentives for the use of health information technology and establishing the position of the National Health Information Technology Coordinator. *The White House.* Retrieved from http://georgewbush-whitehouse.archives.gov/news /releases/2004/04/20040427-4.html

Wilensky, G. (2018, June 19). The need to simplify measuring quality in health care. *The JAMA Forum.* Retrieved from https://jamanetwork.com/journals /jama/fullarticle/2685141

SECTION II

HIS Strategy, Planning, and Governance

CHAPTER 4

HIS Strategic Planning

LEARNING OBJECTIVES

By the end of this chapter, the student will be able to:

- Describe terminology and concepts associated with strategic planning for healthcare organizations, and ways these concepts apply to health information systems (HIS).
- Relate HIS strategy and strategic planning processes to organizational strategy, strategic planning processes, and support of patient care and the health professions.
- Align HIS strategy with the mission, vision, values, and strategic plan of any type of healthcare organization.
- Describe elements of the HIS Strategic Planning Hierarchy Model.
- Identify multiple key components to HIS strategic planning, including organizational strategy, portfolio of application software, internal and external networks and connectivity, data, interoperability, and technology such as hardware and devices.

▶ Introduction

This chapter focuses on the HIS Planning Framework, and to understand how best to use that framework we will explore strategy and planning for organizations as well as for HIS. HIS should be nothing more and nothing less than a reflection of the organization itself, including its character and embedded values, in its structure and service components, as well as its strategies. In order to achieve this, we will take it from the top—first understanding what strategy means and what planning principles and techniques are, and then relating those concepts and processes to HIS and to creating HIS strategy and planning processes that inextricably intertwine the organization and its HIS capabilities. We will cover in detail the HIS Planning Framework, which provides an organizing construct for defining the HIS software portfolio to support the strategies, goals, and objectives of the organization and the health professionals who comprise its services, practices, and management. Thus, these tools and principles guide the successful development of a HIS Strategic Plan that reflects the organization's strategic business plan, capable of successfully propelling the organization, whether large or small, into the future, including population health management, value-based reimbursement, and the dynamics of health care, which are not crystal clear to any of us at this time, given the current challenges.

▶ # HIS Planning Framework

The four quadrants of the **HIS Planning Framework** provides us with the conceptual structure needed to conduct HIS planning discussions that include all key stakeholders, not just information technology (IT), vendors, or consultants driving the HIS agenda. Clinical, administrative, transactional, and analytical systems are described relative to the types of *activities* and *services* of the organization. No significant technical expertise is needed to understand the HIS Planning Framework, hence its usability. The process it describes highlights the interdisciplinary nature of HIS and is based on nontechnical dialogue grounded in technology architecture. The framework begins with the "what we want to do" not "how" or "who" (meaning which function or vendor). The HIS Planning Framework exemplifies the whole concept of this text. It supports the imperative that all disciplines of health professionals become well versed in HIS so they can aptly participate, contribute, and lead in HIS initiatives. After all, HIS exists not for the sake of technology, but for the sake of enabling healthcare organizations and professionals to reach their goals.

Principles of Planning

The universal principles of planning should guide the HIS planning process and HIS strategy. The importance of planning is cross-disciplinary: Benjamin Franklin's quote, "If you fail to plan, you are planning to fail," applies as readily to HIS as it does to any other industry. Perhaps more. Despite this common-sense advice, a common issue is the urge to buy new software in a rush to solve problems that often compels good managers, normally sensible stewards of organizational resources, to take radical departures from those habits and sign contracts that are barely negotiated, committing millions of dollars of the community's resources for ill-defined requirements and nonexistent documented strategies and plans. Submitting to these urges can spell disaster for an organization, so do not do it, under any circumstance. A factor in failed implementations is the fact that most publicity and conference content focus on HIS successes; little time is given to failures, in part because of the stranglehold vendors have on organizations' ability to be transparent about what went wrong. Vendor contracts typically strictly prohibit organizations from saying anything negative about commercial software packages, even if they have errors in them or the vendor provides poor support (Leviss, 2013). We will cover vendor negotiations and contracting guidelines in Chapter 5 and vendor management in Chapter 6. Interestingly, the very few books published on this topic include only anonymous case examples, due to organizations' desire to avoid retribution for exposing failed implementations in hospitals, ambulatory, and community settings. The most important lesson to remember and follow is that *there are no shortcuts in HIS planning.*

🔍 CASE EXAMPLE: NO DECISION IS A DECISION

Let's look at a six-hospital health system in the Midwest, with about 3,000 physicians on its medical staffs, in a variety of community, independent, and group practices plus a large integrated clinic. The implementation of an enterprise-wide, integrated electronic health record (EHR) system for the hospitals took place from 2005 to 2007 to amalgamate a nascent health system that had been recently formed through merger and acquisition. The large integrated clinic had a different, purely ambulatory EHR system that had served them well for many years: this was planned to be replaced as a next step. Following leadership changes (during a time of political unrest between the large integrated group and the new health system), the newly combined organization struggled to cooperate to do the planning and coordinated selection of an EHR solution for the clinic, because the questions about how integrated the large clinic with its long independent history would be with the health system loomed large in the process. As they say, "no decision is a decision," and the planning process was stuck.

Then the health system acquired a provider group with about 30 physicians from a local competing health system. Because that new clinic had already recently implemented an EHR system, the decision was made to use that software license and implement that EHR system for the entirety of the existing integrated clinic. Thoughtful consideration of requirements, coordination and integration of workflows and data, and myriad other considerations were dashed aside, and non-decisions resulted in a peculiar, almost nonsensical implementation of an unevaluated system that floated in during an acquisition. This is how the system for a prestigious integrated clinic was chosen, with no planning or comparison and consideration of alternatives.

What was the outcome? The doctors and nurses of the large clinic were unhappy: it was a clunky, difficult-to-use system, implemented with little input from the end users, so IT just showed up and installed workstations on the walls of the examination rooms with no place for the doctors and nurses to set anything such as their stethoscopes, notebooks, or other equipment. Clinicians had to hold things in one hand and type with the other. In addition, the workstations were affixed to the wall in such a way that the clinicians using the system had to almost completely turn their backs on the patient while they entered data. The new system also required a full hour of extra work for both the physicians and nurses of a practice to finish the additional clerical work that other people used to do, now required of the providers by the new system.

A vendor-based consulting group came in and took control of the implementation. The vendor is now in control of the entire EHR function, and thus the organization, as well. The health system has spent an ungodly amount of money on this implementation. The budget was supposed to be $500 million. It has ballooned to $750 million. One has to take a deep breath hearing numbers like that. After all, this is a community, not-for-profit health system. Nurses with 25 years of experience were fired for missing a question on one of three vendor-administered proficiency tests. And then, after all this effort, all this money and time, the implementation stalled after one hospital go-live. There were too many issues to be tolerated or ignored. The next hospital's implementation is yet to take place. Of course, it doesn't take a rocket scientist to understand why the budget slipped from $500 to $750 million, nor is it hard to figure out who is benefitting: it's certainly not the health system and the providers who practice there, serving the patients and community. Unfortunately, only the vendor and their consulting group are reaping the rewards.

🔍 CASE EXAMPLE: THINKING ABOUT SHORTCUTTING HIS PLANNING? THINK AGAIN

In 2005, after $34 million and several years were invested in planning and developing a new, electronic medical record, physicians at Cedars-Sinai Medical Center in Los Angeles revolted after three months of using the new EHR system, demanding that it be abandoned (Connolly, 2005). Of course, in a disastrous situation like this, it becomes painfully clear that the physicians who admit patients to a hospital have the power to get their voices heard, especially in regard to new ways of taking care of patients. If most members of the medical staff had decided to admit their patients

(continues)

🔍 CASE EXAMPLE: THINKING ABOUT SHORTCUTTING HIS PLANNING? THINK AGAIN *(continued)*

to a different hospital, Cedars-Sinai would have been in dire straits clinically, financially, and from the standpoint of reputation and service to the community. Cedars-Sinai found itself in this very predicament and made the decision to abandon this major HIS project at great financial, operational, cultural, and reputational cost.

At the time, many other healthcare organizations across the U.S. were also in the midst of EHR implementations or considering investing in these expensive, transformative systems. Fear loomed in the hearts of these people who watched the Cedars-Sinai situation unfold, who were undoubtedly saying something like, "There but for the grace of God go I." The Cedars-Sinai EHR failure attracted national and international attention, and those who were in the process of EHR implementations learned from this story. Many hospitals most assuredly took on additional efforts and special care in engaging and involving their medical staff members and other clinicians in the process of introducing a new computer system into a patient care environment.

From the standpoint of lessons learned for HIS planning, involving members of key functions within healthcare organizations is vital to the successful definition and accomplishment of HIS plans. In this example, the medical staff departments were merely glanced at as part of the planning process. Individuals from all disciplines must be key participants on steering committees, task forces, process redesign initiatives, and implementations of new HIS. Engagement can make a major difference in how those staff members feel about the changes they are being asked to help define and implement. Change is not easy for any organization but supporting and involving staff members "into the fray" of an HIS implementation is truly a role that cannot be overlooked in carrying out HIS plans.

To avoid disastrous outcomes, EHR project teams must avoid working *only* through the medical staff *leadership*: the project plans must always infiltrate the ranks of the *total medical staff* through involvement in process redesign, communications, orientation, and engagement in the EHR project. In the Cedars-Sinai example, only about 15 percent of the total medical staff knew much about the project or felt as if they had a voice in the system's design and plans. Even though medical staff leaders were involved, receiving word about the project on a secondhand basis was insufficient for the remaining 85 percent of the medical staff, and this mistake ultimately led to the project failure.

Since the Cedars-Sinai revolt, many healthcare organizations throughout the U.S. have taken clear note, wisely deciding to invest the time, money, and energy needed to reach as many of their own medical staff members as possible, as well as other department members, regarding their EHR implementations. Successful organizations do their best to involve line physicians in the design of their new EHR systems, and then seek to proactively orient and train all clinicians on the new system before it goes "live." Successful HIS implementations now recognize that these key users— the physicians, clinicians, and other healthcare professionals essential to the minute-to-minute functioning of the hospital—have a choice whether to use the new system, and accept that each and every one of these professionals must be given the opportunity to learn about and participate in the planning, design, and development of the new system. As a happy footnote, since this trying experience at the renowned institution, the Cedars-Sinai Medical Center and Cedars-Sinai Medical Group have successfully implemented a new comprehensive, integrated EHR.

The importance of a well-disciplined HIS planning process cannot be overemphasized, given, among other things, the expensive nature of HIS—they are costly to acquire, implement, and maintain. Once in place, these systems have just begun to exact the financial toll on an organization, which, over the long-term (including annual support fees paid to each software vendor), for the software maintenance alone, generally totals 20–25 percent of the total license cost of the software. Typically, in three to four years, the software maintenance fees alone exceed the original purchase fees for the license itself. Plus, this does not include other operational costs for training, backfill of operational staff during the project, internal IT support, help desk expansion, training, upgrades, and other ongoing costs. So, a careful detailed plan is essential, to avoid unhappy financial surprises, missed project deadlines, suffering for the organization's culture, missed financial targets, and redirected budget funds such as using resources intended for personnel wage increases or other important expenses to make up for the shortfall. This is not a desired scenario, and yet it can easily happen without a careful, forward-looking plan that includes detailed implementation plans including a five-year cost estimate for each HIS project in the context of all HIS within an organization. HIS plans should be intertwined with other principles, such as patient-centric, mission-supporting care; the health of patients, practices, and organizations; the facilitation of trusted relationships and interactions with external parties; and the creation of a promising future for the organization and the community it serves.

▶ HIS Strategy: Using Organizational Strategy as a Roadmap

The term "**strategy**" is a word we often hear, readily applied to many different arenas, especially when discussing organizations and their work or important activities. It is easy to dilute the meaning of this term into something amorphous or general, so that the term "strategies" is often used interchangeably (and erroneously) with terms such as "goals," "tactics," "policies," "schemes," "agendas," "plans," or "objectives." At the uppermost levels of an organization's agenda are directional statements or overarching aims directly tied to mission and vision, the large-scale ways that the organization will be able to

successfully move itself forward toward its purpose over a period of years. These are strategies.

Strategies are defined and developed by first reflecting on the organization's reason for existing (its **mission**) and examining the organization in the context of its market; outlining a long-term and evolving view of its place in that environment or market in the future (its **vision**); and then understanding the ways it wants to behave, the philosophies it wants to support, its guiding principles, and the ways it wants to do its work (its **values**). The organization's mission, vision, and values are communicated widely throughout the organization and to its constituents at all levels. These guideposts are often written down, placed on posters on the walls of employees' offices and walkways of the institution, discussed and dissected at great depth and at all levels of the organization, published on the website, and established as official resolutions by the organization's highest level—the board of directors or trustees—as well as communicated to customers, clarified to management, reviewed with employees, and so on. Every action the organization takes should be consistent with these pillars of the organization's purpose (**FIGURE 4.1**).

Note that we have not defined anything yet, named any strategy, or outlined any specific actions: all effort up to this point is spent fully engaging to clarify and define the mission, vision, values, and hoped-for future of the organization. These are the "why" questions that must come ahead of the "what" answers.

Steps in Determining Strategy

The first step in understanding where an organization ought to put its efforts and resources, and which types of efforts or strategies those might be used toward, is for the organization to define its mission, vision, and values. When these overarching and most essential statements of purpose and principle are agreed upon, they become the beacons that guide the organization through its many decisions and

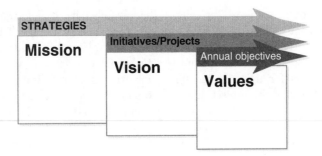

FIGURE 4.1 Organizational pillars. The organization's mission, vision, and values drive its strategy and actions.

challenges. The mission, vision, and values are essentially the compass by which the organization sets its direction for long-term growth and moves to adapt to ever-changing environmental and market conditions. Once these tenets are defined, and then collectively and officially embraced, the organization knows the direction in which it should be trying to go. The next step is to determine how the organization should go about doing so and which activities will get it moving in that direction.

Determining the course for the organization and criteria for decisions about where it invests its precious resources involves: (1) framing a vision for the organization (answering the question, "What does this organization look like in 10 years?"), (2) carefully documenting all currently existing HIS and technology in the organizations, (3) designing a 10- to 15-year view of a desired vision for the organization, and finally (4) mapping out a migration path between this **current state** of the organization and the desired vision or **future state** (**FIGURE 4.2**). The organization can then describe major directional strategies and enterprise-wide actions that will move the organization in the desired direction.

Relationship Between Organizational Strategy and HIS Strategy

Why is this discussion about organizational mission, vision, values, strategies, goals, and objectives important to **HIS strategy**

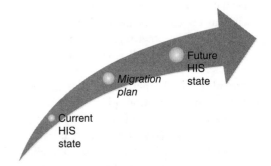

FIGURE 4.2 Current state → future state. HIS strategic growth should move the organization from its current HIS state to its desired future HIS state.

development? The answer to that question is an easy one: the HIS strategy should be to build the IT capabilities and systems necessary to enable the organization's strategies and support these business and clinical goals and objectives. The HIS strategy will encompass its own set of HIS strategies, projects, goals, and objectives, all of which directly tie back into the organization's overall strategies and goals. The HIS strategy is the interpretation of the organization's strategic plan into the IT language of systems, infrastructure, data, expertise, information, and connectivity. To build systems and HIS infrastructure that do not align in this way—or, worse yet, that run counter to these forward-thinking evolutionary steps—hinders the capacity and forward movement of the entire organization and threatens to waylay its trajectory toward its vision state.

The organization's strategic plan thus serves as the roadmap for its HIS Strategic Plan.

🔍 *CASE EXAMPLE: HYPOTHETICAL VISIONING FOR A HEART HEALTHCARE PROVIDER*

If the vision for the organization is to meet the needs of an aging community that includes significant numbers of people with cardiovascular conditions, it may decide to become the number one provider of heart health care in its community or region, providing such care to all patients regardless of their ability to pay (future state). Key strategies to accomplish this might include the following: (1) within 10 years, build a new, comprehensive, state-of-the-art heart care hospital; (2) create a charitable foundation to fund care for the uninsured or underinsured on a needs-based system; (3) negotiate a partnership with health plans to provide incentives for preventive population-based or chronic illness management initiatives and good heart care outcomes; and (4) initiate grant proposal efforts to create funding opportunities to draw researchers and key physicians to the hospital to provide excellent heart care, conduct research, and develop new knowledge around the care and prevention of heart disease. These four strategies are then further broken down into initiatives and projects, which are the actual work that the organization must do to move itself toward its desired future state, in accordance with its mission, vision, and values. In this way, the organization can accomplish what it sees as its purpose and reason for existence. It assures that the finite resources and energies of the organization are used to move the organization toward its desired future. These initiatives and projects can be described in the form of a multiyear agenda for the organization. To ensure that the initiatives and projects are accomplished, the organization must build them into strategic capital budgets; annual operating budgets; and specific, assignable, actionable, annual objectives—the measurable steps and assigned tasks by which each goal is pursued and accomplished and to which people in the organization are held accountable (**TABLE 4.1**).

TABLE 4.1 Example of an Organizational Strategy and Enabling Strategic Initiatives

Organizational strategy: "In 10 years become the #1 provider of heart health care in the area for all patients regardless of their ability to pay" Key strategic initiatives might be …	Build state-of-the-art heart hospital.
	Implement digital health platform to achieve personalized chronic care management, and patient engagement.
	Create charitable foundation to fund care for uninsured or underinsured.
	Work with health plans to provide coverage and incentives for population health initiatives and good heart care and health outcomes
	Engage the community in defining outreach requirements and social support mechanisms for population health initiatives and chronic care management.
	Create research funding opportunities to attract researchers and key physicians.

The HIS Strategic Plan should directly reflect the strategies of the organization and should not stray one iota from enabling the organization to move in its desired direction. It should be absolutely focused on supporting the accomplishment of those organizational strategies and initiatives. In other words, the HIS strategy is a mirror image of the organizational strategy. There is no need for a separate or isolated HIS strategy: that would be meaningless, wasteful, and counterproductive. Rather, the HIS strategy requires the availability of an organizational direction and strategic plan—otherwise, the HIS strategy could be based on something as random as the last conference someone attended, inertia, what the organization across town is doing, or the influence of a convincing software salesperson (think snake oil). If this happens, the expensive investment of time, resources, and energy put into building the organization's HIS and technology infrastructure would be a wasted or misguided effort that does not help the organization reach its desired state. Clearly, then, it is important to make time for organization strategic planning and for HIS strategic planning. Do not skip or short-change these highly related processes. To do so will result in costly HIS misalignment,

which *will* be (not *can* be) devastating to the accomplishment of the organization's strategic plans, in spite of all of its worthy effort.

One last question: what happens if your organization does not have a strategic plan and you need to develop a HIS Strategic Plan and make major HIS decisions and investments? Take charge and create the strategic organizational plan as best you can before launching off to develop and implement the HIS strategy. The strategic organizational planning *must* come first. Document everything you can about what people are thinking about the future directions and plans of the organization. Be a leader. Pull a group of people together, interview people from all disciplines and levels of the organization, and write down everything you learn according to the outline provided in **EXHIBIT 4.1**. Circulate what you document and get people's reactions—and then adjust your documentation based on this feedback. In addition to getting guidance from executive management, ask entry-level employees, grassroots workers, nurses, physicians, departmental process experts, patients, senior leaders, people in the community, board members (might want to get permission on that one first), and administrative assistants (especially!) what they think.

EXHIBIT 4.1 Outline of a Strategic Plan for a Healthcare Organization—Community Physicians Primary Care Group

Strategic Plan

This document lays out a thorough and thoughtful analysis of the long-term future plans for an organization, taking its environmental conditions and community into consideration.

Example: The Strategic Plan for Community Physicians Primary Care Group contemplates the future of the community and defines the plans and funding necessary to address the community's future healthcare needs over the next 10–20 years.

Executive Summary

This section summarizes the essential points contained within each section of a strategic plan, with the intention that decision makers who are asked to consider approving a strategic plan, such as members of a board of directors, can quickly and easily access the primary considerations and issues contained in the plan. (The executive summary is typically one to two pages long and single-spaced.) The executive summary for the Community Physicians Primary Care Group concisely summarizes the main points from each section of its strategic plan for each element listed.

Sample Text

The Community Physicians Primary Care Group plans to grow to at least twice its current size over the next five years to meet the growing and unmet needs of its community, which has doubled its population in the last decade.

Organization History

This section describes the organization's background, including any relevant themes that set the backdrop for the strategic direction for the organization.

Sample Text

The Community Physicians Primary Care Group was established in 1969, at a time when funding from Medicaid provided the means to begin to address the healthcare needs of Greentown's growing numbers of migrant worker citizens, many of whose family incomes were below the federal poverty line. These citizens also were often uninsured or underinsured.

Vision Statement

This section expresses the long-term vision of the organization.

Sample Text

The Community Physicians Primary Care Group aims to provide for the comprehensive healthcare and wellness needs of its community, especially targeting those who cannot pay for those services, in a manner that sustains and enables these people and families to thrive.

Mission Statement

This section describes the organization's purpose and the way that its vision will be carried out.

Sample Text

The Community Physicians Primary Care Group is committed to high-quality, compassionate, and sustaining care that meets the healthcare and wellness needs of all members of its community, regardless of their ability to pay.

Target Population

This section defines the people whom the organization intends to serve within the scope of this strategic plan, which may be a different or expanded population than the one it currently serves.

Sample Text

The Community Physicians Primary Care Group serves the citizens of Greenfield and all new inhabitants within a 50-mile radius of the town.

Community Served

This section defines the characteristics and demographics of the population and community served by the organization.

Sample Text

The Community Physicians Primary Care Group serves members of its target population who come to the clinic for care, regardless of their financial or demographic status. The community's patients and community consist of a diverse combination of people who represent all major ethnic groups, with the low-income population comprising a growing segment of the community and one that is particularly

(continues)

EXHIBIT 4.1 Outline of a Strategic Plan for a Healthcare Organization—Community Physicians Primary Care Group   *(continued)*

in need because many are displaced from areas nearby where economic conditions have worsened in recent years. This population is predominantly in professional service, agricultural, and educational occupations.

Future Issues

This section describes the characteristics and considerations that influence the direction of the organization.

Sample Text

The Community Physicians Primary Care Group faces significant challenges inherent as a result of its rapidly growing population and reduced levels of reimbursement based on the decreasing percentage of its population that has health insurance, due to an expanding low-income demographic.

SWOT Analysis

The *S*trengths, *W*eaknesses, *O*pportunities, and *T*hreats section of the strategic plan describes each of these possibilities as they relate to the organization's market share, competition, facilities, programs, services, medical staff, operations, finances, and other key elements.

Sample Text

In market share, the Community Physicians Primary Care Group's strengths include a growing population that needs the types of services it offers; a weakness in terms of market share is its vulnerability to insufficient revenues if Medicaid reimbursement is not achieved for all those who are eligible for it based on their family income. There is an opportunity for more people from Greentown's socioeconomic demographic segments to obtain health insurance through health reform in addition to Medicaid. However, a threat exists in the potential shift of those newly insured citizens obtaining care in settings other than the Community Physicians Primary Care Group, thus reducing volume below planned-for levels.

Assumptions

This section lists the key assumptions that inform and potentially drive strategic decisions and plans, which are estimations of future characteristics and thus will vary to some degree as reality unfolds and must be watched closely as time progresses.

Sample Text

The Community Physicians Primary Care Group will be one of three major group practices in the community for the foreseeable future.

Goals and Objectives

This section identifies multiyear goals and a process for establishing annual objectives that form the basis of annual operating budgets.

Sample Text

Goals for the Community Physicians Primary Care Group include the implementation of a digital health platform to enable communication between providers and engagement of patients through an easy to use app that connects them from their homes and places of work to their provider. Objectives would be to define the requirements for the digital health app and study the marketplace for systems that might meet these requirements, send a **Request for Proposal (RFP)** to vendors in year one, select and plan the implementation of the digital health platform in year two, and go live with this new patient engagement solution in year three.

Implementation Strategies

This section describes potential strategies for execution of the contents of the strategic plan, including approaches to key goals.

Sample Text

In accomplishing the goal of remodeling its interior and updating the exterior of its buildings, the Community Physicians Primary Care Group will establish focus groups from the community that participate in the remodeling and renovation design and plans.

Organizational Structure Future Plans

This section describes changes to the organization that will need to accompany and enable the strategies contained in the strategic plan.

Sample Text

To support the implementation of the HIS plan including an EHR system, the Community Physicians Primary Care Group will recruit key IT professionals and create a robust HIS department.

Plans: Buildings, Technology, Renovation

This section describes the changes and developments necessary for the physical plant and buildings to meet the needs described in the strategic plan.

Sample Text

The Community Physicians Primary Care Group will add three new satellite practice settings over the next 10–15 years to provide access to its growing patient population near where they live and work.

Marketing Plans

This section establishes a brand in accordance with the mission, vision, and values of the organization and identifies the approach to marketing its services and capabilities to its community.

Sample Text

The Community Physicians Primary Care Group will establish its brand as "reconnecting patients and physicians" and communicate this message and the services that reflect it to the various locales and segments of its patient population and community.

Key Relationships

This section describes the key organizational and community relationships necessary for the organization to succeed in accomplishing its strategic plan.

Sample Text

The Community Physicians Primary Care Group seeks to develop relationships with the primary employers, churches, and schools within its service area as a means of connecting with the people in its patient population and engaging them in managing their health and wellness.

(continues)

EXHIBIT 4.1 Outline of a Strategic Plan for a Healthcare Organization—Community Physicians Primary Care Group *(continued)*

Future Organizational Polices

This section describes key policies that the organization must adopt in order to successfully meet its strategic plan and future vision.

Sample Text

Human resources policies will be adapted to allow for flexibility in hiring practices to provide maximum employment opportunities for Community citizens, in concert with its vision of "reconnecting patients and physicians."

Governing Board Plans: Structure, Roles, Responsibilities

This section defines the governance structure and responsibilities, identifying key roles and types of expertise and representation needed to properly guide the organization through the opportunities and challenges of its future development.

Sample Text

The Community Physicians Primary Care Group Board of Directors will consist of 15–20 members who possess expertise in key disciplines reflecting the needs of the organization. The Board of Directors will form subcommittees for closely overseeing plan execution, such as in the areas of finance, IT, strategic planning, operations management, human resources, and clinical leadership.

Feasibility Plan/Pro Forma

This section estimates the financial, human, and other resource requirements needed to accomplish the strategic plan.

Sample Text

A 5-year financial pro forma estimating revenues, capital requirements, and operating expenses for the 5- to 10-year time horizon contemplated in the Community Physicians Primary Care Group strategic plan.

Contingency Plans

This section describes possible directional changes from the expressed strategic plan and its assumptions, including changes in that plan based on those deviations as reality unfolds over the planning time horizon.

Sample Text

The Community Physicians Primary Care Group plans to hold 15 percent of all revenues in reserve to provide for changes in reimbursement, its economic condition, and the financial well-being of its citizens.

The reason the example was chosen for Exhibit 4.1 is because this is a solid, mainstream organization that differs from the high-profile, marquee names that draw attention. While these marquee name hospitals may be leading in certain groundbreaking aspects of their work, they do not represent the vast majority of healthcare organizations.

Data from Washington State Hospital Association. Importance of strategic planning. http://www.wsha.org/files/62/Gov_Board_Manual_strategic_planning.pdf

You will likely be pleasantly surprised at what you learn. Thoughtful people know the truth about what is going on; they know how to make things work more efficiently and effectively. Everything you learn in this process will be important input for your work of HIS strategy development. Be organized as you go about this process: systematically interview a subset of the people in each category with a structured set of questions and all others you think have a perspective on the work of the organization. This research will paint a picture of what is important to various constituents in the organization and in the community, whose interests all need to be served by the organization and, therefore, by its computer systems and information capabilities. The bottom line is that the HIS strategy should be like a reflection in the pool of the organization's future—it should contemplate the present and lay a path to its desired future.

▶ HIS Strategy: Where Do We Begin?

Four essential themes feed into a solid understanding of HIS strategy: (1) the organizational strategy, which serves as the foundation for HIS planning; (2) the HIS Planning Framework; (3) the HIS decision making processes; and (4) the context of the changing national HIS strategy, including consumer expectations and realities of the HIS marketplace for products and services. These four themes underlie all HIS strategy development and planning.

Organizational Strategy Provides the Foundation for HIS Strategic Planning

The HIS Strategic Plan should be a direct reflection of the organization's strategic plan. How is this accomplished? First, as described earlier, for HIS computer systems, networks, and automation of processes to have a beneficial effect on the organization and be a cost-effective investment of financial, human, and physical resources, the HIS and technology plan must support and enable the organizational plan, from both business and clinical perspectives, in consideration of internal and external drivers. The previous section explained this relationship in terms of strategy and planning, but we emphasize here that the development of the HIS Strategic Plan must be based on that organizational strategic plan. The HIS Strategic Plan serves its purpose when it supports and enables the organization to achieve its vision for the future, based on strategies rooted in its mission, vision, and values.

How does the organization know its desired future state and proper forward direction? How does it improve its processes to achieve new, streamlined ways of delivering services to its customers and supporting its business and administrative functions? It knows these things—or rather, it discovers them—by investing the time, energy, and expense to produce a strategic business plan that is then used to formulate a consistent HIS plan. This strategic planning process consists of the systematic examination of the organization's current state or condition, as well as the changing internal and external dynamics and conditions. The organization's strategic planning process defines a 5- to 10- to 20-year desired future state based on the organization's mission, vision, and values (sound familiar?), identifying strategies that will move the organization in this desired direction, setting specific goals based on those strategies, and then breaking those multiyear goals into measurable annual objectives against which organizational performance can be measured and budgets set. The strategic business plan guides annual goals, objectives, budgets, and projects. These can be specified at a great level of detail yet still understood in terms of how they relate to the higher-level strategy. As the old Irish saying goes, "Keep your head in the clouds, and your feet on the ground."

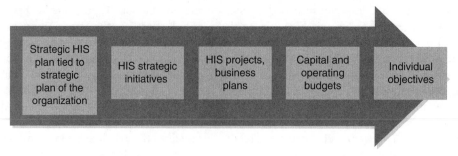

FIGURE 4.3 How HIS supports strategic progress.

Because the HIS strategy uses this organizational strategic plan as its roadmap as well, it logically devises initiatives and projects that establish information technologies and computerization aligned with the strategic direction of the overall organizational plan. Thus, investments in HIS, set upon this foundation, are guaranteed to not only automate the organization but also focus that automation in ways that propel the organization gradually and surely toward its desired future state (**FIGURE 4.3**).

Many HIS strategies focus primarily on selecting a software vendor to provide whatever solutions an organization seeks. This is a mistake. While picking good vendors to provide **software** and **hardware** products is paramount to creating a successful HIS portfolio for an organization, which vendor is chosen is less important than determining whether and how the implementation of that vendor's software product will address the right types of IT capabilities for the organization's needs at that time and into the future. (See the Case Examples in this chapter.) In other words, are the ways a vendor's products can be applied to the structure, functions, and connections of the organization relevant to the structures, functions, and connections that will take the organization into the future successfully? Will the vendor be able to work collaboratively with the people in the organization to design and build specific workflows that meet the organization's needs? Will they support effective and efficient business and clinical processes? Will they

be good partners when things go awry? The answers to all these questions should be "yes." Even an only moderately impressive or semi-sophisticated set of software capabilities that is properly placed—in alignment with the organization's strategy—will be vastly more helpful than an elegant, high-capability software package that is misplaced or inadequately tailored to the needs and preferences of your organization's **knowledge workers**. Poorly applied software, no matter how impressive or fancy, hinders an organization's forward movement. If the vendor software products purchased and implemented are sophisticated but misaligned with the future design and direction of the organization, they will hamper the organization's progress in meeting its strategies and goals because the hefty investment of the organization's time, talent, and resources will be spent pushing the organization against its grain, and the yield from those misapplied resources will produce low value results and potential harm. Be careful when a vendor proposes replicating a solution that it developed for another client—that may be easier for the vendor, but it may not be the best bet for your organization. And remember, there are no shortcuts to good HIS implementations. They are slow and painstaking successes that involve the attention, commitment, and hard work of everyone in the organization.

Now that the organization has a sense of its future direction through the development of its strategic business plan, how does the HIS plan get defined and created? Those responsible for the HIS planning process now have what they need to create the HIS roadmap and strategies that marry up with that strategic business plan and help propel the organization in the right direction. HIS planning should be synchronized with the strategic business planning undertaken by the organization. Using the organization's business plan as its guide, the HIS plan documents the current state of its computer systems and IT infrastructure, contemplates a 5- to 10-year desired future state of HIS and technology (**architecture**), and lays out a path of HIS initiatives and projects that will migrate the organization's systems from "where we are" (current state) to "where we want to be in 5 to 10 years" (future state). These HIS initiatives and projects must be accomplished in the right order (the organization should put the foundational IT infrastructure in place first before implementing new software systems that rely on that infrastructure, for example). At that point, the systematic implementation of new HIS should follow the roadmap laid out by the HIS Strategic Plan to migrate the organization's systems to a new set of systems and capabilities that help the organization evolve, innovate, and grow.

It may be overwhelming to think about the entirety of the HIS that an organization needs now and in the future and about how all those systems will fit together into a unified whole. At any given time within any healthcare organization, many different constituencies are sure to request and create demand for their functions, departments, or processes to be automated with new computer systems. Typically, the demand for new systems serving various areas of the organization is enormous—exceeding the capacity for change within the organization at any one time. Thus, HIS strategic planning must prioritize the introduction of new systems carefully. Further, the demands and requests often deal with functionality oriented to a certain department or service, such as cardiology or billing. The key is to get those requesting the new systems for their areas to see the larger picture and understand the opportunities to

integrate systems. The benefits of implementing enterprise-wide systems rather than creating silos of information—isolated systems that address the work of only one department or function of the organization—are profound. **Enterprise systems** help the organization move forward in a coordinated, comprehensive fashion—silos do not.

How does HIS leadership manage these many needs and organize the computer system implementations in ways that balance the needs that must be addressed with the resources required for these implementations in a way that makes sense from a computerization perspective? The answer lies in thoughtful HIS planning, working collaboratively in multidisciplinary groups according to a disciplined methodology, documenting, and then prioritizing all the information and computerization needs of the organization's many constituents. This work is done according to an HIS architectural framework, the subject of the next section of this chapter and the second pillar in HIS planning. The HIS planning process involves first a top-down view of the organization as seen through the eyes of its senior leadership, who establish the vision, set the direction, determine the resources available, and develop structures and responsibilities for the HIS planning process. It assumes a bottom-up, grassroots perspective to contemplate how work can be done better and what is actually necessary to get the new HIS in place at a very detailed level. It is this combination of "top-down" and "bottom-up" perspectives that makes for a realistic, comprehensive, and forward-thinking HIS plan.

As described in the previous section, sound HIS strategy is a direct reflection of the organization's strategic plan and, as such, will be an enabler of the organization's strategic evolution. Thus, the planned HIS must support all existing business and clinical strategies, as well as enable some business and clinical strategies that would not be feasible using outdated or paper-based processes. An example of this type of enabling HIS is

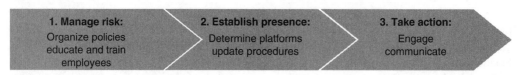

FIGURE 4.4 Social media strategy in health care.

Data from Hewlett-Packard (June 2013). Social Media in Healthcare–Why hospitals, health systems, and practices need to take a proactive approach—now. HP Whitepaper. http://h20195.www2.hp.com/V2 /GetPDF.aspx%2F4AA4-7062ENUS.pdf. Accessed March 10, 2014.

the use of wireless technologies and social media platforms for engaging patients and the community in wellness initiatives and population-based health strategies, as well as for giving researchers and analysts helpful data and insights into population-based ways to help manage chronic conditions and health promotion (**FIGURE 4.4**).

A good HIS plan also advances the organization's performance—for example, by reducing costs, reducing waste, improving revenues, enhancing service, improving the quality of care, and increasing patient, employee, and provider satisfaction. When the HIS strategies and systems support the organization in doing all these things, they are aligned with the strategic and operational needs of the organization. To do *all* these things and not just *some* of these things, the HIS plan should be designed using a systematic approach to planning a "balanced" HIS architecture. If the HIS strategy does only a few of these things, the organization may be partly—but not fully—successful in achieving its future state vision. If the HIS agenda is misaligned, or even partially incorrect, significant organizational resources will be misdirected and wasted because the resources consumed while implementing the HIS will not further the organization's strategies. This is true regardless of which type of healthcare organization it is. Perhaps most serious of all, without an effective, aligned HIS plan, the organization might cease to exist in the future, given the cost of HIS and the evolution of all commerce and interaction to electronic forms. These principles apply to creating HIS plans for physician practices, hospitals, hospital systems, long-term care organizations, home

healthcare agencies, hospice settings, and public health organizations alike.

▶ HIS Planning Framework: An Aligned, Architectural Approach

The HIS Planning Framework provides a way of thinking about HIS in clinical and business terms, yielding a nontechnical, non-vendor-specific method for thinking about HIS. It is very important to think in terms of what HIS do and the data they provide, and not who the supplier is, when evaluating HIS capabilities. Developed originally as a consulting tool, it also presents a way to visualize the totality of application systems needed in an organization's application portfolio. This helps not only the technical planning of those systems, but also the determination of budgetary requirements, staffing needs, and sequencing of the introduction of systems in a logical, feasible series of initiatives over time.

Represented in the HIS Planning Framework is a four-box quadrant, two columns and two rows, labeled as thus:

- Column 1: Transactional/Functional Support Systems

Transactions

QI	QIII
HIS	
QII	QIV

- Column 2: Analytics, Decision Support, Intelligence Systems

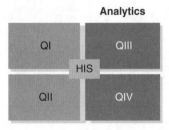

- Row 1: Clinical, Patient, Provider Support Systems

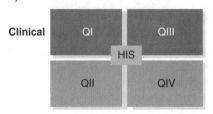

- Row 2: Administrative/Business Support Systems

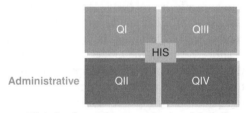

This leads to four quadrants, labeled as thus:

- QI: Clinical Transaction/Functional Support Systems
- QII: Administrative/Business Transaction/Functional Support Systems
- QIII: Clinical Analytics/Clinical Intelligence (CI)
- QIV: Administrative/Business Analytics/Business Intelligence (BI)

To begin, the HIS Planning Framework lays out the types and categories of software systems needed by a healthcare organization on a two-by-two, four-quadrant grid, based on the functional area or analytical purpose each system serves (**FIGURE 4.5**).

The framework is intended to be used to strategize and plan the balanced portfolio of software application systems needed to support the clinical and business functions and capabilities on an institution-specific basis. The framework planning process should take into consideration the market, community, provider capabilities, and population(s) served by an organization. That will create the services model that drives the need for systems to support the various clinical services and business, administrative, and analytical capabilities. Thus, in an ideal state, the organization would have the systems and applications to support those clinical, business, administrative, and analytical capabilities. The model works equally well for health systems, community hospitals, provider groups, clinics, home health, hospice, federally qualified health centers, and so on. Different business models can be planned using the HIS Planning Framework, such as **accountable care organizations (ACOs)**, population health management efforts, and the like.

The HIS Planning Framework is a generic format to be used to engage in interdisciplinary dialogue to estimate the systems needed to support various organizational configurations that might be contemplated, such as the following:

1. Groups of practices or an additional hospital or clinic as might be brought together through acquisition;
2. An example for educational purposes for groups of professionals who might be entering a planning exercise together; or
3. When considering various options for organizational priorities and budgetary allocations.

The HIS Planning Framework can also be used in planning for population health management initiatives to gain perspective on what HIS exist for organizations along the continuum of care that might or might not share certain systems such as EHR systems. This helps groups working together to understand the HIS requirements associated with managing

Transaction/Functional support systems	Management/Decision support systems (BI/CI)
Clinical Quadrant I (Clinical Transaction Systems)	Quadrant III (Clinical Management/Clinical Intelligence Systems)
Administrative Quadrant II (Administrative Transaction Systems)	Quadrant IV (Administrative Management/ Business Intelligence Systems)

FIGURE 4.5 HIS Planning Framework: The four quadrants.

Modified from Jay McCutcheon's Systems Planning Framework.

the scope of a defined population, what information, data, systems, and connectivity are available for managing that population. The framework helps identify where gaps exist or choices need to be made about which sources of data and information will be used or need to be developed and specifics about the information requirements for each quadrant. It can also be helpful for this interplay of strategic organizational and HIS planning to consider the relationship between HIS and the landmark work of Donabedian regarding healthcare quality.

HIS and Donabedian's Model: Structure, Process, and Outcomes

A landmark piece of work in the healthcare quality arena, **Donabedian's Health Care Quality Framework**, offers a complementary framework with which to examine HIS. To begin, Donabedian's conceptual model for evaluating the quality of health care identifies three major areas: Structure, Process, and Outcomes (Ayanian & Markel, 2016). This framework shows key components of health care that must be measured and addressed individually but also comprehensively and cohesively

to evaluate and improve quality of care. Donabedian's model communicates the idea that structure affects process, which in turn affects outcomes. In addition to providing a conceptual model depicting the key elements of healthcare quality, the model is used to guide the measurement of those elements in order to evaluate and provide a roadmap to improving quality. *Structure* and its measures include attributes of the providers and services, such as facilities, infrastructure, technology, education, demographics, or other "inputs" to care. *Process* and its measures apply to the ways work gets done, with people, systems, treatments, and workflows used to deliver the care that yields the *outcomes* (**FIGURE 4.6**).

Examples of process measures include wait times, time to appointments, guidelines adherence, employee training practices, documentation standards use, employee hand-washing rates, communication practices with patients, and others. Outcomes and their measures include the net effect of the care on the patient and ultimately populations and community. Examples include mortality, immunization rates, length of stay, hospital-acquired infections, patient satisfaction, provider satisfaction, and many others (A model of measuring quality care, n.d.).

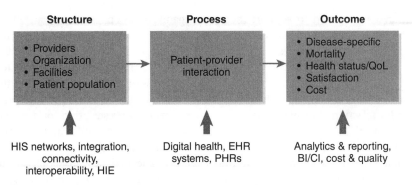

FIGURE 4.6 Donabedian's healthcare quality framework and HIS.

So, now the question becomes, "How do HIS affect and interact with these elements of Donabedian's well-accepted Health Care Quality Framework?" The obvious answer is that data and information are used to measure process and outcomes for all the metrics defined for these areas, measures that can be clinical or administrative and service in nature.

Processes occur in Quadrants I and II of the HIS Planning Framework, since QI and QII systems support day-to-day workflows and transactions. Additionally, outcomes are measured and analyzed in Quadrants III and IV HIS such as clinical intelligence (CI) and business intelligence (BI) reporting and analytics systems. For metrics agreed upon for the processes and outcomes to be evaluated, the QI and QII systems can be designed and implemented to yield the data elements needed for these measurements, which can then be straightforwardly tracked in the appropriate QIII and QIV systems. These areas touch every aspect of healthcare delivery and management, and ultimately, the goal of systems is to support improved processes, provide good data integrity, and deliver accurate, timely, and reliable information for the desired metrics. This is where it is helpful, in measuring the relationship of HIS to these measures, to employ the Five Rights of clinical decision support: making sure the information is where it is needed (right place), for whom it is needed (right person), in the form required (right format), through the right medium or method, (right channel), and when it is needed (right time) (Campbell, n.d.).

What is less obvious is the relationship between HIS and structure, with new organizational models being established in order to transition to value-based care and population health management, such as ACOs, patient-centered medical homes, and provider-patient interaction outside institutional settings. Therefore, HIS influences the structure element of the Donabedian Health Care Quality Framework, as well.

▶ HIS Planning Framework in Practice

The HIS Planning Framework defines each quadrant and the types of HIS software applications and systems that fit into each. On the surface, it does not include specific infrastructure or hardware. However, the applications and capabilities to be supported drive the requirements for those infrastructural requirements, so this is the starting point. No other components should be defined outside this framework's guidance and direction. That would neither make sense nor be cohesive in creating a balanced, integrated, enterprise portfolio of software systems and HIS capabilities. The framework is oriented toward information requirements, functionality, and identification of software systems needed to support those requirements and functionalities. Connectivity, devices, hardware capabilities, networks, security requirements, and other technical and operational requirements can be determined from that basis readily, as can hardware, devices, vendor selection sequencing, etc.

The framework's left-hand column represents transactions, or day-to-day activities and repeatable tasks necessary to conduct the clinical and business work of the organization. These activities embody the "real-time," transaction-based production work of the organization, when efficiency and consistency are essential to productivity of employees and high-quality clinical and administrative work.

The right-hand column represents the information based on "post-production" or retrospective reporting and analysis necessary to manage the clinical and business aspects of the organization, including the following types of capabilities:

- Managerial and clinical reporting
- Analytical activities assessing the efficiency and effectiveness of processes and tasks taking place on the "production" or functional side of the organization
- Outcomes analytics
- Predictive analytics assessing the risk anticipated among patient populations, groups, practices, diagnoses, contracts, and other categories of interest
- Decision support systems for planning and evaluating clinical services and outcomes, financial performance, and operational effectiveness

Following the first step of matching HIS to services and structures, the next question is, "What specific requirements do the systems in these quadrants need to perform for the organization in question?" Certain types of computer system software applications are built to support certain functional areas, departments, or types of transactions, processes, or analytics required to either deliver clinical care or support the business processes of a healthcare

organization. For instance, an EHR system supports processes essential to taking care of patients, such as registering a patient, scheduling an office visit, placing an order for a diagnostic test or treatment, delivering the results of a diagnostic test to a patient's provider, or submitting a prescription for a patient to the pharmacy. These clinical activities are day-to-day transactions that fit within Quadrant I—clinical and patient transactions. Examples of Quadrant II business processes supported by computer software applications include populating a bill with claims data and electronically submitting that claim to a payer and using computer software to track inventory and reorder medical supplies used within the organization. More categories of these types of functions are shown in Figure 4.9.

Other types of software help clinical and business analysts, researchers, and other subject matter experts in healthcare organizations understand the costs or clinical outcomes associated with various types of patients with certain conditions or tally the most frequently seen types of patients in a physician office or hospital or clinic, for example. When using this generic HIS Planning Framework, these types of software and computer systems would reside in Quadrant III (management information and analytics and **clinical intelligence (CI)** associated with evaluating the clinical effectiveness of care provided within the organization). Use of an analytical software tool to evaluate budgeted expenditures versus actual expenditures is an example of an analytical system that would reside in Quadrant IV (management information and **business intelligence (BI)** associated with managing the business side of the organization). In this manner, we can trace our way from the functions or processes of an organization that reside in each quadrant to the types of computer systems, information requirements, and software applications needed to automate those processes and functions. The planning framework shown in **FIGURE 4.7** helps us see the balance needed in the architecture of an

	Transaction/Functional Support Systems	Management/Decision Support Systems (BI/CI)
Clinical	I Patient/Provider/Clinical Care Activities	III Clinical Reporting, Data Analytics, Outcomes Analysis
Administrative	II Institutional Business activities	IV Business Reporting, Data Analytics, Key Performance Indicators Analysis

FIGURE 4.7 HIS Planning Framework: Scope of quadrants.

Modified from Jay McCutcheon's Systems Planning Framework.

	Transaction/Functional Support Systems	Management/Decision Support Systems (BI/CI)
Clinical	I • EHR, EMR, PHR, Medical intranet • Outpatient systems • Radiology, Laboratory, Pharmacy • Transcription/Dictation • Cardiology, ECG, ECHO • Maternity monitoring • Home health • PACS for imaging • Surgery • ICU systems, Monitors, Devices	III • Case mix analysis • Decision support systems • Quality analysis and reporting • Outcomes analysis • Clinical intelligence • Data warehouse • External reporting: » Joint Commission, Leapfrog, CHART, other
Administrative	II • General financials • Patient accounting • Contracts management • HRMS/payroll • Materials management/supply chain • Credentialing	IV • Financial, supply chain, HR management reporting • Cost accounting • Business intelligence, analytics • Financial decision support • Enterprise data warehouse • Budgeting, financial modeling, and forecasting

FIGURE 4.8 HIS Planning Framework with examples of software applications in each quadrant.

Modified from Jay McCutcheon's Systems Planning Framework.

entire portfolio of HIS used by an organization to support all the functions, processes, and information needs of that organization.

What types of clinical and business-related computer systems and software packages or applications support healthcare organizations? **FIGURE 4.8** shows the same HIS Planning Framework with examples of the types of computer software applications that fit into each of the four quadrants, identifying which types of processes are supported by these computer system capabilities.

What is relevant about this categorization schema is not just a listing of computer systems and software applications, but also groupings and relationships between these systems and applications. Most of each quadrant's software systems are related and tend to make use of many of the same data elements. For instance, a software application supporting laboratory test processes and functions needs patient name and medical record number, diagnosis, physician order, correct location of the patient for gathering specimens, which test should be performed, and ordering physician(s) to whom to deliver the lab test result. These same data elements (i.e., patient ID, patient diagnosis, physician order, patient location, physician names and orders) are needed for other clinical therapies and processes, such as medication administration and dispensation, radiology examinations, physical therapy, and other patient care activities. Thus, there is a high degree of overlap between the numerous clinical HIS applications and the data elements and functions they deploy. Additionally, clinically related software applications are typically supplied by software vendors specializing in a particular quadrant, for instance, as part of a comprehensive EHR system (as identified in Quadrant I of the framework).

When data elements are shared by more than one application system, and these applications operate using data stored in the same database, they are **integrated**. This is the real definition of integration. Software applications that share data from separate databases are **interfaced**. For our purposes now, note that this differentiation between integration and interfaced systems is an extremely important distinction that needs to be taken into account in planning HIS architectures. Due to the sharing of many common data elements between systems and applications residing in the same quadrant, integrated systems within a quadrant are highly preferable to interfaced systems. We will explore integration and interfaces in more depth in Chapter 9.

The planning framework depicted in Figure 4.9 is helpful in categorizing systems according to the other applications they relate to and share data with frequently and, therefore, should be integrated (sharing the same database) and not interfaced (functionality bridged between different databases). Software applications, when they will share large amounts of data, should be planned together to maximize opportunities for integration. This is especially true for functions that reside in the same quadrant, as vendors tend to provide systems related to one quadrant or another, such as clinical care (Quadrant I) or business-related financial and administrative systems (Quadrant II). Decision processes for system selection need to prioritize integration between like applications, due to the value this brings in terms of data integrity and the quality of the information produced by these systems.

The HIS Planning Framework provides a nontechnical way to discuss, visualize, and document the software application systems needed by an organization to do its work and provide the services to its patient population. It can be used to ensure that the HIS application architecture is "balanced"—that is, provides computerized support evenly to the various clinical and financial departments and workers whose work processes are being automated. The framework also provides a visual, nontechnical means of documenting the HIS that align with organizational strategy and support organizational activities—no computer science or engineering degrees required!

FIGURE 4.9 portrays the layering and hierarchical order of organizational planning elements, in an organized fashion, from the highest-level concepts and principles, such as mission, vision, and values, cascading gradually through and shaping the phases of Organizational Strategy, HIS Strategy, Strategic Initiatives, Projects, Departmental Functions, all the way to the activities of Individual Contributors. This figure shows the progressive relationships between increasingly detailed activities, beginning at the top with the overall purpose of the organization driving the purpose, content, and activities of each subsequent layer. Following this hierarchy carefully throughout the HIS planning process assures that the efforts

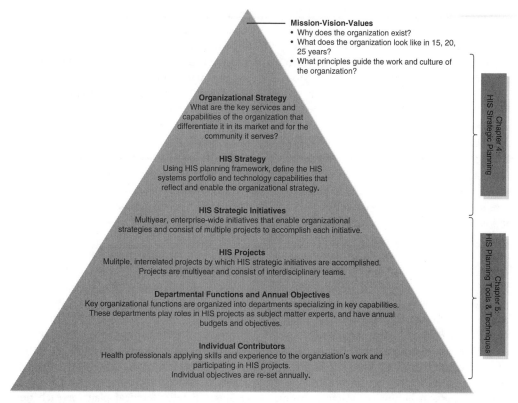

FIGURE 4.9 HIS planning hierarchy.

and resources of the organization are unified in sequence, purpose, and activities. This unified, coordinated approach creates momentum and steady progress toward the organization's desired future state, minimizing waste, confusion, and chaos in the process.

HIS Strategic Planning Process

By rooting the HIS strategic planning process in the organization's overall strategic plan, the time, effort, and resources expended on HIS initiatives, systems, and resources are assured to propel the organization toward its intended role in its community, position in its market, and cultural identity. The HIS Planning Framework guides the systematic definition of increasing levels of detail through the process from the highest mission-vision-values to

strategy to HIS Strategy to Strategic Initiatives, to HIS Projects, and so on, all the way to the work of individuals, whose work will then contribute to the desired forward movement of the organization toward its future.

The HIS Strategic Plan provides the rationale, core systems, and technology necessary for the organization to accomplish its strategic plan which takes it toward and enacts its vision for the future. The HIS Strategic Plan consists of a systematic documentation of the HIS requirements of the organization for systems, technology, data, information, and connectivity for all of its functions, including clinical, business and administrative, and analytical activities of the organization. The approach is a thorough, logical step-wise progression, beginning with a documentation of the current state of the HIS, clinical and administrative workflows, and information processes that are conducted in the organization. This is indeed a global look at and documentation of everything that the organization does in delivering its services, managing the organization, studying its market and community, connecting with outside entities with which it engages for supplies, services, and other outreach needs, and describing those activities and workflows in descriptive and detailed flowchart format. This "current state analysis" provides the starting point for any change to a new HIS. It is the baseline from which the HIS Strategic Plan builds. Remember, the HIS Strategic Plan uses the organizational Strategic Plan as its guide and is a mirror reflection of that organizational Strategic Plan in a systems and technology version. It is therefore the HIS portfolio intentionally designed to thrust the organization forward toward its organizational desired future state, as expressed in the organization's Strategic Plan. The current state analysis is the set of baseline HIS capabilities the organization sets out to replace or integrate into more expansive and capable enterprise-wide systems for the key, core clinical, business/administrative and analytical activities of the organization, designed, developed, and implemented with improved, future workflows in mind.

Migration Plan

So where does that leave us, if we have defined for the organization its HIS Strategic Plan, rooted in the organization's own strategic plan, documented the current state of the organization's HIS portfolio, and designed the future HIS state desired to meet the organization's future strategies? We then need to connect the current state (where we are) with the future state (where we want to be). The way we connect those two states is via a migration plan. Migration, the movement from one place to another, is the Herculean task facing the organization, but hopefully is in the hands of the organization's capable leadership. What is needed here is a chief information officer who thinks in terms of

these overarching strategic terms, as well as the capabilities tactically needed to specify strategic initiatives and the projects inherent to those, to lead the changes and orchestrate, step by step, the organized, understandable sequencing of projects and activities to implement the migration plan to move the HIS portfolio from current state to future state.

Once the HIS and technology *strategic* plans are in place, HIS and technology *tactical* plans must be developed in great detail. A good deal of preparation then occurs before those tactical plans can be carried out. Capital and operating budgets for each project must be established. Project teams and specialized task forces for the HIS and technology initiatives are formed. These teams consist of IT staff, clinical and administrative knowledge workers, and often external resources such as vendor experts and consultants who have familiarity not only with the computer systems but also with the functional areas of the organization being automated. Under the leadership of an experienced IT project manager, each group creates a detailed tactical plan for each new system to be implemented. This tactical plan documents requirements for the new system, analyzes current workflows, and designs new workflows and processes intended to streamline how work is performed. Ways of caring for patients or conducting administrative functions are analyzed, identifying strengths, weaknesses, opportunities, and threats vis-à-vis current methods (SWOT analysis) (Exhibit 4.1). New paths that streamline clinical and administrative workflows are designed and documented as part of the requirements for the new systems. Many ideas for improvement will be readily available from those employees who have been working in those areas and are painfully aware of areas of inefficiency, ineffectiveness, or risk. They are usually eager to participate in the design and implementation of a new computer system intended to improve those areas of weakness or inefficiency and often become the project's greatest supporters and assets.

Once the requirements for a new system are developed, a business plan including budgetary requirements will be prepared for the new project's preliminary approval and committee presentations. Only when the project is approved internally does it move forward through the detailed, tactical planning phase, and interaction through the **Request for Information (RFI)** and **RFP** processes as the ways to engage with vendors of these systems and technologies—and then only under very controlled circumstances. The days of random software vendors pedaling their wares to various department heads should be over, as well as trips to conferences and ski trips for clinical leaders. The disciplined, carefully orchestrated RFI and RFP activities lay the groundwork for the future decisions about which vendor and system will carry the organization into the future. Remember, always, there is no such thing as a free lunch.

Business Plans

A business plan must accompany each project that accomplishes each of the synchronized and interrelated steps that build the portfolio of HIS and capabilities defined using the HIS four-box Planning Framework. The HIS project business plan must be prepared in collaboration with and signed-off by others in the organization whose buy-in, input, cooperation, and resources must be sought, available, and used for the HIS project. Business projects must be approved within the culture for this buy-in and validity to clinicians and business types alike. Business plans, depending on the size of the project, will need various approval levels ranging on the impact and cost of the project to the organization. The outline for a business plan can vary from setting to setting, but generally the format includes the following:

- Executive summary
- Introduction of the problem to solve and why the business plan is being created

- Organizational need
- Information and systems capabilities requirements
- Features and functions
- Connectivity and networking requirements
- End users involved
- Expected financial requirements, five-year capital and operating budgets
- Expected staffing requirements
- Five-year cost estimate for software, hardware, networking, training, support, and maintenance over five years
- Implementation plan
- System contracting guidelines

All of this work is guided by interdisciplinary steering committees that oversee HIS and technology project efforts, help with staffing decisions about internal and external project resources, and provide communication and budgetary support. Once plans for the HIS initiatives coalesce and gain momentum, they motivate the organization to coordinate capabilities, expertise, points of innovation, and energies to begin the process of change through the implementation of new systems. Changes start to occur not only through the acquisition of new systems but also in the ways people think and envision doing their work. Once this shift starts to happen, the culture and mindset of the organization are never the same again. The transformation into the digital age has begun at this point, despite the fact that no new system has been selected as yet. What *has* changed are people's expectations of how they will do their work and care for patients: a new vision begins to take hold among those who work in and care deeply about the organization, the quality of care delivered in the institution, and the role it plays in serving the needs of the community now and well into the future.

HIS Strategic Initiatives

Thus far, we have discussed the use of the HIS Strategic Planning Framework as the guide to conceptualize and document the scope of the

HIS application portfolio. The product of this work is a global view of all HIS applications either existing, as in the case of the current state of HIS or desired, ideal HIS application portfolio. The next step once the desired, planned, directional HIS planning portfolio is laid out is to span it out over the next 5–10 years of making it a reality by the well thought out roll out of the new HIS Strategic Plan. Following the documentation of the desired HIS Strategic Plan, a reality check and feasibility analysis goes on to test the capacity of the organization to actually procure, design, build, implement, update, and support all these systems. Because of the magnitude of this phase, and the reality that organizations can only implement so many HIS at one time, and the interdependencies between the many systems and their data are very complex and must be treated with the utmost care and rationality. This is where keeping the organizational Strategic Plan and the HIS Strategic Plan in synch comes to life. The two should be married not just at the initial definition and creation stage, but also throughout the entire planning life cycle, which is continuous.

The way to break down the HIS Strategic Plan into the next level, following the HIS Planning Hierarchy (Figure 4.10), is to define HIS Strategic Initiatives and the projects that comprise each Strategic Initiative. Examples of this include using the information in HIS Planning Framework quadrants to identify common vendor suppliers of software and services to combine disparate applications and modules into core systems and an integrated enterprise system. As will be discussed later, integrated, enterprise-wide systems are far superior to the organization for many reasons, including data integrity, streamlining of workflows, vendor management, minimizing interfaces, and overall cost-effectiveness. So, the quadrants of the HIS Planning Framework become a useful tool for organizing the global HIS Strategic Plan into recognizable, digestible Strategic Initiatives, the next step toward implementation and bringing the HIS Strategic Plan to life.

Each quadrant represents unique categories of systems, as discussed earlier in this chapter. Clinical systems populate Quadrant I where all software applications of clinical transaction systems have workflows and data elements shared across the many clinical processes they support. We walk through how this detailed planning process and movement toward system acquisition works in more detail in Chapter 5.

▶ HIS Alignment and Strategic Planning

Good HIS strategy and planning rely on and require a linkage to the overall strategies and activities of the organization. In fact, today all business strategies and clinical initiatives the organization might consider must be addressed from an HIS perspective. Sometimes HIS will operate in a support or process-improvement mode (i.e., providing streamlined and improved processes); at other times HIS is the enabler (in other words, the strategy is not doable without HIS technology). The organization is able, through the planning process, to identify new strategic and operational opportunities that are facilitated by HIS.

For example, the organization might have a strategic objective of growing its outpatient cancer care services. With HIS enabling technology, it can integrate its hospital services with its outpatient imaging and cancer care services, making for a more complete and seamless care experience for patients. Alternatively, the organization might use HIS to integrate operations in hospital and university research settings, thereby connecting the "bench to the bed" in ways that help scientific advancements reach patient care settings more quickly. An opportunity to use HIS to enable new efficiency-oriented organizational strategies might apply HIS to improve supplies management by shifting this operation to "just-in-time" inventory control. Each of these three strategies would be implemented very differently if the organization did not have available modern, streamlined HIS and technology that support new streamlined processes or enable brand new models of care.

But this essential alignment—between the strategic plan and the HIS plan—extends beyond HIS supporting and enabling previously known strategies. Some strategies can be imagined only when systems and technology planning is integrated with organizational planning: when synergies between these two forces occur, brand new ideas can be conceived. For this reason, *all* strategic discussions should include an HIS element, and vice versa. That is, all HIS projects should include a calibration with strategy to assure proper strategic alignment as well as tactical objectives associated with the HIS project. This effort should include, for example, a process redesign initiative to streamline workflow and develop new processes through automation.

During this planning process, the aligned organizational and HIS strategies can be developed into detailed tactical HIS plans including HIS initiatives, project descriptions with timetables, capital and operating budgets, staffing plans, and metrics for achieving the desired benefits and mitigating inherent risks. These detailed plans and budgets then become the organizational fodder for organization-wide communication and cultural support for the demanding teamwork associated with HIS implementations and projects.

▶ HIS and Technology Strategy: Advancing Public Health

The uses of HIS and technology, especially the areas of reporting capabilities and communications networks, can have a remarkable effect on public health, the scope of which extends to the next level of the "continuum of care"

when thinking about the relationship between health and access to providers or information emanating from the provider community. Care-providing entities such as hospitals, clinics, and physician practices are striving to reach patients as closely as possible to their homes and places of work—wherever people are every day—so that they may engage in their care, maintain their health, or be cared for and monitored for chronic illness outside of institutional settings. Public health extends beyond the reaches of these healthcare organizations to educate, address, intervene, promote health, and prevent illnesses such as diabetes, heart disease, and cancer, while simultaneously seeking to address conditions, habits, or lifestyle choices that impact health such as behavioral issues related to violence, sexual behaviors, eating, sleep habits, and stress management. Additionally, public health extends to all people, whether healthy or ill, insured or uninsured—striving to keep healthy people healthy and helping people who are not well retain the good aspects of their health that they have and manage their illnesses. For people who are ill, public health's aims are to provide education and support to them and their families, slow the progression of negative health-related behaviors, and prevent the adoption of habits, exposures, or behaviors that might exacerbate their conditions.

The elements of HIS and technology such as planning, systems and their management, software applications, informatics, data and analytics, and opportunities for research have important implications for public health. Public health goes well beyond provider organizations' scopes, with access to public health initiatives being extended into rural regions, statewide, national, continent-wide, and global settings.

How we think about public health HIS and technology is a variation of how we think about HIS and technology strategy and planning for organizations as described earlier in this chapter. Public health HIS and technology have several facets that influence the ways these systems and technology are planned and implemented. Stated another way, the impact of networks and connectivity is profound in HIS and technology uses in all types of healthcare settings, but connectivity provides new means to access needed data and information for purposes of public health HIS and technology. For example, thinking about heath care as a physical, organizational construct, a person can walk across the street to the hospital emergency room or to a doctor's office or clinic to get his or her healthcare needs met. HIS planned and designed in support of public health, in contrast, means building awareness and providing access to information about health-related issues, immunization clinics, safe water, outbreaks of infection, and other major public health concerns in remote areas and undeveloped regions or countries, to uninsured or underinsured segments of the population, across states, or through global initiatives. Without enabling HIS and technology, these far-reaching elements of public health cannot be achieved.

Summary

Effective HIS strategy and planning rely on and require a linkage to overall strategies and activities of the healthcare organization. In fact, today all business strategies and clinical initiatives the organization might consider must be addressed from an HIS perspective in addition to other components. The HIS Planning Framework provides a template for engaging in meaningful dialogue about how to create a balanced application architecture and HIS portfolio for the organization. Its four quadrants display transactional clinical systems (QI), transactional administrative systems (QII), clinical reporting and analytical systems (QII),

and administrative reporting and analytical systems (QIV). The HIS strategic planning process commences with the documentation of the organization's current state of HIS, then defines a 5- to 10- to 15-year desired future state of HIS in alignment with the organization's strategic business plan. The migration plan can then be developed, articulating the roadmap for moving from current to future state. The HIS Strategic Plan breaks down into HIS Strategic Initiatives, projects, business plans, and capital and operating budgets, all the way to individual assignments. This is how the HIS Strategic Plan comes to life and moves the organization surely toward its desired future state. There is no substitute for this thoughtful and aligned HIS planning process. The time spent doing this is well worth it: preventing HIS missteps and assuring alignment between the investment in HIS and the strategic strength will support the success of the organization. The relationship between HIS as examined through the lens of Donabedian's Framework of Health Care Quality including structure, process, and outcomes is also an important aid to planning and implementing HIS and technology to improve healthcare quality. Additionally, well-constructed HIS strategy propels healthcare organizations into the future knowledge-based economy and helps them catch up, if not keep pace, with the rest of societal expectations and norms. Lastly, HIS in organizations devoted to delivering healthcare services as well as those providing for the public's health are converging in many ways. The data and information created and captured in healthcare organizations provides important input to global HIS, research, policy, and public health processes more than ever before, and this synergy stands to help improve health status across populations, an urgent and ultimate goal.

Key Terms

Accountable care
  organizations (ACOs)
Architecture
Business intelligence (BI)
Clinical intelligence (CI)
Donabedian's Health Care
  Quality Framework
Enterprise systems

Future state
Hardware
HIS Planning Framework
HIS strategy
Integrated
Interfaced
Knowledge workers
Mission

Request for Information
  (RFI)
Request for Proposal (RFP)
Software
Strategy
Values
Vision

Discussion Questions

1. Define the term strategic planning in terms of HIS.
2. Describe the HIS Planning Framework, distinguishing between each column, row, and quadrant.
3. How might the strategic planning process differ between a small clinic and a large, multihospital provider? Is the process any less important at the smaller facility?
4. Why do you think Donabedian's Framework has had such a significant impact on understanding the field of healthcare quality?
5. How do models help expand the understanding of complex, interrelated, multidisciplinary concepts, like HIS?

References

A model of measuring quality care. (n.d.). *Act academy: Online library of quality, service improvement and redesign tools.* NHS. Retrieved from https://improvement.nhs.uk/documents/2135/measuring-quality-care-model.pdf

Ayanian, J. Z., & Markel, H. (2016, July 21). Donabedian's lasting framework for health care quality. *The New England Journal of Medicine, 375*(3), 205–207. www.nejm.org/doi/full/10.1056/NEJMp1605101

Campbell, R. (n.d.). The five rights of clinical decision support: CDS tools helpful for meeting meaningful use. *Journal of the American Health Information Management Association, 84*(10), 42–47. Retrieved from http://library.ahima.org/doc?oid=300027#.W5IJOZNKgWo

Connolly, C. (2005, March 21). Cedars-Sinai doctors cling to pen and paper. *Washington Post.* Retrieved from www.washingtonpost.com/wp-dyn/articles/A52384-2005Mar20_1.html

Leviss, J. (2013, March 1). *HIT or miss: Lessons learned from health information technology implementations.* Bethesda, MD: AHIMA.

Weier, M. H. (2009, January 22). Software maintenance fees: Time for this model to change? *Information Week.* Retrieved from www.informationweek.com/software/software-maintenance-fees-time-for-this-model-to-change/d/d-id/1075860

CHAPTER 5

HIS Tactical Planning

"When the organization controls its own destiny and exerts the discipline to define detailed requirements based on strategic needs, the selection of a vendor will be more successful and better position the business relationship while also being future-reaching."

Jean Balgrosky

LEARNING OBJECTIVES

By the end of this chapter, the student will be able to:

- Connect a Health Information Systems (HIS) Strategic Plan with organizational strategy and decision making processes.
- Describe HIS planning principles and the relevance of each to successful implementation of the HIS Strategic Plan.
- Apply HIS principles through policy, governance, and planning methods.
- Use planning tools such as the HIS Planning Framework, HIS business plan template, five-year HIS cost estimate, contracting guidelines, policies, and communications for HIS initiatives and projects.
- Recognize and encourage a learning culture and apply it to HIS planning and initiatives.
- Be attentive to and aware of lessons learned and choices to be made while progressing through the build-out of the HIS Strategic Plan using HIS tools and techniques.

▶ Introduction

In Chapter 4, we covered the topic of HIS strategic planning, addressing it at the strategic level. Once the organization's **HIS Strategic Plan** is complete, or near complete, the tactical level of work is ready to be started, using planning techniques and applying principles and governance structures to the work of planning in preparation for acquiring and implementing systems. This chapter describes this next level of hands-on planning work and introduces pragmatic tools and techniques so that they can be applied to the real work of HIS planning at a detailed, action level. Why? For the written words of the HIS Strategic Plan to come to fruition, rigor and principles must infuse the effort every step of the way. The discipline of process will yield efficiency and assure success in putting the HIS Strategic Plan into reality. How is this assured? Set guiding principles. Systematize organizational progress toward its goals (clinical, business, community, and otherwise). Avoid disasters. Engage patients. Be compliant. Create a learning organization. Be adaptive and agile. Support and enable new organizational models. Change. Adapt. Evolve.

There is no longer any type of initiative in a healthcare organization that does not include HIS. Sometimes HIS will operate in a support or process-improvement mode (i.e., providing streamlined and improved processes); at other times HIS is the enabler (i.e., the strategy is not doable without HIS technology). Through the planning process, the organization is able to identify new strategic and operational opportunities that are facilitated by HIS.

For example, in today's healthcare environment, an organization will likely have a strategic objective to develop and grow its care management services, to support chronically ill patients with care outside the institution. With HIS enabling technology, the organization can integrate its primary and specialty physician practices and connect with patients in their homes and as they go about their daily lives through an app accessed on mobile devices: this makes for a more complete and seamless care experience for patients between office visits, ensuring gaps in care are filled and are minimized. Alternatively, the organization might use HIS to integrate operations and data flow between university hospital and research settings, thereby connecting the "research bench to the bed" in ways that speedily identify candidates for clinical trials and research as well as help scientific advancements reach patient care settings more quickly. An efficiency-oriented organizational strategy might apply HIS to improve supplies management by shifting an organization to "just-in-time" inventory control rather than the older "first-in-first out" or "first-in-last-out" materials management methods. Each of these three strategies would be implemented very differently if the organization did not have access to capable, modern HIS and technology that support new streamlined processes or enable brand new models of care.

The essential alignment between the organization's strategic business plan and the HIS Strategic Plan extends beyond HIS supporting and enabling previously known strategies. Some strategies can be imagined only when systems and technology planning is integrated with organizational planning. When synergies between these two forces occur, brand new ideas can be conceived. For this reason, *all* strategic discussions must include HIS considerations, and all HIS initiatives must connect with strategic considerations. That is, all HIS projects should include a calibration with strategy, to assure proper strategic alignment as well as tactical objectives associated with the HIS project. This project effort for design and implementation of a new system should include, for example, a process redesign initiative to streamline workflows and develop new types of processes through automation. **FIGURE 5.1** shows the strategic planning components. This chapter covers HIS planning tools and techniques.

During these planning processes, the aligned organizational and HIS strategies can be articulated as detailed tactical HIS plans including HIS initiatives, project descriptions with timetables, capital and operating budgets, staffing plans, and metrics for achieving the desired benefits and mitigating inherent risks. These detailed plans and budgets then become the organizational fodder for organization-wide communication and cultural support as well as individual annual

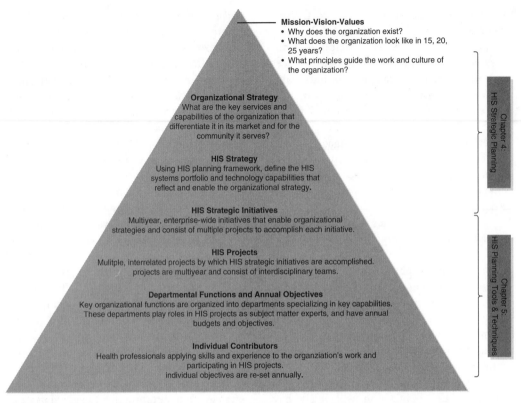

FIGURE 5.1 HIS planning hierarchy: strategic stages and planning techniques.

objectives for the demanding teamwork associated with HIS implementations and projects.

▶ HIS Planning

HIS planning tools and techniques covered in this chapter include the following:

- Guiding principles
- Tactical HIS planning
  - Architectural planning metaphor
  - Connect HIS to the Strategic Business Plan
  - Build HIS Business Planning processes and teams
  - Pursue progressive levels of detail and translate the HIS Strategic Plan into multiyear initiatives, projects, and capital/operating budgets

- Planning governance structures, including leadership, **chief information officer (CIO)**, chief medical information officer (CMIO), steering committees, project teams, and task forces
- Tools and techniques
  - Create a HIS high-level architecture
  - Business Plan template
  - five-year cost estimate template
  - Capital and operating budgets
  - Contracting guidelines
  - Policy, including governance, decision rights, and memorializing these practices and processes to assure organizational teamwork and unity

Once the important work of creating the HIS Strategic Plan is complete, the HIS guiding principles and planning tools and techniques come into play.

Guiding Principles

At the outset of work to implement the HIS Strategic Plan, **guiding principles** must be developed and agreed upon by the group of leaders and participants of these initiatives that carry out the plan's intent. Guiding principles are statements about the things the group agrees on at principles and high level of thinking—statements that the group goes back to as it struggles with decisions, priorities, habits, inertia, or methods, which it will, often. These principles point us back to true north, to the higher purpose and ideas that, at the outset, all parties agreed upon. Make no mistake about it: the work of implementing a HIS Strategic Plan is challenging, as organizational work goes. People often have had a vested interest in doing things a certain way, and have been doing so for many years and for reasons that were very good in the past: moving toward new places and new ways of doing things is uncomfortable. Power and influence and control, once wielded by a few, is distributed more evenly with information science. These changes go against the nature of many people's personalities or chafe at past definitions of success, and such change can be very difficult. The guiding principles remind the group of what they agree on and seek to do on a higher level, and help the group get past the tight spots as it navigates priorities and decisions, in spite of the self-interest of individuals or departments or functions that have "owned" certain work or functions in the past. Guiding principles help us get back on the road when we stray into the weeds.

Managerial and decision making research shows that the *status quo*, or widely held norms hold organizations back when they are operating within a high-velocity environment (Oliver & Roos, 2005). With the advent of value-based care, we have the opportunity to shed ourselves of things that veer us from our vision and try new things. This is where guiding principles can come to the rescue.

With good leadership and facilitation of discussions, these higher-level and rational directions will guide the process, rather than habit, power-mongering, or fear-based decision making. Successful development of guiding principles relies heavily on dialogue, with stages of inquiry, divergence, and convergence. This process works best with excellent facilitation by someone not part of the organization and its culture. These dialogue-intensive processes are similar to those described for facilitating development of a culture of a learning organization (Oliver & Jacobs, 2007). By its very nature, HIS initiatives portend change, movement, redesign, and new ways of doing new things. Creating a culture of collaboration in the organization around HIS means finding the balance between flexibility and control, access and security, discipline in managing information and systems and freedom in insight, information, and knowledge. These dynamics are essential to the successful navigation of HIS strategy to achieve organizational strategic goals and success. And, of course, all of this is enabled by transparency and communication.

Steps in Developing Guiding Principles

Properly facilitated, the steps in a group developing guiding principles, such as an HIS Steering Committee (Chapter 6), begins with talking about the common denominator and shared values, no matter what role someone plays in the organization (Make a Dent Leadership, n.d.). One of the most important features of these discussions (and the HIS Steering Committee) is that they are broad and interdisciplinary. These discussions include representation from every sector of the healthcare organization: from food service to customer care to billing specialist to clinician to executive management.

Here are four broad steps to creating guiding principles (Glandon, Smaltz, & Slovensky, 2010).

- Step 1: *Articulate the organization's values.* A number of core values drive the organization and define it. These values are things that draw people to working in the organization in the first place. The values don't necessarily relate to individuals' personal expertise: they relate to their motivation and purpose for working in health care. This forms the common denominator to engage in dialogue about specific issues and choices in the activation and execution of the HIS Strategic Plan and its many initiatives. There are typically six to eight core values that drive an organization toward its reason for being. These values are applied in every decision this leadership group makes. How HIS is done in an organization should absolutely be consistent with these values. The output of this step is a clearly stated summation of these values that is distributed through the planning committee or organization.
- Step 2: *Document the current state.* Identify how things are done now and explore how that harms the organization and its people's ability to perform the intended purpose. What barriers prevent hard-working professionals from meeting the mission of the organization, harm the quality of the product and services, and keep the organization from its intended purpose? This is the opportunity to identify (and eliminate) irrational practices that impair the organization's ability to meet its goals and provide services in accordance with the shared values.
- Step 3: *Develop the guiding principles.* This step emanates from the previous two and reflects the core values shared by all. The principles must be consistent with the values, address the intended level of service to patients, and speak to the experience of key stakeholders such as nurses and physicians. One pitfall to avoid is that of solution-jumping: keep the discussion on what is important to the organization's ethos. Sample phrasing may include language as follows: "People will be ____ when they ____;" or, "Service will be ____ when it ____."
- Step 4: *Apply the guiding principles.* When people are asked how they apply the values and principles to their decisions or activities, the principles and actions should align. This is a good test of HIS strategic decisions as they are being discussed and before they are finalized. Every decision arrived at by the HIS Steering Committee and along the way in performing HIS planning and decision making should be consistent with these values and principles. This is how guiding principles work: gotta use them!

Examples of guiding principles that might apply to HIS planning include the following:

- *The patient comes first.* This principle is typically one that those working in health care arrive at first and agree on.
- *Be flexible.* To what degree are people willing to adjust their habits, tendencies, and methods that have worked for them in the past to meet a shared goal of the future? HIS strategies and projects should always challenge the status quo and current ways of doing things, otherwise, there is missed opportunity in a major way. So, flexibility could be a very important principle to guide decisions and help people remain connected to their values rather than their habits or current methods or job descriptions.

HIS-Related Guiding Principles

Now let's turn to some HIS-related principles to guide HIS decision and enactment of strategy.

- ***Integration*** over ***interfacing*** *for enterprise systems.* The investment of money, opportunity, energy, and time to define, acquire, build, test, train, implement, and support over the long haul for core HIS should be done with the long-term in mind. Synergy, safety, and simplicity accompany an integrated enterprise system. Thinking interfaces can create these benefits over time is foolhardy and usually motivated by self-interest, resistance to change, and perhaps loyalty to a commercial vendor versus the organization's overall best interest.

■ *Say no to silos.* This guiding principle is related to the "integration over interfacing" principle above, yet "say no to silos" spans not only the systems themselves, but also as a way of thinking and architecting HIS. Silos are defined as a tower, pit, or chamber designed to hold one type of thing: examples of siloes in health care may be a departmental HIS that only communicates with itself, or a department culture that makes decision independently rather than collaboratively. These silo systems, or islands of data, produce information in a vacuum, isolated from other systems and data, and requiring some form of interfacing, integration, or manual combining and comparing with other sources of information. Worse yet, these silos often overlap with the content of other systems, causing arguments and confusion about which source of the same type of information is correct, sanctioned by the organization, and should be used for decision making. These sources also are hazardous, in that they can be used to prepare beautiful reports and graphics, but the data may be only a subset of the total picture that should create that information, thus misleading the clinical or business decision maker. At a minimum, these siloed data sources cause consternation and ineffectiveness organizationally because meetings that should be productive are usually spent debating whose data are right, rather than getting to the task at hand and making good decisions for the organization and patients. At their worst, silos can create bad or misinformed business decisions and clinical errors. Be courageous. Address the tough issues and follow your guiding principles that put the patient first. Avoid silos.

■ *Manage the vendor; don't let the vendor manage you.* Doesn't matter what the product is—software, hardware, services, consulting. Vendors have a way of gaining undue influence in an organization, or at least with certain groups within an organization. Influence within groups is usually due to their connection to that area, there being some sort of mutual interest. For instance, a billing department might align with and therefore be unduly influenced by a vendor of patient billing and accounts receivable software and services. Or, a clinical department, such as cardiology, might be largely in favor of a silo vendor of software that addresses the needs of cardiology exclusively. Another way that healthcare organizations occasionally allow vendors to manage them, rather than the other way around, is accepting contracts written by the vendor. Every vendor contract should be thoroughly negotiated, to the point of it being re-written, to service the needs of the healthcare organization. It takes open dialogue, interdisciplinary involvement, and effective communication and education about the HIS Strategic Plan and guiding principles to navigate these discussions. It can be tricky business for an organization to traverse the shoals of political energy, HIS planning, and timely execution to maintain momentum needed to keep pushing forward toward successful implementation of a HIS Strategic Plan that serves the whole.

■ *Transparency is required in all matters.* Borrowed from the physical world, meaning clear or translucent, the word transparency in management and business means being open and honest, both in commission and omission of the facts and truth. We all know when transparency exists in a relationship or dialogue, and we know when it does not. These dynamics make or break a group and the goals it is trying to achieve. Setting transparency as a guiding principle and then holding the group to it (another thing altogether) is one of the skills of a good facilitator: one who can achieve this dynamic in the culture of a group earns their keep!

■ *Use interdisciplinary decision making processes.* This applies especially to the process of including patients in decisions, in addition to the clinical, administrative, and support subject matter experts in those disciplines. The voices of key disciplines must be represented for holistic decisions.

■ *Adhere to standards; be compliant.* HIS is tied closely to regulations, both in requirements for programs such as **Meaningful Use (MU)** and **Medicare Access and CHIP Reauthorization Act of 2015 (MACRA)**. It is also a completely creative, free process, left to the ingenuity of information technology professional who choose to apply their time and expertise to improving health care. It is somewhere between proscribed and free-form that HIS lives and prospers. We have utterly lacked the discipline and selflessness to embrace universal standards in HIS in the U.S. This is something we pay for every day: the result is expensive financially, clinically, and in terms of human suffering. It is time to wake up and smell the coffee, and adopt relevant HIS standards for technology, data, and processes.

■ *Be adaptive and agile in HIS development methods.* Agile HIS development is based on collaborative and integrative requirements: this method works in short sprints to create HIS development agendas that allow for continuous and flexible progress. This is in contrast to traditional waterfall methods that seek definition of longer-term phases that lock in requirements and then allow developers to work for many months to move HIS products and capabilities forward.

■ *Picking a vendor is not a strategy.* So much attention is paid these days to which electronic health record (EHR) or enterprise resource planning (ERP) system vendor will be selected and implemented by an organization. But this is not the highest priority. Nor does this result in an organization-driven strategy being achieved. The organization must develop *its own* HIS Strategic Plan as a reflection of its strategies and goals, as outlined in Chapter 4, to populate its well thought-out and balanced portfolio of application software to propel it to its desired future state. Too much focus too early on which vendor "should" be selected spoils that comprehensive and strategic aim. When the organization controls its own destiny and exerts the discipline to define detailed requirements based on strategic needs, the selection of a vendor will be more successful and better position the business relationship with the vendor while also being future-reaching. If the selection of a particular vendor for its EHR system is seen as the primary strategic target, the vendor has the organization in its hand: the organization is about to get twisted in the wind, and it'll pay for the privilege. Anytime a true selection is taking place (meaning there are minimum of two vendors for any HIS that could be chosen and be acceptable to the organization), the organization wins. Anytime the converse is true, meaning there is only one vendor the organization has its heart set on, there is not a real negotiation. When that happens, the vendor wins. Buyer, beware.

■ *Be thorough in definition of principles.* Additional guiding principles may be designed by the steering planning group, depending on the particulars of the situation. Examples of other types include technical principles, such as *The HIS Strategic Plan will be constructed using open, standard technologies, not proprietary or closed technologies.*

▶ HIS Plans and Projects Follow the HIS Strategic Plan

The HIS Strategic Plan that reflects the strategic direction of the organization, covered in Chapter 4, is the precursor to the detailed HIS planning that then commences. The overall plan is broken down into **Strategic Initiatives**, linking strategy and actionable projects, each of which consists of numerous projects that together comprise the initiative. When architecting the Strategic HIS portfolio, remember the need for balance and relentless connection to the organization's strategic business plan. Any effort spent otherwise is not only wasted, it also pulls the organization away from its vision and strategic goals.

HIS and Technology Strategy: Architecture Builds a Strong House

Just like planning and building a strong, purposeful house that meets the needs of the people living in it, HIS and technology strategy can be thought of and expressed architecturally. It can be designed to support and enable the functions essential to the purpose, strategy, activities, and structure of the healthcare organization, supporting its services, functions, and relationships.

The first step in creating a strong, useful house is to spend time planning and thinking through the activities and needs of those living in the house, taking its community and surroundings into consideration. One must then draw up detailed plans, blueprints,

specifications, and cost estimates, which are reviewed and approved by all interested parties, before one shovel is shoved into the ground and construction begins. The same architectural approach applies, whether developing HIS and technology plans for a healthcare organization or for public health needs.

Once an architectural plan is devised and approved, "construction" commences. The first step in the construction process is preparing the land and laying a good foundation. It is no different with HIS and technology plans: once the overall plans are approved and funded, the first step is to lay the foundation, consisting of a robust HIS and technology infrastructure. The systems and networks rely on a strong foundation or infrastructure. **Infrastructure** is the "electronic highway" that carries data, images, voice, and information traffic between the myriad users of the systems and technology, all at the speed of light. Clearly, there is nothing more important than a reliable, robust network infrastructure as the foundation of an organization's HIS and technology plan.

Adequate infrastructure must be in place (and constantly maintained) to support the data communications, software, devices, and hardware used to automate all organizational services and functions, and to create and collect all the essential data and information as outlined in the HIS and technology plans. Riding upon this infrastructure are data and images communicated between users of the systems and the data centers where the hardware servers and network monitoring systems reside. Infrastructure also supports the communications between software systems used by clinicians and business people responsible for day-to-day services and management of the organization.

In health care, nothing is more important than having reliable systems that are up to the task of supporting processes and workflows associated with caring for patients and their families, and meeting the needs of busy employees and clinicians. In other industries, and even on the business side of healthcare organizations, if a billing system or human resources management system goes down for a few hours, the organization can quickly adapt and recover. The worst that happens may be that an extra day's work is added to the accounts receivable function, or a recruiting report is not available for a management meeting that can be rescheduled for tomorrow. In health care, however, if a system supporting a clinical function such as the laboratory, the surgical suite, or the EHR goes down for a few hours, *patients' lives can hang in the balance.* When this happens, clinicians must be well trained in immediately turning to temporary manual systems until the computers are back up and running. Such system failures can be harrowing experiences for all involved and are to be avoided at all costs. Computer systems supporting business functions must be accurate, robust, and available 10–15 hours per day; computer systems supporting patient care must be accurate, robust, and 100 percent reliable on a 24 × 7 × 365 basis. Mission-critical clinical systems cannot go down! In the remote chance they do, well-practiced plans must be in place. In turn, HIS and technology—especially that supporting clinical care—must be well funded, robust, reliable, and well supported by internal HIS staff and software and hardware vendors. The number one priority is system "up-time;" clinical systems must always be up and running.

What does this mean for HIS and technology plans and budgets? It means they must be practical, realistic, rooted in good stewardship, and not based on "projections" or wished-for budget commitments. It means that the totality of all the systems running in the organization must be balanced in such a way that sufficient resources are assured not only for their building and implementation, but also for ongoing support of the systems in all essential areas. Investment in one system should be in balance with others. The HIS plans must provide a detailed and realistic accounting of what it will take to meet the HIS and technology needs

of the entire organization and all of its strategies, projects, and workers over the long haul. In other words, returning to the house metaphor, you cannot talk about getting the marble bathtub with waterjets on the second floor of the house until you are sure you can afford running water. You must establish basic plumbing and electrical systems, mark out adequate space, and consult with the family to ascertain its needs. Such is the nature of HIS and technology planning: plans for the total organization must be laid out and collectively agreed upon before becoming super-specialized or esoteric and directed toward any one department or function. Specialization too early often comes at a price—namely, the neglect of other areas that need automated systems to support their work as well. HIS planning must take a balanced, holistic approach so that the total effort and costs to build and maintain all the needed systems and technologies are understood and approved on a feasibility basis *before* the first projects are approved and under way. This is an HIS planning *cardinal rule.*

Other key facets of an HIS and technology plan are mapping out the data plan—that is, who needs to share what data with whom among the various functions and departments within the organization, and who inside the organization needs to share what data with which outside business and clinical partners and suppliers. The data interactions between departments and systems within a healthcare organization are often likened to a bowl of spaghetti, and rightly so. With so many interrelationships within the complex and multidisciplinary nature of healthcare processes and clinical workflow, sharing and communicating cross-divisionally are key.

Balanced Application Portfolio

When thinking about the types of systems that a healthcare organization should have, remember the bottom-line principle: no essential part can be left out. If the household cannot fully function, the people living in the house will not be happy! When considering the various types of systems that must be implemented to support a healthcare organization, the agile HIS planning framework presented in this chapter and in Chapter 4 provides a straightforward approach: systems in all four quadrants must be considered and built into the plan as needed. Major categories of HIS include the following:

- *Clinical care*: Supports day-to-day activities clinical involving patients, providers, ancillary support services, and families (Quadrant I).
- *Institutional business*: Supports day-to-day administrative transactions for financial, billing, human resources, and supply and inventory functions (Quadrant II).
- *Clinical intelligence and quality*: Supports clinical analytics, reporting, and measurement of clinical outcomes and quality improvement (Quadrant III).
- *Business intelligence and management*: Supports business analytics, reporting, management controls, and measurement of budgetary and cost outcomes (Quadrant IV).
- *Infrastructure*: Includes the networks, technology, devices, interface engines, Internet- and web-based systems, and machine environment necessary to house and support all four quadrants of application software systems and services supporting the organization's end users.

A balanced HIS and technology plan and portfolio address the needs of all these areas in a judicious, even-handed manner.

Staffing Plan

In addition to the systems and technology portfolio outlined previously, the HIS and technology plan must identify the IT staffing and talent needed to properly design, build, and support the wide variety of systems and myriad end users of those systems throughout the organization. Each of these systems and technologies requires information systems and technology professionals who possess the highly specialized expertise required for planning, building, implementing, and supporting these systems and end users. A common misconception is that software vendors or consultants can come into the organization and provide all the necessary services to design, build, and implement new systems for the organization. That is just not so. While qualified external players are a very important piece of the puzzle, there is no substitute for in-house experts in the areas of HIS and technology who know *both* the technology *and* the organization, including its people, culture, and processes. It is through these relationships between HIS experts and clinicians and business people of the organization that successful implementations and ongoing support of these systems and their end users take place.

Additional HIS and technology staffing includes people from various disciplines who are recruited to serve on HIS project teams, task forces (charged with accomplishing a single initiative or objective), and steering committees (charged with overall decision making for a major aspect of HIS and technology topics). Their time is essential for interdisciplinary collaboration on the teams and groups that work together to plan, select, design, develop, implement, and evaluate systems and technologies in the organization. The membership of these groups will vary based on the area each system addresses. For instance, a clinical system project, such as a project to select a new software system for the healthcare organization's laboratory, would require participation by individuals with recognized expertise in IT as well as laboratory disciplines such as pathology, blood bank, cytology, and laboratory management. It would also be important to have representation from functions that use the services of the laboratory, such as nursing, medicine, patient billing, inpatient and ambulatory clinical settings, and others. The time spent on these types of initiatives varies, but such efforts can consume a significant portion of a person's full-time-equivalent availability for a period of many months or even years on larger projects, such as projects for a new EHR system or financial systems for the organization. These experts' careers can ultimately shift completely to HIS implementation and support.

Sometimes the addition of HIS expertise and know-how to a healthcare professional's skills set opens up an exciting branch on that person's career path. Many people who have significant experience in various areas in health care (from any of the many clinical or administrative departments such as nursing or finance) truly enjoy the new challenges associated with implementing HIS and technology. Some people just seem to have an affinity for HIS and technology, even if they have worked in other areas for their entire career and have no formal HIS education. They may make the complete transition to specializing in HIS and technology for their functional area (e.g., laboratory systems) and embrace the professional development and stimulation associated with that growth, or they may blend their expertise with HIS in a shared role.

Data Plan

In addition to the software, hardware, and network infrastructure associated with HIS and technology, an essential consideration in HIS and technology planning is **data**. It is critical to develop a data plan that becomes as active a part of managing HIS and technology as keeping the systems and devices up and running. After all, the many systems and expensive technology investments are all for naught if the data being created, stored, and transmitted throughout the organization for patient care and business purposes are inaccurate. A data plan establishes principles and policies by which data will be managed and stewarded by the organization as part of the implementation

and use of its HIS and technology. It consists of these agreed-upon principles, such as identified, single sources sanctioned for each type of data (e.g., an EHR system for clinical data). Also needed are data standards, a data dictionary, and a data model/map, showing the relationship between the various data elements created and captured by all the systems on the HIS plan and in the organization's HIS portfolio.

Documenting and communicating the data plan makes everyone in the organization aware of and part of proper data stewardship, which is the careful and responsible management of something entrusted to one's care. **Data ownership** is an important part of data stewardship; the responsibilities associated with the quality and consistency of the data elements emanating from a particular system are assigned to the individuals who use that system. For instance, the quality and consistency (collective data characteristics constituting what is thought of as "data integrity") of laboratory data are the responsibility of those managing and working in the laboratory, who use the system every day to do their work. If a problem arises with laboratory reports or laboratory billing claims, then the laboratory professionals who "own" the responsibility for laboratory data (in other words, the individuals who are the data stewards for that area) are the ones who, with the assistance of the IT professionals who support the lab system, investigate the causes of the data integrity issues and ensure the problem is corrected. This is the case whether the data integrity problem was due to technical issues, a faulty interface, user training needs, or another factor. Whatever steps are necessary to correct the issues and satisfy both the organization as a whole and those who rely on absolute accuracy of these life-essential laboratory data are treated as the number one priority until the problem is resolved. (This also involves going back into the system and identifying flawed data and double-checking everything that system touches to make sure there are no "collated" or processing data errors.)

Let us describe these data-related terms briefly. (Refer to the Data chapter for further discussion of the uses and attributes of data.) **Data structures** are the methods and formats used to organize data in a computer, often described in terms of records, files, and arrays. IT professionals such as programmers, interface analysts, systems analysts, database specialists, and systems engineers rely heavily on data structures to do their work. The ability to move a data element from one computer system to another, or combine like data elements from source systems with different data structures, relies on properly managing and programming the commands to accurately take these data structures into account while moving or interoperating data.

The **data dictionary** is a directory or database that contains data about the data elements in the systems of an organization, also referred to as metadata ("data about data"). Maintaining the data dictionary is an important way that an organization's IT department does its part for data stewardship. Knowing which data elements exist in all the various systems, where the data elements are located in those systems' databases, what the data elements' structures are, and other key "data about data" or **metadata**, (explored in more depth in Chapter 10) is essential to being able to manage, combine, transmit, and accurately steward data in an organization. Otherwise, confusion and error prevail.

A **data model** is a map or visual representation showing the way data are organized according to their relationship to one another and to key elements of a process or function. In healthcare organizations, these key elements would include patients, providers, employees, and suppliers, among other constituents. A data model is helpful in the systems engineering and programming processes to show the branches on the tree-like structure of the data layout.

Each of these data terms is key to proper data management and stewardship, which is one of the essential parts of an HIS and technology plan. Another key part is the practice of keeping all systems up-to-date in terms of the version of that system that is being used at any point in time. If allowed to lag behind regular vendor updates, the software and technology will not work properly, which can lead to major problems not only in that one system, but also in any other system with which that system interacts or shares data. Keeping HIS software and technologies current is akin to what users of personal computers and word programs call "updates and version control," including the essential habit of making sure you stay current with software updates and apply them to your personal computer and its applications as they become available. In personal computing, sometimes the new versions or updates work very well and add needed or desired functionality. At other times, however, they seem to add features that do not make sense or, worse yet, do not work correctly. In such a case, the vendor must then send out another update or "patch" to correct the problems introduced by the problematic update or version of the software program. It is no different with the large software systems that organizations rely on for clinical and business applications and processes. The only thing that changes is the scale!

Keeping up to date with vendor software versions and updates is part of sound HIS and technology management and stewardship; this requires proper planning and budgeting, open communication, and a good working relationship with the vendor. It is one of the ways that healthcare organizations rely on their suppliers of software, hardware, devices, and services related to HIS and technology, and one of the reasons why having high-quality suppliers of these products and services is so very important to successful HIS and technology efforts within healthcare organizations, and essential to the viability of the organizations themselves.

▸ HIS Planning Tools and Techniques

Progressive layers of detail breaking down/ translating HIS Strategic Plan into multiyear initiatives, projects, and capital/operating budgets is what's involved in implementing the HIS Strategic Plan. Following the overall approach outlined in Chapter 4, this further breakdown of HIS Strategic Plan relies on the definition of HIS Strategic Initiatives to bring phases and stages to each massive or HIS Strategic capability. What must be remembered is that a principle discussed in the last section—a vendor does not equate to a strategy—applies here. The organization takes its future into its collective hands through the implementation of its HIS Strategic Plan. The ability to enact this approach evokes an architectural metaphor, that the principles followed are akin to those used to build a house. No one vendor can provide for all these needs for a balanced HIS portfolio. Architectural principles apply here to create a balanced HIS portfolio of applications for the organization as designed using the HIS Planning Framework with its four-quadrant structure.

The following tools and techniques are tried and true methods to use when getting into the detailed levels of HIS Planning.

HIS Planning Framework: An Aligned, Architectural Approach

A sound HIS strategy is a direct reflection of the organization's strategic plan and, as such, will be an enabler of the organization's strategic evolution. Thus, the planned HIS must support all business and clinical strategies, as well as enable some business and clinical strategies that would not be feasible using paper-based processes. An example of this type of enabling HIS is the use of wireless technologies and social media platforms for engaging patients and the community in wellness initiatives and population-based health strategies, as well as for giving researchers and analysts helpful data and insights into population-based ways to help manage chronic conditions and health promotion.

A good HIS plan also advances the organization's performance—for example, by reducing costs, reducing waste, improving revenues, enhancing service, improving the quality of care, and increasing patient, employee, and provider satisfaction. When the HIS strategies and systems support the organization in doing all these things, they are "aligned" with the strategic and operational needs of the organization. To do *all* these things and not just *some* of these things, the HIS plan should be designed using a systematic approach to planning a "balanced" HIS architecture. If the HIS strategy does only a few of these things, the organization may be partly—but not fully—successful in achieving its future state vision. If the HIS agenda is misaligned, or even partially incorrect, significant organizational resources will be misdirected and wasted because the resources consumed while implementing the misaligned HIS will not further the organization's strategies—they will in fact detract. This is true regardless of which type of healthcare organization it is. Perhaps most serious of all, without an effective, aligned HIS plan, the organization might cease to exist in the future, given the cost of HIS and the evolution of all commerce and interaction to electronic forms. These principles apply to creating HIS plans for physician practices, hospitals, hospital systems, long-term care organizations, home healthcare agencies, and public health organizations alike.

The HIS planning process involves first a top-down view of the organization as seen through the eyes of its senior leadership, who establish the vision, set the direction, determine the resources available, and develop structures and responsibilities for HIS planning. It then assumes a bottom-up, grass-roots perspective to contemplate how work can be done better and what is actually necessary to successfully get the new HIS in place at a very detailed level. It is this combination of "top-down" and "bottom-up" perspectives that makes for a realistic, comprehensive, pragmatic, and forward-thinking HIS plan.

It is important to remember that in HIS and technology, "everything touches everything." In other words, it is impossible to do something in one area of the HIS portfolio that does not affect another, for better or worse. Consequently, leadership within each healthcare arena (whether organizations, government, or clinical/business), coordinated with leadership of each layer and the "whole" is essential to HIS success. Additionally, there is a leadership role within each layer of the HIS model: infrastructure, systems and management, data and informatics, people and processes, analytics, BI, CI, and AI, and global HIS, research, policy, and public health.

The HIS Business Plan

The first tool in **FIGURE 5.3**, high-level architecture, has been explored earlier in this chapter. The second tool, **HIS Business Plan**, is closely linked to the HIS Planning Framework (**FIGURE 5.2**). The purpose of this framework is to provide the structure to conceptualize and document a balanced HIS application software portfolio based on the purpose, clinical and business activities, and information requirements of your organization. Using the framework, it is straightforward to organize and design an application portfolio for any type of healthcare organization. This framework provides a nontechnical, visual tool to help with education and communication about HIS and the planning process for any healthcare organization. The output of this framework tool is a basic, simple, but thorough conceptualization of the operational and management needs of your organization and how HIS and applications

	Transaction/Functional Support Systems	Management/Decision Support Systems (BI/CI)

Clinical	I
	• EHR, EMR, PHR, Medical intranet
	• Outpatient systems
	• Radiology, Laboratory, Pharmacy
	• Transcription/Dictation
	• Cardiology, ECG, ECHO
	• Maternity monitoring
	• Home health
	• PACS for imaging
	• Surgery
	• ICU systems, Monitors, Devices
		III
		• Case mix analysis
		• Decision support systems
		• Quality analysis and reporting
		• Outcomes analysis
		• Clinical intelligence
		• Data warehouse
		• External reporting:
		   » Joint Commission, Leapfrog,
		     CHART, other

Administrative	II • General financials • Patient accounting • Contracts management • HRMS/payroll • Materials management/supply chain • Credentialing	IV • Financial, supply chain, HR management reporting • Cost accounting • Business intelligence, analytics • Financial decision support • Enterprise data warehouse • Budgeting, financial modeling, and forecasting

FIGURE 5.2 HIS Planning Framework with examples of software applications in each quadrant.

Modified from Jay McCutcheon's Systems Planning Framework.

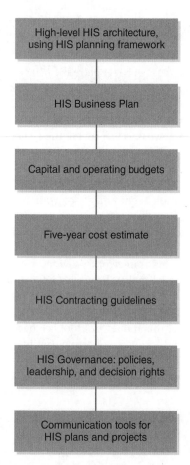

High-level HIS architecture, using HIS planning framework

HIS Business Plan

Capital and operating budgets

Five-year cost estimate

HIS Contracting guidelines

HIS Governance: policies, leadership, and decision rights

Communication tools for HIS plans and projects

FIGURE 5.3 HIS plan techniques and tools.

should be architected and prioritized to support those needs. The information culled from the HIS Planning Framework will be the fodder for the HIS Business Plan.

The basic outline for a business plan includes the description of the HIS project and then breaks it down into specifics so that by the end of the document, the reader understands the project thoroughly including connection to the HIS Strategic Plan and HIS Planning Framework, and is informed about what is required to accomplish it, use case(s), requisite technology needs, staffing, and financial resources, as well as risks and contingencies associated with the project.

The outline for a business plan can vary in specifics, but generally the format, presented in **EXHIBIT 5.1**, includes the following:

■ Executive summary: the executive summary explains the project from top to bottom in one-to-two pages. It should be written in the voice of a nontechnical professional, and transparently and concisely include key facts necessary for the decision maker or a person with a brief time investment, to understand the project costs, benefits, timeframe, risks, and relationship to strategy. The executive summary includes key points of each of the detailed sections of the business plan described as follows.

■ Introduction of the project: this section provides an in-depth description of the project and problem it is intended to solve, in other words, why the business plan is being put forward. Project goals and objectives are articulated in detail, giving background leading up to the definition of the project, connection to other initiatives underway or planned for the organization, and rationale for proceeding.

■ Organizational need: this section describes the needs of the organization for the project, including the functions it is unable to perform without the project and benefits that will be attained by funding and implementing it.

■ Information and systems capabilities requirements: this section defines detailed HIS and project requirements including features and functions, technology, connectivity and networking, and business attributes of the successful HIS and vendor(s).

■ Interdisciplinary involvement: this section lays out the governance structure for the project, including steering committee, task groups, and other roles for multiple disciplines and stakeholders involved in the HIS project.

■ Expected financial requirements, five-year capital, and operating budgets: this

EXHIBIT 5.1 HIS Business Plan Template

HIS Business Plan

Project Name:	
HIS Planning Framework Quadrant	
Date:	
Project Sponsor:	
Primary Project Contact:	
Data Owner/Data Steward:	
Estimated Number/Scope of Users?	
Is this an ASP/Cloud Provider?	Yes ❏ No ❏
Is this project connected to the HIS Strategic Plan? Describe below.	Yes ❏ No ❏

Executive Summary:

Include connection to the HIS Strategic Plan.

Project Description:

Include connection to the HIS Strategic Plan and location and data relationships within HIS Planning Framework

Problem Statement:

What processes will be supported?

Use Case(s):

Please include list of key stakeholders affected by this system.

(continues)

EXHIBIT 5.1 HIS Business Plan Template *(continued)*

Current State	
Proposed Future State:	
Cost Benefit Analysis/ROI : Please attach five-year cost estimate template and summary	
Are there overlaps with existing tools/applications/ software/data?	Yes ❑ No ❑
If yes, please identify overlaps and rationale/issues:	
Are there connections to Key Performance Indicators (KPIs)?	Yes ❑ No ❑
If yes, explain:	
Is there potential for ePHI?	Yes ❑ No ❑
If yes, explain:	
What reporting requirements and metrics will be produced?	
What data elements will be required?	
Evaluation Criteria	
Include project risks.	
Date vetted through HIS Steering Committee	
Committee comments and feedback	
Approved	Yes ❑ No ❑ Disposition:

section includes a summary of all costs needed to carry out the project, including a five-year cost estimate detailing start-up capital expenditures as well as operating expenses for all areas, and HIS participating in the project, such as software, hardware, networking, training, support, and maintenance.

- Expected staffing requirements: this section details project requirements for personnel and consulting resources needed for the project, for all phases, including implementation as well as on-going support and operational support.
- Implementation plan: this section describes the approach recommended for implementing the HIS, including project phases and key milestones.
- Project Summary, needed approvals, and next steps: this section of the business plan summarizes the project, the process for presenting the project to various stakeholders, and what the needed approvals are from stakeholder groups, steering committees, management, and the board of trustees.

Capital and Operational Budgets for HIS

The HIS strategic planning process should include budgeting, and good budgeting begins with policies surrounding the process. Continuous planning and budgeting is part of a well-managed HIS function. This HIS planning and budgeting deserves dedicated staff and attention, including participation in the overall organizational planning and budgeting processes. This requirement should be memorialized in organizational policy; HIS is never an afterthought, but a proactive, detailed set of plans, budgetary requirements and projections, so the financial department can anticipate and build the financial resources into the short- and long-term financial picture overall. The HIS Strategic Plan keeps HIS knitted into the financial fabric of the organization, since it proactively identifies HIS budgetary needs going

forward. This way budgets are anticipated and can be allocated one, three, and five years out for HIS and initiatives. The HIS Strategic initiatives that comprise the HIS Strategic Plan are typically funded in large part through **capital budgets** of organizations, plus the operating budgets that accompany them. Capital budgets are expended for start-up items such as major hardware and multiyear software licenses with greater than a three-, four-, or five-year useful lives, although a few organizations interpret items with greater than a one-year useful life as capital. This is up to the finance leadership of the organization to establish as a policy, applied uniformly across all areas. Items that meet the requirements to be classified as capital expenditures according to **Generally Accepted Accounting Principles (GAAP)** rules, qualify to be funded out of capital budgets.

Budget line items, such as project management, training expenditures, or consulting hourly expenses, are defined as operating expenses and must be funded from the organization's **operating budget**. Operating expenses do not have a useful life of over five years: they get used and then they are gone (like a day's work or food in the cafeteria), with no further useful life from an accounting perspective. It is important to work carefully with the finance department to determine which project expenditures are capital expenses and which are operating, so that proper accounting and budgeting for the project are achieved.

HIS Project Five-Year Cost Estimate and Template

The **Five-year cost estimate** is one of the most informative and revealing exercises in the overall work of HIS planning. Assumptions about the full cost of a project are usually underestimated due to an over-reliance on vendor input and fixation on software license fees, until this thorough estimation of all categories of cost associated with the acquisition and implementation of a new system into the organization is completed. The five-year cost estimate includes not just software license fees, often discussed throughout the organization as the "cost" of a new system, but software maintenance, hardware and devices plus maintenance, implementation and training costs, and a thorough list of all start-up and one-time capital costs and operating expenses with annual increases for inflation and wages, for all identifiable components of the project. This is one of the most eye-opening tasks of HIS planning, and one that must not be skipped. The five-year cost estimate is the best way to avoid cost over-runs in this type of project that is notorious for such calamities. Project risk is reduced by a disciplined adherence to this exercise, which admittedly begins using just estimates, and then as actual bids are received from the various vendors involved in a project, actual contracted numbers can be substituted for estimates. Of course, a contingency for unplanned circumstances is always added to the bottom line total as well. Boards of Trustees will expect that as part of normal careful planning and will be concerned if the total estimate does not take unplanned events into consideration. After all, their responsibility is a fiduciary one, to ensure the continuation of the organization for the benefit and safety of the community for the future. This five-year cost estimate and providing the best estimates possible are the responsibility of the IT department as a normal part of their departmental function, with input from all necessary parties, both internal and external. End-users not trained in HIS and technology participate through their IT department, and all inputs to the process must go through the IT process owners. Vendors must not be allowed to interact with anyone outside IT unless requested as part of the process. IT is also responsible for keeping stakeholders informed as to the process and its status along the way. This is one important insurance policy against runaway HIS costs (**FIGURE 5.4**).

HIS Contracting Guidelines

Another indispensable tool in the HIS planning workshop is HIS contracting guidelines. These tie directly into, "Manage the vendor; don't let the vendor manage you," the guiding principle discussed earlier. The steps described below apply to any HIS project that involves the selection of a vendor or the renewal of a contract, no matter the size of the organization or type of project.

1. *Conduct detailed due diligence on the finalist vendors.* In this step, the organization's internal project team conducts detailed research on each finalist vendor in all three categories: usability, technology, and business relationships. As part of this process, a high-level implementation plan is developed with each finalist vendor as part of the comparisons, and their responses to the contract terms and conditions initiate the beginning of negotiations with the top contenders.

2. *Negotiate agreement(s).* Initiate contract negotiations with the top two vendors, to see how the negotiations proceed and what the yield is from a contractual perspective. If only one vendor is involved, then the organization and vendor are not really negotiating; the vendor knows it is just having its way with the process and the healthcare organization because it is the only choice. Negotiating with a single vendor is a grave mistake on the part of the healthcare organization: the healthcare organization should *always* have two viable vendors emerge from the first nine steps of the system selection process. Generally, a favorite will emerge, but always ask the selection committee to pick two vendors

	Capital costs		Operating expenses						
	Year 1	Year 2	Year 1	Year 2	Year 3	Year 4	Year 5	Subtotal	Assumptions
Software									
Licenses									
Maintenance									
Third-party software									
Interfaces									
Subtotal software									
Hardware and devices									
Network infrastructure									
Cabling									
Wireless									
New hardware									
PCs and other devices									
Disaster recovery									
Data center upgrades									
Other									
Subtotal hardware and devices									
Implementation									
Project management									
System installation									
Data conversion									
Training and conferences									
Contracted resources and temporary staff									
Additional staff resources									
Travel and lodging									
Other									
Subtotal implementation									
Total capital									
Total operating									
Contingency (10%)									
Grand total									

Estimated HIS project cost: Categories of capital and operating expenses

FIGURE 5.4 Five-year cost estimate template.

they can accept. When the first-choice vendor knows there is another competitor waiting in the wings, hoping to win the contract, the organization will have greater leverage and the vendor is more likely to compromise and cooperate where needed for terms favorable to the organization and a deal.

3. Create and send **contractual guidelines** to the finalist vendors as part of their finalist packet of information. Few things are as important

as these contractual guidelines for increasing the probability of a successful systems implementation, because among other things, the guidelines, if built into the agreement with the vendor, tie vendor payments to accomplishment of project milestones. See **EXHIBIT 5.2** for a sampling of contractual guidelines. These help prevent the organization from spending their allocated funds without the project being completed and encourage the vendor to hold up their end of the bargain. Including these contracting guidelines in the negotiation of the agreement with the vendor forces both parties to discuss responsibilities for the implementation and sign on the dotted line, legally committing them to perform those responsibilities.

Remember, the healthcare organization should *never* sign the *standard* agreement of the software vendor. Doing so most assuredly commits the healthcare organization to paying for the entire system based on the passage of time instead of based on the system working or the accomplishment of milestones toward achievement of that goal (a **milestone payment structure**). A standard vendor agreement also likely includes many other terms and conditions that put the vendor company at an advantage and ignore important rights of the healthcare organization. Payment for vendor software based on the passage of time means that the healthcare organization will likely pay for as much as 50 percent of the system upon signing the contract, with the remainder due typically within 1 year of that date, or by the end of the vendor's fiscal year, so the vendor company can book the revenue. Payment for software based on accomplishment of milestones leads to a successful implementation and protects the organization from paying for a system that is never implemented.

If you do not feel comfortable negotiating the contract with the vendor, find a lawyer and a consultant qualified in HIS contract negotiations, and pay those specially qualified professionals to do it either for you or, better yet, with you. Hiring an expert in contract negotiations is money well spent and it is far less expensive than buying software that never works—an outcome that will result in a reimplementation project or the purchase of more software to replace the failed implementation.

EXHIBIT 5.2   Crucial HIS Contractual Guidelines

1. What percentage of the vendor's revenues/resources is spent on research and development (R&D), year over year? The vendor should be transparent about these annual figures and on what they are being spent. Is the vendor pumping margins into the vendor's product or into profit? The statistics and trend will tell you something important about what the maintenance fees is worth.
2. The vendor's stability and longevity. Broach the topic of change of control: what happens if the vendor is sold to another company? Retain the right to change or retain use of the version of the product you bought a license to, even if the vendor is sold to another company, or merges, or does a stock transfer, or the contract is assigned, or other change of control option, if possible.
3. Spell out how the company responds to issues that develop over the long term, as well as in production. What are the escalation procedures? What are the specifics of the service level agreement? Define specific escalation processes and time thresholds for solving problems when they occur—up to CIOs and Chief Executive Officers (CEOs) of the respective organizations.
4. Research the vendor's reputation for meeting its obligations and conducting business according to contract terms and conditions. Check out what current clients say during site visits and

references. Do research and find out who has the software and isn't on the vendor's list: it's worth hearing what they have to say, as well.

5. Require conformance to overall contracting guidelines. This requirement should go out with the **Request for Proposal (RFP)** to the vendors so they know they are expected to work within these contracting guidelines as a prerequisite of participating in the RFP response, proposal, and evaluation.

6. Attach the RFP response to the contract. Make sure the language of the agreement specifies that the attached responses are what the vendor is obligated to deliver into production. This is the only way to hold the vendor accountable to what was promised in the sales cycle. If it is not written down and committed to in the contract, it doesn't exist, and the organization is paying for nothing.

7. Attach the detailed implementation plan to the contract, including a milestone-driven payment schedule. Insist that the vendor work with you to write down the implementation expected plan, and attach payments to the accomplishment of each milestone, reserving at least 25 percent for the final production system test, with everything working together across all modules, applications, interfaces, reports, and functionality.

8. Ensure the agreement includes developing a training plan and resources for training from the vendor.

9. Support and maintenance fees should range from 15 to 25 percent, with annual cost-of-living/ inflation increases only. Ensure levels of support expected and included are clearly defined. Also make sure the types of support not included in annual maintenance fees are defined as well.

10. Document in the agreement the expectations for the vendor's product life-cycle support, including new releases and versions, for 10–15 years. The vendor should reveal, under proper non-disclosure, their roadmap for the duration of the contract term.

11. Spell out in the agreement clear and acceptable expectations for system maintenance by the vendor and service response escalation procedures including a promised time-to-response based on the severity of the problem for the client organization.

12. Hardware specifications tied to system performance metrics must be defined and documented, including system performance criteria. The system must operate a subsecond response time with all interfaces, other data feeds, for peak volumes, and so on, with the proposed configuration. The accountability must be spelled out in the agreement, and if the system does not meet the performance criteria for system performance such as response time and other metrics, the vendor must pay for the hardware and other upgrades necessary to meet the performance criteria.

13. Mutual responsibilities for the project should be defined and spelled out in the agreement.

14. Regarding the ownership of data, the provider organization owns all its data and the vendor may not use those data unless permission expressly approved for specific limited purposes in writing by the organization's CIO or CEO.

15. Interface requirements must be spelled out in detail for the entire system as proposed to function in the RFP and then attached to the contract as an exhibit. The exhibits and attachments must be declared as part of the agreement in the initial definitions and whereas' of the contract, so that everything attached to the agreement is defined as an official part of the agreement.

16. The vendor must commit to maintaining compliance with all relevant regulations and quasi-regulatory requirements (e.g., Health Information Technology for Economic and Clinical Health [HITECH] Meaningful Use, Health Insurance Portability and Accountability Act [HIPAA], The Joint Commission).

17. Upgrade path expectations must be shared, and minimum upgrade expectations set in writing in the contract.

18. Vendors must agree in the contract that they will cooperate with other vendors to connect system interfaces and other cooperative efforts and requirements on behalf of the organization.

▶ HIS Governance: Policies, Leadership, and Decision Rights

Issues of Change and the Need for Governance

In addition to HIS strategic planning, HIS governance and decision making must be taken very seriously and properly managed—a feat requiring a whole new level of discipline and self-control in the organization. HIS and technology planning and implementation are expensive, time-consuming, and mission-critical processes through which the organization seeks to achieve its long-term vision and strategies. They are also highly disruptive. For reasons and in ways that are never fully clear or predictable, when ideas about changes in how people work start to occur and gain momentum, it can be a trying time in even the most forward-thinking organizations. This shift in expectations creates stress in the organization, and there will always be some who react negatively to proposed changes.

Even when the majority of the group agrees that new systems are needed and there is growing enthusiasm around streamlined and new ways to work and care for patients and a new vision for the future, many choices exist in how to approach these activities. Tough decisions must be made and priorities set throughout the implementation of the countless changes that a HIS strategic and technology plan suggests and implementations require. In turn, the organization must prepare itself for structured guidance through all these decisions. **Governance**—the process of thoughtful, balanced decision making for these projects and arbitration of issues that arise during the processes of change—is essential to success. Without effective and timely decisions on issues that arise during the course of these projects, the strategic goals that the HIS plan envisions and supports may never be realized. Thus disciplined, active HIS governance is a crucial part of successful implementation of the HIS and technology plan.

HIS governance focuses on (1) the stewardship of organizational and HIS resources on behalf of the stakeholders who expect a return on their investment and (2) protection of the organization from excessive risk. Governance is conducted:

- at the highest levels of decision making in the organization at the board level for major expenditures and strategic changes;
- at senior management and clinical leadership levels for establishing priorities and allocating precious financial, human, and technology resources;
- to assure regulatory compliance;
- to oversee the evaluation and selection of new application software systems and technologies to bring into the organization;
- to determine which existing systems, processes, and data are retired from use and assure this is done properly;
- for resolving conflicts and solving problems that inevitably arise;
- for communicating throughout the organization; and
- to oversee the roll-out and timing of significant modifications to the ways that administrative and clinical work is conducted.

In the case of the board of trustees or directors, Nolan and McFarlan (2005) state that, "A board needs to understand the overall architecture of its company's IT application portfolio. [...] The board must ensure that management knows what information resources are out there, what condition they are in, and what role they play in generating revenue." The governance structure must also specify **decision rights** and outline the accountabilities to establish the guideposts needed to boost forward progress and appropriate performance in the use of IT (Weill & Ross, 2004). In addition, governance encompasses decision mechanisms throughout the organization needed to weigh in and oversee the many decisions that need to be made throughout an HIS and technology project. HIS governance includes the leadership and organizational structures and processes to make sure the organization's HIS and technology plans and projects sustain and extend the organization's strategies and objectives, while being compliant with regulatory and other requirements (IT Governance Institute, 2003).

Thus, HIS governance occurs at the board level *and* within organizational executive management and committee structures. It includes internal capital allocation and project prioritization committees. It is highly interdisciplinary, because HIS and technology touch every corner of the organization, and good decisions demand that all key perspectives are considered. No detail is too small to overlook in this type of work. Further, interdisciplinary aspects of governance are important because the education, decision making, and orientation about which types of changes are about to commence need to be embedded in the minds and skills sets of those people who are charged with managing the organization on an ongoing basis. This is not to say that additional expertise should not be brought in to assist in that process. Often external expertise is highly valuable, as long as it is aligned with the needs and soul of the organization. Ultimately, however, change is not just about computer systems; it also includes how the organization does its work and delivers its services, and those are the responsibilities of the core leadership, management, and clinical personnel of the organization, as they are the ones who will be there, moving the organization forward and stewarding its resources, long after the consultants have moved on to their next project.

Effective governance, then, serves four purposes. HIS governance:

- Provides assurance that the HIS and technology plans align with the strategic goals of the organization.
- Protects the organization from taking on too much risk with the HIS and technology projects and is compliant with applicable regulations.

- Ensures adequate personnel resources and skill sets are available to these disruptive initiatives.
- Ensures itself that the job is getting done properly and in a timely fashion (Smaltz, Carpenter, & Saltz, 2007).

HIS Steering Committee

In addition to the board of trustees (in not-for-profit organizations) or board of directors (in for-profit organizations), an essential governance group is an interdisciplinary and enterprise-wide HIS and technology steering group. This committee consists of leaders from management, medical staff, nursing, finance, human resources, strategy and marketing, ancillary clinical departments, revenue cycle, facilities, supply chain, and other disciplines, including end users and the patient. It is typically chaired by the CIO of the organization (or whatever the lead IT position in the organization is called, such as IT Director or Manager of HIS). (A good CIO, in addition to having managerial and technical expertise, is a leader who effectively organizes and ensures proper HIS governance.) In some cases, the Chief Operating Officer (COO) may serve or co-serve in that role, depending on the knowledge-base about HIS of the individual involved. The purpose of this HIS steering committee is to develop and oversee adherence to guiding HIS principles and to steer or make key interdisciplinary evaluations and decisions that the project requires. Guiding principles are essential—they are the overarching ideas that, when push comes to shove, will help the group discern and find its way through difficult decisions and debates on a timely basis. Although these decisions often seem difficult and sometimes unresolvable, the organization must deal with them effectively if the project is to move forward. As mentioned in Chapter 4, no decision is a decision.

One important principle that deserves emphasis in guiding the organization through numerous tough HIS decisions is the recognition that integrated systems are superior to interfacing disparate applications. At this point in our society's automation evolution, many healthcare organizations are facing a thorny problem: they are chock full of disparate systems and silos of information that must be integrated to streamline processes and improve efficiency and effectiveness. In these cases, the principle of integration is paramount to guide systems decisions and rethink processes and organizational structures.

Another purview of the HIS steering group is establishing and upholding HIS policies and external regulations in areas of data security, privacy, and confidentiality of information; acquisition and use of hardware, software, infrastructure, and devices; use of the Internet; and other key aspects of HIS and technology plans, decisions, and implementations. These policies must be discussed, and education and training surrounding them conducted, written down, and made part of the mainstream policy manuals and accountabilities of the organization and its managers and employees. Additionally, HIS standards must be established for application software, middleware, devices, hardware platforms, infrastructure, and data. The same levels of education and training must accompany incorporation of these standards into the fabric of the organization and its HIS capabilities.

Perhaps the most important and difficult role of the steering committee is, once those standards are established, enforcing adherence to them. The HIS steering group must establish and exert the discipline needed to relentlessly manage the organization's information systems and technology in accordance with integration versus interfacing, internal controls, external regulations, and organizational integrity, all in a fashion that advances the organization toward its strategies, goals, and objectives. This work always goes against the grain of progress's primary enemy: inertia (Kouzes & Posner, 2007). This work is not for the faint of heart, but it is purposeful and rewarding, as it truly helps the organization continue to grow and evolve, as well as enhance the skills and careers of those working within it.

Governance Within and Outside Organizations

Effective HIS governance is essential to achieving stable, successful HIS and technology that support and enable the organization in achieving its mission and vision. HIS governance and decision making are highly disciplined, documented practices and policies that involve representatives of all major functional units of the organization. These rely on the leadership of the CIO and senior management, including the CEO and the board of directors, as well as the leadership and collaboration of medical staff, nursing, and other clinical disciplines. The work of governance must be collaborative, cooperative, and rooted in a willingness to uphold HIS planning principles and policies on an equitable basis to properly steward the systems, data, standards, and information resources of the organization. It is only when HIS efforts are well planned, governed, and implemented *within* organizations that a *national* HIS and technology strategy can hope to succeed *between* and *among* organizations.

External drivers such as government regulations (e.g., HIPAA and the HITECH Act), consumer expectations and engagement, and general societal progress are exerting considerable pressure on healthcare organizations to develop and implement advanced HIS and technology plans that will advance the strategic position and digital capabilities of those organizations. Once HIS strategies are in place, they can be broken down into a rolling set of strategic initiatives that are executable as manageable projects. No more than five of these strategic initiatives should be under way at any one time. These initiatives give rise to process redesign, systems projects and implementations, specific detailed requirements of functionality to support new electronic capabilities connections and roles, integration, and

HIS-supported processes. From these efforts, data are created and captured and the organization begins to pull itself into a world of improved processes and knowledge. Let the change begin!

Governance Policies

Internal policies memorializing the practices and processes described above assure organizational teamwork and unity around standard practices used by all groups participating in HIS plans, projects, and budgeting activities. Policies should be in place for HIS strategic planning, capital and operating budgets, and decision processes, such as committee oversight of HIS planning and system selections.

Because of the amount of change and expense implied in any HIS activity, the tools and techniques used in HIS Planning must also be spelled out in departmental procedures. HIS planning and projects involve not only the IT department, they also permeate all functions of the organization, including activities such as staffing initiatives, management of projects, and, as mentioned above, capital and operating budgeting rules and practices.

Policy: Staffing Initiatives

Staffing is obviously a key component of any project, and HIS projects typically require staffing by many different disciplines. Organizational policies will also be in place for HIS staffing for projects and on-going operational support and must be followed carefully in accordance with Human Resources policies and leadership. Careful planning, communication, and coordination of staffing must be part of HIS project planning as well as consideration of backfilling for those roles that are pulled from their regular duties, such as patient care, to participate in the HIS project. A particular area of attention must be for training for an HIS project, especially prior to an implementation, when large numbers of end users must be trained in an intensive approach to the activation, or go-live, of a new system. For critical healthcare functions, such as nursing, every hour of nursing time that is pulled off the floor to go to training, sometimes for several weeks, must be backfilled to keep patient care and staffing levels intact. So, these backfill hours and expenses must be added to operating budgets for the nursing departments and allocated carefully to the HIS project. This is just one example of the types of nuances of HIS project budgeting—the budgets for HIS projects are not only for HIS and technology resources.

Policy: Project Management

Policies should be in place to guide project structure and decision making. This encompasses project approval and oversight structures such as board of trustees, senior management, and steering committees, depending on the project scope and magnitude of financial and human resources required to accomplish the project. Each project should be held to standards for documentation requirements, steering groups, operational oversight, and methods. HIS **project management** is a key component of accomplishing successful HIS projects and initiatives, and policy must be in place to require proper leadership and methodology for HIS project management through the HIS department. Project management is an organizational capability that makes or breaks successful coordination and accomplishment of organization-wide projects. These generalizable project management skills apply across various HIS projects, and skilled project managers are a precious organizational resource as they are the "swiss army knives" of HIS initiatives. An HIS project management office is an essential capability in large organizations. The cadre of HIS project managers (PMs) follow consistent project management techniques and communication methods, aiding the organization in knowing where a given project is at any time, and keeping the resources of the organization transparently and properly stewarded.

Depending on the size of the projects, a good PM typically handles several projects at once, as well as projects that span a number of years and cross departmental and organizational lines. So, knowing that these projects follow policy-driven protocols allows for standardization of processes and assurance that policies of finance, human resources, and operations are followed throughout all project activities.

Policy may also define governance, processes, and decision rights for **Program management** in order for HIS projects to be integrated into the overall programs of the organization. This is discussed in greater detail in Chapter 8. It is important to note that policy governing Program Management is particularly important for HIS projects in large organizations, projects that may be part of larger *programs*. Program management functions or "offices" coordinate the myriad of projects that organizations take on, involving different areas, multiple stakeholders, and varying characteristics. The Program Management Office (PMO) is responsible for managing and coordinating all aspects of very complex projects and initiatives with multiple subprojects that comprise separate initiatives. For example, a hospital might be opening a new clinic or building that has many unique elements to the initiative, several of which might be HIS projects. Policies document the authority and processes necessary for a PMO to function in concert with strategy and operations of the organization.

HIS Governance: Leadership

This topic encompasses HIS governance structures and leadership including the CIO, CMIO, steering committees, project teams, and task forces (the "WHO").

HIS Leadership

Leadership and adoption of HIS and technology are multifaceted. That is, HIS leadership involves more than just one type of role, one type of healthcare venue, one method of management, or one vendor's HIS product. HIS leadership occurs throughout the wide variety of healthcare organizations, at all levels, among all disciplines within those organizations, using myriad evolving technologies. In addition to the obvious contributions made by information technology experts, crucial leadership roles are summoned from health care's knowledge workers of today: clinicians, managers, suppliers, vendors and consultants, government workers, researchers, informatics experts, and public health personnel.

Leadership in HIS and technology emanates from several perspectives, including organizational, governmental, and professional views, initiatives, and interests. Leadership in HIS and technology for organizations includes management responsibilities, policy, and governance programs needed to properly oversee, manage, and steward HIS, technology, data, and projects.

Effective HIS leadership comes from a variety of arenas that we will discuss in this chapter: organizational, governmental/presidential, and clinical/business. Effective HIS leadership requires not only expertise in its own arena, but also an understanding of the various layers of the HIS model and the relationships between them. That arena expertise can then take each of the layers of the HIS model into consideration in ways that create maximum synergies within and between each layer, for all parties involved and for the whole of HIS. When this state is achieved, true HIS integration and synergy become possible.

Role of the Chief Information Officer

The most typical lead role of the management positions dealing with HIS and technology in a healthcare organization is the role of the CIO or its equivalent, regardless of the name (in a smaller organization, it might be Director of IT, IT Lead, or HIS Manager, or something similar). For the purposes of this chapter, this position will be referred to as CIO. No matter what the title given to this position, the requirements of the role are similar, just scaled appropriately to the organization's size.

The role of CIO is multifaceted, complex, challenging, and highly interesting. An organization's CIO performs a broad range of responsibilities, including HIS governance; communicating effectively with those who understand HIS and those who do not; assuring strategic and business alignment with HIS plans and strategies; reaping value from HIS investments (more on this later, but remember the terms *transformation renewal*, *process redesign*, and *change management*); managing HIS department services and performance including decisions related to centralization of services and ways to cost-effectively "source" the myriad HIS functions; creating strong and synergistic relationships with the CEO and clinical and business stakeholders; implementing HIS and technology successfully; and building a knowledge-based organization.

The CIO is a member of the senior management team of the organization and participates in the organization's strategic business discussions and decisions as well as operational and tactical activities. The CIO should always be part of the senior circle of leaders because HIS and technology are strategic to the organization—and the CIO needs to be part of those essential discussions to inform and communicate HIS perspectives and opportunities on key issues. Also, HIS touches and is critical to each and every function in the organization, so placing the CIO under one of the leaders of a department or division—for example, finance or operations—results in the HIS and technology decisions being biased in the direction and viewpoint of that particular function. It is infeasible for the CIO to support all functions in the organization in a balanced fashion working from within *one* of those functions, just as it is infeasible for other functions or disciplines to have adequate input into the HIS agenda if

the CIO reports to only one of those departments or functions. The CEO is responsible for guiding and seeing the organization from the most comprehensive perspective possible, and HIS is essential to that overarching organizational perspective—so the CIO should report to the CEO. As discussed earlier in conjunction with HIS strategic planning, alignment of HIS with the organization's overall strategy is critical. Otherwise, the HIS and technology investment could take the organization off course or be wasted (time, money, and effort). Also, the capital and operating expenditures associated with HIS are so significant that they need to be fully considered and prioritized from the inner core leadership group of the organization.

The CIO is responsible for HIS strategic and tactical planning, department management, staffing and sourcing, budgeting, projects, implementations, and services delivery. **Steering committees** form an integral part of HIS management, given that HIS projects are almost always interdisciplinary efforts. Committees provide the organizational forums for collaborations among multiple disciplines to take place outside the normal "hierarchical" organizational structure and reporting relationships. As HIS projects are initiated, conducted, and closed, the CIO is responsible for setting up, running, and retiring steering committees, project-specific task forces, interdepartmental work teams, and the like.

CIO leadership involves engaging others in the organization in dialogue and structured discussions to establish the all-important HIS principles and standards that the organization agrees to in its disciplined approach to HIS management and stewardship. While it is everyone's responsibility to work according to these principles and standards, one executive—the CIO—must have primary responsibility and authority for systems projects and adherence to these important principles (e.g., integration versus interfacing of HIS). The CIO is also responsible for three main functions or branches of the HIS department or function: planning, development and implementation of new systems, and operational support of existing systems and end users. He or she plans, leads, and manages HIS people, projects, services and services quality, budgets, and support over the long term. The CIO makes sure that HIS investments and projects take the organization in *one* concerted direction—and the introduction of EHRs into healthcare organizations requires this directional integrity more than ever.

Ultimately, the CIO is responsible for guiding HIS and technology systematically in the direction desired and required by the organization and advising the CEO and others of the types of support the organization will need and can expect from HIS to accomplish its goals and objectives. Significant emphasis in the CIO's work is placed on the following elements: (1) HIS vision and plans; (2) HIS budget and costs, because the HIS plans and budgets must be affordable over the long haul; (3) assured security of information not only from HIPAA compliance and operational perspectives, but also for purposes of business continuity and disaster recovery in the event of a catastrophic occurrence; and (4) engaging externally with others in the community regarding local or regional HIS initiatives, in addition to meeting internal organizational needs.

CIO leadership is a highly collaborative process, especially since many key stakeholders in projects typically are not HIS professionals but rather are **subject matter experts (SMEs)**; thus, a balance must always be struck between HIS, clinical and business requirements, budgets, and priorities. The nuances involved in this balance are very interesting—namely, holding responsibility for a balanced agenda, while also holding responsibility for guiding the organization in its intended direction (recall the enabling capabilities of HIS and technology). Open communication, active listening, education and sharing by the CIO about the important elements of a system for

each stakeholder, and a structured requirements definition process guided by overarching principles are all necessary elements of a successful, balanced HIS agenda. The elements of the HIS strategy come in handy here: engaging in multidisciplinary leadership, communicating the vision, running a disciplined process, documenting a migration path from the current state to the desired future state, redesigning workflows and processes as part of the HIS implementation, managing vendors, and keeping people all pulling in the same direction through the challenging but rewarding change and implementation process.

When it comes to implementing an EHR system, nothing is more important than active participation of physician, nursing, and other clinical leadership. These people are the stewards of clinical care in the organization, and their expertise, insights, commitment to the process, and plain old hard work are essential to successful EHR implementation. This brings us to the next types of organizational leadership essential to HIS and technology—namely, the CMIO and chief nursing officer (CNO).

Role of the Chief Medical Information Officer

Rule number one in initiating an EHR project or other clinical system implementation is to fully engage physicians and nurses. Physicians need to hear the purpose, rationale, and story behind these projects from a respected peer—that is, another physician who is held in high esteem by physician colleagues. They need to be able to ask their questions and get straight answers from someone who knows medicine and what it means to be a practicing physician, someone who sees things from their perspective. The physician who fills this physician leadership role and becomes a member of the HIS department is typically called the **chief medical information officer (CMIO)**. She or he should also have an affinity for—and perhaps some training in—informatics. In the case of EHR implementations in large, complex organizations, the CMIO position or role may be filled by one of a few physicians who join up formally with the EHR effort on a part-time or full-time basis. The CMIO works as a part of the HIS organization, typically reporting to the CIO, but also may continue to practice medicine on a roughly part-time basis. The CMIO is often a physician who still cares for patients while becoming a member of the HIS team for clinical system implementations, keeping a peer relationship with other practicing physicians, which enhances his or her credibility with this important group. Additionally, a CMIO who still practices medicine stays in touch with the reality of using the new systems and technologies, such as an EHR, and keeps her or his medical skills honed. This is all very helpful in providing guidance to the HIS group as well as the physicians and other clinicians in the design, development, and implementation of new HIS.

The CMIO is a key player in the presentation of new ideas and HIS initiatives to other clinicians. The person who fills this role listens to and addresses concerns about changing the ways things are done clinically. Key CMIO functions include the following:

- Help translate the process of using computers for those who did not learn to practice medicine with automated support.
- Run physician discussions, question-and-answer sessions, and workshops for workflow redesign as part of the design of a new system.
- Lead physician **advisory groups** for clinical HIS projects, such as the multiyear process of implementing and refining an EHR.
- Research external sources such as other organizations, conferences, and published materials about new ways of using systems to support clinical care, while participating in EHR system selections and implementations.

- Engage other physicians in these projects who can bring their energies, ideas, and areas of specialty into the process and encourage adoption of the new system.
- Aid in detecting and resolving clinical and strategic issues in the EHR implementation.

Nursing Informatics and Role of the Chief Nurse Executive

Nursing leadership is especially important in leading collaboration among nurses for HIS implementations; this role is often filled by the **chief nursing officer (CNO)** or Chief Nursing Informatics Officer (CNIO). Nurses possess exceptional clinical workflow knowledge because of their close relationship to the specifics of daily and hourly patient care processes. Their collaboration and leadership are essential to defining key elements of EHR design and implementation from nursing and patient care perspectives, such as medication administration records and standardized clinical documentation methods. Add to this the fact that a significant percentage of clinicians who will be interacting with the EHR system will be nursing professionals and it becomes clear that nursing will drive the EHR implementation in many important aspects. Nursing leadership is required for confirmation of patientcare workflow and documentation methods developed for use within the EHR, as well as for engaging with a broad spectrum of nursing perspectives and disciplines, all which need to be supported and addressed by EHR functionality. Bottom line: if the nurses do not support the EHR implementation, it will not develop beyond the basic functions of registration, scheduling, orders communication, and results reporting, and much of the content of the EHR will not reach the development goals of the EHR vision, as much of that documentation and population of the EHR with data are accomplished by nursing processes. Graduate degrees in **nursing informatics**—the use of computers to support and enhance nursing workflow, documentation, and care processes, as well as the use of information for analysis of clinical quality and effectiveness properties of clinical care—are becoming increasingly available in university-based graduate nursing programs.

Role of the Chief Executive Officer

The CEO and the CIO have a key connection in preparing the organization and its resources for HIS plans to be implemented. The CEO must engage in HIS planning as part of the overall strategic planning and management process. It can sometimes be tempting for busy CEOs to avoid the topic of HIS and technology because chances are they did not receive much if any training in this discipline, especially in comparison to their training in other areas such as operations, finance, human resources, and other more traditional management functions. Eventually, this lack of familiarity of CEOs with HIS and technology will become less of an issue. The most important thing a CEO can do for the HIS and technology agenda is to actively participate in the HIS planning process and place HIS on the executive management team's agenda on a regular basis, just as that team regularly discusses financial issues, human resources, operations, strategic planning, clinical quality, and marketing strategies and tactics. Then the CEO and other senior management team members can engage in meaningful ways with others in the organization regarding HIS plans and implementations. The CEO-CIO working partnership is key to the success of HIS and technology investments, plans, and implementations, all of which are significant to the future of the organization, as well as its ability to perform efficiently and effectively from quality and cost perspectives, and achieve value.

Role of Department Managers

Managers of departments and key functions within healthcare organizations are vital to the successful definition and accomplishment of

HIS plans. The departments for which these managers are responsible exist for a reason: they are essential parts in the healthcare processes that support patients and the communities served by these organizations. Managers and directors are key participants on steering committees, task forces, process redesign initiatives, and implementations of new HIS. Their leadership and encouragement of those staff members who are asked to work and participate in HIS implementations can make a major difference in how those staff members feel about the changes they are being asked to help define and implement. Change is not easy for anyone, and in busy healthcare organizations managing change, even if desired, is often the toughest challenge. Supporting and leading staff members "into the fray" of an HIS implementation is truly a leadership role that cannot be provided by anyone other than those people already managing those departments within the organization. No external consultant or HIS vendor can meet this leadership requirement for a successful HIS implementation.

Clinical Leadership and Medical Staff Leadership

One category of leadership in HIS and technology that deserves special mention is leadership by clinical and medical staff. The clinical and medical staff departments that make up healthcare organizations are the groups necessary to provide care processes provided by the organization. Especially significant in HIS projects is medical staff leadership as a means of reaching the majority of the physicians providing care in the organization. Also essential is the need to reach each and every physician who treats patients in a clinical setting.

Quality and Safety Leadership

Quality and safety officers in healthcare organizations are also key players in the design and implementation of new computer systems, especially in the clinical arena. Certainly, those

🔍 *CASE EXAMPLE: FAILURE TO COMMUNICATE*

"What we've got here is a failure to communicate." This famous line from the 1967 movie *Cool Hand Luke* sums up the unfortunate current state of the majority of EHR implementations, according to recent survey statistics. When queried whether their EHR system was "worth the effort," 79 percent of physicians responded "no." Among large practices, 73 percent said they would not choose the same system again: 66 percent of specialists in internal medicine, and 60 percent of family practice physicians responded the same way. Of course, this question implies that some might think that another system would be better, but there was no differentiation in this question between systems: these providers used a wide variety of EHR software systems. Provider dissatisfaction with the EHR system stems from disruption to workflows, time spent on clerical tasks, and high rates of physician burnout. In 2016, Sinsky et al. (2016) reported for *every one hour* of face-to-face clinical time spent with patients, physicians spent *two or more hours* on EHR documentation and other tasks, plus an additional one to two hours of personal time after hours on clerical tasks, mostly EHR related. When measuring up the negative impact of EHR systems on hospitals, in 2016, greater than 88 percent of total ransomware attacks were in the healthcare sector, compared to 6 and 4 percent in education and finance, respectively. Overall, more than half of the physicians surveyed reported the EHR system had negative impact on their practice's costs, productivity, and efficiency (Green, 2017). This, by any definition, is less than adequate, and if the main users—the physicians—are saying if they had it to do over again, they would not use the same system, that is failure by any rational definition.

Data from "10 EHR Failure Statistics: Why You Need to Get It Right the First Time." (2017, October 31). *EHR In Practice*. https://www.ehrinpractice.com/ehr-failure-statistics.html.

who are responsible for measuring and assuring quality of care should take part in the definition of data elements needed to populate those measures and make sure those data elements are built into the new systems. Thinking about the outcomes of care as the workflows and processes supported by the new HIS are designed and developed assures that the programs written for the new computer system will support the measurement and tracking of those outcomes of care. This is one of the most exciting areas of implementing new computer systems— the ability to think about the desired end state of the work and processes of the functions being automated, so that the quality and effectiveness measures are seamlessly woven into the fabric of the workflows and processes they support.

Change Management Leadership

The term **change management** is often used in other industries, but was not part of the training of many people working in healthcare organizations. Nevertheless, this concept determines the ability of healthcare workers and organizations to successfully meet their goals and for such organizations to successfully adapt to forces in their environment. Change management is the carefully planned move from a current way of doing work or caring for patients, to new ways; it requires involvement of the involved disciplines in the planning of these new methods, followed by the systematic introduction of these methods supported by HIS and technology (Austin, Klasko, & Leaver, 2009). Lessons in change management include that successful HIS and technology implementation must have strong leadership, commitment to addressing the details ensconced in healthcare workflow and processes, involvement of knowledge workers from clinical and business domains, and the will to pursue the implementation of new systems while the organization continues its busy work of caring for people at a particularly vulnerable time in their lives.

🔍 CASE EXAMPLE: THE ROLE AND IMPORTANCE OF CHIEF QUALITY OFFICERS

What earlier was termed quality assurance or quality control is now elevated and emphasized culturally in healthcare organizations within the role of Chief Quality Officer (CQO). This role sits in the C-suite, held usually by a professional trained in nursing who has expanded their perspective and authority in the organization to oversee events that occur not just at a departmental level, but also pervasively through all aspects of the organization.

An example of the importance of quality monitoring, detection, and analysis during the roll-out of a new EHR at a large metropolitan hospital. The new system had been implemented and used for about six to nine months, and quality reporting showed an increase in medical errors. This caused alarm: was this new system and all the effort that went into implementing it worth it? Or was the new system detecting and providing evidence of errors that had already been occurring and only now detected? To make things more complicated, this was occurring in the politically charged situation of a recently acquired hospital (now part of a health system initiative).

The errors were analyzed and leadership came together from the IT, Quality, Compliance, Medicine, and Nursing departments. The total number of errors had indeed gone up. But the quality experts calmly and objectively pointed out in the tense room, that it was the number of Level 1 and Level II errors had gone up: Level III (patient harm but not death) had gone down, and Level IV (sentinel event or death) had no occurrences whatsoever. In fact, the proportion of Level 1 and II errors had increased and Level III and IV went down. The quality experts explained that the new system had enabled nursing and other clinical staff to get early warnings and intervene, preventing harm to patients in more situations than before. They concluded that the new system was helping prevent overall patient harm and thus improved quality. The hospital and quality staff were able to keep errors to lower level issues because the system was identifying them or prompting staff earlier in the processes and thus giving them the chance to intervene and prevent, rather than the errors going undetected and turning into Level III and IV errors. This is an example of (1) the value of transparency and reporting, and (2) the importance of quality monitors and committees and discovery of ways to replicate and permeate these lessons learned through the EHR system into other areas, all the while tracking the metrics and occurrences through the Quality function to improve patient safety and quality overall.

▶ Communication Tools for HIS Plans and Projects

Effective communication is an important accompaniment to rolling out the HIS Strategic Plan through initiatives and projects. All reaches of the organization must be included in a comprehensive, clear, inviting description of the goals, process, and components of the plan. The elements, timing, and expectations should be clear. This may include progressively updated visual aids permeating the corridors, webpages, special newsletters, in-person presentations, and updates to different (and combined) disciplines and groups. Different ways of communicating and re-communicating the vision—such as pictures, documents, mottos, in-person talks—helps clinicians, employees, and others using new systems stay motivated and on-course. A good communication strategy requires participation from diverse leaders representing major disciplines of the organization.

For major projects, such as the implementation of an EHR system, monthly newsletters focused solely on the project, details about the teams working on it, features about what's upcoming, and educational information about the system and how it will affect those working in the organization are important facts to keep sharing. These communiqués are also effective project management tools to announce upcoming activities that employees will be asked to participate in and to offer sources for answers to questions, concerns, and information to be shared with the project team and leadership. The size of the initiatives and organization will dictate the extensiveness or simplicity of the communication strategy, but transparency in the communications about the plan and initiatives and projects to accomplish the plan is an important aid to regularly orient participants and develop confidence and trust in the people and processes behind the work. It is important to have the people who are part of the organization be the focus of the initiatives and keep vendors and consultants in the background.

Global organizational communications give way to specific department by department, project by project, and individual by individual communications about roles and responsibilities for helping the plan come to fruition. This level of specificity and sophistication in communications requires the expertise of true communications specialists. The importance of this effort and content to be conveyed is a full-time effort throughout the entire planning process and implementation. Transparency in communication is a valuable guiding principle. When professionals and employees are being asked to change how they do their work, trust is essential among all parties involved, and a sound communications plan is one key element in living up to this principle. This is an important but sometimes overlooked line item in project budgets, should be funded according to a well thought-out communications plan, and should be managed and staffed as a project unto itself.

▶ Lessons Learned in HIS Planning

Policy, governance, methodology, standards, and expertise all play a critical role in successful roll-out of a HIS Strategic Plan in the form of HIS initiatives and projects. "Lessons learned" that make a difference are derived from experience and important organizational considerations follow.

- Create an HIS culture of learning. Creating a culture of curiosity and collaboration in the organization about what might be, what might work, and new ways to do work calls for finding the balance between collaboration and control, access and security, discipline in systems and freedom in insight, information, and knowledge. Encourage openness and active listening of differing perspectives, which will hopefully meld into brand-new solutions, using really good technology. The author calls this *teachnology*—learning from each other through enabling technology.

- Transparency is key! Use of the word "transparency" in business and organizations became popular in the 1990s when back-room deals and hoarding of information to a privileged few were how power was maintained. In today's world, transparency is a value that harkens back to an original meaning, which is to view something by shining light through it, such as a picture or image. This definition creates an image of clarity and truth in organizational dialogue and dealings and is a value that produces the best results.

- Strive for good communication. Akin to transparency, communication brings all people who are affected by a project into the circle of trust and knowledge about what is about to happen. People appreciate being communicated with and can be informed, active participants as a result.

- Remember history. What might seem a new idea with new technologies, especially amid urgency surrounding recent major legislative and regulatory thrusts to stimulate the adoption of HIS and technology in the U.S., one might think this was a brand-new idea. But this is not the case. Innovation using technology has been around for more than half a century. Most would be surprised to learn that the development and introduction of new information technologies for use in health care has been vigorously and continuously taking place since the 1960s in hospital data processing departments, clinical computer laboratories, home offices, garages, and other humble, dedicated origination points of innovation. So, let's pay attention to lessons from the past that come in the form of HIS fundamentals, standards, and tried-and-true methodologies. This is *not* all new.

- Value interdisciplinary balance, fairness, and collaboration. HIS, by definition, is a team sport. It involves multiple disciplines and should have a sense of organizational community at its heart. Arrogance around technical or any other type of expertise is a detractor and diminishes possibilities for success of an HIS initiative. Listen to other viewpoints and to professionals from other disciplines, all experts in their own rights. Be balanced and fair in how decisions are approached. Collaborate with many disciplines, with external parties, and with competitors. You might be surprised at what happens. Health care is changing, and being open to others and to their ideas will help us find out new and better ways to do things, with HIS providing exciting tools and possibilities.

- Keep vendors in their proper place. Always remember the difference between the role of vendors (selling a product for profit) and the role of the professionals and employees working for the healthcare organization and devoted directly to patients and their professions. Motivations and reward systems are inherently different between vendors and a healthcare organization's health professionals. For vendors, it is monetary profit, the bottom line; for health professionals, the reward system is built around good financial and clinical outcomes. Boards of Directors for vendor companies are rewarded monetarily in the form of dividends and increased value of their options and shares of stock for those in publicly traded companies. Boards of Trustees for not-for-profit, community, and teaching healthcare organizations are rewarded sometimes with some remuneration, but mostly with the prestige and satisfaction of knowing that they are upholding the fiduciary responsibility that the healthcare organization remains solvent and strong for the community and its future. Those are very different business models, and to manage vendors effectively, one needs to keep that context ever present in mind-sets and processes governing the relationship between these divergent parties. These differences are reflected in the difference in what they are called: Board of Directors in the for-profit world vs. Board of Trustees in the not-for-profit community, entrusted with the organization's and community's best interests and welfare in mind.

- Do not neglect to establish good, milestone-driven contracts with vendors that fairly balance responsibility and payment. To do so is a sure path to failure and disappointment.

- Count on collaboration. Encourage shared problem solving and ability to share lessons learned with other organizations. To be sure, during site visits to other healthcare organizations early in the HIS software system selection process, information can be shared among colleagues from the different organizations honestly and discretely.

Why do HIS initiatives fail? Remember common reasons contributing to failure of HIS projects. Ensure proper, even-handed governance, qualified leadership and management, and excellent contracting practices with vendors of software and services. These areas maximize the ability to hold vendors accountable for deliverables, technical competency, and products that perform as advertised. Engage clinical and business expertise and leaders to create first-rate workflows and process design, exercising diligence in planning and design. Ensure accurate and thorough budgeting, especially for related costs beyond software and technology. Most importantly, engage clinicians and other knowledge-workers in HIS planning, initiatives, and projects.

Summary

HIS planning tools and techniques provide methods essential to the predicable and effective accomplishment of HIS projects comprising the building blocks to the HIS Strategic Plan. After all the hard work done to create a great HIS Strategic Plan, carrying out the initiatives and projects to successfully implement it are not miracles or secrets. These reliable tools and techniques assure success. Use them, follow them, and the results will speak for themselves. These tools and techniques for implementing the HIS Strategic Plan include the following:

- *High-level HIS Architecture Using HIS Planning Framework.* Remember, the framework provides the agenda for conversations in nontechnical language about the connections between the needs of clinical and business stakeholders in the organization and the HIS Strategic Plan. It allows HIS planning to be everybody's business.

- *HIS Business Plan template.* Adopt as an organization this easy and straightforward explanation of any HIS project to document a balanced set of facts, resource requirements, and risks for decision makers and other interested parties.

- *Five-year cost estimate template.* No other single planning tool tells a bigger story than this thorough exposure of the full cost of an HIS project, including capital start-up and on-going operating cost estimates. This tool puts a dose of reality on what it takes to implement and sustain a viable HIS for its life-cycle so the organization can make good, informed decisions. This brings clarity and helps the organization avoid HIS project cost overruns and devastating budgetary mishaps.

- *Capital and operating budgets.* Following organizational policies and processes for forecasting keeps HIS in the mainstream of the organization, integrated into the overall discipline of financial stewardship. Work with the planning and finance departments to prepare HIS budgets in accordance with all other disciplines in the organization.

- *Contracting guidelines.* This is the other "most important" tool to use in HIS. These guidelines all but ensure a successful implementation, all while keeping the organization's best interest in the forefront. Much of this has to do with holding vendors accountable and preserving the financial, human, and technical resources of the organization for measurable, *promised,* results from the vendors who are being paid incredible sums of money for their products and services. These guidelines will assure they work for it and deliver the expected results to the organization.

- *Policies to establishing governance and decision rights.* Policies are the organization's rules of engagement, i.e., how it oversees all activities and sets rules that everyone follows. HIS is part of this organizational governance palette and operates within these rules and methodologies. Establish needed HIS-specific policies within the umbrella of organizational policy and follow them.

- *Communication tools for HIS plans and projects.* The hard work involved in HIS initiatives touches all reaches of the organization. Excellent communications practices and skills ensure the organization's professionals and employees are fully informed regarding the HIS initiatives that affect them all.

Once the HIS and technology *strategic* plans are in place, HIS and technology *tactical* plans are developed in great detail. The planning tools described in this chapter should be used as essential parts of those tactical plans.

A good deal of preparation occurs before tactical plans can be actually carried out and put into action, despite the pressure to jump to the end of planning and enter the implementation phase of HIS work. This pressure comes from many pockets of the organization, usually from those who aren't close to the project and therefore not attuned to the depth and breadth of HIS planning work. Capital and operating budgets for each project must be established and folded into the organization's overall capital and operating budgets. Project teams and specialized task forces for the HIS and technology initiatives must be formed and have time for their "storming," "norming," and "conforming" stages. These teams consist of IT staff, clinical and administrative knowledge workers, and often external resources such as vendor experts and consultants who have familiarity not only with the computer systems but also with the functional areas of the organization being automated. Under the leadership of an experienced IT project manager, each group creates a detailed tactical plan for each new system to be implemented. This tactical plan documents requirements for the new system, analyzes current workflows, and designs new workflows and processes intended to streamline how work is performed. Ways of caring for patients or conducting administrative functions are analyzed, identifying strengths, weaknesses, opportunities, and threats vis-à-vis current methods (strengths, weaknesses, opportunities, and threats [SWOT] analysis). New paths that streamline clinical and administrative workflows are designed and documented as part of the requirements for the new systems. Many ideas for improvement will be readily available from those employees who have been working in those areas and are painfully aware of areas of inefficiency, ineffectiveness, or risk. They are usually eager to participate in the design and implementation of a new computer system intended to improve those areas of weakness or inefficiency and often become the project's greatest supporters and assets.

Once the requirements for a new system are developed, a business plan including budgetary requirements is prepared for the new project's preliminary approval and committee presentations take place. Only when the project is approved internally does it move forward through the detailed, tactical planning phase, and interaction with the outside providers of these systems and technologies—and then only under very controlled circumstances. These activities lay the groundwork for the future decisions about which vendor and system will become part of each project to carry the organization into the future.

All of this work is guided by interdisciplinary steering committees that oversee HIS and technology project efforts, help with system selections and staffing decisions about internal and external project resources, and provide communications and budgetary support. Once plans for the HIS initiatives coalesce and gain momentum, they motivate the organization to coordinate capabilities, develop new areas of expertise, identify opportunities and points of innovation, and expend tremendous energies to begin the process of change through the redesign of how work is performed and implementation of new systems. Changes start to occur not only through the acquisition of new systems, but also in the ways people think and envision doing their work—and the culture and the mindset of the organization are never the same again. What have changed are people's expectations of how they will do their work and care for patients: a new vision begins to take hold among those who work in and care deeply about the organization, the quality of care delivered in the institution, and the role it plays in serving the needs of the community now and into the future.

Key Terms

Advisory groups
Capital budgets
Change management
Chief information officer (CIO)
Chief medical information officer (CMIO)
Chief Nursing Informatics Officer (CNIO)
Chief nursing officer (CNO)
Contractual guidelines
Data
Data dictionary
Data model

Data ownership
Data structures
Decision rights
Five-year cost estimate
Generally Accepted Accounting Principles (GAAP)
Governance
Guiding principles
HIS Business Plan
HIS Strategic Plan
Infrastructure
Integration
Interfacing

Meaningful Use (MU)
Medicare Access and CHIP Reauthorization Act of 2015 (MACRA)
Metadata
Milestone payment structure
Nursing informatics
Operating budget
Program management
Project management
Request for Proposal (RFP)
Strategic initiatives
Subject matter experts (SMEs)

Discussion Questions

1. What are guiding principles? What are some examples for guiding principles in HIS implementation?
2. Describe the concept of a "balanced HIS portfolio." How does the HIS planning framework provide insight into that arena?
3. How important is the contract between a vendor and a healthcare provider?

Explain what might be covered in the contract guidelines.
4. Explain the phrase, "no decision is a decision," in terms of the budgeting process.
5. What is the different between an HIS Strategic Plan and an HIS tactical plan?
6. Who are some of the potential department and organization leaders who will make way for new HIS initiatives?

References

Austin, G. L., Klasko, S., & Leaver, W. B. (2009). *The art of health IT transformation*. National Center for Healthcare Leadership. Retrieved from www.nchl .org/Documents/Ctrl_Hyperlink/NCHL.2009.HIT .whitepaper_uid12142009258592.pdf

Glandon, G. L., Smaltz, D. H., & Slovensky, D. J. (2010). *Austin and Boxerman's information systems for healthcare management* (7th ed.). Chicago, IL: Health Administration Press.

Green, J. (2017, October 31). 10 EHR failure statistics: Why you need to get it right the first time. *EHR in Practice*. Retrieved from www.ehrinpractice.com/ehr -failure-statistics.html

IT Governance Institute. (2003). *Board briefing on IT governance* (2nd ed.). ISACA. Retrieved from www.isaca.org/Knowledge-Center/Research /ResearchDeliverables/Pages/Board-Briefing-on-IT -Governance-2nd-Edition.aspx

Kouzes, J. M., & Posner, B. Z. (2007). *The leadership challenge* (4th ed.). San Francisco, CA: Jossey-Bass.

Make a Dent Leadership. (n.d.). Why developing guiding principles is an important step when creating a high performance workplace. *Make a Dent Leadership*. Retrieved from www.makeadentleadership.com /developing-guiding-principles.html

Nolan, R., & McFarlan, F. W. (2005, October). Information technology and the board of directors. *Harvard Business Review*. Retrieved from https://hbr.org/2005/10/information-technology-and-the-board-of-directors

Oliver, D., & Jacobs, C. (2007). Developing guiding principles: An organizational learning perspective. *Journal of Organizational Change Management, 20*(6), 813–828. doi:10.1108/09534810710831037

Oliver, D., & Roos, J. (2005, June 1). Decision-making in high-velocity environments: The importance of guiding principles. doi:10.1177/0170840605054609

Sinsky, C., Colligan, L., Li, L., Prgomet, M., Reynolds, S., Goeders, L., ... Blike, G. (2016). Allocation of physician time in ambulatory practice: A time and motion study in 4 specialties. *Annals of Internal Medicine*. Retrieved from https://adfm.org/media/1476/ann-2016-time-study.pdf

Smaltz, D. H., Carpenter, R., & Saltz, J. (2007). Effective governance in healthcare organizations: A tale of two organizations. *International Journal of Healthcare Technology and Management, 8*(1/2), 20–41. Retrieved from http://inderscience.com/info/inarticle.php?artid=12106

Weill, P., & Ross, J. (2004). *IT governance: How top performers manage IT for superior results.* Boston, MA: Harvard Business School Press.

© Kheng Guan Toh/ShutterStock, Inc.

SECTION III

Managing Health Information Systems

CHAPTER 6

Application Systems and Technology

James Brady, PhD

LEARNING OBJECTIVES

By the end of this chapter, the student will be able to:

- Understand how the software/systems development life cycle (SDLC) is used to develop Health Information Systems (HIS) applications.
- Determine the relationship between HIS programming languages, applications, and databases.
- Describe inpatient and outpatient clinical and administrative HIS applications.
- Identify the benefit of application integration over application interfaces.
- Explain how computer networks work, their importance in supporting HIS applications, and the different network architectures in use today.
- Understand how emerging technologies, such as voice over Internet Protocol (VoIP), unified communications (UC), and video/web conferencing, are affecting HIS initiatives.
- Identify why data center infrastructure, cloud computing, backups, and disaster recovery are critical to properly maintain HIS applications.
- Define the essential components of modern server computing, including unified computing systems (UCSs), server virtualization, and single sign-on (SSO).
- Describe the key benefits of client, device, and mobile computing that are being used specifically to enhance HIS deployments.
- Understand the importance of technologies that deliver privacy and security benefits to HIS applications.

▶ Introduction

In this chapter, we examine the applications and technology requirements needed to support the HIS and technology environment. There is little doubt that healthcare delivery is complex and that HIS can deliver considerable value in improving the quality of care and reducing the costs of care. However, the technology being used to support HIS has been viewed as complicated and, in many instances, well beyond the understanding of nontechnical individuals. As sophisticated as HIS applications and technology may appear to be, when they are examined at their more fundamental levels, HIS can be (and should be by any healthcare administrator or user) readily understood.

Understanding how HIS applications are developed is essential to ensuring they produce the desired functionality. In this chapter, we review one of the primary HIS application development methods in use today—the **SDLC**. We also look at the relationships between HIS programming languages, applications, and databases. The benefits of application integration over application interfaces are also reviewed. To clearly understand HIS, we discuss the clinical and administrative HIS applications being used by healthcare organizations today.

HIS applications require a robust, high-performing, and highly available underlying technical infrastructure. Unless this technology is deployed correctly, HIS users will not be able to access their systems to perform their work—the HIS applications will perform slowly, be inaccessible, or experience data corruption. In this chapter, we examine how computer networks work, consider their importance in supporting HIS applications, and outline the different network architectures in use today. We review emerging technologies that are affecting HIS applications, such as **VoIP**, **UC**, and video/web conferencing. Data center infrastructure, cloud computing, backups, and disaster recovery—all aspects that are critical to properly maintain HIS applications—are discussed as well. The essential components of modern server computing, including **UCSs, server virtualization, and SSO,** are analyzed, along with other key client, device, and mobile technologies. Finally, this chapter highlights the importance of technologies that deliver privacy and security benefits to HIS applications.

▶ HIS Applications

An important concept to understand is that all HIS applications are developed using a programming language, which allows them to operate by executing programming code. Data can be created or modified by programs based on input received from end-user input devices or other software programs and are stored in computer-based files. Large instances of data are normally stored in a database, which offers distinct advantages over other file types, such as documents, spreadsheets, and various forms of graphic and multimedia files. Some of these benefits include support for very large file sizes, the ability of multiple users to edit data at the same time, advanced data recoverability security, and data normalization (i.e., organizing and distilling data). While responsibilities for process redesign and implementation depend on resources within organizations, in healthcare environments, the technical work of developing and maintaining application programming is most often delegated to the vendors who own the application product or to consultants who focus specifically on application programming. Relying on the software vendor to manage software application development, upgrades, and customization allows healthcare organizations to focus on their core business objective of delivering quality health care.

Traditionally, healthcare organizations have purchased licenses for many of these vendor applications, or **commercial off-the-shelf (COTS)** products, causing healthcare data centers to be filled with many "best of breed" applications. Although best-of-breed applications provide healthcare organizations with advanced application functionality for specific service lines or departments, they are generally not developed to integrate or interoperate with other applications. Today, application integration is one way to eliminate application and data silos and to help organizations achieve efficiencies and healthcare reform criteria. For those healthcare environments large enough to require their own customized application development, programmers are typically added to the internal information technology (IT) department to build

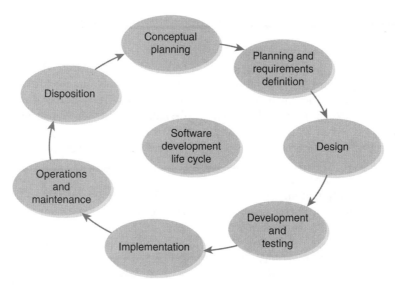

FIGURE 6.1 Software/systems development life cycle.

customized applications that are specific to their organizations. Web services, Microsoft's .NET, and Sun's Java development platform are three prevalent programming languages in use at many health systems today.

Regardless of the programming platform used to develop application programs, one of the standard development frameworks in use today is the **software/systems development life cycle (SDLC)** methodology. When applied to the development of HIS applications, the SDLC process is designed to ensure end-state solutions meet user requirements in support of the healthcare organization's strategic goals and objectives. The SDLC methodology includes seven stages (**FIGURE 6.1**) (StudyMode .com, 2008–2009):

1. *Conceptual Planning.* This phase involves the identification and assessment of the system requirements and enhancements, feasibility, costs, and risks.

2. *Planning and Requirements Definition.* This phase involves identifying functional, support, and training requirements, as well as developing the initial life-cycle management plans, the project plans, and other operations requirements.

3. *Design.* This phase comprises developing the preliminary and detailed designs, including how the system will meet functional requirements.

4. *Development and Testing.* This phase includes the system development, testing, and validation activities, which are designed to ensure the system works as expected and that the project sponsor's (i.e., customer's) requirements are satisfied.

5. *Implementation.* In this phase, the system is installed in the production environment, the training of users is completed, data conversions and system issues are resolved, and the newly designed system is turned over to the project sponsor (the healthcare organization and its appointed employees).

6. *Operations and Maintenance.* During this phase, the new or upgraded system is operationalized, with routine maintenance, upgrades, feature

enhancements, and bug fixes completed.

7. *Disposition.* This phase represents the end of the system's life cycle, when the system is decommissioned and retired. The emphasis of this phase is to ensure that the system is disposed of in accordance with proper procedures.

HIS applications are software programs of similar functionality that are used to support and facilitate work in a given area within a healthcare setting. HIS applications have historically been developed according to the healthcare organization's functional departments, divisional areas, or service lines, as opposed to being developed for the organization as a whole. Some of these applications include laboratory systems, nursing systems, patient billing and accounting systems, payroll and time and attendance systems, and human resources information systems. As a result, most of the early HIS applications were specific to the functional unit for which they were developed, causing the proliferation of many non-integrated systems operating within the same organization.

The development of application **interfaces** (bridges between one program or independent system to another) was the initial attempt to bridge these various systems in hopes that common data sets could be leveraged by multiple departments and functional areas. However, maintaining interfaces— essentially data-translation programs— between disparate applications has proven to be expensive, time consuming, and inefficient. System developers soon found that application **integration**, the process of developing different applications to share data and use a common database, is much more efficient. Essentially, integration avoids building applications in silos, which in turn eliminates the need to build and maintain interfaces on a regular basis after the initial development. Application programs that are integrated use

data from the same shared data repository, whereas application programs that are interfaced exchange and maintain data repositories between separate databases for each application using one- or two-way data transfers. Middleware is a type of software that is designed to provide application interfacing between two existing application programs that are already fully developed and in use.

Clinical Applications

One of the most important types of applications in healthcare organizations is clinical applications. A clinical application can be defined as any system that supports clinical care (e.g., electronic health record (EHR) systems), **ancillary clinical support processes** (e.g., laboratory testing, radiology), clinicians (e.g., **computerized physician order entry (CPOE)**, **clinical decision support**, and **patient flow** (e.g., registration, scheduling). Clinical applications are designed to improve the quality of care; increase efficiency; provide better patient services; reduce medical record transportation costs; and improve a number of processes, including workflow, patient communications, accuracy for coding evaluation and management, drug refill capabilities, charge capture, and claims submissions.

An EHR application is an example of a clinical application that supports clinical care. EHR applications enhance communication and enable the computerized documentation of patient care activities and health services from myriad settings. Key functions supported by EHR applications include electronic capture of data for subsequent storage in a data repository, real-time order entry and results reporting, administrative processes linked with clinical activities, **electronic data interchange (EDI)** with agencies and partners, clinical decision support for diagnosis and care management, performance reporting internally and to external agencies, and individual patients' access to their own records (HMD, 1991, 1997).

Another clinical application commonly found in healthcare organizations is a **clinical information system (CIS)**. A CIS application is a computerized system that supports clinical diagnosis, treatment planning, and medical outcomes evaluations. This computerized system organizes, stores, and double-checks all of a patient's medical information. Such an application keeps health history, prescriptions, doctor's notes and dictation, and all other information together electronically, and replaces the paper charts of the past. Examples of departmental and service lines systems that are considered CIS applications include quality management, laboratory testing, radiology, endoscopy, nursing, surgery, operating room, and pharmacy. Nursing and physician documentation are also CIS applications. CIS systems include embedded clinical guidelines and treatment protocols, establish rules and alerts, and provide evidence-based treatment plans. An important success factor for achieving future CIS viability and integration throughout the organization's HIS applications is the need for enterprise-wide HIS strategic planning.

A **laboratory information system (LIS)** is a CIS application that supports chemistry, pathology, blood bank, instrumentation, calculations, calibrations, and results management areas within clinical settings. Core functions of a laboratory system include test requisition processing, scheduling and cataloging specimen collection, and test processing; delivering results of completed tests that have been verified and recorded, and results directly reported into patient records; identifying abnormal results and alerts; providing statistical reports for laboratory management and patient summary reports; performing quality control and charge capture functions; and supporting laboratory operations management.

A **pharmacy information system (PIS)** is a complex CIS application that is tightly integrated with clinical care, particularly with nursing personnel and workflows. Because medication errors are always a concern with pharmacy systems, integration is a high priority to ensure the proper delivery of care. **Workflow redesign** is especially important when implementing medication administration management processes; pharmacy system automation requires a different approach than automation of paper-based processes. It is critical that pharmacy applications are tightly integrated with nursing **medication administration records (MARs)** and other order management processes to ensure patient safety. Additional areas that pharmacy systems automate as part of their effort to improve the quality of care and patient safety are drug inventory management, charges, medication error tracking, profile orders, performance management, drug-drug interactions, allergies, and other screenings.

Radiology information systems (RISs), **medical imaging systems (MISs)**, and **picture archiving and communication systems (PACSs)** are all CIS applications that provide clinical support processes. MISs support image management, image processing, enhancement, visualization, and storage. RISs provide functionality that manages test requisitions, schedules procedures, manages test results, identifies charges, and delivers patient test and department management reports. In addition, radiology systems are capable of performing image enhancements, computed tomography (CT) scans, ultrasound imaging, angiography, magnetic resonance imaging (MRI) scans, nuclear medicine functions, radiation therapy, computerized patient-specific treatment planning programs, and surgery. PACS applications manage image storage, local and remote retrievals, and distribution and presentation of PACS files. Recent advances with PACS applications have added features such as improved turnaround time for results, elimination of film loss, support for teleradiology, and reduction of physical space requirements for storage.

Outpatient systems are CIS applications designed to assist in the delivery of care for patients who are hospitalized for less than 24 hours. These **ambulatory care systems**

are CIS applications that assist caregivers in performing consultations, treatments, or interventions in an outpatient setting, such as a medical clinic. Examples of the types of procedures that are performed in this environment include minor surgical and medical procedures, dental services, dermatology services, and diagnostic procedures such as blood tests and X-rays. Ambulatory care settings have needs similar to those served by inpatient clinical and business applications, but slightly different priorities. Two important areas of emphasis in ambulatory care settings are financial and administrative systems—which include billing, eligibility determinations and authorizations, claims processing, general financial, human resources, and materials management applications—and clinical systems—which support scheduling, appointment reminders, EHRs and **personal health records (PHRs)**, transcription, prescription management, disease management, and patient communications.

Long-term care (LTC) systems are CIS applications designed to aid in the delivery of care for patients who are older than age 65 or who have a chronic or disabling condition that needs constant supervision. LTC facilities can provide nursing home care, home health care, and personal or adult day care for individuals. LTC systems include clinical, financial, and administrative management functionality that is designed to address the unique requirements of the LTC environment. Adoption of CIS applications in LTC settings has been slow to date, but transitioning to computerized systems in these environments has been shown to improve care delivery. Two special challenges are encountered in LTC environments: (1) they are not tightly integrated with health systems and (2) physicians are not routinely present at LTC facilities.

CPOE systems are CIS applications that directly support clinician workflow requirements. CPOE comprises the electronic entry of medical practitioner instructions, referred to as "orders," for the treatment of patients under that practitioner's care. Typically, these orders are communicated within and through an EHR application to departments such as pharmacy, laboratory testing, or radiology, where they will then be filled. CPOE applications have the benefit of decreasing delays in order completion, reducing errors related to handwriting translation or transcription, allowing order entry at the point of care or off-site, enabling error checking for incorrect or duplicate doses or tests, and streamlining the posting of charges and inventory management.

CIS applications have many benefits for both healthcare organizations and patients. These advantages include reduction of staffing requirements over the long term, attaining eligibility for pay-for-performance payments, recruiting and retaining physicians, enhancing the legibility of clinical documentation notes, reducing spelling errors within CIS applications, improving access to medical charts, reducing costs associated with transcription and facilities used for storing paper, and improved recovery of medical data following a disaster. Additional benefits include allowing multiple clinicians to simultaneously access medical charts, having laboratory and X-ray results returned automatically, checking for drug-drug and drug-allergy interactions, integrating physician dispensing software, and improving patient safety. **FIGURE 6.2** summarizes the key CIS applications that healthcare organizations are seeking to deploy in their efforts to achieve technology adoption and meaningful use of EHRs (Hanover, 2010).

Administrative Applications

Historically, health care has lagged behind other industries in the development of robust administrative and financial systems. Healthcare reform has brought increased pressure on healthcare organizations to take a more strategic approach to managing these systems. In response, healthcare providers and payers are now deploying systems that integrate administrative and financial systems. These include

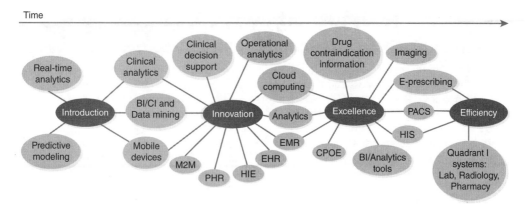

FIGURE 6.2 Healthcare provider technology adoption map.

Data from IDC Health Insights, Nov 15, 2010.

EHRs, along with **enterprise resource planning (ERP)** systems, **customer resource management (CRM)** systems, and **supply chain management (SCM)** systems. **Patient accounting** is an administrative application that manages billing and accounts receivable and is often integrated into a health provider EHR application. ERP systems are bundled applications that manage a healthcare organization's financial and accounting applications. They can include general ledger, accounts payable, materials management, human resources management, and facilities management applications, which have been traditionally installed at healthcare organizations as separate or "point" solutions (silos).

In the Robert Wood Johnson Foundation's annual report, *Health Information Technology in the United States: Better Information Systems for Better Care* (2013), 44 percent of hospitals reported having a basic EHR system as of 2012 (Stalley & DesRoches, 2013). This was a 17 percent increase from 2011, demonstrating that hospitals, physicians, and other providers have made significant strides in the adoption of health IT and the integration of healthcare data. Physicians were reported to have also made substantial progress, with 38.2 percent having adopted basic EHR functionalities by 2012. Despite these advances, many organizations have not taken steps to achieve

an integrated ERP solution and, therefore, may face challenges in generating comprehensive reports due to the existence of data silos and data integrity issues.

Home health care is an evolving method of care delivery that is increasingly using administrative applications of HIS. With the advent of healthcare reform and technology advances, including mobile devices that are being used by nurses in the field, delivery of care outside of traditional hospitals and clinics is becoming more feasible and widespread. With a laptop computer and Internet access, a nurse can make home visits, enter updates into his or her laptop, and automatically update central medical office systems. Home healthcare organizations require the same types of administrative, financial management, and clinical applications as other healthcare organizations. The only difference is that **home health HIS applications** need to be customized to meet the unique requirements found in the home health environment. This functionality includes monitoring patients for specific conditions, developing treatment plans, identifying measures that can be taken and communicated to the home health site, and communicating with caregivers in homes between visits using mobile technology. Home health care is a highly regulated arena of healthcare delivery, so automation saves caregivers the time associated with filling

🔍 *CASE EXAMPLE: A TICKET TO RIDE*

Through Kaiser Permanente, home health and hospice staff often provide care to patients in urban areas where driving and parking is a challenging, stressful, and time-consuming process. Time spent navigating to and searching for parking near a patient's residence compromises the time available for providing quality health care to the patient. In 2017, Kaiser Permanente initiated a staff ride share program using Uber to address this. Several alternative methods were evaluated, including map-finding, alternative transportation connections, and electronic parking assistance, and this program was determined to most effectively meet the transportation needs of staff and their ability to meet the care needs of their patients. Employees are able to access these rides using the requisite apps connected and supported through Kaiser Permanente. The piloted program increased staff job satisfaction/ retention (due to reduced stress while driving, increased sense of personal safety, and reduced potential of personal auto accidents and damage) and lowered overall staff transportation expenses. Additionally, the ability for staff to chart, plan, and communicate while being an Uber passenger increased staff performance. Kaiser is now looking to spreading this type of capability across the organization.

Case Example by James W. Brady.

out the many required forms by hand, leaving more opportunity for caregiver-patient interaction, an outcome that is satisfactory for caregivers and patients alike.

▶ **Technology**

Essential to the success of an HIS deployment is first ensuring that the basic building blocks of data communication are architected and maintained properly. Many HIS implementations risk failure or high user dissatisfaction if the infrastructure supporting the transfer of voice and data is outdated, unstable, or not managed efficiently. Two related important areas that we will cover are **telecommunications** and **networking**. Each of these technology areas is one of the most complex topics in the computer-related field.

Telecommunications and Networking

Telecommunications is defined as the electrical transmission of data among systems, whether through analog, digital, or wireless media. Data transmissions can occur across a variety of media types, such as copper wires, coaxial cable, fiber, or airwaves. Both large and small healthcare organizations today utilize these data transmission types and mediums. Data communication networks consist of three basic hardware components: servers, clients, and circuits. A **server** is a host computer that stores data or software and is accessed by clients. While a server resides at one end of a communication circuit, a **client** is the input/output hardware device at the user's end of a communication circuit. A client typically provides end users with access to the network and a server. A **circuit** is the pathway by which messages between servers and/or clients travel. Copper wire, fiber-optic cable, and wireless transmissions are three of the most common circuit types deployed today, with switches, routers, and gateways being three of the many devices used to enable circuits to transmit information.

An example of these three components in a healthcare setting can be seen with an LIS. The LIS servers hosting the data and providing the application processing will be located in the organization's data center. The doctors and nurses who need to access the LIS information will use their client computers—usually a personal computer (PC) or mobile device.

The hospital or clinic's wireless or wired network, along with the Internet, can be considered the circuit that is used to transfer data between the client and the server.

Types of Networks

Networks are commonly categorized into four different types: **local area networks (LANs)**, **backbone networks (BNs)**, **metropolitan area networks (MANs)**, and **wide area networks (WANs)**. LANs are groups of devices located within the same geographical area, such as one or more floors within a building, or multiple buildings in close proximity to each other. BNs are designed to connect LANs, WANs, and other BNs at high data transfer speeds and typically span several miles. MANs connect LANs, BNs, and WANs that are usually located within 3–30 miles of each other and are often referred to as **campus networks**. WANs connect BNs and MANs and can connect devices that are located around the world. Whereas healthcare organizations can create and maintain their own LAN, BN, and MAN infrastructure, commercial carriers are the primary providers of WAN infrastructure, which consists of fiber-optic cable, switching equipment, and microwave towers or satellite equipment. LANs, BNs, MANs, and WANs support data transmission speeds of up to 10 gigabits per second (Gbps) between each other, with higher speeds currently being developed. Data transfer rates via devices connected to LANs can range from 10 megabits per second (Mbps) or 10 million bits per second to 1 Gbps or 1 billion bits per second.

Networks may also be classified as intranets or extranets. **Intranets** are LANs that function similar to the Internet, providing web-based technologies that are accessible only to internal users of an organization. Vendor-developed and internally customized web-based applications can be found on an intranet. Examples of web-based applications that are often found in healthcare organization intranets include company directories, user account request systems, collaboration and file sharing sites, human resources information systems, purchasing systems, and help desk ticketing systems. **Extranets** are similar to intranets but provide web-based content and access to applications and databases for users who are outside of the organization—for example, business partners, patients, vendors, and students/faculty.

Both intranet and extranet content are most efficiently maintained using enterprise web content management (EWCM) systems, which allow individual departments to easily update their content made available on the network without knowledge of HTML programming or use of web design skills. In many cases, health organizations are leveraging **remote hosting** by engaging a third-party web-hosting company to manage their external web content. This is often done by entering into a contract with a professional EWCM vendor, who then supplies all the necessary hardware, software, website address information, and website development. The healthcare customer simply needs to provide the Internet connectivity to the external website, along with supplying the web content.

Network Models

Networks perform the basic function of transferring data from a sending device to a receiving device. To make this process efficient and modular, the various functions necessary to complete the data transfer operation are divided into network layers. The two most important network models useful to describe these network layers are the **Open Systems Interconnection model (OSI)** and the Internet model. The OSI model was developed in 1984 and defines seven network layers (**FIGURE 6.3A**) (Online Browsing Platform (OBP), 1984):

- *Layer 1: Physical Layer.* The Physical Layer is designed primarily to transmit data bits (0s and 1s signifying positive and negative electrical charges) over a communication circuit.

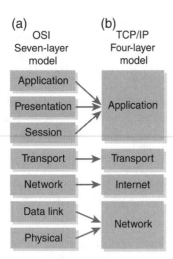

FIGURE 6.3 (a). The seven layers of the OSI model and (b). The four layers of the Internet model.

Data from Hitchcock (May 8, 2008). OSI Reference Model: Layer 1 Hardware. http://www .windowsnetworking.com/articles-tutorials/common/OSI-Reference-Model-Layer1-hardware.html. Accessed March 10, 2014.

- *Layer 2: Data Link Layer.* The Data Link Layer is responsible for the physical transmission circuit in Layer 1 and converts it into a circuit, ensuring the transmission is error free.
- *Layer 3: Network Layer.* The Network Layer is responsible for routing—that is, identifying the best path through which to send the data—and ensuring the message arrives to the destination address.
- *Layer 4: Transport Layer.* The Transport Layer manages end-to-end network issues, such as procedures for entering and departing from the network. This layer establishes and manages the logical connections between the sending device and the receiving device, performs error checking, and, if necessary, breaks up the data packet into smaller packets for more efficient transmission.
- *Layer 5: Session Layer.* The Session Layer is responsible for initiating, maintaining, and terminating the logical sessions between end users. These functions can be best explained by considering how a telephone call is made: a phone generates

a dial tone, a number is dialed, and the receiving phone answers the call, creating the logical call session where both parties can talk to each other. The session layer also manages security checks and file transfers. Again, this can be best explained by comparing the process to a telephone call: picking up the phone and dialing to connect to another phone initiates the session and the session is then maintained until it is terminated by one of the parties hanging up.

- *Layer 6: Presentation Layer.* The Presentation Layer manages the formatting of the data being transferred so that it can be presented to the end user, regardless of the type of device the end user is using. Layer 6 is also responsible for compressing the data, if necessary.
- *Layer 7: Application Layer.* The Application Layer is designed to manage the end user's access to the network. This includes applications and programs used by the end user. In addition, network monitoring and network management are two important functions that are performed at the Application Layer. Both of these functions keep track of how the network is operating and allow network administrators to ensure that the network is working optimally.

Although the OSI model is the primary model used to describe how networks work, the **Transmission Control Protocol/Internet Protocol (TCP/IP) or Internet model** is a simpler model that is used with today's hardware and software; it is also the model that defines the Internet. Understanding both the OSI and Internet models is important for healthcare professionals, as they are wonderful examples of how complex HIS are made of multiple independent layers or modules, each functioning autonomously within their own context, yet working together with other self-contained modules to create a fully functional, multifaceted HIS. The Internet model (**FIGURE 6.3B**) keeps the same OSI model for layers 1–4, but combines the OSI model layers 5–7 into the Internet model layer 4, which is labeled the application layer.

It is also common to further classify the OSI model and the Internet model into the following groups of layers (Outcome 1: IP addressing):

- *Application Group Layer.* The Application Group Layer consists of the OSI model Session, Presentation, and Application Layers.
- *Internetwork Group Layer.* The Internetwork Group Layer comprises the OSI model Transport and Network Layers.
- *Hardware Group Layer.* The Hardware Group Layer includes the OSI model Data Link and Physical Layers.

Finally, it is important to understand how each network layer communicates with the other layers. When two computers are transmitting data to each other, both the sending computer and the receiving computer will use software to perform different functions at each network layer. As such, each network layer uses a formal language or protocol that defines how it will operate at each layer.

To see how this works, imagine that an end user creates a message (e.g., an e-mail) using a web browser and sends that message to another user, who will also receive and read the message using a web browser. In this example and using the Internet model, the **Hypertext Transfer Protocol (HTTP)** is used at the application layer to create an HTTP request packet, which includes the message from the sender. The TCP is used at the transport layer to break the HTTP packet into one or more smaller-sized HTTP packets, place each of these smaller HTTP packets into TCP packets, determine the destination server address, and then open a connection to the destination server for the transfer of the TCP packets. The IP at the network layer then determines the next stop on the way to the destination server, packages the TCP packet into an IP packet, and sends the IP packet to the next stop. The Ethernet protocol is used at the Data Link Layer to format the message, provide error checking, add the IP packet into an Ethernet packet, and then instruct the physical hardware to transmit the Ethernet packet to the next stop. The Physical Layer takes the Ethernet packet and transmits it over the network cable as a series of positive and negative electrical impulses.

When the destination server receives these electrical impulses, the preceding steps are carried out in reverse order: the Physical Layer translates the electrical impulses into Ethernet packets, the Data Link Layer converts the Ethernet packets into IP packets and checks for errors, the Network Layer converts the IP packets into TCP packets, the transport layer converts the TCP packets into HTTP packets, and finally the application layer presents the request (or webpage) from the HTTP packet to the end user.

This example demonstrates both the complexity and the elegance involved in sending a simple message between computers over a network. On the one hand, many different software programs and languages are used at the various layers, which allows applications to be built in a modular fashion. Such an approach requires that software and hardware vendors use the same standards when developing their products. On the other hand, the different and multiple layers of the protocol stack can create a level of inefficiency that slows down the transmission of data. This example also highlights the importance of **technical standards** that ensure common protocols for transmitting data along the various steps between layers.

Local Area Networks

LANs are the primary networks used by desktops, servers, and network and other devices to communicate when they are in close proximity with each other. LANs are used for two reasons: *information sharing*, which enables users to exchange data, files, emails, and other types of information; and *resource sharing*, which refers to a computer sharing an attached device or software application such as a printer or fax application. LANs can be set up to operate in a client-server or peer-to-peer configuration. In a peer-to-peer network, computers share information and resources equally, and there are no dedicated network servers in place. In a client-server network, one or more dedicated servers provide the client computers with various types of network services, such as web services, application services, and database services.

LANs are composed of a number of components. A **network interface card (NIC)** is a hardware component in each computer that enables that computer to physically connect to the network and transfer data over a network cable. Network cables connect the NIC to a wall jack or directly to a network switch using a copper or fiber-optic cable. Desktop computers typically connect using a Category 5 (CAT5) or higher copper cable, and server computers or other networking devices can be connected with either copper or fiber-optic cables. Copper cables, as the name implies, are constructed with universal twisted pair (UTP) or standard twisted pair (STP) copper wires. These can be twisted or bent and support transmission speeds between 10 Mbps and 100 Mbps. Fiber-optic cables are made of very fine layers of glass and use light to transmit data at speeds of 10 Gbps and higher; unfortunately, they are more apt to malfunction if bent or twisted. Due to cabling length restrictions, LANs must be interconnected by using hubs or switches.

LANs are the basic building blocks that interconnect desktops, servers, and other devices. When setting up a new LAN, it is important to ensure that the LAN is designed to operate at high speeds, the network traffic is optimized and controlled, and redundancy and high availability are built into the architecture. Having an unstable or slow-performing LAN will negatively affect end-user computer performance. When designing a new LAN, attention should be given to assessing and remediating any shortcomings with how the LAN is configured. This is vital to healthcare

organizations, as end-user satisfaction with HIS application depends on the network connectivity being robust and available on a 24/7 basis. Several areas to consider in this regard include replacing old, legacy network hubs with modern network switches, installing network patch panels to reduce lengthy cabling runs, eliminating "daisy-chained" network switches, replacing slower copper network cabling with higher-speed fiber-optic cabling between intermediate distribution frame (IDF) and main distribution frame (MDF) network closets, upgrading desktop computer network connections from 10 Mbps or 100 Mbps speeds to 1 Gbps speeds, replacing "flat" or statically addressed network segments with virtual LANs (VLANs) using dynamic addressing, and implementing advanced LAN management and monitoring tools.

Wireless LANs

Wireless local area networks (WLANs) are perhaps one of the fastest-growing network technologies in today's healthcare environment. Clinicians and other healthcare workers are increasingly seeking to use mobile workstations on wheels (WOWs), laptop computers, tablet computers, smart phones, and other wireless devices to do their jobs faster, more efficiently, and with greater flexibility. WLANs operate by transmitting data from a wireless access point (WAP) through the medium of air using radio frequencies. WAPs are typically distributed on or inside the rooms and hallway ceilings requiring wireless coverage, but they are physically connected to network switches using CAT5 or higher cabling. Of the various wireless technologies in use today, the **Institute of Electrical and Electronics Engineers (IEEE) technologies** known as IEEE 802.11a, IEEE 802.11b, IEEE 802.11g, and IEEE 802.11n are four of the most widely adopted WLAN technologies, with IEEE 802.11n being the most recent technology developed that supports the highest speeds and the largest ranges.

WLANs have the benefits of faster, easier, and less costly deployment requirements, as there is no need to go through the time-consuming and expensive process of deploying cabling to each computer. Important WLAN implementation considerations include replacing old and legacy IDF switches with **power-over-Ethernet (POE)** switches; ensuring POE switches have ample available and unused ports to support future growth; resisting the temptation to configure stationary computers for wireless access, thereby avoiding the additional performance limitations and complexities involved with wireless protocols; performing WLAN site surveys and staggered WAP placement to eliminate dropped- or low-coverage areas, as well as WAP contention; deploying redundant and properly distributed wireless access controllers; and implementing wireless network access control technology to support the increasing demand for guest, physician group, vendor, patient, and other non-employee access.

Wide Area Networks

Wide area networks connect users on LANs to other LANs or other WANs. As healthcare reform continues to drive healthcare organizations toward greater reliance on EHR and other computerized HIS, various configurations are increasingly necessary to connect with other computers over greater distances. Many healthcare organizations encompass facilities at multiple locations. A WAN is used to connect the LANs at disparate locations to each other. If an organization is large enough to have multiple WANs, these can also be linked together to form an even larger WAN. The largest WAN in existence today is the Internet. WANs are interconnected using high-speed fiber-optic cabling and typically support data transmission rates of 10 Gbps or higher. They utilize network devices called routers to connect or route data traffic from one LAN or WAN to another LAN or WAN. Routers send information through network devices called gateways.

A reliable WAN with sufficient bandwidth or capacity to handle end-user network traffic is critical for the successful operation of HIS implementations. Important areas to review to attain a high-performing WAN include replacing slower, legacy WAN circuits, such as T1 lines (also referred to T-carrier lines), asynchronous transfer mode (ATM) lines, or other copper-wire point-to-point telecommunications with high-speed fiber-optic multiprotocol label switching (MPLS) circuits (Internet Engineering Task Force, n.d.); using multiple commercial carriers and redundant pairs of networking devices for high availability; eliminating all single points of failure along the WAN physical path; and implementing network link-load balancing (NLLB) and WAN optimization technology.

Wireless Wide Area Networks

Another wireless technology increasingly used within healthcare environments is **wireless wide area networks (WWANs)**, often referred to as broadband or cellular network technology. WWANs are wide area networks that provide service to large geographic areas through separate areas of coverage, referred to as cells. Cell phones, smart phones, tablet computers, and hot spots are mobile devices commonly used to connect to WWANs. Three families of WWAN technologies are prevalent today: (1) Global System for Mobile Communications (GSM) and Universal Mobile Telecommunications System (UMTS); (2) Code-Division Multiple Access (CDMA) One, CDMA2000, and Wideband CDMA (WCDMA); and (3) Worldwide Interoperability for Microwave Access (WiMAX) and Long-Term Evolution (LTE). The GSM/UMTS and CDMA One/CDMA 2000/WCDMA standards are referred to as second-generation (2G) and third-generation (3G) technologies, as they were designed to replace the slower, more limited analog cellular networks with higher-speed, digital cellular networks. The WiMAX and LTE standards are high-speed fourth-generation (4G) technologies that are now gaining increasing market share on a global scale. T-Mobile, AT&T, Sprint, and Verizon are four major WWAN service providers.

The consumerization of IT has given rise to the **bring-your-own-device (BYOD)** phenomenon, in which increasing numbers of end users seek to use their personal smart phones and/or tablets for both personal and work use (Bent, 2012). Many healthcare organizations have responded to the complexities involved in supporting both personal and corporate data on a personally owned mobile device by deciding to officially support only corporate-owned mobile devices. Other organizations have developed appropriate BYOD policies and deployed mobile device management technology. Many organizations have recognized the need to provide uninterrupted cellular network coverage to doctors, nurses, and other healthcare workers for functions such as voice, texting, web browsing, and other mobile applications; for those organizations, **distributed antennae system (DAS)** technology can eliminate dead spots and other areas of poor cellular signal coverage within hospital buildings. Recent advances in 5G cellular technology are enabling organizations to leverage Wi-Fi access points as a platform for indoor small cell technology. This is a lower-cost alternative to DAS and enables coverage and data access outside the main wireless network, improving seamless connectivity.

Storage Area Networks

Storage area networks (SANs) are dedicated back-end computer systems designed to efficiently and cost-effectively store and transfer a healthcare organization's server data. These high-speed networks are dedicated to centrally store and provide access to data from multiple server systems. They have the distinct benefit of providing high availability with no single hardware component (a so-called single point of failure) being able to disrupt access to data. Traditional methods of storing data

involve using directly attached storage, where each server stores its associated data to **hard disk drives (HDDs)** directly attached to itself. This method has many limitations in today's environment, where end users are demanding ever-greater storage capacity and performance. Directly attached storage systems still exist today, but they are largely giving way to SAN systems, which boast higher capacity, faster access, greater availability, and stronger security at less cost. The different types of SANs in use today include fiber channel (FC) SANs and network attached storage (NAS) devices.

At a basic level, data are stored on an HDD and can be written or read. To ensure that the data will be available in the event the hard disk fails, hard drives can be placed into a **redundant array of independent drives (RAID)** configuration, with the data copied across multiple drives. A RAID controller is a computing peripheral that keeps the disks in the array in synchronization and manages all the write and read (input/output [I/O]) operations to and from the disks. Four RAID configurations widely used today are RAID 1, RAID 5, RAID 5 with a spare, and RAID 10.

- RAID 1 configurations, also called mirrored disks, use two HDDs, one as the primary HDD and the other as the secondary HDD. This configuration provides redundancy if an HDD fails and boasts fast read performance, as the data can be read from either disk. Unfortunately, it has slow write speeds to the HDD and is more expensive because two HDDs are required.

- RAID 5 distributes the common or redundant information (called parity) to all HDDs in the configuration. If a block or HDD fails, the parity information ensures that the lost information can be restored when a replacement HDD is inserted into the array. RAID 5 requires a minimum of three HDDs and has the advantage of performing fast HDD reads.

- RAID 5 with a spare configuration contains an additional HDD, called a hot spare; it remains unused until an HDD in configuration fails, at which time the array automatically rebuilds the failed HDD to the spare HDD. This scheme has the advantage of providing an additional layer of redundancy should an HDD fail.

- RAID 10 is a combination of RAID 1 and RAID 5, giving it the fastest performance and highest availability, albeit with the highest cost, because only half of the HHD capacity is used for the actual storage of data.

In healthcare server systems today, RAID 1 is often used to configure stand-alone server operating system drives, while RAID 5 is used as a cost-effective and acceptably performing configuration for both directly attached and SAN data storage environments. RAID 10 is used for SANs that require very high performance and availability. Most mission critical databases are stored on RAID 10, as it provides higher levels of availability and write access. However, it costs almost twice as much as RAID 5 because it has almost twice the number of disks.

SANs can be used to support very large amounts of data. To do so efficiently, they allow for the creation of disk pools that vary in size, speed, and cost by using different RAID configurations, HDD sizes, and HDD access times. When a server needs new or additional storage, based on what is needed and how expensive the storage needs to be, logical volumes (LUNs) can be provisioned and presented to the server as a local HDD. SANs communicate with each other using either the Ethernet (also referred to as IP), FC, **Fiber Channel over Ethernet (FCoE)**, or **Internet Small Computer System Interface (iSCSI)** protocol; they also use high-speed fiber-optic cabling and network switches that support the IP, FCoE, or iSCSI protocols. Modern SAN deployments typically use either 10 Gbps FCoE Ethernet or 16 Gbps FC. With the application of aggregation technology, both Ethernet and FC SAN connections can be increased to higher speeds to support increased traffic loads and higher data transfer requirements.

SANs that have medium to high storage capacity requirements but do not have high performance requirements, such as file servers, can be configured as NAS devices. NAS systems use the Ethernet (IP) protocol over standard LAN switches to present storage to servers and other devices on the network. This approach has the benefit of being less expensive than FC-based SANs because it uses less costly LAN switches and cabling and cheaper and larger HDDs. SAN and NAS vendors are continuing to develop easier-to-use management consoles for SAN administrators, reducing the learning curve and skill set needed to troubleshoot and maintain the various SAN technologies.

Voice and Communications

Voice over Internet Protocol (VoIP) and **unified communications (UC)** are emerging technologies that healthcare organizations are beginning to leverage and implement at their facilities. VoIP comprises a family of technologies that enable IP networks to be used for voice applications such as telephony, messaging, and collaboration. With greater reliance on robust data networks, traditional analog-based private branch exchange (PBX) office phone systems that operate over public switched telephone networks (PSTNs) telecommunication circuits are now being replaced with more cost-effective VoIP solutions that run over existing IP networks. With high-speed, robust LAN and WAN connections in place, and with the Internet being capable of supporting voice traffic over data circuits, voice calls no longer need dedicated analog circuits and can leverage the existing data network. This approach requires a VoIP-enabled phone or a computer and headset. Analog voice calls are converted to packets of data, which are then sent over the data network, and converted back to analog signals. The addition of voice to a data network allows organizations to reduce costs, improve productivity, and enhance collaboration.

Voice over wireless local area network (VoWLAN) is a technology designed to integrate mobile devices using the WLAN. It is proving particularly advantageous as more clinical applications are developed for use with smart phones, tablets, and portable computers. Use of VoWLAN offers the following benefits:

- Improves workflow and productivity by delivering ubiquitous, robust coverage;
- Enables roaming of voice clients and high-quality voice communications by using real-time radio frequency scanning and monitoring to minimize interference;
- Minimizes roam time and client connectivity issues; and
- Provides advanced quality of service (QoS), extended talk-time, and call security.

UC is another evolving technology that involves the integration of real-time communication services, such as instant messaging and presence, VoIP and VoWLAN, video conferencing, and web conferencing. Digital signage, wayfinding, and IP television (IPTV) are also considered part of the UC family of services. UC is designed to use a single, consistent user interface to provide one or more of these services, along with transferring data over the IP network. An example of UC in an HIS setting can be seen when virtual meetings are conducted with products such as Cisco WebEx, Citrix Go-To-Meeting, or Microsoft Lync web conferencing software. Although healthcare workers and partners might be located around the world, they can meet via an online session, sharing voice, video, presentations, chat, and other forms of collaboration—all while using only a web browser and computer or mobile device.

Instant messaging or chat is used often in healthcare environments as the real-time communication needs of clinicians and IT personnel expand. Instant messaging allows users to send messages or files to each other. In a healthcare setting, a secured instant messaging application is required to avoid issues with electronic protected health information (ePHI) or other sensitive information traveling over unsecured networks, such as the Internet. Instant messaging has the additional benefit of giving others notice of an individual's presence or status, such as whether he or she is online, offline, busy, or in a meeting.

FIGURE 6.4 illustrates the multiple components in the WLAN protocol that securely support data and voice traffic.

Video conferencing enables two or more individuals to talk and see each other by transmitting audio and video signals. Although this technology has existed for many years, it has not been widely adopted due to the complexity and high costs involved in using analog circuits and deploying proprietary video conferencing equipment. UC, however, enables video conferencing to be performed over IP data networks with significantly reduced costs and complexity. Popular applications of this technology in healthcare environments include

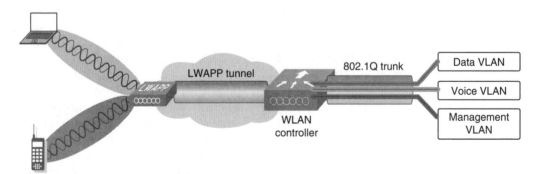

FIGURE 6.4 VoWLAN protocol.

video conferencing over desktop computers and mobile devices, video conferencing in conference rooms using large-screen monitors (which eliminates the need for travel and other expenses involved in face-to-face meetings), and cloud-based video conferencing services (which eliminate the need to buy and maintain expensive equipment).

Web conferencing is used frequently in healthcare organizations because of its simplicity, convenience, and low cost. It enables users at multiple locations to hold audio meetings and share desktop computer applications or applications from their mobile devices over the IP network. Given the never-ending quest to reduce costs, web conferencing is being widely embraced as a solution that enables organizations to reduce employee travel requirements while increasing collaboration between all stakeholders. Web conferencing solutions can be cloud based or deployed using an on-premises architecture.

Digital signage uses server technology and IP networks to electronically display information, such as organizational training or news, advertising, or other healthcare-related messages, using liquid crystal displays (LCDs) or plasma displays that are placed in various public or internal locations within hospitals and work areas. Digital wayfinding uses digital signage technology, but adds touch-screen technology to allow users to interact with the LCD-presented information (Dern, 2013). Examples of digital wayfinding technology commonly found in hospitals include interactive touchscreen LCDs that allow patients to obtain directions to various departments, find information about their physician, see cafeteria information, and look up healthcare education information.

Data Centers and Cloud Computing

Ensuring that HIS applications and data are protected, secured, and always accessible to the end users who need to use them is a very important aspect to HIS. **Data centers** are the facilities where HIS are located and are vital to the successful implementation and ongoing support of providing healthcare applications. With the ever-growing reliance on electronic information, healthcare organizations must ensure that their data centers can provide high availability for their computer systems, are secure and modernized to remain cost-effective, and have ample capacity for growth and expansion. One of the first decisions facing healthcare organizations is whether they will maintain their own data center facilities, lease one or more commercially owned colocation data center facilities, or outsource (remote host) both their data center facility and computing equipment to a third party. Due to the high costs and complexities involved in an organization maintaining its own data center facility, contracting with a co-location facility and remote hosting are increasingly popular options with many healthcare organizations.

Another important decision organizations need to address involves data center consolidation. Newer servers, networking devices, and other equipment located inside data centers are increasing in capacity and performance (referred to as computer density) while requiring less cabinet, rack, and floor space. Organizations are discovering that they no longer need multiple data centers but rather can consolidate their IT infrastructure into a single facility. At the same time, to ensure high availability and disaster recovery capability, healthcare organizations need a secondary data center. This is typically a smaller facility that can support running the mission-critical applications (at a minimum) and is often remotely hosted by a third-party data center vendor.

A third important question is how the organization will position itself with the evolving technology of cloud computing. **Cloud computing**, a recent emergent technology, follows in the footsteps of mainframe, client-server, web, and service-oriented architecture (SOA)—all popular at some point in the past. Cloud computing is a general term associated

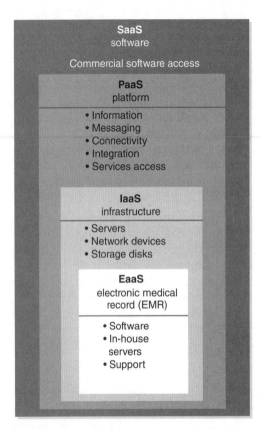

FIGURE 6.5 Cloud computing components.

Data from Venture Beat News. Cloud 101: What the heck do IaaS, PaaS and SaaS companies do? http://venturebeat.com/2011/11/14/cloud-iaas-paas-saas/. Accessed March 10, 2014.

with delivering hosted services, with the goal of providing easy, scalable access to computing resources and IT services. As depicted in **FIGURE 6.5**, these services are organized into three categories: **infrastructure-as-a-service (IaaS)**, **platform-as-a-service (PaaS)**, and **software-as-a-service (SaaS)**, with some healthcare proponents now discussing **EMR-as-a-service (EaaS)** as a future possibility (Ontario MD Inc., 2013). An IaaS-hosted solution involves a vendor supplying a data center with all the server hardware and network connectivity needed to support HIS applications. The HIS customer then needs to install and manage its server operating systems, applications, and databases itself. A PaaS-hosted solution is similar to an IaaS-hosted solution, except that the cloud vendor also supplies the

server operating systems. With a SaaS-hosted solution, the cloud vendor installs and manages all previously mentioned components. With an EaaS-hosted solution, the cloud vendor fully hosts the EMR solution. In all four scenarios, the HIS customer still manages the processes of entering and extracting data from the service.

A cloud can also be categorized as private or public. **Public clouds**, such as Amazon Web Services, sell services to anyone on the Internet, typically consumers. **Private clouds** are proprietary networks and data centers that supply secure, hosted services for use within a particular organization; these are increasingly popular among healthcare organizations.

A number of emerging technologies have been adopted in today's modern data centers. **Software Defined Networking (SDN)** is a type of dynamic configuration that takes place whenever software-based services in a data center network are made accessible through an IP address. **Network Functions Virtualization (NFV)** simplifies data infrastructure by leveraging inexpensive hardware and allowing workloads to be migrated to customer data centers. **Containers**, such as Kubernetes clusters running Docker, are emerging service platforms encapsulating applications in containers with their own operating environment that use SDN to map network addresses to individual workloads. With each workload having its own network address, software load balancers can make it possible for these workloads to be dynamically replicated if more capacity is needed. **Hyper Converged Infrastructure (HCI)** simplifies how modern data centers are operated by managing applications, servers, networks, compute, storage, and memory as a single platform.

Data center facilities have a number of critical components that must be managed appropriately. The most costly operational expense related to a data center, other than the high capital costs required for building or upgrading the facility itself, is electrical power consumption. The green data center concept is an initiative designed to improve the environment by reducing power usage. In a data center, this goal can be accomplished by using energy-efficient equipment and reducing the amount of physical equipment inside the data center by leveraging technologies such as virtualization and consolidation.

Data centers receive their primary power, called utility power, from commercial utility companies. Ideally, this should be supplied by two separate physical paths (or feeds) into the building's main distribution unit to provide redundancy. The typical power path is 1–10 megawatts (MW) or greater. Through a series of electrical transformers, high-voltage electricity is reduced or "stepped down" so that facilities and computing equipment can be supplied with appropriate voltages. Utility power is routed to power distribution units (PDUs), which are distributed throughout the data center. In large data centers, remote power panels (RPPs) route power to one or more data center cabinets. Power is then distributed to each cabinet, which can directly connect to computing equipment or a set of smaller cabinet power strips. Most servers and data center equipment will plug into these data center cabinet PDUs, which can be remotely monitored over the network using a **branch circuit monitoring system (BCMS)** application. Larger facility equipment uses 480- or 220-v capacities, while computing equipment uses 220- or 110-v capacities.

In the event that the utility power feeds fail, data centers should be configured to automatically fail over to use backup power, in a battery-supported form. The typical power path is an **uninterruptable power supply (UPS)**, a flywheel-driven **continuous power source (CPS)**, or a combination of the two. Backup power is important to ensure that HIS applications remain available and accessible, as inevitably electrical components suffer outages from time to time. Any disruption in power will translate into these critical HIS applications going offline, in turn negatively impacting patient care. UPS backup systems use batteries to provide electricity and have the advantages of being less expensive and starting up faster than non-battery backup systems, such as CPS systems. However, UPS systems are not considered environmentally friendly and the batteries require regular maintenance and replacement. CPS systems use a continuously spinning flywheel driven by high-speed turbines to generate electricity. They are robust and considered environmentally friendly, but are more expensive and slower to assume the primary load than UPS systems. Generators, using diesel or gasoline fuel, are needed to provide power to both UPS and CPS systems. Due to the high levels of noise generated by CPS equipment, data center personnel must use earplugs to minimize ear damage.

Data centers should have **service level agreements (SLAs)** with fuel companies to deliver fuel until the utility power is restored, and they often are equipped with local storage tanks capable of holding tens of thousands of gallons of fuel. In many data centers that are large enough to use CPS backup systems, UPS systems are also installed to ensure the primary load is assumed quickly.

In addition to a CPS, cooling is essential to reliably support HIS. Many computer systems are located in densely configured data centers, where a tremendous amount of heat is produced within a confined space. To provide ambient or room cooling, **heating, ventilating, and air-conditioning (HVAC) systems** are used. HVAC systems utilize water to absorb excess heat: **computer room air handlers (CRAHs)** draw in the hot air, and then cold water traveling through large pipes absorbs the heat. Subsequently, roof or wall condensers release the heat outside the data center and large, heavy-duty water chillers cool and recirculate the water. As a contingency, in case commercial or utility water sources become unavailable, many data centers have wells that can hold tens of thousands of gallons of water.

To protect a data center from damage by fire, fire suppression systems—such as water-based dry-pipe pre-action sprinklers or gas-based FM200 fire suppression systems—

are used. Dry-pipe systems fill the pipes with water if a fire occurs. They are less expensive than the gas-based FM200 systems but have the disadvantage of potentially damaging computer systems in the event of a fire. However, because individual sprinkler heads open only after a temperature fuse breaks (normally at a temperature of approximately 175°F), water damage will be limited to just the computer equipment directly below the specific sprinkler head where the fire is occurring. FM200 systems contain a fire retardant that will not damage computer equipment, but tend to cost more and require data center personnel to evacuate the area being treated. To help provide early warning detection of a potential fire, **very early smoke detection apparatus (VESDA)** systems monitor for smoke particles and sound alerts when they are detected.

If a catastrophic and life-threatening event does occur within a data center, in which terminating all electricity is the only option to resolve the situation, an **emergency power off (EPO)** switch should be available. Once this button is pressed, all electricity to the data center is shut off.

BCMS can be deployed in data centers to monitor and manage electrical circuits and provide data center staff with the ability to ensure that data center equipment has sufficient electrical capacity. **Data center management systems (DCMSs)** are hardware and software systems that allow data center personnel to design and proactively manage these and additional data center technologies; they can help reduce unplanned system downtime caused by poor planning or a lack of standardized and documented processes and procedures. A DCMS may include power protection and distribution management, air-conditioning and environmental controls, intelligent cable management, cabinet space management, server and network device remote access, and asset management and tracking (**FIGURE 6.6**).

Business Continuity and Disaster Recovery

Another area associated with data centers is business continuity and disaster recovery. "Business continuity" describes the processes and steps a healthcare organization puts in place to ensure that its essential business functions will continue during and after a disaster (Barnes, 2004). One of the most important areas of business continuity planning is disaster recovery

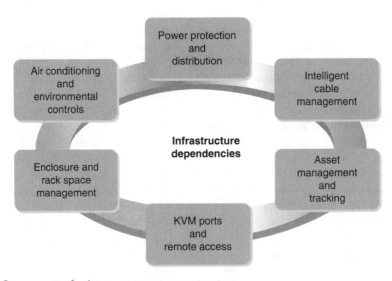

FIGURE 6.6 Components of a data center management system.

planning, which comprises the planning, process, policy, and procedures undertaken to prevent the interruption of mission-critical IT services and to reestablish full IT functioning as swiftly and smoothly as possible.

As EHRs and other HIS technologies become more commonplace in healthcare environments, it is critical that the risk of a system outage or data center disaster be mitigated. Many health organizations today have not fully developed their **business continuity plan (BCP)** or **disaster recovery plan (DRP)**; these organizations should consider performing a BCP or DRP assessment to determine the level of risk that is acceptable. In preparing a BCP, the organization should first identify and prioritize the criticality of the various HIS components and then determine the appropriate **recovery time objective (RTO)** and **recovery point objective (RPO)** for each HIS in the event of a disaster or unplanned system outage. RTO refers to the total time (in minutes, hours, or days) during which a server or service can remain unavailable before it is restored to full functionality, while RPO refers to the total time (in minutes, hours, or days) for which data might be lost. Keeping BCP and DRP at the same level of priority as other projects within HIS is often challenging for healthcare organizations to accomplish, but it is critical to do so. The increasing dependence on HIS and technology throughout health care necessitates investment of time and effort to establish and maintain these protective capabilities.

An examination of important DRP concepts will demonstrate the various steps that organizations can take to reduce this risk. **Redundancy** is one of the simplest concepts that should be implemented at all levels of DRP. Where possible, having two instances of server, storage, or network system components—such as central processing units (CPUs), HDDs, NICs, storage host bus adaptor (HBA) cards, system controllers, and cabling—will enable the hardware system to support the HIS and remain operational should a failure occur that is restricted to any one of the components.

At the next level, servers, storage, and network systems themselves should be clustered, load balanced, or mirrored such that if the primary system fails, the secondary system will continue to provide service. Clustering is typically used with applications and databases, while load balancing is used with web servers, file servers, and various network devices. Mirroring is used to replicate and maintain synchronous copies of data between two or more SANs.

Moving to the highest level of redundancy, data centers themselves should be redundant. To accomplish this in today's environment, each primary data center should be associated with a corresponding secondary or backup data center. Secondary data centers can be configured as cold sites, tepid sites, warm sites, or hot sites, such that they can provide different levels of service in the event that the primary site is unavailable.

- *Cold sites* are facilities that have hardware and software available for use, but are shared with other organizations and contain no data from the primary data center. Should a disaster occur, the cold site systems would need to be configured and the backup data restored to the cold site location. This is the least costly DRP option and has no distance limitation between data centers, but it can take several days to bring an organization's critical systems back online.

- *Tepid sites* are similar to cold sites, but have the data from the organization's critical systems copied over using basic SAN replication. This is the third most costly DRP option, has a distance limitation of 1,000 miles or less, and takes only two to three hours to bring an organization's critical systems back online.

- *Warm sites* improve on the tepid site capability, with the difference being that all systems and data from the primary site are copied over, although noncritical systems will operate in a degraded mode. This is a costly DRP option, has the same distance limitation (1,000 miles) as tepid sites, and requires only one hour or less to bring an organization's systems back online.

- *Hot sites* can provide rapid, automated and full system and data recovery in less than a minute, but are the most expensive option. They have a distance limitation of either 200 miles or a data transfer round-trip time of 10 milliseconds.

Backup systems are another key technology that healthcare organizations can leverage to ensure HIS and data availability. Tape-based backup systems, such as digital linear tape (DTL) and linear tape-open (LTO) models, use magnetic tape, tape drive systems, and stand-alone or centralized backup application software to make backup copies of computer data on tape. Tape backup systems have been used in data centers for many years but suffer from limitations such as unacceptably slow backup and restore transfer times, limited capacity to address the exponential storage growth found in modern HIS, the risk of losing tapes that are stored at remote locations, and the inability to store data indefinitely. Additionally, tape backup systems lack support for advanced features such as encryption-at-rest capabilities.

Disk-based backup systems address many of the shortcomings of tape backups by backing up system and application data to disk. These systems have the benefits of being able to reduce the amount of data that must be backed up by as much as 90 percent through a process called data deduplication. Data deduplication eliminates the need to back up redundant or already backed-up data. As a result, disk-based backup systems have higher backup storage capacities and faster backup and restore times. They more easily move and store data to disparate locations using network and cloud-based technologies and are designed to use advanced security features and both encryption-at-rest and encryption-in-transit.

Virtual tape libraries (VTLs) are backup systems that use disk-based arrays to emulate tape libraries. With these systems, the storage medium can be switched from tapes to disks while continuing to use the existing tape backup software. VTLs lack the advanced features of disk-based backup systems.

Server Computing

Servers are specialized computers that are designed to process or "serve" computing requests, such as requests for database information, application processing, or file transfers and storage. Although they have the basic components found in client or desktop computers, they are architected differently. Servers are designed with multiple high-speed CPUs, large amounts of **random access memory (RAM)**, redundant and high-capacity I/O, internal bus systems, and access to high-speed storage, network, and backup systems. These computers are inserted or "racked" in computer cabinets to allow for high density, and they do not require the individual directly connected monitors, keyboards, mice, or other devices that are common with client or desktop computers. As many as 10–12 rack-mounted servers may be stored in a single computer cabinet (**FIGURE 6.7**). A high-capacity server is so large that it requires an entire computer cabinet on its own.

Keyboard, video, and mouse over IP (KVMoIP) devices are centralized systems that give system administrators keyboard, monitor, and mouse access over the network, eliminating the requirement and additional cost to provide these peripheral devices for each server.

Blade server technology represents an advance in increasing server density and reducing server costs. Blade servers are stored in a compact enclosure called a blade chassis, which has a reduced size and uses less energy. These types of servers boast higher availabilities achieved by sharing common components, such as network, storage, cabling, and power infrastructure. Three-to-four times more

FIGURE 6.7 Data center class servers.
Courtesy of James W. Brady.

blade servers can fit in the same cabinet space as rack-mounted servers. UCS technology is a next-generation data center platform that increases server density, performance, availability, management, and efficiency beyond blade server technology by uniting multiple blade server chassis, networks, and storage infrastructures into a single cohesive system.

Virtualization is another technology advance that has significantly reduced the amount of server infrastructure needed to support today's healthcare environments, thereby greatly smoothing the way for healthcare organization server consolidation initiatives. Physical servers or hosts generally use only 10 percent or less of their processing ability. The virtualization feature takes advantage of a server's unused processing power by creating multiple virtual server instances, which typically increases server density by a factor of 10–15. A **hypervisor or virtual machine monitor (VMM)** is a piece of computer software, firmware, or hardware that creates and runs **virtual machines (VMs)**. VMs run on servers running Windows, Linux, and Solaris operating systems, and on logical partition arrays (LPARs) in UNIX-based servers such as the Advanced Interactive eXecutive (AIX) operating system.

Servers that run one or more VMs are called hypervisors and are defined as host machines. Individual VMs are called guest machines. Hypervisors present and manage the operation of the guest operating systems within the virtual operating platform. By combining or clustering multiple host computers into redundant and highly available server farms so that VMs and LPARs can automatically move between physical hosts, server virtualization significantly reduces server downtime due to hardware failure or planned maintenance. **FIGURE 6.8** illustrates how virtualization is designed to maximize server hardware and software resources.

Despite the many advantages of server virtualization, including the ability to rapidly and easily deploy servers, reduced costs per server, and simplified server management, several challenges need to be addressed when moving forward with this technology. Server sprawl or large numbers of servers may occur due to the relative ease with which systems can be deployed. New charge-back models and processes must be put in place when this approach is used, as most of the server infrastructure must be procured and deployed prior to identifying the need for a

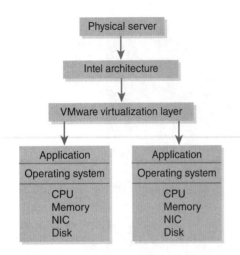

FIGURE 6.8 Diagram of a virtualized server.

Data from Nash Networks, Inc. (2009). Virtualization: A small business perspective. *Executive Summary.* http://www.nashnetworks.ca/virtualization-a-small-business-perspective.htm

new server. Additional care must be given to server architecture and change management because there is increased risk that multiple systems might be negatively affected by any design flaw or problematic configuration change or upgrade.

Servers can be classified in additional ways. Servers that are fully supported and managed by a vendor (usually installed with a proprietary operating system and software) are called **appliances**. Appliances are typically self-contained, requiring only a network connection; are easy and fast to deploy; and can be a preferred method for delivering a server application, as healthcare organizations or customers do not have to address all the complications and delays involved in setting up the server themselves. Servers are also classified as production, development, or test types, with all three types being stored in secured, highly available data centers.

Infrastructure Servers

Infrastructure servers provide core services that support server system functionality and that need to be implemented properly if a

healthcare organization expects to rely on its business and clinical applications. A poorly implemented underlying server infrastructure environment will cause significant issues with HIS application deployments. Understanding the following infrastructure servers and applications will provide insight needed to establish a robust and stable environment that reliably supports HIS applications.

Dynamic Host Configuration Protocol (DHCP) servers assign a unique address to each computer on the network. A misconfigured or inaccessible DHCP server can cause both servers and end users' computers to receive duplicate or incorrect addresses, making them unable to function. **Domain Name System (DNS)** servers enable users and servers to contact websites and other servers by maintaining a directory listing of server and website names. It is important for organizations to ensure that their DNS servers are properly configured, and if an update or modification is required, thorough testing must be performed. Should the DNS service be disrupted, end-user web browsing via the Internet and server-to-server communications can be inhibited. **Active directory (AD)** servers maintain lists of users, computers, and printers, along with any associated passwords and security settings. A misconfigured or inaccessible AD server can cause users and computers to have access, connectivity, and password issues. **Identity and access management (IAM)** servers automate and streamline the management of user, computer, and application accounts and passwords; their use can significantly reduce the number of help desk or IT staff needed for these tasks.

Additional infrastructure servers include **enterprise-monitoring** servers, which are used to monitor servers, applications, storage, and network services. Such servers can send alerts or resolve failed services, thereby greatly increasing system uptime. Systems management servers provide comprehensive management of applications, services, physical resources, hypervisors, and networks.

They also provide centralized services such as desktop imaging and software deployment, antivirus and antimalware protection, application security patching and upgrades, and computer configuration and asset management. Endpoint encryption servers are systems that install and manage encryption on client computers.

Database servers maintain a healthcare organization's database instances; they are frequently clustered or configured with multiple servers to support large database sizes. Most HIS and administrative/clinical applications use transactional databases, such as Oracle 11G, IBM DB2, or Microsoft SQL, whereas EHRs may use high-speed object databases, such as Intersystems Cache.

Enterprise web content management (EWCM) servers enable departments to easily update and manage web-based content on the corporate intranet and, in some cases, on the organization's externally facing website. Finally, application virtualization servers enable users to run applications that are installed on centrally located servers, eliminating the need to install the application locally and, in most cases, improving the performance of the application and overall end-user experience. Application virtualization is being widely adopted in healthcare settings due to its tangible benefits.

Client Computing

Client computing describes the computers and devices used by end users. These can be categorized as either stationary or mobile devices, with mobile computing needs on the rise. Nevertheless, the standard client computer issued today is a PC directly connected to the organization's network using a wired or copper cable network connection. Recent advances in technology have significantly reduced the size and cost of PCs, but additional improvements in wireless technology are needed to transition to a fully wireless environment.

Other stationary computers found in a healthcare setting include **all-in-one (AIO) computers**, wall-mounted computers, thin- and zero-client computers, and electronic tracking board systems. AIO computers are often needed in clinical areas with space constraints, such as in operating room (OR) or emergency room (ER), and are designed with all the computer system components (except for the keyboard and mouse) integrated with the monitor, which is typically a 24- to 27-inch LCD plasma screen. Wall-mounted computers are frequently deployed in patient rooms and other locations where space constraints exist. In patient rooms, care must be taken to ensure that these computers are optimally situated to enhance the caregiver-patient experience, as maintaining eye contact between both parties is vital for the proper delivery of care. In some cases, special construction must be undertaken to create stationary workstation areas in the center of rooms that support multiple patients.

Thin-client computers are increasing in use in healthcare settings. These small machines rely on a server to perform and store all data processing, and can be likened to client dumb terminals from the mainframe era. Thin-client computers typically have a small amount of RAM, a reduced-size CPU, a small hard drive that runs a modified version of the Windows operating system (called Windows Embedded), and an NIC. The benefits of thin-client computing include improved maintenance and security due to central administration of the hardware and software in the data center, and reduced client hardware and energy costs.

Zero-client computers are similar to thin-client computers but offer the additional advantage of having no local hard drive or operating system to secure or maintain (Kleyman, 2013). Like thin-client computers, zero-client computers are gaining in popularity in healthcare settings, as they are well suited to furthering desktop virtualization and integrating with WOWs due to their light weight, small form factor, and ease of management.

Electronic tracking board systems support the real-time tracking of critical information pertinent to the flow of care for individual patients. Tracking board systems consist of room-sized LCD or plasma computer monitors connected to an EHR or another clinical application. They are often used in ERs.

Mobile computers frequently used in healthcare settings include WOWs, laptops, tablets, and smartphones. WOWs, which are also referred to as computers-on-wheels (COWs) or mobile workstations, are mobile carts that integrate with client computers and peripherals. They can function as either a mobile system or, by locking the wheels at the base of the cart, a stationary system. WOWs are often used in clinical areas such as nursing stations, patient rooms, hallways, and other rooms; due to their larger size, however, it is not always possible to deploy them in smaller or crowded areas. WOWs vary in cost, with the more expensive carts having advanced battery power capabilities, lockable drawers or bins for medication administration and other supplies, power assistance, and advanced cart software. Specialized medical-grade keyboards and mice are often deployed with WOWs to improve infection control. WOWs are often deployed using thin-client computers, zero-client computers, or AIO computers.

In some cases, healthcare organizations elect to use laptops and medical-grade tablets with docking stations when deploying WOWs. Laptops and tablets can be readily disconnected from WOWs for easy portability because they have their own battery and operating systems; once disconnected, they can be used as stand-alone devices and later reconnected to WOWs. Tablets are easier to carry than laptops when making rounds but are not as well suited for clinical documentation as laptops and standard PCs. As a result, iPad and medical-grade tablet usage in clinical

settings has seen mixed adoption rates. In a healthcare setting, smartphones are used primarily for communication-related activities such as e-mail, alerting, scheduling, texting, web-based searches, and viewing clinical application data.

Other important client devices and peripherals needed to provide patient care include bar-code scanners, signature pads, printers, document scanners, and identification (ID) badge and access control systems. **Bar-code scanners** are used to automate the input of patient and medical information, including patient ID from bar-coded wristbands or ID tags, and medication administration that uses pharmacy bar-coded labels. Bar-code scanners are manufactured in wired or wireless configurations, with the wireless modality being both more popular and more expensive. Signature pads are designed to electronically accept patient and clinician signatures and are frequently deployed at hospital admission and patient accounting areas. Both bar-code scanners and signature pads are among the peripherals often found on a WOW.

Printing and **electronic document management (EDM)** are two final client computing areas that are critical to a healthcare organization. For large healthcare organizations, centralized print servers can be deployed in the organization's data center; these computers typically support as many as 500 printers. EDM is seeing more adoption in health care due to the transition from paper records to electronic records. It involves scanning paper documents and using **intelligent optical character recognition (OCR)** technology to convert the image into editable text. Low-speed, medium-speed, and high-speed scanners—listed here in order of not only increasing costs but also better scanning speeds and capacities—are essential EDM devices in today's healthcare environment, particularly in **health information management (HIM)** departments.

Portable scanners are commonly used in various clinical areas, such as admissions and nursing stations.

ID badge and access control systems are increasingly widespread in healthcare environments. The important components of badge and access control systems include the ID badge media, **radio frequency identification (RFID)** badge readers, badge printers and cameras, and badge access control hardware and software. Smart-card ID badges uniquely identify individuals who work in a healthcare setting and are now frequently used to log in and out of computers, gain access to restricted areas within a hospital or healthcare facility, and record start and end times of work shifts. Proximity, iClass, and multi-Class smart-card ID badge technologies are pervasive in healthcare environments, with the latter two having the advantage of not requiring any physical contact between the badge media and the reader. In addition to displaying the user's photo and work information, smart-card ID badges can be configured to hold embedded information, such as an employee number or medication administration identifier. Use of smart-card ID badges by clinicians to dispense medications reduces the risk of medical errors. RFID badge readers are often deployed on WOWs or other client computers to allow users to quickly log in and out of their computer session. Specialized badge printers and camera equipment are needed to take individual user photos and print the smart-card ID badges. Badge access control hardware and software is required to maintain the list of users who have been assigned a smart-card ID badge, along with their user and access-level information. Such hardware and software are usually deployed with the server system and database installed in the organization's primary data center, with individual servers or appliances installed in a distributed fashion at each facility that has a geographically disparate location.

Virtual desktop infrastructure (VDI) technology is gaining increased acceptance in healthcare settings, largely due to its direct impact in improving patient care delivery. Desktop virtualization is defined as a client's desktop operating system that is hosted within a VM running on a centralized server in the data center. Thin- or zero-client computers are the most prevalent desktop computers running in VDI environments. However, because VDI desktop client hardware requirements are minimal, legacy PCs can be repurposed with a VDI desktop and used for several additional years. It is also common for organizations to deploy VDI software to mobile devices, such as laptops and tablets, which gives them the ability to operate their local desktop or a VDI desktop. Another strategy used in healthcare organizations is to deploy VDI desktops to PC workstations, thereby giving the users of these computers the option to run either both the local desktop and the VDI desktop, or only the VDI desktop. Server computers hosting VDI desktop VMs require a different configuration than host systems running server- and application-based VMs. VDI VMs demand large amounts of RAM, CPUs, and high-speed SAN storage to provide an acceptable end-user experience. In contrast, VDI desktops generally use a standard desktop image that has all the applications and programs preinstalled. A user's personal settings, such as wallpaper and browser shortcuts, along with information on which desktop applications the user has permission to access, can be maintained centrally. Files and documents used during a VDI desktop session can be stored centrally on a file server.

VDI desktops are categorized as either persistent desktops or non-persistent desktops. When a user logs in to a persistent desktop, he or she receives a new desktop installation each time, along with the user's current personal settings and file sharing information copied to the desktop. If the user then experiences a difficulty with a desktop application or the desktop freezes or crashes, he or she simply needs to log off and then log back in, as doing so will create a new or "fresh" desktop. In healthcare settings, this setup can greatly reduce queries to the help desk. Also, because all users receive the same standard desktop image, significantly less server storage and ongoing maintenance are needed. A downside to persistent desktops is that when the desktop image is upgraded with new applications, care must be taken to ensure that the upgrade will work correctly with the existing applications installed to the desktop.

Non-persistent desktops function much like a non-VDI experience, except that dedicated server storage for each VDI desktop and the user's VDI desktop is not recreated or refreshed when logging in. This approach is not as effective when addressing end-user help desk requests regarding problematic VDI desktop issues, but does more closely simulate the traditional user desktop experience.

Single sign-on (SSO) and **tap 'n go technologies** can provide significant benefits to healthcare organizations that are deploying VDI desktops. SSO has the benefit that users have to remember just one username and password for their desktop session and all applications. It works by requiring users to log in to their desktop session with their username and password. Once in the desktop session, the SSO technology automatically logs the user in to each of the various applications without requiring the user to remember or enter application-specific passwords. In a healthcare setting where many different applications are used, each requiring the use of a separate password, this is a significant time saver and user satisfier.

Tap 'n go technology enables users to quickly log in and out of computers with just the "tap" of their ID badge. When moving from computer to computer, the user's desktop session is transferred seamlessly based on the proximity of the ID badge to a workstation, bringing it over to the next computer exactly as it was left in the previous computer. If an application was opened on one computer, the same application remains open when the user moves to the next computer.

In short, VDI desktops have the potential to improve the desktop experience, reduce desktop support costs, simplify desktop management, increase desktop standardization, and strengthen remote access and data security. Drawbacks to VDI technology are the relatively high up-front capital costs, the more advanced system administrator skill sets needed, the limitations encountered when working offline, and the challenges associated with supporting video and other bandwidth-intensive applications.

Mobile Computing

Mobile computing in health care has emerged as a leading driver for improving the quality, accessibility, and safety of care, as well as increasing the cost-effectiveness of care. For many years, technology adoption in health care has lagged behind that in other industries such as the financial, manufacturing, and retail industries. With the recent development of **mHealth** (i.e., mobile health), there are now significant opportunities to improve how healthcare professionals deliver care. An important benefit of mobile computing can be seen with how it improves the real-time delivery of care. In addition, with the rapid adoption of smart phones and tablets among clinicians, consumers, and employees, the BYOD phenomenon is gaining acceptance within healthcare settings. Providers of care, who traditionally have been slow to respond to technology innovation, are now taking steps to transform how they deliver health care through the use of mobile computing.

To ensure that mobile computing is successfully deployed in an HIS environment, it is vital that healthcare managers understand how an effective mobile computing strategy can be developed. The steps should be considered when developing a mobile computing strategy (Mobile Security Work Group, 2013).

1. Identify the Key Stakeholders

Four key groups of stakeholders who have unique mobile computing requirements are end users, clinicians, management, and IT staff. To appropriately determine each of these stakeholders' requirements, their input is needed prior to selecting and deploying the mobile solution. End-user concerns typically center on if and how they can use their device, how to obtain assistance or training, what their password requirements will be, what they should do if they lose their device, what the rules are for personal versus company data on the device, and what, if any, reimbursement policy exists.

Physicians and nurses need secure point-of-care mobile technology that will allow them to communicate with each other rapidly and in real time to efficiently do their jobs. Secure text messaging functionality and the ability to integrate with Wi-Fi to provide coverage in areas where cellular signals are weak are two critical areas gaining traction in healthcare settings. Recent research indicates that clinician involvement in technology decision making and use of a single mobile device (instead of multiple mobile devices) improves the quality of care they can provide and increase physician and nurse efficiency.

Management will be concerned about the liabilities, costs, insurance, and changing legal and vendor landscape that are associated with mobile computing. In addition, the ownership and protection of corporate data and assets, along with the ability to measure user patterns, will be an area of management interest. Finally, the focus of the IT staff will be on mobile computing device and application deployment, support, and management; application and data configuration and standardization; and ways to address mobile computing incidents and lost/stolen device issues.

2. Create Policies, Procedures, and an End-User Acceptance Agreement

It is vital that healthcare organizations develop a comprehensive mobile computing policy, including language clearly defining their BYOD strategy. An acceptable use agreement detailing the terms and conditions of mobile computing expectations for end users should be developed by the healthcare organization and signed by each end user prior to that person being given access to organizational resources via his or her mobile device. Typically, this can be implemented by including the user acceptance agreement when deploying the mobile computing software to the end-user mobile devices. Incorporating mobile computing into security awareness training is also an important step toward ensuring ongoing compliance.

3. Understand Regulatory, Legal, and Compliance Requirements

A successful healthcare mobile computing strategy must include all pertinent local, state, and federal regulatory, privacy and security, legal, and compliance requirements. Important legislation such as Health Insurance Portability and Accountability Act (HIPAA) and the Health Information Technology for Economic and Clinical Health (HITECH) Act at the national level, as well as state-level regulations, such as California Senate Bill (SB) 13863, which includes notification rules that outline requirements for disclosure of breaches, are important regulations that need to be considered before and monitored after implementing mobile computing in HIS environments.

4. Develop Mobile Management Strategies

A number of mobile management strategies have emerged, with **mobile device management (MDM)** being the most mature in its development. MDM encompasses managing mobility at the mobile device level, with secure e-mail, calendaring, contacts, web browsing, and application store management being standard areas that are typically covered. Enrollment and automatic profile/application capabilities; remote administration; screen passcode settings, remote wipe for lost or stolen devices, and encryption at rest and in transit; secure web browser capability; persistent push e-mail delivery; and compliance/auditing, asset, device, location, and network tracking are additional features that are found in MDM products.

Another mobile computing area that is critical in healthcare environments is **mobile content management (MCM)**, which provides encryption for files and attachments, content expiration, screen capture controls, and online/offline access to secure content. Some MCM products have advanced functionality that restricts data from being physically stored on a mobile device, yet provides full access and functionality to the content. **Mobile application management (MAM)** gives organizations control over mobile application delivery and app store management, blacklist/whitelist functionality, application tracking, and application security. In addition, it provides a framework for managing a healthcare organization's internal customized mobile applications.

5. Define the Technical Architecture

Four important technical areas must be considered as part of the **mobile computing strategy**: (1) what the mobile platform will be; (2) whether enterprise directory integration will be needed; (3) which devices and native applications will be supported; and (4) which telecommunications management capabilities and restrictions will be applied. The benefits of cloud computing, including more robust security and reduced costs, have made hosted or SaaS solutions attractive alternatives to on-premises virtual or appliance mobile computing

solutions. Other areas to review are perpetual versus monthly licensing, single-versus multitenancy architecture, **role-based access control (RBAC)** support, web-based administrative features, and self-service capabilities.

Medium to large healthcare providers typically require AD, Certificate Authority (CA), and **Secure Socket Layer (SSL)**, **virtual private network (VPN)**, and WLAN integration. The ability to support a wide range of mobile devices using their native applications, particularly for e-mail, calendaring, and contact management, is a necessity, especially for users participating in a BYOD program. It is not uncommon for employers to limit company-issued mobile devices to one or two vendor device lines, with the Apple IOS iPad and iPhone having a notably large market share among physicians.

As BYOD gains in popularity, telecommunications management functionality is becoming of increasing importance. This includes controlling and tracking voice and data roaming, cellular and Wi-Fi network data usage and signal strength, and phone call history. Finally, it is important to ensure an optimal and successful end-user experience, avoiding scenarios such as requiring an end user to change his or her existing carrier data plan to a more costly plan to participate in a BYOD program.

Organizations that take a conservative risk-based approach toward BYOD may require users to agree to strict policies regarding privacy and what the organization can view or cannot view. Also, restrictions on using consumer-based cloud storage, for example, can limit users from storing or backing up their mobile device data to popular and free cloud-based services. This can cause users who value their privacy, have a need for convenience, or desire to choose their data storage provider to opt out of a BYOD program.

Information Security

Ensuring and maintaining the security of HIS data, applications, and supporting technical infrastructure are vital to the long-term viability of healthcare organizations. Without appropriate security program, policies, and corresponding controls in place to (1) define how users and computer systems should behave and (2) protect valuable assets such as computers, applications, databases, networks, and data centers, organizations will be vulnerable to data, financial, and reputational loss. Such losses can be the result of unintentional occurrences, such as unplanned system outages due to poor configuration or a lack of change management. They can also result from intentional acts, such as cybercrime, computer hacking, or malware, which target systems that are not updated or lack appropriate security controls. When designing or implementing HIS, security should be considered at the outset— not just after the systems have been developed and deployed in a production environment. Of course, security controls need to be incorporated in all aspects of technology, including mobile devices, client computers, servers and applications, network devices, and data center infrastructure. In addition to taking security considerations into account in the system planning stages, security needs to be reviewed and adjusted on an ongoing basis to properly protect the ever-evolving technology environment.

Many information security-related systems and technologies can be deployed to protect modern healthcare environments. **Firewalls** are network devices that limit access and protect an organization's internal network from unauthorized users and external systems. Traditional firewalls use "stateful" network packet inspection to determine whether a network packet should be allowed through the firewall. A network packet's "state" is related to its source and destination address, but does not indicate whether the data inside the network packet are good or bad. Stateful firewalls are becoming obsolete for this reason, as they are unable to determine the kind of traffic or the data inside the network packet. **Next-generation (NG)** firewalls address the traffic inspection and application awareness drawbacks of stateful inspection firewalls and are now replacing

those traditional firewalls. Two of the most important features of NG firewalls are deep network packet inspection and application awareness. Deep packet inspection examines the network packet payload for anomalies and known malware, while application awareness is a feature that enables NG firewalls to better identify and manage web application traffic. Enterprise firewalls include other advanced network security features.

VPNs allow remote users to connect to applications or services that are accessible only from computers on the internal or corporate network. VPN connections are secure, encrypted remote-access sessions that use either the Internet Protocol Security (IPSEC) or SSL VPN tunnels to encrypt all data traffic that travels between the remote computer and the internal network. **Intrusion detection systems (IDSs)** and intrusion prevention systems (IPSs) are intelligent monitoring and analysis systems that detect irregular or inappropriate data traffic occurring on the corporate network; they generate alerts to network and system administrators describing the offending system or device.

Despite the many benefits provided by network firewalls, additional security technologies are needed to thoroughly protect healthcare organization networks, servers, applications, databases, desktops, and other devices. Web security systems are designed to monitor end-user Internet activity; they block or greatly reduce users' ability to access inappropriate and malicious websites, and restrict usage of unauthorized web services, such as unsecured document/file sharing and music/video streaming services. Web security systems can use the Web Cache Communication Protocol to ensure that no end users can bypass the web security system. In addition, most web security systems have data loss prevention (DLP) capability, which is designed to restrict confidential or unauthorized data from leaving the internal network. A current limitation with DLP technology is that it is unable to inspect encrypted traffic traveling about the Internet.

Encryption-in-transit is an important control that ensures the security of all data traffic containing confidential or ePHI information, such as network traffic, web activity, email messaging, file transfers, text messaging, and instant messaging. Encryption-at-rest is a similar security control that protects data stored in databases, applications, storage and backup systems, and laptops and mobile devices. One of the most often cited reasons that healthcare organizations receive fines for HIPAA violations is lost or stolen laptops containing ePHI that was not encrypted. As such, healthcare organizations need to give attention to encrypting all of their laptops.

Multifactor authentication (MFA) is an easy-to-deploy technology that can be used to provide secure access to remote systems as well as to critical servers or network devices. It works by requiring two forms of identification. The most common form of single-factor authentication in use today is a username and password; this falls under the category of something a user *knows*. MFA commonly includes a username and password, plus something a user *has* in his or her possession, such as a smart card or a randomly generated personal identification number (PIN) that is sent to a small device or mobile phone. MFA can also include something a user *is*. Although not widespread in healthcare organizations, this technology is found in biometric devices, such retinal or fingerprint readers.

Security information event management (SIEM) is a critical technology that is designed to automate and intelligently analyze system logs for anomalies and inappropriate activity. With increasing reliance on EHRs and other HIS applications, and hundreds of thousands of system log entries to review for inappropriate user activity, thereby ensuring that access to confidential or sensitive data is restricted to only those who have a need to know, SIEM technology is often the only practical method by which a healthcare organization can detect these types of violations.

System hardening, vulnerability assessments, and penetration testing are three ongoing security activities that are designed to ensure that network, server, application, and database systems are configured in a highly secure manner, fully up-to-date with security patches, and free from vulnerabilities that can be exploited to negatively impact the confidentiality, integrity, and availability of production systems.

As seen in **FIGURE 6.9**, managed security services are cost-effective information security services provided to healthcare organizations by consulting or vendor companies. These services typically manage many of the healthcare organization's information security technologies, such as IDS/IPS, SIEM, vulnerability assessments, and security incident response. Such services provide value by reducing the number of information security personnel needed by the healthcare organization, thereby allowing the organization to spend more time and resources concentrating on its core mission of delivering quality health care.

Summary

It is important for healthcare professionals to understand the basics of technology, even though it may not be a core component of their field or specialty. With the explosion of digital technology, cloud, mobile devices, and big data, today's healthcare worker is increasingly becoming more familiar and dependent on technology adoption.

HIS applications and their supporting underlying technology infrastructure are complex, yet easily understood when examined through the lens of their smaller, core components (or building blocks). HIS applications are developed using programming languages to define how data will be processed. HIS data are stored in databases that provide advanced processing and reporting functionality. Application integration has been found to be a more superior process for connecting HIS applications than developing and

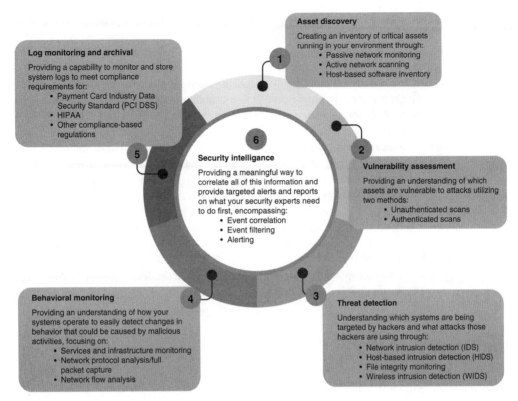

Asset discovery

Creating an inventory of critical assets running in your environment through:
- Passive network monitoring
- Active network scanning
- Host-based software inventory

Log monitoring and archival

Providing a capability to monitor and store system logs to meet compliance requirements for:
- Payment Card Industry Data Security Standard (PCI DSS)
- HIPAA
- Other compliance-based regulations

Security intelligence

Providing a meaningful way to correlate all of this information and provide targeted alerts and reports on what your security experts need to do first, encompassing:
- Event correlation
- Event filtering
- Alerting

Vulnerability assessment

Providing an understanding of which assets are vulnerable to attacks utilizing two methods:
- Unauthenticated scans
- Authenticated scans

Behavioral monitoring

Providing an understanding of how your systems operate to easily detect changes in behavior that could be caused by malicious activities, focusing on:
- Services and infrastructure monitoring
- Network protocol analysis/full packet capture
- Network flow analysis

Threat detection

Understanding which systems are being targeted by hackers and what attacks those hackers are using through:
- Network intrusion detection (IDS)
- Host-based intrusion detection (HIDS)
- File integrity monitoring
- Wireless intrusion detection (WIDS)

FIGURE 6.9 Managed security services.

Courtesy of Sword & Shield Enterprise Security, Inc.

maintaining application interfaces. To develop such applications, the SDLC methodology is typically used as the programming development framework. Healthcare organizations are relying increasingly on vendors to develop HIS applications, thereby allowing them to focus on their core competency—that of delivering quality patient care.

HIS applications are categorized as delivering clinical care (e.g., EHRs), clinical support processes (e.g., laboratory testing, pharmacy, radiology), clinician (e.g., CPOE, clinical decision support), and patient flow (e.g., registration, scheduling). CIS applications can be either inpatient or outpatient systems. Examples of outpatient CIS applications include ambulatory care systems, PHRs, LTC systems, and CPOE systems. HIS applications also encompass administrative applications, such as ERP, customer relationship management, SCM, and home health care. Critical to the success of HIS applications is a smoothly running, properly configured underlying technical infrastructure. This includes technologies such as networks, data centers, server/client computers, and other devices.

Understanding how computer networks operate is essential to ensuring a high level of performance and efficiency for HIS environments. The most important types of computer networks are LANs, WLANs), WANs, WWANs), and SANs. The Internet is a well-known WAN that is being increasing leveraged by HIS applications due to its robust, highly available platform and pervasiveness. For example, many healthcare organizations are now leveraging the Internet as they strive to improve their communication with patients, develop new marketing strategies, and educate their health plan members. Emerging technologies, such as VoIP, UC, video/web conferencing, and mobile computing are providing new ways for clinicians to collaborate with each other and their patients.

The sizes of healthcare data centers are decreasing due to advances in server and storage consolidation, virtualization, and cloud computing. Remote-hosting EHR applications are now more commonplace, with many healthcare organizations becoming increasingly reliant on co-location or vendor-supported data centers to host HIS infrastructure. As organizations struggle to develop acceptable business continuity and DRPs, they are discovering that remote-hosted data centers and cloud

computing boast high SLAs and lower costs. But no matter where the systems are housed, they must be protected by viable business continuity and DRPs. Virtualization and SSO advances in client computing have benefited HIS application usability, greatly increasing end-user satisfaction. Wireless WOWs and other peripheral devices are continuing to expand their footprints in hospitals as demands for mobility by clinicians increase. The consumerization of IT and BYOD models are steadily gaining acceptance in healthcare environments.

Finally, challenges with privacy and security remain, but advances in technology are positioning healthcare organizations to mitigate many of these vulnerabilities, with the promise of successfully delivering and maintaining efficient, secure, and high-performing HIS applications.

Key Terms

Active directory (AD)
All-in-one (AIO) computers
Ambulatory care systems
Ancillary clinical support
    processes
Appliances
Backbone networks (BNs)
Bar-code scanners
Blade server technology
Branch circuit monitoring
    system (BCMS)
Bring-your-own-device
    (BYOD)
Business continuity plan
    (BCP)
Campus networks
Circuit
Client
Clinical decision support
Clinical information system
    (CIS)
Cloud computing
Commercial off-the-shelf
    (COTS)

Computer room air handlers
    (CRAHs)
Computerized physician
    order entry (CPOE)
Containers
Continuous power source
    (CPS)
Customer resource
    management
    (CRM)
Data center management
    systems (DCMSs)
Data centers
Database
Digital signage
Disaster recovery plan
    (DRP)
Distributed antennae system
    (DAS)
Domain Name System
    (DNS)
Dynamic Host
    Configuration Protocol
    (DHCP)

Electronic data interchange
    (EDI)
Electronic document
    management (EDM)
Electronic tracking board
    systems
Emergency power off
    (EPO)
EMR-as-a-service (EaaS)
Enterprise resource planning
    (ERP)
Enterprise-monitoring
Extranets
Fiber Channel over Ethernet
    (FCoE)
Firewalls
Hard disk drives (HDDs)
Health information
    management (HIM)
Heating, ventilating, and
    air-conditioning (HVAC)
    systems
Home health HIS
    applications

Hyper converged infrastructure (HCI)

Hypertext Transfer Protocol (HTTP)

Hypervisor or virtual machine monitor (VMM)

Identity and access management (IAM)

Infrastructure servers

Infrastructure-as-a-service (IaaS)

Instant messaging or chat

Institute of Electrical and Electronics Engineers (IEEE) technologies

Integration

Intelligent optical character recognition (OCR)

Interfaces

Internet Small Computer System Interface (iSCSI)

Intranets

Intrusion detection systems (IDSs)

Keyboard, video, and mouse over Internet Protocol (KVMoIP) devices

Local area networks (LANs)

Long-term care (LTC) systems

Medical imaging systems (MISs)

Medication administration records (MARs)

Metropolitan area networks (MANs)

mHealth

Mobile application management (MAM)

Mobile computers

Mobile computing strategy

Mobile content management (MCM)

Mobile device management (MDM)

Network functions virtualization (NFV)

Networking

Next-generation (NG)

Open systems interconnection model (OSI)

Outpatient systems

Patient accounting

Patient flow

Personal health records (PHRs)

Pharmacy information system (PIS)

Picture archiving and communication systems (PACSs)

Platform-as-a-service (PaaS)

Power-over-Ethernet (POE)

Private clouds

Public clouds

Radio frequency identification (RFID)

Radiology information systems (RISs)

Random access memory (RAM)

Recovery point objective (RPO)

Recovery time objective (RTO)

Redundancy

Redundant array of independent drives (RAID)

Remote hosting

Role-based access control (RBAC)

SDLC (See Software/systems development life cycle)

Secure Socket Layer (SSL)

Security information event management (SIEM)

Server

Service level agreements (SLAs)

Single sign-on (SSO)

Software defined networking (SDN)

Software/systems development life cycle (SDLC)

Software-as-a-service (SaaS)

Storage area networks (SANs)

Supply chain management (SCM)

Tap 'n go technologies

Technical standards

Telecommunications

Thin-client computers

Transmission Control Protocol/Internet Protocol (TCP/IP) or Internet model

UC (See Unified communications (UC))

UCSs, server virtualization, and SSO

Unified communications (UC)

Uninterruptable power supply (UPS)

Very early smoke detection apparatus (VESDA)

Virtual desktop infrastructure (VDI)

Virtual machines (VMs)

Virtual private network (VPN)

Virtual tape libraries (VTLs)

Virtualization

Voice over Internet Protocol (VoIP)

Voice over wireless local area network (VoWLAN)

Web conferencing

Wide area networks (WANs)

Wireless local area networks (WLANs)

Wireless wide area networks (WWANs)

Workflow redesign

Zero-client computers

Discussion Questions

1. Describe the seven stages of the SDLC methodology and explain which functions are performed in each phase.
2. Discuss the pros and cons of using application integration versus application interfaces.
3. Identify the various clinical applications (Quadrant I) that support clinical care, clinical support processes, clinicians, and patient flow, and describe how they differ from one another.
4. List three major inpatient CISs and explain how technology enables these systems to deliver improved care.
5. Identify two outpatient CISs and explain how these systems differ from inpatient clinical information systems.
6. What are the benefits of a CPOE system?
7. Explain the differences between the various computer networks supporting HIS applications today (e.g., LANs, WLANs, WANs, WWANs, and SANs).
8. Identify some of the emerging technologies being used to support HIS and describe how they are benefiting the delivery of care.
9. Which technologies are being utilized today in computer networks, data centers, servers, and applications to provide increased availability and allow HIS to remain accessible, even in the event of a hardware or component failure?
10. Discuss the benefits of server virtualization and describe how it is affecting HIS applications.
11. Identify the various types of client computing devices that are being deployed in hospitals today and explain which types of advantages they bring.
12. How can ID badge and virtual desktop infrastructure technology improve the delivery of care?
13. What are the important steps a healthcare organization should consider before implementing a mobile computing strategy such as bring-your-own-device technology?
14. Why is security information event management an important technology for managing the security of EHRs and other HIS applications?

References

Barnes, J. C. (2004). *Business continuity planning and HIPAA: Business continuity management in the health care environment* (pp. 13–24). Brookfield, CT: Rothstein Associates.

Bent, K. (2012, October 19). How the BYOD phenomenon is shaping the next era in managed print services. *CRN*. Retrieved from https://www.crn.com/blogs-op-ed/channel-voices/240006736/how-to-avoid-the-five-biggest-byod-mistakes.htm use this one

Dern, D. P. (2013, December 9). The benefits of integrating wayfinding with digital signage and who's using it now. *Campus Safety Magazine*. Retrieved from http://www.campussafetymagazine.com/article/The-Benefits-of-Integrating-Wayfinding-with-Digital-Signage-and-Who-s-Using

Hanover, J. (2010). Building the right foundation for long term meaningful use. *IDC Health Insights*, p. 21.

Retrieved from https://electronichealthreporter.com/idc-health-insights-judy-hanover-structured-data-long-term-affects-health-reform/

Health and Medicine Division of the National Academies of Sciences, Engineering, and Medicine (1991, 1997)". *The computer-based patient record: An essential technology for health care.* In R. S. Dick & E. B. Steen (Eds.). Washington, DC: National Academies Press.

Internet Engineering Task Force. (n.d.). Multiprotocol label switching. Charter for working group. Retrieved from http://datatracker.ietf.org/wg/mpls/charter/

Kleyman, B. (2013, October 11). The zero-client: The next-generation in client computing. *Data Center Knowledge*. Retrieved from http://www.datacenterknowledge.com/archives/2013/10/11/the-zero-client-the-next-generation-in-client-computing/

Mobile Security Work Group. (2013). 20 questions to ask about bring your own device (BYOD). *HIMSS*. Retrieved from http://www.himss.org/ResourceLibrary /ContentTabsDetail.aspx?ItemNumber=21437

Online Browsing Platform (OBP). (1984). Information processing systems—Open Systems Interconnection— Basic Reference Model, Addendum 1: Connectionless-mode transmission, Ref. No. ISO 7498: Add.1: 1987(E).

Ontario MD, Inc. (2013). EMR as a service. Retrieved from https://www.ontariomd.ca/idc/groups/public /documents/omd_file_content_item/omd012523.pdf

Outcome 1: IP addressing. The TCP/IP Protocol Suite. HN Computing. Retrieved from http://www.sqa.org.uk /e-learning/NetInf101CD/page_15.htm

Stalley, S., & DesRoches, C. M. (2013). Progress on adoption of electronic health records. In Robert Wood Johnson Foundation, *Health information technology in the United States: Better information systems for better care*. Princeton, NJ: Author.

StudyMode.com. (2008–2009). The seven phases of the systems development life cycle. Retrieved from http:// www.studymode.com/essays/Seven-Phases-Systems -Development-Life-Cycle-163461.html

CHAPTER 7

HIS Management and Technology Services

James Brady, PhD

LEARNING OBJECTIVES

By the end of this chapter, the student will be able to:

- Communicate the importance of technology readiness and gap analysis initiatives.
- Define process improvement in the context of Health Information Systems (HIS).
- Develop an information technology (IT) governance framework using one of the three commonly used methodologies.
- Describe IT service support and IT service delivery using the Information Technology Infrastructure Library framework.
- Understand the key financial management issues affecting HIS.
- Value the skilled talent needed for successful HIS implementations.
- Manage relationships with vendors for optimal support, maintenance, and performance.
- Understand the benefits and principles of contract management, including the importance of milestones, change control, and data ownership guidelines.
- Describe HIS project management methodology and knowledge areas.
- Define the roles and responsibilities for IT-related functions.

▶ Introduction

There is little doubt that managing a healthcare organization's information systems is a complex undertaking requiring many highly qualified healthcare professionals working closely together. Yet, surprisingly, many healthcare leaders do not fully understand the numerous factors involved in planning, developing, implementing, and supporting a comprehensive HIS environment. The *HIS Software* and *HIS Technology* chapters review the importance of developing and maintaining a robust and highly available technology infrastructure. Given the complexities involved with HIS applications, it is imperative that the underlying technology be both stable and consistently available. These characteristics will provide HIS implementation and operational support personnel with the much-needed capacity to focus on managing HIS deployments in order to achieve successful outcomes. To ensure that the technology areas are acceptable and ready to support HIS implementations, it is common for organizations to complete a technology assessment or **gap analysis** well before the HIS implementation begins. Areas in need of improvement that are found in the assessment (i.e., "gaps") can then be addressed or remediated, allowing the HIS deployment to proceed without being hampered by technology issues.

A key indicator of the effectiveness of an HIS program is the ratio of unplanned work to planned work. Unplanned work includes mitigating major system "crashes" and other adverse events that cause systems to become unstable, unresponsive, or unavailable; this is compared to planned work such as system updates or implementation efforts. An effective HIS initiative will have minimal system issues compared to the day-to-day activities of managing HIS activities. Nevertheless, installing hardware and software itself is not enough to ensure success. If HIS are to achieve all of their intended purposes, organizations need to look at the people who manage HIS and the HIS organization's processes from three vantage points: from an operational perspective, from a project view, and in light of how the technology and other IT services are delivered.

For many years, the work of the HIS department in healthcare organizations was seen as filling a purely technical role, with the IT staff often assigned to work in the basement, a data center, or another remote area that left them at a distance from the organization's business and clinical workers. With the advent of healthcare reform and the proliferation of electronic health record (EHR) systems, the HIS department now must establish a proactive and tightly integrated "hand-in-glove" working relationship with business

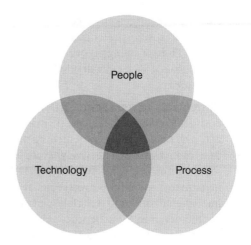

FIGURE 7.1 The people-process-technology paradigm.

and clinical staff. In addition to introducing innovative and transformational technology, HIS departments are discovering that partnering and collaborating with other departments within the organizations is key to long-term HIS success. Having covered the technology areas in Chapter 6, the goal of this chapter is to delve into the remaining two areas in the "people, process, and technology" paradigm— people and process. **FIGURE 7.1** provides a simple description capturing this concept. The following discussion will provide the reader with a comprehensive understanding of how HIS cannot only be deployed successfully but also experience high staff and end-user adoption and satisfaction ratings.

▶ Managing Process

To achieve the successful implementation and ongoing support of HIS, well-defined processes are required. Without structured and formal processes, HIS deployments suffer increased risk of failure, and it is unlikely that high user satisfaction ratings will be achieved once the systems are in place. **Information technology governance (ITG)** is a term used to define this requirement. It comprises the processes that ensure the effective and efficient use of IT in enabling an organization to achieve its goals. ITG can be divided into two additional areas:

- **IT demand governance (ITDG)** is a business investment decision making and oversight process by which healthcare organizations effectively evaluate, select, prioritize, and fund their HIS investment, including overseeing their implementations and tangibly measuring the organizational benefits achieved. In other words, it is what IT should be working on.
- **IT supply-side governance (ITSG)** makes sure the IT organization operates in an efficient and organized fashion. Essentially, it defines who in IT should be doing what.

To implement IT governance in healthcare environments, an ITG framework must be used. Trying to implement governance without a formal and structured framework, or attempting to deploy HIS applications without any ITG at all, will most certainly cause the organization and its HIS initiatives to fail. Several mature ITG frameworks exist today that healthcare organizations can use to develop structured processes for the delivery of HIS. The ITG frameworks that we will discuss here are **Information Technology Infrastructure Library (ITIL)**, **Control Objectives for Information and Related Technology (COBIT)**, and frameworks developed by the **International Organization for Standardization (ISO)** and the **International Electrotechnical Commission (IEC)**.

ITIL is perhaps the ITG framework most widely adopted by healthcare organizations today. It was first developed in the early 1990s by the British government and is made up of a library of books that describe an integrated set of seven process-oriented "best practices" for managing IT services. As seen in **FIGURE 7.2**, ITIL is well suited for organizations that have a

chief information officer (CIO) or HIS leader championing HIS-process improvements. Unlike some of the other process improvement models, ITIL provides high-level "how to" guidance via its many generic process flow diagrams and descriptions. IT service management (ITSM) is a term that describes the two primary best practices or core areas of ITIL: IT service support and IT service delivery, represented in **FIGURE 7.3**.

IT service support is an important process area that an HIS department should consider addressing when deploying or supporting existing HIS applications. As depicted in **FIGURE 7.4**, IT service support encompasses the support processes needed to ensure acceptable service. This area is more process oriented than technical, and its activities are accomplished by managing problems and changes in the IT infrastructure. IT service support can be seen most clearly when organizations need to (1) quickly solve issues encountered by staff when using HIS, (2) train staff on how to best use the software, or (3) manage requests for modifications or upgrades in a non-impactful way that does not negate the many benefits of the HIS applications.

The IT service support process areas in the context for HIS support include the following elements:

- The *service desk* is the single point of contact for users to report incidents and seek troubleshooting resolution. This component is typically called the help desk in healthcare organizations. In addition to handling calls or online/email support requests for issues, the service desk can manage requests for many other types of purchases or services. A request that has been received by the service desk is generally referred to as a "ticket." An example of service desk workflow is presented in **FIGURE 7.5**.
- *Incident management* is the process by which "trouble calls" or system-related incidents are brought to resolution. Trouble calls are usually directed to the

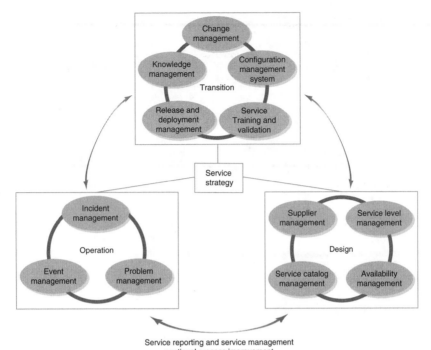

FIGURE 7.2 ITIL model.

Data from TSE & TSE Business & Tech Consulting Inc. ITIL Model - IT Service Delivery Methodology. http://tsetseconsulting.webs.com/tse-and-tse-consulting-identity-access-management-toronto-itil.html. Accessed March 10, 2014.

healthcare organization's help or service desk staff, who will resolve the issue or route it to higher-level IT support personnel for more assistance if they cannot resolve the issue themselves.

■ *Problem management* is the process by which recurring incidents are analyzed to determine their root causes and provide permanent solutions. Root-cause analyses (RCAs) are performed and documented after HIS application outages or other unplanned server downtimes; they describe the problem and identify possible solutions to avoid the problem in the future.

■ *Change management* is the process by which changes are introduced into the computing environment of an organization. Typically, organizations establish a formal process that describes the HIS modifications or updates. The appropriate

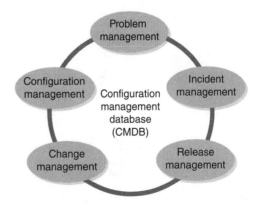

FIGURE 7.3 IT service management.

managers authorize the change request, and a **change management board (CMB)** convenes to formally approve the change request. Changes to systems that are considered "production" or live almost always require CMB approval prior to their implementation, whereas changes to

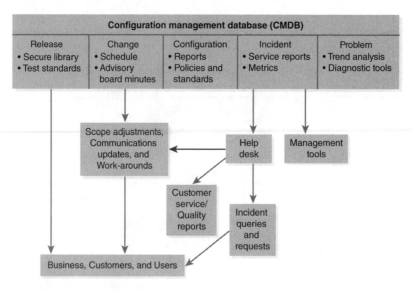

FIGURE 7.4 ITIL service support processes.

Data from the United Kingdom Office of Government Commerce and the Controller of Her Majesty's Stationary Office (HMSO).

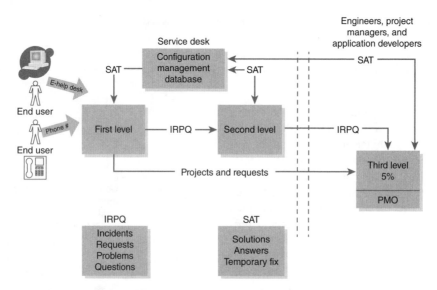

FIGURE 7.5 Sample service desk workflow.

less critical systems, such as test or development systems, do not.

- *Release management* is the process by which major new releases of application or operating system software are implemented. Regardless of whether a vendor or the healthcare organization is responsible for performing the application or

software development work, a predictable methodology is required to ensure the final release product is free of errors or "bugs."

- *Configuration management* is closely tied to all of the previously mentioned HIS service support processes and is the process by which the computing environment is documented, typically in a configuration management database (CMDB). A CMDB is a valuable resource for resolving issues and maintaining inventory, as it can be used to trace the root causes of problems. For example, if the HIS experience a problem, the CMDB can be used as a reference to determine if the issue is with the client computer, the application, the database, the server, or the network.

IT service delivery is the second core process area that is important for the proper implementation and support of HIS applications. This area defines the services; describes the roles and responsibilities of those who pay for services (i.e., the customers), those who use the services (i.e., the users), and those who provide the services (i.e., the service providers); and defines the service quality, availability, and timeliness expectations.

The IT service delivery process areas in the context of HIS services include the following elements:

- *Service level management* is the process by which **service level agreements (SLAs)** are negotiated with end users and tracked for performance adherence. For example, in a typical healthcare environment, SLAs regarding HIS outages can be categorized as critical, high, medium, or low regarding how much time can transpire before the system must return to an operational state. This time span often ranges from less than one hour for the highest SLA (e.g., a mission-critical production HIS such as the Laboratory Information System (LIS)) to seven days or longer for test or development systems.
- *Availability management* focuses on ensuring that the HIS infrastructure and support services are available to the business functions. Frequent auditing and system checks are useful in making sure that HIS remain available and functioning.

For example, database administrators must either manually check or put an automated process in place to ensure that database logs do not grow to a point that all available hard drive space is consumed and the system shuts down.

- *Capacity management* seeks to ensure that the HIS infrastructure has the processing capacity needed by the business functions. Like many other healthcare environments, HIS are often added iteratively without first developing a comprehensive, long-term plan that will factor in future growth requirements. In some instances, the organization may change direction, merge with another healthcare organization, or add a new initiative—all of which will need to be supported by proper capacity management.
- *Financial management* is the process of accounting for the complex nature of HIS services, understanding costs in terms of unit of service, and assisting in management decisions relating to HIS services. Ongoing support and maintenance, software licensing, application upgrades, and hardware refreshes require agile financial management to continue to deliver the needed services.
- *Service continuity management* is the process by which organizations identify their most critical applications and design, test, and maintain alternatives for providing HIS services in the event of a major service interruption. This area is otherwise known as the "disaster recovery" or "business continuity planning" function.

ISO/IEC 38500 is an ITG framework that describes six guiding principles for the effective, efficient, and acceptable use of IT: responsibility, strategy, acquisition, performance, conformance, and human behavior. This framework is organized into three major sections: scope, framework, and guidance. ISO/IEC 38500 was first used in manufacturing, but with the adoption of other ISO/IEC standards in health care, this framework is now seeing greater use in healthcare environments. For example, many healthcare organizations are now using the ISO/IEC 27001 Information Security Standard to comply with HIPAA requirements, successfully attest to the meaningful use (MU) of EHRs, and build their organizational information security policies and ongoing compliance programs. ISO/IEC 38500 allows organizations to become accredited or registered, thereby assuring customers that the organization adheres to the ISO quality assurance standards. One criticism leveled at the family of ISO/IEC standards is that they require a great deal of administrative overhead to deploy them and there is a cost to becoming registered.

COBIT is an international open ITG standard that was first developed in the 1990s by the IT Governance Institute. Its reference framework is useful for HIS governance, oversight, and process audit, and includes requirements for the control and security of sensitive data. At a high level, COBIT consists of an executive summary, management guidelines, framework, control objectives, implementation toolset and audit guidelines, and a list of critical success factors (CSFs) for measuring ITG effectiveness. The control objectives are made up of four main areas: planning and organization, acquisition and implementation, delivery and support, and monitoring. Relative to HIS, two important supporting areas of the standard focus on information and HIT resources. Although COBIT does well in describing what characterizes an organization that has robust internal control mechanisms, it has been criticized for falling short in its "how to" descriptions.

Financial Management

In the age of EHR adoption, managing a healthcare organization's financial areas is as important as ever. Hospital profit margins are being subjected to increasing Medicare rate cuts and

pricing pressures from commercial payers. Healthcare system chief financial officers are facing the challenges of mounting patient "bad debt" loads as patients struggle with higher copayments and other charges that uninsured and underinsured individuals are having trouble paying. The entire healthcare ecosystem is adapting to major changes associated with healthcare reform, struggling to shift to a focus on a health versus sickness model. In addition, HIS costs from EHR implementations, as well as the costs to support EHRs on an ongoing basis, have put tremendous financial pressure on many healthcare organizations. A study in 2011 demonstrated that actual versus projected hospital IT operating expenses as a percentage of total operating expenses are significantly higher for those healthcare organizations that are just beginning to implement EHRs compared to those at a high EHR maturity level (HealthPopuli, 2011).

When it comes to HIS budgeting, CIOs should take a key lesson from their CIO colleagues in other vertical industries when developing HIS budgets: the amount spent on support, maintenance, and labor exceeds the license fees for the software after about four years and continues on for the life of the system. Communicating the cost of software shouldn't stop at the licensing fees but should continue through all the costs of the journey forward. Maintenance and support is often eclipsed by discussions of license fees during negotiations with the software vendor. For this reason, and because it is an essential planning step to understanding the total cost of ownership, this text emphasizes the importance of the five-year cost estimate as part of the business plan for any new system and covers it in detail in Chapter 5.

Meanwhile, technology (both hardware and software) constitutes the easier-to-forecast hard costs in the HIS implementation equation. Another area in which unexpected costs may arise in HIS and

🔍 CASE EXAMPLE: EFFECTIVE IT GOVERNANCE TO ACHIEVE ECONOMIES OF SCALE

Two health systems in the Pacific Northwest were facing the same challenge—implementing an enterprise-wide EHR system. They had some similarities and some differences. Located in the same region, they were similar in that both had selected the same vendor's EHR system, both were in a time-crunch due to the MU Stage 2 deadline, and both were going through the massive challenges of moving away from siloed systems (best-of-breed) and implementing their first integrated, enterprise-wide EHR systems. They were different in that one was an urban health system and the other a community-based health system with a significant rural presence with four rural hospitals in addition to a community hospital and many clinics.

The challenges of launching an entirely new EHR system are vast, and since both health systems had already selected the same EHR platform, they decided to collaborate and combine their two implementations into one. The hope was to streamline the process and project management, as well as achieve economies of scale financially and operationally. The strength and clout of the combined organizations with the vendor created a force that neither could achieve on their own— the combined unit was able to get and keep the attention of the vendor and its key resources for the duration of the implementation. As evidence of this alliance and synergy, the two systems would share EHR settings and workflows.

To begin, they created a combined governance group and shared expertise and vendor relations information. Despite the similarities of the two health systems, and the fact that they got through the joint implementation successfully within their time deadlines, their differences proved challenging. The governance group moved slower than desired, for one thing, though it arrived at good decisions, with input from end users as well as management. Structural differences also created issues for decision making including: (1) differing strategic and operating goals; (2) the larger scope of decisions forced governance to operate at a more global level, diminishing the input of grass-roots, operational levels, which had been a hallmark of the rural system's culture; (3) different levels of governance experience; (4) size and complexity differences; and (5) regional, cultural, and reimbursement regulation differences. Despite these significant challenges, both health systems got their enterprise EHR systems implemented in time for MU Stage 2 as well as adopting ICD-10.

However, following the initial implementation, governance inefficiencies, meeting fatigue, and the need to address priorities became more urgent than the already-completed EHR implementation. The two systems examined the governance strengths, weaknesses, and new objectives post-implementation, which led them to develop a hybrid governance model on behalf of the EHR alliance of the two organizations. This included an executive alliance committee for ongoing EHR oversight and to guide decisions regarding advanced functionality and cooperation between the two organizations, as well as a joint operations committee to address the adoption of new workflows and monitoring operations and quality. Key disciplines were represented on each committee. Each health system established proprietary governance structures to address local issues, as well as communication protocols and standards that guided the work in their individual organizations. This hybrid, or combined governance, approach worked well post-implementation as the two groups worked within their unique cultures and structures to achieve good outcomes for both organizations while taking advantage of the strength and clout of the combined EHR initiative.

Data from Wiedower, J. (2016). Information Technology Governance: Vital to Healthcare Systems. Oregon Health & Science University. Retrieved from https://digitalcommons.ohsu.edu/cgi/viewcontent.cgi?article=16902&context=etd

EHR implementations is related to project duration: EHR implementations often take longer and cost more than HIS application planners expected. For example, during their transition to EHRs, hospitals saw an 80 percent increase in their IT operating expenses, which directly impacted the hospitals' overall operating budget—specifically, increasing this budget by more than 200 percent. Some evidence suggests that those increases could be permanent over the longer term (Accenture, 2011).

The same 2011 study also identified the existence of health IT staffing challenges—specifically, the need to attract and retain the skilled talent required to make HIS implementations happen and to stay on track to meet MU requirements. In addition, the cost to maintain operations was found to be high due to, among other things, training requirements. For example, productivity dips occurred when nursing personnel were taken off their regular assignments to receive training, despite attempts to provide adequate coverage using back-filled personnel. Without a doubt, the pool of highly skilled IT professionals is shallow. Furthermore, healthcare providers are competing for this talent with other vertical industries such as financial services, telecommunications, automotive, and technology companies. This supply and demand gap has driven up the cost to hire an HIS professional, negatively impacting operating costs for providers who are already constrained by limited operating budgets. Skilled talent for HIS is in a shortage situation. According to Accenture (2011), "The war for health IT talent is on." For organizations to qualify for the incentive payments doled out for MU of EHRs, transitioning to a "culture for adoption" is key: 75 percent of hospital clinicians must consistently use advanced electronic medical record (EMR) components, such as computerized physician order entry, if the hospital is to receive the incentive payments. To achieve this goal, healthcare systems must foster employee engagement,

which will in turn lead to effective change management in the organization.

A key indicator of effective ITG is the ratio of unplanned work to planned work. Unplanned work is any activity in the IT organization that cannot be mapped to an authorized project, procedure, or change request (Kim, 2006). Organizations that spend less than 10 percent of their time on urgent and unplanned work have been found to have very high levels of operational excellence, compliance, and security. In other words, better governance and planning will lead to fewer "surprises." Examples of unplanned work at low-performing HIS departments can include failed or unauthorized changes, a lack of preventive work, configuration inconsistency, poor security-related patching and updating, improper access, product failures, release failures, human or user errors, and project failures. Failed changes can occur when the production environment is used as a test environment and the customer serves as the quality assurance team. Unauthorized changes often happen when engineers do not follow the established change management process and make mistakes that are difficult to track and fix. A lack of preventive or root-cause analysis will cause repeated failures, as the same problems will most likely continue to reoccur. Configuration inconsistencies in user applications, platforms, and configurations make appropriate training and configuration mastery difficult. Applying security-related patches and performing system updates will become dangerous if there are inadequate understanding and a lack of consistent configurations. When too many people have user and system access that is not required to perform their job roles, preventable issues and incidents can occur. Product failures often occur when associated software, hardware, and other infrastructure underperform. And, of course, end users' mistakes, whether intentional or unintentional, can be among the largest contributors to unplanned work.

To address financial and budget risks, HIS management should be knowledgeable in the following areas: (1) budgeting and planning; (2) purchasing options such as capitalized and depreciated assets; (3) operating expenses, basic accounting principles, and standards; (4) financial models and methods; and (5) compliance regulations. **TABLE 7.1** outlines four steps developed by Bogacz (2012) that can be taken to reduce financial risk in a healthcare setting. In addition, **TABLE 7.2** presents four steps developed by Owen (2012) to consider when managing healthcare budgets.

Vendor Management

HIS departments are increasingly looking to vendors to implement and manage the many complex HIS initiatives that they must undertake. Although large healthcare organizations may employ full-time application developers and programmers to support their in-house systems, most organizations simply do not have sufficient resources to invest in large and ongoing system development projects or in customized software application development. An increasing number of healthcare organizations are focusing on developing their core competency—delivering quality health care—and leaving the majority of HIS development and deployment to vendors and consultants, who work in concert with in-house personnel to implement these systems and develop new workflows and processes that fit that organization. In such circumstances, the customer-vendor relationship is critical to the success of HIS initiatives. It must be a collaborative, formal, and mutually agreeable relationship that benefits both parties. In this type of outsourcing partnership, vendors will have the necessary core competency in the area of software or application development and support, consultants may be engaged to provide additional development or implementation services, and in-house HIS departments will importantly need to provide direction and guidance, along with staffing resources to collaborate with end users and support future HIS deployments.

Given the many vendor and consulting companies that populate the HIS landscape, it is vital that healthcare organizations establish truly strategic vendor relationships. Whether the HIS and technology environment are

TABLE 7.1 Managing Financial Risk	
Risk Domain	**Steps to Address Financial Risk**
Identification	Involves identifying financial risks that can occur as a result of negative factors or, conversely, as a result of favorable events (e.g., when unexpected success leads to exponentially increased demand for services).
Quantification	Assesses the likelihood or probability of these risks and their magnitude of impact.
Risk response	Involves the organization determining and implementing a response to address the risk, such as acceptance, transference, mitigation, or avoidance.
Monitoring	Involves a continuous review of existing and future risks.

Reproduced from the Winter 2010 issue of *Strategic Financial Planning*. Copyright 2010 by Healthcare Financial Management Association, Three Westbrook Corporate Center, Suite 600, Westchester, Ill., 60154. For more information, call 800-252-HFMA or visit hfma.org

TABLE 7.2 Managing Budget Risk

Plan budgets using best estimates carefully at outset of project.	■ Account for capital expenses. ■ Account for operating expenses. ■ Refine initial budget once specific costs and pricing are negotiated with vendors. ■ Use a milestone-driven, pay-for-performance method in constructing vendor contracts.
Include contingency funds in project budgets.	■ Ten percent is commonly used, but the percentage amount can be below or above that depending on the preferences of your organization. ■ These funds anticipate and protect the project and organization from unplanned costs.
Collaborate with other departments in annual budget processes.	■ This ensures each department understands and budgets for HIS related project expenses. ■ Understand project charges and allocations between departments for HIS services.
Manage budgets closely!	■ Track and report to management the actual versus expected weekly expenses. ■ Communicate quickly when there are budget overages. ■ Be proactive; if you anticipate budget problems or issues, escalate the issue to management right away.
Understand the significant components of the budget.	■ Pay closest attention to the large line items in the budget. ■ Communicate regularly to keep awareness focused on budget adherence. ■ Keep communications about budget awareness and adherence positive: avoid negative messages and warning tones. Instead, build in encouragement, incentives, and rewards when feasible.

Data from Owen J. *The Leadership Skills Handbook*. 2nd ed. San Francisco, CA: Jossey-Bass; 2012, pp. 189–190.

large (several hundred applications) or small to medium (fewer than 100 systems), having too many vendors delivering HIS products and services can be inefficient, costly, and overly complicated. Having too many vendors also results in too many siloed systems and burdens the organization with trying to cobble together disparate systems and varying sources of data and information. Identifying a narrower set of key vendors that will partner with the organization to deliver projects and important initiatives will strengthen the viability of the

healthcare organization and is likely to result in better integration of systems.

Typically, strategically aligned vendor companies will have a large portfolio of products and services that can offer value in tandem with standardization and consistency across the organization. For example, having multiple EHR vendors is not recommended, although some large healthcare organizations now face that predicament, having grown by merger and acquisition or lacked adequate IT governance. Often these strategic vendors

🔍 *CASE EXAMPLE: REDUCING CHANGE INDUCED INCIDENTS*

Kaiser Permanente is very focused on reducing Change Induced Incidents (CIIs), which are a leading cause of missed SLAs, staff/member dissatisfaction, and quality/safety concerns. In a large organization, tens of thousands of IT changes are performed annually. Even a small number of CIIs can impact patient care and have high visibility due to the increasing dependency all clinical systems have on technology systems. Kaiser Permanente's efforts to address this are the following:

- Establishing robust release and change management procedures;
- Ensuring that everyone involved in releases and changes participates in online training;
- Ensuring that separation of duties is adhered to so that all tasks are validated properly; and
- Ensuring that automation and scripting is implemented in the testing and execution of the changes to remove human error.

Case Example by James W. Brady.

will also have a strong portfolio in other HIS areas, such as laboratory services, pharmacy, business intelligence, and data analytics, furthering an integrated systems portfolio. In the supporting technology areas, many of the core hardware and software infrastructure areas (e.g., desktop computers, servers, networking, and databases) can be delivered and maintained by a few companies (e.g., Cisco, Microsoft, IBM, Oracle, Dell). Reducing the number of these vendors will allow both the healthcare customer and the supplier of these systems and technologies to craft competitive and long-lasting contractual relationships.

The vendor management process begins with the vendor selection process. Vendors are needed in healthcare organizations to assist with the delivery of a variety of products—applications, hardware, networks and infrastructure—and services such as implementation, programming, consulting, temporary staffing, and specialized HIS resources. Healthcare organizations should follow four steps to select the right vendor (also detailed in **FIGURE 7.6**):

1. *Formally submit a project request.* This step involves submitting a new project request. HIS planners will create the initial project and

business plan and will involve all needed parties.

2. *Analyze their business requirements.* Activities at this level include defining the system scope, feature, and functions; reviewing integration and technical requirements; defining the reporting features needed; and finally issuing a **Request for Proposal (RFP)** to the appropriate vendors.

3. *Conduct a three-layer HIS vendor evaluation search.* In the first layer (the *functional layer*), features and functions, the upgrade path, the ease of training, the integration benefit, and the workflow supported are evaluated. Here, usability, features, and functions; workflows; and test scenarios are the three areas that need to be reviewed. In the second layer (the *technology layer*), the technical architecture and specifications of the network, databases, and other infrastructure are considered. In addition, the integration benefits and adherence to IT standards are reviewed. In the third layer (the *business relationship and*

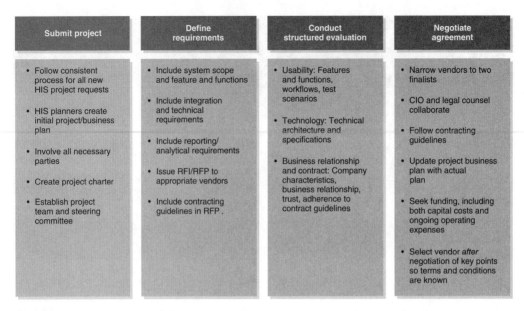

FIGURE 7.6 Structured vendor selection flow.

contract layer), the company characteristics, survivability, contracting guidelines adherence, business relationships, trust, integrity, and commitment to the project and to the industry are examined.

4. *Select the winning candidate and successfully negotiate a contract.* In this step, the potential vendors are often narrowed down to two candidates. The CIO and legal counsel then collaborate to successfully finalize an agreement with the finalist in adherence with contracting guidelines. Lastly, the business plan is updated and the funding source is identified.

A deeper examination of the three layers involved in an HIS product vendor evaluation search can provide additional insights into the vendor selection process. In the functional layer, the product's end-user functionality and usability are addressed. This layer requires the direct involvement of all clinical and business disciplines who will be using

the system, along with the HIS experts. Without this involvement, the most appropriate vendor may not be identified. Some of the questions that are asked at this level are the following:

- Does the product have the generally available features and functions?
- What are the development pipeline and timeline dates?
- Does the product perform the tasks required by the end users?
- Does it integrate well into the existing workflow and improve it?
- Are the modules or applications integrated or interfaced?
- Is the end-user interface easy to understand?
- Is training easily and adequately accomplished?
- Does the product support an efficient workflow for the users?
- Will the workflow need to change with the product's implementation? If so, how?
- Does it permit efficiencies and savings in time/money or both?

Can the system support specialty departments, such as Cardiology, Nuclear Medicine, Dietary, and Oncology?

In the technology layer, it is imperative that all technical aspects of the systems are clearly identified. These include the various *technical components*, such as the hardware platform, operating system, device requirements, network, and security; the *technical architecture*, such as the use of industry-standard technologies and coding/development techniques, modularity design, ease of updates, and disaster recovery; and the *technology standards* and life cycle, along with the availability of resources and expertise necessary to support and maintain technical platform.

In the business relationship and contract layer, all issues with the vendor company should be addressed, including the details of the contractual agreement. In HIS business relationships, issues reviewed during the negotiation include the following:

- The percentage of vendor company resources devoted to this product
- How the company responds to issues that develop over the course of a multiyear relationship, including specific processes for problem resolution and escalation of issues on a timely basis
- The vendor's conformance with HIS contracting guidelines
- The vendor organization's stability and longevity
- The vendor's reputation for completing obligations and conduct according to contract terms and conditions
- The implementation plan
- The training plan
- The support services
- The maintenance agreement and scheduled upgrades and enhancements
- The milestones and payment schedules
- The product life-cycle support

Several common pitfalls need to be avoided to achieve successful vendor management

(Perelman, 2012). First, it is important to not confuse vendor selection with vendor management; just because you have chosen a vendor, it does not mean you can "check out." Equal importance should be given to managing the vendor relationship both during and after the selection and contracting phase. Second, healthcare customer organizations should not necessarily select the vendor that offers its products or services for the lowest price. Typically, a set of criteria should be used in the vendor evaluation and contracting process, with price being only one of several factors that are considered. This will promote a strong and mutually beneficial long-term relationship between the customer and the vendor. Third, neglecting to measure the vendor relationship can produce less than desired outcomes. In addition to measuring the SLAs in the contract, the business value of the vendor relationship should be based on business metrics, including whether the vendor relationship is providing value to the organization.

Horine (2009) identifies 10 vendor-management principles that can enable healthcare organizations to develop and maintain strong vendor relationships:

1. Adopt a structured project management methodology that will support proper planning, project sponsorship, clear roles and responsibilities, and formal change and issue management.

2. Understand the different components of vendor management, some of which include evaluation and selection, contracting, and relationship and delivery management.

3. Pay very close attention to the contract details—specifically roles and responsibilities and the use of incentives and penalties—following the contract requirements.

4. Formalize all the important requirements in the contract, such as project changes and communication modifications.

5. Ensure that the contractual details are equal to the level of project risk. Expect a large complex project to have a very detailed contract.

6. If it is important, put it in the contract. Deliverable specifications, methodology used to create the deliverable, specific resources, roles and responsibilities, planned communications, deliverable acceptance criteria, and project success criteria should all be included in the contract.

7. Obtain senior management commitment and buy-in from both the customer and the vendor at the beginning of the project. This will go a long way toward ensuring vendor management success.

8. Look for ways to benefit both the customer and the vendor. This will help the partners build mutually beneficial resolutions should issues and tensions arise.

9. All terms and processes should be clarified, reviewed, and explained to avoid conflicts and misunderstandings.

10. Clarify internal roles and responsibilities, particularly between key functional and project personnel who must work collaboratively to manage the project and perform team-oriented tasks such as redesigning processes and workflows. Examples include the procurement administrators and project team, the contract manager and the project manager, and the vendor project manager with the internal sales, accounting, and legal teams.

Contract Management

One of the key factors in successful vendor management is contract management. Contract management in the context of HIS can be explained as the execution and monitoring of a contract to maximize financial and operational HIS performance and minimize HIS risks. The HIS contract comprises a written agreement between a healthcare organization and a vendor in which the responsibilities of both parties are outlined to ensure the terms of the contract are clearly explained and followed. Contract management brings a number of benefits to both healthcare organizations and vendors:

- Standardized processes and procedures, which decrease uncontrolled spending and supply risk while increasing purchasing leverage, allowing for less cost to be incurred.

- Expenditure visibility, which lets an organization see if it is purchasing at the right times, quantities, and prices, and if those purchases are standardized with consistent contract terms and conditions.

- Improved compliance management, which, based on the Aberdeen contract management methodology, can increase 55 percent when a contract management system is put in place.

- Enhanced spending and performance analysis, which allows actual delivery to be compared with contracted purchases and helps identify policy or regulation violations.

- Reduced uncontrolled spending, stemming from all the important contractual details having been clearly identified, thereby eliminating scenarios where either party might say, "I didn't know we had a contract" or "I didn't know I wasn't supposed to do that."

- Evergreen contract elimination, where proactive alerts are generated notifying the healthcare organization when it is time to renew the contract, reducing the chance it will be unknowingly locked into the contract for another term.

Understanding contract management guidelines provides a framework for accountability to both the customer and the vendor, with the end result being a successful engagement for both parties. This set of guidelines and the list of terms and conditions serve as the basis of contract negotiation and establish a level playing field between the HIS customer and the vendor. Promises made during the sales cycle are defined in exact specificity and committed to in writing. In other words, if the requirement is not written down and signed as part of the contract, it does not exist. All mutual responsibilities are to be defined and documented. Escalation procedures when problems occur must be agreed to, ending with the chief executive officer (CEO) of each organization if necessary. The implementation plan, RFP, and other requirements and commitments are also attached to the agreement.

Contract milestones are key areas that both parties must carefully review and agree upon to assure contract success. In HIS terminology, milestones can be likened to pay-for-performance expectations: they are significant accomplishments that signify phases within an HIS implementation, and they reassure both parties that the implementation schedule is on course. Many contracts are written so that vendors receive payment when they complete each implementation phase. Once a particular phase is successfully accomplished, the CIO signs off on the invoice and payment for that phase is issued. Hardware specifications and system performance metrics are also defined within a contract. For example, system response time ranges in terms of milliseconds will often be quantified in the contract. This commitment prevents vendors from selling a system for a very low price by under-configuring the hardware and system specifications. The vendor must guarantee that the system will perform as configured according to performance specifications (e.g., the response time during normal usage as well as during a period of peak or maximum user activity).

HIS contracts also typically specify requirements regarding the ownership of data, change control, and maintenance costs. The *ownership of data* will identify if the data in the system belong to the healthcare organization;

if the vendor has a need to use the data for a specific purpose, this point is agreed to in writing by the CIO (for one-time use, in most cases). It is very important for the contract to outline clear ownership of the data by the healthcare organization. If not, the organization may end up having to pay the vendor to obtain its own data for analytics or other uses. It is also important that the vendor not be allowed to use the data from the system they are supporting (and thus have access to the data housed in the system) for any purpose outside providing service to the healthcare organization, such as remarketing of the data or use in another product for benchmarking, without express written permission from the CIO for use of the data for a specific purpose. Additionally, healthcare organizations need to spell out what the mechanism is for accessing data housed in a vendor-hosted system and whether there is a charge for this activity. For example, a hospital may need to generate custom reports from its HIS applications. If those applications are hosted by the vendor but the data belong to the hospital or physician practice, services and fees will often be incurred by the healthcare organization when it asks the vendor to dedicate the time and effort necessary to produce the custom reports.

Change of control is useful to manage all changes that occur in HIS implementation. If a vendor acquisition occurs, the contract might specify that the new owner must obtain the customer's permission before transferring responsibility over to the new vendor organization. This constraint ensures that the healthcare organization maintains the right to self-support the system; if there is source code involved, the healthcare organization is given the right to use the source code.

Maintenance costs, which typically average between 20 and 35 percent of the original purchase price for each additional year following the initial procurement, must be carefully reviewed. In many cases, these costs outstrip the license fee after three to five years and continue for the life of the system. Because maintenance costs can escalate over time, such expenses must be carefully spelled out in the contract and budgeted for by the healthcare organization.

HIS contracts often specify terms and conditions in additional areas, such as interface requirements, regulatory compliance, upgrade path expectations, cooperation with other vendors, and escalation processes. Finally, a healthcare organization rarely signs a vendor's standard agreement (and it never should); in most cases, it is required that the standard terms and conditions be mutually revised to satisfy the requirements of both parties.

For its HIS initiative to deliver the maximum value with the desired outcomes, the healthcare organization must ensure that four core areas are emphasized. First, achieving strategic alignment is critical. This includes developing a strategic plan, along with a yearly project and support agenda that aligns with the needs of the organization. Second, architectural excellence and balance are critical. They ensure that the HIS are designed and built by following proper HIS architectural principles and practices. In addition, the HIS architecture must be balanced and in line with the organization's priorities and issues. Third, value and benefits are goals that, if attained, will demonstrate that the organization is able to achieve the desired and anticipated benefits associated with the HIS implementation. Questions such as, "Is aggressive process redesign intended to be a part of this HIS implementation?" will need to be asked and considered on a case-by-case basis. Finally, service delivery needs to be emphasized. HIS departments should understand that it is imperative that they deliver quality support and services to their users.

Project Management

One of the most important disciplines that plays a major supporting role in HIS implementations is **project management**. Each HIS implementation can and should be categorized as a project: it is critical that organizations have viable and robust project management methodologies in place. Project management is defined as the discipline of planning, organizing, securing, managing, leading, and controlling resources to achieve specific goals. From a practical perspective, a project is a temporary endeavor with a defined beginning and end. The temporary nature of projects demonstrates how they differ from operational or functional initiatives, which consist of repetitive, permanent, or semi-permanent functional activities. Hospital staff members who are dedicated to day-to-day operational or departmental duties (such as laboratory, pharmacy, and other services) are called functional staff, and their sponsoring group is referred to as a functional organization. Staff brought onboard as a dedicated resource for one or more projects are called project staff, and their sponsoring group is referred to as a project-based organization. In most cases, healthcare organizations need both functional and project staff. In a matrixed organization, both departmental staff and project staff, although they may have direct reporting relationships with their respective departmental and project management, also have dotted-line or indirect reporting relationships with each other.

How HIS projects start and wend their way to completion can be understood by reviewing the five project management phases identified by the Project Management Institute (PMI) (2009):

1. *Initiating Phase.* In this phase, the project leadership identifies project stakeholders, develops the project charter and the preliminary project scope statement, and obtains approval of the project charter from the appropriate governance bodies.

2. *Planning Phase.* This phase involves planning the project scope, quality and risk management, and the project schedule. The project scope is defined by

creating the project management plan, developing the project scope management plan, and creating the work breakdown structure (WBS). Quality and risk management planning involves identifying and analyzing risks, along with planning the risk response. The project schedule is developed by defining and sequencing activities, estimating activity resources and duration, determining the project schedule, and planning for the commitment of human resources to the project.

3. *Executing Phase.* This phase involves directing and managing project execution; acquiring, developing, and managing the project team; performing quality assurance; problem solving; and procuring project resources.

4. *Monitoring and Controlling Phase.* This phase involves managing the integrated change control process; controlling quality; controlling changes in cost, schedule, and scope; measuring performance; and monitoring and controlling risks. An effective change control methodology will address both reactive and requested changes; will include a process for categorizing changes; and will include a process for determining how changes are requested, reviewed, and implemented.

5. *Closing Phase.* This phase involves performing project closure and contract closure.

PMI (2009) has also defined 10 knowledge management areas. These project management knowledge areas include all the aspects of project management that are required for the successful completion of a project on time, on schedule, and with the best output. These nine areas of activity complement the five phases of project management, in that they can occur during more than one phase. For example, all of the knowledge management areas may be addressed during the planning phase, whereas only two of these areas play roles during the initiating and closing phases. Successfully run HIS projects will require a good working knowledge of how to apply these knowledge areas. The following explanations summarize each knowledge area:

- *Project Scope Management.* The primary purpose of project scope management is to ensure that all the required work is performed to complete the project successfully. This is accomplished by defining and controlling what is included in the project and what is not. Project scope management activities include the scope plan, scope definition, WBS, scope control, and scope verification.

- *Project Time Management.* The main goal of project time management is to develop and control the project schedule. Project time management components include activity definition, activity sequencing, activity resource scheduling, activity duration, schedule development, and schedule control.

- *Project Cost Management.* The purpose of project cost management is to complete the project within the approved budget. Accordingly, cost management includes cost estimates, cost budgeting, and cost control.

- *Project Human Resources Management.* The focus of project human resources management is obtaining, developing, and managing the project team who will perform the project work. This area includes planning for the commitment of human resources, acquiring the project team members, developing the project team's capabilities, and managing the project team.

- *Project Procurement Management.* Procurement management seeks to manage the acquisition of products and services from outside the project team needed to complete the project. Project procurement management components include planning acquisitions, planning and negotiating contracts with sellers, selecting sellers, administering contracts with sellers, and closing contracts.

- *Project Risk Management.* The intended purpose of project risk management is to identify potential risks and respond to them should those risks become realities. An example of a risk is a shortage of vendor resources necessary to execute the project. This risk can be mitigated by identifying qualified consulting resources familiar with the vendor's software product that could then supplement the resources available from the vendor for the project, allowing it to stay on schedule and within the budget. Project risk management includes planning the risk management, identifying risks, performing a risk analysis, developing a risk response plan, and monitoring and controlling risks.
- *Project Quality Management.* The principal objective of project quality management is to ensure that the project satisfies its objectives and requirements. Project

quality management components include performing quality planning, performing quality assurance, and performing quality control. When managing projects, three critical areas that require attention are project scope, time (or schedule), and cost. A change in one of these three areas will require one or both of the other two areas to change as well. As seen in **FIGURE 7.7**, these three areas—scope, time, and cost—have a direct relationship to project quality. For example, if the project scope increases, either the project cost or the project schedule will need to increase to achieve the desired project quality.

- *Project Integration Management.* The main goal of this area is to manage the integration of the various project activities. Project integration management includes developing the project management plan, directing and managing project execution, monitoring and controlling the project work, and closing the project.
- *Project Communications Management.* Project communications management focuses on ensuring that project information is generated and distributed promptly. It includes planning communication, reporting the project performance and

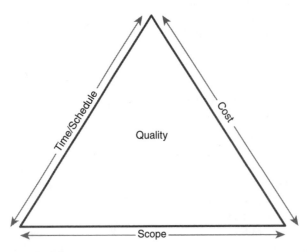

FIGURE 7.7 PM cost scope schedule.

the project status, and communicating to resolve issues among the stakeholders.

- *Project Stakeholder Management.* A new knowledge area on the PMI list, project stakeholder management defines all stakeholder activity that occurs within a project. Much of this new knowledge area is derived from the project communications management knowledge area, with the principal difference being that stakeholder management seeks to not only identify the project stakeholders, manage their concerns and issues, and communicate with them, but also keep them engaged throughout the life of the project.

An HIS implementation project, whether it be a complex, multiyear EHR deployment or a much shorter-term, narrower-scoped laboratory information system upgrade, requires the addition of key project-based personnel. These individuals can be full-time employees (FTEs) of a healthcare organization who will work on the HIS project, either as part-time or dedicated, full-time project resources. Alternatively, outside services—such as consultants, contractors, or vendors—may be hired to perform the required project tasks. In either case, it is important to understand the roles and responsibilities of the various project-based positions that most HIS projects demand. A failure to properly assess the area of human resources management can cause an HIS project to become severely hampered or come to a halt partway through the schedule due to resource constraints. **FIGURE 7.8** depicts the relationship between the PMI project phases and knowledge areas.

Of the many roles that are observed in projects today, the project manager has the most critical role related to bringing the project to successful completion. The project manager has the following responsibilities:

- Working with project sponsors, the project team, and others involved in the project to meet project goals
- Delivering specific project objectives within budget and on schedule

Project processes

Project aspects	Project life cycle
• Communication • Time • Scope • Risk • Procurement • Human resources • Integration • Quality • Cost	• Initiating • Planning • Executing • Controlling • Closing

FIGURE 7.8 PM stage and knowledge area overview.

- Controlling the assigned project resources to best meet the project objectives
- Managing project scope, schedule, and cost
- Reporting on project progress
- Facilitating and resolving issues, conflict, risks, and other items detrimental to a project

FIGURE 7.9 depicts the internal project coordination relationships of the project manager.

In any HIS project, numerous *customer roles* are likely to exist—for example, executive sponsor, project board member, information systems director, project manager, change manager, application analyst, operational analyst, design analyst, workflow analyst, system administrator, network administrator, operations/systems manager, business analyst, security administrator, testing coordinator, training coordinator, core trainer, go-live coordinator, physician advocate, clinical advocate, user liaison, and project coordinator. Depending on how the project is being staffed, it is possible for consultants or contractors to fill some or many of these roles.

Typical *vendor roles* in HIS projects are the executive sponsor, project manager, financial engagement leader (FEL), revenue-cycle consultant, implementation consultant, analytics and/or decision support systems backload consultant, technology team lead, technology consultant, application or technology delivery

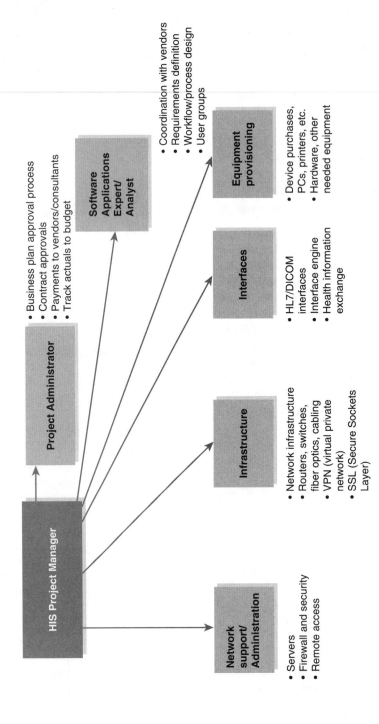

FIGURE 7.9 HIS department: Internal project coordination.

Data from http://projectmanagementau.com/

consultant, device integration consultant, database administrator, conversions consultant, integration consultant, interface consultant, and project team member. It is important for project teams to understand that successful project completion and accomplishment of the project objectives require that all project team members work together—whether they are HIS department employees, consultants, contractors, or vendors.

Compliance Management

The Health Insurance Portability and Accountability Act (HIPAA) of 1996 and the Health Information Technology for Economic and Clinical Health (HITECH) Act of 2009 are significant federal laws regulating how healthcare organizations manage the protected health information (PHI) and electronic protected health information (ePHI) of their patients. The HIPAA Security Rule specifies that administrative, physical, and technical safeguards be developed to ensure the confidentiality, integrity, and security of ePHI. HITECH was established with the primary purpose of requiring HIPAA covered entities (CEs) and their business associates to provide notification following a breach of unsecured protected health information. A *breach* is defined as an acquisition, access, use, or disclosure that is not permitted by the HIPAA Privacy Rule and that compromises the security or privacy of PHI. The Breach Notification Rule requires healthcare providers and other HIPAA CEs, to promptly notify the affected individuals of such a breach.

In addition to protecting the privacy and security of PHI, HIPAA prevents healthcare fraud and abuse and simplifies billing and other transactions, thereby reducing healthcare administrative costs. The Privacy and Security Rules apply to a broad range of healthcare organizations, including health plans, healthcare clearinghouses, and any healthcare provider who transmits health information in electronic form. CEs include all healthcare providers, regardless of practice size, provided that they

transmit health information electronically. Such providers can include doctors, hospitals, clinics, psychologists, dentists, chiropractors, nursing homes, and pharmacies. If an individual is part of a CE, he or she is responsible for safeguarding all PHI, whether it is transmitted electronically, in paper format, or verbally.

PHI is defined as information that meets the following criteria: (1) relates to the past, present, or future physical or mental condition of an individual, and provisions of health care to an individual or for payment of care provided to an individual; (2) is transmitted or maintained in any form, such as electronic, paper, or verbal representation; or (3) identifies, or can be used to identify, an individual. Examples of PHI or **individually identifiable health information (IIHI)** include patient's name, address (including street, city, parish, ZIP code, and equivalent geocodes), name of employer, various dates (e.g., birth date, date of admission, or discharge date), telephone and fax numbers, electronic (email) addresses, Social Security number, and medical records. HIPAA mandates that healthcare employees do not use or disclose an individual's protected health information, except as otherwise permitted or required by law. CEs, however, may share PHI for certain purposes, such as treatment, payment, and healthcare operations; disclosures required by law; and public health and other governmental reporting. When doing so, CEs must use or share only the minimum amount of PHI necessary. Exceptions to this rule can be made, but only for requests made by the patient or as requested by the patient to others, by the Secretary of the Department of Health and Human Services (DHHS), as required by law, or to complete standardized electronic transactions, as required by HIPAA. Prior to releasing PHI, CEs must obtain a signed authorization from the patient.

When employees of a healthcare organization are interacting with PHI, they should follow several guidelines. First, individuals should look at or use a patient's PHI only if they need it to perform their job. A patient's PHI should be given to others or discussed only during occasions when it is necessary for those persons to perform their jobs. If it is necessary to discuss PHI, it is recommended that individuals speak in soft tones and do not discuss PHI in public hallways or in elevators. Employees who breach their organization's HIPAA policies and procedures can be subjected to disciplinary action, up to and including termination. When faxing information, it is recommended that individuals verify the receiver, double-check the fax number, and call to confirm that the fax was sent and received. PHI should not be left in HIS department conference rooms, on desks, on laptop hard drives, or on counters where the information may be accessible to the public, to other employees, or to individuals who do not have a need to know the PHI.

The HIPAA Security Rule requires that ePHI be protected by ensuring the confidentiality, integrity, and availability of that information through safeguards:

- *Confidentiality* refers to not disclosing ePHI to unauthorized individuals or processes.
- *Integrity* refers to ensuring that the condition of the information has not been altered or destroyed in an unauthorized manner, and that data are accurately transferred from one system to another.
- *Availability* refers to ensuring that specific information is accessible and usable upon demand by an authorized person.

Healthcare organizations can take a number of practical steps to ensure the confidentiality, integrity, and availability of ePHI. One safeguard entails implementing access control. Access control specifies that all users have unique user IDs. Users should be assigned a unique user ID for computer system log-in purposes, and individual user access should be limited to the minimum information needed to do that person's job. A user's ID should never be shared with or used by another person. Once employees are terminated, their access should be immediately removed.

A second safeguard is password protection. Passwords should not be shared with or used by others and should be changed periodically. Passwords should not be written down, but rather committed to memory.

A third safeguard is workstation security. Workstations include electronic computing devices, laptop and desktop computers, and other devices that perform similar functions; they may also contain electronic media stored in or nearby the device. Physical security measures that can be taken to protect workstations include disaster controls (e.g., surge protectors), physical access controls (e.g., screen savers, locks, or ID badge readers), device and media controls (e.g., backups), and **malware** controls (e.g., software that protects the workstation from viruses, worms, spyware, Trojans, and suspicious emails).

Although a compromised user account or workstation can potentially disrupt one or more HIS user or application, malware has the potential to significantly impact a healthcare organization's network and mission-critical systems. As a result, it is important to understand the various types of malware present today. **Viruses** are programs that attempt to spread themselves throughout workstations, servers, and the entire network; their proliferation can be prevented by installing client **antivirus software**. **Worms** are malicious programs similar to viruses that spread without any user action. Worms take advantage of security weaknesses in the workstation or server operating system or software package; thus, their spread can be prevented by ensuring that each computer system has all required security updates installed. **Spyware** is a class of programs that monitor a user's computer usage habits and report this information back to an external computer for storage in a marketing database. Spyware is typically installed unknowingly when end users are installing programs or browsing the Internet. This form of malware often opens advertising windows and slows down the computer's performance; its acquisition can be prevented by installing and running an updated spyware scanner. Remote access **Trojans** are malicious software programs that allow remote users to connect to a client computer without the user's permission. These programs can take screenshots of the user's desktop, assume control of a user's mouse and keyboard, and access client programs at will. Most antivirus software programs can detect and remove Trojans. Suspicious e-mails, often blocked or "picked up on" by protection software, may include any e-mail that is received with an attachment, any email from someone whose name the e-mail recipient does not recognize, and phishing e-mails. **Phishing emails** contain web links

that appear to be legitimate but, when clicked on, redirect the user to a malicious website where the user's username, passwords, and credit card details can be compromised.

In summary, malware includes a variety of dangerous programs that can significantly diminish the productivity of healthcare workers. Malware can cause client workstations to have reduced performance (e.g., the computer slows down or "freezes"), windows opening by themselves, missing data, slow network performance, and unusual toolbars added to client web browsers. When these symptoms are noticed, the affected end user should contact his or her organization's help desk. To properly

🔍 CASE EXAMPLE: PROTECTING YOUR ORGANIZATION FROM RANSOMWARE

Managing cybersecurity threats, such as ransomware, is an important area of concern for healthcare organizations. Ransomware is a type of malware (e.g., malicious software) that denies access to data by encrypting an organization's data with a key known only to the attacker who deployed the ransomware. After a user's data are encrypted, the ransomware typically directs the user to pay a ransom in order to receive the key to decrypt the user's data. This is usually done in a cryptocurrency, such as Bitcoin. Even if a ransom is paid, the ransomware attacker may not provide the key to decrypt the data or may increase ransom demands. In order to prevent a ransomware attack, healthcare organizations should follow the five steps listed below:

1. *Implement security awareness and training.* These efforts should include processes to detect and guard against malicious software, as well as training of the workforce on how to detect and report malicious software.
2. *Perform a risk analysis.* This involves identifying the risks and vulnerabilities to the confidentiality, integrity, and availability of ePHI at the organization. ePHI is a healthcare organization's "crown jewel." Knowing where ePHI is located and who the owners of these data are is critical to responding quickly and minimizing the impact in the event of a ransomware attack.
3. *Develop a risk management program.* The organization should implement security measures sufficient to reduce identified threats and vulnerabilities to a reasonable and appropriate level.
4. *Assure access controls are in place.* It is important to ensure the access rights granted are not excessive, assuring that only people who need access to a system for their job related to the care or administrative matters, are allowed.
5. *Create Business Associate Agreements (BAA) for all vendors involved with ePHI.* This includes defining processes—including responsibilities—to prevent, manage and report security incidents and breaches.

Data from U.S Department of Health & Human Services. Retrieved from https://www.hhs.gov/sites/default/files/RansomwareFactSheet.pdf

protect workstation computers and HIS data, recommended best practices include the following measures:

1. Use client firewalls.
2. Use end-point protection software (e.g., antivirus, antispam, antimalware software) and keep it up-to-date.
3. Install computer software updates, such as Microsoft Windows and third-party patches.
4. Encrypt and password-protect portable and mobile devices, including smartphones, tablets, and laptops.
5. Enable automatic disconnect or log-off features.
6. Use password-protected screen savers.
7. Keep computing equipment locked up and in secured locations.
8. Do not store sensitive or confidential information on portal devices.
9. Back up critical data and software programs.
10. Sanitize and safely dispose of old or unneeded hard drives and portable media such as compact discs (CDs), and Universal Serial Bus (USB) sticks (or "thumb drives").
11. Use encryption when transmitting emails, files, text messages, or other information that contains sensitive or confidential information.
12. Report any suspicious activity to HIS management immediately.

In addition to addressing HIPAA privacy and security requirements, data breach regulations, as specified by the HITECH Act, must be carefully considered by CEs. One of the most significant changes to HIPAA that is found in the HITECH Act is the inclusion of the Federal Breach Notification Law for health information. The Federal Breach Notification Law, which applies to all ePHI, mandates that CEs immediately notify the federal government in the event of a data breach if more than 500 individuals are affected, or annually provide notification if fewer than 500 individuals are affected. Such notifications must be also made to a major media outlet and listed on a public website once reported. In addition, CEs are responsible for providing notice to all individuals affected by the breach, to all their business associates, and to the Secretary of Health and Human Services. HITECH requires that all CEs be trained to ensure that they are aware of the importance of timely reporting of privacy and security incidents, and of the consequences of failing to do so. Recent estimated costs from fines and other penalties for data breaches have averaged more have $200 per patient affected, or approximately $3 million per data breach.

As a part of its continued efforts to assess compliance with the HIPAA Privacy, Security, and Breach Notification Rules, the HHS Office for Civil Rights (OCR) began its second phase of audits of covered entities and their business associates in 2016 (U.S. Department of Health & Human Services, 2018a). As of June 2018, OCR has received over 184,614 HIPAA complaints and has initiated over 902 compliance reviews, with 96 percent of these cases (177,194) being resolved. Over 110,000 cases were deemed not eligible for enforcement, and 25,972 cases were resolved by voluntary compliance or correction action. 11,478 resulted in no violation, and 684 were referred to the Department of Justice as criminal referrals, leaving a total of 56 resolution agreements with monetary settlements or Civil Money Penalties (CMP). To date, $83.4 million has been paid, with $19.4 mission paid in 2017 and $7.9 million paid in 2018 through June (U.S. Department of Health & Human Services, 2018b).

The HIPAA compliance issues investigated the most (in order of frequency) are:

- Impermissible uses and disclosures;
- Lack of safeguards of PHI;
- Lack of patient access;

- Lack of administrative safeguards of ePHI; and
- More than the minimum necessary (U.S. Department of Health & Human Services, 2018b).

Finally, to better understand the sources of data breaches in health care, one should look at the most common causes of breaches. According to the Department of Health and Human Services, these are:

- Stolen security credentials;
- Inadequate access controls;
- Failure to put up firewalls;
- Misdirected mail or email;
- Unencrypted media;
- Improper disposal of paper records or films; and
- Untrained workforce members (U.S. Department of Health and Human Services: Office for Civil Rights, 2018).

▶ Managing People

The increased adoption of technology in HIS has expanded the role of IT. In addition to traditional or general IT functions, the field of HIS has created new roles and responsibilities. These can include, but are not limited to, roles involved in electronic coding, accounting, and billing systems; EMRs or EHRs; networks for digital imaging such as picture archiving computing systems (PACS); and informatics. Informatics roles include medical informatics, nursing informatics, clinical informatics, and biomedical informatics. Managing these diverse roles is at least as complex and delicate a matter as managing the organization's hardware and software.

HIS-related careers can be found in many different types of organizations—for example, hospitals and healthcare provider systems, healthcare payer organizations, regional extension centers, health information exchanges, community health centers and long-term care facilities, ambulatory centers and small physician practices, education institutions and academic medical centers, government agencies and the military, vendor organizations, and consulting companies. Both IT and HIS roles exist in these organizations. Individuals with a clinical background who are interested in a career in HIS will find excellent opportunities in most of the previously mentioned organization types. Those from IT transitioning to HIS without prior medical or clinical experience may find job opportunities difficult to attain, largely due to the intense competition and large numbers of applicants for some positions (Santiago, 2013).

Senior Management Roles

Board of directors, executive management, and medical executive committee support are essential for the success of HIS initiatives. The CIO is generally the most senior-level IT executive. In many health systems, this role also carries the vice president or senior vice president designation. Additional IT-related leadership roles can include the chief medical information officer (CMIO), the chief nursing information officer (CNIO), the chief technology officer (CTO), the chief information security officer (CISO), HIS department directors and chairs, and physician and nurse champions. Recently, health systems have developed new roles, such as the chief innovation officer and chief applications officer positions, to meet the needs of the evolving technology environment.

Information Technology Roles

HIS departments are staffed with internal FTEs or outsourced personnel who support traditional IT-related roles. Job descriptions for these roles are categorized as senior level, mid-level, and junior level, and typically include titles such as director, manager, architect, analyst, engineer, technician, administrator, programmer, and developer. Common areas that these roles cover include applications, business intelligence, data warehouses, databases, data centers, directory services, help desks, IT security, mobile applications, servers, networks, telecommunications, storage, systems integration, backup systems, messaging, collaboration, technical documentation, virtualization, and websites.

HIS Roles

To meet the evolving technology demands of healthcare organizations, particularly in light of the increased usage of EHRs, many clinical, business, and project-related roles now require HIS knowledge and expertise. Some of the more in-demand clinical and business positions are analyst roles. These include specialty roles covering systems, administrative support, applications, clinical systems, reports, financial services, the supply chain, human resources and payroll, the revenue cycle, decision support, interfaces, and business intelligence. Two critical roles required to support EHR implementation projects are application analysts and operational analysts.

Application analysts translate the healthcare organization's business requirements into a complete and fully tested system that successfully integrates automation with workflow. Application analysts tend to have more technical or IT backgrounds and are responsible for performing system configuration for one or more of the EHR modules. Operational analysts are the focal point for communication of functional departmental/unit needs, requirements, specifications, decisions, and issues between the user departments, users, and implementation project team. These analysts perform less technical functions but understand the clinical or business workflow from an operational perspective.

Other important healthcare IT roles include positions in informatics, clinical engineering, go-live events, implementation consulting, integration, project management, quality assurance, and usability. **EXHIBIT 7.1** (from Essentials) presents a comprehensive list of the types of IT and HIS department roles commonly found in large healthcare organizations.

EXHIBIT 7.1 HIS Job Titles

Active Directory Engineer	Electronic Mail Administrator
Application and Technology Specialist	ERP Programmer/Analyst I
Cable Technician	ERP Programmer/Analyst II
Clinical Content Analyst	ERP Programmer/Analyst III
Clinical Systems Engineer	ERP Specialist I
Data Technician	ERP Specialist II
Data Technician per Diem	ERP Specialist III
Data/Cable Technician	Executive Assistant
Database Administrator	Field Operations Supervisor
Database Analyst	Health System Director
Department Computer Technician	Health System Manager
Departmental Financial Coordinator	HIS Application Coordinator
Deskside Services Tech Team Lead	HIS Application Specialist I
Deskside Services Technician I	HIS Application Specialist II
Deskside Services Technician II	HIS Business Systems Analyst
Deskside Services Technician III	HIS Equipment/Stock Coordinator
Desktop Engineer	HIS Financial Team Lead
Desktop Specialist	HIS Liaison Analyst
EHR Security Analyst	HIS Principal Trainer

HIS Project Engineer	Senior HIS Application Specialist
HIS QA Engineer	Senior HIS Liaison Analyst
HIS Report Analyst	Senior HIS Project Engineer
HIS Report Specialist	Senior HIS QA Engineer
HIS Security Specialist	Senior HIS Test/Doc Specialist
HIS Sys Test/Document Specialist	Senior HIS Administrator
HIS Administrator	Senior Electronic Mail Administrator
HIS Manager	Senior EHR Security Analyst
HIS Technologist Team Leader	Senior Interface Analyst/Developer
Interface Analyst/Developer	Senior Network Engineer/Data Networks
Interface Testing Coordinator	Senior Network/Systems Engineer
Knowledge Engineer	Senior Server Engineer
Lead Active Directory Engineer	Senior Programmer/Analyst
Lead Desktop Specialist	Senior Project Coordinator
Lead HIS Application Specialist	Senior Systems Analyst
Lead Project Coordinator	Senior Telecomm Project Engineer
Lead Project Engineer	Senior Telecomm Supervisor
Management Assistant I	Senior Web Technology Specialist
Management Assistant II	Systems Access Coordinator
Medical Domain Expert	Systems Analyst
Network Engineer/Data Networks	Systems Integrator
Network Operating Systems Engineer	Systems Support Specialist
Network/Systems Engineer	Telecomm Analyst
PBX Technician	Telecomm Customer Service Rep
PeopleSoft System Administrator	Telecomm Operator II
Programmer/Analyst	Telecomm Operator Per Diem
Project Coordinator	Telecomm Project Engineer
Project Support Technician	Telecomm Supervisor
Senior Active Directory Engineer	Telecomm Systems Engineer
Senior Applications and Technology Specialist	Telecomm Team Leader
Senior Business Systems Coordinator	Time and Effort Report Analyst
Senior Database Administrator	Time and Effort Systems Coordinator
Senior Database Analyst	Video Conferencing Technician
Senior Desktop Engineer	Web Technology Specialist
Senior HIS Application Coordinator	

Career Opportunities

To assist those individuals looking to transition into HIS careers, the **Office of the National Coordinator for Health Information Technology (ONC)** developed a program designed to educate and train potential HIS workers. The ONC program has identified six healthcare IT workforce roles that healthcare providers will need as they transition to EHRs (HealthIT.gov, n.d. a, b). These roles, which provide a good understanding of the types of duties needed in HIS, include the following:

■ *Practice Workflow/Information Management Redesign Specialist.* Workers in this role assist in reorganizing the work of a provider to take full advantage of the features of health IT to improve health and care.

■ *Implementation Manager.* Workers in this role provide on-site management of mobile adoption support teams for the period of time before and during the implementation of health IT systems in clinical and public health settings.

- *Implementation Support Specialist.* Workers in this role provide on-site user support for the period of time before and during the implementation of health IT systems in clinical, administrative, and public health settings. These individuals provide support services above and beyond what is provided by the vendor, ensuring that the technology functions properly and is configured to meet the needs of the redesigned practice workflow.
- *Clinician/Practitioner Consultant.* This role is similar to the practice workflow and information management redesign specialist, but brings to bear the background and experience of a licensed clinical and professional or public health professional.
- *Technical Software Support.* Workers in this role support the technology deployed in clinical and public health settings. They maintain systems in clinical and public health settings, including patching and upgrading of software. They also provide one-on-one support in a traditional "help desk" model to individual users with questions or problems.
- *Trainers.* Workers in this role design and deliver training programs to employees in clinical, administrative, and public health settings.

Staff Development

Staff development is a key component in assuring that HIS employees attain competency in information and management system tools and skills. Staff improvement programs provide employees with the proficiencies and qualifications needed for advancement within the organization, and they help staff form the necessary attitudes and interpersonal skills to work effectively. Organizations can provide employee development through training

and in-service programs, certification classes, community college or university educational courses, conferences and workshops, and professional association involvement. HIS management teams can also promote self-study in HIS employees through books, industry magazines, videos, and online resources.

Training and *in-service programs* are two types of development activities that many healthcare organizations provide for their employees. These can originate from several sources:

- The organization's *human resources department* typically has responsibility for organization-wide training requirements (e.g., HIPAA, security and safety regulations, nondiscriminatory practices, and quality improvements).
- Supervisory, management, and leadership development may be designed and offered by a *leadership department* within the organization or through the human resources department.
- The *department or group in which the employee works* may provide programs such as in-service or line training.
- *Specific HIS projects* for information and management systems usually include a budget for training for system developers, administrators, and end users who will be supporting and using the product.

HIS certifications are another area of interest for both healthcare providers (who are implementing HIS products) and healthcare professionals (who are looking either to transition to an organization that has a specific HIS product or simply to increase their HIS product skills set and knowledge). IT-based certifications have long been a mainstay of IT education and professional credentials. Certification has two main advantages. First, it provides a framework by which technical staff can learn and gain a level of proficiency in a specific HIS-related topic. Second, certification provides the recipient with a credential showing that he or she has a defined body of knowledge in a specific area. Although certification by itself will not qualify a person for a new job or promotion, it does demonstrate that the individual has mastered the basic level of a specific knowledge area and has the desire to increase his or her skill set. Certifications are most often viewed as a positive contributing factor when organizations are making decisions about who to hire. It is recommended that clinicians keep their clinical licensure and certifications active and up to date, even if they are no longer in a clinical role. HIS professionals should also consider keeping their IT certifications active, particularly those certifications that are in high demand in HIS.

Many of today's highly sought-after HIS certifications can be obtained only by employees of organizations that are engaged in a specific vendor-product deployment, such as an EHR or other HIS project. However, healthcare systems also prefer generally available certifications that develop the employee's overall competency and value, particularly if a company is in the process of deploying a certain methodology throughout its organization. These include certifications such as **Certified Professional in Healthcare Information and Management Systems (CPHIMS)**, **Project Management Professional (PMP)**, ITIL, and Lean Six Sigma.

Other avenues that exist for HIS professionals' advancement are *professional development* and *education*. The expenses for these activities are typically borne by the employee, but in many cases are reimbursed by healthcare provider organizations as a benefit of employment. Several of the more often used avenues are the following:

- Healthcare IT conferences and workshops
- National and regional professional association program events
- University bachelor, master, or doctoral degree programs, as well as community college certificate programs, in HIS, informatics, information management, or information systems
- Self-study using books, industry magazines, videos, and online resources

Steering Committees

When it comes to moving HIS initiatives forward, bringing closure to projects, selecting systems, and addressing ongoing system needs, steering committees are an essential tool. In today's healthcare environment, strategic priorities and key stakeholder collaboration are required to ensure that the right decisions are being made and that HIS projects and goals stay on course. According to the Computer Economics IT Management Best Practices 2011/2012 study, nearly 80 percent of all HIS organizations have steering committees and 69 percent of those organizations make full use of their committees (Trembly, 2012). Of the 15 practices covered in the study, the use of HIS steering committees ranked as the single most important HIS management practice. Regardless of whether an organization is looking to go forward with a large-scale HIS project or just better manage the existing HIS operational environment, steering committees are useful in driving these areas forward.

A **steering committee** is an advisory committee that is usually made up of high-level stakeholders and experts who provide guidance on key issues such as company policy and objectives, budgetary control, marketing strategy, resource allocation, and decisions involving large expenditures. HIS steering committees are the best practice approach in healthcare organizations for aligning strategic business and HIS priorities. These committees, which usually include executives and departmental heads, focus on three main tasks: HIS strategic planning, project prioritization, and project approval. Clear mandates and a real ability to influence decision making through executive participation increase the value of IT steering committees.

To ensure success in this important area of ITG in HIS, healthcare CIOs should consider adopting a number of recommended strategies (CTG, 2005). First, it is important to select another name for the committee. For example, rather than calling it the "IT Steering Committee," this group might be named the "HIS Information Management Planning Council"—a name that reflects the organization's work culture and the committee's specific purpose. A committee charter should be developed that includes the desired outcomes. Such a document will help everyone understand the role and purpose of the group, which includes promoting improved communications and recognizing the partnership required for a successful HIS deployment and success. The steering committee should also ensure that its scope reflects a corporate-wide perspective. This broader focus will be helpful when mediating conflicts in priorities or departmental perspectives that may not be in the best interest of the entire organization. The role of the steering committee in ensuring optimal decision making should be identified up front. For example, the committee might be designated as a coordinating body that will resolve priorities, endorse proposals prior to approvals, and monitor progress of major HIS initiatives in lieu of exercising budgetary approval or other departmental expenditure decision making.

Someone other than the CIO may be selected to chair the HIS steering committee. In some organizations, depending on the role of the CIO or IT leaders, assigning a non-IT person, such as the chief operating officer (COO), CMIO, or chief financial officer (CFO), to chair the group communicates the message that HIS is accepted as a critical resource and recognized as such by the entire organization. Best practices regarding how to conduct meetings should be put in place, including scheduling the meetings in advance, sending out meeting agendas, recording meeting minutes, and following up on issues, risks, and action items.

To form an effective HIS steering committee, three essential steps should be considered (InfoTech Research Group, n.d.):

1. Build a case for HIS steering by aligning strategic business and HIS priorities. Focus on core HIS *steering objectives* (strategic in nature), rather than HIS *resource allocation responsibilities* (operational spending decisions). In addition, include shared decision making and foster a culture of communications between business units.

2. Establish a steering committee charter. This document should outline the key tasks and responsibilities for the committee along with important roles and responsibilities.

3. Keep the HIS steering committee small and meet on a monthly basis. Make sure that the membership communicates regularly and is engaged to address important issues. Also ensure that it includes executive decision making authority, which is critical to the success of the HIS steering committee.

HIS steering committees are a valuable tool to drive HIS initiatives and align HIS direction with the organization's business objectives. This is especially true in the area of ITG, strategic planning, and project management. By forming HIS steering committees with clear goals, strong senior management participation, and consistent interaction, HIS leadership can accomplish its goals in an enhanced fashion.

Summary

Managing HIS implementations and providing ongoing support for HIS is a complex undertaking. Paramount to this endeavor is clear understanding that HIS applications require a robust and highly performing underlying technical infrastructure. When the technology supporting HIS areas is flawed, system disruptions (e.g., system crashes) and end-user difficulties result. Before all large system deployments, technology assessments should be performed, with sufficient time allotted to remediate any significant gaps or deficiencies. To achieve a highly performing HIS environment, however, additional areas will need attention to ensure they are operating at the required levels; these involve process and people.

IT governance frameworks, such as the Information Technology Infrastructure Library, Control Objectives for Information and Related Technology, and standards established by the International Organization for Standardization and the International Electrotechnical Commission are important process improvement methodologies that enable organizations to formally manage their HIS assets. ITIL is an ITG framework that many healthcare organizations have adopted; it offers the benefits of IT service support and service delivery. One key area within IT service support is the service desk (also known as the help desk), which is critical for the proper support of HIS applications. A key area within IT service delivery is service level agreements, which are important for defining the performance of HIS applications and tracking end-user satisfaction.

Financial management, including proper budgeting and maintaining adequate staffing, is critical for HIS deployments to be successful. Adherence to best practices with vendors and contract management are important areas and management needs for healthcare organizations and vendor employees alike. All HIS contracts should specify requirements regarding milestones, the ownership of data, change control, and maintenance costs.

Project management is another key process area that must be formally addressed for HIS implementations to be successful. As both healthcare customers and vendors work together to complete HIS projects, it is vital that they follow the five project management phases and understand the 10 project management knowledge areas as defined by the Project Management Institute.

Nevertheless, technology and process are not enough to deliver and sustain effective HIS initiatives. Equally important is the requirement for new roles and responsibilities in the field of HIS. HIS implementations require appropriate clinical, administrative, and IT resources and expertise, with healthcare experience, advanced skills sets, certifications, training, and professional development opportunities noted as important areas of need. Whether the emphasis is on the individual, or individuals collaborate together through vehicles such as HIS steering committees, it is evident that HIS success relies on "people, process, and technology" to achieve the healthcare organization's goals.

Key Terms

Antivirus software
Certified Professional in
    Healthcare Information
    and Management Systems
    (CPHIMS)
Change Management Board
    (CMB)

Chief information officer
    (CIO)
Control Objectives for
    Information and
    Related Technology
    (COBIT)
Gap analysis

Individually identifiable
    health information (IIHI)
Information technology
    governance (ITG)
Information Technology
    Infrastructure Library
    (ITIL)

International Electrotechnical Commission (IEC)

International Organization for Standardization (ISO)

IT demand governance (ITDG)

IT service delivery

IT service support

IT supply-side governance (ITSG)

Malware

Office of the National Coordinator for Health Information Technology (ONC)

Phishing email

Project management

Project Management Professional (PMP)

Request for Proposal (RFP)

Service level agreements (SLAs)

Spyware

Steering committee

Trojans

Viruses

Worms

Discussion Questions

1. Why is performing a technology assessment or gap analysis before deploying an HIS application important, and how can this mitigate future system problems or crashes?
2. What are the benefits of IT governance?
3. Discuss the differences between IT service support and IT service delivery as defined by Information Technology Infrastructure Library.
4. Why is it important to have a CMB?
5. Which financial challenges related to budgeting and staffing should hospital CIOs be aware of, and why?
6. Describe the process that healthcare organizations should undertake when selecting a vendor to deliver a product or service.
7. Discuss the important principles and areas to avoid when managing vendors.
8. Explain the benefits to both the customer and the vendor from using formal contract management.

9. Elaborate on why HIS contracts should specify milestones, ownership of data, change control, and maintenance costs.
10. Why is project management important in delivering HIS implementations?
11. Describe the five project management phases, and explain how they relate to the nine knowledge management areas.
12. For individuals looking to pursue a career in HIS, which differences in opportunities exist between candidates with clinical backgrounds versus candidates with IT backgrounds?
13. How valuable are certifications in the HIS field, and what are some additional avenues that HIS professionals can utilize to advance their career options?
14. Discuss several strategies that can be used to ensure that HIS steering committees are successful.

References

Accenture. (2011, January). *Secrets of success on the EMR journey to meaningful use: Leading hospital CIOs reveal key lessons learned.* Retrieved from https://www.accenture.com/no-en/blogs/blogs-secrets-emr-success-demystified

Bogacz, P. A. (2012). Four-step process for identifying and managing financial risk. Retrieved from https://www.trintech.com/blog/compliance-solution/4-steps-to-managing-corporate-financial-risk-with-automation/

CTG. (2005, April). IT steering committee: Advocate or adversary? Retrieved from https://itgov.ucsf.edu/care-technology-governance-committee-ctg

HealthIT.gov. (n.d.). Get the facts about Health IT workforce development program. Retrieved from https://www.healthit.gov/sites/default/files/get_the_facts_workforce_development.pdf

HealthIT.gov. (n.d.). Preparing skilled professionals for a career in health IT. Retrieved from https://www.healthit.gov/sites/default/files/2017-09/workforcefoa1292015.pdf

HealthPopuli. (2011, January 24). Don't underestimate the costs of adopting health IT. Retrieved from http://healthpopuli.com/2011/01/24/dont-underestimate-the-costs-of-adopting-health-it/

Horine, G. (2009). *Absolute beginner's guide to project management* (2nd ed.). Indianapolis, IN: Que Publishing.

InfoTech Research Group. (n.d.). Establishing an effective IT steering committee. Retrieved from http://www.slideshare.net/Info-Tech/establish-an-effective-it-steering-committee

Kim, G. (2006, April 10). Unplanned work is silently killing IT departments. Retrieved from http://www.computerworld.com/s/article/110242/Unplanned_Work_Is_Silently_Killing_IT_Departments

Owen, J. (2012). *The leadership skills handbook* (2nd ed.). San Francisco, CA: Jossey-Bass.

Perelman, D. (2012). Six steps to successful vendor management. Retrieved from http://www.eweek.com/c/a/IT-Infrastructure/Six-Steps-to-Successful-Vendor-Management/

Project Management Institute. (2009). *PMBOK guide: A guide to the project management body of knowledge* (4th ed.). Newton Square, PA.

Santiago, A. (2013). How to break into a career in healthcare IT. Retrieved from http://healthcareers.about.com/od/administrativeandsupport/p/HealthITjobs.htm

Trembly, A. (2012). IT steering committees: Do they have any power? Retrieved from http://www.insurancenetworking.com/blogs/it_steering_committee_ce_it_management_best_practices-28649-1.html

U.S. Department of Health & Human Services. (2018a, July 31). Numbers at a glance Retrieved from https://www.hhs.gov/hipaa/for-professionals/compliance-enforcement/data/numbers-glance/index.html

U.S. Department of Health & Human Services. (2018b, July 31). OCR Launches Phase 2 of HIPAA Audit Program. Retrieved from https://www.hhs.gov/hipaa/for-professionals/compliance-enforcement/audit/phase2announcement/index.html

U.S. Department of Health and Human Services: Office for Civil Rights. (2018). Breach Portal: Notice to the Secretary of HHS Breach of Unsecured Protected Health Information. Retrieved from https://ocrportal.hhs.gov/ocr/breach/breach_report.jsf

CHAPTER 8

Managing Change— HIS Implementation

LEARNING OBJECTIVES

By the end of this chapter, the student will be able to:

- Describe the role of the Health Information Systems (HIS) Strategic Plan in HIS implementations.
- Explain and apply the Phases and Stages of implementation.
- Define the disciplines of and distinctions between project management, program management, and portfolio management.
- Describe the importance of interdisciplinary participation in HIS implementations, especially in terms of process and workflow redesign.
- Explain electronic health record (EHR) system implementation, including system selection and contract negotiation.
- Understand the difference between comprehensive and basic EHR system functionality and scope, and what that means for implementation planning.
- Portray the realities of HIS implementations and key issues and methods to ensure project successes and reduce failures.

▶ Introduction

As presented in Chapters 3 and 4, the HIS Planning process yields a board-approved, organizationally socialized HIS Strategic Plan for the organization. The overall plan consists of a documented current state connected to a defined future state by a migration path. The migration then breaks down into Strategic Initiatives comprising Projects that ultimately achieve the total HIS Strategic Plan. Each of these Projects, creating links to the future, must be defined and funded in the proper sequence, carefully coordinated with and intersecting with other Projects to build a strong foundation and HIS fabric for the organization.

In this chapter, we will explore change management in terms of HIS **implementation**. The moment of implementation is typically the first thing that people think of when the topic of a new HIS is broached. However, as the previous chapters have iterated, this is a moment that depends on all other moments (planning, strategy, collaboration) that came before it. That said, let's explore the challenging and exciting phase of implementation.

▶ Implementation

So now that the HIS Strategic Plan is approved and defined at a high level, it becomes time to face down the monumental challenge of actually *doing* what everyone in the organization has been *talking about* for quite some time. It is time to implement the systems conceived in the HIS Strategic Plan, which means defining the extreme detail of every system and Project required, and putting new systems, processes, and technologies into actual use. This is a significant shift in focus for the organization, yet every bit of work that went into the organization's disciplined and thorough planning process will pay off, as detailed implementation planning commences including project management detail, organizational readiness, interdisciplinary participation, and technology usability (Beeson, 2017). While systems are being implemented, every health professional participating will use everything they ever learned in their lives and professional development to get them through the trials and tribulations of HIS and technology implementation. This work is not for the faint heart—but nor is it to be avoided, because it's critical to the HIS advances that will get our industry to the promise of value-based care. Many people like to talk about which HIS and capabilities would be best to support the organization, but far fewer, and you know who you are, are those who live in the reality of systems implementations.

But all the courage and hard work in the world can't make up for a poorly planned and weakly structured implementation. Stated in the positive, systems implementations require thorough and proper planning, and well-structured governance, budgets, Initiatives, process redesign, and programs to engage clinicians and all the health professionals involved in the major cultural shift that occurs when a new system is implemented. If systems are not implemented well—or implemented at all—all the talk about the promise of HIS and technology is for naught and can be a massive waste of time, money, and energy for the organization and everyone in it (Bresnick, 2014). Implementation is the opportunity to truly do something that can improve the quality of health care for individuals both receiving and delivering care, as well as help health professionals improve their effectiveness. These aspirations for implementation are achieved through skilled discipline. A well-planned and managed implementation produces better quality of care and service, offering improved value and cost outcomes over those available today. The converse is also true. Scores of failed implementations have occurred in excellent healthcare organizations, due to lack of discipline encompassed in careful, comprehensive planning, adherence to principles and processes of governance, and competent management of the Projects and Initiatives embodied in the HIS Strategic Plan and the details that must follow. Successful implementations are well-planned Initiatives that follow lessons learned from those that failed. Key principles of successful implementations including ensuring the EHR system is based on a comprehensive HIS plan and integrates across all related clinical functions, minimizing silos of information and functionality, engaging physicians, other clinicians, and other employees using the system, all done in a culture of trust (Beeson, 2017). The goal of this text is, in part, to alter the course of these failures that are due not to lack of intention or commitment, but lack of availability of education and practical tricks of the trade. When the good people who devote their professional lives to health care are armed with information and insight, they can fully participate in the HIS Planning and Projects in their organizations. That is how change and improvement in these HIS implementations happens.

The Challenge of Implementation

Implementing systems is tough work, even for the seasoned HIS and technology devotees among us. While many organizations have implemented innovative and properly functioning HIS portfolios of systems, the non-structured approach of organizations implementing systems customized to various silos and departments—doing what they felt best and what they were ready for on a one-by-one basis—has resulted in a great deal of variability between organizations and implementations (Pearl, 2017). Healthcare organizations throughout the U.S. have been planning and implementing new HIS application software and technology over the past 50 years, but it's been more recently that we've recognized that the lack of standards in technology, data definitions, features, functions, and capabilities associated with clinical and administrative systems and abilities threaten the efficacy, safety, security, and usability of that data. The recognition that HIS wasn't delivering on the better care it had promised prompted the Meaningful Care program, the American Reinvestment and Recovery Act of 2009 (ARRA) and the Health Information Technology and Clinical Health (HITECH) Act of 2009 stimulus funding to provide incentives for physician practices and hospitals to implement EHRs. While these incentives have made a watershed difference in moving up stubbornly low EHR implementation rates in healthcare settings and in health information exchanges (HIEs) in the U.S., the road to ubiquitous availability of secure, patient-centric

healthcare data continues to be a long and hard one. Building upon the progress fueled by ARRA, HITECH, and Meaningful Use (MU), the Medicare Access and CHIP Reauthorization Act of 2015 (MACRA) has added new layers of definition to reporting and metrics to quantify progress toward quality improvement and cost reduction goals. In other words, these programs promulgated by Medicare regulations are driving the U.S. health system toward value-based care and value-based reimbursement. Additionally, excellent peer-reviewed research has helped frame needed definitions about the depth and breadth of EHR functionality. For as anyone who has had their hands on one of these systems can attest to, the often-said truism, "you see one EHR and you've seen one EHR," is accurate—the range of EHR functionality is immense (Pearl, 2017).

The era of customization as an enticement to clinicians from various specialties to adopt the new system has found itself drowning in the impracticality of supporting those silo systems. The sheer weight of trying to keep those systems synchronized, let alone widely varied data definitions and clunky interfaces, has made the information contained within those systems unobtainable by the knowledge workers attempting to use them. A lack of definition of EHR functionality has resulted in the mythology around percentages of EHR system adoption that permeates literature even today. This mythology is based on the fact that simply to say that an organization has an EHR gives no specificity about the range and types of functionality actually implemented and in use in that institution (**TABLE 8.1**). DesRoches et al. (2013) have dutifully tracked the levels of functionality adopted in the EHR system over the course of post-HITECH incentives, showing basic versus comprehensive and MU Stage 2 adoption levels: true EHR adoption rates vary widely among the different types of provider organizations. Adler-Milstein et al. (2015) showed early increases in at least a basic system from 59 percent in 2013 to 75 percent

TABLE 8.1 Basic and Comprehensive EHR Functionalities

EHR Functions Required	Basic EHR without Clinician Notes	Basic EHR with Clinician Notes	Comprehensive EHR
Electronic Clinical Information			
Patient demographics	✓	✓	✓
Physician notes		✓	✓
Nursing assessments		✓	✓
Problem lists	✓	✓	✓
Medication lists	✓	✓	✓
Discharge summaries	✓	✓	✓
Advance directives			
CPOE			
Lab reports			✓
Radiology tests			✓
Medications	✓	✓	✓
Consultation requests			✓
Nursing orders			✓
Results Management			
View lab reports	✓	✓	✓
View radiology reports	✓	✓	✓
View radiology images	✓	✓	✓

(continues)

TABLE 8.1 Basic and Comprehensive EHR Functionalities *(continued)*

EHR Functions Required	Basic EHR without Clinician Notes	Basic EHR with Clinician Notes	Comprehensive EHR
Results Management			
View diagnostic test results	✓	✓	✓
View diagnostic test images	✓	✓	✓
View consultant report			
Decision Support			
Clinical guidelines			✓
Clinical reminders			✓
Drug allergy results			✓
Drug-drug interactions			✓
Drug-lab interactions			✓
Drug dosing support			✓

Reproduced from Charles et al. (2012, February). ONC Data Brief No. 1: Electronic health record systems and intent to attest to meaningful use among non-federal acute care hospitals in the United States: 2008–2011. Retrieved from https://www.healthit.gov/sites/default/files/page/2018-07/ONC_Data_Brief_AHA_2011.pdf

Basic EHR adoption requires each function to be implemented in at least one clinical unit, and comprehensive EHR adoption requires each function to be implemented in all clinical units.

= identifies EHR functions included in each category of EHR: Basic without clinician notes, Basic with clinician notes, and comprehensive.

in 2014. (Note: this topic is discussed in detail later in this chapter and in Table 8.1.) At the same time, the variety of ways for sharing data among providers and institutions on behalf of patients has become a labyrinth of possibilities, since the starting and ending points between connections have countless variations now.

If only getting more EHR systems implemented was the goal, the HITECH Act had its desired effect, with at least a basic level of EHR system now in place in more than 83 percent of U.S. healthcare organizations (Henry, Pylypchuk, Searcy, & Patel, 2016). Also, 9 out of 10 physicians have adopted electronic record keeping

(Stanford Medicine, 2018). Progress in adoption has been made. The larger goal, standards in care and quality, remains elusive, and health outcomes metrics seriously lag in this country, making the required road to value-based care and reimbursement—improve outcomes and stem the unsustainable cost increases in health care—a daunting one. Before we get ahead of ourselves, let's examine the implementation of an HIS Strategic Plan, of which the EHR system is but one, albeit a core, component (**FIGURE 8.1**).

Multiyear Phases of the HIS Strategic Plan

Given that it takes years for most organizations to implement their HIS Strategic Plan, a good approach to breaking this mission-critical effort for the enterprise into recognizable, executable portions is to create **Strategic Plan Phases**. Each Phase contains Strategic Initiatives and key related Projects, each with multiple **Strategic Plan Stages** that encompass early foundational work. Placed then upon this foundation are the basic enterprise application systems of the plan, followed with increasingly advanced types of systems and functionality that the organization gradually and painstakingly reaches on its implementation "journey." For each *Phase* of

the HIS Strategic Plan, there are *Stages*, including (1) planning, (2) development/selection, (3) implementation into production, (4) ongoing support and evaluation. Each of these Stages must be accomplished with planning and discipline and each is a Project unto itself, with progressive steps that are highly related to the next. These Phases and Stages are represented in **FIGURE 8.2**. This integrated patchwork forms the pathway to achieving the portfolio of core HIS defined in the HIS Strategic Plan, defining an uppermost agenda for the organization, approved by the Board and socialized with other stakeholders as the proper HIS Portfolio of systems for the organization's future.

Each Phase of the HIS Strategic Plan consists of multiple Strategic Initiatives. For example, to create Foundational Infrastructure (Phase I), multiple interdependent capabilities are required—which are, by the way, Strategic Initiatives because they are the building blocks of the HIS Strategic Plan. It is wise to think of all of these Initiatives in terms of how each fit into the strategic picture, properly painted by the HIS Strategic Plan. Any effort spent otherwise is a deviation from the creation of a robust Strategic HIS Portfolio destined to take the organization toward its intended future state.

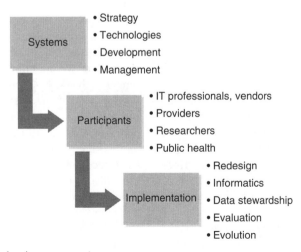

FIGURE 8.1 HIS and technology progression.

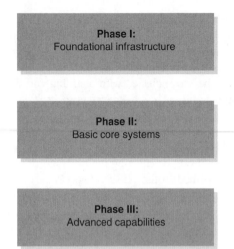

FIGURE 8.2 Stages per Phase of HIS Strategic Plan.

Let's break down this process for each Phase. Generally speaking, every organization needs the following:

1. Phase I: Foundational Infrastructure
2. Phase II: Basic Core HIS
3. Phase III: Advanced HIS Capabilities

Phase I: Foundational HIS Infrastructure Description

Phase I: *Foundation HIS Infrastructure* consists of network infrastructure, internet/intranet/extranet capabilities, devices for connecting end users to the network and systems, and establishment of secure computing environments needed to support the software applications and technologies to be implemented as well as those currently in use. (This is one of the tricks to HIS strategic thinking—always think forward and backward at once, since existing systems and capabilities must be well supported while new ones are going in place.) **FIGURE 8.3** describes generally needed Initiatives for each Phase of implementation. The specific systems and capabilities will vary according to the particulars of each organization, but the overall goal is to create enterprise-wide, core systems that give the organization the opportunity to build HIS that

last. From there, slowly but surely and properly, definition of data structures, processes, and reporting capabilities that can stand the test of time is built, with an eye toward enterprise data structures and stewardship. The culture of these organizations as it faces these Phases should be one of agile, data-driven care, one that embraces the relationship of data as way to establish competitive and collaborative edge.

Phase I: Foundational Infrastructure, including the data center and other computing environments, includes a medical intranet for sharing data from existing systems while Projects to replace them are pending or under way. This is for systems that are in greatest need, the oldest systems, and systems that help sustain the effort by delivering information in the meantime. Another key component of Phase I is the development of the **master patient person index (MPI)**, a unique patient identifier or corporate medical record number that allows data on the same patient from disparate systems to be correctly identified and pulled together. All three Phases need the MPI for full functionality of the medical intranet, although it may not be feasible to implement the MPI until Phase II and the implementation of the EHR, during which the conversion of data from disparate systems being replaced by the integrated EHR

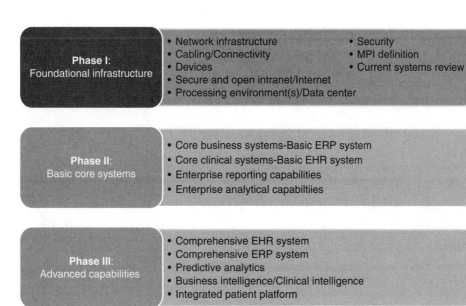

FIGURE 8.3a Phased HIS Strategic Initiatives—Phase I.

is accomplished with the activation of the MPI. Additionally, the suppliers and vendors of various pieces of equipment and products are all to be determined as part of the detailed business planning and system selections associated with each Initiative and Project.

Phase II: Basic Core HIS Capabilities Description

Phase II: Basic Core HIS Capabilities includes implementing the basic elements of the EHR, a core capability of any modern healthcare organization; the enterprise resource planning (ERP) system; and enterprise reporting and analytical systems and capabilities. Phase II relies heavily on the work done in the strategic planning process, especially regarding the HIS Planning Framework (Chapter 4). The already completed, thorough analysis and documentation of the *current state* of how all core clinical and administrative processes are performed informs the new workflows built into new systems in Phase II. The current state review is the starting point of the migration path and will be the roadmap from today to tomorrow—a new future state, the goal of the

new systems implementations. These systems are complex and their initiation into the fabric of an organization is a seismic undertaking.

Phase III: Advanced Core HIS Capabilities Description

Phase III: Advanced Core HIS Capabilities includes increasingly advanced Initiatives, building upon the foundational basic systems put in place in Phase II. These advanced capabilities typically involve quality management, outcomes analysis and reporting, business intelligence, clinical intelligence, computerized provider order entry (CPOE), and other advanced EHR capabilities such as enhanced user interface for clinical documentation. Phase III Initiatives build upon the foundation of infrastructure and basic EHR and other software capabilities implemented in Phases I and II.

Defining Phases Within Strategic Initiatives and Projects

It is important to recognize that each Phase must be broken down into Strategic

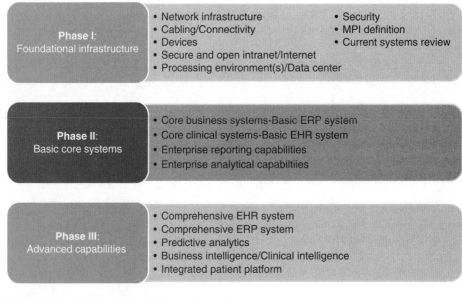

FIGURE 8.3b Phased HIS Strategic Initiatives—Phase II.

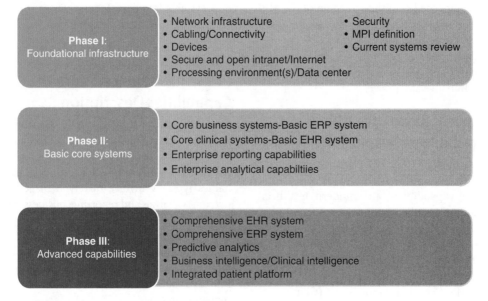

FIGURE 8.3c Phased HIS Strategic Initiatives—Phase III.

Initiatives, which then are broken down into Projects. Similar to the HIS Strategic Plan, a Phase is too large to be broken down simply into Projects. Rather, Phases consist of multiple Strategic Initiatives which consist in many cases of multiple interrelated Projects, all of which fit together to create the strategic capability envisioned for that Strategic Initiative. As an example, see the hierarchy of Phase I in **FIGURE 8.4**. Each Phase of the HIS Strategic Plan consists of an analogous hierarchy.

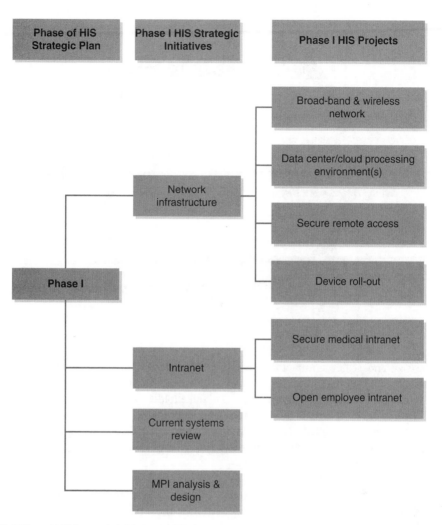

FIGURE 8.4 Phase I HIS Strategic Initiative and Projects.

The next section presents the progression of four Stages that each Phase goes through as it matures from initiation to completion as depicted in **FIGURE 8.5**.

Each Phase, as previously stated and portrayed in Figure 8.2, is made up of Initiatives with multiple interdependent Projects. In other words, to accomplish a Phase, it is easiest to break it down into Initiatives. To be accomplished, each Initiative and each Project go through the same, normal four Stages, described below. For a new HIS or technology, these Stages include (1) planning, (2) system development/selection, (3) implementation/production, and (4) ongoing support and evaluation of the new system capability.

Each Phase, Initiative, and Project Goes Through the Same Stages

Stage 1: Planning. Planning, the first Stage, breaks down the Phase (I, II, or III) into a logical series of Initiatives and Projects that comprise a major Phase of the HIS Strategic

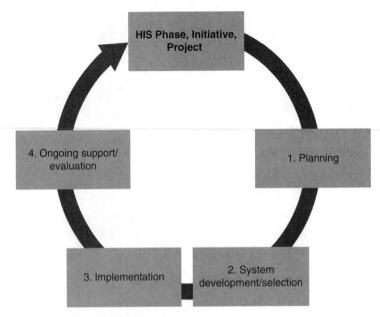

FIGURE 8.5 Four Stages of HIS Strategic Plan Phases, Initiatives, and Projects.

Plan. The size and scale of implementing a plan insists that it gets broken into organized, bite-size pieces that are digestible by the organization. This is one of the main reasons the landscape is littered with failed HIS Projects that have resulted in, at least, dashed expectations, and at worst, catastrophe for the organization due to a lack of essential structure to the Project or Initiative. These Projects need structured plans, structured budgets, structured governance, structure task forces or workgroups, structured training, and overall project management. Lack of these structures means lack of leadership, and this is the common theme to failed Projects (Bresnick, 2014). Each Initiative is comprised of more than one Project, and for each Project, detailed planning at the first Stage must be properly conducted. Such planning includes documentation of the Initiative's or Project's connection to the HIS Strategic Plan; definition of related business and clinical goals; requirements definition; alternative solutions evaluation; process redesign requirements and Projects; estimation of required capital, operating, and staffing resources for the long term, such as five years;

estimation of timetable and synchronization with other Projects; and interaction with stakeholders to ensure buy-in culturally and operationally. Refer to Chapter 5 of this text for more details on this topic, including planning templates.

Stage 2: System Development/Selection. Once the Project is planned and approved, work commences to define, then develop or select the application system or technology capabilities needed to accomplish the Project goals and objectives. System requirements are documented in detail, a **Request for Information (RFI)** and a **Request for Proposal (RFP)** are issued and evaluated, or development Project commences, the system is developed or procured, and the organization prepares for implementation. A preliminary component of this Stage is examination and redesign of the workflows and processes involved in the scope of the implementation. Process redesign precedes system development, as part of requirements definition, to ensure the new system features and functions

FIGURE 8.6 What we want versus how we get it.

are capable and programmed to support the new processes and workflows, thus moving the organization forward by implementing systems that hard-code and systematize the streamlined processes. Implementing new HIS to recreate processes that already exist because "this is the way we do it" is a terrible mistake, wasting the opportunity to rethink and enable more efficient and effective processes and workflows. This process redesign is often resisted by many people in organizations, some of whom have made a career of doing things a certain way. Sometimes their resistance is due to feeling threatened by technology changing the ways things are done and therefore adding risk, in their minds, to these processes. Sometimes they simply don't

like change (**FIGURE 8.6**). Either way, implementation of new systems and technologies enables the organization to seize opportunities to modernize and improve the organization's clinical processes and business services. *Carpe diem*! (Figure 8.6)

The HIS selection process is one that has been tried and tested for many years, and it has become known and accepted industry wide. Numerous healthcare information systems professional organizations, such as the **Health Information Management Systems Society (HIMSS)**, have published methodologies for this process. Most HIS and technology consulting firms have a consistent methodology that their consultants follow for this type of work (Ammenwerth, Graber, Herrmann,

Bürkle, & König, 2003). The steps are generalizable to various types of HIS Projects and healthcare settings—hospitals, clinics, physician practices, long-term healthcare facilities, community clinics, public health organizations, and others. Moreover, regardless of the type of HIS and technology product, with certain modifications in the content or emphasis of the methodology, the HIS selection process can be used by any organization for software, hardware, services, or other HIS and technology products.

The system selection process should follow an agreed upon methodology that is used by the healthcare organization consistently for all of its HIS and technology Projects. This way, the organization can create familiarity with the process throughout the organization, consistency in the application of criteria, and equity among the various groups seeking systems for the organization. Importantly, this process involves input from all stakeholders in the system and its eventual implementation.

As an example, consider the selection process for a new software system such as an **enterprise resource planning (ERP)** system. An ERP system is a suite of software applications that support financial, human resources, and supply chain/inventory management. For clinical HIS, these vendors operate in the healthcare software marketplace exclusively. For business application software systems, such as ERP or business intelligence and analytics tools, sometimes healthcare organizations consider products from outside the healthcare systems and technology marketplace as well as from within that arena. In addition, many vendors of non-healthcare-specific software companies have divisions that specialize in healthcare implementations because the processes being automated that are ubiquitous to all types of industries—for example, finance systems such as the general ledger, accounts payable, and supply chain management—have specific ways of being used in different industries. Such software is applicable to any industry.

The software selection process follows a series of essential steps, outlined in **FIGURE 8.7** and **EXHIBIT 8.1**.

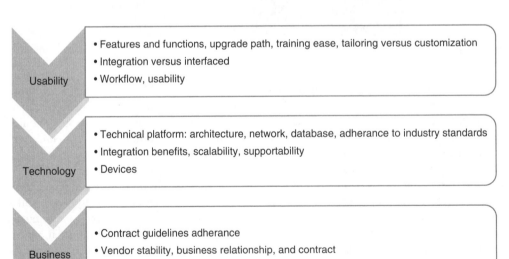

• Features and functions, upgrade path, training ease, tailoring versus customization
• Integration versus interfaced
• Workflow, usability

Usability

• Technical platform: architecture, network, database, adherance to industry standards
• Integration benefits, scalability, supportability
• Devices

Technology

• Contract guidelines adherance
• Vendor stability, business relationship, and contract

Business relationship

FIGURE 8.7 Qualifying a vendor: categories of criteria for system selection.

EXHIBIT 8.1 Steps in the System Selection Process

1. Approve business plan
2. Establish planning assessment and communication with organization
3. Document requirements, technical parameters, business requirements, and constraints
4. Determine selection criteria
5. Identify qualified eligible vendors
6. Create and send an RFI
7. Narrow field; send detailed RFP
8. Evaluate responses, hold scripted demonstrations, and conduct site visits
9. Identify 2–3 finalists
10. Negotiate agreement
11. Finalize Project Plan and final budget
12. Launch Project

Steps in Selecting an HIS

1. *Develop the HIS Project Plan and communicate it to the organization.* This step involves taking much of the work that was accomplished in the HIS Planning process and using it to document why the new system is needed, where it fits into the overall HIS Plan for the organization, and what the goals are for implementation of the new system. A detailed Project Plan with a timetable and work plan can be a very useful tool for informing managers and employees about the new system selection process and setting expectations for when the new system might be implemented (in general terms). This communication step marks the beginning of an ongoing communication process that should accompany every step of the selection process and continue through the implementation and go-live point for the new system.

2. *Establish the selection committee.* The selection committee should consist of experts in software and systems (IT personnel with software, hardware, and implementation expertise) along with **subject matter experts (SMEs)**—in this case, business analysts who are experts in the systems as they are used in the functional areas for which the new system will be selected. In the ERP system selection example, the SMEs include people with finance, human resources, payroll, and materials management expertise and roles in the organization.

3. *Define the system requirements.* This task involves the documentation of all system requirements and forms the basis of the evaluation process. These requirements fall into three categories: software features and functions, technology requirements, and business relationship requirements. These three areas represent very important categories of requirements that deserve discussion with the selection committee and others throughout the organization, as well as with the vendors competing for the business as part of the communication process. Often

individuals who have a particular interest in the new system quite naturally tend to believe the selection criteria should be more heavily weighted in the direction of their focus. End users tend to assign a higher value to software features and functions (usability); IT professionals tend to love the technology; and chief information officers (CIOs) and contract negotiators tend to value a solid business relationship (HIMSS Usability Task Force, 2011). The education process, therefore, needs to explain how each category of selection criteria (usability, technology, and business relationship) is equally important. While different people in the organization may value one category over another, criteria in all three areas (software functionality, technology, and business relationship) must be successfully satisfied by the vendor for the vendor to be considered a finalist for selection. It is up to the CIO to make sure a balanced decision is made.

4. *Develop selection criteria.* Selection criteria are the specific requirements within each category that reflect what is important to the selection process for the organization. *Usability* includes desired features and functions and ease of use. *Technology* includes the criteria for specific technical capabilities, supportability, and scalability. *Business relationship* includes the levels of trust between the organization and the vendor, and the contractual negotiation, reflecting the ongoing condition of the working relationship between the vendor and the organization as well as legally binding terms and conditions that will guide the rights, relationship,

and interaction between vendor and organization for many years to come. Selection criteria spell out what exactly is important in each of these categories.

5. *Identify potential vendors.* With each HIS Project, a host of potential vendors must be considered as candidates during the software selection process. The organization can identify a full list of potential contenders through industry connections and research, which will be narrowed through the RFI process.

6. *Develop an RFI, including the desired rules of engagement, and send it to potential vendors, including the desired rules of engagement.* The RFI is a concise description of the healthcare organization, the system requirements, timing, scope, and expectations. It is sent to the full list of possible software vendors, with this list then being narrowed through the RFI evaluation process. The RFI process is intended to gather enough information about each potential vendor to make an initial assessment regarding their viability as a candidate for the in-depth selection analysis without putting both the organization and the vendor through an exhaustive evaluation process. The goal of this step is to narrow the field to five to seven vendors who will be sent the RFP and earn the opportunity to propose their system to the healthcare organization for possible selection to make an initial assessment regarding their viability as a candidate for the in-depth selection analysis without putting both the organization and the vendor through an exhaustive evaluation

process. The goal of this step is to narrow the field to seven or so vendors who will be sent the RFP and earn the opportunity to propose their system to the healthcare organization for possible selection.

7. *Develop an RFP, including contracting guidelines, and send it to the narrowed field of vendors.* The RFP is a more thorough document that outlines, in great specificity, the requirements of the system from usability, technology, and contractual standpoints. The proposal from the vendor in response to the RFP represents a greater commitment than the more cursory response to the RFI. The HIS Project team within the organization digs into the details of the RFP responses to validate each specific response. The vendors are held to their representations not only in the evaluation against the criteria and comparisons to other vendors but also contractually. RFP responses are attached to the agreement with the vendor as part of the contractual obligations. This keeps the vendor honest about what is represented during the proposal and sales cycle; both parties sign on the dotted line and commit to these terms contractually and legally.

8. *Evaluate the RFP responses, narrow the field of vendors, hold scripted demonstrations, and conduct site visits.* This step includes the exhaustive process of evaluating the RFP responses from the various vendors, comparing the responses, and beginning to size up how vendors compare to one another. Ultimately, a field of 7–10 vendors that responded to the RFP should be narrowed to two or three finalists. These are the only vendors

that proceed to the next step. The other vendors should be sent a concise, diplomatic, and clear one-paragraph letter notifying them that they have been eliminated from the competition and that the decision is final.

9. *Conduct detailed due diligence on the finalist vendors.* In this step, the organization's internal project team conducts detailed due diligence on each finalist vendor in all three categories: usability, technology, and business relationships. As part of this process, a high-level implementation plan is developed with each finalist vendor as part of the comparisons, and their responses to the contract terms and conditions initiate the beginning of negotiations with the top contenders.

10. *Negotiate agreement(s).* Initiate contract negotiations with the top two vendors, to see how the negotiations proceed and what the yield is from a contractual perspective. If only one vendor is involved, then the organization and vendor are not really negotiating; the vendor knows it is just having its way with the process and the healthcare organization because it is the only choice. Negotiating with a single vendor is a grave mistake on the part of the healthcare organization: the healthcare organization should *always* have two viable vendors emerge from the first nine steps of the system selection process. Generally, a favorite will emerge, but always ask the selection committee to pick two vendors they can accept. When the first-choice vendor knows there is another competitor waiting in the wings, hoping to win the contract, the organization will have greater

leverage and the vendor is more likely to compromise and cooperate where needed for a deal.

Send the contractual guidelines to the finalist vendors as part of their finalist packet of information (**EXHIBIT 8.2**). Few things are as important as these contractual guidelines for increasing the probability of a successful systems implementation. Including these guidelines in the negotiation of the agreement with the vendor forces both parties to discuss responsibilities for the implementation and sign on the dotted line, legally committing

them to perform those responsibilities. The healthcare organization should *never* sign the *standard* agreement of the software vendor. Doing so most assuredly commits the healthcare organization to paying for the entire system based on the passage of time instead of based on the system working or the accomplishment of milestones toward achievement of that goal (a **milestone payment structure**); a standard agreement also likely includes many other terms and conditions that put the vendor company at an advantage and ignore important rights of the healthcare organization. Payment for vendor software

---

EXHIBIT 8.2   HIS Examples of Contractual Guidelines

1. Percentage of company resources devoted to research and development
2. Vendor organization stability and longevity; change of control—what happens if vendor is sold to another company? Retain right to change if possible.
3. How company responds to issues that develop over the course of long term
4. Vendor reputation for meeting obligations and conduct business according to contract terms and conditions
5. RFP response attached to contract
6. Detailed implementation plan attached to contract: including milestone-driven payment schedule
7. Training plan developed and resources available to support training from vendor
8. Support service 25 percent or less, appropriate increases only
9. Conformance to overall contracting guidelines
10. Product Life-Cycle Support: for new releases and versions for 10–15 years
11. Maintenance agreements expectations clear and acceptable—time-to-response based on severity of problem.
12. Hardware specifications and system performance metrics well defined, including system performance criteria; the system must operate a subsecond response time with all interfaces, other data feeds, for peak volumes, etc. *with proposed configuration*
13. Mutual responsibilities defined and spelled out
14. Ownership of data: the provider organization owns all its own data, and vendor may NOT use it unless expressly approved in writing by the organization's CIO or CEO
15. Interface requirements spelled out in detail and attached to contract
16. Regulatory compliance: the vendor must commit to maintaining compliance with all relevant regulations, e.g., HITECH Meaningful Use criteria and other requirements, HIPAA, Joint Commission, other
17. Upgrade path expectations must be shared, and minimum upgrade expectations set in contract
18. Cooperation with other vendors: both vendors cooperating to connect system interfaces and other cooperative efforts
19. Escalation processes: define specific processes and time thresholds for solving problems when they occur—up to CIOs and CEOs

based on the passage of time means that the healthcare organization will likely pay for as much as 50 percent of the system upon signing the contract, with the remainder due typically within one year of that date, or by the end of the vendor's fiscal year, so the vendor company can book the revenue. Payment for software based on accomplishment of milestones that leads to a successful implementation protects the organization from paying for a system that is never implemented, thus never gaining the benefit of the bargain with the vendor. If you do not feel comfortable negotiating the contract with the vendor, you should find a lawyer and a consultant qualified in HIS contract negotiations, and pay those specially qualified professionals to do it either for you or with you. Hiring an expert in contract negotiations is money well spent, and it is far less expensive than buying software that never works—an outcome that will result in a reimplementation Project or the purchase of more software to replace the failed implementation. Note: the milestone payment method eliminates any payments based on the passage of time, i.e., we sign the contract on x date and on x date plus 30 days, we must pay y, and x date plus 60 days we must pay z, regardless of whether any project activities have taken place. So, the milestone payment process attaches payments NOT to dates, but to successful accomplishment of Project milestones, such as hardware and software installation, Project Plan development, IT staff training, system design and build, and so on, as outlined in **FIGURE 8.8**. This is absolutely one of the most important contractual elements that the organization MUST insist upon with their vendors, whether that is a vendor for hardware, software, middleware, reporting tools, etc. (Figure 8.8).

11. *Finalize the Project plan and budget based on the negotiated prices, cost estimate spreadsheet, and specifics of the implementation plan. This step puts the Project plan into complete form and allows roles,*

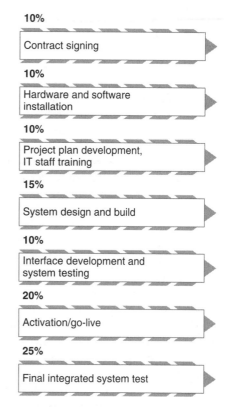

FIGURE 8.8 Milestone payment structure.

responsibilities, timing, and tasks to be identified and assigned to the people who will be participating in the Project. Once the Project plan is complete, it should be clearly and thoroughly communicated throughout the organization so that all departments and people working on the Project can plan accordingly. The time period when a new system is being implemented should be preserved for that activity predominantly—during go-live Stages, no other major activities should be attempted in the organization. Systems touch every nook and cranny of the organization, so other Projects must go into "freeze" mode as the activation of the new system nears.

12. *Launch the Project, including the organizational communication plan.* Now that the system selection and planning Phase is complete, it is time to launch the Project. Typically, this is an exciting and somewhat harrowing time for those close to the Project, because they are responsible for a very disruptive, potentially high-risk, high-reward endeavor for the entire organization. But if the planning has been thorough, the team is qualified and committed, and the budget for the Project is adequate, the only thing between the starting line and a successful outcome for the Project is a lot of hard work.

Stage 3: Implementation and Production. Implementation consists of activating a new system, beginning with readying the designed and programmed new software systems, preparing and training the organization, and interfacing the connecting systems and processes for the introduction of the new system into the mix of the HIS portfolio. Goals and measurable objectives are established for success measures of the new system and its impact on the organization. The work of Stage 3, implantation and production, is covered in the *Project Management* and *Implementation of an EHR System* sections.

Stage 4: Ongoing Support, System Maintenance, and Evaluation. Once the new system is successfully activated and in production, the IT department supports the new system and end users, in coordination with and managing the vendor(s) for the system, according to the roles and responsibilities, support responsibilities, and escalation protocols defined in the agreement with the vendor(s). Once the new system is in production, the work is not done; rather, the journey is just beginning. The evaluation component continues on, and the goals and objectives for the Project continue to be tracked, measured, and reported, continuously updating and setting new objectives, so that progress continues in providing input into the design functionality and enhancing the workflows. In a well-managed Project, all issues on a typically lengthy issues list are worked until resolved, and as each objective is accomplished, new objectives are set so that the new system gains a life of its own in advancing clinical, administrative, and analytical functions to support attainment of the organization's strategies, business and clinical goals, and operational support. Evaluation becomes a continuous process, part of the organization's culture of excellence, measuring specific objectives to see if they have been attained, and adjusting processes and system features, functions, capabilities, training, and data accordingly. Chapter 7 of this text covers HIS services in depth.

Rollout of the Multiphase HIS Strategic Plan

Further Details on Phase I: Foundational Infrastructure

Phase I of the HIS plan most likely consists of and should begin with a **network infrastructure Initiative**. Associated with the HIS Strategic Plan, this network infrastructure Initiative is the upgrade or rebuild of the infrastructure necessary to provide the strong foundation and "electronic highway" for the new portfolio of application software systems to be implemented. In Chapters 4 and 5, we invoke architectural concepts and compare building a strong house to creating a balanced HIS architecture upon the sturdy foundation of robust network infrastructure: all systems, connectivity, and data capabilities in the HIS Strategic Plan rely upon this foundation.

While many organizations may be still developing their HIS capability and prowess, the process outlined here is ideally intended

🔎 CASE EXAMPLE: FALL DOWN, GO BOOM: IT WITHOUT INFRASTRUCTURE

In 2001, Harvard Medical School was ranked first among healthcare IT capabilities, according to InformationWeek. Then a disaster occurred that took them by storm. The network upon which the entire system of Harvard healthcare organizations depended, including the EHR system, faltered. Network engineers managed what was thought to be a temporary problem and had initial results that made it seem like the problem was easily resolved.

However, things got gradually worse. The straw that broke the camel's back was a simple intra-network email of a file from one colleague to another across campus. The network was down for a week. No part of the HIS—software or application—was available to anyone. Vendors of the network equipment—Cisco and others—jumped into action to help in this disaster. The IT staff involved went without sleep repeatedly for over 24 hours as they tried to diagnose and problem-solve. Meanwhile, health care marched on: nurses old enough to have worked years ago in the pre-EHR paper era taught the younger nurses how to fill out a paper laboratory test request and other diagnostic request forms. The CEO of the Harvard health system put on his running shoes and dashed laboratory requests and results to and from the hospital. The vendor companies and healthcare organization worked together to rapidly rebuild the network. Within a couple of weeks, life within the organization was up and running.

Ultimately, a combination of poor architecture, missed upgrades, and circumstance was diagnosed as the problem that brought the entire network down. Priorities for other important (more visible) needs had superseded the "invisible" network maintenance and, ultimately, that lack of attention to a network that seemed led to major, highly publicized consequences. The lesson of not ignoring essential infrastructure was learned by many through this experience: the Harvard team deserves tremendous credit for openly and actively communicating this experience to others, through the media and conferences. In retrospect, the transparently reported incident was used as a teaching moment for all healthcare organizations (Berinatos, 2003).

for organizations that may be considering a rebuilding of their HIS architecture, or better yet, contemplating the purchase and implementation of a *major* new system, such as an enterprise EHR system or ERP system. When an organization has a gaping hole in its HIS portfolio, it behooves the organization to look at the whole landscape and assess the proper prioritization, interdependencies, foundational work, and overall strategic expenditure that will be required over 5, 10, and 15 years, in order to accomplish its near-term as well as long-term goals. It is only in this broader, more comprehensive context that a major new system should be considered and decisions made. So as part of this, the initial Phase should always consider first the infrastructure

or foundational electronic highway needed to implement any new application system to ride upon it. Years ago, one of the main reasons for early EHR system failures was inadequate network infrastructure: application software capabilities rely upon the capacity and ability of all end users to be attached to the system at any one point in time and receive sub-second response time performance, as well as meeting other parameters, such as security requirements and connectivity to all other connected necessary parties. Modern organizations, take heed. Not only does network infrastructure need to be initially constructed, but it also needs to be maintained. This is a "silent" area, meaning that when it's working properly, it's invisible. When it is not working adequately, or fails, the organization that relies upon this network for its daily clinical and administrative operations comes to a disruptive and screeching halt. Those who think of infrastructure as an afterthought or not worthy of highest priority consideration at the beginning of any capital budgeting process are directed to read the adjacent case example. Wise CIOs take heed and invest in large, broadband network infrastructure. The author has heard a steering committee, comprised largely of physicians, say, "spend the rent money on network infrastructure" and they were right.

In addition to network infrastructure—which includes not only the network but also Projects such as devices rollout, cabling, and wireless infrastructure—other Projects to be included in Phase I depend on the organization's overall priorities for clinical, business, and analytical systems, as identified in the **current systems review**. The current systems review documents all existing systems in the organization as the baseline for creating an HIS migration plan that will boost the organization from its current state to its desired future state in HIS. The future state comprises a 5- to 10-year view of which

$\mathcal{Q}$ CASE EXAMPLE: HIS STRATEGIC PLANNING FOR A MULTIHOSPITAL HEALTH SYSTEM

The Northwest Regional Health System (NWHS) had grown by merger and acquisition, as hospitals and provider practices throughout the region had struggled to survive. The pressures of increasingly difficult reimbursement circumstances, cutting costs while implementing new programs and services, adapting to HITECH MU quality metrics and capabilities, the shift of financial risk from payers to providers, the high cost of implementing the HIS needed, all while the MACRA and Merit-based Incentive Payment System (MIPS) reporting periods ticked by and incentives turned into penalties, proved to be too much for some healthcare providers. NWHS had previously included only a teaching hospital and a community hospital, but now had also acquired two additional hospitals and numerous provider practices, all experiencing protracted financial difficulties, aging systems, and leadership challenges. This challenging period of acquisition resulted in the genesis of opportunity for this community-enhancing regional resource: a four-hospital, multi-clinic, regional provider network, pulling in rural and community providers throughout the entire county. These providers and hospitals now were a corporate entity and legally one organization, but their processes, services, and systems as well as their cultures and staffs were as disjointed as if they were isolated from one another. The Board of Trustees directed new management and internal thought leaders supported by qualified consultant facilitators to develop a strategic enterprise business plan to lay out a vision and roadmap for the new health system to achieve a positive margin for the enterprise in total within a five-year time period. This effort was made in order to preserve and enhance the mission, services, and practice settings of these collective organizations to their communities. As part of this planning process, an HIS Strategic Plan was also created to enable the new enterprise and support the five-year future state clinical and financial goals for the new NWHS.

The NWHS HIS Strategic Plan created directly reflects the strategies, timing, and structure of the new health system's plan. Within this five-year planning horizon the entities of the new health system needed to be completely connected with one another and their new enterprise trading partners. Thus, as a prelude to automation of enterprise-wide systems, intensive redesign of NWHS's clinical services and administrative support processes were designed, with metrics for planning volumes, reimbursement, and margins associated with their footprint in their region. Because these organizations that came together to create the new health system had no relationship to one another previously, by definition, their systems and processes were completely disparate. Also, the portfolios of HIS and the technology of the two new hospitals and many of the provider practices brought together into the new enterprise were in many cases aging and in need of replacement, since when provider organizations are struggling financially, they are typically not in the position to replace or implement new systems. And by definition, all data structures were foreign to one another among the four hospitals and provider organizations. This is the condition many new health systems find themselves in across the U.S., as consolidation of hospitals and providers has occurred over the past 10–15 years, along with a massive push to connect with and engage with patients where they live and work in an effort to care for them outside the hospital setting (Landro, 2018).

The NWHS HIS Strategic Plan called for moving forward with enterprise-wide HIS and technology infrastructure to help create this new health system. The HIS Strategic Plan was presented in three Phases, spanning the five-year planning timeframe. Phase I included creation of secure, broad-bandwidth network infrastructure and updated end-user technology for the new health system, thus connecting the four hospitals and major clinical settings into the same technology network, along with infrastructure support for the provider groups and clinics that were now part of or allied with this new enterprise. Establishing this secure, reliable connectivity, along with communications systems such as secure email and medical intranet capabilities, went a long way to nurturing the budding new culture of the new health system. These efforts enabled new clinical services to be developed across the NWHS by providing secure access to and exchange of clinical data and administrative information among the hospitals, clinics, providers, and corporate administrative support functions across the entire system. Once the Phase I foundational infrastructure and medical intranet capabilities were in place, NWHS could commence to implement Phase II enterprise-wide core systems. Planning for the Phase II included new, enterprise-wide revenue cycle systems, including patient accounting and accounts receivable as well as an integrated ERP system. The initial implementation of these systems included a *basic* scope of functionality across these applications, since the sheer magnitude of implementing new systems for the expanded administrative and business functions of the health system. As well as the new administrative systems, reporting capabilities and basic decision support and business analytics had to be put in place. Implementation of the enterprise-wide core clinical and EHR systems commenced once the new health system's administrative and business support systems were in place. Phase III of the HIS Strategic Plan brought advanced capabilities in the clinical and business information portfolio, such as clinical decision support, predictive analytics, advanced ERP systems capabilities, cost accounting, and other business and clinical intelligence systems. Phase III also capitalized on the well-planned and forward-looking Phase I network infrastructure and technology, enabling the design and implementation of provider-patient connectivity and applications to engage patients more actively in the management of their medical care and health. Thus, over a five-year period, a nascent health system that started as a new health system on paper only was able to become a connected enterprise, bringing new integrated clinical and business services to the entire region, and thrive more fully for all communities involved by achieving economies of scale, clinical and business integration. NWHS's advanced information capabilities allowed the organization to adapt to value-based reimbursement methods and new organizational models including a new Accountable Case Organization and integrating care and work among the four hospitals and numerous provider and clinical settings. This robust five-year plan created a viable foundation and core systems to carry this new health system to a strong and successful future, in line with the mission, vision, and values of its Board, providers, and constituents throughout the region.

systems will be in place after the HIS plan is implemented and a new computing environment has been achieved in accordance with the organization's vision. This desired future state reflects the organization's business plan strategies and goals that form the basis of the HIS strategies and plans, as described in Chapter 4. As the organization's strategies evolve, so does the HIS plan. The two should always be in synch, keeping the planning process continuous and active. To this end, the HIS leadership and function in a healthcare organization should have a planning capability that continuously works on assessing needs, defining requirements, planning systems implementations, developing and reconciling budgets, and integrating that work with the planning function and processes of the organization overall.

Once the HIS Strategic Plan's Phase I Initiatives are identified, each Project comprising the Initiatives needs to be defined in the form of a business plan, approved through the organization's capital planning and operating budget processes, formalized, communicated throughout the organization (not just to those participating), and initiated. The kickoff is just what the name implies—the formal initiation of the implementation Project. During this process, a number of decisions must be made. For example, who is the project manager and which personnel will be included in each project team? For each Project, the team membership should possess the necessary skills sets for that Project as well as provide for representation from key disciplines that will be using the new system. This facilitates an even exchange of inputs from the various perspectives and enables everyone on the team to learn from one another.

For a network infrastructure implementation Project, for example, the project team might consist of three subgroups, led by a project manager. The first subgroup includes technical experts in the areas of networks, technical infrastructure, network monitoring technology, and devices that need to be connected to the infrastructure. The second subgroup includes representatives from the organization's facilities management department, who are essential to the construction aspects of this Project: the implementation may require opening up walls and ceilings of the physical plant to allow cabling and other infrastructure components to be built out. The third subgroup comprises representatives from the clinical and administrative areas that will need to be entered and involved to install the infrastructure cabling, routers, and switches into the ceilings, walls, patient rooms, and office areas. Such is the nature of infrastructure Projects; they are complex and closely akin to capital construction Projects. This type of implementation Project moves the technology infrastructure into the patient care and administrative areas so that the network foundation and electronic highway for the other systems are in place; once established, this highway will move increasing amounts of data at subsecond speed so that new clinical and administrative systems can be implemented and workers have ready access to the systems and data they need to do their jobs.

Other Projects that might be included in Phase I are establishing a secure medical intranet for provider access to data from existing systems while new, more advanced, integrated systems are going through the definition, business planning, approval, and readiness work required preceding their implementation, and other important priorities that the organization is ready to implement, such as MPI definition. At a health system where the author served as CIO, the organization happened to have a license to a decision support system software (acquired during the mergers and acquisitions portion of the health system's formation) (**EXHIBIT 8.3**). This access had been "turned off" while integrating the hospital into the new health system. So, we took the opportunity during our Phase I of the HIS Strategic Plan to reimplement that basic decision support system (a case mix system) for the whole health system under that license. This is an example of how

Phase I may have certain Initiatives that can clear the path for more disruptive Initiatives coming down the path during Phases II and III.

Further Details on Phase II: Basic Core HIS Capabilities

Phase II of the HIS plan implementation will include basic systems and technology that introduce core, enterprise systems such as the Core Clinical Systems and Basic EHR System. All of this requires Phase I basic systems and infrastructure to be in place. Therefore, the kickoff for the EHR Project will occur in Phase II, because it requires the presence of a robust and high-speed network infrastructure and very involved planning Phase to initiate these steps. When an EHR Project kicks off, it must include a multidisciplinary project team with representation from IT; clinical departments such as laboratory, radiology, pharmacy, and therapies; physicians; nursing; finance; human resources; inpatient and outpatient settings; and other involved functions or clinics. Phase II will also include core business systems, such as a basic System including general ledger, accounts payable, materials management or supply chain, and human resources management applications. ERPs are an interdisciplinary Initiative, as they encompass departments such as finance, human resources, materials management, IT, operations, and other disciplines. The point is to include not only those who will directly use the system but also those who will be affected by the information produced and used from the system, such as clinical departments, human resources, strategic planning, and others, as a means of transparency in information usage, disclosure, and collaboration. Additionally, basic, core enterprise reporting and analytical capabilities will be established during Phase II. These basic capabilities are designed and built with the larger, longer goal in mind, built to adapt and expand to future and more advanced information functions and requirements that the organization will be mature enough in its use of these basic systems to which it can now envision, design, implement, and adapt.

Further Details on Phase III: Advanced Core HIS Capabilities

Phase III includes the advanced systems and capabilities that bring the organization into journey of collaboration, innovation, and additional functions used to improve clinical and business outcomes. It takes time to recover from Phases I and II and ready the organization for Phase III, but this is always the goal. It is important to plan the resources and priorities around this Phase as well as just getting the basic systems in place. In Phase III, the comprehensive EHR System functions are implemented in accordance with the operational needs of the organization; the regulations governing HIS, such as Health Insurance Portability and Accountability Act (HIPAA) and HITECH; and the ambitions and innovations of key clinical leadership. Likewise, Phase III includes the implementation of advanced, enterprise and comprehensive ERP system functions, taking stock of the use and opportunities created by implementing the basic ERP system in Phase II, then enhancing and advancing those capabilities as the journey toward excellence in capabilities and service continues. Equally important in Phase III is the advanced enterprise reporting and analytics capabilities needed to continue to keep the organization forward-looking and challenging itself to learn, anticipate, and get ahead of patient conditions or business issues to improve outcomes, and gain deeper insights into how and why those clinical and business outcomes occur and what can be done to improve them. Building upon all these HIS capabilities, the health organization can turn toward the patient, making both clinical care and administrative services more accessible. Patient engagement is essential to management of care outside the institution and is the key to connecting with patients, managing the health of populations, and connecting with

EXHIBIT 8.3 A Note to CIOs

The key to being a good CIO or leader of HIS and technology in an organization is to engage and involve many people with appropriate representation around you as you lead the charge. Once the vision (five-year "future state") for the organization's HIS and technology is agreed upon and established, then the HIS strategic planning process commences. The first step is to document the "current state" of systems. In one comprehensive electronic health record (EHR) system project I was in charge of overseeing, to document the "current state" baseline for the HIS planning process, we engaged nine management engineers full time for six months to walk the corridors and doorways of our hospitals and scores of clinics to document through interviews, flow charts, and narrative descriptions, the current ways we took care of patients. Every key clinical process that would be supported by the new EHR—registration, scheduling, orders management, results reporting, laboratory, pharmacy, radiology, and therapies such as occupational therapy and respiratory therapy—was documented, flow charted, and discussed so that actual steps in the workflows were clear. Frontline workers were interviewed—registration clerks, schedulers, nurses, physicians, therapists, laboratory technicians, etc.—and asked for insights regarding strengths, weaknesses, opportunities, and threats they were aware of in the current ways of providing care and doing their work. The resulting work, which was printed and published in very large foldouts housed in large three-ring binders, became our roadmap and source of the truth for developing streamlined and hopefully improved processes in the design phase of the EHR system project. This information served as the baseline for the migration from "where we are" (current state) to "where we want to go" (future state). This documentation was very interesting since, in many cases, it reflected people's concern for changing things—often the workers interviewed would ask to remain anonymous, concerned that their ideas for change might upset others.

Bottom line, it was very important to get stakeholders to participate in the process. Every minute and dollar invested in this planning phase is well worth it. So much truth and intelligence lies in the voices of the grassroots workers. Never forget, they are just as intelligent as the people in the C-suite—they just have different jobs. Take the time to listen to them, and it will be some of the best information you can get about a better way to do things.

Go to the ambulatory settings that will be integrated with the inpatient setting. Find out what is important to them and what issues they experience and would like to correct. Make sure these ambulatory processes are documented and understood as well as those of the powerful departments in the hospital. Make the effort to determine how clinics and ambulatory settings will be integrated into the integrated enterprise system and workflow of the EHR. Remember to follow the flow of the patient, not just the departments providing various services.

Once the HIS Plan is in place, break down the total effort into **Strategic Initiatives**, each of which then can be broken down into phases, each having individual project that takes the organization along its migration path from the current state to the future state. Remember that this migration includes the entire HIS portfolio—infrastructure, financial systems, clinical systems, EHR systems, human resource systems, business intelligence, and decision support systems. EVERYTHING gets updated, rebuilt, replaced, and revamped as needed. Many older, decrepit systems, left to languish and drag along the workers who rely upon them, will finally be managed and dealt with according to a unified, integrated, and updated HIS Plan. People will be happy to get updated technology to support their work, and they will work very hard to help bring these systems into reality.

Start with the infrastructure component, including the data center. Develop a project plan, get funding, define the network bandwidth capacity requirements needed to all the new systems and data that will be transmitted over that electronic highway, and ensure everyone and everything gets what they need. It is essential to get stakeholder engagement and inclusion in the process.

After performing a requirements analysis, the next step is the software product selection process. This is where the importance of detailed plans, like a blueprint is important to the construction of a new house, will be magnified. Each Strategic Initiative comprising the HIS Plan needs to be assessed for the level of effort required so that appropriate staffing can be added. Limit the Strategic Initiatives to three to five at any given time, but keep three to five in the pipeline at all times. This makes things manageable for the organization to move forward with change, while supporting existing systems at the same time.

the health and needs of the community in meaningful, new ways.

Summary of Multiphase HIS Strategic Plan Efforts

Implementation of such a multiphase plan means starting at the beginning and growing from there. Any attempts to skip steps or rush the process are usually exercises in futility, and more time and money are wasted with missteps in such a case than if the organization follows the steps in order and stays in touch with the reality of what it takes to revamp an entire HIS architecture and automate new workflows for its employees and processes. Implementing an HIS plan takes years. That is why the future state is a 5- to 10- to 15-year view of what the organization would like to look like. It takes that long to implement such massive change and then curate it to a point of maturity and total immersion of the culture in the new ways of doing things and actually changing the core of the organization. In the following sections we look at each of the three Phases in more detail.

This work, both technically and culturally, becomes a point of connection and mission for the organization, creating energy and collaboration between functions and professions that have done their work in a more isolated fashion previously. This type of advancement of capability challenges even the most highly trained professionals to learn, innovate, and change their ways for the better. Development

of new workflows, streamlined processes, and value-added insights are what is at stake. Organizations of the future must enable themselves to adapt to a more patient-centric and cost-effective future. HIS is part of that solution.

Next, we shall dig into implementation of Projects that comprise Strategic Initiatives described above, and remember, these insights and techniques apply to all Phases, Initiatives, and Projects. Once Strategic Initiatives have been articulated into the approved, planned Projects that comprise them, implementation begins. As always, in HIS work, nothing is simple, and must be systematically broken down into a sequence of logical steps that are then systematically accomplished.

▶ Implementation: Project Management

The discipline of project management is a capability essential to the successful implementation of not only an HIS Strategic Plan but also any type of Initiative or Project. The HIS Strategic Plan defines what type of HIS Initiative or Project is to be done, while project management defines how to manage these Initiatives and Projects, seeing them through to full implementation. Recall that all of this activity takes place *after* the HIS Strategic Plan is created and approved by as many groups— from senior management to staff nurses to the board of trustees—as practicable and socialized among the many stakeholders of the organization. Once the HIS plan is in place, initial Projects that get the plan launched need to be defined in detail, approved in the form of business plans, and initiated. In most cases, the rolling list of Strategic Initiatives can be used for this purpose and are very effective; this method provides a useful format for not only organizing and initiating systems Projects but also communicating to keep the organization up to date on how the HIS plan will be implemented in Phases, Initiatives, and Projects.

The Discipline of Project Management

Project management is a universal skill set that has certain areas of focus, HIS software systems and technology being a major specialization within project management. To implement software systems and technology, project management requires expertise not only in how to manage a project, and the tools and techniques necessary to do that but also an understanding of HIS Project scope definition, systems analysis and requirements definition, system design, building, testing, implementation, evaluation, and support. The project life cycle includes initiating, planning, executing, monitoring, controlling, and closing projects (**FIGURE 8.9**).

To boil it down to its basics, project management is defined as the use of knowledge, skills, and tools to accomplish objectives and tasks of a project, allowing the organization to meet its goals through these carefully planned collaborative activities designed to achieve a particular aim. Project management in the HIS context is not limited to software or technology Initiatives: project management skills are equally important to

the successful accomplishment of a planning project, such as developing an HIS Strategic Plan, as well as other HIS elements, such as orchestrating an RFP process, selecting a new application software system, or redesigning clinical or administrative workflows as part of an implementation.

A multifaceted discipline, project management requires technical skills and tools for managing projects, as well as soft skills of communication, group dynamics, interpersonal, conflict resolution, negotiation, and other types of "softer", but nonetheless important, leadership skills. Project managers are responsible for developing project plans as part of the project planning process, including careful definition of HIS project scope, timetable, and resource requirements. It is always important to include stakeholders in the definition process and build their roles into the project plan. Project manager responsibilities include allocating work tasks, setting expectations for project roles, tracking tasks and accountabilities, addressing issues, communicating effectively to management and stakeholders, and controlling project activities according to milestones set collaboratively.

Key Steps in Implementation for Project Managers

Key steps in the implementation of a new HIS can be defined as follows. These steps occur in sequence, but as part of a whole, through the lens of project management.

1. Kickoff and Project Planning. Create the project planning team and task forces.
2. System Selection. Select the system to be implemented using a disciplined process.

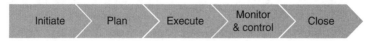

FIGURE 8.9 Project life cycle.

3. Contract Negotiation. Negotiate agreements for all necessary system components and services, such as software, hardware, devices, consulting services, infrastructure, and others as needed.
4. Design. Perform system design in concert with process redesign, including interfaces required for sharing data between systems feeding data to those receiving data.
5. Development. Develop the system and "build," including creation of all system files reflecting the organizational specifics, such as numbering systems, providers, sites, and elements.
6. Testing. Perform system-wide testing for each module and connections between modules and applications.
7. Training. Train IT staff and project participants initially while the system is being developed and built and then train end users closer to time of the system's go-live or deployment point.
8. Deployment. Prepare the system site, go-live, and roll out the system into the production environment for end users to utilize in their work.
9. Evaluation. Test and validate systems after going live to make sure everything is working the way it should. Feed the results of the evaluation, and issues identified, back in an organized manner through the steps in the process until the system is working perfectly and any issues are resolved.

Projects differ from operations in that projects have a beginning and an end, are temporary, and vary in how they are budgeted and staffed from ongoing operational support in that projects are one-time processes and are not repetitive. For this reason, those attracted to the role of project manager are those who are comfortable not "belonging" to any one part of the organization or functional unit (aside from perhaps a project management office), and those who seek variety, enjoy tackling new problems, and thrive on learning new things and on change, as well as interacting with new groups of people on a regular basis. This is not to say that they do not become experts in certain areas, such as HIS software implementations of a clinical or business nature, but they are comfortable applying their skills to many different projects in different areas of the organization or perhaps in different organizations on a regular basis.

Portfolios, Initiatives, Programs, and Projects

Initiatives and programs involve multiple Projects with beginnings and ends. Programs differ from Projects in that programs comprise multiple Projects not one of which alone could accomplish the goals of a program. Portfolios include multiple Initiatives and programs that support the strategies and goals of the organization, such as a series of phased and prioritized HIS Strategic Initiatives. A project manager's focus is on the goals and tasks of a particular Project, while the focus of a program manager is on bringing benefits to the organization through the accomplishment of multiple aligned Projects and Initiatives. Multiple programs and Initiatives roll up into a portfolio for the organization. So, the HIS Portfolio consists of programs, Initiatives, and Projects. One way to envision this structure is presented in **FIGURE 8.10**. **FIGURE 8.11** fills out this diagram to encompass the HIS Strategic Plan and the entire HIS capability of a healthcare organization.

Project Management Training and Skills

Certified project management professionals have completed a prescribed program,

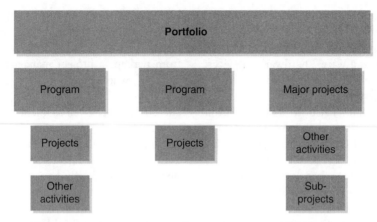

FIGURE 8.10 Portfolio, Program, Project, and activities hierarchy.

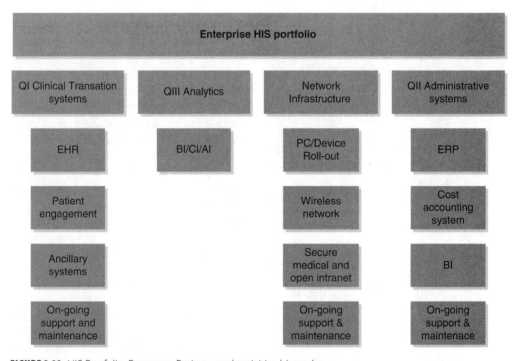

FIGURE 8.11 HIS Portfolio, Programs, Projects, and activities hierarchy.

qualifications including bachelors or high school education, and a required number of months of direct hands-on experience managing projects (4,500 and 36 months, and 7,500 and 60 months, for bachelors and high school graduates, respectively), as well as training and successful testing in the tools, techniques, management, and leadership of projects. The key process areas of training are initiation planning, execution, monitoring and controlling, and closing of projects. The education and training for project management focuses on content areas including project integration, scope management, schedule management, cost planning and management, quality control, resource management, project communications and risk management, procurement management, and interaction and management of stakeholders (PMBOK, 2008). While a certification in project management is a good qualification to see on the resumé of a candidate, many intangibles accompany a highly effective project manager, and those do not show up on paper—they are seen in practice. As the saying goes, the proof is in the pudding, and the success or tepid performance or abject failure of a project, relies on project management tangibles and intangibles equally.

While good **project managers (PMs)** come with varied training, backgrounds, tools, and personalities, it usually doesn't take long to identify a good project manager from an ineffective one in the heat of a project. There are a variety of project management methods, and often lively debate about which is best, but methodology is only part of the equation. It takes a project manager whose innate talent is balancing multiple, dynamic attributes of a project skillfully and artfully. The author has observed project managers who didn't attend any formal training in project management, but rather they learned over the course of their experience doing this type of work and are inherently good at it. Sometimes PMs use complex, sophisticated tools and methods for managing their projects, but sometimes they use an Excel spreadsheet and do a great job. So, it is important to not judge exactly on the formality and initials behind someone's name, rather, judge based on results and on successful project leadership and management. When done well, the organization is enhanced and management satisfied with the results, as are the people involved in the project. Conversely, when project management is ineffective, the

organization is at a minimum frustrated and no doubt harmed by lack of results and what is usually a waste of time, money, and other resources, as well as the opportunity cost to the organization of what could've been done with that time which was now wasted, never to be recouped.

While the attributes displayed in **FIGURE 8.12** are widely accepted, the weight of each attribute is up for discussion. While each skill set is important, effective project management tools and techniques are essential, and without those a project manager cannot be effective. And certain business skills can be enhanced or provided by a project team member working in close collaboration with the project manager. But without the core project management expertise in terms of methodology (which can vary), tools, and techniques, the basic capabilities of a project manager are lacking, and that person should not be given the responsibility for this important activity for the organization.

For every step in the process of managing a project, continuous planning efforts are required, including initiating, planning, executing, monitoring and controlling, and closing the project. Planning ensures a thoroughly detailed work effort, helps with communication, provides clarity to roles and responsibilities, identifies potential issues in advance, and defines evaluation objectives so that success is measurable. Projects can be planned in their entirety or by Phase, but for dynamic, changeable, and new design work, agile planning methodology is a collaborative approach that allows for planning in brief cycles, or sprints, and the ability to adapt based on evolving requirements and dynamic, adaptive scenarios. The role of a **Project Management Office (PMO)** is to provide the policies, coordination, planning, integration, management tools, techniques, compliance, and communication to multiple projects on behalf of the organization and the benefits it is seeking from the investment of

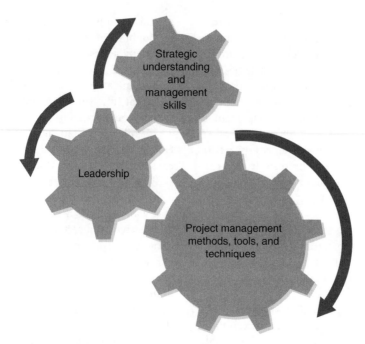

FIGURE 8.12 Project management skills and abilities.

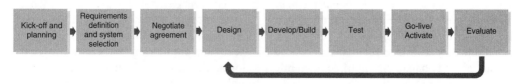

FIGURE 8.13 Steps in HIS implementation.

time, energy, consistency, methodology, and resources in projects. The hierarchy of projects, programs, and portfolios is displayed in Figures 8.10 and 8.11.

Project life cycle vs. *product* life cycle: a project has a beginning and an end, and is not the entirety of a program or organizational objective, but is instead just one key part that helps the organization move toward that objective. A product life cycle is longer in timespan than a project, and through numerous projects over the course of a product life cycle, the product can evolve and grow, especially with the adoption of agile project thinking and

methodology. In HIS, product life cycles for software application systems and technologies can span many years and many projects that help that product attain additional capabilities, stay current, and evolve with changing clinical and business needs, often through the use of projects to help upgrade and sustain the product's life cycle.

Implementation progresses step by step, leading up to the profound moment of "go-live" or activation of a new system (**FIGURE 8.13**):

1. Implementation planning (including system selection, elements of

contract negotiation, system specification, and documentation of the setting in which the system will be implemented)

2. System design (including creation of computer functionality that accomplishes redesigned workflow and processes in user-friendly ways)

3. System or application programming (including the technical aspects of systems engineering and writing computer programs that reflect the system design)

4. Development or "build" (including the creation of applications, interfaces, and interaction between those applications so that the resulting overall system performs desired functions in a smooth and integrated fashion)

5. Testing (including system and integration testing challenging and perfecting the system programs and interfaces to weed out and correct any errors in the development Phase)

6. Rollout or deployment (including detailed implementation and go-live system activation planning and execution)

7. Evaluation (including measurement of system functioning against performance and user satisfaction metrics)

This progression of steps is continually repeated in a feedback loop as enhancements and functionalities are added to the system being implemented. Implementation is a lively, active process that never ends once a system is "live" and being used in the support of real work in an organization (otherwise referred to as the system being in "production"). Once a system is in use, there begins the iterative process of continually making improvements, fixing issues, adding new

functionalities or capabilities to the existing platform, adding new end users and new reports, updating and upgrading the system, and so on. Once a system is "live" and stabilized, the addition of more users, more functionality, and additional process redesign become the journey that use of a system truly is. The system becomes a part of the daily work and life of the organization and the people who work there and, as such, needs continual care, attention, energy, and resources to sustain it and move down the path of growth and evolution for the organization. Conversely, if a system is not given the attention, resources, and nurturance it requires, the consequences can be dire for the organization, its providers, and its patients: faulty systems or data may result in faulty processes and inaccurate information, which in health care can be disastrous, potentially leading to medical errors. Take heed of this and be courageous, be diligent, and read on about HIS and technology implementation—where the rubber does, indeed, meet the road. The process of implementation is similar whether the system is an enterprise system or a standalone system, and whether it is deployed in a hospital system, physician practice, clinic, home health organization, hospice, community health center, public health clinic or organization, research organization, or any other type of healthcare organization. The steps of an implementation effort are consistent—it is only the content, scope, technology, and participants of the implementation that will vary based on the organizational setting and type of system being implemented. These steps and lessons are generalizable and can be tailored to any system implementation scenario.

Projects are successful when stakeholder expectations are satisfactorily met, the project comes in on time and on or under budget, business objectives are met or exceeded in accordance with the project business plan, end-user adoption is high and sustainable, the quality of service to end users is consistently high, the project is conducted according to governance criteria and processes, and an effective benefits realization component is implemented as part of the project and evaluated on an ongoing basis following the project's completion.

▶ Electronic Health Record (EHR) System Implementation

While most hospitals and providers have adopted at least a basic EHR system, the baseline goal of most organizations has been accomplished, but more advanced types of functionality to achieve critical outcomes elude most at this point. Nor is it known if certain types of organizations, such as smaller, safety net, or rural organizations, have the capacity to achieve beneficial advanced EHR functions. The next challenge is to move from Basic to Basic with documentation to Comprehensive EHR functionality—this is the long road of EHR implementation, which, for those organizations that have made it, takes tremendous focus and resources, and years. Attention must now turn to this advanced function usage, and track which types of institutions are able to achieve this level of EHR system adoption, and why others are not in order to address this lag.

EHR System Definition

To understand what is involved in EHR implementation, we should address some important definitions regarding how EHR adoption is currently measured. A **basic EHR system** is a system that uses EHR functionality on at least one clinical unit and includes patient demographics, physician notes, nursing assessments, patient problem lists, laboratory and radiology

reports, and diagnostic test results, as well as computerized ordering for medications. By comparison, a **comprehensive EHR system** includes the basic functionality described previously plus 14 other clinical functionalities (Table 8.1) and is used throughout the entire hospital (Jha et al., 2011).

Let's face it. The bar is markedly different for meeting the definition of basic EHR adoption versus a comprehensive EHR, and most of us think "comprehensive" when we hear that a provider or health system has "an EHR system." A basic EHR requires each function to be implemented in at least (or only) one clinical unit, while comprehensive EHR adoption requires each function to be implemented in all clinical units. More advanced functionalities such as CPOE, electronic generation of quality measures, and patient electronic access to their records are more challenging to implement for all hospitals (Jha, DesRoches, Kravolec, & Joshi, 2010). Comprehensive functions include those categorized as performance measurement and patient engagement, two areas essential to improving outcomes and achieving value-based care. The HITECH stimulus incentives called for these functionalities to be implemented in Stages called MU Stages 1, 2, and 3, with Stage 3 now replaced with the MIPS program, as discussed in Chapter 3.

EHR System Adoption
Status of EHR Adoption in the U.S.

Research since the HITECH Act was enacted shows progress in EHR adoption, although comprehensive adoption continues to elude all but a handful of healthcare organizations. As of 2015, total EHR system adoption including basic and comprehensive is presented in **FIGURE 8.14**.

FIGURE 8.15 shows the increases in adoption of basic and comprehensive EHR systems and reflects a more serious statistic—a divide developing between the "haves" and "have-nots" of advanced functionality. Adoption of comprehensive EHR systems is associated with large not-for-profit hospitals and those hospitals participating in accountable care organizations (ACOs) and patient-centered medical homes, adoption with a high level of

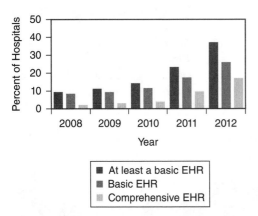

FIGURE 8.14 EHR adoption in U.S. hospitals from 2008 to 2012.

Data from DesRoches, C. M., Charles, D., Furukawa, M.F., et al. (2013). Adoption of electronic health records grows rapidly, but fewer than half of U.S. hospitals had at least a basic system in 2012. *Health Affairs, 32*(8), 1478–1485.

variability among types of advanced functions adopted, with about 25 percent of hospitals adopting all performance management functions, and 15 percent of hospitals adopting all patient engagement functions (Adler-Milstein et al., 2017). While notable progress occurred in the adoption of basic EHR systems by rural and critical access hospitals, from 22 percent in 2011 to 80 percent in 2015, the increase of about 20 percent from 2011 to 2014 slowed to a 5 percent increase from 2014 to 2015. And other types of hospitals such as psychiatric and children's hospitals lagged behind the other groups with EHR adoption (The Office of the National Coordinator for Health Information Technology, n.d.). As time passes from the initial implementations, the hospitals able to adopt the advanced EHR functions are enabling performance measurement (quality and efficiency) and patient engagement, as well as clinical decision support, the types of advanced functions that accompany comprehensive EHR systems (Figure 8.15 and Table 8.1).

MU adoption for physicians and other providers includes adoption of the following

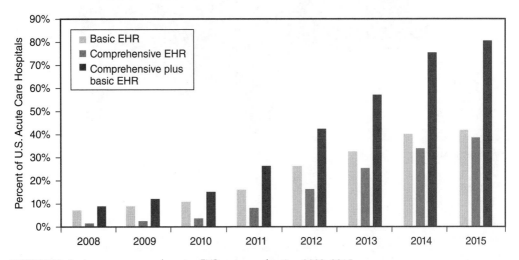

FIGURE 8.15 Basic versus comprehensive EHR system adoption 2008–2015.

Data from the Journal of the American Medical Informatics Association, Adler-Milstein, J., Holmgren, A. J., Kralovec, P., Worzala, C., Searcy, T., & Patel, V. (2017). Electronic health record adoption in US hospitals: the emergence of a digital "advanced use" divide. Journal of the American Medical Informatics Association, 24(6), 1142–1148.

EHR capabilities for use in their practices and clinics (**FIGURE 8.16**) (Henricks, 2011):

1. Computerized provider order entry.
2. E-prescribing (eRx).
3. Report ambulatory Clinical Quality Measures to **Centers for Medicare & Medicaid Services (CMS)**.
4. Implement one clinical decision support rule.
5. Provide patients with an electronic copy of their health information, upon request.
6. Provide clinical summaries for patients for each office visit.
7. Drug-drug and drug-allergy interaction checks.
8. Record demographics.
9. Maintain an up to date problem list of current and active diagnoses.
10. Maintain active medication list.
11. Maintain active medication allergy list.
12. Record and chart changes in vital signs.
13. Record smoking status for patients 13 years or older.
14. Capability to exchange key clinical information among providers of

Percent of all Office-based Physicians that have Demonstrated Meaningful Use through Medicare | December 2015

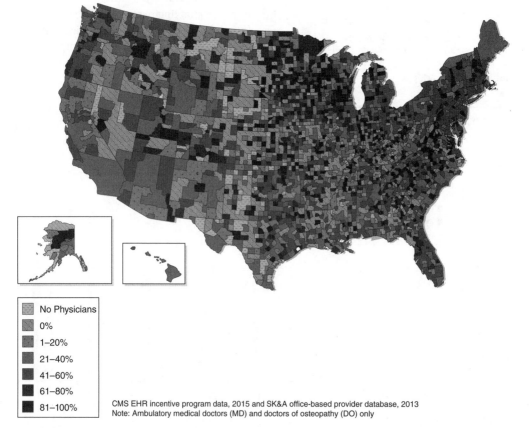

No Physicians
0%
1–20%
21–40%
41–60%
61–80%
81–100%

CMS EHR incentive program data, 2015 and SK&A office-based provider database, 2013
Note: Ambulatory medical doctors (MD) and doctors of osteopathy (DO) only

FIGURE 8.16 Office-based physicians demonstrating MU (2015).

care and patient-authorized entities electronically.

15. Protect electronic health information.

Additionally, as of 2015, 87 percent of office-based physicians reported using at least a basic EHR system, increasing from 35 percent in 2007 (**FIGURE 8.17**); of these physicians, 40.6 percent reported using a fully functional EHR system in 2015, compared to 3.7 percent in 2007 (Office of the National Coordinator for Health Information Technology, 2016).

Participation in HIEs has also been increasing, with progress reported in 2013 statistics at 30 percent of hospitals and 10 percent of ambulatory practices now active in 1 of 119 HIEs found across the U.S. At the same time it was also reported that more than 70 percent of these exchanges are struggling to find a sustainable business model and are at

risk of failing once the governmental stimulus funds are no longer available to help sustain them (Snell, 2018). Today, physician participation in HIEs is growing, as well as the overall viability and collaborative HIE efforts through multiple mechanisms, including greater cooperation on the part of EHR system vendors, state-wide HIE efforts that are maturing in an effort to exchange useful data to increase access to care via telemedicine and other outreach methods, research showing productivity gains and cost savings such as the Notre Dame study showing HIE use and federal incentives could benefit the government through Medicare savings of $3.2 billion per year (Adjerid, Adler-Milstein, & Angst, 2016). Results vary based on the maturity of the HIE, with longer-established data exchange groups able to demonstrate greater, and more predictable cost savings, and public health uses are evident, including epidemiologists ability to expand disease investigation

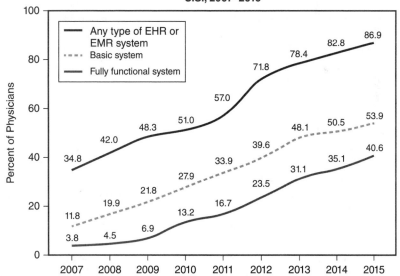

Office-based physicians with an electronic health record or electronic medical record (EHR or EMR) system: U.S., 2007–2015

NCHS, National Ambulatory Medical Care Survey and National Electronic Health Records Survey, 2007–2015.

FIGURE 8.17 Office-based physicians with an EHR system.

and disease management without spending more time, using HIE data, yielding time and cost savings (Snell, 2018).

These data show that the HITECH Act of 2009 has had the intended effect of stimulating the adoption of EHRs and data exchanges among healthcare providers, yet also has reflected some indication of the difficulty associated with these implementations. This scenario provides us with the backdrop for discussing HIS and technology implementations.

▶ Lessons Learned on Projects

Reasons for Project Failures

Reasons for project failures are numerous and range from technical and quantitative (science) reasons to qualitative (art). Some of the most pronounced are the following:

1. Unqualified project manager or frequent change in project manager. Successful projects are staffed with qualified talent who manage and motivate people, creating an atmosphere of support and excellence throughout the life of the effort.

2. Poor or misunderstood project definition, and allowing the scope of the project to grow randomly and uncontrolled, commonly referred to as "scope creep." Successful projects define clear metrics for assigned accountabilities.

3. Lack of control of project cost or schedule. The best project methods include well-defined checkpoints and quality-centered mechanisms that measure productivity and quality data. In this way, costs, schedules, quality metrics, and other project factors can be assessed and properly estimated, ensuring the project has the tools and resources it requires.

4. Weak project sponsorship. This includes uninvolved project sponsors who do not provide the necessary leadership and subject matter expertise for the function in which the project is occurring. Customer and end-user involvement at each Stage of the Project is essential to bringing value to the organization and to solving problems encountered during the course of the effort.

5. Poorly constructed project plan, including poorly defined, undocumented project team roles and responsibilities. Effectively managed projects have consistent methodology for planning and execution of the work.

6. Unclear definition of benefits the project is expected to bring the organization and the relationship of project tasks or deliverables to those benefits. Fruitful efforts tie key strategic processes and business value to the project, measured through benefits realization processes.

7. Poor change control, meaning when an appropriate, agreed-upon change in scope or tasks to the project is to take place, the project scope, definition, requirements, tasks, costs, timetable, and team activities are not properly documented, communicated, and socialized among project participants and stakeholders. When necessary change occurs during the course of a project, interdependencies between project activities, benefits, and accountabilities are tied to success criteria. This allows for normal learning that occurs in the course of the project to be

integrated into the work, without losing control of cost, time, or scope (Discenza & Forman, 2007).

Ensuring HIS Project Success

HIS and technology implementations are complex projects, requiring careful and smart strategic and tactical planning. Success begins with a carefully thought-out, well-documented, and effectively communicated HIS Strategic Plan that lays the groundwork for the sequencing and timing of HIS Phases, Initiatives, and Projects.

HIS and technology projects require motivated, qualified IT personnel and interdisciplinary staff representing the functional disciplines whose areas will be touched by the new system. The types of IT staff needed include HIS planners, project managers, trainers, communication specialists, systems analysts, programmers, network engineers, hardware experts (such as for workstation or mobile device rollouts and other "projects within the project")—and the list goes on. The organization depends on the IT department to provide qualified, well-trained personnel who are familiar with the systems and technologies being introduced into the organization. IT staff must be encouraged to not fall into their own silos and always be directed to serve the needs of the organization, rather than simply embracing the technology with which they are comfortable or in which they have become experts during their years in the organization's HIS department. When managing the HIS department, it is important to keep these very specialized staff continuously learning new technologies and systems, working on a variety of projects, using new programming languages, and adapting to new ideas and ways of doing their work. Likewise, it is essential to keep discussing the organizational vision with these professionals so that even as particular individuals specialize in a particular area of HIS and technology, they retain a clear picture of the entire HIS architecture and remember their work touches all

systems that support the well-being of patients, as well as those who support the clinicians and administrative knowledge workers of the organization—not for the sake of the information technology itself.

Remember why we are here. Almost every HIS professional is a "healthcare person" at heart. If IT staff become stressed with long hours laboring over a large project or problem, a good practice is to have them take a break and walk to the patient care areas, talk with a few caregivers, and see their systems in use. Doing so immediately regrounds them in the purpose of their work and can be amazingly effective at bringing new energy and perspective to their highly technical jobs. Conversely, when nurses and other clinicians have a chance to see and learn what the HIS staff do each and every day, they gain an incredible respect for the intricacy and depth of the work done by HIS professionals on the systems in daily use by clinicians and other members of the healthcare organization. A true epiphany can occur when IT and clinical professionals learn about one another's work, thereby helping to build cooperative relationships that will come in very handy during the trying times of an implementation.

Good contracts are keys to success. Solid, well-negotiated agreements that hold vendors and suppliers accountable to milestones for project deliverables and clarify responsibilities are worth every minute invested in their creation. When negotiating contracts, do not be intimidated by anyone. Do what you know is right for the organization and, most importantly, for the patients and clinicians by locking in favorable, risk-mitigating terms and conditions into the contracts signed with software vendors. There is always more than one solution to any problem and don't let anyone convince you or the organization otherwise. Software salespeople can be very convincing—but they are not your friends, even though they definitely want you to think so during the sales cycle. One lesson the author was taught as a young, budding CIO by her first boss, then chief financial officer (CFO) of Holy Cross Health System (now Trinity Health), Sr. Geraldine Hoyler, CSC, was this: "If you go to dinner or lunch and a vendor is present, you pay." It was her way of making sure the CIO was empowered and motivated to keep the power and independence on her side of my business relationships with vendors, and never feel even the slightest bit beholden to anyone. Another saying is, "*Remember—there's no such thing as a free lunch.*" Good business practice and compliance rules restrict members of organizations from accepting any sort of gifts from vendors. In a business scenario, if someone buys something for you, that person will no doubt expect something in return. Do not allow yourself to be compromised by accepting gifts or favors from someone who wants something from you (in this case, a software salesperson wanting a contract). Doing so might just soften your resolve on a difficult contract term negotiation, or make you feel as if you need to give something back. Keep your objectivity and fight hard for a favorable contract for your organization.

Link payments of the software license fee (the primary method of payment for use of a software package) to successful accomplishment of key milestones in the project that are not payable until both parties' senior project executives sign off on them. In the healthcare organization's case, that person is the CIO or CEO; for the vendor, it is the senior account executive. Spell out in the contract the mechanism that attaches portions of the total license fee to key steps in the system development and implementation. This milestone-based payment process ties each payment to the accomplishment of real progress in the project; it is also the best way to keep the attention of the vendor throughout the course of the implementation and make sure the vendor is incentivized to perform as promised. If the agreement does not specify a milestone-based payment structure, it will likely oblige the healthcare organization to pay for the software license based on dates, which is a very dangerous approach from the customer's point of view. If the payments are due based on the passage of time (meaning a certain percentage of the license fee is paid on specified dates), the vendor simply has to watch the days of the calendar tick off until it receives payment—it does not have to perform and accomplish project work to get paid. In such a case, there is no incentive for the vendor to push forward on the hard work of working with the organization in building and implementing the system and solving the problems that always occur along the way (Figure 8.7).

Fund projects with adequate resources to succeed. Properly resourced projects (in terms of both money and time) are the ones most likely to succeed. This is not to say that project budgets should be padded or excessive in funding, but rather that projects should be carefully planned at a very detailed level and realistic cost estimates based on those details. This can be challenging sometimes, because HIS and technology projects require resources for many line items that are not related to software licenses. (Figure 5.4 in Chapter 5 provides details on the typical line items for a software implementation project.) It can be a startling reality check to see the enormous difference between just the license fees (which is what the vendor emphasizes) and the total cost of an implementation. Take special care to think of every single necessary category of license fees—for example, the license fees required for third-party software packages that may be needed to run the software system on the hardware, or do reporting, or connect devices to the network, or upgrade the interface engine software to handle a new volume of interfaces. The devices connected to a new software system need to be new in most cases, because older devices typically do not have the capabilities necessary to extract all the benefits from the new software. Go through the cost spreadsheet in a step-by-step manner, counting all of the users and the square feet of hardwire and wireless coverage needed for nomadic clinical workers and business personnel. Do not be wasteful, but plan for ample resources to get the whole job done. User departments should not be expected to have budgeted funds for a new IT system being implemented in their area. Instead, the HIS project budget must contain all funds needed to implement the project throughout the organization. End users expect their new systems to be fully implemented, with proper network coverage and bandwidth for moving massive amounts of data quickly. This is critical for adequate training, support, and end-user enthusiasm as the organization adapts to the new system. Users will work hard with you to make the implementation a success if they know you have planned properly on their behalf.

Watch out for silos. Failed implementations or major problems in the completeness or integrity of data can occur if plans for systems projects are too general or do not "fit" together properly. Poor implementations are often planned with a "silo mentality," in which synchronization between other projects and the implementation project is lacking. Imagine making changes to two interconnected computer systems at the same time without informing both parties and then expecting them to work perfectly afterward: it is highly unlikely that the systems would both work properly or that the integrity of the data would

be intact afterward. Unfortunately, unless the people who are responsible for supporting each of those systems are communicating actively and are exceedingly careful about planning and synchronizing necessary changes, changes might be made to individual systems independently, resulting in unintegrated systems and out-of-sync data.

The organization owns all its own data and must keep it that way. Make sure the contract states and standard business practice upholds that the vendor may *not* use data to which it has access by virtue of supporting and even housing the system, or otherwise. The only condition under which this is allowed is if the organization expressly approves in writing by the organization's CIO, the one-time use of a subset of de-identified data for a specific purpose (not general usage). Beware: vendor standard contracts contain language that gives them the right to own or use the healthcare organization's data for other purposes, including reselling de-identified data to other organizations for benchmarking purposes and marketing. You must remove this language and replace it with language that clearly lays out that the organization and the organization only, owns the data. Note: patients of course always have a right to a copy of their data.

HIS projects require cooperation with other parties. When implementing systems and

🔍 CASE EXAMPLE: DATA OWNERSHIP

A community hospital had a long-standing contract with a third-party billing service that provided off-site software and billing services for a major payer (Blue Cross). The hospital needed to get its billing data for another purpose but was told it could not have the data unless the organization paid for it. The hospital's contract with this third-party billing system service gave the vendor the data-ownership rights, so ultimately the hospital had to pay $50,000 to the third party (that was already profiting from the relationship) to get a copy of its own billing data. This example makes a key point: contracts with software vendors and any third parties that process data for the healthcare organization as a service must spell out that the healthcare organization owns its data and the software vendors and third-party data processers do not. This consideration is becoming increasingly important as the popularity of cloud-based software-as-a-service for processing organizations' data grows.

building interfaces, there will be other vendors on the other sides of those interfaces; the new system vendor must work and cooperate with those vendors to construct the two-way interfaces that act as bridges between the new system and the other systems with which it shares data. This collaboration is necessary to accomplish the tasks demanded of this new system. The contract should spell out the behavioral and cooperative elements of this type of work, in addition to listing the interfaces, and the vendor must agree to be held to this level of cooperation. Often vendor personnel balk at the prospect of cooperating with their competitors; such intransigence merely hurts the customer—the healthcare organization implementing these software systems. Vendors may try to displace other vendors rather than cooperate with them on behalf of the customer, so the expectations for cooperation must be spelled out and agreed to in the contract. Vendors have financial incentives to sell more software, of course, and the software marketplace is highly competitive. Thus, it is necessary to obligate the vendor contractually to play nicely with others.

Freeze or minimize other priorities during the period of the implementation. Other implementations and projects should be frozen while a new system is being implemented, especially the large ones. Minimize the number of changes attempted simultaneously to stabilize the environment so that problems can be quickly isolated and solved. This will reduce the number of variables the implementers are trying to handle at any one time; during a time of change, this sort of narrowed scope is crucial.

Devote time and effort to getting the organization's culture ready for the change. A cooperative, forward-thinking collaborative environment among the various disciplines affected by the new system's implementation is not only effective but also represents a growth opportunity for everyone involved. A well-functioning team is paramount in these challenging projects, and team building can

help get the group prepared for productively and successfully working through the inevitable challenges of a system implementation.

Build in and celebrate interdisciplinary coordination, the essential ingredient for a transforming implementation. The promise of HIS and technology is locked in through willingness to redesign processes and workflows as part of the system implementation project, followed by building the new software to support the new, streamlined workflows and processes. This type of effort requires strong interdisciplinary teams to check their egos at the door and work together for the good of the cause. Do not allow the system implementation project to be hijacked by those stuck in their ways, who seek to muscle the implementation to replicate paper-based processes or traditional processes with the new computer system. Workflows are becoming increasingly more integrated, which requires everyone—including IT, management, clinical and business user communities, vendors, and consultants—to coordinate their efforts and cooperate.

HIS leadership, or lack thereof, can make or break HIS implementations. HIS management professionals with appropriate qualities, qualifications, and backgrounds are essential to HIS implementation success. When the HIS plan identifies many projects to be carried out simultaneously, HIS management must be able and willing to run consistent, formal processes for system selection and implementation. Important characteristics of HIS managers include steady HIS governance, independence from vendors, non-favoritism, and egalitarian leadership in selecting systems, determining how they are made available to users, and prioritizing projects. Also important is the ability to minimize risk to the organization by picking reliable HIS software and hardware products and services, and keeping vendors at arm's length. The best interests of patient care and the organization must always remain uppermost in HIS leaders' minds.

🔍 CASE EXAMPLE: STREAMLINING IN ACTION

A large academic teaching hospital in the Midwest redesigned its medication administration process in preparation for a new clinical information system implementation. The original legacy process had 20 steps, including decision trees, handoffs, and additional steps; the redesigned process had only nine steps and fewer handoffs. The hospital's new workflow resulted in a more efficient and effective process for medication administration, an area in which far too many errors occur, which can have devastating effects on patient safety. As the *To Err Is Human* report revealed, these errors tend to occur during handoffs in workflow. The redesign work at the Midwestern hospital resulted in 11 fewer steps and thus fewer opportunities for errors to occur in the medication administration process. The new process was built into the new computer system programs and workflows, and most probably created a better, safer environment for patients. If the software had merely mimicked the then-current, legacy way of doing things, it would not have simplified the process, saved time, reduced the potential for errors, or moved the organization forward toward its desired future state of safer care. The end result was only possible through interdepartmental cooperation: with the collaboration and hard work of physicians, nurses, pharmacists, informaticists, supply chain personnel, process redesign experts, technology staff, trainers, other SMEs, and project management, the new nine-step process became reality. The lesson is clear: nurture collaboration, courage, and unselfish attitudes in process redesign work, insist on cooperative approaches, ditch the urge to hold on to legacy processes, address toxic mindsets, and use HIS implementation to support safer, streamlined workflows (**FIGURE 8.18**).

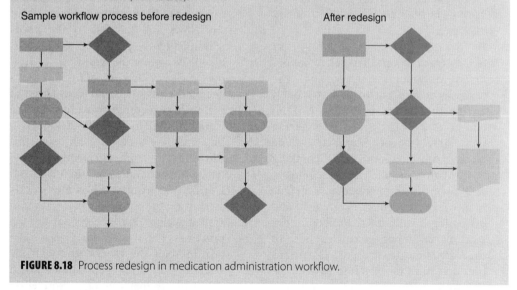

Sample workflow process before redesign   After redesign

FIGURE 8.18 Process redesign in medication administration workflow.

Parting Thoughts About Implementation

- *"Development begins where you are."* This quote (whose source is unknown) seems so obvious, but often when launching a plan or project, we can become so focused on where we are going that we forget that we must begin where we are. That is the starting point and anything that is implemented must be so from that point of origin, training, and culture. What is perhaps most important is that it is often easy to forget where the thought processes are of the people who we are expecting to adapt to such a new system and workflow, and where they are in their work and knowledge base. As much as we might want to change this fact, we cannot. They see things the way they see them. The current state of HIS is the place from which we must venture out to make our way to the desired, future HIS state; we cannot just take a leap and land in the new place. We must acknowledge the starting point of people, processes, and technologies, and build the migration path to the new place *from there*. The starting point skills, ideas, comfort zones, processes, or perspectives are what they are, and awareness of this starting point is the first step to understanding the task at hand to implement a new HIS. But if we get on point with them, acknowledge the current state, and then present a path to the goal, others will likely be much more amenable to joining the effort.

- *Do not turn over one shovel of dirt in constructing this new HIS "house" unless you know the whole plan.* The best way to run out of budget money, or flub up a design, is to start work on one part of a big plan without having thoroughly thought through the whole plan from beginning to end. "Thinking it through" includes interdisciplinary, well-documented requirements definition, writing the entire plan down, and discussing it with others to obtain their reaction and input (essential fodder of the HIS Strategic Plan). It also means breaking down the plan into its composite project parts and making an honest budget estimate and projection for each of those projects for approval so that the organization can live within its means. An HIS strategy and plan, then, must be thought through from beginning (meaning the current state) to end (meaning

the desired future state) before launching into the first project of a multiyear effort. Enough will be changing around you as it is—everything you *can* understand about this whole plan, you *should*.

- *Software systems "out of the box" are raw conglomerations of thousands of capabilities, none of which, at the project's outset, have yet been shaped to conform to a cohesive whole or to the specific organization's characteristics and desired workflows for key processes.* This shaping takes place during the system design and build portions of the project. When viewing a vendor demonstration, take heed: that is a canned presentation, running off of their laptop, not connected to any real or live system anywhere. It is not apparent during these demos that software packages from vendors consist of raw and unshaped features and functions that need to be programmed into cogent workflows and tailored to the needs identified by the project team responsible for designing the workflows to support each key process. Many questions need to be answered and ideas tested to define these requirements and shape the workflow designs for each organization implementing a new system using this software. This applies to any type of system, whether clinical or administrative. During this process, it becomes starkly evident that the people participating in system design "own" the system and the processes, not the vendor. It is a mistake to allow the vendor to design the workflow for the organization—which is not to say that vendor personnel do not have good ideas, cannot suggest workflow innovations, or should not share what has worked at other organizations. To the contrary, great gains can be realized through collaboration with other organizations using the same vendor's software package, especially via user groups. Nevertheless, the system ownership must reside with those inside the organization implementing the system. Design of the system and workflow must be driven internally by people who are accountable for quality patient care and functional business processes. When systems are activated, the end users should recognize what they are being asked to use to care for patients or perform their administrative responsibilities.

Summary

The implementation of an HIS Strategic Plan requires intense planning including the HIS Strategic Plan and HIS Strategic Initiatives, project management, successful system selection and contract negotiations, organized introduction of the new system into the organization, and ongoing support, maintenance, and enhancement for the long life of that system. The HIS Strategic Plan, along with the HIS Planning Framework and four-box quadrants, provides the guideposts for deciding which systems and technology should be implemented, and in what order. The HIS Strategic Plan also cannot be implemented without being broken down into a series of manageable Phases, Initiatives, each of which has Initiatives and Projects that allow the organization to build the complex enterprise HIS architecture in manageable chunks, and in the proper order, beginning with the foundational infrastructure (Phase I), basic core systems (Phase II), and then more advanced capabilities (Phase III). Viewing each portfolio, objective, and activity through the lens of "Phases" can help break this enormous undertaking into bite-sized chunks and keep the work on task. System selections must take the three areas

of vendor capability and relationship into account before a vendor can be deemed worthy of spending the organization's precious resources on these expensive and taxing projects: usability/features and functions, technology, and business relationship including satisfactory contract terms and conditions. HIS, services, and technologies procured from vendors must be accompanied and preceded by a careful negotiation process, in accordance with the HIS contract guidelines. Process redesign expertise and project management competency become key organizational capabilities when it comes to HIS, often resulting in the establishment of a PMO in larger organizations. Implementation of EHR systems is a uniquely high priority in healthcare organizations, demanding a comprehensive, multidisciplinary effort from all facets of the organization. Implementation is interdisciplinary, challenging work that defies organizational sophistication, resource availability, and prowess. It can be a humbling experience. But armed with the right understanding of what is involved and how to think about it, health professionals can successfully collaborate and implement new HIS.

These transforming projects are linked together through the HIS Strategic Plan, creating abundant opportunity for the organization to achieve its strategic aims and improve its clinical and business processes. Many lessons can be learned—in vendor product surveillance, sharing with organizations, and preparation before and along the way—to improve the probability of success in these implementations. In the end, few things are more satisfying in the world of HIS and technology than achieving the hard-fought goal of implementing a new system and witnessing the improvements to clinical and business efficiency and effectiveness that result from a successful implementation.

Key Terms

Basic EHR system
Centers for Medicare &
    Medicaid Services (CMS)
Comprehensive EHR
    system
Current systems review
Enterprise resource planning
    (ERP)
Implementation

Master patient
    index (MPI)
Milestone payment structure
Network infrastructure
    Initiative
Project management
Project managers (PMs)
Project management office
    (PMO)

Request for Information
    (RFI)
Request for Proposal
    (RFP)
Strategic Initiatives
Strategic Plan Phases
Strategic Plan Stages
Subject matter experts
    (SMEs)

Discussion Questions

1. What are the important elements of implementing an HIS Strategic Plan?
2. Project management expertise can be applied across many types of projects. What are the tradeoffs of generic project management versus project management specific to a certain area, such as EHR system implementation?
3. What elements are most important to a successful HIS implementation? Include your thoughts on a sound HIS Strategic Plan, project management

expertise, good HIS contracting, organizational readiness, and other factors.
4. Has the HITECH MU program been a success in meeting its original objectives? Why or why not?
5. What are some reasons for HIS implementation failures? What can organizations do to prevent these points of failure?
6. What do you think is success in HIS implementation? What do you think is failure?

References

Adjerid, I., Adler-Milstein, J., & Angst, C. M. (2016, April 14). Reducing medicare spending through electronic information exchange: The roles of incentives and exchange maturity. *SSRN*. Retrieved from https://papers.ssrn.com/sol3/papers.cfm?abstract_id=2765098

Adler-Milstein, J., DesRoches, C. M., Kravolec, P., Foster, G., Worzala, C., Charles, D., ... Jha, A. K. (2015, December). Electronic health record adoption in US hospitals: Progress continues, but challenges persist. *Health Affairs*. Retrieved from www.ncbi.nlm.nih.gov/pubmed/26561387

Adler-Milstein, J., Holmgren, A. J., Kravolec, P., Worzala, C., Searcy, T., & Patel, V. (2017, August 22). Electronic health record adoption in US Hospitals: The mergence of a digital "advanced use" divide. *Journal of the American Medical Informatics Association*. Retrieved from https://academic.oup.com/jamia/article/24/6/1142/4091350

Ammenwerth, E., Graber, S., Herrmann, G., Bürkle, T., & König, J. (2003). Evaluation of health information systems: Problems and challenges. Research Group Assessment of Health Information Systems, University for Health Informatics and Technology, Tyrol. Retrieved from www.ncbi.nlm.nih.gov/pubmed/14519405

Beeson, K. (2017, September 12). EHR implementation plan: Your 8-step checklist. *EHR in Practice*. Retrieved from www.ehrinpractice.com/ehr-implementation-plan.html

Berinatos, S. (2003, February 25). All systems down. *Computer World*. Retrieved from www.computerworld.com/article/2581420/disaster-recovery/all-systems-down.html

Bresnick, J. (2014, June 9). Why do so many hospital EHR implementations continue to fail? *EHR Intelligence*. Retrieved from https://ehrintelligence.com/news/why-do-so-many-hospital-ehr-implementations-continue-to-fail

DesRoches, C. M., Charles, D., Furukawa, M. F., Joshi, M. S., Kravolec, P., Mostashari, F., … Jha, A. K. (2013, August). Adoption of electronic health records grows rapidly, but fewer than half of US hospitals had at least a basic system in 2012. *Health Affairs*. doi:10.1377/hlthaff.2013.0308

Discenza, R., & Forman, J. B. (2007). *Seven causes of project failure: How to recognize them and how to initiate project recovery*. Paper presented at PMI Global Congress 2007—North America, Atlanta, GA. Newtown Square, PA: Project Management Institute. Retrieved from www.pmi.org/learning/library/seven-causes-project-failure-initiate-recovery-7195

Henricks, W. H. (2011, February 11). "Meaningful use" of electronic health records and its relevance to laboratories and pathologists. *Journal of Pathology Informatics*. Retrieved from www.ncbi.nlm.nih.gov/pmc/articles/PMC3049251/

Henry, J., Pylypchuk, Y., Searcy, T., & Patel, V. *Adoption of electronic health record systems among U.S. non-federal acute care hospitals: 2018–2015*. (2016, May). The Office of the National Coordinator for Health Information Technology. Retrieved from https://dashboard.healthit.gov/evaluations/data-briefs/non-federal-acute-care-hospital-ehr-adoption-2008-2015.php#figure2

HIMSS Usability Task Force. (2011). *Promoting usability in health organizations: Initial steps and progress toward a healthcare usability maturity model*. Retrieved from www.himss.org/files/HIMSSorg/content/files/HIMSS_Promoting_Usability_in_Health_Org.pdf.

Jha, A. K., Burke, M. F., DesRoches, C. M., Joshi, M. S., Kralovec, P. D., Campbell, E. G., & Buntin, M. B. (2011). *Progress toward meaningful use: Hospitals' adoption of electronic health records*. Harvard School of Public Health, Department of Health Policy and Management. Retrieved from www.ncbi.nlm.nih.gov/pubmed/2221677

Jha, A. K., DesRoches, C. M., Kravolec, P. D., & Joshi, M. S. (2010). A progress report on electronic health records in U.S. hospitals. *Health Affairs*. Retrieved from www.ncbi.nlm.nih.gov/pubmed/20798168

Landro, L. (2018, February 25). What the hospitals of the future look like. *The Wall Street Journal*. Retrieved from www.wsj.com/articles/what-the-hospitals-of-the-future-look-like-1519614660

Office of the National Coordinator for Health Information Technology. (2016, December). *Office-based physician electronic health record adoption: Health IT Quick-Stat #50*. Retrieved from www.dashboard.healthit.gov/quickstats/pages/physician-ehr-adoption-trends.php

Pearl, R. M. (2017, June 15). What health systems, hospitals, and physicians need to know about implementing electronic health records. *Harvard Business Review*. Retrieved from https://hbr.org/2017/06/what-health-systems-hospitals-and-physicians-need-to-know-about-implementing-electronic-health-records

PMBOK. (2008). *PMBOK guide: A guide to the Project Management Body of Knowledge* (4th ed., p. 12). Newton Square, PA: Project Management Institute.

Snell, E. (2018, May 21). How increasing EHR adoption, HIE use fuels healthcare industry. *EHR Intelligence*. Retrieved from https://ehrintelligence.com/news/how-increasing-ehr-adoption-hie-use-fuels-healthcare-industry

Stanford Medicine. (2018, September). White paper: The future of electronic health records. *Stanford Medicine*. Retrieved from http://med.stanford.edu/content/dam/sm/ehr/documents/SM-EHR-White-Papers_v12.pdf

The Office of the National Coordinator for Health Information Technology. (n.d.). *Basic EHR adoption among children's and psychiatric hospitals is significantly lower than general medicine hospitals*. Retrieved from https://dashboard.healthit.gov/evaluations/data-briefs/non-federal-acute-care-hospital-ehr-adoption-2008-2015.php#figure3

SECTION IV

Harvesting the Fruits of Your Labors

© Kheng Guan Toh/ShutterStock, Inc.

CHAPTER 9

Adopting New Technologies

You never change things by fighting the existing reality. To change something, build a new model that makes the existing model obsolete.

Buckminster Fuller

LEARNING OBJECTIVES

By the end of this chapter the student will be able to:

- Understand why new technologies are adopted and what the potential pitfalls are.
- Develop an awareness of the value and trade-offs of evolving Health Information Systems (HIS) and technology.
- Apply Rogers's Theory of Diffusion of Innovation to adoption of new technology and HIS.
- Create a culture for the successful adoption of new technologies and systems.
- Describe the importance of the user interface (UI) and user experience (UX).
- Describe and understand new and existing data sources.
- Explain the levels of automation achievable in electronic health record (EHR) adoption.
- Be aware of unintended consequences associated with the introduction of new technologies into clinical care and administrative processes.
- Emphasize technology, HIS, and digital health education for health professionals.
- Discuss health profession education as it relates to HIS.
- Understand the importance of employing HIS technology standards.

▶ Introduction

Embracing innovation involves a number of key factors and, certainly in health care today, HIS and technologies play a significant role. In order to innovate, the industry must seize opportunities to improve on current, mainstream technologies and build on them: better UI and UX for our providers using EHR systems, greater patient engagement, solid security, data controlled by owners, and the ability to deliver on the promise of health information technology. These innovations will lead to excellent clinical and business outcomes and improved health for patients and populations. As demonstrated by the HIS Model, new technologies and HIS must be anticipated, piloted, tested, and adapted to. In most cases, new HIS must fit in with existing HIS: rare indeed is the unicorn invention, the new, stand-alone capability that can exist on its own or in an isolated fashion and still add value to health care.

In this chapter, we will explore why new technologies and systems are needed, the risks and benefits adoption of such new processes brings, and the tools and mind-sets that help adoption succeed.

▶ The Context of HIS Innovation

Innovation in health care is borne of forces driving change in health care: unsustainable costs, the move to value-based care and reimbursement, and patient-centric consumerism. These trends push healthcare organizations, providers, and payers to seek technology-driven solutions as they seek to adapt to new business models, respond to value-based reimbursement methods, meet evolving consumer expectations based on services and products they experience in other areas of their lives, and become more efficient and effective in the process. To do so, healthcare organizations and providers must ascend steep learning curves as they try new methods and find ones that work. A lot is at stake as providers and organizations try, fail, and learn, and in some cases make significant financial and cultural bets on new technologies, directions, and solutions. The lessons and methods presented in earlier chapters in this text provide important structure to making sure these investments are tied directly to capabilities and activities that will propel the organization to its desired future state and successful achievement of its strategies.

New Technologies and Existing Problems

It is easy to get swept up in technology hype, whether or not the use case or business case for a new system is clear. It's best to try to avoid the love of new technology for newness sake and remember that a well-thought-through workflow supported by less-than cutting-edge technology that creates safe care or efficient business processes is better than new technology thrown at a problem that doesn't extend to the goals of the enterprise. With that in mind, we must ask the question, "Why do new technologies matter?"

While this chapter is not about the problems of current HIS, it is useful to consider persistent challenges as we begin the conversation about adopting new technologies: the problems that we are searching to solve may meet their match in adopting new technologies and HIS. For some examples of deep-rooted problems in health care today, consider the following issues that healthcare organizations, providers, and patients wrestle with every day, to their detriment:

1. Security breaches and ransoming are rampant and completely out of control. This exacts immeasurable harm on organizations and individuals.

2. In the past 10 years, billions of dollars and hard work have been invested in difficult-to-use technologies and systems dominated by assembly-line workflows and profit-minded vendors, not with the end-user (clinician) experience nor ease of use in mind. This has resulted in wasted clinician time and goodwill as well as underutilized EHRs. EHR system UIs and UXs are seriously subpar to the point that many providers are so disillusioned they are, in many cases, considering leaving their practice—in fact, many are doing just that, at great cost to their dreams of helping people and to society overall.

3. Patients remain on the outskirts of the very activities and information intended to help them. Information is controlled by organizations

and, in many cases, payers, not by people and patients whose lives and bodies it reflects.

4. The costs of these HIS and technologies are a hefty burden for organizations and society to bear.

When considering adopting a new technology, always begin with the same discipline and planning processes discussed in earlier chapters. Consider what creates value for organizations, providers, and patients.

▶ The Value of Adopting New Technologies

Realizing the expected benefits from adopting a new system or technology can be an elusive goal that requires strong and persistent leadership. Historically, while the benefits to be achieved from HIS and technology have been debated, the "promise" of HIS and technology has certainly been widely touted. For example, the Meaningful Use (MU) criteria of the Health Information Technology for Economic and Clinical Health Act (HITECH) Act of 2009 for EHR implementations and incentive payments were expected to spawn the achievement of HIS benefits that fall into three categories: (1) improving the accuracy, timeliness, and availability of health information to care providers; (2) improving access to information, thereby allowing providers to better anticipate the diagnostic and health needs of their patients and share this information among other providers as appropriate; and (3) empowering patients to more actively participate in their health care and wellness, and have access and input to their health data (HealthIT.com., n.d.). Reality has proved that achieving these benefits has been too far a reach for many organizations, and for those who achieve the functionality associated with the promised benefits of performance improvement, clinical decision support, and patient engagement, this requires a longer journey and more funding

than most imagined or planned at the outset. The discrepancy between reality and plans also paints a picture of what is meant by the challenge of "achieving the value or promise" of HIS and technology in health care.

Realizing Value

Regardless of the type of new technology used, the value in HIS and technology aligns around four areas: strategic alignment, architectural excellence and balance, realization of intended system benefits, and HIS services delivery. Here, we look at four areas critical to **value realization**: strategic alignment, architectural considerations, post-implementation evaluation, and excellence in HIS service delivery.

Strategic Alignment

When the HIS and technology plan directly supports the intended direction of the organization and, likewise, it does not take the organization's momentum in any different direction, the chance of success drastically increases. This harkens back to the earlier concept of creating a balanced HIS portfolio so that the various needs of the organization are addressed more or less equivalently by the components of the HIS architecture. HIS and technology are expensive, strategic investments, and misalignment of these resources and "hardwired" clinical and business processes would be disastrous for the healthcare organization. Clearly, then, strategic alignment of HIS plans and organizational strategy is essential to the short- and long-term well-being of the organization and, by extension, the community it serves.

Architectural Considerations

Architectural excellence and balance means that the HIS and technology are designed and built according to proper HIS architectural principles and practices. This builds on the notion of strategic alignment and emphasizes proper construction of the HIS and technology architecture. It means building systems according to open systems standards, not proprietary technologies that do not integrate or interface easily. Also, systems must be designed to meet the HITECH Act's MU criteria, data and security requirements, and technical standards.

Post-Implementation Evaluation

The third element of HIS value realization involves verifying that the implementation's intended objectives are actually being achieved. Of course, this implies serious interdisciplinary dialogue among those involved in the implementation as well as those responsible for overall organizational performance. Post-implementation evaluation helps make the connection between newly automated workflows and processes with the benefits to be achieved. It points to processes or workflows that have the opportunity to be streamlined through aggressive process redesign. Disciplined metrics associated with desired yet realistic objectives and measurement of their accomplishment or failure are the only way to measure, manage, and know the progression of HIS and technology. In this way, the organization can realize the hoped-for value and benefits from the investment of time, money, and talent in that implementation.

Excellence in HIS Service Delivery

Lastly, high-quality HIS and technology services delivery must never be overlooked. It is wonderful to talk about, plan for, and invest in the implementation of new HIS and technology for healthcare organizations, but new systems do not work by magic. At the end of the day, having properly trained HIS staff plentifully available to support the new system and end users through their struggle to adapt to a new HIS is crucial to ongoing clinical and business activities. Remember, we are not talking about building widgets here—we are talking about taking care of people in their most vulnerable

state, as patients needing lifesaving healthcare services and support. This topic of HIS service delivery is covered in-depth in Chapter 7.

The HIS Value Proposition

Few true cost/benefit studies have been published regarding EHR systems, comparatively speaking, considering the hundreds of thousands that have been implemented over the years. One exception is the U.S. Department of Veterans Affairs (VA), which is well known to have implemented a very successful EHR and established a track record of leadership in EHR adoption over the last several decades. In a comparison of the IT investment and value derived at the VA versus private-sector healthcare systems based on estimated costs and benefits, it was shown that the VA spent proportionately more than private-sector health systems but achieved higher adoption and quality of care, with the value of the VA's IT investment estimated at $3.09 billion net of cumulative costs (Byrne et al., 2010). This methodology provides a framework for estimating the benefits and costs of HIS resulting from the federal health IT stimulus efforts as well. The VA estimates it costs approximately $68 per patient per day to build, support, and maintain the department's system. This amount is roughly the cost of a laboratory test; thus, if the system saves the organization from performing just one duplicated laboratory test per patient per day, the system pays for itself and the cost is justified in the organization's eye (Caroline, 2012).

Realizing the benefits of HIS and technology depends on creating a deliberate, organized system implementation focused on defining the benefits the organization hopes to achieve through the adoption of the new system, broken down into measurable, realistic objectives for each benefit or goal. These objectives (steps toward each major goal) must be set in ways that recognize the organization's starting point in pursuit of its desired outcomes and must be achievable within the established time frames;

once accomplished, the objectives must then be reset to new levels. If the targeted benefits are too lofty, nonspecific, or unrealistic to accomplish in the designated time frame, they will be ignored or avoided and progress will be thwarted. An important, ever true working principle is to keep targeted objectives realistic and within reach. Otherwise busy workers, facing the prospect of trying to implement a new HIS and change their work processes while still performing their normal duties, can easily become discouraged or overwhelmed. It is better to go a little more slowly and make steady progress in the changeover and implementation process than risk such overload of employees. Benefits can be identified and measured in numerous areas, such as patient, provider, or employee satisfaction, clinical quality, efficiency and patient safety, sharing and reporting of electronic information and data, patient education and prevention, and cost savings (HIMSS, n.d.-c).

Use Technology to Simplify Processes and Access to Information

The increasing complexity of information compels us to involve key subject matter experts (SMEs) and key stakeholders in introducing any new technology, underscoring the fact that this is not about introducing technology for technology's sake, but to improve something.

Informatics techniques to evaluate and dissect the work and processes of decision making can improve the decision maker's ability to move forward in the clinical or business process to help the patient or organization. Intuitively, we know that *more* information is *not* necessarily better. The ways that the quantity and quality of information available to a decision maker can be optimized are the subject of a great deal of work in informatics, with roots in information science and its intersection with clinical medicine. In complex

situations, which is increasingly the norm in medicine and healthcare settings, people typically choose a less complex option than they would otherwise decline if fewer options were available. Thus, the greater the complexity of a situation and the more options available to a decision maker, the more likely the decision maker is to gravitate toward a simpler option—and paradoxically, the more options available to contemplate or digest, the more attractive the status quo option becomes. Despite all the development of more sophisticated diagnostic tests and sources of biomedical information supported by new devices and other sources of data, under the assumption that getting all relevant information to a decision maker is wise, it turns out that we may be detracting from that person's ability to process relevant information because of excessive complexity and volume of information. If not properly introduced to the knowledge worker, more information sometimes defeats its very purpose—to assist those using the information to make better decisions.

Additionally, findings reflecting on clinical decision making nuances indicate a dynamic tension between policy or group-level considerations and the decision making of a physician when treating an individual. The clinician is more likely to exhaust a broader array of options when treating an individual than when looking at the same information across a group (Chaudhry et al., 2006). Many of these tendencies or nuances occur in clinical decision making, creating an impetus for informatics researchers to find out how, why, and when people are influenced differently by varying amounts and presentation formats of information. The intricacies of the relationships between people, systems, and information are profound when one considers the massive rollout of EHR systems and other forms of information availability in health care. This is not to say that the increased availability of information for clinical decision making is necessarily either better or worse, but evidence strongly suggests it will be different.

Adopting new technology takes on characteristics of the different types of work it is applied to—work done by clinical knowledge workers such as physicians, nurses, therapists, researchers, public health experts, and others. As long ago as 1990, David Eddy asserted, "The complexity of modern medicine exceeds the inherent limitations of the unaided human mind." This is drastically compounded as an issue since that time. It is known that there is too much new information being produced every year for physicians, nurses, and others working in health to keep up with using traditional methods—that is, by reading professional peer-reviewed journals and other publications. There simply is not enough time in the day or the capacity in the human mind to hold and process all of this information and still perform one's daily work. Thus, clinical decision support, artificial intelligence (AI), and knowledge workers who understand informatics and process design and integration become alchemists in their work to manage the science and art of introducing new technology into already complex clinical and business processes, which begs the question, "How much information is the right amount?"

Thus, the science and art of adopting new technologies means bringing to bear problem solving skills in the content and structure of data and information as well as the application of new technologies. This requires nurturing and investing in SME in disciplines and departments being automated—this is not a job for the IT department alone. Understanding how new technologies can be adopted *to solve problems* involves not only technology but also workflows and processes, data content for key performance indicators, measurements related to achieving desired outcomes, and discovering how new technology gets integrated with clinical workflows. These are the ways to improve efficiency, effectiveness and improved, more satisfying work processes and

results. Clearly, we have moved in the wrong direction with our current iterations of EHR systems. When we think of the variety of types of specialized work this includes, the challenge we face reflects its importance: making sure that the data and information presented to clinicians and others are accurate, timely, and appropriate while streamlining workflows, resulting in a choice between confident decisions or confusion and frustration.

At the end of the day, new processes and information sources must also be carefully conceived and designed so that hopefully the new technologies enable new, streamlined, and better ways of delivering care and providing service. That is when adopting new technology makes sense.

▶ Rogers's Theory of Diffusion of Innovation: Adoption of New HIS and Technology

I believe we're on a series of "change curves"—one for adopting the technology and another for actually using it.
—Mike Painter (2013)

Make a better mousetrap, and the world will beat a path to your door.
—Ralph Waldo Emerson*

For all its virtues, health care has been markedly slower than other industries (often industries with simpler processes and fewer complexities) to use information technology ubiquitously to accomplish its work. Such use

---

* https://en.wikipedia.org/wiki/Build_a_better_mousetrap,_and_the_world_will_beat_a_path_to_your_door

of HIS and technology is called **adoption**, meaning that the providers and healthcare industry change the ways that clinical care is provided and the work of health care is done. To adopt disruptive HIS and technology also means that organizations adapt to automated work processes—a huge change from the paper-based processes and workflows that typically take much longer than anticipated with even the most conservative of estimates. Adding to the dynamic nature of this change, adoption of HIS and technology occurs amidst the hustle, bustle, and stress of today's dynamic healthcare environments, which are normally fast-moving, unpredictable settings of high priority to the patients and clinicians involved. As far as the drive to develop business intelligence and analytics in health care is concerned, the ability to use information to adapt to changes in the environment quickly is essential—whether responding to changes in the health status of a population, or to shifts in the major regulations governing health care, or to competitive pressures in the healthcare marketplace. The adoption of HIS and technology within a highly dynamic backdrop of complex relationships, clinical advancements, and human realities takes on special meaning and risks. And, of course, there is always the added layer of complex change in the development and evolution of technology itself: new types

of hardware, software, wireless devices, telecommunications, and biomedical technologies are being launched every day. It is no wonder, then, that when the question "Why does it take so long for health care to change or adapt?" is asked, the answer is often that health care and the adoption of HIS and technology are more complex than the environments found in other industries or lines of work.

Adoption Patterns

Before discussing the history and current status of adoption of HIS and technology in the U.S., it is necessary to explore the term "adoption" and the theory behind it. The adoption of HIS and technology is thought to follow the pattern of the diffusion of innovation and adoption of disruptive technologies, as described by Rogers in 1962 in his landmark book, *Diffusion of Innovations*. This book was published when computer systems and other new electronic technologies capable of "disrupting" traditional work processes were being developed and introduced with increasing regularity into our world (Rogers, 1963). Studied by many, Rogers's theory is as much about social structures and communication as it is about technologies. The **adoption curve** (**FIGURE 9.1**) Rogers describes has five groups or segments that play roles in the adoption of disruptive,

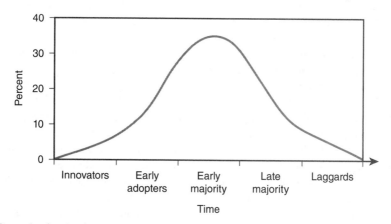

FIGURE 9.1 Rogers's adoption/innovation curve.
Data from Rogers, E. M. (1963). Rogers' adoption/innovation curve. In: *Diffusion of innovations*. New York: Free Press.

new technologies such as HIS into an organization or other setting: Innovators (2.5 percent), Early Adopters (13.5 percent), Early Majority (34 percent), Late Majority (34 percent), and Laggards (16 percent) (Robinson, 2009).

Innovators are the initiators of the change—the curious, restless, brave types who enjoy being on the cutting edge, who are comfortable with uncertainty and failure, and who always want to try something new, get a new tool, or experiment with new methods to do their work. Innovators are important communicators to others in the organization about the attempted change or modernization.

Early Adopters (a term often used in many venues other than technology adoption) are often respected opinion leaders of the organization, accepting of change and new ideas, who use the experience of the Innovators to inform their decision to attempt the adoption of the innovation. They are often knowledgeable and savvy—people who are interested in trying new technologies and new ways of doing things, but are not reckless in how they approach the innovation. Rather, they make carefully thought-out, well-informed decisions.

The *Early Majority* is the group of careful, cooperative, attentive people who embrace the innovation as part of a move toward a positive change and the desired direction of the leaders. They have strong connections with their compatriots and are satisfied to observe the experience and listen to the communications of the Early Adopters and Innovators, basing their decisions to embrace the change on others' opinions and input. While they are careful about change, they adapt more quickly than average.

The *Late Majority* consists of people who will eventually adjust to the change or use the new technology, but usually only after most others have already done so, and when it becomes more trouble to not change than to change. Late Majority members can be the skeptics of the organization, with low tolerance for risk and uncertainty.

Laggards are described as traditionalists, resistant to change, who prefer the old ways of doing things. They adapt to the innovation only when it has become the norm and is not seen as complying with anything radical or drastic (Diffusion of Innovation Theory, 2012; Rogers, 1995).

The adoption of innovation is led to the point of Early Majority adoption by the actions and communications of opinion leaders, meaning the Early Adopters and Innovators of the group. This achievement of Early Majority adoption is also popularly referred to as the tipping point, sociologically rooted in the more gradual progression through the phases described by Rogers. Recent further interpretation of Rogers's adoption curve and diffusion theory speaks to the "chasm" between the Early Adopters and the Early Majority, noting that as the progression of change moves through these categories, jumping across this chasm is very difficult, much more so than surviving the Innovator and Early Adopter phases (Spagnulo, 2008). Getting past this chasm to the point where the change gains critical mass momentum is where many innovations fade or fail, and making it to the Early Majority phase is seen as the true determinate of widespread adoption and recognition of the change as the "new normal."

With the backdrop of Rogers's diffusion of innovation theory in mind, we next review the lengthy evolution and adoption of HIS and technology in health care—a process that has been actively under way since the 1960s. Along the way, we will draw some connections between and insights into the theory of diffusion of innovation, and the adoption of HIS and technology in health care.

Rogers gives us timeless insight into the sociocultural aspects of adopting any type of new technology, with a strong reality check that no matter what type of incredible new capability might be developed, it takes time to put it into practice. Some segments of the end-user community will never adopt the new innovation—thus, the sociology and culture of organizations must change, as well as the training, orientation, mind-set, education, understanding of how to best use a new technology in a clinical, business, or technical discipline. Willingness of end users—to change how they do their work, interact with others, and practice their profession, whether they are patients, professionals, technologists, caregivers, or administrators—is critical.

▶ Historical Sources of HIS and Technology Innovation

Early innovations and documented advancements in the use of HIS and technology over the course of the past 25 or so years occurred at a small number of noteworthy healthcare organizations: Intermountain Health Care (IHC) (Utah), U.S. Department of Veterans Affairs, Regenstrief Institute (Indianapolis, Indiana), Partners Health (Boston, Massachusetts), El Camino Hospital (Mountain View, California), and University of Pittsburgh Medical Center (UPMC). In fact, in a comprehensive review of original high-quality literature in HIS and technology from 1995 through 2007, the first four of these organizations published a full 25 percent of all studies of HIS, most of which addressed the use of clinical decision support HIS capabilities and computerized provider order entry (CPOE) (Chaudhry et al., 2006; Goldzweig, Towfigh, Maglione, & Shekelle, 2009). To this list today, we would add Geisinger Health and a few others. The point it, HIS innovation occurs in a handful of organizations whose cultures and capacities are fertile grounds for trying new HIS and technologies and applications. These pioneers blazed the trail, publishing research results for other healthcare organizations to learn from—other organizations that might not have the appetite for risk or innovation, or the HIS expertise, needed to accomplish this type of advancement. Many healthcare organizations continually struggle to maintain even the slimmest of positive financial margins, so the innovation

process and investment in pilot projects in HIS and technology or inventing new ways of doing work are often left to a handful of organizations whose cultures and bottom lines are better suited to tackle these types of high-risk research and development efforts.

▶ The History of HIS Innovation

Since the 1960s, hospital data processing departments, clinical computer laboratories, home offices, garages, and other humble, dedicated offices have all been origination points of innovation. *During those early beginnings,* the few hospitals able to afford expensive mainframe hardware and programmers to write software developed the early healthcare computer application software. These huge machines required massive infrastructure for power and cooling and the early software applications focused primarily on the accounting and financial applications arena. Generally accepted accounting principles (GAAP) and the "data" of finance lent itself easily to HIS.

In the 1970s, with the advent of air-cooled minicomputers, things began to change. The first vendors emerged to support hospital financial software. Many hospitals that made the independent decision to invest in hardware, programmers, and data centers developed much of their own software for financial, patient accounting, and order communications systems. This early HIS work gave rise to the first HIS professional organizations: Hospital Information Systems Sharing Group (HISSG) and Electronic Computing Hospital Organization (ECHO). These hospital members developed, shared, and collaborated on software among themselves. A culture of innovation flourished.

The first HIS were really extensions of charge-capture systems for patient billing system purposes. The first comprehensive medical information system (akin to today's EHR systems) was designed and built through a federal grant from Lockheed Martin; it was eventually commercialized and named Technicon, and it was initially implemented at El Camino Hospital in Mountain View, California, in 1971. The people who developed this software came out of the aerospace industry and worked with those who understood hospitals and health care. Also in the 1970s, Science Applications International Corporation (SAIC)—a large, successful employee-owned company with expertise in information systems work for the defense industry and federal government—developed an early clinical information system for VA hospitals. (This system was replaced in 1982 with a newer version system called Veterans Health Information Systems and Technology Architecture [VistA], an integrated EHR that is currently in use in more than 1400 VA hospitals and ambulatory clinics across the U.S. [World VistA, n.d.].)

The 1980s ushered in the era of the minicomputer: Hewlett-Packard, Digital Equipment Corporation, and IBM developed highly competitive air-cooled minicomputers which required less infrastructure and made the business of HIS more affordable. As the market grew, vendors came into being, many commercializing software that had been developed in hospitals in the 1970s. Some vendors created their own software packages, but that was less common. The early adopters among healthcare providers began to buy and implement computer systems to support their financial systems, and increasingly some ancillary clinical (e.g., laboratory, radiology, pharmacy) and practice management (e.g., registration, scheduling, and billing) systems.

Innovation in Clinical Systems and the EHR

Clinical HIS have their roots in charge-capture systems for patient billing system purposes, rather than systems with functionality truly grounded in clinical care processes. As noted earlier, Technicon developed the first comprehensive medical information system—a system focused on clinical care—in the mid-1970s. The

requirements document for this system reads very much like the requirements documentation for one of today's modern EHR systems. This was truly an innovation that disrupted the healthcare industry. The VistA system, described in depth in Chapter 2, was another early HIS that is still in use today in VA hospitals across the U.S. Specialized niche ancillary clinical systems—such as laboratory, radiology, and pharmacy management—began to emerge especially in the 1980s seeking to provide automation of profitable hospital departments such as laboratory, radiology, and pharmacy management. These niche systems often competed to be recognized as "best-of-breed" systems. Also blossoming were physician practice management systems for large medical practices. At this point, software was still very proprietary and hospital programmers would interface the many siloed "in-house" and vendor-provided systems. Initial clinical information systems included "order entry" systems, early versions of CPOE.

In the 1990s, the advent of the Internet transformed healthcare computing, just as it transformed computing in all industries. In lockstep with this disruptive innovation, the federal government enacted the Health Insurance Portability and Accountability Act (HIPAA) to protect the security and privacy of citizens' data in anticipation of the significant increase in use of the Internet along with an increasing scope of electronic systems and technology in healthcare processes (U.S. Department of Health and Human Services, n.d.).

▶ Role of Professional Organizations in Adopting New Technologies

The world of health care includes several organizations that provide professional development for key leadership roles in HIS and technology, clinicians and informatics, vendor and services companies, and healthcare management and administration. These leadership functions cover a wide range of activities, such as designing, provisioning, implementing, using, and improving HIS and technology.

Health Information Management Systems Society

The roots of the **Health Information Management Systems Society (HIMSS)** lie in an organization originally established in 1962 for management engineering professionals in health care called Hospital Management Systems Society (HMSS). HMSS morphed into HIMSS in 1986 as the organization modified its "systems" purpose from a focus on process alone to a focus on information systems. The new focus on information systems represented an opportunistic shift from the more general "systems" and processes that management engineers in health care historically sought to improve by applying their industrial engineering techniques and expertise (HealthTech Wire, n.d.). Thus, the HIMSS was born. It has since evolved into the primary HIS and technology professional organization in the U.S., with a growing international reach.

HIMSS's mission statement expresses a not-for-profit philosophy aimed at developing and advocating for HIS professionals and their roles, in an industry full of highly profitable vendor products. The mission statement implies a commitment to objectivity and the needs of healthcare organizations striving to successfully adopt HIS and technology systems. This stance is necessary given that HIS and technology vendor selections in provider organizations should be made without bias or undue influence. HIMSS seeks to improve health care and patient safety: "HIMSS is a cause-based, not-for-profit organization exclusively focused on providing global leadership for the optimal use of information technology (IT) and management systems for the betterment of healthcare." (HIMSS, n.d.-a).

Worldwide, HIMSS has more than 70,000 individual members; more than two-thirds of those members work in healthcare provider, governmental, and not-for-profit organizations. HIMSS also has more than 600 corporate members and 450 not-for-profit associations as members. It holds annual national and regional meetings, which typically include extensive educational sessions. The organization also maintains an analytics database containing data about use of HIS and technology in provider organizations and publishes reports on HIS and technology including the annual statistics on its electronic medical record (EMR) adoption model. HIMSS operates both regional and international chapters (HIMSS, n.d.-b).

American Health Information Management Association

Originally known as the Association of Record Librarians of North America (ARLNA), the **American Health Information Management Association (AHIMA)** aims to "elevate the standards of clinical records in hospitals and other medical institutions" (AHIMA history, n.d.). This farsighted recognition of the importance of medical record quality to patient care and research underlies the organization's strength today. The American Medical Records Association (AMRA) was founded in 1928 to improve health record quality and provide a professional organization for medical record librarians. Since then, these roles have gradually evolved through the 1960s to the 1990s, when the accreditation title for health information management professionals was changed to Registered Record Administrator (RRA), and eventually updated to Accredited Health Information Administrator (AHIA). AHIMA provides strict accreditation and certification tests as well as processes for achieving and maintaining **Registered Health Information Administrator (RHIA)** accreditation for health information professionals and **Registered Health Information**

Technicians (RHITs) certifications for coders. AHIMA has consistently played a leadership role in the effective management of health data and medical records needed to deliver quality health care to the public (AHIMA facts, n.d.). The professionals accredited by this organization are the managers (RHIAs) and coding experts (RHITs) of health information departments found in hospitals and clinics (traditionally the "medical records department"). They also provide critical skills regarding medical records and EHRs to others in the healthcare and HIS industry such as patients, HIS vendors, payers, researchers, and legal entities. Their responsibilities include proper documentation, and diagnostic and procedure coding of data in the medical records using classification systems and medical terminologies and upholding standards related to clinical activities, administrative functions, and the privacy of protected patient information.

As computerization of health records has occurred gradually over the past few decades, AHIMA has evolved as well to provide education, training, certification, and accreditation for its professionals to achieve expertise in EHR systems plus reporting, medicolegal, research, analysis, and business uses of the data in the medical record for healthcare organizations.

American Medical Informatics Association

The **American Medical Informatics Association (AMIA)** promotes and develops the science and practice of informatics in health care. Its focus is the practice of informatics—the clinical application of health IT and data analytics in health care, with the intent to improve healthcare delivery, practices, and outcomes. Formed in 1989, AMIA is the result of the combination of three organizations with complementary missions: the American Association for Medical Systems and Informatics (AAMSI), the American College of Medical Informatics (ACMI), and the Symposium on Computer Applications in Medical Care (SCAMC) (AMIA, n.d.). Through conferences, education, meetings, research, and policy, AMIA strives to educate, promote, and support the science of five informatics domains: translational bioinformatics, clinical research informatics, clinical informatics, consumer health informatics, and public health informatics.

Alliance for Nursing Informatics

Supported by both AMIA and HIMSS, the **Alliance for Nursing Informatics (ANI)** represents more than 2000 nurses and brings together 18 independent nursing informatics groups. ANI provides leadership and productive relationships between its various nursing informatics organizations with the aim to transform health and health care through nursing informatics (Alliance for Nursing Informatics, n.d.).

The common theme among the organizations described in this section is a devotion to professional development, leadership, and collaboration among those in the HIS and technology-related disciplines. These groups have been in existence for decades and were often formed through a cooperative decision to combine separate, smaller organizations that developed simultaneously during the early years of HIS and technology development. This is analogous to the early development of HIS and technology software, hardware, and services companies—an initial proliferation of products and services with similar purposes eventually merged or were acquired into larger organizations (i.e., big fish eating little fish). Thus, although the development of HIS and technology might seem like a recent, attention-grabbing movement, it is not: it has been under development and in action in healthcare organizations in the U.S. for the past 60 years.

Medical professional organizations promote the development of HIS and technology and its integration into clinical practice. These organizations include the American Medical Association (AMA); Medical Group Management Association (MGMA); American Hospital and Health Network Association (AHA); Health Care Management Association (HFMA); American College of Health Care Executives (ACHE); and other national, state, and international organizations. They provide professional leadership support, and development for those in the clinical disciplines of medicine, nursing, clinical therapies, radiology, laboratory, pharmacy, and others; they have added HIS and technology to their agendas for education, collaboration, research, conferences, and other activities. Leadership provided by these professional associations develops, promotes, and evolves the productive and safe use of HIS and technology in health care through the integration of HIS into the normal activities and research conducted by these professional development organizations.

▶ Impact of New Technologies on Existing HIS

Adoption of new technologies for new or existing use cases has an effect on existing HIS plans and architectures; thus, this adoption must be thought through not only in terms of any new technologies being used but in terms of existing systems, processes, and plans as well. Innovation begins with solving problems and often, in the haste and hype of new technologies, the focus on identifying how the technology solves a problem is either lost or gives way to limited planning to understand how the innovation should fit in with existing technology and HIS, which took great effort, time, and money to implement. You can be certain the massive EHR systems in place now following the flurry of implementation

over the past 15 years is here to stay for the duration, so one must carefully nurture that infrastructure, knitting in new technologies to improve and enhance EHR workflows. That is the ballgame we are in. Carefully plan, using the HIS Planning Framework as the guidepost to enhance, and fix what exists: *do not* plop additional technologies atop the core systems. They must be carefully connected, using the new technology to augment and enrich that which exists. It's always important to carefully plan use cases, using the same interdisciplinary planning processes used for the rest of the HIS portfolio of systems, when integrating new technologies, devices, and data sources into HIS architecture, systems, workflows, and capabilities. Sometimes new technologies are the means to a new use or innovation, and sometimes it is a matter of building upon the HIS that are in place, creating enhancements and new capabilities upon an existing platform. This is where the "journey" of an organization's EHR system or enterprise resource planning (ERP) system comes into play. Great expansion is possible by building upon these core systems, and in health care, the EHR system provides levels of capabilities leading up to paperless clinical environments as described in the next section.

Electronic Medical Record Adoption Model

In addition to the DesRoches and Jha definitions of "basic," "basic with documentation," and "comprehensive" EHR system functionality, another model that defines different levels of EHR adoption is the **Electronic Medical Record Adoption Model (EMRAM)**. EMRAM was developed over a decade ago by HIMSS as part of their analytics division, with the intention of assisting hospitals and outpatient healthcare organizations to measure and track their progress toward more robust EHR systems. This model consists of eight gradually

STAGE	EMR Adoption model cumulative capabilities
7	Complete EMR; external HIE; data analytics, governance, disaster recover, privacy and security
6	Technology enabled medication, blood products, and human milk administration; risk reporting; full CDS
5	Physician documentation using structured templates; intrusion/device protection
4	CPOE with CDS; nursing and allied health documentation; basic business continuity
3	Nursing and allied health documentation; eMAR; role-based security
2	CDR; internal interoperability; basic security
1	Ancillaries-laboratory, pharmacy, and radiology/cardiology information systems; PACS; digital non-DICOM image management
0	All three ancillaries not installed

FIGURE 9.2 EHR adoption stages.

Reproduced from Healthcare Information and Management Systems Society (HIMSS). EMRAM A strategic roadmap for effective EMR adoption and maturity. Retrieved from https://www.himssanalytics.org/sites/himssanalytics/files/HIMSS percent20Analytics percent20EMRAM percent20- percent20web_2.pdf

increasing levels of EMR functionality, beginning with Level 0 (an EHR system without the three main ancillary systems installed, i.e., laboratory, radiology, and pharmacy information systems) to Level 7 (complete EMR, including governance, analytics, external health information exchange (HIE), Disaster Recovery, Privacy and Security capabilities) (**FIGURE 9.2**).

Results of current participants in the program for the approximately 5,500 hospitals participating, as of 2017, are presented in **FIGURE 9.3**.

In 2010, HIMSS introduced EMRAM criteria developed for outpatient organizations in a program called Outpatient EMRAM (O-EMRAM). The eight levels for O-EMRAM are displayed in **FIGURE 9.4**.

The mission of this program is to help provider practices and clinics increase adoption and utility of their EHR systems capabilities. HIMSS has worked with over 45,000 outpatient organizations, and as of 2017, over 5,700 of these have achieved Stage 6 and 3,600 are at Stage 7, the highest levels of EHR adoption (Introducing HIMSS Analytics O-EMRAM, n.d.).

Market Forces

Trends in investments in the health information technology market are indicators of where interest and progress lies. Progress is being made across numerous fronts of investment and, therefore, so is hoped-for technology innovation as displayed in **FIGURE 9.5**. Investment ranges widely, and the list that follows arranges categories of investment from most to least: patient-centric solutions, provider-centric solutions, clinical

STAGE	2017 Q3	2017 Q4
7	6.1%	6.4%
6	32.7%	33.8%
5	33.5%	32.9%
4	10.1%	10.2%
3	12.6%	12.0%
2	1.9%	1.8%
1	1.5%	1.5%
0	1.6%	1.4%
	N: 5,480	N: 5,487

FIGURE 9.3 Percentages of hospitals at EMRAM levels 0–7.

Reproduced from Healthcare Information and Management Systems Society (HIMSS). Retrieved from https://www.dicardiology.com/article/himss-opposes-congress%E2%80%99-call-suspension-ehr-incentive-program

data analytics, spending and revenue analytics, and productivity solutions. Interestingly, investment to help patient-centric technologies as well as spending and revenue analytics are taking off, while the more settled disciplines of provider-centric technologies (think EHR systems) and clinical analytics are diminishing in levels of new money going into them, as those markets are more saturated. Now the vacuum of patient-centric technologies used to engage patients in the management of their own health is a growing market. One could tie this trend to the need to address these things when the patient is between visits to the physician practice or hospital, address population health and chronic care management.

This makes sense, as we are getting to the point of efficiencies in the more traditional areas of work in revenue cycle and productivity, as supported by **FIGURE 9.6** which displays the maturity of various types of HIS and technologies in their adoption. Over time, the maturity of technology applications and organizational expertise needed to capitalize on their use is displayed.

▶ Unintended Consequences of Adoption of New Technologies

Through the efforts of healthcare organizations throughout the U.S., HIS and technology are being increasingly used to achieve safer patient care, greater patient and provider satisfaction, improved efficiency of care, better analytics and reporting through the secondary use of data, and streamlined processes supported by automation. But that is not the whole story. The detection of all the effects of automation has, quite naturally, lagged behind its implementation. Thus, while counting the number of organizations that have implemented HIS and technology, the depth, breadth, and quality of the actual functionality of those systems is less well understood. Additionally, as more research is being conducted on HIS and technology implementation, evidence is emerging that the consequences of introducing these systems into healthcare organizations are not always positive or benign—that, in fact, harm can be attributed in some cases to the ways chosen to automate healthcare processes (HMD, 2012).

Initially, in the zeal to implement EHR systems throughout practices and hospitals in the U.S., the assumption was always that the promise of automating paper records would hold so many benefits (which of course it can)

STAGE	Outpatient EMR adoption capabilities
7	Complete EMR; external HIE; data analytics, governance, disaster recovery
6	Advanced clinical decision support; proactive care management, structured messaging
5	Personal health record, online tethered patient portal
4	CPOE, use of structured data for accessibiliy in EMR and internal and external sharing of data
3	Electronic messaging, computers have replaced paper chart, clinical documentation and clinical decision support
2	Beginning of a CDR with orders and results, computers may be at point-of-care, access to results from outside facilities
1	Desktop access to clinical information, unstructured data, multiple data sources, intra-office/informal messaging
0	Paper chart based

FIGURE 9.4 O-EMRAM: outpatient EMR adoption capabilities.

Reproduced from Healthcare Information and Management Systems Society (HIMSS). O-EMRAM. https://www.himssanalytics.org/sites/himssanalytics/files/image/HIMSS percent20Analytics percent200-EMRAM percent20Criteria percent20sheet.pdf

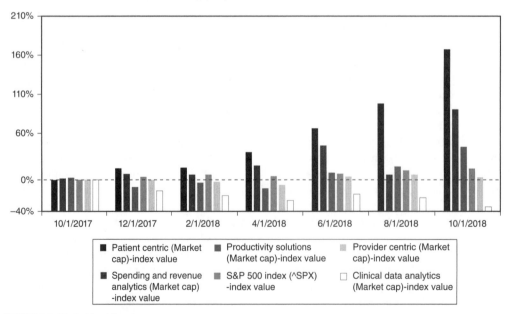

FIGURE 9.5 Digital health subsectors.

Data from Novahill Partners LLC.

that the negative effects or difficulties for some more than others in successfully implementing simply weren't anticipated or known. Once enough time passed for results to be measured and research to be conducted on the range of impacts of EHR systems on outcomes, first anecdotes and then reports and research have reflected a range of outcomes and detected harm as well as benefit due to these implementations. Coined "unintended consequences,"

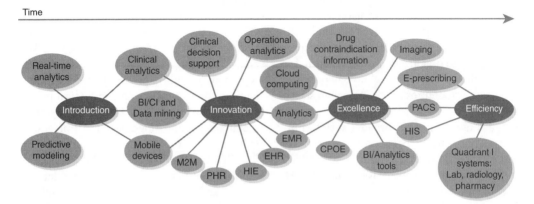

FIGURE 9.6 HIS and technology adoption map.

🔍 CASE EXAMPLE: CHALLENGING FINANCIAL EFFECTS OF EHR IMPLEMENTATIONS

In our zeal to implement new EHR systems, it is important to present the other side of the realities of implementations for organizations. Vanderbilt University has historically enjoyed a leadership role in medical education surrounding use of EHR systems, in large part because Vanderbilt hospital had a home-grown EHR system, which could be appropriately tailored for medical education as well as patient care, while maintaining compliance for HIPAA and other regulations. This bolstered the education of medical students compared to other teaching institutions because other settings depended on vendor systems provided by third parties, who did not prioritize establishing a separate environment for students and medical education on their roadmaps. Due to confidentiality requirements, a separate processing environment must be made available for students so that they are not accessing records of patients. Hence, medical education for EHR has been a strong suit for Vanderbilt. This is a strong, financially successful, clinically excellent, and EHR leadership and teaching organization, and they owe their success in medical education for EHR to their in-house developed and supported system.

However, that system was replaced recently with an Epic installation. As a result of this Epic rollout, the organization also has had to withstand a 60 percent reduction in operating revenues per year, and has planned for further reductions in operating revenues in future years due to increased operating expenses associated with supporting the new Epic EHR system (Ellison, 2018). This is an example of the other side (the downside) of new systems. This implementation changed at least two very important elements of an esteemed teaching institution and medical education program. One, it changed the flexibility and control of an in-house system able to also support medical student training on EHR systems, and two, this new system has sustained operating losses that extend beyond the implementation period, no doubt affecting other programs as well.

these negative effects attributable to the computers and implementations bubbled up and are now more clearly understood. Another landmark Health and Medicine Division (HMD) Report was published in 2011, called *Health IT and Patient Safety: Building Safer Systems for Better Care*, pointing out emerging evidence of the known effects of HIS and technology on patient safety and making recommendations to organizations, federal agencies, and suppliers of HIS and technology products and services to improve their impact on safety. The report describes safety as a system property, a consequence of a broader sociotechnical system consisting of technology (hardware and software), process, organization, external environment, and people (**FIGURE 9.7**) (HMD, 2012). The nature and degree of harm that may be caused by unintended consequences of HIS and technology, including EHRs, while not fully known, is now evident. Reasons for difficulty in pinpointing cause and effect are in part due to the fact that health IT products are varied; not standardized, they have wide-ranging and diverse impacts on healthcare environments, processes, and workflow. Perhaps most devastating to knowing what errors are attributable to computer systems

and thus being in a position to begin to solve them, vendor-favoring contracts contain legal language forbidding open disclosure of system problems, thus blocking transparent reporting of software product-related problems, as does "inadequate and limited" evidence for the variance in the literature (HMD, 2012).

Crossing the Quality Chasm describes features of safer HIS and technology in key areas, including features of health IT such as workflow, usability, balanced customization, and interoperability; design and development including software, UIs, testing deployment, maintenance, and upgrades; and implementation characteristics such as careful planning, benefits realization, system stabilization, and optimization. The report identifies a lack of hazard and risk reporting data on health IT as a factor hindering the construction of safer systems; it also warns that current market forces are contributing to the risks that may accompany HIS and technology. The key to addressing these safety risks is to be thorough and careful when planning HIS and technology implementations, use multidisciplinary project teams to design and implement these systems, create a transparent system of reporting system issues and quality problems attributable to the HIS, and develop standards for HIS and technology safety.

As sobering as these types of recommendations are, we would be wise to heed the reality that anything as powerful as HIS and technology also has the power to do harm if improperly designed, implemented, used, or maintained. Anyone who works in the arena of HIS and technology will tell you that these cautions are valid—thus those working in healthcare organizations must be realistic and exceedingly careful as systems are implemented. While this does not mean everyone should be paralyzed with fear, it does mean that healthcare organizations must be very disciplined, detail oriented, patient, and systematic in how these systems and technologies are introduced.

FIGURE 9.7 Sociotechnical system underlying health IT-related adverse events.

Data from Institute of Medicine. (2012). *Health IT and patient safety: Building safer systems for better care.* Retrieved from http://www.iom.edu/Reports/2011/Health-IT-and-Patient-Safety-Building-Safer-Systems-for-Better-Care.aspx. Accessed July 22, 2013

🔍 CASE EXAMPLE: BLOCKCHAIN: TO ADOPT OR NOT TO ADOPT

Blockchain is a digitized, decentralized, public ledger of transactions. The goal of blockchain is to make transactions (or information) trackable and accurate while staying completely anonymous: it allows market participants to keep track of digital currency transactions without central recordkeeping. This is the technology that makes something like Bitcoin possible. More recently, this HIS leaders and vendors have begun to theoretically apply blockchain to healthcare information.

It's clear there is in an appeal: there will be personalized, precision data for everyone in the future. How do we amass the right data at the primary care practitioner from all these other sources, while still maintaining privacy? It's about evolving with these new models—central authorities will go away, with distributed authority of blockchain. The current HIS model has been centered on the EHR system as the source of truth, but that model will be challenged by new technologies giving control back to the patients: with something like blockchain, central authorities go away.

An interesting question when considering the risks of introducing new errors as a result of automating healthcare processes is, "How does one determine the cause of the errors?" Are they due to problems within the computers or to problems with the humans who are using those computers? One study reported of the total number of errors studied, 56 percent were computer system related and 44 percent were attributable to human error (Sparnon & Marella, 2012). Of particular note was the finding that workflows that use *both* paper-based and electronic records (a very common practice) seem particularly problematic as more organizations transition between paper-based and electronic systems.

Another word of caution regarding HIS and technology is to be realistic about the cost of adopting HIS and technology. As enthusiastic as organizations typically are about implementing HIS and technology, and as carefully as those projects might be planned, this effort almost always takes longer and costs more than expected. In fact, during the transition, hospitals often see an 80 percent increase in IT department expenses (Sarasohn-Kahn, 2011). Hospital chief information officer's (CIO) and chief financial officer's (CFO) estimates also differ by about 75 percent regarding the cost

of implementations. This significant variance is because CIO estimates include support costs and other operational expenses associated with HIS implementations that CFOs generally underestimate. The amount spent on labor to support and maintain the new system increases by four times over the average implementation time frame (Sarasohn-Kahn, 2011). Thus, the total cost of ownership of HIS and technology usually varies significantly from initial estimates, especially considering that project implementations typically take much longer than expected before expected outcomes become reality.

Provider Dissatisfaction with EHR Systems

One of the most pronounced untoward and presumably unintended consequences of adoption of new technologies is physician burnout. While several factors contribute to this alarming phenomenon, in one large survey by Medscape, to which 15,000 physicians representing 29 specialties responded, three of the four top complaints were time spent in bureaucratic, clerical tasks, too much time spent at work, and increased computerization of their practices (Peckham, 2018). The September 2018 Stanford Report: the Future of Electronic Health Records reports that physicians spend 62 percent of their total time with a patient documenting in the EHR system. Scathing commentary about EHR systems' effect on the practice of medicine: the EHR systems get in the way of provider-patient interaction—"We've turned physicians and nurses into data-entry clerks" is one that breaks this author's heart—it is underestimated how much professional angst and moral distress the use of this tool, the EHR system, has created for physicians (Stanford Medicine, 2018). There are select, long-time pioneer organizations that have seen the benefits of EHR system achieved, and who feel they improve the quality of care. The early research of Goldzweig et al. showed that a great proportion of research regarding early EHR systems came from a handful of organizations: the Veterans' Administration, Intermountain Healthcare, Regenstrief Institute, Brigham and Women's/Partners, Permanente, Vanderbilt, and a few others (Goldzweig, Towfigh, Maglione, & Shekelle, 2009). This dichotomy is portrayed in the KLAS (a research company that evaluates health IT products and services, founded by Kent Gale, Adam Gale, Leonard Black, and Scott Holbrook, thus the acronym) results that state that while less than half of physicians feel that their EHR systems enable quality care, there are about six organizations in which 75 percent of physicians feel that their EHR systems enable high-quality care (Stanford Medicine, 2018).

As we move past the basics of HIS and EHR implementations, digital health and future uses in new ways of emerging technologies call for additional education of all health professionals and health administration professionals in the areas of digital health, patient involvement in design, UI/UX and human-centered design, interdisciplinary teams and projects, hands-on experiential learning using the tools being learned, and

new models of care connecting providers and patients between visits (The Medical Futurist, 2018). More on digital health innovations in Chapter 12.

▶ Building HIS and Technology into Education of Health Professionals

While most health professionals have been trained to use systems, few have been afforded the opportunity to formal education in health information technology and HIS. Building HIS and technology into the curricula of professional schools such as schools of medicine, nursing, therapies, management, policy, and other dimensions of the fabric of health care is imperative to competently managing the avalanche of automation that has befallen health care. This discipline and the ability to oversee activities of organizations and vendors of HIS products and services—as well as discern the correct way to plan, implement, and manage systems—is essential to not only optimal but adequate use of HIS and the data and information produced by them. While informatics is a discipline emerging in many of the health professions such as medicine, nursing, and other areas, the vast majority of clinicians and managers in health care have little experience and no education in this arena. It bears mentioning that this lack of formal training overall puts health professionals and the organizations in which they practice at a disadvantage in making excellent and proactive use of the systems that now are implemented in their organizations. The HITECH Act of 2009 devoted $2 billion out of $36 billion allocated to providing incentives for the implementation of EHR systems in healthcare organizations and practices. But the training programs these dollars were granted to were mostly community colleges for rapid training of health IT technical professionals who could help implement the wave of new EHR systems that were being installed across the country. Most of the educational programmatic support was for new programs at the technical level, not as part of the formal education of health professionals and health managers, as additions to their curricula. As of 2012, it was estimated that less than one-third of medical schools had health information technology classes as part of their curricula (Graham-Jones, Jain, Friedman, Marcotte, & Blumenthal, 2012). Further, the education that is called for regarding the wave of implementations stemming from the HITECH Act and MU is geared more toward the use of systems, including clinical decision support, MU requirements and clinical outcomes analysis. It is necessary for healthcare managers and professionals to have a broad and in-depth understanding of HIS so that they might be in the driver's seat and work collaboratively to plan, purchase, implement, and make use of these new technologies to accomplish the goals of the organization and on behalf of improved quality and cost performance overall.

How do we support and facilitate professionals and organizations adaptation to an automated clinical and digital health environment that extends far beyond the four walls of any healthcare institution? Nursing informatics and medical informatics degrees are now available in a handful of postgraduate programs in nursing and medical education programs. This is a wonderful addition to the education of health professionals, although the numbers of graduates are still very small, every step forward helps. What is needed is the addition of a few key classes as part of the required curricula in the education and training of all health professional programs and for health management and policy students in schools of public health, public policy, and graduate schools of management.

▶ Cultural Change Comes with New Technology and HIS

Our world continues to be changed. There are new ways to think about information in a technology-enabled, knowledge-based economy. No longer are assembly-line processes with specialized workers isolated into workgroups performing one type of task sufficient or functional in today's world. A knowledge-based, connected economy has emerged in other industries, and health care lags behind in adoption of new technologies to streamline and advance how work is done and to improve outcomes. Expectations are fully upon us that health care should follow suit. This is true for both the conduct of commerce and consumer expectations.

Similarly, we think differently about the definition of assets now—a value migration from visible, tangible assets including financial and physical capital to intangible knowledge resources has occurred (Murray, 2016). Organizations are valuing, managing, and nurturing their knowledge and human assets with a different view: these talented people should be rightly recognized as the source of creating and delivering the services that result in financial and physical resources—services much needed to compete successfully in the marketplace with excellent services and products. Intellectual capital is gaining importance as the means of improving organizational performance and market position (Bhatti & Zaheer, 2014). Attaining talent and allowing it to thrive is the imperative now. This is based on the creation of a work environment dependent on state-of-the-art HIS and technology that acknowledges and allows knowledge workers to create new solutions and activities that improve the ability of the organization to adapt to its new environment and meet increasing demands for improved quality and efficiency. This is a much different mind-set than a traditional strict set of known methods, rules, and benchmarks against which worker performance and productivity are measured. This is not to say that performance and productivity are not important—they most certainly are as part of good management. But they alone are not enough. The problems and capabilities of today's modern world insist on improvements based on human creativity, process enhancement, and new solutions to problems.

Emergence of the Knowledge-Based Economy

HIS and technology will most certainly play a central role in the emergence of the knowledge-based economy, and especially in health care as it finds its way through this developmental, evolutionary phase. What does this trend mean for health care? Patients will no longer be passive recipients of medical services; rather, they must be active participants in achieving the mutual goal held by those working in health care and those consuming healthcare services. This goes beyond the mere hope for the absence of disease or injury, but extends to achieving and maintaining optimal health and wellbeing.

Additionally, HIS and technology have changed the format of information itself. Digital technology is **"dematerializing" information** (eliminating paper, having paper stored out in the "cloud") and enabling separation of information from the physical structures and objects used to carry it (Spender, 2015). In essence, this trend is "taking geography out of the equation." In other words, whether it pertains to a patient or a testing or therapeutic facility, essential information is no longer isolated to a physical location, but rather can be shared at the speed of light to any professionals or people who need or should have access to that piece of information simultaneously. This is an enormous change from the days of the "central records room" or the "corporate office" mentality that implied, "All the important information resides within a central office of an organization, and so does all the real intelligence." Now, within the constraints of the roles-based security and access mandated HIPAA, information can be anywhere we desire it to be with the help of computerization. Geography, then, is no longer a primary issue. With the aid of systems and technology, information sharing and collaboration can take place across a large building, a city, a country, or even internationally. Traditional work clusters and assembly line-based processes can be decoupled with the right types of systems support, in terms of place, time, and performance of the work.

Changing Organizational Models

The idea that HIS and technology "take geography out of the equation" or that information or connection between humans or machines is no longer confined to a physical space makes revolutionary changes possible for organizations and their structures. Organizational configurations are free to transition from strict, defined, hierarchical structures designed to control and facilitate the flow of information from bottom to top, to fluid, social, adaptable networks and organizational forms that can move and adapt to changing circumstances with greater ease (Aaronson, 2016). Organizations can now be what is called "flat," meaning information sharing and collaboration occur between any and all "team members" who need to interact to achieve the work of the organization. In the case of health care, that means work on behalf of the patient and the mission of the organization. This fluidity (all with proper roles-based security and confidentiality, of course) represents a sea change from the restrictive, power-based availability of information inherent in traditional, hierarchical structures. This is not to say that hierarchy does not have its place: many, if not most, organizations today are structured this way, and without structure, roles, and responsibilities, chaos would prevail. Nevertheless, within this discipline of hierarchy, function, and process, the ready access to information and connection between the humans working in those organizations is changing due to the automation of information—and changing for the better. A greater ease of sharing of ideas and information between knowledge workers within a trusted, secure environment can create a greater synergy between the work and ideas of those workers. It is recognized that not all good ideas must come from the top layers of an organization—in fact, generation of actionable ideas is encouraged from every part of an organization. This empowers individuals through access to information and enables the development and implementation of processes and systems that can lead to greater effectiveness and productivity for the organization overall.

What does this mean for health care? Imagine patient care in a traditional, hierarchical organization, where power—through access to information—exists predominantly with those at the top of the hierarchy (think physician leaders and administrators) but patient care (the product) is delivered at the ground level, through other knowledge workers (think nurses, technicians, and therapists) who handle the day-to-day, hands-on work of caring for the patients (in other words, delivering the product and determining its quality). Before automation could connect the various roles and players on this knowledge train, the hierarchy served this purpose. But along with that rigid discipline and restricted access of information came a certain required, measured pace of process and progress. When health care was simpler, and fewer professionals and therapies were involved, this schema worked well in well-run organizations. In today's complex healthcare environment, where multiple parties may need access to patient and business information

regarding a patient simultaneously, a single thread of information passed along from person to person via paper or word of mouth cannot possibly keep up. Adaptability, prompt action based on real-time feedback, and fluidity are crucial elements in the interactions taking place between the many different professionals charged with responsibilities in today's healthcare organizations. Systems and technology can boost positive interaction, enabling healthcare organizations to become more adaptable and responsive to changing requirements of patient care and administration responsibilities.

Will this transformation magically take place simply as a result of buying and installing new computer systems and software? Not at all. It is a painstaking process involving thorough planning and a careful analysis of workflow, where all these activities maintain a close connection to the purpose and meaning of care in that organization. In addition to streamlining and redesigning work processes, we must successfully build systems and technology to support those improved processes that span across organizational structures to create new connections, openness of communication, and access to information to support the knowledge workers involved.

Facilitating Organizational Evolution

Despite being absolutely essential to communities, hospitals can no longer be treated as the center of the healthcare universe. With changing demographics, including an aging population and skyrocketing rates of chronic illness such as diabetes, obesity, cancer, Alzheimer's disease, and heart disease, increased focus is being placed on primary, personalized care. This type of care fits with *prevention*, while hospitals are intended for *acute care needs*. Innovations such as medical homes and accountable care organizations

🔍 CASE EXAMPLE: BINDERS VERSUS AUTOMATION

Automation creates opportunities for streamlining workflow to gain efficiencies, focus on service, enhance communication, and improve timeliness and quality of care. What is revolutionary about this chance is we have the chance in health care to consider the impact of process and workflow on efficiency, effectiveness, and quality in ways that have not been imaginable heretofore. For instance, an earlier way of working on quality assurance and process improvement relied on figuring out how to make sure the paper documents with the most up-to-date guidelines for care were printed and kept in binders on each and every nursing unit in a hospital, accompanied by regular in-service training to review these ever-changing guidelines that each and every worker must follow to be effective (and somehow this activity must be tracked to see if, in fact, the guidelines were followed). Now, patient care can be supported by computerized prompts that guide caregivers as they use these systems to use evidence-based processes of care and document these activities along the way. Of course, successful use of such a system requires close collaboration between the IT professionals who build and support these computer systems, individuals familiar with current clinical guidelines, and the clinicians who use the systems in providing care. That close collaboration is the hallmark of successful systems implementations.

(ACOs) take to heart the need for coordination across the continuum of a person's life (the medical home) and the continuum of care; ACOs coordinate care ranging from primary to acute care, depending on the needs of the patient. These innovations rely on, among other things, "geography being taken out of the equation"—that is, using HIS and technology to connect clinicians, care settings, patients, and administrators involved in that continuum. The long-term integration and aggregation of patient information into a lifetime patient record enables the medical home scenario to become reality, and careful integration using HIS and technology facilitates a patient-centric view of information across various healthcare settings along the continuum of care. This continuum reaches from the hospital to the doctor's office to the patient in his or her home or workplace; it involves managing risk factors associated with a chronic illness as well as taking great care of patients in the hospital or clinical settings. Neither the medical home concept nor the ACO model would be feasible without computerized patient care records and networks connecting these settings of care.

The fee-for-service, volume-based, payer-driven healthcare system currently found in the U.S. does not begin to address the true determinants of health that exist in a person's community, environment, and home. These health determinants—such as education, diet, stress levels, exercise habits, exposure to pollution and violence, and other lifestyle characteristics—factor mightily into a person's total health and wellness picture, along with access to healthcare services. These more personal touch points along the "continuum of care" do not occur primarily in traditional bricks-and-mortar healthcare services settings, but they have everything to do with the personalized behaviors, care, and health of individuals. So how do caring healthcare organizations begin to integrate these settings—from home, to school, to places of entertainment, worship, work, and community—to support the pursuit of health, by minimizing the development and effect of factors that lead to chronic conditions in the first place? HIS and technology, organized into "digital health" platforms through social media, mobile devices, and other means, can provide gateways to more integrated care that

🔍 CASE EXAMPLE: ACO VERSUS A HOSPITAL FOR A PATIENT WITH DIABETES

If a chronically ill patient—such as someone with diabetes—arrives at the hospital for the first episode of care, it is too late for effective control of the disease; the condition by that time has become severe and expensive to treat. It is clear that both the patient and the healthcare organization are in losing situations. Of course, healthcare organizations will always approach each patient as he or she presents under the circumstances, but it is far better for the patient and far more cost-effective for the organization to address the care of a patient with a chronic condition early in the progression of that chronic condition. At this stage, it may be possible to reverse that progression or keep it from occurring by treating it early, before devastating effects take place. By the time, a chronic disease manifests and reaches the later stages, more aggressive and expensive forms of care are required, which often are directed at controlling symptoms, rather than effecting a cure.

ACOs are intended to create fully coordinated clinical care methods in which doctors, nurses, and therapists provide healthcare services in the appropriate venues to effectively manage the health of populations. Claims for this care are submitted to insurance providers, and the entire process of healthcare services delivery and business dealings takes place as cost-effectively as can be managed, i.e., value based. Traditional methods of care and reimbursement are evolving rapidly, with new arrangements between hospitals, clinics, and physicians emerging to support these new models of care and chronic disease management. The new business relationships and clinical models should be designed to support shared objectives of improving patients' and populations' health, rather than simply seeking reimbursement for an approved set of services according to the rules of an insurer-based healthcare system (Durovich & Roberts, 2018).

is "nearer" to the patient. Lifestyle, determinants of health, environmental conditions, and social context all matter here.

What is the role of HIS and technology in these considerations? Answering this question requires a shift in our thinking—from the inpatient, hierarchical organizations of the past as the "centers of medical care" (think hospitals), to flexible, diverse networks of community and organizational settings, many of which are "healthcare related" in the traditional sense, but others of which are not. All of these "nodes" on the network of community, health, and healing can play a vital role in the long-term health and well-being of the people who live in those communities and frequent these environments. The types of networks and platforms found in this model will be just as different as they are similar, and will include a diversity of participants, community settings, customers, educators,

recreational facilities, food sources, governmental participants, suppliers, retailers, and all the relationships between them. In addition, each of these nodes on this type of network will have its own systems and connectivity to the ultimate social network, the Internet. Such a connected "community" network can be local, regional, national, or international in scope. It will be supported by a combination of organizationally based systems, personal digital assistants (PDAs), smartphones, and other mobile devices, all of which can connect to digital health platforms and to one another, to provide real-time feedback to the people using them and to create personalized health-related information (Pritchard et al., 2017). Some might call this a "non-system," but as our society adapts to the ubiquitous use and availability of information technology, it will become obvious that this network of social connections that ebbs and flows with the very fabric of our lives is, in fact, a digitally enabled social system that has many variations and a powerful effect on the quality of our lives and health. Lifestyle, environmental context, and social determinants of health begin and end here.

All of these current realities, ideas, and possibilities will require and inspire a shift from a sole focus on traditional inpatient, hierarchical, bricks-and-mortar organizations to the inclusion of diverse networks between intra- and interorganizational settings, suppliers, customers, relationships, and communities where people live, work, and play. Empowered consumers in this type of social milieu of health will be enabled by information technology. Although some of this technology—such as social media—is often excluded when defining "health information systems and technology," the empowered consumers who use it are more directly participating in their health and health care. Taking part in this evolution of healthcare delivery and information sharing represents a generational shift, a radical shift in disease trends, and a shift of the burden of coordinating and integrating care from the patient and family to an interorganizational and personal collaboration. This collaboration will include physicians, patients, families, and the holistic combination of emotional, wellness, nutritional, exercise, social, and education services. Empowered HIS- and technology-enabled knowledge workers become active collaborators in this process as well. This evolution of health care is part of the greater societal revolution fueled by systems and technology experienced by each of us, each and every day. Where it leads us is up to us.

Extending the concept of starting with the end user in mind a step further, we are entering the era of personalization of health care, in which medicines, treatments, wellness regimens, prevention strategies, and therapies can be personally customized based on genetics, evidence-based practices, personal desires, and clinical characteristics of an individual's conditions. HIS and technology are intrinsic to this evolution; these HIS are the engines that bring together the predictive, individual and diverse data sets to support the **clinical intelligence (CI)** necessary to unleash the focus

🔍 CASE EXAMPLE: HUMAN-CENTERED PROCESS

Primary care through physician offices has been a mainstay pillar of the U.S. healthcare system for many years. Generationally, things are changing. Millennials and others today are showing a strong preference for convenience, and about half as many millennials (those born between 1981 and 1996) do not have to a primary care provider compared to those a decade older (Vartorella, 2018). A function of overall societal expectations and norms (such as online banking), as well as convenience and age-related preferences, providers are working to provide additional professionals available, such as nurse practitioners, and new online tools to increase ease of access for their practices by millennials. Rather than thinking the solution is a shift away from primary care provider practices to minute clinics or other retail solutions, practitioners are seeking to make their practices more user-friendly to millennials by changing their ways of communicating with them, not abandoning this age group or refusing to see the signs of the times. In this case, the new tools of secure messaging (like texting) and other online connections with this age group is solving the problem because the practitioners understand the value of a longitudinal record of care, since care is safer this way since the provider knows what medications the patient is on and other relevant history, as well as the benefit of establishing a relationship with their patients through the means comfortable for those patients. This is the "use of new tools" in action, applied to a problem to solve, not just used for the sake of technology, but also based on the preferences of the patient, taking the end user in mind and working backwards from there. This is an example of **human-centered design**.

and creativity of well-minded clinicians, working in concert with patients and families, to develop customized preventive and therapeutic programs specifically tailored to the needs of each patient. Individuals receiving care wish to shape their care experiences. Doing so not only gives patients a voice in the process but also leads to their full engagement with caregivers and active participation in their care, which evidence tells us leads to improved outcomes (James, 2013).

This HIS- and technology-powered personalization is essential to helping people manage and alter risk-inducing behaviors that might lead to chronic illnesses such as diabetes, heart disease, Alzheimer's disease, and cancer. Such digital health solutions will become commonplace, because health care today requires coordination across institutions, professionals, services, and communities, and direct engagement by patients in their care and health preservation. Stated another way, the chronic conditions that will plague the majority of us will be prevented, controlled, and managed only when people modify their behaviors leading to diseases caused by those behaviors. The view that therapies (e.g., drugs and surgeries) targeting acute infections, illnesses, or injuries can also be used to treat chronic, behavior-induced illnesses is a misconception. Moreover, the only way to change a person's behavior is to involve that individual directly in the information feedback loop associated with the behavior—such as a person's nutrition, levels of physical activity (exercise), and sleep habits.

HIS strategy must adopt new technologies to enable these new clinical and organizational directions into account if healthcare organizations are to cope successfully with the new reality. At this time, health care is in a state of major flux, as healthcare organizations adopt the transformative strategy of moving away from paper to electronic processes and strive to shift from a purely medical model to one that sustains health. This is challenging work, all done while the everyday important work of healthcare providers continues in a complex world of providers, payers, patients, and medical advancement. One can envision a new future state in which IT-enabled organizations and empowered knowledge workers and patients are able to collaborate using the best of medical science, patient-provider engagement, and clinical intelligence to support their efforts. Unfortunately, some organizations will never get there: the transition will require a larger step than they are able to sustain or afford by themselves, and they will have to either become part of a larger health provider organization or gradually become less relevant to the changing complexion of health care and chronic disease processes. This is not a good outcome for the communities those organizations serve; the preferred outcome is for organizations to learn to adapt and integrate HIS and technology into the evolutionary processes that healthcare and public health organizations and communities are navigating today.

Management of Information Resources

Knowledge management—the strategic management of information resources—is an essential part of this evolutionary process, which depends on HIS and technology strategy as an enabling factor. Quadrants III and IV of the HIS planning framework comprise clinical and business intelligence systems, respectively (Figure 4.12 in Chapter 4). These systems, and the data and information that are housed and produced within them for use by clinical and business knowledge workers, add an entire layer of HIS and technology to the architectures and mix of systems supporting healthcare management. Health care comprises an information-intensive set of activities. It encompasses interactions between highly trained experts such as physicians and nurses, as well as the information these knowledge workers need to ensure the best treatment for people who happen to be particularly vulnerable at this point in their lives.

In addition to creating information system capabilities within the organization, healthcare organizations must conduct environmental or market analyses, an essential component of the strategic management of knowledge resources. This type of analysis challenges the existing assumptions about providers and consumers of health care based on traditional usage (i.e., the current state of the market) to predict and plan for its future status. It enables business analysts to make new assumptions about the possible future states of the patients and community that the organization will serve; these states cannot be perfectly predicted, of course, but they can be estimated or modeled using these assumptions. This type of anticipatory analysis helps healthcare organizations understand the possibilities associated with their futures, and plan and manage their services and processes to produce desired outcomes.

Clearly, HIS and technology involve much more than just automated support. They are an integral part of the care process and part of the organizational evolution in communities. HIS- and technology-enabled information and knowledge provide the bases for continuous innovation and organizational adaptation as the healthcare landscape evolves. Such information and knowledge facilitate new inter-organizational connections and provide the underpinnings of competitive and collaborative advantage—namely power in the marketplace and support to the community.

Summary

Adopting new technologies is a topic steeped in theory and based in the earthy reality of solutions that become tried and true or fail. Adoption of new HIS and technology takes several forms consistent with the HIS model and can be considered from a variety of perspectives, including the organizational, presidential/political, and professional organization arenas. The adoption of HIS and technology can be seen as rooted in the overall social system theory known as Rogers's diffusion of innovation, and as progressing through five stages of adoption demarcated based on the types of personalities and social systems within the organization, driving and responding to change: Innovator, Early Adopter, Early Majority, Late Majority, and Laggard.

The 50-year history of HIS and technology adoption has taken U.S. health care through a series of developments and technological innovations originating mostly within hospitals and other healthcare delivery organizations. Vendors of software emerged as a result of these hospital software development innovations, a fact that often surprises those individuals with a more recent exposure to the health information technology industry.

Successful HIS and technology adoption faces numerous challenges, including barriers such as high capital and ongoing costs, concerns with vendor stability, ability to select software that will meet the organization's needs, disruption to workflows, and productivity dips during implementation cycles. Trends toward adoption of such systems and technologies are gaining momentum, in part due to HITECH financial incentives to physician practices and hospitals for EHR implementations and achievement of MU. The HITECH Act has resulted in achieving desired EHR system adoption rates, and attention has turned to stubbornly low interoperability capabilities to enable needed data exchange so that the hard-fought implementations of EHR systems can yield greater value. Recent evidence points to unintended negative consequences to patient safety associated with implementing HIS and technology, and cautions are becoming more pronounced as all parties seek to develop safety standards for HIS and technology products, medical devices, projects, and risk reporting processes. Additional realities of HIS and technology implementations should also be kept in mind, such as the toll they are exacting on health professionals who are spending inordinate amounts of additional time in the documentation process, entering data and doing clerical tasks EHR systems in their current iterations demand. Also needing greater attention, solution finding, and education are the tendency to underestimate the costs associated with these implementations and the fact that both computer and human errors contribute to these unintended consequences.

Discussion Questions

1. What forces drive the perceived need to adoption new uses of HIS and technology?
2. What are the five persons and their key characteristics as described in Rogers's Theory of Diffusion of Innovation?
3. In what ways are the lessons learned in the early years of HIS adoption relevant to today's problems to solve? In what ways do they differ from today's systems and issues?
4. Professional organizations have contributed to the overall development and adoption of new technologies in health care. What are the best ways for these organizations to evolve and continue to meet the educational and professional support needs of health professionals in today's technology-rich environment?
5. Is HIMSS' EMRAM framework describing the progressive adoption of EHR systems helpful? In what ways is it helpful and in what ways is it not helpful or irrelevant?
6. Describe what the market forces and investment categories are telling us about true priorities for healthcare organizations and health professionals.
7. How does the sociotechnical system affecting HIS adoption apply to new technology adoption? What is the most important bubble on this construct and why?
8. What is an intangible knowledge asset? What are some examples of these in health care?
9. Have you experienced an unintended consequence of HIS and new technology adoption? What was this experience and how did it make you feel about your role and about the technology?
10. How does the adoption of new technologies use the HIS strategic planning lessons covered in Chapters 4 and 5?

Key Terms

Adoption
Adoption curve
Alliance for Nursing
    Informatics (ANI)
American Health
    Information Management
    Association (AHIMA)
American Medical
    Informatics Association
    (AMIA)

Blockchain
Clinical intelligence (CI)
Dematerializing information
Electronic Medical Record
    Adoption Model
    (EMRAM)
Health Information
    Management
    Systems Society
    (HIMSS)

Human-centered
    design
Registered Health
    Information
    Administrator
    (RHIA)
Registered Health
    Information Technicians
    (RHITs)
Value realization

References

Aaronson, A. (2016). Try Google Way to start culture of innovation in healthcare. *Modern Healthcare.* Retrieved from https://www.liebertpub.com/doi/full/10.1089/pop.2017.0015

AHIMA. (n.d.). AHIMA facts. Retrieved from http://www.ahima.org/about/facts.aspx

AHIMA. (n.d.). AHIMA history. Retrieved from http://www.ahima.org/about/history.aspx

Alliance for Nursing Informatics. (n.d.). About ANA. Retrieved from http://www.allianceni.org/about.asp

AMIA. (n.d.). AMIA mission. Retrieved from http://www.amia.org/about-amia/mission-and-history

Bhatti, W., & Zaheer, A. (2014, December). The role of intellectual capital in creating and adding value to organizational performance: A conceptual study. Retrieved from https://www.researchgate.net/publication/270505923_The_Role_of_Intellectual_Capital_in_Creating_and_Adding_Value_to_Organizational_Performance_A_conceptual_study

Byrne, C. M., Mercincavage, L. M., Pan, E. C., Vincent, A. G., Johnston, D. S., & Middleton, B. (2010). The VA experience: The value from investments in health information technology at The U.S. Department of Veterans Affairs. *Health Affairs, 29*, 629–638.

Chaudhry, B., Wang, J., Wu, S., Maglione, M., Mojica, W., Roth, E., … Shekelle, P. G. (2006). Systematic review: Impact of heath information technology on quality, efficiency, and costs of medical care. *Annals of Internal Medicine, 144*(10), 742–752.

Diffusion of Innovation Theory. (2012, January). News-on-mobile: NEWSLAND. Retrieved from http://quipuapps.com/wp-content/uploads/2012/01/diffusion_of_innovation_theory_.pdf

Doxey, W. (1889). *Borrowings: A compilation of helpful thoughts from great authors.* http://historiesofecology.blogspot.com/2012/11/build-bettermouse-trap-and-world.html

Durovich, C., & Roberts, P. (2018). Designing a community-based population health model. *Population Health Management, 21*(1). Retrieved from https://www.liebertpub.com/doi/full/10.1089/pop.2017.0015

Ellison, A. (2018, May). Vanderbilt University Medical Center points to Epic rollout for 60% drop in operating income. *Becker's Hospital CFO Report.* Retrieved from https://www.beckershospitalreview.com/finance/vanderbilt-university-medical-center-points-to-epic-rollout-for-60-drop-in-operating-income.html

Goldzweig, C. L. (2012, May). *HIT and quality improvement: Summary of the evidence and a case study.* Presentation at UCLA Health Policy and Management 440A Health Information Systems and Technology.

Goldzweig, C. L., Towfigh, A., Maglione, M., & Shekelle, P. (2009). Costs and benefits of health information technology: New trends from the literature. *Health Affairs, 28*(2), 282–293. doi:10.1377/hlthaff.28.2.w282

Graham-Jones, P., Jain, S. H., Friedman, C. P., Marcotte, L., & Blumenthal, D. (2012, March). The need to incorporate health information. Retrieved from https://www.healthaffairs.org/doi/full/10.1377/hlthaff.2011.0423

Health and Medicine Division of the National Academies of Sciences, Engineering, and Medicine. (2012). *Health IT and patient safety: Building safer systems for better care.* Retrieved from http://www.iom.edu/Reports/2011/Health-IT-and-Patient-Safety-Building-Safer-Systems-for-Better-Care.aspx

HealthIT.com. (n.d.). Benefits of meaningful use. Retrieved from http://www.healthit.gov/policy-researchers-implementers/meaningful-use

HealthTech Wire. (n.d.). HIMSS celebrates 50 years. Retrieved from http://www.healthtechwire.com/himss/himss-celebrates-50-years-2529/

HIMSS. (n.d.-a). About HIMSS. Retrieved from http://www.himss.org/AboutHIMSS/index.aspx?navItemNumber=17402

HIMSS. (n.d.-b). Frequently asked questions about HIMSS and its members. Retrieved from http://www.himss.org/himss-faqs?navItemNumber=18017

HIMSS. (n.d.-c). HIMSS health IT value suite. Retrieved from http://www.himss.org/valuesuite?src=smor http://himss.files.cms-plus.com/HIMSS%20Health%20IT%20Value%20Suite%20Executive%20final.pdf

Introducing HIMSS Analytics O-EMRAM. (n.d.). HIMSS. Retrieved from https://www.himssanalytics.org/news/introducing-o-emram

James, J. (2013, February). Health policy brief: Patient engagement. *Health Affairs.* Retrieved from https://www.healthaffairs.org/do/10.1377/hpb20130214.898775/full/

Murray, A. (2016, April). The world of intangible asset valuation. Retrieved from http://www.kmworld.com/Articles/Column/The-Future-of-the-Future/The-world-of-intangible-asset-valuation-110580.aspx

Painter, M. (2013, June). *Electronic health records: Are we there yet? What's taking so long?* Robert Wood Johnson Foundation. Retrieved from http://www.rwjf.org/en/blogs/culture-of-health/2013/06/electronic_healthre.html

Peckham, C. (2018, January). *Medscape National Physician Burnout & Depression Report 2018.* Retrieved from https://www.medscape.com/slideshow/2018-lifestyle-burnout-depression-6009235#13

Pritchard, D., Moeckel, F., Villa, M. S., Housman, L. T., McCarty, C. A., & McLeod, H. L. (2017, January). Strategies for integrating personalized medicine into healthcare practice. *Personalized Medicine, 14*(2).

Retrieved from https://www.futuremedicine.com/doi/full/10.2217/pme-2016-0064

Robinson, L. (2009, January). A summary of diffusion of innovations. *Enabling Change*. Retrieved from http://www.enablingchange.com.au/Summary_Diffusion_Theory.pdf

Rogers, E. (1995). *Stanford discussion of diffusion of innovation*. Retrieved from http://www.stanford.edu/class/symbsys205/Diffusion%20of%20Innovations.htm

Rogers, E. M. (1963). *Diffusion of innovations*. New York, NY: Free Press.

Sarasohn-Kahn, J. (2011). Don't underestimate the costs of adopting health IT. *Health Populi*. Retrieved from http://healthpopuli.com/2011/01/24/dont-underestimate-the-costs-of-adopting-health-it/

Spagnulo, C. (2008, October). EdgeHopper: Approaching technology with mindfulness. How to cross the chasm. Retrieved from http://edgehopper.com/%E2%80%A8-what-geoff-recognized-was-that-there-is-more-to-this-curve-he-recognized-that-there-is-a-difference-between-disruptiveinnovations-those-that-are-changing-the-game-altogether-and-gard/

Sparnon, E., & Marella, W. M. (2012, December). Safety implications of HER/HIT. Pennsylvania. Retrieved from http://www.patientsafetyauthority.org/ADVISORIES/AdvisoryLibrary/2012/Dec;9(4)/Pages/113.aspx

Spender, A. (2015, February). Three emerging trends driving business. *Smarter with Gartner: Digital Business*. Retrieved from https://www.gartner.com/smarterwithgartner/three-emerging-trends-drive-digital-business/

Stanford Medicine. (2018, September). White paper: The future of electronic health records. Retrieved from http://med.stanford.edu/content/dam/sm/ehr/documents/SM-EHR-White-Papers_v12.pdf

The Medical Futurist. (2018, July). How to prepare the future generation of physicians. Retrieved from https://medicalfuturist.com/how-to-prepare-the-future-generation-of-physicians

U.S. Department of Health and Human Services. (n.d.). Health information privacy. Retrieved from http://www.hhs.gov/ocr/privacy/

Vartorella, L. (2018, October). Millennials are upending the primary care model: 4 things to know. *Becker's Hospital Review*. Retrieved from https://www.beckershospitalreview.com/patient-flow/millennials-are-upending-the-primary-care-model-4-things-to-know.html

World VistA. (n.d.). VistaA history. Retrieved from http://worldvista.sourceforge.net/vista/history/

CHAPTER 10

Data

Ric Speaker

LEARNING OBJECTIVES

By the end of this chapter, the student will be able to:

- Describe data, how data can lead to information creation, and data's importance to health care.
- Name the 3V's of data and describe Big Data and Thick Data.
- Comprehend how government initiatives such as Medicare Access and CHIP Reauthorization Act (MACRA) are shaping healthcare data collection, use, and protection.
- Understand the sources and the evolution of data.
- Appreciate the challenges and opportunities that increased volumes of data present.

▶ Introduction

This and the next chapter may seem to be inherently technical, dry, and perhaps obscure; however, the near future of analysis and uses of data will be exponentially more pervasive. Data users will include providers, patients, and consumers of health care; government, payers, software applications, and devices; and risk-bearing entities. No healthcare industry participant or interested party will remain untouched by contemporary and historical clinical and business process data. Understanding the scope of health care's data explosion, its potential relevance to improving the quality of care, and its assured contribution to cost containment measures may make these chapters more compelling.

Data and its close relative derived analytics have the potential to offer more knowledge and insight into improving patient care and economic efficiency than all of the other current noise in the industry. With the ever-expanding use of technology in our daily lives, the term data is usually perceived to be an abstraction and not commonly touched or needed in everyday life. Or, many believe in the notion that data at a base elemental level may seem trivial. This is especially true in health care. More and more, healthcare software, devices, and business processes depend upon data. Within this chapter, healthcare data will be exposed for its value, use, sources, and magnitude, as well as data's potential contribution to improving the industry's operational challenges and patient care.

Additionally, as a result of several converging trends—including the adoption of mobile devices with hundreds of thousands of iOS (Apple) and Android-based software applications, the expanding use of electronic health record (EHR) systems, diagnostic imaging technologies, privacy legislation, and dramatic changes in the assignment of financial risk—it is clear that data's value is increasing exponentially.

Other industries depend upon the security, veracity, and granularity of data. Notably and peculiar to health care, the need for data accuracy and interdependencies of aggregated data is essential for a clinical caregiver's daily "life and death" decision making. For example, if the tagging of a hospital laboratory's electronic specimen result is somehow inaccurate or the electronic resultant messaging from the laboratory equipment to an EHR is wrong someone may die and they do. As validated and published in *The Journal of American Medical Association*, there are approximately 1 million deaths in the U.S. due to adverse drug reactions, many of which are attributable to inaccurate data pertaining to an order (Lazarou, Pomeranz, & Corey, 1998). Again, data is important.

▶ Exponential Growth of Data

Yet the U.S. healthcare industry is profoundly fragmented, lacks uniformity, and operates on conflicting financial incentives and objectives. The definition and measurements for the quality of clinical outcomes, while generally humane and nobly inspired, struggle for consistency and consensus. These issues of discrepancy extend into the collection, care, and use of data. In its daily processes of patient encounters and treatments, every healthcare institution small and large generates extraordinary volumes of data. Yet, how these data are recorded, stored, organized, and eventually made available to all the disparate users of data-based analytical information has no universally accepted methods. We are talking about an estimated 50 percent annual increase in annual healthcare data generation leading to more than 2,300 exabytes (1 exabyte = 1 billion gigabytes) likely generated by the year 2020. When considering the complexity of data, one needs to factor in data for population health, medical research, pharmaceutical development, military health care, and other stakeholders. The challenge for accepted standards is obvious. The opportunity for data's use is boundless.

Our current healthcare system is unsustainable. U.S. healthcare spending grew 4.3 percent in 2016, reaching $3.3 trillion or $10,348 per person. As a share of the nation's gross domestic product (GDP), health spending accounted for 17.9 percent (Centers for Medicare & Medicaid Services, 2016a). Centers for Medicare and Medicaid Services (CMS) projected that healthcare spending will on average rise 5.5 percent annually and by 2026 will reach 19.7 percent (Centers for Medicare & Medicaid Services, 2016b). By comparison, in 2016, the U.S. military war expenditure, often remarked as incredibly high, amounted to 3.1 percent of GDP (The World Bank, 2017). The cost of health care is huge, whether viewed comparatively or alone. Better use of our treasure trove of data to lower the cost of care must become an imperative. Data logically leads to information, which should lead to more focused decision making, which can lead to improved clinical outcomes and new care delivery models (**FIGURE 10.1**).

This is the definition of data used in this text: *Data is base-level computer information that may consist of numerical or word elements, facts, values, or combinations of stored information that can be either qualitative or quantitative, and from*

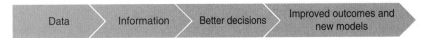

FIGURE 10.1 How data improves health care.

which knowledge is derived and decision making may be made better and more logical.

In defining data, one must first understand that it may be a singular and/or a combination or plural use of words, values, numbers, and/or various amalgamations of these elements. For example, a patient's last name is a singular notion for a computer, and at the same time the discrete letters comprising that name are each unique data elements. Similarly, a single magnetic resonance imaging (MRI) has its own visual data identity while all the millions of **pixels** (as with television viewing acuity) are each discrete data elements as well as the brand, age, and location of the equipment, who ordered, and who "read" the image. A patient's electronic or written prescription is one data element with myriad sub-data elements including the clinician's order, drug's manufacturer, age, production batch, dosage, supply chain history, and other relevant information.

Some of the most significant and voluminous sources of healthcare data are profiled here:

Clinical

- Electronic health records/electronic medical records/personal health records (EHRs /EMRs/PHRs)
- Images and image management systems (e.g., picture archiving and communication systems [PACSs], digitized X-rays, CT scans, and PET scans)
- Case mix, care management, and disease management systems
- Independent laboratory and other clinical results (e.g., blood, tissue, and fluids)
- Monitoring systems (e.g., maternity, cardiology, and ICU)

Transactional/Operations

- Hospital information systems (e.g., admissions and emergency department [ED] visits)
- Hospital departmental systems (e.g., radiology, laboratory, pharmacy, surgery, ED, and order entry)
- Materials management, supplies, and cost accounting systems
- Physician practice management systems (e.g., scheduling and billing)
- Revenue-cycle processes (e.g., provider billing, claims, and patient accounting)
- Post-acute clinical and billing systems (e.g., skilled nursing and home care)

Payer

- Payer claims and contracting systems (e.g., benefit rules, risk calculations, and claims adjudication)
- Care management systems (for coordinating transitions of care and discharges to home or other facilities)

Third Party

- Research systems (e.g., universities, human, and animal)
- Clinical trials systems (e.g., pharmaceutical companies and universities)
- Satisfaction surveying systems (e.g., patients, providers, and staff)

External

- Internet resources
- Registries, population management, statistics, and risk adjustments
- Industry reporting (e.g., benchmarks, score cards, and report cards)

- Cellular devices and applications
- Personal monitors and watches

Government

- Federal government programs (e.g., CMS, State Children's Health Insurance Program [SCHIP], Department of Defense TRICARE and TRICARE for Life programs, Veterans Healthcare Administration [VHA] program, and Indian Health Service [IHS] program)
- State and local government programs (e.g., Medicaid, MediCal, State Health Insurance Assistance Program [SHIP], Children's Health Insurance Program [CHIP], Health Resources and Services Administration Primary Care: the Health Center Program, and healthcare marketplace regulatory programs)

Types of Organizations

Listing the principal participants in creating healthcare data will set the stage for understanding the kinds of data sources they require. The following groups all generate and process data in different intervals, including real time, daily, and monthly:

- Providers (e.g., physicians, nurses, and other clinicians)
- Hospitals and hospital systems
- Outpatient care facilities (e.g., imaging, urgent care, and physical therapy)
- Payers and third-party administrators
- Government, including military organizations
- Post-acute care facilities (e.g., skilled nursing and hospice)
- Home health
- Patients (i.e., consumers)
- Pharmaceutical companies and laboratories
- Research centers (e.g., universities and government)
- Public health organizations

There are hundreds of discrete revenue-cycle and health record operational systems or data sources used among, hospitals, physician groups, clinics, and other provider environments. Some of these systems may be very small, used in a single department or for a specific application producing small packets of data, creating an information "silo." Conversely, enterprise-wide and larger mission-critical applications serve to accomplish multiple functions and applications that are used by all personnel creating voluminous data output. For example, CMS and CHIP have management of beneficiaries covering about 35 percent of the U.S. population and the VHA picks up over 20 million military veterans. These data are used internally for a host of measurements and patient care. The same data are the underpinnings for communications to insurance companies, numerous governmental agencies, and other healthcare institutions. These very different **data sources**—places from which data emanate—have applications for both clinical and business processes and analyses (Chapter 6).

Historically, most of the focus on healthcare data was on information in revenue-cycle systems, supporting processes such as billings and insurance claims processing, scheduling, etc. These systems operated at the departmental level and there were few clinically related software applications. But because they were first, the limited data within modified managed care and fee-for-service financial models have been the foundation for operational, mission-critical software systems for the provider and payer sides. Before the contemporary EHR systems, these data were sufficient for providers to assess their respective measures of success at least along financial performance lines. Without internal or external pressure to make painful decisions about the better alignment of risk for all healthcare stakeholders, it is nearly universally agreed that this status quo payment model may not continue. Providers', payers', and patients' economic risks must be rebalanced, which will affect all healthcare stakeholders. None of this may be accomplished without expanded and efficient use of data.

With more than 1,045,910 (Statista, 2013) licensed physicians in the U.S., 2,995,200 (Bureau of Labor Statistics, 2017) registered nurses, more than 500 versions of healthcare insurance companies (and many more health plans offered by provider groups), 5,534 (American Hospital Association, 2018) registered hospitals, 43,749 (IBIS World, 2018) outpatient facilities, and myriad government programs, one can begin to imagine the interrelated dependencies and the complexities of healthcare data.

▶ The Three Big Data Sources

While we have established that the volume of data is ever increasing, it is also important to note the three biggest contributors.

EHR Systems

Aisles and drawers full of folders with paper notes and records have slowly been replaced by EHRs over the last several decades, principally in the last two decades, documenting patient visit and event. Hundreds of software vendors and many healthcare institutions have developed their vision for the perfect software to be able to create and store the patient record. Arguably, this application of HIS has been the most controversial automation tool in health care's history. It has affected the patient's experience and the clinician's time, has necessitated myriad data interfaces, and has been the greatest challenge for design architects, physician consensus for functionality, and resulting disparate use provider by provider practice. This disparity is not surprising, considering that there are 141 M.D. and 30 D.O.

medical schools (AAMC, website) that don't share the same software within their teaching environments. Further, it continues to be contended (while it may well be a myth) that the clinician's age has affected willingness and adaptability to all the aforementioned issues for EHRs.

Irrespective, the amount of data produced while using an EHR is exponentially greater than within the traditional scheduling, billing, and insurance processing systems that practices depended upon early in HIS adoption. Within the American Recovery and Reinvestment Act (ARRA) of 2009 legislation, there is a significant financial and compliance incentive to install and use EHRs. ARRA established mandated timelines forcing practices to accelerate use of their already chosen EHR or finally make a purchase decision. Implementing and using an EHR system is an enormous undertaking. It involves teams of deciding influencers, hardware selection, interfaces to legacy software, use design with the vendor of choice, development of various new patient/clinician workflows, and extraordinary enterprise staff training. As a beneficial by-product, there will be a voluminous amount of new electronic data to manage.

Mobile Communication and Devices

As the healthcare industry is wrestling with "patient engagement," the cellular phone may be leading the way in affordable ways of communication. There are currently over 3,800,000 Google Play (Android) and 2,000,000 iOS (Apple) (Statista, 2018) certified cellular healthcare applications, not to mention other platforms. Cellular is reliable, portable, affordable, and there is meaningful software to use. Clearly, there are numerous trivial and/or infrequently used applications, but millions of Americans use their cell phone for related healthcare purposes. Millions of people are using wrist, heart, and other cellular compliant

🔍 *CASE EXAMPLE: MOBILE DEVICES CREATING DATA WHILE MANAGING DIABETES*

Clinicians request that patients with Type II diabetes test their glucose (a quick blood stab) and record the results about twice each day. The patient is then instructed to keep track of a written record and/or take action when a glucose reading has an unfavorable result. With a device that integrates glucose testing capability with a cellular phone platform, the patient may test, get an immediate result, and have the results electronically sent to their clinicians, care givers, parents (in the case of juvenile diabetes), or other clinical resources. The patient's clinical resource may preprogram prompts providing advice messaged on the phone's screen to take a particular action based upon the glucose reading.

Were all of the Type II diabetics in the U.S. to use such a device the data produced would be impressive. With 30.3 million Type II diabetic patients or about 9.4 percent (Centers for Disease Control and Prevention, 2017) of the U.S. population testing twice daily, this cellular technology would produce more than 22 billion discrete tests annually. Each test would include who, when, what, messages from/to the patient, messages to the caregiver, and more. The message to the patient may communicate a testing trend (if the clinician so dictated) and so on. Holistically, there could be a significant cost containment for the same diabetic patient and the health system with these automated clinical advice messages as an alternative to having the patient present at a clinic or an expensive hospital ED.

Case Example by Ric Speaker.

communications as well as standalone devices. These devices produce real-time data and batch data acquisition multiple times during the day, daily or on an *ad hoc* basis.

Imaging

Imaging includes various means of radiology such as MRI, X-ray, CT (computed tomography) scanning radiology, and digital photography combining to be another huge data source. Imaging uses are evolving as an ever-enhancing, noninvasive tool for diagnostic care management. More and more test results are taking the form of digital images. For example, with biopsy results, a picture may accompany the written pathology report. Because digital imagining is precise, it conserves precious physician time. Additionally, compared to radiological films, it's more portable, may occupy myriad storage modalities, and its retrieval is far more facile. There is, however, a direct correlation between enhanced imaging

technologies and a noteworthy increase in data proliferation.

As imaging technologies continue to be enhanced through optical granularity and visual acuity, there are proportionately greater data volumes. Images take up more storage space than other types of data. A single X-ray image will be duplicatively required within the imaging center, the referring clinician's and the local hospital's EHR systems, and at the cloud-based software vendor's site, and may be stored at a research facility. Inopportunely, the translation of the image's detail into any sort of a granular bit-mapped data set can currently be stored only as retrievable location of the image in aggregate. So, an X-ray image or scan is stored as a single picture, but you cannot extract any data other than that picture as a whole. For example, an X-ray of a foot "No.9.20.18.ABC" is without judgment, bone description, dimension, or any data narrative. (Plus, with potentially disparate naming conventions within imaging and EHR systems, there may be duplication in the naming or numbering convention for an X-ray requiring a difficult normalization process.) The X-ray data storage and retrieval would be based upon the code "NO.9.20.18ABC." Importantly, future developments will make these static data references (images) available with more data analytics based upon technology. In turn, a very large data volume will be required for a single diagnostic element such as the aforementioned diabetic glucose reading or X-ray.

Also, with the predicable proliferation for **telemedicine**, imaging will be an invaluable tool requiring visual acuity, reliability, and security. Telemedicine will allow a clinician who may be 100 miles distant to read an image, evaluate test results and their trends, and observe on her computer's EHR other bodily function measurements without having to touch the patient. For rural Americans, the attributes of telemedicine are clear. Combining the growing U.S. population with the paucity of physicians and certified nurses, even urban areas may benefit from telemedicine's diagnostic attributes as a method for primary care triage.

▶ Data Technology

Oracle defines a **data dictionary** as "a collection of tables with metadata." IBM's definition is a "centralized repository of information about data such as meaning, relationships to other data, origin, usage, and format."

Healthcare data dictionaries, as with all data dictionaries, are fundamentally rule-sets for how all the collected and stored data are expected to behave. This rule-set describes data types, structure, formatting, and use. An imperative goal for the compliance of these rules is to achieve semantic **interoperability**—the ability to play nice in the sandbox. For example, two different clinicians may describe a disease or procedure slightly differently, but for data interoperability to occur, among numerous requirements, the data dictionary must have resolved this disparity

and adjudicate this semantic debate to make either data element usable.

Metadata is additional information about data itself. Essentially, it's data about data. The data dictionary may provide an organizational method to extract and systematize metadata for specific reasons. With the demands for clinical data exchanges involving EHRs, **Accountable Care Organizations (ACOs)**, **health information exchanges (HIEs)**, Meaningful Use (MU), and MACRA, data dictionaries will need to become undeniably reliable and compatible across the market.

As a relevant part of **data modeling** and with the proliferation of patient engagement, **democratization of data** (accessibility of digital information) must occur. The healthcare consumer will need to better acquire and analyze their state of health within what is clearly an industry that is technical and specialized. So, the vast nonspecialist patient population—with varying educational backgrounds and medical experiences—will require a relatively facile method for accessing medical histories, assessments for treatment options, and determinations for cost alternatives. This last notion is to have available, web-based, universally published transparency for health care's fees and patient financial responsibilities. These are not small tasks.

As aforementioned, clinicians use various visualization methods for diagnoses including X-rays, MRIs, laboratory results, clinical analytics, and more. All of these visual impressions presuppose high data availability. An important part of data democratization will include **data visualization** heretofore reserved for the "profession." We all respond to visual aids when trying to understand something and much more so when we have little training of the subject matter before us.

▶ Data Security

As previously stated, the security, veracity, and granularity of data are particularly important in the healthcare industry. These data are used in life and death decision making.

From a policy standpoint, The Health Insurance Portability and Accountability Act (HIPAA) and Protected Health Information (PHI) legislation has codified the security of healthcare data. These preventive laws are necessary when one is dealing with contemporary attacks on valuable data and for controls of confidential clinical information. In spite of these security efforts, more than half of U.S. hospitals have had their operational systems illegally accessed and data has been stolen only to be ransomed by clever thieves (hackers) (Centers for Disease Control and Prevention, 2017). To prevent a wholesale disclosure of patient and operational financial data, hospitals have more often than not quietly paid for the return of the patient's property (data). This obvious vulnerability makes healthcare institutions distressfully open targets. Furthermore, when data is stored and is internally made available to clinical or operational personnel, security must be assigned at the most elementary data level to prevent unauthorized personnel from accessing confidential clinical information. Just because one works in a clinic or hospital does not allow them access to patient information.

In regard to the security part of the ARRA, a provision called the Health Information Technology for Economic and Clinical Health (HITECH) Act was enacted to promote the adoption and MU of health information technology. Subtitle D of the HITECH Act addresses the privacy and security concerns associated with the electronic transmission of health information, in part, through several provisions that strengthen the civil and criminal enforcement of the HIPAA rules. There are stiff penalties for breaches of noncompliance for securing data transmissions and disclosure of PHI. ARRA has allocated a $25.9 billion spend by the Department of Health and Human Services (HHS) to encourage the adoption of security precautions and implementation of EHRs.

Another security measure in the field of medical research is that of "blind" data. This is where the specific patient identity is undisclosed, yet the clinical and/or financial data is used in an aggregate manner that allows broader statistical modeling discovery and decision making.

▶ Data Ownership

There are two notions of data "ownership" and uses. First, the legal, *de facto* ownership of clinical and financial data should always be with the patient. The patient should maintain the rights to all of their medical history; however, they may assign access for various uses such as care or research.

Second, the notion of control and ownership of data varies within the provider community, internal operating departments, and software vendors. Legally, none of these entities may use a patient's medical information without the patient's codified permission. However, there is often a bifurcation of internal belief regarding who "controls" the data within an institution or enterprise. Generally, the information technology (IT) department controls or stewards the data due to operational responsibilities for software application operations, necessary data interfacing, storage, and data organization. Pervasively, there is a belief that with IT training they have better competency and understanding of the data. Some alternative models give control of data to the purview of finance. As data and the resulting opportunity for analytics take a more critical and central importance, some institutions are assigning data ownership to an analytics group.

This text suggests, as with progressive business models, that the institution or enterprise must embrace the certainty that it has internal customers (operational departments) as well as external customers (patients, providers, etc.). We'll focus more on internal customers in the next data chapter (Chapter 11), but all employees and operational partners require myriad uses of data to perform their daily responsibilities. For some, they may need specially tailored content acquired from the singular or aggregate data stores. So, IT's role is to "mother" the institution's data so that its internal customers may use resulting data content that is reliable, timely, available, organized as requested, and based upon the roles each individual plays. The liaison of what internal customers need and how IT may fulfill delivery of these requests is essential in achieving healthcare efficiencies. The role of a data analyst who can synchronize their in-depth knowledge of the data with the internal customer's functional needs is an invaluable skill to any healthcare institution. Therefore, the concept for the control of data will be measured by every employee's ability to use the data effectually.

One significant challenge involving healthcare data is the plethora of software and device applications that generate data on a regular basis. An individual hospital may have dozens of disparate clinical and business processing applications. Some very large systems' vendors may provide the majority of mission critical operations for hospital or clinic operations, but no one vendor has proven to offer one software platform for all needs. There may always be narrow-use and point software applications that will need interfacing with these large systems vendors.

Further, mobile healthcare applications (apps), now numbering in the hundreds of thousands, often provide important critical patient data. Therefore, the data from these devices must be integrated into a central data repository for any approximation of a holistic clinical patient view.

None of the above is easy work. Software is inherently imperfect. Health care is experiencing the dubious distinction of being on new ground involving so many new data sources and lack of definitive standards. As a parallel, in the auto industry's rush to deploy driverless cars we have seen the malfunctioning of

software leading to fatalities. With health care's equivalence in human vulnerability, we need to appreciate that software's improper performance and uses of data may lead to human injury or worse.

So, we all need to appreciate the complex responsibilities for programmers and technical personnel charged with "mothering" data. Healthcare institutions have created large data stores and have in many instances provided their internal customers with invaluable information. However, with health care's long-standing reputation for slow technology adoption and its omnipresent demands regarding legacy systems and contemporary software integration, the demands on IT's time are oppressive.

To support this challenge, a 2015 *Health-Leaders* Media survey indicated that 81 percent of healthcare institutions rely on an EHR, while 95 percent expect to do so within three years. Yet it is estimated that the EHR today only contains 50 percent or less of available patient data, presenting, at best, an incomplete view of the patient record even though institutions indicate that they rely on an EHR for clinical and business decision making. Unstructured and fragmented data across multiple systems, and even paper records, will continue to block even the most committed institutions from success until they are able to retrieve all forms of information and assemble those data in a form that is clinically actionable. In addition, the expense of maintaining **legacy systems** will continue to siphon away the resources needed to move forward.

Technology alone is merely a tool, and without proper analysis and workflow, data cannot improve patient health outcomes or lower costs. Systems and processes that manage this information in a way that optimizes data's value are needed, and having them in place is among the most fundamental change providers and organizations must adopt before they can distinguish between value and merely a data "dump."

🔍 CASE EXAMPLE: DATA IN ACTION

One of the most fundamental healthcare transactions is a provider office visit. Today, from this visit, there will be a simple or multifaceted entry into an EHR system. Many, but not all, providers have a single vendor for health records and for their financial purposes. For the patient and insurance billing process, the medical practice must document one or more procedure codes (that may include modifying codes), diagnostic code(s), who, when, where, the practice fees, and any insurance-related patient payments made at the time of service. In aggregate this encounter contains a coded record comprised of dozens of discrete data elements. The EHR and office billing systems will provide internal software programming that links this single visit with historical visits and clinical synchronization of the patient's medical trends. The data from the single patient visit must be normalized and be available for the practice's internal use as well as made available for myriad exterior healthcare organizations.

For an acute care (hospital) episode, it may be an outpatient emergency visit, a same-day procedure, or an extended inpatient stay. The enormous amount of data generated for any of these above care circumstances must be available for certain real-time clinical decision making.

Case Example by Ric Speaker.

Data is prolific in a hospital environment whether from an inpatient or outpatient experience. There are a number of scenarios for the inception of a hospital ED visit. **FIGURE 10.2** shows the transactional flow of a hospital emergency visit. Having spent 25 years as an emergency physician in Denver, Colorado, Mark Radlauer, M.D., estimates that a hospital's ED may provide 35–60 percent of its inpatient admissions. It may begin with a referral from a community physician, a lesser-equipped emergency facility, or just as a patient walk-in. If the patient's presentation came from a provider or other clinician, it is likely that some sort of medical documentation will accompany the patient. Electronic documentation may have preceded the patient's physical arrival. In any case, if there is not an existing data interface established between the referring environment and the hospital's information systems, a new medical record will begin at presentation.

Insurance, demographic, and the patient's complaint information will create the foundation for a detailed record for both clinical and billing information. Dependent upon the ED's staff the patient's record will be built with

observations and diagnostics. Further, it may be additionally populated with imaging, laboratory, and other medical device results. Eventually, the patient will either be discharged with advice, drug prescriptions, or, in more severe cases the patient may be admitted within the hospital for subsequent care. The hospital may have an integrated single vendor software system or it may have a separate ED system that is most likely interfaced to the hospital's acute care system (Admit, Discharge, Transfer system or ADT).

A patient's experience that begins in the ED and continues to admission to the hospital will assuredly create a substantial collection of clinical and financial data. Indeed, if printed out, the electronic data may contain hundreds to thousands of pages. Also, the hospital must aggregate and maintain longitudinal data from each patient experience or stay after-the-fact as demonstrated by a recent individual's extended stay in a Colorado located hospital that generated over 9,000 pages of history.

One of the greatest challenges for the industry is the fact that data is often not **normalized** and may be siloed in disparate

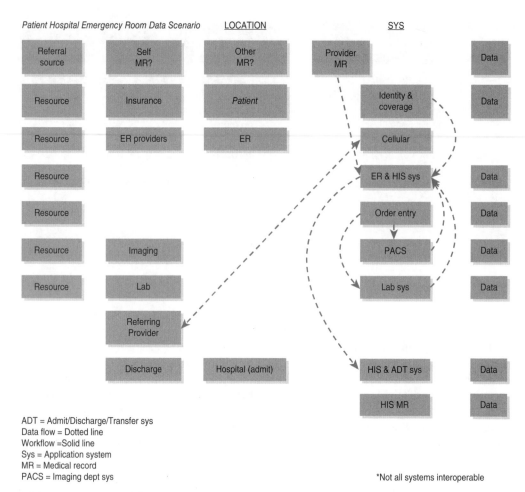

Patient Hospital Emergency Room Data Scenario   LOCATION   SYS

ADT = Admit/Discharge/Transfer sys
Data flow = Dotted line
Workflow =Solid line
Sys = Application system
MR = Medical record
PACS = Imaging dept sys

*Not all systems interoperable

FIGURE 10.2 Transactional flow and data creation from an ED visit.
Courtesy of Ric Speaker.

software applications. Integrating data from literally hundreds of software applications used in various providers and payers systems is laborious and expensive. On top of that, data is often housed within uncooperative entities or system from different and uncooperative vendors. Unless a functioning HIE is in place, there is no real incentive to share data across organizations—other than, of course, patient outcomes—and so organizations and vendors can remain chronically unaligned, thereby facilitating an environment where the most beneficial use of data may suffer.

▶ Medicare Access and CHIP Reauthorization Act

The **Medicare Access and CHIP Reauthorization Act (MACRA)** of 2015 is a cogent example of data's importance in the nation's struggle to address improved quality care and control costs. Federal legislation for the Department of HHS and CMS is applying efforts to measure the quality of care and to create incentives to compensate providers for their respective compliance and energies to affect this. To this end, MACRA principally addresses Medicare beneficiaries through various initiatives. In addition to modifying physician compensation, it establishes new federal advisory groups, new requirements for data development and testing, technical assistance to providers, and mandates for data sharing. Each of these initiatives represents consensus building and complicated programming and technical efforts in an industry that traditionally doesn't adopt change well, especially when there will inevitably be financial winners and losers. Compiled, organized, and reported data will be central in this new economic paradigm.

Participating Medicare providers will be formulaically compensated for the effectiveness and quality of their care: in other words, value. As described on CMS's website, MACRA repeals the sustainable growth rate (SGR) formula that has determined Medicare Part B reimbursement rates for physicians modifying these rates through new payments for care based upon effectiveness and the quality of care. Theoretically, traditional compensation that has been significantly influenced by volume of care is being subordinated to quality and value measurements of care.

This creates a situation where providers will need to know what occurs outside of their offices and within the totality of the patient's care network. Providers will be reliant on dependable and accurate data to effectively manage patient care. Abstractly, it means the provider's office EHR patient record will potentially need to share data with several disparate and competitive EHR systems. The central aggregation or accurately integrated collection of a patient's data must be accessible and minable for the provider to appropriately report information that CMS requires. A rather daunting task, as the current EHR application software systems do not communicate cross-vendor satisfactorily, much less commonly share integrated patient history. To fully implement MACRA, formidable new work by practices, programmers, database architects, and software vendors will be necessary, including the development of new electronic communication methods and security software.

Reporting requirements from CMS are included in the **Merit-based Incentive Payment System (MIPS)** quality, resource use, clinical practice improvement, and **Meaningful Use (MU)** of Certified EHR Technology. These measurements will lead to a variable incentive payment or loss of payment starting in 2019 at 4 percent and increasing to 9 percent in 2022. In parallel to MIPS, **alternative payment models (APMs)** will provide a method whereby Medicare may compensate higher rates to healthcare providers for their Medicare beneficiaries. Most providers who participate in APMs will also be subject to MIPS, but will receive favorable scoring with compatible higher reimbursement rates. Providers participating in the most advanced APMs (including Accountable Care Organizations, patient-centered medical homes and bundled payment models) may be designated as Qualifying APM Participants (QPs), which are not subject to MIPS yet provide for added financial incentives. All these rules from Medicare Part B will require provider observance for compensation. The results of this whole MACRA initiative will allow transparent public review.

Just imagine all the real-time data being transmitted between competitive providers, insurance businesses, and individual patients to make these government-sponsored initiatives work. There will be lots of fingers in lots of eyes in the unfolding.

▶ Big Data and Thick Data

One does not have to be technically inclined to have heard about Big Data. Big Data products and services are touted between car and food TV commercials. It is pervasive throughout all industries and our day-to-day lives.

Big Data is not about large individual data elements such as "elephant," "mountain," or such. It refers to the contemporary phenomena of having a massive amount of discrete data elements, thoughts, audio/video, social media, transactional applications, and more. As with other industries, Big Data has created data sets whose magnitude and construct have stressed traditional hardware and storage capabilities as well as databases that were not necessarily configured or architected to capture, manage, and process such copious amounts of data. Fortunately, hardware processing is faster, data storage including cloud storage is more affordable than traditional local storage methods, and in many cases database architecture is now perfecting the usage of these masses of data. Other industries—petroleum, consumer goods marketing, and social media—are all ahead of health care in wrangling and capitalizing on Big Data.

Health care will benefit from technological advances and models of Big Data use. However, health care is not just about numerics, words, or algorithms. The center of health care is the patient, a very subjective stakeholder. For improved quality of care, the patient's behaviors, motivations, perceptions, and observations must be included within the subject of outcomes and quality measurement. Therefore, to add to Big Data we must include **Thick Data**. Thick Data is by nature more subjective, visceral, and intuitive. The term refers to the murkiness or difficulty in the measurement of these data sets (e.g., how the patient feels about his progress in physical therapy). Quality measures will involve anthropological and ethnographical intelligence. For example, if a post-surgical orthopedic knee patient complies with all range of motion allowances, yet extreme pain persists, we will not have accomplished a quality outcome. The patient's perceptions and motivations will come into play. Intuitively, the industry will need even more subjective and patient-supplied data to satiate Thick Data's appetite.

Additionally, data reflecting issues of public health concern not only personal data but also environmental, social, acts of violence, and other systemic data. Our discussion for Thick Data is too new to imagine the variability of questions and answers with resulting data sets.

▶ **Velocity, Volume, and Variety (3Vs)**

Worldwide, health care is one of the larger contributors to creating its own Big Data due in part to high Velocity, high Volumes, and wide Variety of necessary data creation. The description of the **3V's of data** encourages a broader understanding of how data moves and works.

Velocity

Velocity suggests that data have momentum through applications, consumer uses, and business uses. This momentum is virtually exponential. Everyone who has used cellular technology has experienced this velocity of data through their phone's enhanced technology. Just a few years ago, consumers could not track their exercise performance, research extensive disease narratives, or communicate with their providers by digital means. Now consumers can perform all these tasks with personal electronic devices, portals, and websites.

Volume

Volume suggests similar exponential growth of accessible and seemingly necessary data. Earlier in this chapter, we discussed a volume example based on imaging; it is extremely relevant for understanding the ramifications of the increasing amounts of data in health care. Data growth in the future will likely be larger in health care than in any sector other than global security and social media.

Variety

Variety suggests that data are associated with, and will continue to take on, seemingly limitless descriptions. The use of new personal electronic devices will make fluid, organ, and almost any other bodily function measurement feasible. Cellular devices will serve up various health data such as blood glucose, blood pressure, cholesterol levels, and other essential measures in an attempt to improve the quality of medicine and disease management. Comparing other varieties in Big Data sets, there are an estimated 30,000 human diseases known to medicine. This makes the variety of healthcare data greater than that of home loans, for example. When adding in comorbidity issues and Thick Data, it is difficult to wrap one's mind around.

Analyzing Big Data allows analysts, researchers, and business users to make better and faster decisions using data that was previously inaccessible or unusable. Using advanced analytics techniques—such as text analytics, machine learning, predictive analytics, data mining, statistics, and natural language processing—businesses can analyze previously untapped data sources independently or together with their existing enterprise data to gain new insights resulting in better and faster decisions. We'll address Artificial Intelligence in Chapter 11 (**FIGURE 10.3**).

▶ Challenges for Data and Best Practices

Disparate Data

Healthcare organizations use these data as an integral part of their daily work. They are constantly developing and managing data interfaces between their own multipurposed applications as well as in between third-party

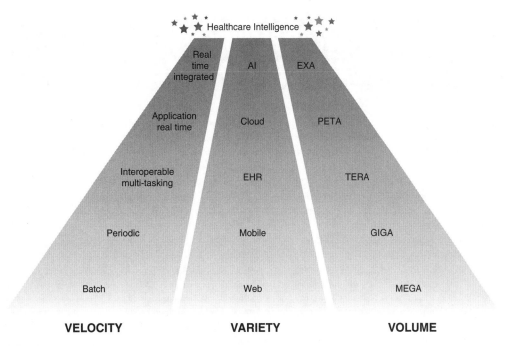

FIGURE 10.3 The 3Vs: The base of healthcare intelligence.

software applications. Many have centralized databases that aggregate these transactions along with alternatively sourced data from potentially hundreds of disparate clinical and business applications.

Financial Risk Associated with High Volume of Data

Health care's history includes iterative reinvention in adapting to trends and political aims. New technologies and care delivery methods are contributing to exponential increases in data volumes. At a macroeconomic level, the discussion for different financial risk assumption models has accelerated operational introspection from both clinicians and business leaders.

Clinician Time and Patient Experience

The focus on healthcare data is so profound that some would debate that it may be cluttering the experience of patient care where its ultimate value may prove to be incalculable. Clinicians consistently report spending as much time completing the electronic documentation of a patient encounter as they spent with the patient interaction itself. The math for having the most expensive and limited human resource typing on a keyboard vis-à-vis spending more time with the patient is inexcusable. Further, as consistently expressed, these clerical-like duties are breeding dissatisfaction within the physician community. The production of all these great data has some unintended consequences.

Security

With health care's vulnerable security history, one wonders about the prospective volumes of personal healthcare data. In the words of Amazon's CEO, Jeff Bezos, the conflict between privacy and security is the "issue of our age (Tsukayama, 2016)." Noted healthcare lawyer Paul Ohm puts it this way: "Data can either be

🔍 CASE EXAMPLE: COMPLEXITY IN CODING HEALTHCARE DIAGNOSES AND PROCEDURES

The complexity of health care becomes clear when one considers that the kernels for healthcare billing and revenue cycle management include **International Statistical Classification of Diseases and Related Health Problems** (ICD-9 and ICD-10) codes, **Current Procedural Terminology (CPT)** codes, and **diagnosis-related groups (DRGs)** coding. There are approximately 14,000 ICD-9 and 68,000 ICD-10 unique codes, each three to seven characters in length, along with potential modifiers that must be used by providers to attain contractual reimbursement for their services. Recently in the U.S., ICD-9 codes were replaced by ICD-10 codes. This process led to tremendous changes in personnel training and software systems—the transition has had a deleterious cash-flow effect on providers, while the greater specificity of ICD-10 codes will allow for more precise matching of codes to complete diagnoses and conditions. There are 7,800 CPT codes with even more potential modifiers. DRGs are used in acute care as a bundling method for multiple patient care activities grouped and based on similar consumption of resources. All of these codes may be used by employers as methods to compensate providers; project income; plan for facilities and materials; and serve as input for population management, evaluation, and trend prediction. Tens of thousands of coders must translate what providers do into these diagnostic and procedural codes to properly complete and adjudicate an insurance form. These codes must be retained and must be available for extensive periods of time for a host of analytical and legal reasons.

Case Example by Ric Speaker.

🔍 *CASE EXAMPLE: ARRA AND ITS IMPACT ON DATA*

There are so many facets of health care's woes and many insiders wish that the industry would take the painful steps to cure itself. However, there has been little progress in doing so. Therefore, the government is taking action as demonstrated by the following:

ARRA was enacted on February 17, 2009. ARRA includes many measures to modernize our nation's infrastructure, one of which is the HITECH Act. The HITECH Act supports the concept of EHR-MU, an effort led by CMS and the Office of the National Coordinator for Health IT (ONC). HITECH established the MU of interoperable EHR systems throughout the U.S. healthcare delivery system as a critical national goal. MU is defined by the use of certified EHR technology in a meaningful manner according to criteria specifying the adoption of functionality and capabilities (for example electronic prescribing); ensuring that the certified EHR technology is connected in a manner that provides for the electronic exchange of health information to improve the quality of care; and that in using certified EHR technology, the provider must submit to the Secretary of Health and Human Services information on quality of care and other measures.

The concept of MU rested on the "5 Pillars" of health outcomes policy priorities, namely:

1. Improve quality, safety, efficiency, and reduce health disparities.
2. Engage patients and families in their health.
3. Improve care coordination.
4. Improve population and public health.
5. Ensure adequate privacy and security protection for personal health information.

Case Example by Ric Speaker.

useful or perfectly anonymous but never both (Ohm, 2009)."

Summary

Data provide an increasingly essential resource for healthcare organizations and providers. Data support clinical work and business processes, and they offer the necessary tools for information creation and analytical opportunities. Data are created and captured in transaction systems, from contemporary devices, and from cellular software applications that support the daily activities of health care, both clinically and from a business perspective. Healthcare data continue to exponentially increase in terms of their velocity (usefulness), volume (amount), and variety (types). Ultimately, these combine to form a resource yet to be defined, called Big Data and Thick Data, which creates notions of limitless possibilities for insight, information, imagination, and intelligence. None of these goals will be reached easily, as the challenges and barriers to intelligent information usage are many. Critical technology standards, disparate source systems, and silo processes continue to challenge healthcare organizations and it will be many years before this disintegration is overcome. There are mandates that are supporting the needs for data security, privacy, and confidentiality. Efforts for all these data requirements are still fragmented, but with appropriate realignment of financial incentives and empirically measured clinical outcome measures, health care will benefit.

By considering the technical and analytical needs and uses of data, the healthcare industry can accelerate implementation of the long-standing belief that the economics and efficacy of health care may be enhanced through evidence-based medicine. Predictive capabilities driven by Big Data and Thick Data will allow healthcare risks to be anticipated, shifting health care from reactive to proactive more of the time. The exponential growth of data production will be both foundational and a technological challenge to manage. Systems must be developed to more efficiently collect, normalize, and integrate data to be analyzed on both a real-time and a retrospective basis.

A growing number of healthcare institutions, however nascent, have undertaken the monumental task of providing a solution for the data explosion. In the long run, this discipline will provide an opportunity for the growth of organizational cultures into learning organizations, as well as individual employee development and career growth.

Key Terms

3V's of data

Accountable Care Organizations (ACOs)

Alternative payment models (APMs)

Big Data

Current Procedural Terminology (CPT)

Data

Data dictionary

Data modeling

Data sources

Data visualization

Democratization of data

Diagnosis-related groups (DRGs)

Health information exchanges (HIEs)

International Statistical Classification of Diseases and Related Health Problems (ICD)

Interoperability

Legacy systems

Meaningful Use (MU)

Medicare Access and CHIP Reauthorization Act (MACRA)

Merit-based Incentive Payment System (MIPS)

Metadata

Normalized

Pixels

Telemedicine

Thick Data

Discussion Questions

1. Write your own definition of data. How does your daily life intersect the world of data?
2. What about data is mysterious to you? Describe the areas you do not understand.
3. Can you envision any other new data source that might become part of the healthcare arena?
4. Are there any roles described within this discussion on data that are of interest to you?
5. If sharing data between healthcare organizations may have a macro industry benefit, how do you think this could happen?
6. Have you worked or are you currently working in a healthcare organization that has emphasized data as being strategic? How has the organization communicated this idea throughout its entire team?
7. Describe how disparate data might be converted into a single vocabulary.
8. Have you personally experienced an encounter with a provider and felt it beneficial that the provider might have access to or use real-time data to assist the provider with your care?
9. What, in your opinion, are the three biggest data challenges in health care?
10. Do you believe that other industries that have been using data for their own operational efficiencies may help the healthcare industry better navigate the adoption and use of data for both business and clinical benefit? If yes, how so?
11. Is there a single best source of data for health care to start with, in terms of managing the inherent responsibilities to collect, aggregate, and store data? Or do all the data sources need to be tapped at once?

References

American Hospital Association. (2018). *Fast facts.* Retrieved from https://www.aha.org/statistics/fast-facts-us-hospitals

Bureau of Labor Statistics. (2017). *Registered nurses.* Retrieved from https://www.bls.gov/ooh/healthcare/registered-nurses.htm

Centers for Disease Control and Prevention. (2017, July 18). *New CDC report: More than 100 million Americans have diabetes of prediabetes.* Retrieved from https://www.cdc.gov/media/releases/2017/p0718-diabetes-report.html

Centers for Medicare & Medicaid Services. (2016a). National health expenditure data. Retrieved from https://www.cms.gov/Research-Statistics-Data-and-Systems/Statistics-Trends-and-Reports/NationalHealthExpendData/NationalHealthAccountsHistorical.html

Centers for Medicare & Medicaid Services. (2016b). National health expenditure projections 2017–2026: Forecast summary. Retrieved from https://www.cms.gov/Research-Statistics-Data-and-Systems/Statistics-Trends-and-Reports/NationalHealthExpendData/Downloads/ForecastSummary.pdf

IBIS World. (2018, July). Emergency & other outpatient care centers in the U.S. *IBIS World.* Retrieved from https://www.ibisworld.com/industry-trends/market-research-reports/healthcare-social-assistance/ambulatory-health-care-services/emergency-other-outpatient-care-centers.html

Lazarou, J., Pomeranz, B. H., & Corey, P. N. (1998). Incidence of adverse drug reactions in hospitalized patients: A meta-analysis of prospective studies. *JAMA, 279*(15), 1200–1205.

Ohm, P. (2009). *Broken promises of privacy: Responding to the surprising failure of anonymization.* Electronic Privacy Information Center. Retrieved from https://epic.org/privacy/reidentification/ohm_article.pdf

Statista. (2013). Statistics and facts on U.S. Physicians/Doctors. *Statista.* Retrieved from https://www.statista.com/topics/1244/physicians/ (Statista, physician topics, 2018)

Statista. (2018). Number of apps available in leading app stores as of 1st quarter 2018. *Statista.* Retrieved from https://www.statista.com/statistics/276623/number-of-apps-available-in-leading-app-stores/

The World Bank. (2017). Military expenditure (% of GDP). Retrieved from https://data.worldbank.org/indicator/ms.mil.xpnd.gd.zs

Tsukayama, H. (2016, May 18). Amazon CEO Jeffrey Bezos: Debate between privacy and security is 'issue of our age.' *The Washington Post.* Retrieved from https://www.washingtonpost.com/news/the-switch/wp/2016/05/18/amazon-ceo-jeffrey-bezos-debate-between-privacy-and-security-is-issue-of-our-age/?utm_term=.3a481967ad70

CHAPTER 11

Analytics, Business Intelligence and Clinical Intelligence

Ric Speaker

LEARNING OBJECTIVES

By the end of this chapter, the student will be able to:

- Appreciate the historical foundations of healthcare business intelligence (BI) and clinical intelligence (CI).
- Understand the concept, purpose, and potential of healthcare analytics.
- Describe the myriad stakeholders who need BI and CI information to perform their jobs in the healthcare arena.
- Identify the methods for receiving, organizing, storing, mining, and formatting data for BI and CI purposes.
- Be introduced to the technological advances that may benefit health care's dire need for useful analytics.

▶ Introduction

Analytics is the art and science of applying information, derived from data, to a given situation. This is where data gets exciting and extremely relevant. Additionally, at the time of this writing, the field of analytics is on the verge of changing the healthcare industry for the better in major ways.

The generic definition of **business intelligence (BI)** is a set of theories, methodologies, processes, architectures, and technologies that transform raw data into meaningful and useful information for business purposes. This term—and the practice—is applied widely throughout various industries. In line with health care's deserved reputation of slow adoption and implementation of integrated data, purposeful data mining lags behind other industries. Like BI, the term **clinical intelligence (CI)** refers to data sets turned into useful information; unlike BI, CI is healthcare specific. For a host of reasons—review Chapter 10: Data—the entire healthcare industry must accelerate the use of both clinical and business data.

The urgent tone in this chapter reflects the climate in the healthcare industry at large. The Centers for Medicare and Medicaid Services (CMS) Administrator Seema Verma wrote, "We must shift away from a fee-for-service system that reimburses only on volume and move toward a system that holds providers accountable for outcomes and allows them to innovate. Providers need the freedom to design and offer new approaches to delivering care." Key notions suggested by Verma are "allows them to innovate" and "providers need the freedom to design and use new approaches." Healthcare providers must lead in a transformation of their industry. It should not be payers, the government, or the profit-taking suppliers who do not actually practice patient care. Providers will never accomplish meaningful change until they can use and value the prodigious amount of historical (and currently escalating production of) data. The imminent adoption of the market's value-based financial risk paradigm shift, clinician compensation incentives and disincentives, cost transparency, population health management, and other industry changes that are affecting all stakeholders will force leveraging historical and real-time data. Further, advances in software, hardware, and data storage methods will facilitate data mining. Technology innovations such as **artificial intelligence (AI)**, **machine learning (ML)**, **cloud-based data storage**, **deep learning (DL)**, and application software capabilities are all promising developments that will assist in health care's quest to leverage data for the purpose of analytics and innovation of care.

▶ Health Care's BI and CI

A Definition and Overview of BI/CI Complexity

BI handles large amounts of data and information to help identify and develop new opportunities. Making use of new opportunities and implementing an effective strategy can provide a competitive market advantage and long-term stability. BI technologies provide historical, current, and predictive views of business operations. Common functions of BI technologies include reporting, online analytical processing, analytics, data mining, complex event processing, business performance management benchmarking, text mining, predictive mining, predictive analytics, and prescriptive analytics (Mulcahy, n.d.).

CI is emerging adjunct to BI and is focused on the healthcare industry. With the mandated proliferation of various forms of electronic clinical data use, as well as industry and political pressures to obtain and utilize clinical measurements, BI is the obvious technological foundation for CI. The aforementioned BI definition works perfectly as CI's mechanics and functionality underpinning. Thus, a generic definition of CI is a set of theories, methodologies, processes, architectures, and technologies that transform raw data into meaningful and useful information for clinical purposes. Specific uses for health care's BI and CI include statistics, scorecards, quality metrics and reporting, multipurpose presentation dashboards, outcomes-based compensation, longitudinal care management, **key performance indicators (KPIs)**, alerts, supply-chain analysis, experience-based rating engines, and population management.

There is no convenient singular description to create a cogent definition for the many meanings and types of health care's BI and CI. Health care's BI and CI are very subjective—remember, "Health care is local," and so is data use. As with the practice of medicine and the extremely competitive environment for operational software, there is a paucity of standards that affects data, its organization, and its mining. The application of an intelligence process may be static and trivial, or it may be dynamic and extremely complicated. Thousands of discrete software applications, cellular software tools, and data collection devices, and tens of

🔎 CASE EXAMPLE: HYPOTHETICAL BI

A CEO wants a **dashboard** that is refreshed nightly. A single dashboard screen presentation includes all of the organization's profit and loss data, accounts receivable (A/R) status, insurance payment denials, patient throughput volumes, prospectively booked appointments, and additional KPIs. The CEO will be able to review the insurance payment denials graphic and hover her computer mouse over the bar chart for the Blue Cross/Blue Shield (BCBS) payer indicator, double-click, and open the details for all the claims without outstanding denied payments. She may then tag this detailed report and send it to her chief financial officer (CFO) with questions and a requested response expectation.

Case Example by Ric Speaker.

🔎 CASE EXAMPLE: HYPOTHETICAL INTEGRATED BI/CI

A clinic administrator is negotiating with an insurance company over an at-risk contract for the insurer's largest business client's employee population. The administrator searches the BI/CI data for the same population (including subscriber family dependents) currently seen in the practice. Then the administrator sorts the list of patients by diagnostic procedural codes, stratifying them by age, weight, ethnicity, comorbidities, charges and payment history, IDC-10 and CPT codes (International Classification of Diseases, Tenth Revision, and Current Procedural Terminology), and prescriptions. The administrator produces the same summary for three other payers and large employer contracts and subsequently produces a comparison to these existing contracts and the proposed compensation by the new insurer.

Case Example by Ric Speaker.

thousands of discrete data elements are used daily by providers, payers, and related health organizations, all of which would have their own description for what and how data intelligence is relevant for them.

There are a nearly infinite number of current and imagined health care's BI and CI content examples. We will review some next.

Assembling and preparing all these data for specific subsequent use is hard, technical work. Adoption of BI/CI has been slow—slower even than electronic health record (EHR) adoption. (It did not hurt to have significant financial incentives from CMS to accelerate the latter.) It is estimated that 30 percent of U.S. healthcare providers have implemented data warehouses and BI/CI software to support clinical decision making, pay-for-performance (P4P) programs, **comparative effectiveness research (CER)**, and to track clinical outcomes

as part of healthcare quality measurement initiatives (Agosta, 2010). Given the government mandates for information from providers, increasing sources of clinical data from EHR systems, reimbursement increasingly tied to value, needs to manage the health of populations, greater transparency through public reporting of healthcare outcomes, and a host of other circumstances, in the near term BI/CI will become more pervasive and vendor tools will become easier and more robust to use.

Healthcare organizations have had very mixed experiences in regard to BI/CI. With the support of sophisticated internal information technology (IT) departments, the more advanced healthcare providers have created valuable **central data repositories (CDRs)**, or data warehouses, through diligent attention to quality, organization, and maintenance of those new data storehouses. Where nascent

BI/CI solutions were designed for accuracy, performance, and breadth of purpose, these organizations have achieved marked successes.

Conversely, where data have been contained in silos and where either an IT or finance department has restricted use of those data to a chosen few parties, there have been some black eyes for vendors and for BI/CI initiatives. Expectations often are not met by actual outcomes of those projects: expectations may be inflated due to the vendor overselling its methods, an organization misunderstanding the level of expertise, investment and commitment necessary, or both parties failing to appreciate the complexity of BI/CI. "We have overpromised and under-delivered," says Dr. Brennan Spiegel of the University of California, Los Angeles (Fry & Mukherjee, 2018).

CI is a term that has only recently been coined, in conjunction with the increased adoption and use of the EHR, EMR, and personal health record (PHR), all of which overlap to some extent in terms of their functionality and usage. Their differences generally reflect who collects the data, the setting where this occurs, and the comprehensiveness of the application (Fry & Mukherjee, 2018). In spite of myriad estimates that only as much as 50 percent of the total patient's health history, an EHR system comprises the broadest description of a patient's medical and health history, covering a large collection of clinical data including ambulatory, acute care, and holistic care information. Also, EMRs are used to facilitate clinical care processes in real time. An EMR is often employed in a singular ambulatory or acute care setting, such as a freestanding physician's office or hospital, and may or not have any or have little electronic connection to another facility such as an ambulatory or hospital setting. EMRs lack functionality with regard to offering a longitudinal view across multiple settings of care. The PHR is managed by the patient (or a parent or guardian) and populated with personally acquired medical and health-related information. The varying terminology and need to integrate these dissimilar platforms create a significant challenge when attempting to implement analytics using data from these and other systems. Such issues as data normalization will always be a challenge (**FIGURE 11.1**).

There is a correlation between the number of users for intelligence and analytics and the complexities for creating content. The vast number of users generally require more mundane and more easily created content. More complex content is utilized by smaller audiences created by more technical personnel. For example, overdue payment records are easier and more widely distributed than comorbidities for Parkinson's disease and depression.

CI, when properly implemented, will not only support more focused clinical analysis than BI but should also be designed and managed to integrate "business data" for broader analysis, including, for instance, cost accounting data within a clinical analysis. A longitudinal patient medical history combined with the business history (e.g., charges, payments, pharmaceutical prescriptions, or disposable medical equipment consumption) for the same patient would provide invaluable insights for outcomes measurement and monitoring as well as process effectiveness. Consider the following example of BI/CI integration to see how this works: suppose a patient with cardiovascular disease receives a stent in a catheterization procedure. Future and concurrent caregivers might like to know the stent's source, cost, stockkeeping unit (SKU) identification, and date of manufacture and installation (as well as by whom and where); provider follow-up observations; patient-reported experience; related diagnoses and other therapies provided; patient outcome including complications; and other related medical issues. Hypothetically, in the event of the patient's continued complaints or a manufacturer's recall, the organization could search the patient's integrated data and take appropriate action.

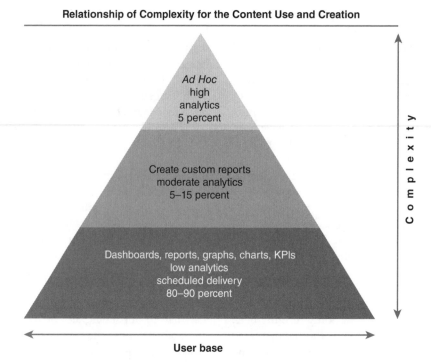

Relationship of Complexity for the Content Use and Creation

Ad Hoc
high
analytics
5 percent

Create custom reports
moderate analytics
5–15 percent

Dashboards, reports, graphs, charts, KPIs
low analytics
scheduled delivery
80–90 percent

Complexity

User base

FIGURE 11.1 Relationship of complexity for content use and creation.

In spite of tremendous industry and governmental attention—as well as technology advances—healthcare organizations' adoption of comprehensive BI/CI has been disappointingly slow. Some components of reporting, analytics, and data presentation are being used, but usually in siloed application environments. Siloed application environments—such as revenue-cycle or laboratory systems that pull data from separate repositories—tell only part of the story of what is going on for the patient or the organization, rather than providing a more holistic or comprehensive viewpoint. These silos can deter progress and syphon off resources that could be devoted toward more integrated BI/CI implementation projects.

Cost, limited staff experience, restricted implementation resources, numerous competing mandates and industry requirements (e.g., the mandates for EHR use, and ICD-10 conversions), data store architectural efficiency, hardware/cloud-based performance concerns,

and a host of other considerations are some of the valid reasons for lowering the prioritization for BI and CI. Nevertheless, surveys of chief information officers (CIOs) and other organizational executives by the Healthcare Information and Management Systems Society (HIMSS), the Medical Group Management Association (MGMA), and other member groups consistently indicate that healthcare organizations plan to become proactive in tackling more relevant and dramatic projects within their landscape of data. Such expanded capabilities would be consistent with the burgeoning development of data warehousing and BI initiatives in other industries.

It must be noted that there is a scarcity of data analysts. More work will lead to better industry recruitment for hiring BI and CI talent. Challenging as this work might be, it is both exciting and rewarding. Given the current crises in cost and quality, health care stands to gain as much as, if not more than, any industry by increasing its secondary use of data for BI and CI insights and improvements. These data analytics platforms will offer essential capabilities to help better manage and improve the quality of care delivered by healthcare organizations.

🔍 CASE EXAMPLE: A WELL-DESIGNED BI/CI SOLUTION FOR MULTI-PROVIDER OBGYN CARE

A relatively small obstetrics/gynecology practice had problems tracking compliance in its administration department and inventorying Gardasil. The Gardasil vaccine is used to prevent human papillomavirus infection, which may lead to cervical cancer; for maximum effectiveness, it needs to be administered as a series of doses in the same patient. This drug has a limited shelf life, so an expensive inventory must be destroyed if not used.

Using health information systems (HIS) and technology systems to provide a BI/CI solution, the practice combined data from its purchasing, scheduling, electronic medical record (EMR), and provider productivity systems to stratify by provider which patients were receiving Gardasil. To better manage the inventory of this vaccine, it then calculated the drug volumes that would be necessary based on trending appointments and the targeted patient population demographics. The data provided (1) a list of patients for scheduling and (2) an order process for Gardasil. The resulting analytics provided a quality factor to ensure proper patient scheduling and administration of the drug (including a potential recall) while saving the practice hundreds of thousands of dollars in wasted inventory. This example demonstrates the many different disciplines involved in improving a single clinical process, along with the resulting impact on cost management and clinical quality (**TABLE 11.1**).

TABLE 11.1 BI/CI for Gardasil at a Northeastern Healthcare Provider

Provider	All Female Patients, Ages 11–26	Three Shots Given	Two Shots Given	One Shot Given	No Shots Given	Cost	Revenue
	29	1		2	26	$9,840	$15,170
Aggarwal	188	18	14	35	121	$53,640	$82,695
Chang	35	2		3	30	$11,520	$17,760
Churchill	304	63	32	19	189	$76,440	$117,845
Cooper	124	25	8	11	80	$32,400	$49,950

(continues)

🔍 CASE EXAMPLE: A WELL-DESIGNED BI/CI SOLUTION FOR MULTI-PROVIDER OBGYN CARE (continued)

Provider	All Female Patients, Ages 11–26	Three Shots Given	Two Shots Given	One Shot Given	No Shots Given	Cost	Revenue
Cohen	328	158	25	17	121	$50,640	$78,070
Demartino	23	8	1	1	13	$5,040	$7,770
Gorman	73	17	3	6	46	$18,360	$28,305
Iannini	720	276	100	71	260	$122,640	$189,070
Jakmczyk	81	20	11	8	41	$18,000	$27,750
Knights	15	2	2	3	8	$3,840	$5,920
Kovacs	245	69	22	24	130	$55,200	$85,100
Oh	140	19	8	12	100	$39,840	$61,420
Paparello	144	7	1	2	134	$48,480	$75,295
Rodman	117	26	8	18	65	$28,680	$44,215
Rubinstein	721	325	95	51	233	$107,520	$165,760
Simon	610	218	59	57	268	$117,240	$180,745
Steger	10	1		1	8	$3,120	$4,810
Talland	64	18	11	3	32	$13,560	$20,905
Travassos	714	264	76	79	286	$131,040	$202,020
Tripp	282	139	28	31	82	$40,320	$62,160

Way	4	1			3	$1,080	$1,665
Werner	349	74	38	28	202	$84,000	$129,500
Wong	16	1		1	14	$5,280	$8,140
Zentz	24	5	2	3	14	$6,000	$9,250
Totals	5,360	1,757	544	486	2,506	$1,084,080	$1,671,290

Case Example by Ric Speaker.

▶ History of BI and CI

The healthcare industry has come a long way in data collection and processing. As demonstrated in Chapter 10, there is a massive collection of business and clinical data. Nevertheless, healthcare organizations have a long way to go in effectively organizing and analyzing these data to realize workplace efficiencies and better medical outcomes.

When computers entered the marketplace in the late 1960s and early 1970s, healthcare-related data were generally focused on processing billing and automating the byzantine world of insurance claims. At that time, the landscape for the dominant fee-for-service model for charges, payments, and adjustments was straightforward. Getting paid as providers and paying as payers according to the appropriate procedure and diagnostic codes worked rather well. The financial environment was characterized by straightforward fee-for-service reimbursement rather than today's complex risk arrangements, with concomitant detailed contracting and productivity measures. Interestingly, the notion of using small apartment refrigerator–sized computers for coding and sending off insurance claims both stressed and fascinated healthcare providers during that era. Principally, the adoption rate for computerization was slow because it required a significant resource investment—too much for many self-employed physicians and investment risk-adverse hospitals. Pharmaceutical companies just needed to count things they sold, laboratories sent out results and bills on paper, and payers used massive computers to enroll subscribers and adjudicate claims with fewer contracting rules than today. Hospitals had paper census lists, paper bills, and paper medical records (and overused photocopy machines).

In the early 1980s, an MGMA vendor exhibit hall had fewer than five software vendors extolling the virtues of their applications. The majority of vendors had paper products, book publishers, disposable clinical supplies, and the like. Today the same national and regional MGMA meetings are principally software vendors with well over one hundred. As transactional software began to capture data sufficient for providers to file claims and for payers to adjudicate those claims, the art of functional reporting emerged. Reporting became an important part of the promise of HIS through the advent of early healthcare software. Those reports are the ancient predecessors of analytical intelligence. Limited tabular screen shots provided some breakthrough efficiencies in an environment that was conditioned to use paper and pencil. For example, aged trial balance reports and computer-based appointment registries empowered physicians and became the staple reports for receivables management.

These reports also amplified the ensuing friction between payers and providers arguing about whose pocket the money should be in and when. Insurance claims began being printed by providers as a significant time saver. In contrast, insurance company personnel scanned or manually entered the claims. When providers and payers conducted contract negotiations, weeks might pass while IT departments tried to figure out inputted (but difficult to retrieve) costs and payment history. Few data processing directors (the forerunners of today's chief information officers) spent any time with "information," but rather treaded water while trying to keep hardware working and prevent software and hardware from crashing. Accessing data was profoundly difficult.

Reports were typically structured or "**canned**." User requests for report changes joined a queue of reporting enhancements to be eventually delivered by IT departments and software vendors. With fewer software offerings available, reports were produced for specific applications for specific operational audiences. If some executive at hospital X wanted to see information across her fiefdom of departments and within her niche computer applications, she would likely call upon someone from her IT or accounting team to populate a basic spreadsheet. Over time, the spreadsheet started to overtake reports as an analytical tool.

During the early days of computing, multitasking software and PCs were not available. Terminal screens were gray, orange, or green. A storage capacity of 10 megabytes might suffice for a busy 10-provider group practice; 400 megabytes would carry the day for a small hospital. Larger institutions often used service bureaus with larger computers along with slow phone line connections to run their businesses. To meet the need for reporting, a programmer who knew COBOL, FORTRAN, or early MUMPS (early software programming languages still in use as the foundation within many systems worldwide) would have to manually program each report. Adding an unforeseen data element to the application at a later date meant going back to the programming cubicle and rewriting code. There was no such thing as email or the Internet; likewise, networks (either hardwired or wireless), now such a familiar part of life, were not broadly available.

As with many innovations in the computer and software world, an evolutionary development occurred in the mid-1990s. The notions of early **executive information systems (EIS)** and **decision support systems (DSS)** were introduced in the healthcare industry. These types of application software brought together data from multiple sources. As their names suggest, EIS and DSS were designed to help management teams at healthcare organizations make decisions by providing relevant information from data acquired from transaction systems. In spite of the fact that this BI effort was still generally static, it represented a quantum leap forward. Unfortunately, producing these reports took an inordinate amount of time, and they were primarily focused on BI rather than CI. After the advent of EIS and DSS, universities, pharmaceutical companies, and laboratory testing companies started to provide some analysis for limited clinical measures, mostly for internal knowledge. For example, disease management gained some theoretical traction in trying to predict better clinical care and apply early cost-control measures. Managed care had progressed to the point that payers wanted better information principally for the purpose of actuarial and underwriting for risk evaluation—a relatively narrow area of concentration.

All of these efforts were limited by the computer power of the time and constraints associated with the older programming languages. However, this was also a point in history when an uncomfortable political focus on quickly rising healthcare costs began, which helped prepare the way for early EHR systems, increased computing power, use of Internet technologies, and less expensive data storage. Little could these early adopters and innovators possibly imagine the world of healthcare computing today!

▶ Current Challenges for Analytics

Analytics and Thick Data

Most healthcare processes can be described and managed at a very scientific level. Chemistry, biology, radiology, and other macro disciplines in the practice of medicine should be "black and white." By extension, one might assume that science would breed objectivity. However, there is a great deal of subjectivity in the delivery of health care and BI/CI. Reasons for this subjectivity and variability include the constant growth of evidence-based medicine, opinionated and differently trained human practitioners and managers, inherent patient uniqueness, and challenges in communication. In our Data chapter (Chapter 10), we discussed Thick Data, which reflects this notion of subjectivity, how clinicians interpret the science of medicine, and the variability of patients' motivations and tolerances. Therefore, for analytics, there may be a needed, bifurcated agreement that (1) analytical content might be scientifically true or 99 percent defensible while (2) clinical decisions that incorporate Thick Data will need necessary wiggle room or conclusions that are at best 80 or 90 percent right. This conundrum is reflected in the computer and software systems that attempt to support these divergences.

Vendor Choice

No single computer hardware or software system has controlled the industry, becoming the standard, dominant selection. For almost any application, there is a handful of leading competitive systems that vie for customers in the niche. The hospital world has replaced a number of mission-critical operational (including EHRs) systems titrating the acute care world's choices down to about five major vendors. The physician market for practice management systems (PMS) is far more fragmented and there remains a plethora of vendors, many of which are aging. Available to any healthcare organization are well in excess of 1,000 vendors espousing their singular superiority while running on different hardware platforms, relying on different operating systems, and using a host of programming languages, many of them proprietary and all of which are modified, enhanced, and upgraded on a regular basis, thereby affecting the continuity of data, interfaces, and operational use. One could walk through any metropolitan city's hospitals and medical clinics and find disparate vendor software packages, computer configurations, and strategies for IT and business management. These organizations' views of the world and the purpose of HIS are manifested in very different ways. As a result, it might be argued that many of health care's macro inefficiencies are inherent in the confusing landscape of software and derived from the independent methods of delivery utilized by the healthcare industry's participants. This discordant landscape is certainly relevant to the discussion of analytics. Interoperability, data normalization, transferable skillsets, and interfacing are all examples that create challenges for the successful architecting and implementation of analytical solutions in health care.

Adoption of Technologies and Process

In the retail, manufacturing, and banking industries, for example, the adoption of BI, analytics, modeling, and forecasting has outpaced that in health care. None of these other industries is modest in its complexity, and information system implementation and data use are certainly no small tasks. One interesting comparison as voiced by Dale Sanders of Health Catalyst is that health care compiles an average of 100 MB of data for every patient every year while Tesla monitors operating data in every one of its autos to the tune of 25 GB per car per hour (Burton, 2018). That is one reason why Tesla's data, analytics, and AI are much better: they collect so much more information (more types of information, more data points, more continuously) than a healthcare provider collects on a patient one or two times a year.

In defense of the healthcare industry's relatively slow embrace of BI/CI, its amorphous and complex nature brings about a number of profoundly challenging issues when it comes to the subject of analytics. Health care is extremely fragmented. As stated elsewhere in the text, common entities, professionals, and components in this industry more often than not "doing the same thing differently." Following are some major reasons why healthcare analytics can be a challenging environment:

- Health care is a $3+ trillion industry, fast on its way to accounting for almost 20 percent of the U.S. gross domestic product, and has lots of moving parts (Centers for Medicare & Medicaid Services, 2016).
- Only recent CMS legislation provides financial incentives for coordination of medical care among competitors.
- More than 4 million healthcare providers of various types provide services in the U.S.
- In the U.S., there are more than 5,500 hospitals (American Hospital Association, 2018), more than 200 insurance payers (Heilbrunn, 2013), 141 medical schools (Association of American Medical Colleges, n.d.), and more than 16,000 nursing homes (Centers for Disease Control and Prevention, n.d.)—many of whom are "doing the same thing differently."
- Dozens of "legacy" (meaning old) and contemporary programming languages

and operating systems are contemporaneously in use throughout the healthcare industry.

- From single departments to enterprise-wide applications, there are more than 1,000 commercially sold and "home-grown" software offerings for healthcare practices, including over 100 disparate EHR/EMR/PHR solutions with potentially 10 times more discrete data elements than a revenue-cycle software system.
- Several, rather than a single *de facto*, communication and formatting standards exist.
- Disparate terminologies and entry errors in data entry are commonplace and require difficult data normalization that can never be assumed to be static.
- Software systems must adapt to ever-changing healthcare laws and industry operations, which affect data elements, functionality, security and interoperability requirements, interfaces, and operational use.
- Public health and population management's access to nongovernmental health delivery is limited.

Despite these hurdles, healthcare organizations must use their data to help solve and improve all facets of the industry. A plethora of solutions must be adopted or invented, with their varying degrees of success and failure only then becoming clear.

Next, we walk through some models for an enterprise architecture and strategy that might lead to better healthcare analytics.

▶ Models for Data Architecture and Strategy

FIGURE 11.2 illustrates the critical components necessary to arrive at a usable analytics solution.

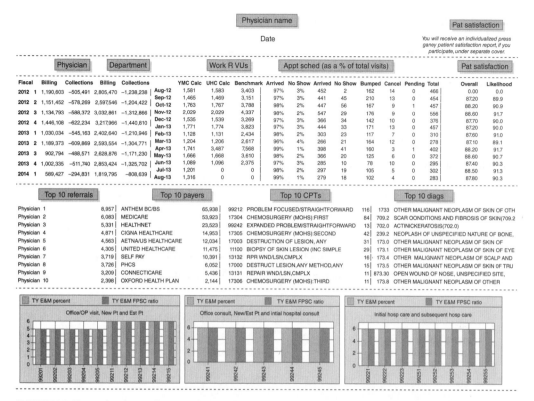

FIGURE 11.2 Example of an architectural map. This illustrates critical components necessary for any usable analytics solution.

Courtesy of Yale University School of Medicine.

A few terms and acronyms require definition:

■ **Source data.** Operational or transactional software applications may be used as a "point" solution (laboratory, radiology, or materials management) or may serve as a multipurpose, mission-critical solution, such as the hospital's admit, discharge, and transfer (ADT) system; revenue cycle management (RCM); or EHR. Data are entered for that application's operational use, with those data then becoming available for subsequent extraction to a CDR (discussed later) or BI/CI system. Data from materials management involves purchasing, inventorying, and pricing. "E-Apps," any of the myriad web-based and cellular software applications, also are data sources.

■ **Extraction, transformation, and load (ETL).** ETL is a generic term used across industries that refers to the process for creating data repositories for analytical purposes. This process starts with a host software application into which data have been entered through use of that application. These data can be formatted for extraction by the developer or a third party. In either case, the data need to be transformed, which may include normalization, organization, redefinition to ensure aligned vocabulary, and assurance of referential integrity. The source data may then be imported or loaded into the target repository, typically a BI/CI solution or other applications software. New extraction methods are being developed, but ETL is the most widely used method at the current time. ETL work is laborious programming work and it is an iterative process as application software updates occur or when the customer elects to modify the tables and/or tools designed within a software vendor's architecture.

■ **Metadata**. The literal definition of metadata is data about data. In the study of BI/CI, metadata refers to data identifying where the source data were created, when (time and date), by whom, and for what purpose; where they are located within the computer architecture; and whether standards were used in the data creation process. Metadata may be modified and created by nontechnical personnel and

may provide grouping and logical similarities and/or differences among the data.

■ **Central data repository (CDR)**. In years past, the CDR might have been called a data warehouse. It stores larger amounts of information, provides a replication of data from the source systems, organizes the data for extraction for analytics, and may provide an environment for **disaster recovery (DR)**. The CDR supports a system's ability to replicate and rebuild data if the original hardware is destroyed (**FIGURE 11.3**).

■ *Utilities and rules.* Within the IT solution, one will find administrative utilities, object management, and rules such as those governing distribution or content scheduling. The functionality for analytics, *ad hoc*

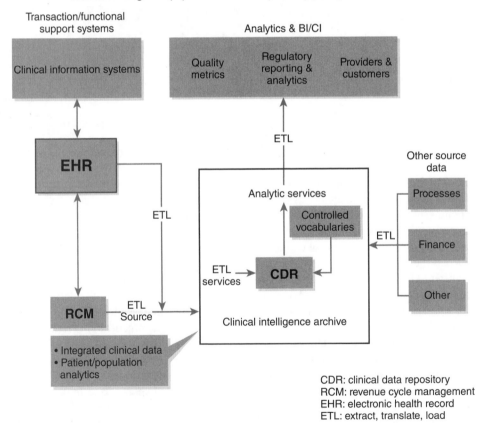

Clinical intelligence (CI) / Clinical data repository (CDR) model

CDR: clinical data repository
RCM: revenue cycle management
EHR: electronic health record
ETL: extract, translate, load

FIGURE 11.3 How a CDR works.

reporting, dashboard tools, KPIs, score card methods, and other application software capabilities are programmed here.

As healthcare analytics is more broadly adopted and matures, certain outcomes will be accepted as means to measure their value. Following is a list of requirements and functional attributes for a viable BI/CI solution.

Requirements for BI/CI Solutions

- *Secure*. Whether combined within a CDR or in a BI/CI solution, all data must be secure. For personal health information (PHI) and Health Insurance Portability and Accountability Act (HIPAA) compliance, the system's architectural environment must ensure that each data element maintains a secured utility to limit access, use, and improper exposure. Thus, each data element is tagged to control its use and to provide an essential audit trail indicating when, how, and by whom the data have been accessed.
- *Extensible/scalable.* Considering the expanding direction of healthcare data, the BI/CI solution must be able to scale up and extend to new areas. Just as the adoption of EHRs has proliferated over the last decade, so newly expanded uses for the Internet and mobile technologies will require more data as they are developed. Additionally, the government's role is still rather fluid, but it seems relatively safe to assume that government agencies will demand increased care measurements and reporting in the future. Lastly, like most maturing industries, the healthcare industry is consolidating: smaller shops are coming together to create mega-organizations that will be combining huge amounts of historical data during their mergers.
- *Integrity*. Health care is a professional industry populated by a highly educated workforce. Science and pragmatism are pervasive throughout the healthcare arena. Nevertheless, there is always a level of subjectivity and variability for the reasons discussed earlier; additionally, there is great emphasis on humanity in sustaining a patient's health. From both of these vantage points, accuracy and integrity are imperative. Data must have high integrity, meaning its accuracy and consistency must be assured. For users to trust the system there must be a high degree of veracity and authenticity across software applications, the resulting data sets, and any analytics and reporting. You do not have to look far to find voluminous anecdotal history of software systems failing to be adopted because providers did not trust the output.
- *Performance*. EHR, laboratory, and other clinical point of care systems must provide real-time information for healthcare providers. Their clinical decision making depends on the timeliness of this information. Conversely, BI/CI is inherently a retrospective analysis of transactional and clinical systems. Different data feeds to the BI/CI system may be real time, daily, monthly, or even quarterly. Well-timed performance is a subjective observation: each output must be timely (whether the information is needed immediately or periodically). When an output from a BI/CI system is required, it must be readily accessible. Depending on the form of output, the system should provide the information in a few seconds to a few minutes. A responsive solution will have automated utilities for the scheduled delivery of many objects such as KPIs, dashboards, statistics, or other predetermined requirements. *Ad hoc* demands will take longer in the first run of an inquiry.

Functional Attributes of BI/CI Solutions

- *Accessibility*. All modern workers are knowledge workers who require information to perform their jobs most effectively and a properly designed BI/CI system should make access to data relatively easy for those who have been trained in its use. Most internal consumers or users will never create intelligence content but they or their managers should understand the concept of how the system works if they are to have properly trained personnel develop content to their needs. From a control standpoint and to satisfy general security concerns, a healthcare organization may choose to program utilities that identify improper commands or inordinate demands from the **central processing unit (CPU)** to control illogical or improper personnel access. In environments where operational personnel are dependent upon a small IT or analytics group to develop content, there will be an untenable bottleneck. For the creation and daily use of data for most roles-based users, a team lead or the expedient access to broader analytics-trained personnel will be more productive.

- *Usability.* One reason for the relatively slow adoption of BI/CI solutions is that many are still rather complex to use. The more content that can be built or modified by nontechnical personnel, the greater the likelihood of success. For example, a clinician doing the hands-on work of health care may appreciate which kind of BI/CI is usable "in the field" better than an IT staff member: if they can drill down into the information themselves, the clinician can harvest information with more responsiveness and agility than would be otherwise. In addition to tables and spreadsheets, graphic and visual representations of data are invaluable. Because of its functional value, a BI/CI solution may regularly generate hundreds of unique content displays at any provider environment.
- *Actionable.* If the content from a BI/CI solution is not "actionable"—that is,

if it does not improve decision making, enhance day-to-day performance, solve relevant problems, or improve processes—then it will undoubtedly be discarded onto the giant heap of unrealized clever information. A BI/CI solution can only provide visibility into an organization's data; by itself, it will not make decisions. The BI/CI solution must provide clear evidence so that appropriate personnel feel comfortable in changing methods, managing their function, doing their work, and making decisions to improve health care in ways that matter based on those data.

- *Asking from the answers.* This principle is based on the adage, "You don't know what you don't know." Once a BI/CI solution is in the hands of healthcare workers, they may know better which kind of questions to ask. A competent analytics solution will allow an inquiry's "answer" to be queried time and again. In the world of BI/CI, you do not know the next question until you see the answer to the first. In theory, this may occur ad infinitum, especially as the questioning audience grows and multiple thoughts begin to challenge the results. In turn, an analytical result may promote a follow-up question or the addition or deletion of data to better refine the original inquiry. It becomes a circle of better investigation based on digging and creatively using stages of analytical output.
- *Roles-based use.* DSS and EIS are antiquated concepts as every worker—not just executives—needs some level of actionable information to perform his or her job or role. The dissemination of information is imperative and no longer valuable only to management and executives. Such distribution may consist of the presentation of small, daily refreshed tactical data such an insurance denial report or an appointment follow-up list. Also appropriate to her or his role, an executive may want to

review more sweeping views of different tactical or strategic business operations, with the ability to drill down into highlighted areas of interest or concern. There may conceivably be as many daily, weekly, and monthly analytical outputs as there are users in the enterprise.

■ *Data Visualization.* Humans tend to relate or understand visual narratives, explanations, or general information when displayed in a visual presentation. Graphs, charts, tables, colors, and more should be used for data and its content presentation. Dashboards allow often-used data sets to be graphically presented in one or a few locations on a regular basis where the user has unlimited access and may toggle between information with just a few keyboard or mouse clicks (**FIGURES 11.4–11.6**). This is a form of data visualization. The idea is to centrally locate lots of information, according to agreed-upon KPIs. A first glance gives a summary level, which can be clicked on to access supporting detailed data.

■ *Retrospective nature of BI and CI.* Real-time clinical decision making is based on a combination of the clinician's experience, the information available within the EHR, and other data tools available in the practice. While more real-time analytic innovations are under development, with today's technology, the traditional frequency of updating a CDR or pure BI solution is daily. Therefore, analytical reports, dashboards, and other outputs are generally produced for the various users the morning after systems have been updated on the prior evening. This gives end users data to inform decisions going forward in the new day.

Technology

Successful healthcare analytics is dependent upon on number of technology capabilities: suitable hardware, sufficient data store architectures, interoperability of various data source software applications, software innovation to accomplish dynamic mining functionality, and new software that will deal with Big Data and Thick Data. Heretofore, there have been a number of technology impediments to deal with. Speed, storage, interoperability, facile mining and presentation tools, software to manage growing data, and the notion of Thick Data have all lagged as necessary competencies. However imperfect, wonderful advances have been made on a number of technological fronts. Astounding stuff happens along the way in technology's progression. Remember IBM's Watson? It's been dusted. On June 9, 2018,

🔍 CASE EXAMPLE: BI/CI AND DASHBOARDS

A busy, university-based practice combined a dozen data sets relating to provider productivity, comparative patient satisfaction feedback, benchmarked relative value unit (RVU) measures, and other data sets. The ultimate goal was to deliver a month-end summary of each provider's compensation. Heretofore, this exercise necessitated more than eight unique report formats, took many employee hours, and was delivered more than a week after the month-end closing.

The new BI/CI-driven single-page summary included an information dashboard with nine different windows combining all of the former discrete reports. The process was completely automated, was deliverable in the provider's preferred modality (email, fax, or hard copy), and was customized for each department reflecting the specialty nuances of measures. This combination of data to present timely, actionable information was challenging to create, but once it was in place, it became a valuable management tool, useful to many.

Case Example by Ric Speaker.

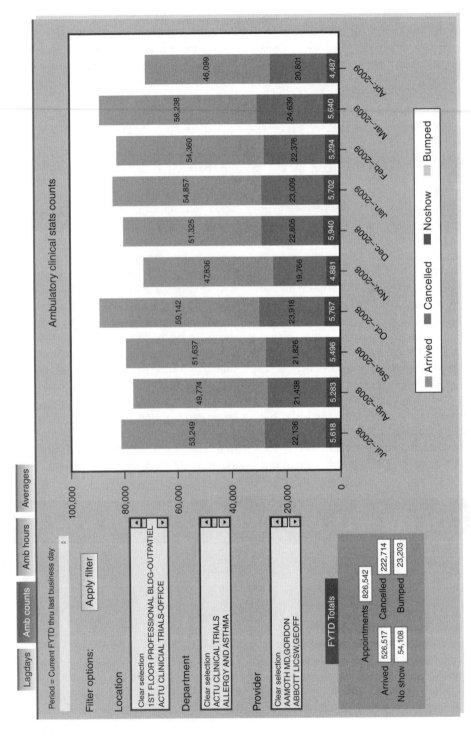

FIGURE 11.4 Example of patient workflow or measurement dashboard, demonstrating provider productivity.

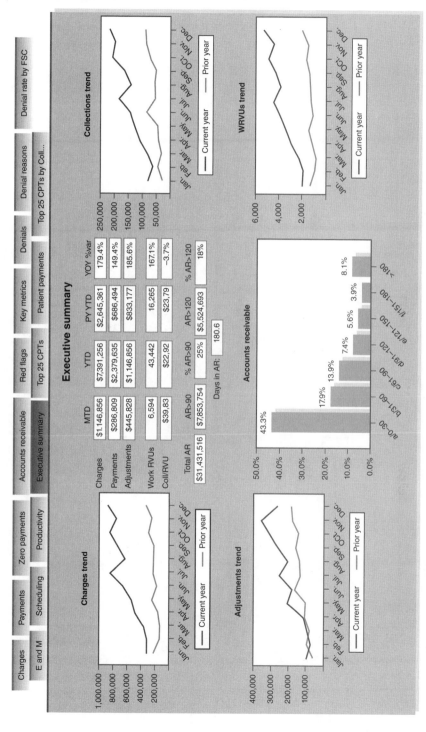

FIGURE 11.5 Example of a financial office dashboard, demonstrating reporting analytics.

Courtesy of Precision BI.

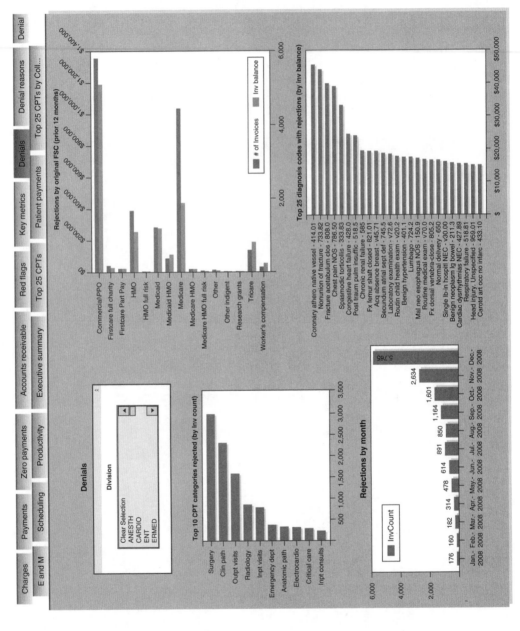

FIGURE 11.6 Example dashboard portraying accounts receivable and denials management.

The Wall Street Journal reported that IBM's latest supercomputer, Summit, can perform 200,000 trillion calculations a second while processing 250 petaflops of storage. The current world champ is a less powerful Chinese 93 petaflop computer, TaihuLight. According to Moore's Law, this horserace is long from being over, but these kinds of exponentially boosted speeds and storage capacities will have a positive impact on health care's quest to push around its Big Data. Decisively, since health care is very dependent upon images and graphic visualization, these speeds will accelerate analytics. As with most first-generation computer advances there will be a price inelasticity for most healthcare providers, but there will soon be a cost crossover point for this kind of performance and the mandate to change the cost of the healthcare system.

For most early BI/CI offerings, the ease of use has been a limiter for adoption. Legacy vendor offerings were and remain relatively cumbersome, slow, and in some cases, required specialized arcane software language expertise (these issues persist today). Today there are far more user-friendly tools that may be layered on top of a legacy system or used as the front end of a data repository. These tools are intuitive, may be learned by quasi-technical personnel, and the use cost is reasonably affordable. Time will tell as to their scalability and ability to deal with health care's intricate security demands. Since this chapter has espoused that without easier data content creation capability and roles-based content deliverability to *all* provider employees, these tools may be as important as any other technological advance.

As with better data mining and presentation tools, data repository architecture needs are critical. Much of this potential lies within the programming staff. The recruitment for these highly specialized skills will be demanding as all industries are in need of similar engineering experience. Again, providers were (are) dependent upon their legacy vendor's data storing methods. The data architecture

for revenue-cycle purposes or EHR data collection and storage has proven to be somewhat different than for the needs of BI/CI. Technical debates occur over methods of data storage and organization. For BI/CI purposes health care's vast amount of data must be able to be queried across disparate data sources in a unified manner. Some hospitals may have over 50 discrete applications making the repository analytical functionality most difficult. Also, security remains a challenging component that is different from knowing where a barrel of oil may have been harvested in the petroleum industry or how many SKUs for men's size 32 white underwear are currently in stock for the "big box" retailer. We do have providers who have accomplished necessary features for healthcare data architecture and one wonders if these will become commercially valuable intellectual properties or shared throughout the industry.

The late Stephen Hawking opined that AI "could spell the end of the human race." Once smart enough, computers and robots might fulfill science fiction's wondrous imagination of taking over the world. Notwithstanding, amongst the excitement for computers to think like (or better than) humans is the wonderment for what great things they might offer for health care. There is an overlapping of terminology including AI, DL, and ML. This subject matter could be a chapter unto itself because health care is, in fact, a universe of opportunity for leveraging computer software to solve so many clinical applications. If computers, with our growing and aging population along with the paucity of trained caregivers to care for them, could be layered into such things as rapid and accurate diagnostics, imaging interpretation, pharmaceutical drug matching of a patient's genome, and other care requisites, then it is worth tempting fate.

Irrespective of using AI, ML, DL, or an algorithm, the source data must be true, clean, and meaningful for valuable, reliable analytics. Much like human thinking, the more data that is being processed the better. As AI is used it must have been fed voluminous precedent data. GE Health care's imaging business has been working for years with provider organizations with as much as 10 years of CT scanned images. One exercise includes trying to find patient data with Stage 1 lung cancer because if they can intervene before Stages 3 or 4, the treatment can have a radically better outcome. This clearly differentiates between human memory and probable decision making. With early AI and DL, the programming can be made to report probable accuracy and if the software report any level of insecurity a radiologist may arbitrate the diagnosis. Similarly, an acute care environment using AI to monitor vital signs and detect delicate changes would aid staff nurses in prioritizing care. The computer's AI is dispassionate and has no ego. In programming with AI you don't predetermine a hypothesis, you feed true data and allow the data to generate the hypotheses.

While the excitement for using AI is palpable, one needs to complicate its application in health care with Thick Data. The behavioral science of medicine will be much harder to model. Images, vital signs, measureable body movements, and more are nearly "black and white" as compared to human perceptions and motivations. Moreover, some of these human characteristics are dishonestly reported. Gradually, however, even Thick Data will be "learned," and AI will save diagnostic and treatment decision time as well as preserving valuable physician resources. This evolution of transforming a nearly infinite amount of historical and every increasing patient data to consequential intelligence will take many years to validate, but this technology holds enviable promise to help cure some of the terrible problems facing health care today.

▶ The Future of BI/CI

There will undoubtedly be tremendous opportunities for individuals who understand the complexities of health care's BI/CI. For example,

Forbes recently wrote about the "Best Jobs in America": #1 actuary (compiling and analyzing data to assess risk and premiums); #4 Statistician; #6 data scientist; #8 software engineer, and #10 computer systems analyst (Adams, 2015). Every other position in the top 10 either shapes or is affected in one way or another by BI/CI: audiologists (#2), biomedical engineers (#5), dental hygienists (#7), and occupational therapists (#9) will all have their fields ameliorated by good BI/CI, and mathematicians (#3) may help crunch the numbers to create it. Prospective provider organizations and BI/CI application vendor roles will include the following:

- *BI/CI executives and SMEs*: operations, quality, planning, medical staff leadership, nursing leadership, strategy, and management who understand the problems inherent in each discipline and, therefore, what the information solutions might be.
- *Systems architects*: personnel who are generally highly technical and create the environment for acquiring, storing, and accessing the data necessary for BI/CI.
- *Programmers*: personnel who program or create software applications and then support and enhance these programs once the software is developed and used in production.
- *Data analysts*: personnel who work with data and often act as the liaisons between technical and nontechnical users of data and information.
- *Content creators*: personnel who format and structure data in a desired or logically deliverable design for all roles in the organization.
- *Implementation*: trainers and personnel who deal with interface creation, data translations, rollout to users, updates, and issues resolution.
- *Project managers*: the people who help organize, roll out, and guide projects and act as a liaison between care providers, executive staff, and IT departments.

The notion of intelligence and analytics is profoundly useful and beneficial to the quality of health care at so many levels. Considering the healthcare industry's size and influence on the U.S. economy as well as its dependency on the voluminous amounts of data and types of BI/CI for its operational efficiency and clinical performance, it must and will accelerate the adoption of better methods in leveraging those data. Talented data analysts and architects are the key to organizing the detailed tasks into projects, persevering to pull together the many threads inherent in BI/CI solutions, and helping users adopt their use. As in other healthcare IT pursuits, BI/CI work is not without significant challenges, but it is greatly rewarding once accomplished. Despite the structural and logistical limitations that must be overcome to reach this goal, there is now enough political, consumer-based, and industry demand to support its achievement.

Summary

If we all agree that making current, practicable information available to workers will likely improve performance within the healthcare workplace environment, then BI/CI is a viable concept. Health care has an inordinate number of moving parts and an incredible plethora of raw and uncoordinated data. In lay terms, bringing all those data into a single location, harmonizing them, and making the results available to the masses of potential users is a very good thing. Beyond good, it is necessary. Health care's unsynchronized and unaligned methods of providing care have become untenable and unaffordable as organizations attempt to effectively manage their businesses. As the government, quality watch groups, employers, and patients demand necessary change, the healthcare industry must put into practice proven methods of gathering and distilling information into intelligence. Other industries have already demonstrated the value of BI, and so, in growing ways, has health care.

All healthcare organizations have limited capacity to implement IT investments. Currently, there are mandated priorities, such as with EHRs; organizations are developing Internet strategies, e-mobile integration, security solutions, consumer-based focuses, and other competing initiatives as well. However, recent surveys of C-level and IT executives, as well as industry member groups such as the HIMSS and the MGMA, consistently espouse the need for better BI. There are no precise data on the use of BI in health care, but best estimates would suggest fewer than 35 percent of all provider organizations have implemented a true BI/CI solution and even fewer have done so on an enterprise-wide level.

In addition to the pure logic of using analytics, the BI/CI paradigm has a very intellectually rewarding and creative side. The process of identifying what needs better workflow process and obtaining distinct business and clinical answers, plus the ability to dig around and present data solutions, can be deeply fulfilling. With properly designed and implemented data architecture and intelligence mining software, one can discover empirical answers to both mundane and extraordinarily complex healthcare questions.

Key Terms

Analytics
Artificial intelligence (AI)
Business intelligence (BI)
Canned
Central data repositories
  (CDRs)

Central processing unit
  (CPU)
Clinical intelligence (CI)
Cloud-based data storage
Comparative effectiveness
  research (CER)

Dashboard
Decision support
  systems (DSS)
Deep learning (DL)
Disaster
  recovery (DR)

Executive information systems (EIS)

Extraction, transformation, and load (ETL)

Key performance indicators (KPIs)

Machine learning (ML)

Metadata

Source data

Discussion Questions

1. Who might use and benefit from healthcare BI/CI?

2. What do you think might be the preferred way of structuring a BI/CI group within a hospital? For a multispecialty ambulatory group?

3. How might you describe the differences between non-healthcare industries' and the healthcare industry's use of analytics?

4. If applicable, how have you used analytics as part of your work in a healthcare organization? Did you use BI or CI?

5. Do you believe that healthcare organizations might "push" personal analytics out to patients for their own monitoring and improvement of health and quality of life issues?

6. Would you use more personalized health information in your own life? How might you do so? What would be your preferred method of communication?

7. Do any of the roles described in relation to the use of BI/CI interest you, and why?

8. Are the existing HIPAA, PHI, and other security measures sufficient to allow you to trust healthcare organizations in aggregating, mining, and analyzing data?

9. Do you believe that BI/CI should be mandated and controlled by the various government agencies that are involved in health care? Why or why not?

References

Adams, S. (2015, April 14). The best jobs for 2015. *Forbes*. Retrieved from www.forbes.com/sites/susanadams/2015/04/14/the-best-jobs-for-2015/#2f5793fc31c8

Agosta, L. (2010, June 7). Healthcare business intelligence systems: An IT laggard no more? *Search Business Analytics*. Retrieved from http://searchbusinessanalytics.techtarget.com/news/2240019450/Healthcare-business-intelligence-systems-an-IT-laggard-no-more

American Hospital Association. (2018). *Fast facts on U.S. hospitals, 2018*. Retrieved from https://www.aha.org/statistics/fast-facts-us-hospitals

Association of American Medical Colleges. (n.d.). *Medical schools*. Retrieved from https://www.aamc.org/about/membership/378788/medicalschools.html

Burton, D. (2018, April). The future of healthcare AI: An honest, straightforward Q&A. *HealthCatalyst*. Retrieved from https://www.healthcatalyst.com/insights/future-healthcare-ai-q-and-a

Centers for Disease Control and Prevention. (n.d.). *Nursing home care*. Retrieved from http://www.cdc.gov/nchs/fastats/nursingh.htm

Centers for Medicare & Medicaid Services. (2016). *National health expenditures 2016 highlights*. Retrieved from https://www.cms.gov/Research-Statistics-Data-and-Systems/Statistics-Trends-and-Reports/NationalHealthExpendData/downloads/highlights.pdf

Fry, E., & Mukherjee, S. (2018, March 19). *Tech's next big wave: Big data meets biology*. Retrieved from http://fortune.com/2018/03/19/big-data-digital-health-tech/

Heilbrunn, E. (2013). U.S. News & World Report Health Insurance Top Health Insurance Companies. Retrieved from http://health.usnews.com/health-news/health-insurance/articles/2013/12/16/top-health-insurance-companies

Mulcahy, R. (n.d.). Business intelligence definition and solutions business intelligence topics covering definition, objectives, systems and solutions. *CIO*. Retrieved from www.cio.com/article/40296/Business_Intelligence_Definition_and_Solutions

SECTION V

A Changing HIS World

CHAPTER 12

HIS and Digital Health

"The brain is by far the most complex piece of highly excitable matter in the known universe by any measure. We don't even understand the brain of a worm."

Christof Koch, Chief Scientist and President of the Allen Institute for Brain Science, on challenges involved in artificial intelligence design.

LEARNING OBJECTIVES

By the end of this chapter, the student will be able to:

- Define digital health and explain digital health technologies and approaches.
- Portray potential uses of new technologies such as artificial intelligence (AI), machine learning, telemedicine, telehealth, mobile devices, and personal genomics.
- Outline the risks and rewards associated with the technologies explored.
- Explain the relationship between digital health and value-based care and value-based reimbursement.
- Evaluate ways to encourage patient engagement through the use of new technologies and health information systems (HIS).
- Describe major HIS-related regulations and their relevance to digital health.
- Describe the progression of security standards, from the Health Insurance Portability and Accountability Act (HIPAA) to the Health Information Technology for Economic and Clinical Health Act (HITECH) to Health Information Trust Alliance (HITRUST).
- Portray regulatory trends and future directions and expectations.

▶ Introduction

This chapter is intended to explain and provide examples of ways that new categories of technologies—such as AI, telehealth, telemedicine, medical devices, and others—can be applied to improve outcomes on the dimensions of quality of care, cost, service, and satisfaction.

Ideas abound for digital health solutions in myriad formats for care, communication, connectivity, data capture, and interactions between providers and patients that can benefit both parties. Patient engagement, a watchword for digital health, often results in solutions designed with the provider in mind, so that care can be supported or delivered between in-person visits to the provider office or clinic.

Equally important in engaging patients is making sure the communication needs and desires of the patient are prioritized as requirements in developing digital health solutions. It makes sense but bears repeating that for the demographics of an aging and increasingly chronically ill population (at all ages), giving patients reasons to want to engage with technology couldn't be more important—because if those needs are met, the patient will be able to engage with the provider to meet the needs to address value-based care and other organizational and external shifts and pressures, so the practice or clinic or health system can survive the changing reimbursement landscape. More on patient communication preferences a little later in the chapter.

Why does digital health matter? Is the use of new technology always associated with improved quality, better service, happier providers, streamlined processes, and efficiencies? Is the goal the cool new technology itself, to ensure being the hippest health provider on the block, or does technology help us solve deeper issues of quality and cost? The question answered for any digital health initiative must be, "What specific plan assures that the investment of time, energy, and money into this particular digital health initiative achieves measurable results to improve a healthcare process or develop a new service, integrated with existing systems and processes?"

▶ Approaches to Digital Health in HIS

In many cases, "approaches to digital health" can be reworded as "new ideas and new technology applied to old problems in health care." As discussed in Chapter 3, the challenges that healthcare professionals face today are numerous; some are vast. To get our digital health terminology handled, this section sets out definitions often discussed as "new technology" that hold promise of helpful application and innovation in health care.

Artificial Intelligence

Artificial intelligence (AI) is a category of analytical capability that in its purest form refers to using computers or machines to perform analyses in ways that mimic human intelligence. AI rests with the notion that learning or problem solving are skills of the human mind, which when done with technology, become "artificial" intelligence. Problem solving, understanding human speech, autonomous operation of machinery or devices, and content delivery such as clinical decision support are examples of types of AI capabilities. As in many types of technologies, AI is often solving the next problem that hasn't yet been solved, such as optical character recognition. In other words, AI makes possible the impossible before the mainstream has even been able to ask the question. Therefore, AI is continually breaching its own definition: what was once thought of as AI is no longer.

Controversy surrounds AI: it clearly can be helpful, such as anticipating diseases before clinical symptoms or signs appear by analyzing language and context of individuals, but many fear AI as a harbinger of dangers, as it can be readily used for harmful, powerful purposes that do not help patients. It all depends on what your perspective is and what the intention is. For example, AI is being used now by insurance companies to scoop up data about patients from nonsecure sources such as social media to predict health risks, and denying access to coverage today based on an anticipated risk in the future. Also, AI can now present themselves through voice and reasoning, appearing to be human. However, the conscious human mind is complex and includes things like empathy, trust, context, and emotion. In mimicking humanity, AI may intrude on the humanness of interaction without people knowing it, thus tricking them and falsely confusing the line between human intention and reality. To keep this fine line in perspective, consider this quote from Christof Koch, Chief Scientist and President of the Allen Institute for Brain Science explaining challenges associated with AI design: "The brain is by far the most complex piece of highly excitable matter in the known universe by any measure. We don't even understand the brain of a worm (The New York Times, 2018)." It will be a long time before AI replicates anything close to human thinking. In the meantime, what do we expect of AI in health care, and are we able to identify problems for which AI realistically would be the solution?

Setting the challenges of AI aside for the moment, this technology is at the center of HIS innovation, piloting advanced analytics to improve quality, reduce costs, improve organizational performance, and proactively address population health management. AI technologies include subsets of **natural language processing** and **machine learning**. AI use cases are helping redefine health care and how information is approached. AI efforts are not without issues, and like the adoption of other evolving technologies, the promise of AI will occur via a normal curve of fits and starts, as health care learns how to apply this technology, but optimism is warranted given AI's contribution and uses in other industries: early successes will eventually yield efforts to fully realize AI's enormous potential.

Implementation challenges within HIS portfolios and organizational capacities that are a mismatch for expertise in knowing how to operate the AI processing and systems, as well as expertise in putting it into actual use challenges slowing AI advancement include inaccurate, incomplete, inconsistent, and messy data; use of nonstandard local terminologies; use of specialized terminologies without adequate mapping to industry standards; difficulties with context, disambiguation, and negation. The following sections explain various facets of AI.

Machine Learning

Machine learning is a branch of AI that uses data analytics of data obtained through processes, to automate models that improve as they are increasingly fueled with data. Machine learning is based on the idea that computers can learn from data through the identification of increasingly precise patterns and then base decisions on those learnings.

Deep Learning

Deep learning is a way that machine learning employs brain simulation, creating artificial neural networks that learn and become deeper with multiple layers by being fed with data and training algorithms, making them sharper and easier to use and improving machine learning and steps toward real AI. A key aspect of deep learning is that these layers of features are not designed by human engineers but they are learned from data using a general-purpose, computer-driven, learning procedure.

Predictive Analytics

Applications of machine learning in health care include **predictive analytics**. Predictive analytics are algorithms based on more and more data being fed through them, then pinpointing the type of analysis to provide actionable information so that performance and outcomes can be improved. An example is identifying patients who comprise the top risk in terms of condition and cost in the near future and are likely to be readmitted within 30 days or present to an emergency room, and why they are at risk so that pre-emptive interventions can be defined and accomplished. The range of topics and areas of predictive analytics is limitless—it all depends on defining the types of questions that are relevant to the organization, provider, patient, and end user, and the programmatic objectives intended to address the results of the analyses. For example, predictive analytics is an essential capability as part of management of a population's health and in achieving value-based care.

Personal genomic sequencing: **genomic sequencing** is now affordable for many individuals, and many innovators and start-up companies are developing solutions for using genomic information for treating or preventing various types of conditions. Easy and increasingly accessible, personal genetic sequence technology now can be used for innovative healthcare applications, such as precision in determining cancer therapies based on the genetic sequence matched with the analysis and literature on cancer therapies to determine the best course of action.

Blockchain: emerging technologies are always present in the healthcare marketplace, but the **blockchain** craze has surely captured health care, evolving even as this book is written. Blockchain is middleware, a distributed, immutable ledger for transactions and data, with applications anticipated in everything from supply chain to patient identity. The hope is that blockchain, or distributed ledger, or "the blockchain" depending on one's vernacular can be transformative in solving some of health care's most persistent problems: identity, data integrity, patient control over their own data. Use cases and persistent issues to which blockchain might be applied that are identified as particularly promising, including assuring patient identity and data with 100 percent accuracy, storing certain key clinical data elements and making them readily available where needed *under the direct control of the patient*, and business applications such as supply chain management for identifying medical devices for recall, are the commonly discussed use cases with promise.

Blockchain is not a solution to every problem in healthcare IT, and like all new technologies, it must be pointed at the right target. Concerns of the potential for unintended consequences are voiced by many due to the need for a blockchain standard, without which this new technology might create more of the very problems of privacy and security it is hoped to solve (Forbes, 2018).

Blockchain and Digital Cryptocurrencies

Implications of blockchain should be considered alone as its own technology, especially the implication of digital **cryptocurrencies**. Blockchain and cryptocurrency are two different, but related, capabilities. It is important to understand carefully what blockchain might do in health care, according to the plans, organizational strategies, and current issues and problems. Sound familiar? Yes, just like any other new technology or HIS initiative, it has promise, but the result lies in the application.

And we must ask ourselves, is blockchain a hype or is it really a solution itself to real problems? If we use blockchain with the same kind of thinking we have used today's technologies, will the results be any better? What are the issues with blockchain we must remember as we run toward this new technology? (CB Insights, 2018)

🔍 CASE EXAMPLE: BIG DATA, BIG POSSIBILITIES

Through a working relationship between the Maine Health Information Network (healthinfonet.org) and HBI Solutions, Inc., the network has amassed data from 90 percent of the provider electronic health record (EHR) systems of the state of Maine. Initially sought for purposes of exchanging patient data amongst providers as Health Information Exchanges (HIEs) are intended to do, this initiative has also yielded a data warehouse and environment for analysis of the data. This environment provides

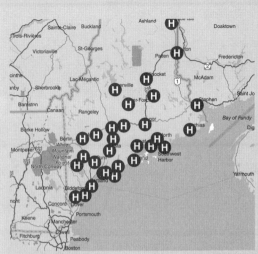

Current HIE statistics

Health information exchange statistics

Inbound clinical messages received today 645,422

Users who have accessed the HIE today 357

Population Included

Active HIE users	6,578
Patients included	1,631,067
Maine residents	1,205,450
Non-maine residents	425,617
Opt-out rate	1.35 percent
Crossover rate	61 percent

Percent of patients who have been to two or more different facilities parlities participating in the HIE

FIGURE 12.1 An HIE statistics snapshot from participating providers in Maine.

Reproduced from Health Info Net. Retrieved from http://hinfonet.org/

capabilities so that predictive analytics and other helpful analyses are created to guide providers and interventions to prevent the onset of disease or allow for timely intervention to manage this population's care, reduce risk of disease progression, and avoid unnecessary cost. (See **FIGURE 12.1** for an overview of the Maine HIE usage statistics.)

The power of this health information network is multiplied, doing double duty: first enabling dynamic data exchange *and* then also creating a database for analytics to predict impending disease so that interventions can be implemented. This is predictive analytics, warding off disease before it advances among the patient population. Results from one peer-reviewed published study from this effort showed successful prediction of the transition from pre-diabetes to diabetes over six months—combined with appropriate pre-emptive actions, resulting in the disease being halted for many patients through interventions *before* traditional physiological markers could be detected and the diabetes diagnosis confirmed (Jin et al., 2017).

To manage the health of a population, it is essential to identify the pre-disease states for high-incidence, preventable conditions such as diabetes. This can be accomplished through predictive analytics techniques and algorithms applied to the robust and continuously increasing data set housed in HIEs' data warehouses. This also speaks to leveraging the investment and effort expended standing up an HIE, adding value beyond the use of the network to exchange data between providers and other relevant parties. Results of this project show that the shift from pre-diabetic condition to diabetic condition, a critical clinical event in the long-term clinical and cost outcome of a patient, can be detected six months prior to its occurrence through the application of predictive analytics techniques. This published result adds to available medical knowledge so that effective interventions can be enacted to improve outcomes (Jin et al., 2017) (**FIGURE 12.2**). This is a wonderful example of adopting new technologies to address a specific and actionable problem, with the promise of significant results for both populations and individual patients.

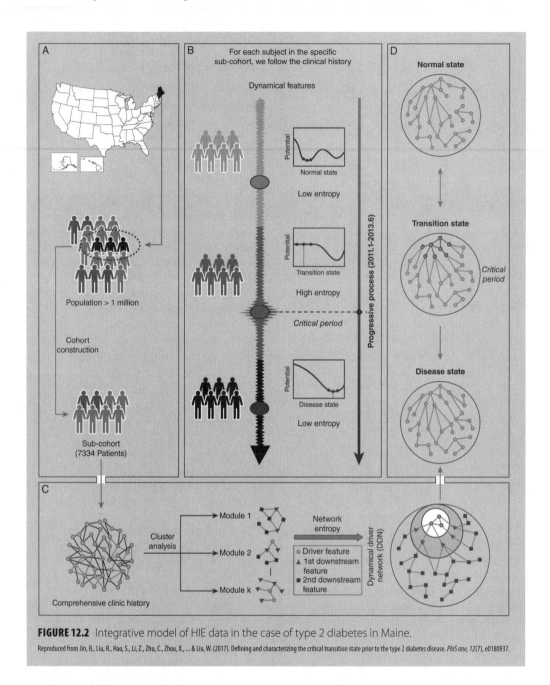

FIGURE 12.2 Integrative model of HIE data in the case of type 2 diabetes in Maine.

Reproduced from Jin, B., Liu, R., Hao, S., Li, Z., Zhu, C., Zhou, X., ... & Liu, W. (2017). Defining and characterizing the critical transition state prior to the type 2 diabetes disease. *PloS one, 12*(7), e0180937.

Perspective on Adoption of New Technologies

Organizations such as PWC and Accenture report that although health care trails other industries in innovation using new technologies, there is reason for optimism, predicting an interconnected global healthcare industry by 2020, making creative use of innovations that have been used in other industries such as telecommunications (PwC Health Research Institute, 2016). To do so will require use of these technologies for health care to become more patient-centric, cost-effective, and convenient from the patient's or consumer's perspective. Gone are the days of organization-centric dominance in what good outcomes comprise. These innovations and improvements will require changes in perceptions of what is normal in health care, investments in technology innovations, and new skillsets and workflows among HIS solutions (Meissner, 2013). This change of mind extends to healthcare trading partners, providers, patients, payers, and suppliers. How this factors beyond large, complex healthcare institutions into rural and small practice environments and patient settings will also need to be solved.

▶ Digital Health: Connecting the Unconnected

Telemedicine and Telehealth

At its core, **telemedicine** is the remote delivery of clinical services using these types of technologies and the remote delivery of health-related information from one site to another via electronic communications, with the goal to improve a person's health awareness and access to information in the broader context of health promotion and prevention of illness or harm (American Telemedicine Association, n.d.). The World Health Organization (WHO) adds to that definition by stating that **telehealth** includes the exchange of valid clinical information in situations where geographic distance is a factor for the purposes of diagnosis, treatment, and prevention of disease and injuries, research and evaluation, and the continuing education of healthcare providers (WHO, 2010). WHO describes four key elements of telemedicine—namely, its intent to provide clinical support, overcome geographical barriers, connect users who are in different physical locations using the variety of types

of modern information and communication technologies, and improve health outcomes. Establishing a telehealth "platform" includes the virtual care component and video but adds integration with EHRs and workflow optimization. Telemedicine and telehealth have many applications and use a variety of technologies, including smartphones, the Internet, secure email, video transmission, and other telecommunications capabilities.

New HIS technologies and their increasing ubiquitous availability, accompanied by a continuous drop in costs, are contributing to the current growth of telemedicine and telehealth. These capabilities are increasingly being adopted and refined as useful and cost-effective means of delivering clinical treatments, health services, and enhanced provider-to-provider interactions across distances that were previously challenging, if not infeasible, to surmount. Certainly, telemedicine and telehealth can improve access to medical and health services for those populations currently lacking ready access to health practitioners and information. Also, some populations, for example parents with young children, house-bound individuals, Millennials, and other groups, prefer telemedicine and telehealth services whenever possible for convenience, as these types of methods mimic the shift in the economy to web-based services, such as Amazon prime versus the traditional mall, Instacart versus grocery shopping, and the like, and personal services such as therapist apps and other typically in-person, human-to-human interactions.

Barriers to adoption of telemedicine and telehealth solutions include the following:

- The complexity of human and cultural factors is a major challenge, including departure from traditional work and communication methods for clinicians, patients, and people receiving the health information. A related barrier is a lack of the necessary technical proficiency to connect and use these various technologies to communicate and conduct care processes remotely.

- The cost of sustaining telemedicine and telehealth initiatives originally started with a grant or some seed funding can prove problematic. These ventures often fail for lack of sustained funding, despite the fact that telehealth almost always reduces organizational overhead and that the costs of technologies are consistently declining.

- A shortage of studies evaluating costs and benefits, and a lack of business cases documenting the cost-effectiveness of these telemedicine initiatives, diminishes their ability to raise investment monies. Such evidence is needed to win support for establishing the necessary infrastructure and funding program start-up costs.

- Legal issues around the crossing of transregional boundaries may create significant barriers to implementing telemedicine programs. Notably, healthcare providers are challenged by the lack of international law in this area and complexities and differences in interstate laws governing the transmission of healthcare information across national and state lines.

- Technical challenges create barriers to the integration of the various types of systems, devices, and networks needed to conduct telemedicine and telehealth. Many areas that need these types of services are rural or remote, and they may not have the requisite expertise to implement and support the technology platforms (WHO, 2010).

While telemedicine and telehealth definitions overlap with definitions of **mHealth** and **eHealth**, the former terms are typically used to describe HIS that eliminates geographical and physical proximal barriers to care. Telemedicine provides the needed medical and health services to patients and citizens separated by distance from the clinicians and healthcare providers. These technologies are also hugely useful in providing connections between providers for purposes of consultation, research, education, and training.

Telehealth and Telemedicine Applications

Before describing telehealth and telemedicine progress and activities, it is relevant to define each, and differentiate them, as the two terms are often used interchangeably. The goals of digital health include improving outcomes, supporting behavioral change, and improving efficiencies and cost performance. Under the umbrella term of digital health, telehealth is a subset of eHealth, and telemedicine is a subset of telehealth. This is similar to the distinction between EHR systems (the longitudinal electronic record for both medical and health-related activities and interactions between providers and patients, including preventive services and education, as well as medical encounters) and electronic medical record (EMR) systems (the episodic electronic record of medical encounters between patient and providers, focused on point-in-time medical interventions and visits of patients to providers). Telehealth includes not only clinical services but also nonclinical preventive and health-related activities such as education, provider training, continuing education, meetings, and other activities that contribute to the health system overall, while telemedicine includes remote clinical services, including follow-up, management of chronic conditions, specialist consultation, and medication management, without an in-person visit, both enabled by telecommunications technology such as video-conferencing and other media (Smith, 2015).

Implementing Telehealth and Telemedicine. Implementing digital health systems and initiatives has been met with many challenges including scalability within an organization beyond the pilot phase, unclear reimbursement practices and rules, lack of widespread advocacy and support within or beyond the organization trying to implement it, unclear success metrics and lack of their measurement, and technical issues (Lovett, 2018).

Due to the current state of implementation of digital health solutions, many digital health projects never make it beyond the pilot phase. The American Medical Association (AMA) has published a Digital Health Playbook, with a perspective on digital health implementations and a 12-step sequence to help make sure projects are successful. Students will recognize these 12 steps, consistent with the Phases, Stages, tools, and techniques of HIS planning, selection, contracting, process redesign, integration, project management, implementation, and post-implementation evaluation and ongoing support covered in earlier chapters (Chapters 3, 4, 5, and 6) of this text. As this text emphasizes, HIS fundamentals apply, no matter what the technology and type of initiative. In this case, the arena happens to be digital health, including telehealth and telemedicine. The 12 steps in the AMA Playbook for Digital Health Implementation emphasize something as critical success factor currently lacking in many digital health initiatives, namely, the clinical integration of digital health tools. These steps include the following:

Phase I—Pre-implementation Planning
    Step 1: Identifying a Need
    Step 2: Forming the Team
    Step 3: Defining Success
    Step 4: Evaluating the Vendor
    Step 5: Making the Case
    Step 6: Contracting

Phase II—Implementation of Remote Patient Monitoring
    Step 7: Designing the Workflow
    Step 8: Preparing the Care Team
    Step 9: Partnering with the Patient
    Step 10: Implementing
    Step 11: Evaluating Success
    Step 12: Scaling

Phase III—Post-implementation Support and Resources

Additionally, data driven telehealth and telemedicine initiatives portend a critical success factor, where clinical and performance indicators are defined and measured, helping these initiatives transcend the pilot phase and become viable, sustainable digital health services, supporting and integrating with clinical processes and EHR and EMR systems (Lovett, 2018).

Telehealth: An Increasing Market. Telehealth is reaching levels of massive growth, with a market for virtual health applications and activities expected to reach $3.5 billion by 2022 according to Verify Markets (Verify Markets, 2016). This growth is supported by clinicians who see the applicability of telehealth and telemedicine to helping provide the clinical support necessary to manage patient care needs and also provide support between visits to the provider and in-person clinical setting. A recent 2018 survey of physicians and nurses estimates that 45 percent identify telemedicine as high priority and 86 percent want to use telemedicine to improve outcomes (Roth, 2018).

Digital health trends, including telehealth and telemedicine applications, are increasingly embraced by large organizations on an enterprise-wide basis, moving away from the typical pilot initiative that was isolated into a niche or department, as these types of initiatives were first emerging on a test or trial and error basis. More than 50 percent of hospitals are planning and implementing telehealth initiatives across all areas, moving away from initial departmental projects. The range of digital health initiatives requires enterprise coordination, so that standards and scope can be carefully planned, and enterprise, consistency of approach achieved, just like other HIS. These digital health initiatives are not immune to the need to make sure they follow the HIS Planning Framework, ensuring integration with overall clinical and service processes. It doesn't matter what the technology is, the HIS planning framework and methodologies apply, and these initiatives must fit within the HIS Strategic Plan, just like any other. Progress is being made in identifying and developing initiatives for specialties such as emergency department (ED) services management, outreach to mothers for prenatal care, and expansion of access to specialty services such as ophthalmology and child abuse assessment and prevention (Roth, 2018).

Telehealth Initiatives. Examples of telemedicine and telehealth include remote radiology interpretations and intensive care monitoring by clinicians for hospitals located remotely or smaller organizations that cannot afford full-time specialists 24 hours a day; clinician-patient consults over live video; and remote patient monitoring for heart disease, diabetes, or other common, chronic conditions that need to be tracked closely but that do not require the patient to be institutionalized (Steciw, n.d.).

Telemedicine also encompasses education and networking, allowing remote healthcare professionals to earn continuing education credits and giving patients access to online support groups and specialized health information.

🔍 CASE EXAMPLE: USING REMOTE MONITORING TO REDUCE INFANT MORTALITY RATES

As discussed at points earlier in this chapter, it is important to exert discipline, when faced with a problem or an issue, to not "solution-jump," but rather to study and carefully define the problem in great detail before coming up with alternatives to potential solutions. And the first part of any alternative solution ideas should always be to look at current systems and technology resources available to adapt those to yield needed remedies and capabilities to address the situation. One example of this is work being done to attack the persistent and, in some cases, worsening problem of infant mortality in the U.S. In 2016 in the U.S., the infant mortality rate was 5.9 for every 1,000 births, ranging from 3.6 percent among Asians to 11.3 percent among African-Americans (Centers for Disease Control and Prevention). In response to these statistics—higher than many other countries—The Healthcare Information and Management Systems Society (HIMSS) issued a challenge to health software developers to see what ideas could be generated to help address this situation (Erreger, 2018). This is an example of health IT professionals asking themselves what they can do to help a complex problem with a multiplicity of economic, physical, and social factors. For this problem of infant mortality, variation by state is shown in **FIGURE 12.3**. Numbers of infant deaths are highest in the South and in Indiana and Ohio. This information is important for generating ideas for how HIS might target its efforts to help reduce these numbers (Erreger, 2018).

Areas where health IT can help include different uses of HIS and connectivity, for example, two-way communications capabilities for monitoring, detecting, and communicating changes in infants associated with sudden infant death syndrome (SIDS), which occurs in 33 percent of infant deaths between 27 days and 11 months after birth. A pulse-oximeter-equipped, Bluetooth-enabled smart sock provides one such hopeful tool to prevent infant mortality, using two-way communication to signal connected parents if any interruption in breathing occurs. Of course, the ability to afford the $300 device, as well as the connection devices such as smart phones, is required and is a barrier for some parents. Thus, these problems are more than technology-related issues and include socio-economic, educational, and demographic factors. Expanded access to information will raise awareness as well as inform providers, policy makers, technologists, researchers, and others to support the development of ways to address these multifaceted problems. Essential information such as local, state, and national statistics, surveillance data, population health and outcomes analysis, and other types of decision support information can provide pre-emptive insights as well as analytical depth to providers and policy makers working to determine effective, multipronged solutions to this problem.

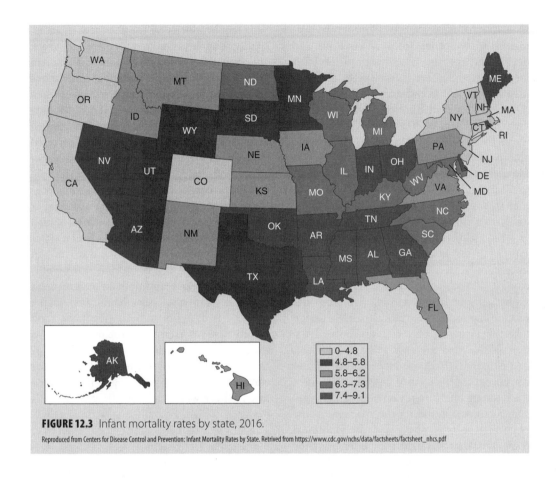

FIGURE 12.3 Infant mortality rates by state, 2016.

Reproduced from Centers for Disease Control and Prevention: Infant Mortality Rates by State. Retrived from https://www.cdc.gov/nchs/data/factsheets/factsheet_nhcs.pdf

▶ **Human-Centered Design: User Interface and User Experience**

The crucial connection between systems, data, and knowledge workers is at once an opportunity and challenge given the work done to date to roll out new EHR systems and other HIS at record pace over the past 10 years. The opportunity is that in place now are the EHR systems and essential foundations they provide for advancing digital health, clinical decision support, population health management, and other advanced initiatives intended to improve the quality of care and cost-effectiveness of services. The challenge is that these foundational

EHR systems and the workflows they have hard-wired into existence are burdening the physicians and other clinicians who must use them with too much typing and other clerical work, to the point now where a cultural and professional crisis among providers is upon us. We are now faced with what can accurately be described as the unintended consequence of frustrated and disillusioned physicians and other clinicians with the **user interfaces (UIs)** and **user experiences (UXs)** of EHR systems. Let's first examine the definitions of human-centered design: UI and UX.

UI is the visual and physical environment in which humans interact with machines or computers, including the design of that interaction and its sequencing, the devices involved, and a variety of mechanisms such as keyboards, mouse, screens, voice-activation, visual elements such as menus, icons, and buttons, and devices such as pens. The design of the UI is ideally something that is pleasing to use or at least helpful to the end-user. Usability of the interface is designed in anticipation of the activities the user will want accomplish, using elements that make it easy to access, understand, and complete the desired tasks. The UI enables the user to employ all these elements to communicate with the computer using commands, menus, and instructions embedded in the UI design to perform tasks they seek to accomplish.

UX includes the attitudes, emotions, and satisfaction experienced by the end-user in interacting with a computer product, in the context of usability, access, and pleasure of individual interactions as well as the broader relationship with the product. UX design takes all elements of the interaction of the user so that they are easy, relevant, efficient, and pleasant. UI/UX are often spoken of and considered together, since together they form the resulting total interaction between the user and computer, including the mechanics, the physical aspects involved, and the emotional response to that overarching experience. While it sounds "soft," this total UI/UX is what determines an essential component of the return on the investment of the computer system and its implementation. When automating already taxing and serious clinical processes, the creation of additional burden and strain to clinicians already stretched to the max physically and emotionally is extremely challenging. Anything vendors and healthcare organizations can do to improve UI/UX is critical to improving health-determining and life and death situations. In the U.S., too little pressure is put on vendors regarding innovation in UI/UX.

Human-centered design is a term that emerged in application to computer systems UI/UX over the past decade to address methods for creating not computer interactions that would not only produce accurate, automated work but also create interactions between humans and computers that are useful and pleasant.

This requires focus on the preferences, accessibility, usability and requirements of users, and employing ergonomics and other human factors. This section in particular emphasizes the importance of these design principles when talking about clinicians as users, including physicians, nurses, other care providers, as well as patients. The goal of the human-centered approach is to enhance the user's overall experience, efficiency, effectiveness, satisfaction, and sense of wellbeing, while diminishing negative consequences of the user of the computer such as adverse effects on performance, human health, safety, and sustainability.

User-centered design focuses on an understanding of the user, informed by ethnographic research and domain expertise. It's essential to involve users (clinicians) in the process, and perform both qualitative and quantitative research about the user as well as the customer, all while testing design assumptions. This changes over time based on the user community, and provides a good, integrated way to check work and help HIS professionals design and plan. Empathizing with users will go a long way in them being helped rather than burdened by the system.

The Problem with UI/UX Today

While automation of health care is booming, with now a majority of providers and organization using computers to do the majority of their work, we must ask what is working, and what isn't, and what are the solutions? A problem plaguing arguably the most precious and highly-trained knowledge-workers of our society is the major step backwards their roles have been forced to take in order to interact with awkward and inefficient UI/UX as end-users of "modern" EHR systems. This massive problem has launched a tsunami of dissatisfaction and disillusionment amongst healthcare professionals, since the majority of hospitals, clinics, and practices are now using—*wed* may be more apt than using—to these EHR systems for a long, long time. This is creating a despondence and exhaustion among physicians. A poorly designed, hard-coded end-user experience is taking the time needed to care for patients—their lives' goal—and siphoning it to administrative tasks. They feel trapped. As articulated in a recent white paper published by Stanford Medicine, physicians spending time using EHR systems have lost precious interaction time (looking at and talking with patients), added time to their already demanding schedules, and cut into personal time with family and friends. What are they are doing? Typing, pointing and clicking, and using dropdown menus to document and direct care (Stanford Medicine, 2018).

The major problem of EHR systems with poor UI/UX is sometimes attributed to issues of aging of the population served and of the provider users, UI/UX expectations, generational talent gap among providers, and lack of human-centered design in the design of the computer's workflows and UI, creating a sub-par UX. In the opinion of this author, burdensome UI/UX

is *the* major problem in health care that must be solved in this next wave of HIS and EHR system work, now that the core systems are implemented and surely will be in use for decades. It must be addressed as we rush to implement new technologies to meet the requirements of population health management, care management, and patient engagement.

▶ New Technologies and the Hype Cycle

In an evaluation of potential benefits and future directions of more than 2,000 new technologies, the Gartner Group created a **hype cycle** figure for 2018 that shows the continuum of adoption and innovation of new technologies (**FIGURE 12.4**). This work is done by economists, futurists, and others to identify passing, lasting, and nascent trend in technology. The term "hype cycle" refers to a

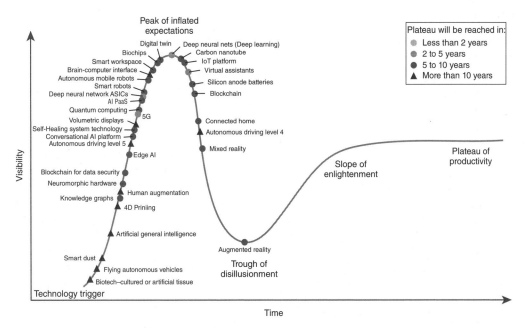

FIGURE 12.4 Gartner hype cycle, 2018.

Data from Panetta, K. (2018). Trends Emerge in the *Gartner Hype Cycle* for Emerging Technologies.

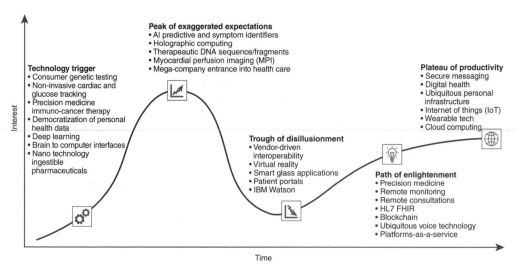

FIGURE 12.5 Phases of evolution for new health technology.

Data fom Lloyd Price (2018). The Digital Health Hype Cycle 2018. Retrieved from https://www.healthcare.digital/single-post/2018/02/20/The-Digital-Health-Hype-Cycle-2018

visual representation of the life cycle stages a technology goes through from conception to maturity and widespread adoption. Many of the technologies on this curve will be meaningful parts of the future in health care and public health; others will not. Of the 17 technologies analyzed, five categories or trends are identified: democratized AI, digitalized ecosystems, do-it-yourself biohacking, transparently immersive experiences, and ubiquitous infrastructure.

What does this mean for health care? Technologies that have been the targets of some serious exploration, if not traction or adoption, for use in health care and public health include those reflected in a healthcare interpretation of Gartner's Hype Cycle. This **FIGURE 12.5** identifies the almost-universal phases of evolution of new technologies including the technology trigger, peak of exaggerated expectations, trough of disillusionment, path of enlightenment, and plateau of productivity, presented in the following figure presents a hype cycle for health care. Examples of digital health opportunities realistically applied in the near term include precision medicine, **Health Level 7 (HL7)** and data standardization, **Fast**

Healthcare Interoperability Resources (FHIR) and health data sharing, blockchain, and **voice technology**. Technologies that will reach productive use in health care include secure messaging, telehealth, personal health assistants, remote monitoring using digital medical devices, **Internet of things (IoT)**, and **wearable technologies**.

Emerging technologies are only as useful as their practical application and demonstration of value in achieving hoped for results in the form of benefits and creative goals designed into each pilot project or trial testing a new use of HIS. As HIS progresses into new phases of digital health, it is fueled by research, pilot projects, and intentions of improving health outcomes and health care. HIS research and grant projects focus on areas in information and decision support, clinical workflow improvement, care coordination, and understanding the impact of HIS on outcomes. The shift to value-based reimbursement will put emphasis on application of digital health initiatives on patient involvement and engagement, care management, cost, quality, and provider and patient satisfaction. Assumption of risk by providers will be reexamined, enabled by technology.

▶ The Importance of Informatics in Adopting HIS and New Technologies

How we put technology to work to enable new, safer, streamlined workflows and processes is the key to getting good results from adopting new technologies and new HIS. The purpose of the informatics discipline is to understand the relationship of computers and technologies to humans to do their work, in ways that make this work easier, better, and serve to create synergies between knowledge-workers and enabling technologies. In some instances, we have had great successes in using new technologies to improve effectiveness and efficiency of health care—take picture archive communication systems (PACS) as an example. These automated image management systems have revolutionized the access and quality of radiologic and other images in health care, such as magnetic resonance imaging (MRIs), CT scans, pathology studies, and other results, more and more of which are being created and captured in the form of an image. The convenience associated with being able to share an MRI with consulting physicians who might be on the other side of the country or world, to help in the diagnosis and care of patients, the reduction in lost X-rays, and the elimination of delays in getting these important CT studies to surgeons and other critical providers in the event of an emergency is unparalleled. PACS has been a technology-enabled success, without question, also improving the use of knowledge-workers precious time as well as reducing time to treatment for many diagnoses, surely saving lives in the process. And further advances are now being taken as AI is being applied to radiology processes to interpret these digitized images. Technologists working with providers and informaticists including radiologists to achieve these advances have

improved care, provider and patient satisfaction, and assuredly, outcomes in the process.

However, the need for serious work by informaticists and other side of the coin is apparent in the effect of EHR systems' documentation processes requiring massive amounts of time typing by our highly trained and experiences knowledge-workers, physicians, turning them into data entry clerks, is an abysmal stain on the promise of innovation and the current state of the EHR system story. It is well documented that physicians are spending far too much time staring at a computer screen and typing at the expense of their time spent connecting with patients, their personal time, and professional schedules. As displayed in **FIGURE 12.6**, every hour spent with patients requires two hours interacting with the EHR system, such as typing documentation. Of time spent with patients, 62 percent is spent interacting with the EHR system (Stanford Medicine, 2018). Moreover, the amount of professional angst and moral distress caused by these systems is underestimated according to Christine Sinsky, Vice President of Professional Satisfaction at the AMA (Stanford Medicine, 2018).

Stanford EHR Report: How Physicians Spend Time per Patient

This is where informatics comes in. The correct solution is not to throw more technology at the problem. To do so would probably only make the problem worse. For instance, recently the company General Electric (GE) has come up with an approach, probably a very expensive one, called a command center to take all the information in the various systems and data sources and combine it, apply third-party algorithms, and then tell clinicians and managers what to do. This concept is terrible to this author on many levels: strategically, architecturally, culturally, and economically. Rather than adding another layer of technology, process, and management to address the lack of

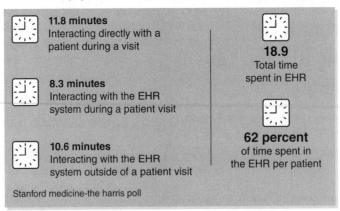

FIGURE 12.6 How physicians spend their time.

Data from Stanford EHR Report: How Physicians Spend Time Per Patient, Stanford University, Retrived from https://med.stanford.edu/content/dam/sm/ehr/documents/EHR-Poll-Presentation.pdf

process and information integration in current EHR architectures, the true solution is to work together within the organization to redesign and streamline workflows, processes, apply the organization's influence with vendors such as Epic, Meditech, and Cerner to rethink the end-user interface with the EHR system implementations to support the new, more efficient, and hopefully, more pleasing workflows. Process redesign can make all the difference: knowledge workers who understand both the technology and the workflows being redesigned (clinical documentation in the GE case) should be at the center of that redesign. Another layer of technology, process, and expenditure atop the already inefficient documentation process of the EHR system might feed the revenue stream of the vendor, but it only adds complexity for the user and makes the problem worse for providers. How we solve problems makes all the difference, and this is where informatics come in. Informaticists are the knowledge workers who understand the system and the processes and its goals and objectives, so they are able to develop expertise in taking advantage of system capabilities to create a *streamlined*, better process and thus experience of the clinicians involved. This is the answer. This work must be guided by the goal of regaining the satisfaction of providers in their work.

The Role of HIS and New Technology in Clinical Innovation

As organizations work to identify issues and problems that deserve their concerted efforts to solve, they are often spurred on by the promise of technology-enabled innovations and digital health solutions. The hype cycles described above can be applied in this process to help health professionals and their organizations determine the viability of an idea based, in part, on where in a new technology category resides in the technology and digital health hype cycles. If a new technology is very early in the hype cycle, chances are smaller that it can be applied for productive use across an organization, and it needs to travel through the additional work of testing and trying before betting on application with real patients. But if the category of technology innovation under consideration has moved past the trough of disillusionment to the path of enlightenment or plateau of productivity, it is viable to consider for real-world application and sustaining. To show how this might work, below are presented the top 10 medical innovations of 2019, ranked in order of importance by the Cleveland Clinic innovation arm, with this author's comments below each

🔍 *CASE EXAMPLE: HOW WORKFLOW REDESIGN CAN WORK*

Overly burdened by the documentation required by the multi-monitored EHR system, doctors at Kaiser were fed up with the added stress upon an already stressful job: dissatisfaction among clinicians and others who needed their attention, such as patients and families of patients, was mounting. Then came along the COOL Team, and everything changed. The COOL Team—whose members consisted of technology-savvy nurses, clinical informaticists, and IT experts—worked side by side with the intensive care unit (ICU) nurses to redesign and streamline the EHR system documentation process. The end result was nothing short of phenomenal. After the documentation process was redesigned, and using the EHR system tailored to support this new process, the ICU nurses spent 25 percent of the time after the COOL Team did their work as before, in other words, by smartly redesigning the ICU clinical documentation process and building that into the existing EHR system, the informaticists reduced the time spent documenting complex ICU care by 75 percent. No new systems or technology needed—simply process redesign by knowledgeable informaticists. It changed the lives of the ICU nurses who were no longer tethered to the EHR system documentation screens. The team attacked the problem of an unworkable interface with the right mix of clinical and technical expertise, solving the problem and massively improving the satisfaction of the ICU nurses, some of Kaiser's most precious knowledge workers, and likely improving patient care by making these knowledge workers more accessible to direct interaction.

This type of work can be replicated across any type of process and system. If the vendor was engaged to solve the problem, the result would almost certainly require spending more money to buy additional programming or modules (remember, the vendors' business models only reward increasing revenues, not end-user satisfaction or improved quality of care), or "train" the end-users to "make better use of the system." The idea that the solution to this pervasive problem is "better training" and adaptation on the behalf of clinicians is repugnant. *Always* approach problems with EHR systems and other HIS with process redesign in mind.

item to help identify potential applications of technology innovations to these types of initiatives. This vital prioritization of innovation within an organization, as it decides which issues and problems to pursue, focuses the leadership and its finite resources on key initiatives and ensures that innovation silos are minimized. Worth noting is that innovation does often start in a single practice or area, but to become relevant, scalable, and socialized throughout an organization, it must become part of the organization's overall mechanics for planning, IT standards and integration, funding, process design and clinical integration, implementation, and on-going support and evaluation. This medical innovations list includes (Rege, 2018):

1. Planning tool for pain management therapies. Smart, local tools that can be used by providers to detect opioid blood levels and intercede with early warning that a pain management issue might exist. This helps plan intervention and appropriate care necessary.

2. The advent of AI in health care. A broad digital health category that requires prioritization within it to identify areas of focus. Examples include:

3. Expanded window of time for acute stroke intervention. May include a smart device and digital communications to immediately detect stroke or imminent event so that earlier intervention may commence.

4. Advances in immunotherapy for cancer treatment. Noted on Figure

12.6, at the point of technology trigger is **Immuno-Oncology**, the study and development of treatments that take advantage of the body's immune system to fight cancer. A digital health relationship to this type of initiative may include genomic sequencing and advanced computer processing and analytics to identify and match candidate therapies and patients.

5. Patient-specific medical devices created through 3D printing, such as finger splints, organ models, and implants for parts of the body, such as a piece of the skull (Meissner, 2013).

6. Virtual reality programs to enhance medical education, as presented in Chapter 14.

7. New tools and technologies for prehospital stroke diagnosis. This digital innovation applies to wearable technology, remote monitoring, predictive analytics, a smart phone app, and telehealth capabilities using a medical device and/or sensor to detect pre-stroke physiological changes and immediately alert patient, family, first responders, and providers for intervention to commence before a stroke occurs.

8. Innovation in robotic surgery. This technology-enabled innovation area continues to develop new, more advanced capabilities such as cutting away cancer tissues from sensitive areas such as blood vessels or organs of the body.

9. Innovation in cardiac surgery, specifically mitral and tricuspid valve percutaneous replacement and repair.

10. RNA-based gene therapies. May employ haplotyping, advanced analytics, and other technology innovations.

Leaders in the Field

What stands out about this list is the fact that all of the innovations are tech-enabled and involve integration with existing HIS, such as the EHR system and adoption of new technology in various forms. Most of them use many of the technology innovations called out on Figure 12.6. What may be a hefty agenda for one leading organization is the hope for others that are less well-endowed and cannot afford the capacity, resources, and cultural nurturing necessary to attempt to invent new solutions to problems experienced in all institutions. Many of these organizations rely upon and will ultimately benefit from organizations with "innovation departments" and forward-thinking, readily available IT staff to conceive and perform the innovation projects, pilot new applications in real-world settings, measure results, and transparently share lessons learned and results. These leading organizations are able to increase IT-related efforts beyond Meaningful Use (MU) and operational excellence. Focusing on other IT-related initiatives enabling strategies for value-based care, new organizational models, and digital business and clinical innovation will result in improved clinical care, engaged patients, improved provider experiences, more effective service offerings. This helps all healthcare organizations, over time, improve their service levels, patient and provider satisfaction, cost, and quality of care.

Progress is a journey, and digital health innovators will lead the way to many exciting and game-changing capabilities. In the meantime, for most organizations, this means a focus on MU, Merit-based Incentive Payment System (MIPS), cost reduction, and bread and butter capabilities. While 99 percent of providers are able, for example, to access EHR data remotely, including clinical results, documentation, images, computerized physician order entry (CPOE), operative reports, care plans, medication reconciliation, and other core clinical capabilities, only about half of them are able to do so using mobile devices, secure messaging and other communications infrastructure that is necessary to support remote access from places other than other hospitals and owned practices. Clinical communications between EHR systems and other care settings such as rehabilitation facilities, home health, hospice, and other less connected care settings other than hospitals and physician practices also lag (EHR Intelligence, 2018). Further, data exchange and integration of HIS falls short of what is needed for most provider organizations presently, making the basic requirements of population health management a struggle, as reported by College of Healthcare Information Management Executives (CHIME) from data gathered for their 2018 Most Wired Survey (College of Healthcare Information Management Executives, 2018). Thus, innovation will spawn from centers dedicated to that type of activity and deserve all due credit for moving the digital health agenda and all it portends for improving patient service, clinical outcomes, and cost-effectiveness of care across the board.

▶ New Data Sources

Additional data sources are available as advances in technology mature, such as HIEs and access to legacy data stores and warehouses. When available, both these approaches make existing data available and useful, thus avoiding the need to add additional systems or re-create the same data in order to get access to it, such as repeating lab tests or radiological studies. In addition, HIEs can make existing data that resides in a different organization's systems available to a broad, qualified group of providers participating in the HIE who only access it on a need-to-know basis. The data available through the network of HIE participants can be accumulated into a data warehouse and analyzed, using predictive analytics and other techniques, to gain intelligence about which patients may be at immediate or near-term risk for disease progressions, hospitalization, or trips to the ED. These analytics can identify which

interventions should be used to intervene and pre-empt those occurrences, resulting in prevention, improved quality of care, and reduced costs, thus a return on investment of the time, money and effort to create the HIE. Analytics environments can also be created as part of stewarding legacy data, creating warehouses of historical data, whose value can be synergistically enhanced by creating data warehouses and adding analytic and reporting tools to make the data usable and accessible to providers, analysts, researchers and others whose roles can benefit from ready access to historical data. Predictive analytics, clinical and business intelligence, and AI are all possibilities to harvest great yield from existing data for purposes of effectively managing a population's health and guiding preventive interventions based on the knowledge that can be gleaned from existing and legacy data.

Medical Devices

New data sources in the form of mobile, wearable, and implantable medical devices as well as numerous consumer, commercial devices capable of monitoring personal physiological parameters are now available to the mainstream to monitor personal physiological parameters for many conditions as well as personal health monitoring. This can be a source of needed data for preventive and population health efforts. These types of precise and reliable devices include smart medical devices and wearables that monitor, for example, cardiac function and blood sugar levels and give immediate early warnings of changes and problems for these patients. Commercially available devices, such as Apple watches, provide a near ubiquitous infrastructure for personalized quantification of relevant physiological data, which, when combined with organizational medical data existing in EHR systems, can help stave off clinical events with early intervention. These patient-provided data can also sharpen algorithms running against those data in institutional data stores. Heart rate, weight, oxygen levels, blood glucose levels, and other physiological data assist providers in identifying patients who need contact to address a condition that can be accurately diagnosed or predicted as worsening, such as heart failure, diabetes, hypertension and stroke, and other chronic illnesses that require regular monitoring.

Additionally, new technologies can take data from these various devices, consolidate and present them in a patient-centric fashion from multiple types of devices (another version of data silos) to keep track of the condition of a patient. Pulling all these various data sources together into a user-convenient format and medium takes great care and effort but, when done properly, adds great value to clinical workflows and patient-provider communications. For example, busy ICU nurses can lose critical time checking multiple device manufacturers' websites to pull data for their patients with implantable heart-monitor devices. Now, there is an interface that is available to ICUs regarding implantable heart-monitor devices that consolidates data from multiple manufacturers. By consolidating streams of data from different types of manufacturers, the data can be presented in a convenient UI to clinicians and other knowledge workers who can make use of those data to anticipate issues with patients and avert worsening conditions from occurring, without having to jump from one manufacturer's website to another. See the adjacent case example for details.

Internet of Things

Generally speaking, the Internet of things (IoT) is the collective network of computer-embedded devices, appliances, vehicles, and other connection points that contain sensors, software, computing electronics, and connectivity to perceive, connect, and exchange data, used across all industries. When one thinks of health care and potential use-cases of IoT, these uses are many and have the ability to support

🔍 CASE EXAMPLE: THE HEART OF DATA AND UX

Several different manufacturers provide widely used, implantable cardiac monitoring devices. While this technology may sound like it makes caring for the patient in the cardiac care unit (CCU) or ICU easier in the event of a cardiac event, it often ends up in a hectic and difficult time for the nurses and clinical staff working there. Medical devices are usually developed with the device and monitoring important physiological parameters for individual patients in mind. These devices are very important for monitoring heart conditions such as heart failure and arrhythmias, but can become problematic when considered from the CCU or ICU frame of mind. Tracking the same parameters from implantable devices from different manufacturers is problematic for these units unless perfectly integrated with their HIS, which typically is not the case. An innovative system developed by a new company called Geneva Health, consolidates and provides helpful data visualization for cardiology practices, device clinics, CCUs, and ICUs, overwhelmed by the deluge of data from multiple implantable devices for cardiac monitoring for these busy clinicians. Their product enabling providers to take advantage of the data from multiple different manufacturers' devices in an easy-to-use use UI, thus improving the UX. Expecting care providers to track individual data streams from multiple cardiac monitoring devices is illogical and works against high quality care. Again, UI and UX are paramount to make sure the value of the data can be achieved as originally envisioned by developers of these important devices. When considering that half of hospital admissions are cardiac related, namely heart failure and arrhythmias, enabling these important critical care unit knowledge workers to focus on care should be paramount. They shouldn't be inconvenienced with time-consuming visits to multiple websites to print off results, wasting time and other resources, in order to use the data from these life-saving devices. Advances through UI/UX design is critical to critical care and the wellbeing of patients.

and improve important workflows, especially considering the clinical monitoring and convenience for patients in acquiring and communicating useful physiological data to providers. As a reflection of the value to health care, the IoT market is expected to grow worldwide from $41.2 billion in 2017 to $158.7 billion in the following five years. Use of IoT in health care often is described in terms of the quantified self, where data and monitoring of physiological parameters on a regular basis can provide needed information for providers and alerts if a value is reaching an out-of-normal range. All of this hopefully improves patient outcomes.

Example uses of IoT include (Sharma, 2017):

- Personalized treatment plans that can be monitored remotely by physicians and platforms connecting patient with providers between visits, such as for chronic care management of conditions such as diabetes, using smart glucometers and blood pressure cuffs to transmit regular readings to providers.
- Preventive care using IoT technologies enables a bigger picture than the feedback from annual or biannual checkups. Patient parameters—specific to disease prevention for conditions they may be at risk for—can be monitored and clinical as well as lifestyle-based guidance, such as nutritional advice provided based on data gathered.
- Smart pills have been developed by a number of innovators and pharmaceutical companies to monitor medication levels, health problems, and medication compliance. These pills, once taken by the patient, send physiological data to sensors worn by the patient, data that is then sent to mobile apps or platforms for review and action by providers and the system which can analyze and detect problems.
- Also in the medication compliance arena, smart pill bottles can signal when the less than prescribed amount of medication is taken by a patient, alerting providers and family members so that adherence

of needed medicine can be improved. This helps solve the persistent problem of less than 50 percent adherence to needed medications, which could help patients manage or ameliorate their conditions.

- IoT capabilities allow for improvement of communications by creating connections between providers and patients and their families. A good example of this is in the surgical process: IoT connections can alert family members when a patient is done with surgery and remove the need for communications to be limited to when the family and provider are physically present or one the telephone with one another. This helps providers and family members alike.
- IoT is a valuable enabler of care management capabilities, helping to monitor physiological parameters from home to the provider, based on the condition of the patient, such as heart rate, blood pressure, blood glucose levels, and other important data to assist caregivers and providers work with patients to manage their conditions without having to go into the clinic or to the hospital to be monitored.
- When done securely and properly, IoT protects patient data by keeping it securely transmitted to their EHR system with their provider, rather than written in paper logs at home or other nonsecure means over the Internet. As with all HIS capabilities, security must be held paramount in IoT communications and connectivity.

To take this last point further, before we run forward adopting IoT in myriad uses, one must take a step back and be realistic about a major issue with the Internet of things: security. In health care, devices developed for a specific purpose may or may not have security provisions protecting them from hacking and other intrusions. The question for health care is to what degree is the IoT useable in handling sensitive, personal data according to good practices and regulatory requirements of health care? The same principles apply in use and connection of devices to healthcare networks and systems whether one considers this the IoT or HIS in the traditional sense. Before IoT concepts should be applied in health care, chief information officers (CIOs) and other IT leaders must embrace the notion that the normal security measures to protect networks and HIS are not adequate to protect those networks and HIS when connected to the host of devices and connection points developed for focused use cases in mind: these security measures must be built into the design process. Healthcare organizations are increasingly vulnerable as devices are added to the nooks and crannies of organizations, sometimes without the involvement or appreciation of the IT professionals supporting that organization. Better to emphasize security training and educate for the IT function and organization overall to assure adequate security measures are applied across all HIS, network, technology, and devices. Hacking and hackers are becoming more intrusive and capable, to the point where specific use cases involving devices connected to the internet and the organization's network should be considered carefully, and secured, one initiative and device at a time. The whole enterprise and patients depend on it. Clinicians using devices that might become connected to the network are part of this effort as well, and must be provided support and information to protect not only patient data individually, but the organization's network upon which all core, enterprise systems operate.

▶ Using New Technologies to Engage Patients: The Holy Grail

Enabling and encouraging patient engagement is the goal, as it is well-established that an engaged patient is a healthier patient who has a more satisfying experience of care and connection with providers as a consumer of those services. As the population ages and chronic illness grows along with unsustainable costs of healthcare services, the healthcare marketplace is compelled to adapt, with three drivers disrupting how HIS and new technologies are being applied to enable new types of services and organizational models as it evolves: cost pressure, value-based care, and consumerism (IDC Health Insights). These trends push health care in the direction of digital health, with unsustainable costs and the move away from fee-for-service, in support of new organizational models grounded in the proper mix of acute care and digital care needed to achieve value-based care. This of course is driven by the fact that the U.S. spends over $3.2 trillion on health care annually, with 90 percent spent on preventable chronic conditions such as diabetes, obesity, heart disease, and cancer, diseases that lend to digital health forms of care management (Burke et al., 2015).

Coupled with this situation is the fact that there are too few physicians to meet the demands of a growing Medicare population as the Baby Boomers have reached Medicare age and continue to do so at the rate of about 3.5 million per year (CMS.gov). Given these dynamics between supply (number of physicians) and demand (increasing non-acute disease burden) two trends are evident and must be addressed: (1) the application of technology to support patients through digital health capabilities, connecting patients who can be supported with monitoring of chronic conditions and care management between visits to the provider; and (2) the need to prepare physicians for digital health through new approaches to enhance medical education as it evolves (The Medical Futurist, 2018). Digital health capabilities can be effective in managing chronic conditions and the signals are strong for organizations to adopt these capabilities as they adopt new organizational models in the move to value-based reimbursement and value-based care (Jepson, Harris, Platt, & Tannahill, 2010; Riegel et al., 2017; Tuomilehto et al., 2001).

Patient Communication Preferences

Seventy-nine percent of Americans with chronic health conditions say it's extremely or very important for their healthcare provider to give individualized, patient-specific recommendations. Nearly all healthcare providers (95 percent) agree. The West Group researched the wish list of patient communication preferences with their healthcare providers presented in **FIGURE 12.7**.

Care Management

Care management connects patients with providers in ways that personalize the interaction based on the preferences and conditions

Top ten communication priorities patients desire from providers

Patients wish for communications centered around **prevention, disease management** and **billing transparency**.

Routine & preventive care	**Patients would like providers to communicate about routine healthcare and prevention, such as:** Help patients track laboratory and other diagnostic results. Recommend & schedule tests and preventive screenings. Text or communicate digitally with patients between visits. Send reminders to patients for appointments and medications.
Chronic care management	**Patients would like providers to communicate with them about chronic disease management, such as:** Recommend personalized care based on individual needs. Develop understandable & relevant health goals with the patients. Send reminders for prescription refills and fulfillment. Monitor chronic conditions between visits, including key metrics & care needs of patients.
Patient financial service	**Patients want healthcare providers to clearly define and help them manage financial responsibilities, such as:** Clarify for patients what their insurance does and does not cover and the portion they are responsible for paying. Make it easier for patients to understand and pay their medical bills.

FIGURE 12.7 Patient communication wish list.

Data from West Corporation (2018). Beyond the Appointment Reminder: Leveraging Technology to Benefit Your Practice.

and/or diagnoses of the patient. **FIGURE 12.8** displays a general layout of digital health for care management, the practice of connecting provider practices with patients and caregivers. Key characteristics include a digital health platform connected to patients, their family, and caregivers, integrated with provider EHR systems and patient medical devices. A healthy care management platform makes way for regular patient interaction with remote providers who provide medical advice based on a personalized care plan as well as behavioral, nutritional, and preventive support.

Figure 12.8 depicts characteristics of care management, including the dimensions of patient-centric care, based on clinical and patient goals; an interdisciplinary care plan managing documentation and communications; and the important ability to escalate to the provider if a chronically ill patient's condition changes in a clinically significant way. Connected devices monitor the patient's key

parameters regularly, and analytics support the refinement of care processes and predictive analytics identification of those at risk in the near term so that clinical interventions to keep them out of risk of advancement of their condition.

Digital Health and the Social Determinants of Health

Evidence has validated that involving patients outside institutional settings must be accomplished in order to address social factors, as these are outside the capability of healthcare institutions. Thus, technology-enabled innovation identifying the social, economic, and environmental factors affecting patients' health and connecting them with needed support such as nutrition, transportation, mental health services, safe housing, and clothing is critical. This must be a priority for health systems and payers, recognizing that health and value-based care require digital connectivity

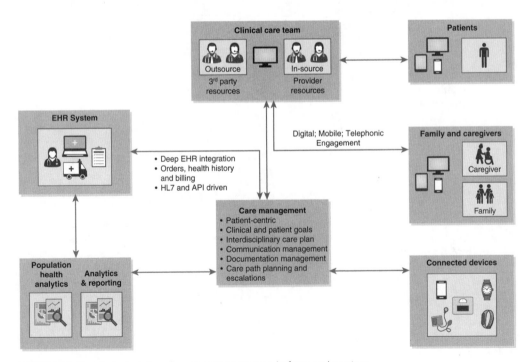

FIGURE 12.8 Key characteristics of a care management platform and services.

between patients, providers, and health services. A University of Wisconsin study found that social and economic factors comprise a full 40 percent of determinants of health, *twice that of the role of medical and health services* (Truong, 2018) (**FIGURE 12.9**).

One issue from the perspective payer organizations is that the traditional fee-for-service system is not set up to financially incent dealing with social determinants. But the barrier is starting to change with the shift toward value-based care, with more executives seeing the value of addressing social and economic factors as a way to significantly improve health outcomes. This is one way the traditional fee-for-service model for reimbursement did this

country's care a disservice. Moving into a new paradigm—that of value-based care—is challenging but necessary.

▶ Ubiquitous Infrastructure: The Power of Texting and Smart Phones

At the heart of health care is the ability to communicate. The relationship between provider and patient is based on interaction and communication. Enter ubiquitous connection and

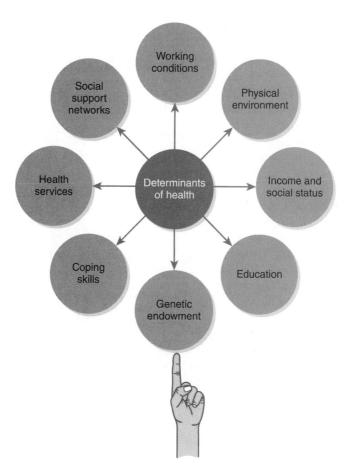

FIGURE 12.9 Social determinants of health.

communication through smart phones and the accessibility of them around the world—no longer are computers relegated to the water-cooled rooms of the 1970s. Cell phones and smart phones provide ubiquitous infrastructure for an ever-increasing host of uses and capabilities. In health care, it makes sense to use smart phones—within security and privacy considerations—to interact with the multiplicity of end-users, in particular, providers, other clinicians, patients, and their families or caregivers. Additional value for this diffuse and ubiquitous infrastructure derives through their application for preventive, population health management, research, outreach, and public health purposes. Clearly, the value of these devices is not isolated to their use as end-user devices for HIS in healthcare organizations. Rather, consistent with their purpose, smart phones bring capabilities to people wherever they live, work, and play. In fact, some of the most powerful uses of ubiquitous infrastructure include the ability to reach people in all reaches of the globe who do not have access to traditional institutional care—thus, reaching them in meaningful ways with information that helps them maintain their health or get information about treatment opportunities. In fact, the use of texting in rural areas and developing countries has made life-saving advancements with this essential and basic ability to communicate between sources of information and people internationally.

So much of "computing" in health care today is structured around the needs of an organization, e.g., hospital, clinic, payer. Infrastructure throughout our world now enables personalized interaction between and engagement with patients and provider. This replaces organizational workflows established for the purpose of controlling, creating, and moving information within an organization or business in the era before ubiquitous information technology. Many new technologies appropriately adapt to this shift from provider- or payer-centered computing to patient-centered computing by connecting people to health information and their providers at the right time, in the right format, to the right person, all while meeting the "rights" of information sharing.

However, just because a smart phone is used for a new capability doesn't ensure success for a clinical or business idea, or successful adoption of a well-thought new workflow, process, technology or system that integrates with clinical or business processes. The same diligence about the use case and its appropriate connection to the goal of the use case and integration of applies. The fundamentals always apply. See the adjacent case examples to explore this further.

▶ The Big Tech Companies from Other Industries in Health Care

Entrance of new players in health care is once again upon us. This time it is the biggest industry-agnostic technology vendors: Google, Amazon, Microsoft, IBM, Oracle, and Salesforce. Six of the world's largest technology giants have thrown their sizable weight behind advancing interoperability in health care. Microsoft, Amazon, Google, IBM, Oracle, and Salesforce issued a joint statement vowing to remove the barriers to interoperability by promoting the "frictionless exchange of healthcare data" through open standards and active engagement with the healthcare industry.

With shared goals of improved care, lower costs, and improved patient satisfaction, these massive companies have committed themselves to unleash and enable frictionless data exchange. They aim to accomplish this through new developments; using open source and open standards; empowering developers; and coordinating collaboration among participants in the healthcare ecosystem including providers, researchers, device manufacturers, employers, payers, scientists, pharmaceutical companies, and others.

🔎 CASE EXAMPLE: UBIQUITOUS TECH: TWO SUCCESS STORIES

One idea that has made use of the functionality of a cell phone is a notion developed by an emergency medicine physician. The physician's sister, a new mother at the time, texted him in the middle of the night during a December snowstorm, not only worried about her two-month-old daughter who had a slight fever but also worried about the risk of taking the baby out in the ice and snow to the emergency room. Her brother and she texted back and forth on their cell phones, until the physician finally texted, "Just let me see the baby. I know if I can see her, I will be able to tell if this is of concern, or if she just needs a cool washcloth, some liquids, and rest." The two made a face-to-face call through an app, and once he saw his niece, the physician knew that the baby was fine. "Just push the liquids and call me in the morning." This is an example of telehealth in its nascent stage: now, many payers refer patients to face-to-face apps with remote providers, thereby saving EDs and urgent care facilities for truly urgent care.

In the same vein, a different ED physician noted, like many before him, that when the ED gets overwhelmed with patients, a common practice is for physicians and nurses to walk out into the waiting room and quickly assess whether patients really need emergency care, or if there is some quick advice and care that can be given to get patients handled and out the door, making way for truly emergent cases.

These experiences gave rise to a new company, called CirrusMD, established to exploit the capabilities of a smart phone, especially secure messaging to replace traditional nurse triage in EDs. Panels of ED physicians, as well as other types of physicians within organizations, are now connected with patients and members of organizations, without charge, so that they can use primarily texting (actually secure messaging) to ask questions and interact with physicians. This way the patients and provider can quickly determine whether they should come into the ED, wait and see their primary care or other provider, or stay home and do a few home-care remedies. Using this app, the interaction between these physicians and patients is 70 percent texting and has had extremely positive results.

🔎 CASE EXAMPLE: UBIQUITOUS TECH: LEARNING FROM FAILURES

One innovation that didn't work as intended—resulting in unintended consequences—involved a use of smart phones to get patients in the U.K. to schedule appointments using their smart phone, rather than calling in to provider practices. The premise was that technology could be used to reduced general practitioner (GP) appointments by screening symptoms. A symptom checker using AI was used to evaluate whether or not the patient's condition could be solved with an online interaction or if the patient would need to see a provider and how soon they would need to see a provider. An unintended consequence of this approach was that patients figured out how to use the technology to get an appointment more quickly. Access to appointments in the U.K. can at times be an issue, and so patients involved in the pilot project quickly learned how to outsmart the system (reporting more severe symptoms) for appointment scheduling in order to get an earlier appointment. The pilot had to be abandoned. It was determined that the symptom checker was being used to obtain an earlier appointment with a provider in a system where this can be an issue sometimes. Thus, the pilot was abandoned (Wickware, 2017).

This is not the first time large, successful companies from other industries have entered the huge healthcare market—this has been tried numerous times by others such as American Express, Federal Data Corporation (FDC), and 3M, to name a few. Time will tell if the designs of mega-companies quite successful in other areas can succeed in health care, and if the needs of healthcare organizations and patients will benefit from that involvement. The expectation of profit from the huge healthcare market (nearing 20 percent of the gross domestic product) will bend to the will of companies accustomed to working in areas not requiring security at the same levels as health care, and being focused primarily on the well-being of patients and their families.

▶ Issues of Change and the Need for Governance

Regulations have heavily influenced the development and direction of HIS over the years. The names and alphabet soup are probably familiar to readers by now: **Health Insurance Portability and Accountability Act (HIPAA)**, **Health Information Technology for Economic and Clinical Health Act (HITECH)**, **Health Information Trust Alliance (HITRUST)**, Medicare Access and CHIP Reauthorization Act (**MACRA**), **MIPS**, **Quality Payment Program (QPP)**. This section will describe these regulations and the development of regulations and their influence, which has been sizable, on HIS over the years, in particular HIPAA and the HITECH Act and MU. Note that new major legislation has been issued every few years—2008, 2009, 2012, 2016—and the industry has had to adapt to every new iteration of regulation. Health care and the professionals who work within it will have to continue to be responsive to the needs of consumers and demands of

government agencies and changing administrations. Unfortunately, the care of people has been politicized. These are issues the students of today will be facing head on in their careers: it's best to know now that every four to eight years there will some radical change in how health care is administered.

In addition to HIS Strategic Planning, HIS governance and decision making must be taken very seriously and properly managed—a feat requiring a whole new level of discipline and self-control in the organization. HIS and technology planning and implementation are expensive, time-consuming, and mission-critical processes through which the organization seeks to achieve its long-term vision and strategies. They are also highly disruptive. For reasons and in ways that are never fully clear or predictable, when changes in how people work start to occur and gain momentum, it can be a trying time in even the most forward-thinking organizations. This shift in expectations creates stress in the organization, and there will always be some who react negatively to proposed changes.

Even when the majority of the group agrees that new systems are needed and there is growing enthusiasm around a new vision for the future, many choices exist in how to approach this process. Tough decisions must be made and priorities set throughout the implementation of the countless changes that an HIS strategic and technology plan suggests and implementations require. In turn, the organization must prepare itself for structured guidance through all these decisions. **Governance**—the process of thoughtful, balanced decision making for these projects and arbitration of issues that arise during the processes of change—is essential to success. Without effective and timely decisions on issues that arise during the course of these projects—decisions that have significant impact clinically, financially, and operationally—the strategic goals that the HIS plan envisions and supports may never be realized. Thus, disciplined, active HIS governance is a crucial part of successful implementation of the HIS and technology plan. Ultimate definition of governance requires that HIS governance must not be a "one-off" activity that is not grounded in policies and practices consistent with overarching governance of the organization, starting with the Board of Trustees on down.

HIS governance focuses on (1) the stewardship of organizational and HIS resources on behalf of the stakeholders who expect a return on their investment and (2) protection of the organization from excessive risk. Governance is conducted at the highest levels of decision making in the organization: at the board level for major expenditures and strategic changes, and at senior management and clinical leadership levels for establishing priorities, selecting software systems, resolving conflicts, communicating throughout the organization, and overseeing significant modifications to the ways that administrative and clinical work is conducted. In the case of the board of trustees or directors:

> A board needs to understand the overall architecture of its company's IT application portfolio. [...] The board must ensure that management knows what information resources are out there, what condition they are in, and what role they play in generating revenue.
>
> Nolan and McFarlan (2005).

The governance structure must also specify *decision rights* and outline the accountabilities to establish the guideposts needed to boost forward progress and appropriate performance in the use of IT (Weill & Ross, 2004). In addition, governance encompasses the decision mechanisms throughout the organization needed to weigh in and oversee the many decisions that need to be made throughout an HIS and technology project. HIS governance includes the leadership and organizational structures and processes to make sure the organization's HIS and technology plans and projects sustain and extend the organization's

strategies and objectives (IT Governance Institute, 2003).

Thus, HIS governance occurs at the board level *and* within organizational executive management and committee structures. It includes internal capital allocation and project prioritization committees. It is highly interdisciplinary, because HIS and technology touch every corner of the organization. No detail is too small to overlook in this type of work. The interdisciplinary aspect of governance is important because the education, decision making, and orientation about which types of changes are about to commence need to be embedded in the minds and skills sets of those people who are charged with managing the organization on an ongoing basis. This is not to say that additional expertise should not be brought in to assist in that process. Ultimately, however, this change is not just about computer systems: it includes how the organization does its work and delivers its services, and those are the responsibilities of the core leadership, management, and clinical personnel of the organization.

Effective governance, then, serves four purposes:

- Provides assurance that the HIS and technology plans align with the strategic goals of the organization.
- Protects the organization from taking on too much risk with the HIS and technology projects.
- Ensures adequate personnel resources and skills sets are available to these disruptive initiatives.
- Ensures itself that the job is getting done properly and in a timely fashion (Smaltz, Carpenter, & Saltz, 2007).

In addition to the board of trustees (in not-for-profit organizations) or board of directors (in for-profit organizations), an essential governance group is an interdisciplinary and enterprise-wide HIS and technology steering group. This committee consists of leaders from management, medical staff, nursing, finance, human resources, strategy and marketing, ancillary clinical departments, facilities, and other disciplines. It is typically chaired by the CIO of the organization (or whatever the lead IT position in the organization is called, such as IT Director or Manager of HIS). The purpose of this committee is to develop and oversee adherence to guiding HIS principles and to steer or make key interdisciplinary decisions that the project requires. These guiding principles are essential—they are the overarching ideas that, when push comes to shove, will help the group discern and find its way through difficult decisions and debates on a timely basis. Although these decisions often seem unresolvable, the organization must deal with them if the project is to move forward.

One important principle that will guide the organization through numerous tough spots is the recognition that integrated systems are superior to interfacing disparate applications. At this point in our society's automation evolution, many healthcare organizations are facing a thorny problem: they are chock full of disparate systems and silos of information that must be integrated to streamline processes and improve efficiency and effectiveness. In such a case, the principle of integration is paramount to guide systems decisions and rethink processes.

The other purview of the HIS steering group is establishing and upholding HIS policies in areas of data security, privacy, and confidentiality of information; acquisition of hardware, software, infrastructure, and devices; use of the Internet; and other key aspects of HIS and technology plans, decisions, and implementations. Standards must be established as well for software and hardware platforms, infrastructure, and data.

Perhaps the most important and difficult role of the steering committee is, once those standards are established, enforcing adherence to them. The HIS steering group must establish and exert the discipline needed to manage the organization's information systems and technology in accordance with integration versus interfacing, internal controls, and organizational integrity, all in a fashion that advances the organization toward its strategies. This work always goes against the grain of progress's primary enemy: inertia (Kouzes & Posner, 2007).

▶ Reality Check

And after a chapter full of ideas about digital health and hype-curve technologies, it is probably a good idea to provide a little dose of reality to see what provider organizations and their IT shops are dealing with when it comes to bringing innovation into reality. Assuming the bread and butter EHR system functionality is in place, since CHIME just reported that over 95 percent of providers surveyed have access to EHR data (EHR Intelligence, 2018). *USA Today* just reported (on Daylight Savings Day, naturally) that the Epic EHR system, one of the most-used EHR systems in U.S. hospitals, does not deal with the daylight savings time change, forcing hospitals to perform awkward, if not dangerous, workarounds (USA Today, 2018). Epic's system may delete the records for that hour; many hospitals cope with this by turning the system off, or shifting to paper to writing down the vital statistics and other key clinical documentation for the hour between 1 AM and 2 AM so that those data can be re-entered once the system "falls back." In any hospital setting this is a frightening thought—but in an ICU the amount of critical data and calculations are so extreme that it boggles the mind that the solution is to require caregivers to use paper to jot down vital statistics. Researchers and medical leaders from RAND, AMA, and major healthcare organizations weigh in with dismay and disbelief that, despite the millions of dollars spent by hospital systems on EHR systems, this hasn't been fixed. Cerner, another widely used system does not address this requirement either (**FIGURE 12.10**).

FIGURE 12.10 Falling back (in quality of care).
© Albachiaraa/iStock/Getty Images.

When approaching digital health initiatives and advanced technology innovations, remember that many of the basics one might assume are aren't necessarily there, and vendors, even the wealthiest of them, can't be moved to fix basic things that introduce risk into the patient care process. That is the state of affairs that providers and their IT departments must deal with every day. Clearly, and consistently with HIS history, innovation comes from provider organizations and the clinical and IT professionals working in concert to create new innovation; it does not stem from vendors.

Summary

Adoption of new technologies in digital health has numerous exciting avenues to potentially pursue. AI, machine learning, telemedicine, telehealth, predictive analytics, mobile devices, sensors, blockchain, and other new technologies displayed on the digital health hype cycle (Figure 12.5) are capable of many things. Barriers to adoption include complexities of healthcare processes, costliness of new technologies, legal issues, technical issues, and organizational readiness. Human-centered design, creating great UI/UX for patients, providers, and consumer base system design with the user in mind, should be of high importance. The Digital Health Hype Cycle identifies new technologies emerging in other industries and technology overall and their potential for health care. Informatics in the design of digital health solutions is as important now as ever; just like it is important to apply planning principles consistent with HIS strategic planning methods, informatics must guide the design and use of new technologies in adaptive workflows and processes. IoT is a burgeoning area with worldwide utility, and as other technology applications in other industries, special attention to building new technology uses is to do so to guarantee security of private and personal health information. Patients are now also consumers of healthcare services and digital health capabilities must be designed with their communication preferences as well as their medical conditions and health in mind.

Care management is a category of care that embodies digital health connecting patients with providers between visits. This is particularly important considering the incidence of chronic illness and the growing, aging population, combined with the shift in health care from fee-for-service to value-based, as a means of controlling unsustainable costs. Social determinants of health have a significant effect on health and must be considered as part of the goals and design of digital health solutions. Ubiquitous infrastructure is now available in the form of smart phones and secure messaging, proving to be very useful in enabling care outside institutional settings.

All this change underscores the importance of proper governance of design, decisions, and application priorities for adoption of new technologies. What is important, as with all HIS and technology, is to connect the use of new technologies to the strategic directions and issues to be solved by the organization, using interdisciplinary teams to discern, design, and try new digital health solutions.

Key Terms

Artificial intelligence (AI)

Blockchain

Care management

Cryptocurrencies

eHealth

Fast Healthcare Interoperability Resources (FHIR)

Genomic sequencing

Governance

Health Insurance Portability and Accountability Act (HIPAA)

Health Information Technology for Economic and Clinical Health Act (HITECH)

Health Information Trust Alliance (HITRUST)

Health Level 7 (HL7)

Human-centered design

Hype cycle

Immuno-Oncology

Internet of things (IoT)

Machine learning

MACRA

mHealth

Merit-based Incentive Payment System (MIPS)

Natural Language Processing

Predictive analytics

Quality Payment Program (QPP)

Telehealth

Telemedicine

User experiences (UXs)

User interfaces (UIs)

Voice technology

Wearable technologies

Discussion Questions

1. Define key new technologies being adopted as part of the emergence of digital health. What are the potential roles for each?

2. What is AI? What are potential applications in health care? What areas, business or clinical, are most ripe for uses of AI?

3. Describe telemedicine and telehealth. In what ways are telemedicine and telehealth the same, and how do they differ?

4. Barriers to telemedicine and telehealth include what types of issues?

5. Blockchain is often associated with digital currencies. Are the two always used together? How is blockchain applicable in health care?

6. In what ways does patient engagement relate to digital health? Why is patient engagement so important now?

7. What are the drivers of change for healthcare organizations?

8. Patient preferences are important priorities for how digital health initiatives and solutions are designed. What are the top patient preferences for communications with their providers?

9. What is the role of governance in digital health and adoption of new technologies? In what ways do the normal principles and practices of HIS strategic planning apply to adoption of new technologies? In what ways do they differ?

References

American Telemedicine Association. (n.d.). What is telemedicine? Retrieved from http://www.americantelemed.org/learn

Burke, L. E., Ma, J., Azar, K. M., Bennett, G. G., Peterson, E. D., Zheng, Y., … Stroke Council. (2015). Current science on consumer use of mobile health for cardiovascular disease prevention: A scientific statement from the American Heart Association. *Circulation, 132*, 115–1213.

CB Insights. (2018). Digital health insights. Retrieved from https://us1.campaign-archive.com/?u=0c60818e26ecdbe423a10ad2f&id=00eaeab874&e=a554382e8c

Centers for Disease Control and Prevention. Infant mortality. Retrieved from https://www.cdc.gov/reproductivehealth/MaternalInfantHealth/InfantMortality.htm

CMS.gov. National health expenditure projections 2016–2025. Retrieved from https://www.cms.gov/Research-Statistics-Data-and-Systems

College of Healthcare Information Management Executives. (2018). Most wired trends report highlights gains and challenges for providers. Retrieved from https://chimecentral.org/most-wired-trends-report-highlights-gains-and-challenges-for-providers

EHR Intelligence. (2018). 99% of healthcare organizations fully access EHR system remotely. Retrieved from https://ehrintelligence.com/news/99-of-healthcare-organizations-fully-access-ehr-system-remotely

Erreger, S. (2018). How can technology help address infant mortality? Retrieved from https://bit.ly/2T5XiMU

Forbes. (2018). Blockchain in health care: The good, the bad and the ugly. Retrieved from https://www.forbes.com/sites/forbestechcouncil/2018/04/13/blockchain-in-health-care-the-good-the-bad-and-the-ugly/#614d6ea96278

IDC Health Insights. (2019). Healthcare IT services strategies an IDC health insights research advisory. Retrieved from https://www.idc.com/getdoc.jsp?containerId=IDC_P31350

IT Governance Institute. (2003). *Board briefing on IT governance* (2nd ed.). Retrieved from http://www.itgi.org/Template_ITGIc9a4.html?Section=About

Jepson, R. G., Harris, F. M., Platt, S., & Tannahill, C. (2010). The effectiveness of interventions to change six health behaviours: A review of reviews. *BMC Public Health, 10*, 538.

Jin, B., Liu, R., Shiying, H., Li, Z., Zhu, C., Zhou, X., … Ling, X. B. (2017). Defining and characterizing the critical transition state prior to the type 2 diabetes disease. *PLOS One*. Retrieved from https://journals.plos.org/plosone/article?id=10.1371/journal.pone.0180937#pone-0180937-g001

Kouzes, J. M., & Posner, B. Z. (2007). *The leadership challenge* (4th ed.). San Francisco, CA: Jossey-Bass. Retrieved from http://www.nclp.umd.edu/resources/bookreviews/BookReview-The%20_Leadership_Challenge-Truesdell-2011.pdf

Lovett, L. (2018). *AMA launches digital health implementation playbook*. Retrieved from https://www.mobihealthnews.com/content/ama-launches-digital-health-implementation-playbook

Meissner, A. (2013). The global healthcare industry in the year 2020. Retrieved from www.mddionline.com/global-healthcare-industry-year-2020

Nolan, R., & McFarlan, F. W. (2005). Information technology and the board of directors. *Harvard Business Review*. Retrieved from http://hbr.org/2005/10/information-technology-and-the-board-of-directors/ar/1

PwC Health Research Institute. (2016). Top health industry issues of 2017: A year of uncertainty and opportunity. Retrieved from https://www.pwc.com/us/en/health-industries/pdf/pwc-hri-top-healthcare-issues-2017.pdf

Rege, A. (2018). Cleveland clinic: Top 10 medical trends, innovations in 2019. Retrieved from https://www.beckershospitalreview.com/hospital-management-administration/cleveland-clinic-top-10-medical-trends-innovations-in-2019.html

Riegel, B., Moser, D. K., Buck, H. G., Dickson, V. V., Dunbar, S. B., Lee, C. S., … Council on Quality of Care and Outcomes Research. (2017). Self-care for the prevention and management of cardiovascular disease and stroke: A scientific statement for healthcare professionals from the American Heart Association. *Journal of the American Heart Association, 6*(9). doi: 10.1161/JAHA.117.006997

Roth, M. (2018). 5 Need-to-know leaps in telehealth. Retrieved from https://www.healthleadersmedia.com/innovation/5-need-know-leaps-telehealth

Sharma, R. (2017). How IoT is changing the health-care world forever. Retrieved from http://techgenix.com/iot-health-care/

Smaltz, D. H., Carpenter, R., & Saltz, J. (2007). Effective IT governance in healthcare organisations: A tale of two organisations. *International Journal of Healthcare Technology and Management, 8*(1/2), 20–41.

Smith, A. (2015). Telemedicine vs. Telehealth: What's the difference? Retrieved from https://chironhealth.com/blog/telemedicine-vs-telehealth-whats-the-difference/

Stanford Medicine. (2018). Stanford Report, STANFORD MEDICINE SEPTEMBER 2018 White Paper: The Future of Electronic Health Records. Retrieved from http://med.stanford.edu/content/dam/sm/ehr/documents/SM-EHR-White-Papers_v12.pdf

Steciw, A. (n.d.). What is telemedicine, and how does it affect health IT? Retrieved from http://searchhealthit.techtarget.com/healthitexchange/healthitpulse/what-is-telemedicine-and-how-does-it-affect-health-it/

Sweeney, E. (2018). Amazon, Google, Microsoft and IBM pledge support for healthcare interoperability. Retrieved from https://www.fiercehealthcare.com/tech/amazon-microsoft-ibm-google-interoperability-data-sharing?mkt_tok=eyJpIjoiTkRZME16WmpZV1poTnpnBeSIsInQiOiJPWXFFJem5zeFgyWlA0ZWZldDI2Qk1cL0VCQm55GMUM5STFyddDRua0dGVk42RjdNQ1puME1wOGFHd01vWW4xaU1sYmF3dERTTYkN3Miswclwv WDV0NFJoVFhXbU0xMjV4UWZ5SnNHSlvvRzJ2UlhQMlBTWWpDZGtooSGtKVzFTcmh4 TGliIn0%3D&mrkid=751246

The Medical Futurist. (2018). How to prepare the future generation of physicians. Retrieved from https://medicalfuturist.com/how-to-prepare-the-future-generation-of-physicians

The New York Times. (2018). Quotation of the day: Jeff Hawkins is finally ready to explain his brain research. Retrieved from https://www.nytimes.com/2018/10/14/todayspaper/quotation-of-the-day-jeff-hawkins-is-finally-ready-to-explain-his-brain-research.html

Truong, K. (2018). How to address the social determinants of health—And pay for it too. Retrieved from https://bit.ly/2TXL4Dg

Tuomilehto, J., Lindström, J., Eriksson, J. G., Valle, T. T., Hämäläinen, H., Ilanne-Parikka, P., … Finnish Diabetes Prevention Study Group. (2001). Prevention of type 2 diabetes mellitus by changes in lifestyle among subjects with impaired glucose tolerance. *New England Journal of Medicine, 344,* 1343–1350.

USA Today. (2018, November). Like clockwork: How daylight saving time stumps hospital record keeping. Retrieved from https://amp.usatoday.com/amp/1864579002

Verify Markets. (2016). United States virtual healthcare market. Retrieved from https://www.verifymarkets.com/products/2016-united-states-virtual-healthcare-market

Weill, P., & Ross, J. (2004). *IT governance: How top performers manage IT for superior results.* Boston, MA: Harvard Business School Press.

WHO. (2010). Telemedicine opportunities and developments in member states: Report on the second global survey on eHealth. *Global Observatory for eHealth, 2.* Retrieved from http://www.who.int/goe/publications/goe_telemedicine_2010.pdf

Wickware, C. (2017). Babylon pilot ditched after patients manipulated system to book appointments. Retrieved from http://www.pulsetoday.co.uk/your-practice/practice-topics/it/babylon-pilot-ditched-after-patients-manipulated-system-to-book-gp-appointments/20035712.article

CHAPTER 13

HIS Around the Globe

"What kind of world do we want to live in?"

Tim Cook, CEO of Apple, cautioning all in a speech to European leaders, on the data industrial complex
(Nicas, 2018)

"We do not ride on the railroad; it rides upon us."

Henry David Thoreau, lamenting the U.S. industrial complex in the 1800s (Lyndon, 1846)

LEARNING OBJECTIVES

By the end of this chapter, the student will be able to:

- Describe uses, strategies, and impacts of Health Information Systems (HIS) in countries internationally.
- Explain the context in which these different approaches to HIS occur, including the overall performance of health systems around the world.
- Portray the relationship between cost, outcomes, and HIS in these countries.
- Detail the highlights and lowlights of various countries' HIS infrastructure and strategies.
- Identify the strengths and weaknesses of HIS in various countries.
- Provide examples of the uses of digital health solutions internationally.
- Illuminate the ways that the structure of a health system affects HIS strategy and results.
- Explain lessons learned from the experiences of different countries in the adoption of HIS.

▶ Introduction

The subject of HIS in other countries provides a vibrant opportunity to learn what types of HIS and technology work in other health system structures, providing a view into the ways HIS can improve the support of clinical, administrative, analytical, and population health management processes, as well as cautions about the problems and effects of those uses. It is not lost on students of health care that the U.S. differentiates itself in two conflicting ways: first, some of the most excellent healthcare services are available in the U.S.; second, that care is only accessible on a regular basis to those with comprehensive affordable health insurance or lots of cash, leaving the underinsured and uninsured, and in fact, many with high deductible plans at risk. Additionally, U.S. health outcomes are last among **Organization for Economic Cooperation and Development (OECD)** nations and lag at low standing compared to all nations in important statistics such as maternal and infant mortality (Martin & Montagne, 2017). While progress is being made in many areas, medical errors comprise 10 percent of all deaths in the U.S., serious public health problems have reached crisis proportions, such as the opioid epidemic, and we are far from stemming such problems and failings of the system (Pearl, 2017). Certainly, the combination of health system structure and HIS that support it are important elements of those poor outcomes.

Research and Statistical Foundation of Measuring Health System and HIS Effectiveness

Government organizations, universities, and global organizations such as the **World Health Organization (WHO)**, **The Commonwealth Fund**, **Institute for Health Care Improvement (IHI)**, the **Health and Medicine Division (HMD) of the National Academies of Sciences, Engineering, and Medicine**, and many other respected organizations are devoted to the development of new knowledge, methods, insights, and information related to healthcare quality, cost, population health, and other relevant topics that can be put into action to influence the ways health care is delivered and public health measures are tracking. The reach of these organizations' impact is far and wide and, in some cases, ubiquitous. These organizations perform research—that is, inquiries, studies, and reporting on all manner of health-related topics. Of course, these organizations need data to conduct these activities effectively. Thus, the research, policy, and public health impact of HIS depend on availability of high-quality data from healthcare organizations, health surveillance methods, and direct data collection

techniques. The source systems of these data include the growing base of core HIS described in the HIS and management layer of the HIS model, which in this case, applies to HIS internationally. Without these HIS data sources, research, policy, and public health organizations also conduct primary data collection or find data through other means, which can be difficult and limited in scope. It behooves the cause of advancement of learning in health care around the globe to connect consistent, comprehensive data sources from primary sites of healthcare delivery (that is, healthcare and public health organizations) to these secondary uses of data for research, policy, and public health purposes.

A Nation's Healthcare Philosophy and Structure Influences Its HIS Strategy

In most developed nations, other than the U.S., health care is supported by the government through a variety of programs and mechanisms, but consistent in the principle that health care is available as a right to all its citizens. **Private health insurance** and care is also typically available in these countries with a **national health service** for those who wish to pay for the privilege of on-demand health care. Any discussion of HIS in these countries should be done in the context of the overall structure of the countries' health system. Questions to consider when evaluating HIS adoption and uses in other countries include:

1. Is access to health care universal or selective?
2. Who has access to health care and how are HIS and digital health used to facilitate that access?
3. What role do HIS play in achieving the results in health outcomes and cost in that country?
4. What are the strengths and weaknesses of HIS in this particular country?

5. How widely are new digital health technologies being used in these countries?

6. What highlights and low-lights have occurred in the adoption and use of HIS and digital health in that country?

7. What are some experiences and examples of using digital health such as eHealth, mHealth, and telemedicine used internationally? How are HIS and digital health used to support and facilitate health care in that country?

8. What are lessons learned from these findings and scenarios that can be shared with and adopted in other countries? How does the structure of a country's health system influence the ability to adopt HIS and digital health?

▶ Adoption of HIS in Many Countries

HIS investment and adoption abounds internationally, as technology ubiquitously infiltrates and surrounds our world. As would be expected, countries invest and deploy HIS and technology based on the traditions, structures, and philosophical underpinnings of their own health systems, economics, and strategies for providing (or not providing) for the health needs of their population. Countries vary according to the principles and parameters of their commitment to their populace, fueled by societal forces and markets, governed by public and private regulations and law.

Common goals internationally revolve around efforts to automate, streamline, and innovate within each country's unique health system. Historically, in a 2008 study funded by the Commonwealth Fund, HIS and technology plans and projects in Australia, Canada,

Germany, the Netherlands, New Zealand, the U.K., and the U.S. were examined. More than 90 percent of general practitioners in Australia, New Zealand, the Netherlands, and the U.K. reportedly used electronic health records (EHRs), whereas only 10–30 percent of practitioners in ambulatory settings in the U.S. and Canada used EHRs (Jha, Doolan, Grandt, Scott, & Bates, 2008). These adoption statistics have changed remarkably since that time. A striking finding of the earlier study is that only 10 percent of hospitals in the seven countries studied met the criteria for major elements of an EHR system, a measure comparable to the distinctions drawn between **"basic" and "comprehensive" EHR systems** in studies of U.S. hospitals and ambulatory settings (Jha et al., 2008). Since then, enormous but varied investments of financial resources, time, effort, and organizational energy have been made country by country, and the results are largely the same internationally as in the U.S.—**HIS adoption** is slow and painstaking work. Results vary widely from country to country, which is to be expected, given the varying resources, different political systems, and competing priorities country by country. Still, international comparisons provide an important natural experiment on what it takes to use HIS to achieve desired economic and health outcomes and provides interesting texture to discussions about the effectiveness of various health system structures and funding mechanisms, as well as approaches to HIS strategy.

For instance, various versions of national health systems exist, even if based on a similar construct of a **single payer model**—that is, national health systems in which providers, hospital systems, and the payer are all part of the same unified health system, such as in the U.K., tend to be better positioned to set up standardized HIS and infrastructure, and thus opportunity for effective **population health management programs**. Numerous countries internationally with single payer health systems have viable opportunities to pull together consistent efforts to implement nationwide to HIS initiatives and provide the foundation to support cost-effective health care for their population. In the U.S. system, consisting of a combination of free market and governmental programs, Kaiser Permanente is an example of such a self-contained health system that sets the benchmark for effective population health management, even amid the complicated U.S. health system.

Even so, developing a national HIS strategy is still incredibly difficult work for many reasons. First, a cogent overall **national health system strategic plan** must be created and agreed upon, upon which to base the HIS Strategic Plan. Additionally, the required financial, human, and infrastructural resources must be determined and then allocated to support the development, implementation, on-going maintenance, and enhancement of expensive EHR systems and HIS infrastructure, following methods consistent with those described in Chapter 4: HIS Strategy, Planning, and Governance and Chapter 5: HIS Planning: Guiding Principles and Planning Tools. These efforts are of such magnitude and extended time horizons that if other major circumstances such as economic crises or changes in national leadership emerge at the same time, progress can be slowed or undone altogether. Nonetheless, when a country philosophically believes in health care as a compassionate pledge to its citizens, these social support programs can be quite successful, as evidenced by examples such as Australia, Denmark, the Netherlands, Canada, and Japan. These examples, along with others, are detailed further in this chapter. In all cases, as in the U.S., political, popular, and professional energies and wills must align sufficiently to muster the resources and commitment to plan, implement, and sustain the HIS infrastructure required to support a health system nationally.

Unfortunately, sometimes one of these pillars of progress may falter. For instance, in Germany, a setting in which a national EHR system and "**smart card**" for 80 million

citizens' personal health records made major headway between 2000 and 2010, then ran into strong opposition based on mounting concerns about privacy on the part of citizenry, slowing momentum and progress toward EHR adoption in that country (Versel, 2010). The U.K., Taiwan, and other countries have encountered major difficulties in adopting EHR system for health care. Major transformational systems implementations such as EHRs and required infrastructure are accomplished over a period of years, requiring not just sustained HIS technical expertise and leadership to support these initiatives, but also sustained consistent philosophy, regulation, and social environment— not a common scenario. While creation of HIS and infrastructure and innovative change is desired, the obstacles associated with their implementation and adoption are felt in all types of health systems, whether national or free market in philosophy (Anderson, Frogner, Johns, & Reinhardt, 2006). In addition to the socio-political and HIS infrastructures needed, challenges tied to the establishment of technical standards and discipline in data management have proved to be enormously challenging to health systems in countries around the world.

HIS capabilities of countries are described in the following section, including: the U.K., Netherlands, Canada, Australia, Germany, the U.S., France, and others. A comparison of HIS use in the U.S. compared to other countries is provided, including highlights, lowlights, expenditures, outcomes achieved, and emphases such as clinical or financial. This comparison table is intended to report adoption rates amongst countries and connect the use of HIS to the type of culture and health system structure of each country.

TABLE 13.1 displays the relationship between a country's type of health system, the method of paying for health care, the degree of adoption, and cultural issues such as ethos underlying the HIS, e.g., charge-capture and financial-oriented (fee-for-service in the U.S.)

TABLE 13.1 Health System Financing in 19 Countries

	Health System and Public/Private Insurance Role			Benefit Design	
	Government role	Public system financing	Private insurance role (core benefits: cost-sharing; noncovered benefits: private facilities or amenities; substitute for public insurance)	Caps on cost-sharing[a]	Exemptions and low-income protection[a]
Australia	Regionally administered, joint (national & state) public hospital funding; universal public medical insurance program (Medicare)	General tax revenue; earmarked income tax	~47% buy complementary (e.g., private hospital and dental care, optometry) and supplementary coverage (increased choice, faster access for nonemergency services, rebates for selected services)	Caps for pharmaceutical out-of-pocket expenditure only, dependent on income and total out-of-pocket expenditure in the same year	Low-income and older people: lower cost-sharing; lower pharmaceutical out-of-pocket cap and lower out-of-pocket maximum for 80% Medicare services rebate
Canada	Regionally administered universal public insurance program that plans and funds (mainly private) provision	Provincial/federal general tax revenue	~67% buy complementary coverage for noncovered benefits (e.g., private rooms in hospitals, drugs, dental care, optometry)	No	There is no cost-sharing for publicly covered services; protection for low-income people from cost of prescription drugs varies by region

(continues)

TABLE 13.1 Health System Financing in 19 Countries

(continued)

	Health System and Public/Private Insurance Role			Benefit Design	
	Government role	Public system financing	Private insurance role (core benefits: cost-sharing; noncovered benefits: private facilities or amenities; substitute for public insurance)	Caps on cost-sharing[a]	Exemptions and low-income protection[a]
China	Supervision by health authorities (Health and Family Planning Commissions) at the national, provincial, and local levels; some direct provision through public ownership of hospitals	There are three main publicly financed health insurance types with local-area risk pooling urban employer-based (mainly payroll taxes, for formally employed urban residents), urban resident basic (mainly government-funded, for urban non employed residents), and rural cooperative medical scheme (governmentfunded, for rural residents)	Complementary to cover cost-sharing and gaps, as well as better healthcare quality and/or higher reimbursements; no data on coverage, but growth has been rapid	No	Government subsidies to low-income families for insurance contributions and out-of-pocket costs; emergency assistance by local governments for specific diseases and unpaid emergency department or other expenses

Country	System	Financing	Private/supplementary coverage	Out-of-pocket cap	Exemptions
Denmark	National healthcare system; regulation, central planning, and funding by national government provision by regional and municipal authorities	Earmarked income tax	~39% have complementary coverage (cost-sharing noncovered benefits such as physiotherapy); ~26% have supplementary coverage (access to private providers)	No; decreasing copayments with higher drug out-of-pocket spending	Drug out-of-pocket cap for chronically ill (DKK 3,775 [USD 498D]; financial assistance for low-income and terminally ill
England	National Health Service (NHS)	General tax revenue (includes employment-related insurance contributions)	~11% buy supplementary coverage for more rapid and convenient access (including to elective treatment in private hospitals)	No general cap, but out-of-pocket payments almost exclusively apply to prescription drugs and medical appliances only: for drugs, prepayment certificate with GBP 29.10 [USD 41.10] per three months or GBP 104 [USD 147] per year ceiling for those needing a large number of prescription drugs	Drug cost-sharing exemption for low-income, older people, children, pregnant women and new mothers, and some disabled/chronically ill; financial assistance with transport costs available to people with low incomes; vision tests free for young people, older people, and low-income people
France	Statutory health insurance (SHI) system, with all SHI insurers incorporated into a single national exchange	Employer/employee earmarked income and payroll tax; general tax revenue, earmarked taxes	~95% buy or receive government vouchers for complementary coverage (mainly cost-sharing, some noncovered benefits); limited supplementary insurance	No; EUR 50 [USD 60] cap on deductibles for consultations and services	Exemption for low income, chronically ill and disabled, and children

(continues)

TABLE 13.1 Health System Financing in 19 Countries

(continued)

	Health System and Public/Private Insurance Role			Benefit Design	
	Government role	Public system financing	Private insurance role (core benefits: cost-sharing; noncovered benefits; private facilities or amenities; substitute for public insurance)	Caps on cost-sharing[a]	Exemptions and low-income protection[a]
Germany	SHI system, with 118 competing SHI insurers ("sickness funds" in a national exchange); high income can opt out for private coverage	Employer/employee earmarked payroll tax: general tax revenue	~11% opt out from statutory insurance and buy substitutive coverage: some complementary (minor benefit exclusions from statutory scheme, copayments) and supplementary coverage (improved amenities)	Yes; 2% of household income: 1% of income for chronically ill	Children and adolescents <18 years of age exempt
India	Financing legislation, and regulation by central government; financing regulation, and direct provision of services by state governments	General tax revenue	Limited role (<4% of total expenditure) providing substitutive coverage for the upper-class urban population	No; significant reliance on out-of-pocket payments (~70% of total health expenditure)	Various government financed health insurance schemes for poor and vulnerable population groups to improve access to hospitalization and reduce out-of-pocket payments

Israel	National health Insurance (NHI) system with four competing nonprofit health plans; government distributes the NHI budget among the health plans primarily through capitation	Earmarked income-related tax and general government revenues	Complementary (for benefits such as dental care, drugs, or long-term care) and supplementary coverage (for quicker access and superior service) provided by two types of voluntary health insurance: VHI offered by statutory health plans (HP-VHI) (~87% of adult population coverage); commercial VHI (C-VHI) (~53% coverage): C-VHI tend to be more comprehensive and more expensive	Not overall: caps on out-of-pocket costs for drugs (chronically ill only) and specialist visits (at household level)	Quarterly out-of-pocket caps for drugs for the chronically ill and age, income, and health status-related discounts; copayment exemptions for holocaust survivors; age-, income-, disability-, and health status-related exemptions on copayments for specialist consultations; reduced health tax (3% instead of 5%) for people on low incomes
Italy	National healthcare system: funding and definition of minimum benefit package by national government planning, regulation, and provision by regional governments	National earmarked corporate and value-added taxes: general tax revenue and regional tax revenue	Patients buy complementary (services excluded from statutory benefits) or supplementary coverage (more amenities in hospitals, wider provider choice); a round 5.5% buy individual VHI coverage (1.33 million families), while around 2.5 million people have group coverage	No; max EUR46.15 [USD 61] copayment per outpatient specialist consultation or diagnostic procedure; limited copayment (regional rates) on drugs	Exemptions for low-income older people/children, pregnant women, chronic conditions/disabilities, rare diseases

(continues)

TABLE 13.1 Health System Financing in 19 Countries

| | Health System and Public/Private Insurance Role | | Benefit Design | |
	Government role	Public system financing	Private insurance role (core benefits: cost-sharing; noncovered benefits; private facilities or amenities; substitute for public insurance)	Caps on cost-sharing[a]	Exemptions and low-income protection[a]
Japan	SHI system, with x-3,400 noncompeting public, quasi-public, and employer-based insurers; national government sets provider fees, subsidizes local governments, insurers, and providers, and supervises insurers and providers	General tax revenue; insurance contributions	Majority of population have coverage for cash benefits in case of sickness, usually together with life insurance; limited role of complementary and supplementary Insurance offered separately from life Insurance	Yes: coinsurance reduced to, e.g., 1% after IPY 80,100 [USD 763] monthly cap, depending on enrolled age and income: annual cap of total out-of-pocket payments at between IPY 340,000 [USD 3,238] and IPY 2.12M (USD 20,190) per household, depending on income and ages of household members	Low-income monthly out-of-pocket ceiling: JPY 35,400 [USD 336]; reduced cost-sharing for young children, older people, those with chronic conditions, mental illness, and disabilities: tax-funded health services for those on social

(continued)

Country	System	Financing	Private insurance	Cost-sharing	Exemptions
Netherlands	SHI system, with universally mandated private insurance (national exchange); government regulates and subsidizes insurance	Earmarked payroll tax: community-rated insurance premiums; general tax revenue	Private plans provide statutory benefits: 84% buy complementary coverage for benefits excluded from statutory package such as dental care, alternative medicine, physiotherapy, eyeglasses, contraceptives, and copayments	No, but annual deductible of EUR 385 [USD 465] covers most cost-sharing	GP care and children exempt from cost-sharing; premium subsidies for low-income
New Zealand	National healthcare system; responsibility for planning, purchasing and provision devolved to geographically defined District Health Boards	General tax revenue	~33% buy complementary coverage (for cost-sharing, specialist fees, and elective surgery in private hospitals) and supplementary coverage for faster access to nonurgent treatment	No: reduced fees after 12 doctor visits per year/patient and no drug copayments after 20 prescriptions per year/family	No primary care consultation charges for children under 13; subsidies for low-income, some chronic condition and high-need groups, Maori and Pacific Islanders
Norway	National healthcare system; regulation and some direct funding and provision roles for national government and some responsibilities devolved to Regional Health Care Authorities and municipalities	General tax revenue, national and municipal taxes	~8% holds supplementary voluntary health insurance, mainly bought by employers for providing employees quicker access to publicly covered elective services and choice among private providers	Yes; overall annual cost sharing ceiling is NOK 2,105 [USD 223]	Exemptions for children <16 years somatic, <18 years psychiatric, pregnant women, for some communicable diseases (including STDs), and those with work-related injuries; low-income groups receive free essential drugs and nursing care

(continues)

TABLE 13.1 Health System Financing in 19 Countries

(continued)

	Health System and Public/Private Insurance Role		Benefit Design	
	Government role	**Public system financing**	**Private insurance role (core benefits: cost-sharing; noncovered benefits: private facilities or amenities; substitute for public insurance)**	**Caps on cost-sharing[a]**	**Exemptions and low-income protection[a]**
Singapore	Government subsidies at public healthcare institutions and some providers; Medisave: mandatory medical savings program for routine expenses; MediShield: catastrophic health insurance; Medifund: government endowment fund to subsidize health care for low-income and those with large bills; government regulation of private insurance, central planning and financing of infrastructure. and some direct provision through public hospitals and clinics	General tax revenue	Medisave-approved Integrated Shield Plans (private insurance plans) supplement MediShield coverage to provide catastrophic health coverage for additional ward classes; other types of private insurance are also available, including private insurance provided by employers	No	Subsidized care for low-income population, with income- and asset-based means test to target subsidies; Medifund as safety net to pay for low-income and people with no means to pay for their healthcare bills

| Sweden | National healthcare system; regulation, supervision, and some funding by national government; responsibility for most financing and purchasing/ provision devolved to county councils | Mainly general tax revenue raised by county councils: some national tax revenue | ~10% of all employed individual sages 15–74 get supplementary coverage from employers for quicker access to specialists and elective treatment | Yes: SEK 1,1 OO [USD 123] for health services and SEK 2,200 [USD 246] for drugs | Some cost-sharing exemptions for children, adolescents, pregnant women, and elderly |
| Switzerland | Mandatory health insurance system, with universally mandated private insurance (regional exchanges): some federal legislation, with cantonal (state) government responsible for provider supervision, capacity planning, and financing through subsidies | Community-rated insurance premiums; general tax revenue | Private plans provide universal core benefits: some people buy complementary (services not covered by mandatory insurance) and supplementary (improved amenities and access); no coverage data available | Yes; CHF700[USD549] maximum after deductible | Some copayment exemptions and CHF 350 [USD 274] cap for <19-year-olds; income-related premium subsidies (27% receive); maternity care fully covered |

(continues)

TABLE 13.1 Health System Financing in 19 Countries

	Health System and Public/Private Insurance Role		Benefit Design	
	Government role	**Public system financing**	**Private insurance role (core benefits: cost-sharing; noncovered benefits: private facilities or amenities; substitute for public insurance)**	**Caps on cost-sharing[a]**	**Exemptions and low-income protection[a]**
Taiwan	Single-payer government-administered national health insurance system with mixed private-public, albeit predominantly private, delivery system; government subsidies to disadvantaged populations	Payroll-based premium, supplementary premium based on non-payroll incomes, general tax revenue for premium subsidies, tobacco tax, and lottery gains	National Health insurance provides comprehensive benefits including outpatient and inpatient care, drugs, dental Chinese medicine, dialysis, rehabilitation, home nursing care, care for the mentally ill etc.: private insurance plays at best a supplemental role; main benefit is cash indemnity payments to policyholders to use as they see fit, for example, private rooms, coinsurance for inpatient stays; private insurance plays no substitutive role to the public insurance system	Caps apply to coinsurance for both episodic and annual inpatient stays: for 2015, cap on per episode of inpatient stay was NTD 33,000 (USD 1,022), and the annual cap NTD 56,000 (USD 1,734)	Premium exemptions apply to low-income households, active service military personnel and military school students on scholarships, widows of deceased military personnel on pensions, prison inmates, and veterans; copayment and coinsurance exemptions apply to low-income patients and patients with any of 30 catastrophic diseases or conditions (for example, cancer, chronic mental disorders, rare diseases, congenital diseases, end-stage kidney disease, etc.)

(continued)

| U.S. | Medicare: age 65 and older, some disabled; Medicaid: some low-income: for those without employer coverage. State-level insurance exchanges with income-based subsidies; insurance coverage mandated, with some exemptions (10.4% of adults uninsured) | Medicare: payroll tax, premiums, federal tax revenue; Medicaid; federal state tax revenue | Primary private voluntary insurance covers ~66% of population (employer-based and individual); supplementary for Medicare | Yes for most private insurance plans: $6,600 yearly limit for individuals; $13,200 for families as of 2015 | Low income: Medicaid; older people and some disabled: Medicare: premium subsidies and lower cost-sharing for low- and middle-income families on the exchanges; some affordability exemptions from insurance mandate |

Reproduced from International Profiles of Health Care Systems (2017). Elias Mossialos and Ana Djordjevic London School of Economics and Political Science Robin Osborn and Dana Sarnak. The Commonwealth Fund. Retrieved from https://www.commonwealthfund.org/sites/default/files/documents/___media_files_publications_fund_report_2017_may_mossialos_intl_profiles_v5.pdf

[a]All bracketed figures in USD were converted from local currency using the purchasing power parity conversion rate for GDP in 2015 reported by the Organisation for Economic Co-operation and Development (2016).

vs. clinical- and patient-oriented (national health system in the U.K.). Due to reliance on the fee-for-service reimbursement system historically, systems in the U.S. have been built to support complex documentation, coding, and claims processing functionality, and the underlying nature of much of the software's capabilities reflects these financial objectives. Conversely, in countries where there is a single payer, the financial aspects of HIS are likewise simpler, and the software functionality can be built to focus on clinical workflows and processes. The reduced administrative complexity of a single-payer system places less emphasis on billing, collections, and third parties, while the complicated network of payers associated with fee-for-service health care demands a greater proportion of resources devoted to financial processes. In the U.S., efforts of the majority of providers to adopt EHR systems has been in response to the incentive stimulus of the American Reinvestment and Recovery Act (ARRA) with the Health Information Technology for Economic and Clinical Health (HITECH) Act of 2009 and Meaningful Use (MU) program. Before we examine the HIS frameworks and progress among these different environments, looking at the context of the health system environments within which these HIS are implemented provides a backdrop that sheds light on the HIS strategy and approach in these countries (Jha, King, Patel, Furukawa, & Mostashari, 2013).

Setting the Context: Health System Cost and Performance Variation Among OECD Countries

According to the OECD and the definition used for statistics in **FIGURE 13.1**, healthcare spending is defined by OECD as follows:

Health spending measures the final consumption of healthcare goods and services (i.e., current health expenditure) including personal health care (curative care, rehabilitation, long term care, ancillary services, and medical goods), and collective services (prevention and public health services as well as health administration) but excluding spending on investments. Health care is financed through a mix of financing arrangements including government spending and **compulsory health insurance** ("Government/compulsory") as well as **voluntary health insurance** and private funds such as households' out-of-pocket payments, **non-governmental organizations (NGOs)**, and private corporations ("Voluntary"). This indicator is presented as a total and by type of financing ("Government/compulsory," "Voluntary," "Out-of-pocket"). This indicator is also presented as a total and by share of total spending and in **USD per capita** (OECD, 2018).

In comparing healthcare costs as a percent of **gross domestic product (GDP)**, the U.S. spends the highest percentage at 17.1 percent, followed by Switzerland (12.3 percent), France (11.5 percent), Germany (11.3 percent), Sweden (10.9 percent), Japan (10.7 percent), Canada (10.4 percent), Norway (10.4 percent), Austria (10.3 percent), Denmark (10.2 percent), Netherlands (10.1 percent), Belgium (10.0 percent), the U.K. (9.6 percent), Finland (9.2 percent), Australia (9.1 percent), New Zealand (9.0 percent), and Portugal (9.0 percent) (OECD, 2018).

On the low end of the spectrum of health spending as a percentage of GDP, the following countries have the lowest expenditures per capita, including: Indonesia (3.4 percent), India (3.6 percent), Turkey (4.2 percent), Russia (5.3 percent), People's Republic of China (5.4 percent), Mexico (5.4 percent), Luxembourg (5.4 percent), Columbia (6.2 percent), Latvia (6.3 percent), Lithuania (6.3 percent), Poland (6.7 percent), and Estonia (6.7 percent).

These cost structures are important comparative elements when assessing the overall performance of a country's health system as well as efficiency and effectiveness of HIS within it.

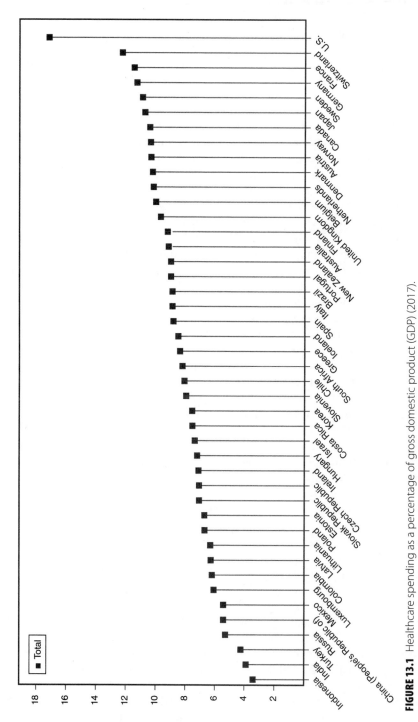

FIGURE 13.1 Healthcare spending as a percentage of gross domestic product (GDP) (2017).

Data from OECD (2017). Health Spending 2017. Retrieved from https://data.oecd.org/healthres/health-spending.htm

Why the High Cost of U.S. Health Care and How Can HIS Be Used to Help?

A far first among the OECD countries with the greatest expenditures per capita, the reasons for the high costs in the U.S. are primarily due to higher prices and greater use of expensive medical technologies than other countries for healthcare services and goods (Bivens, 2018). Contrary to what might seem logical, that these high costs might be the result of overutilization, people in the U.S. are *not* using more healthcare services—they are in fact going to the physician office less and are hospitalized less often than in many other OECD countries. The main driver of these costs is higher prices for the services accessed and supplies such as pharmaceuticals and medical devices, which are more expensive in the U.S. This is not a new trend. Research from 2003 data as well as more current information, provides evidence famously outlined by Anderson et al.'s 2003 article entitled "It's the Prices, Stupid: Why U.S. Healthcare is So Different From Other Countries" including the fact that in 2003 the U.S. had fewer hospital beds and practicing physicians and nurses, and used fewer inpatient days than the median OECD country (Anderson, Reinhardt, Hussey, & Petrosyan, 2003). What the U.S. did then and does today, is pay much higher prices for pharmaceuticals, physician visits, and inpatient stays (Anderson, Frogner, Johns, & Reinhardt, 2006).

HIS has long been identified as an essential element to improving outcomes as well as reducing costs (HMD, Kohn, Corrigan, & Donaldson, 2000), in the U.S. and in OECD countries (Anderson et al., 2006). The existence of a **national HIS network** and capabilities including an integrated EHR system, digital health capabilities such as mHealth and telehealth, as well as robust network infrastructure and connectivity are thought to be key elements of a national HIS. The lack of an integrated, national IT system for health in the future could worsen the U.S.' overall cost and quality performance relative to other OECD countries that lead in implementation of HIS infrastructure (Anderson et al., 2006). Early studies regarding EHR systems estimated that these capabilities could improve cost-effectiveness of the U.S. health system and save $142 billion in physician offices and $371 billion in hospitals over a period of 15 years (Hilstead et al., 2005). Of course, these savings would require tremendous cost and effort, estimated at $156 billion over five years, with an additional $48 billion in operating costs over the same time period to implement the systems and infrastructure to accomplish these benefits, nonetheless achievable. Thus, the lessons in this text are essential to effectively manage these systems and implementations so that the expected benefits are achieved, and to provide motivation for their creation.

Much hope is attached to the idea of patient engagement; the activation of a patient's motivation to participate actively in the management of one's health is evidenced to create lower costs and better outcomes, and is a strategy identified as important to achieving the **Triple Aim** of (1) improved outcomes, (2) better patient care, and (3) lower costs (James, 2013). Certainly digital health initiatives to engage with patients where they live and work are intended to not only reduce in-person, more costly visits to the provider, but also to encourage patients to actively participate in managing their health through these innovations. These initiatives also provide payments to providers who employ digital health services as part of their toolkit, with CMS now providing reimbursement for **CPT codes** for **non-face-to-face, digitally-enabled services** such as **chronic care management (CCM) 99490, CCM initiation pre-work G0506, general care management services at rural health clinics G0511, CCM behavioral healthcare management 20 minutes 99484, annual wellness visit and pre-work G0438 and**

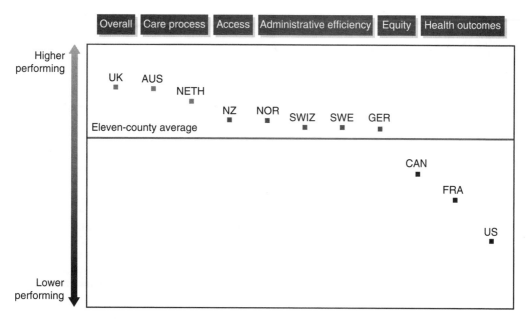

FIGURE 13.2 Performance rankings of OECD countries 2017.

Reproduced from Eric C. Schneider, Mirror, Mirror (2017). International Comparison Reflects Flaws and Opportunities for Better U.S. Health Care. The Commonwealth Fund. Retrieved from https://interactives .commonwealthfund.org/2017/july/mirror-mirror/

G0439, **transitional care management**, **transitional care management services 99495 and 99496**, and **complex CCM 60 minutes 99487**.

Health System Performance— OECD Countries

Comparing overall health system performance among OECD countries, **FIGURE 13.2** presents the results according to a 2017 study performed by Commonwealth Fund Analysis ranking overall performance of health systems, calculating an overall score based on taking care processes, access to care, administrative efficiency, equity, and health outcomes into consideration.

The U.S. system ranks lowest compared with all other OECD countries on Overall Performance, considering cost compared to outcomes, with the U.S. ranking last on dimensions of access, administrative efficiency, equity, and healthcare outcomes (Schneider, Sarnak, Squires, Shah, & Doty, 2017) (**FIGURE 13.3**).

An inverse relationship exists between greater expenditures and outcomes in U.S. health care—these per capita expenditures actually result in the lowest health outcomes on almost every key outcome measure among OECD countries, including—disturbingly, **life expectancy at birth**, which is lowest in the U.S. (Etehad & Kim, 2017). Also, the number of preventable deaths due to conditions that would have been responsive to health care are higher in the U.S. than in all other countries of equivalent advanced economies (**FIGURE 13.4**) (Peterson-Kaiser Health System Tracker).

Performance Pluses and Minuses

While performance for many measures are improving, such as overall mortality (**FIGURE 13.5**), the U.S. underperforms in key quality measures such as overall mortality rate, premature death (Potential Years of Life Lost), life expectancy at birth, mortality amenable to health care, and trauma during vaginal birth as well as others. The U.S. over performs in

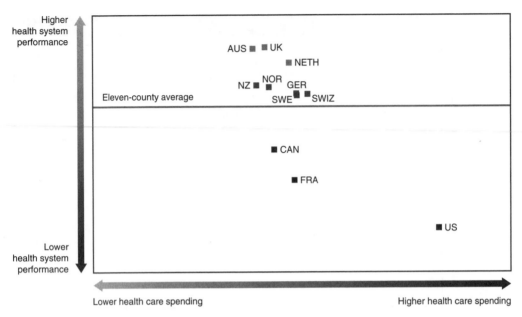

FIGURE 13.3 Healthcare system performance compared to cost.

Reproduced from E.C. Schneider, D.O. Sarnak, D. Squires, A. Shah, and M.M. Doty, Mirror, Mirror (2017). How the U.S. Health Care System Compares Internationally at a Time of Radical Change. The Commonwealth Fund. Retrieved from https://www.commonwealthfund.org/publications/fund-reports/2017/jul/mirror-mirror-2017-international-comparison-reflects-flaws-and

mortality rates and five-year-survival rates for breast and colorectal cancers, and 30-day in-hospital mortality rates for acute myocardial infarction and ischemic stroke (U.S. Population Health Measures, 2015). Compared to other countries, the U.S. excels in a few criteria, such as processes for treatments of in-patient conditions and access to health insurance coverage, and fails in broad measures such as equitable access to care and health insurance, primary care, and prevention (Claxton et al., 2015). In what ways do HIS connect to these results, and in comparing countries regarding cost and quality? Ironically, half of **primary care providers** in the U.S. polled in a survey from The Commonwealth Fund and the Kaiser Family Foundation reported that tracking the many metrics intended to assess their quality of care and assess financial penalties based on those metrics is having a negative effect on quality (Kaiser Family Foundation, 2015).

The following four tables provide details behind measuring and evaluating health systems internationally regarding: (1) financing and insurance coverage, (2) health system indicators, (3) performance indicators, and (4) ownership, payment, and primary care. These provide the backdrop for understanding the HIS strategy and infrastructure in each of these countries (**TABLES 13.2, 13.3,** and **13.4**).

The Course of HIS Adoption Among OECD Countries

Now that the current context of cost and outcomes is described, let's turn to the development of HIS within this host of countries. Are there patterns or correlations between how HIS strategies and infrastructures are invested in and built in these countries and these outcomes? Certainly the degree of HIS adoption must be considered with statistics associated with cost and quality among OECD countries, since HIS is considered a means of improving quality and cost performance. Early proclamations of the association of HIS with quality and cost appeared in the Health and Medicine

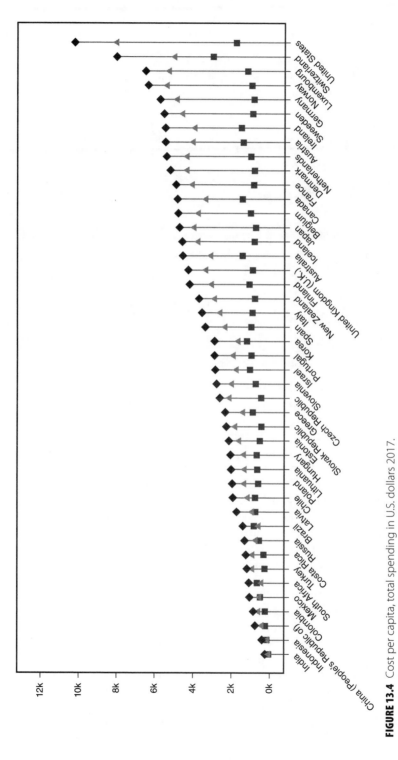

FIGURE 13.4 Cost per capita, total spending in U.S. dollars 2017.

Data from OECD (2017). Health Spending 2017. Retrieved from https://data.oecd.org/healthres/health-spending.htm

Stage	EMR Adoption Model Cumulative Capabilities
7	Complete EMR; external HIE; data analytics, governance, disaster recovery, privacy and security
6	Technology enabled medication, blood products, and human milk administration; risk reporting; full CDS
5	Physician documentation using structured templates; intrusion/device protection
4	CPOE with CDS; nursing and allied health documentation; basic business continuity
3	Nursing and allied health documentation; eMAR; role-based security
2	CDR; internal interoperability; basic security
1	Ancillaries-laboratory, pharmacy, and radiology/cardiology information systems; PACS; digital non-DICOM image management
0	All three ancillaries not installed

FIGURE 13.5 EMRAM EHR adoption framework.

Reproduced from Healthcare Information and Management Systems Society (HIMSS). Retrived from: https://www.himss.eu/healthcare-providers/emram

Division of the National Academies of Sciences, Engineering, and Medicine, formerly the Institute of Medicine (2001) report "Crossing the Quality Chasm: A New Health System for the 21st Century." The study named "inadequate use of information technology" as one of four main reasons for high rates of occurrence of preventable medical errors (diagnostic, medical, preventive, and other types of errors such as equipment failures) and avoidable deaths in U.S. hospitals (HMD, 1999). Since use of HIS is identified as an effective means to reduce medical errors and improve quality through automation, comparing HIS adoption rates among OECD countries provides another dimension associated with overall results connected to quality, cost, and structure of health care in like OECD countries. As early as 2002, studies provided evidence that the U.S. lagged between 4 and 13 years behind other countries in initiating comprehensive adoption of HIS and EHR systems (Taylor & Leitman, 2002).

As of 2003, levels of effort and expenditure toward a national HIS and EHR footprint varied widely between countries. For example, the U.S. only established the Office of the National Coordinator of Health Information Technology in 2004, with expectations to begin a 10-year initiative in 2006, ending in 2016, to create electronic patient records and connectivity nationally. In contrast, Germany began efforts towards the same in 1993, including a smart care initiative for individual citizens' health records and national network of HIS by 2003. Norway and Canada began in earnest in 1997, with Canada's embracing the goal of half

TABLE 13.2 Health System Indicators for 18 Countries

		Australia	Canada	China	Denmark	France	Germany	India	Israel	Italy
Population 2014	Total Population (Millions of People)	23.78	35.85	1,360.72ᵃ	5.66	66.42	81.20	1,295.29	8.31	60.80
	Percentage of Population Age 65 and Older	14.7%	15.7%	9.6%	18.2%	18.0%	20.8%	5.50%	10.7%ᶜ	21.4%
Healthcare Spending 2014	Percentage of GDP Spent on Health Care	9.0%ʰ	10.5%	5.6%ʰ	10.7%ᵇ	11.8%	11.0%ʰ	4.7%ⁱ	7.4%	9.1%ʰ
	Healthcare Spending per Capitaᶠ	$4,207ʰ	$4,728	$420ⁱ	$5,012ᵇ	$4,620	$5,119ʰ	$215ᵃ	$2,353ⁱ	$3,207ʰ
	Out of Pocket Health Care Spending per Capitaᵉ	$532ᵇ	$644		$671	$305	$664		$602	$706
	Spending on Pharmaceuticals per Capitaᶠ	$626ᵇ	$772		$325	$656	$741		$306ᶜ	$544
Physician Capacity and Utilization 2014	Number of Practicing Physicians per 1,000 Population	3.5ⁱ	2.5	1.9	3.7ᵇ	3.1	4.1	0.7	3.5	3.9
	Average Annual Number of Physician Visits per Capita	7.3	7.6ᵇ	5.6ⁱ	4.5	6.3	9.9			6.8ᵇ
Hospital Spending Utilization and Capacity 2014	Total Curative (Acute) Care Beds, per 1,000		2.1ᵇ	4.9	2.6	4.1	6.2		2.3	2.8ᵇ
	Hospital Spending Per Dischargeᶠ	$10,530ᵇ	$16,451		$14,105	$10,591	$5,900		$5,069ᶜ	$12,150
	Hospital Discharges per 1,000 Population	163ᵇ	84ᵇ			159ᵇ	236		156	107
	Average Length of Stay for Curative (Acute) Care in Days	4.7ᵇ	7.5ᵇ			5.8ᵇ	7.6		5.1	6.8
Medical/ Information Technology	Magnetic Resonance Imaging (MRI) Machines per Million Population, 2014	15.2	8.9ᵇ			10.9	30.5		4.0	25.2ᵇ
	Magnetic Resonance Imaging (MRI) Exams per 1,000 Population, 2014	35.3	54.9		75.0	95.5	114.3ᶜ		32.1	
	Primary Care Physicians' Use of Electronic Medical Records, 2015	92%	73%			75%	84%			
Health Risk Factors, 2014	Percentage of Adults Who Report Being Daily Smokers	13%ᵇ	14%	26%ᶜ	17%	22%	21%ᵇ	13%ᶜ	17%	20%
	Prevalence of Obesity (BMI > 30)	28%ᵇ	26%ᵇ	7%ᵍ	14%ᵍ	15%ᵃ,ᵇ	16%ᵃ,ᵇ	5%ᵍ	18%ᵍ	10%ᵍ

(continues)

TABLE 13.2 Health System Indicators for 18 Countries *(continued)*

		Japan	Netherlands	New Zealand	Norway	Singapore	Sweden	Switzerland	U.K.	U.S.
Population, 2014	Total Population (Millions of People)	127.11	16.90	4.60	5.17	5.54[k]	9.75	8.24	64.88	321.19
	Percentage of Population Age 65 and Older	25.1%	17.3%	14.4%	15.8%	11.7%[k]	19.3%	17.5%	17.4%	14.5%
Healthcare Spending, 2014	Percentage of GDP Spent on Health Care	11.4%[h]	10.9%[h]	10.9%	9.3%	4.9%	11.7%	11.4%[h]	10.2%	17.2%
	Healthcare Spending per Capita[i]	$4,152[h]	$5,227[h]	$4,038[b]	$6,432	$2,752[k]	$5,306	$6,787[h]	$4,094	$9,364
	Out of Pocket Health Care Spending per Capita[e]	$126[b]	$649	$263[b]	$882		$787	$1,815	$586	$1,034
	Spending on Pharmaceuticals per Capita[f]	$783[b]	$401		$457		$489	$730	$485	$1,112
Physician Capacity and Utilization, 2014	Number of Practicing Physicians per 1,000 Population	2.4		2.8	4.4	2.0[l]	4.1[b]	4.1	2.8	2.6[b]
	Average Annual Number of Physician Visits per Capita	12.8[b]	8.0	3.7[c]	4.3		2.9	3.9[c]		4.0[e]
Hospital Spending, Utilization and Capacity, 2014	Total Curative (Acute) Care Beds, per 1,000	7.9	3.3[c]	2.7	3.4	2.0[m]	2.4	3.8	2.3	2.5[b]
	Hospital Spending Per Discharge[j]	$14,388[d]	$14,181[c]		$13,923[b]		$12,393	$14,624	$11,663	$21,063[e]
	Hospital Discharges per 1,000 Population	113	115[c]	132[b]	187		139	150	125	
	Average Length of Stay for Curative (Acute) Care in Days	16.9	6.4[c]	5.2[b]	5.5		5.4	5.8	6.0	5.4[b]
Medical/ Information Technology	Magnetic Resonance Imaging (MRI) Machines per Million Population, 2014	51.7	12.9	11.3[b]					6.1	38.1
	Magnetic Resonance Imaging (MRI) Exams per 1,000 Population, 2014	63.0[n]	51.2[n]					76.0		109.5
	Primary Care Physicians' Use of Electronic Medical Records, 2015	98%	98%	100%	99%		99%	54%	98%	84%

Health Risk Factors, 2014								
Percentage of Adults Who Report Being Daily Smokers	20%	19%	16%	13%	12%	20%[c]	19%[b]	13%
Prevalence of Obesity (BMI > 30)	4%	13%[g]	30%	10%[g,c]	12%[d]	10%[g,a,c]	26%	38%

Reproduced from International Profiles of Health Care Systems (2017). Elias Mossialos and Ana Djordjevic London School of Economics and Political Science Robin Osborn and Dana Sarnak. The Commonwealth Fund. Retrieved from https://www.commonwealthfund.org/sites/default/files/documents/___media_files_publications_fund_report_2017_may_mossialos_intl_profiles_v5.pdf

OECD Health Data 2016 unless otherwise noted.

[a]2015.

[b]2013.

[c]2012.

[d]2011.

[e]2010.

[f]Adjusted for differences in the cost of living.

[g]All data self-reported except in Australia, Canada, Japan, New Zealand, U.K., and U.S., where it is measured.

[h]Current spending only, and excludes spending on capital formation of healthcare providers.

[i]China Health and Family Planning Statistical Yearbook, 2015.

[j]China Health and Family Planning Statistical Yearbook, 2011.

[k]World Bank, 2015.

[l]World Bank, 2012.

[m]World Bank, 2011, and may include chronic care beds as well as acute care beds.

[n]Unpublished Commonwealth Fund grant, 2014.

[o]2015 Commonwealth Fund International Health Policy Survey of Primary Care Physicians

TABLE 13.3 Health System Performance Indicators for 17 Countries

Category	Indicator	Australia	Canada	China	Denmark	France	Germany	India	Israel
Access to Care, 2016	Able to Get Same-Day/Next-Day Appointment When Sick	67%	43%			56%	53%		
	Very/Somewhat Easy to Get Care After Hours[a]	44%	63%			64%	64%		
	Waited Two Months or More for Specialist Appointment[b]	13%	30%			4%	3%		
	Waited Four Months or More for Elective Surgery[c]	8%	18%			2%	0%		
	Experienced Access Barrier Because of Cost in Past Year[d]	14%	16%			17%	7%		
Safety Problems Among Older Adults, 2014[e]	Health Professional Did Not Review Their Prescriptions in Past Year	16%	16%			47%	19%		
Care Coordination and Transitions, 2016	Experienced a Coordination Problem in Past Two Years[f]	22%	30%			31%	19%		
	Experienced Gaps in Hospital Discharge Planning in Past Two Years[g]	29%	40%			60%	28%		
Chronic Care Management, 2016[h]	Doctor or Healthcare Professional Discussed Patient's Main Goals or Priorities in Caring for Condition	71%	56%			66%	67%		
	Doctor Healthcare Professional Discussed Treatment Options with Patient Including Side Effects	67%	57%			61%	60%		
Performance Feedback, 2015	Primary Care Practice Routinely Receives and Reviews Clinical Outcomes Data	35%	23%			43%	44%		
	Primary Care Practice Routinely Receives and Reviews Patient Satisfaction and Experience Data	46%	17%			3%	25%		
	Primary Care Practice Routinely Receives Data Comparing Performance to Other Practices	13%	17%			49%	29%		
Healthcare Quality Indicators	Diabetes-related Lower Extremity Amputation Rates per 100,000 Population, 2013	4.5	7.4		8.5	7.5	9.2		15.9
	Breast Cancer Five-Year Survival Rate, 2008–2013 (or nearest period)	88%	88%		86%		86%		88%
	Mortality After Hospital Admission for Acute Myocardial Infarction per 100 Admissions, Patients Age 45 and Older, 2013	4.1[l]	6.7		5.7	7.2			6.7[l]
Avoidable deaths, 2013[m]	Mortality Amenable to Health Care (Deaths per 100,000 Population)	62[n,o,q]	78[q,p]		82[n]	61[n]	83[q,q]		
Preventive Health Care, 2014[r]	Percentage of Children with Measles Immunization	93	95	99	90	90	97	83	96
	Percentage of Population Age 65 and Older with Influenza Immunization		63.1		43	48.5	58.6[k]		63.8
Overall Views of Healthcare System[t]	Work Well, Minor Changes Needed	44%	35%			54%	60%		
	Fundamental Changes Needed	46%	55%			41%	37%		
	Needs to Be Completely Rebuilt	4%	9%			4%	3%		

	Italy	Japan	Netherlands	New Zealand	Norway	Sweden	Switzerland	U.K.	U.S.
Access to Care, 2016									
Able to Get Same-Day/Next-Day Appointment When Sick			77%	76%	43%	49%	57%	57%	51%
Very/Somewhat Easy to Get Care After Hours[a]			25%	44%	40%	64%	58%	49%	51%
Waited Two Months or More for Specialist Appointment[b]			7%	20%	28%	19%	9%	19%	6%
Waited Four Months or More for Elective Surgery[c]			4%	15%	15%	12%	7%	12%	4%
Experienced Access Barrier Because of Cost in Past Year[d]			8%	18%	10%	8%	22%	7%	33%
Safety Problems Among Older Adults, 2014[e]									
Health Professional Did Not Review Their Prescriptions in Past Year			37%	23%	36%	48%	27%	21%	14%
Care Coordination and Transitions, 2016									
Experienced a Coordination Problem in Past Two Years[f]			23%	22%	35%	32%	30%	19%	35%
Experienced Gaps in Hospital Discharge Planning in Past Two Years[g]			47%	31%	61%	52%	45%	28%	22%
Chronic Care Management, 2016[h]									
Doctor or Healthcare Professional Discussed Patient's Main Goals or Priorities in Caring for Condition			59%	62%	41%	26%	64%	61%	63%
Doctor Healthcare Professional Discussed Treatment Options with Patient Including Side Effects			57%	62%	32%	30%	59%	54%	60%

(continues)

TABLE 13.3 Health System Performance Indicators for 17 Countries   *(continued)*

		Italy	Japan	Netherlands	New Zealand	Norway	Sweden	Switzerland	U.K.	U.S.
Performance Feedback, 2015	Primary Care Practice Routinely Receives and Reviews Clinical Outcomes Data			88%	65%	32%	79%	9%	86%	52%
	Primary Care Practice Routinely Receives and Reviews Patient Satisfaction and Experience Data			61%	60%	9%	88%	15%	88%	63%
	Primary Care Practice Routinely Receives Data Comparing Performance to Other Practices			42%	61%	4%	55%	37%	71%	37%
Healthcare Quality Indicators	Diabetes-related Lower Extremity Amputation Rates per 100,000 Population, 2013	2.7		4.7[j]	5.9[k]	5.7	4.1	3.1%	3.1	
	Breast Cancer Five-Year Survival Rate, 2008–2013 (or nearest period)	86%		85%	86%	89%	89%		81%	89%
	Mortality After Hospital Admission for Acute Myocardial Infarction per 100 Admissions, Patients Age 45 and Older, 2013	5.5	12.2[u]	7.6[j]	6.6	6.7	4.5[l]	7.7%	7.6[l]	55%
Avoidable deaths, 2013[m]	Mortality Amenable to Health Care (Deaths per 100,000 Population)	75[n]		72[n]	87[n,o]	64[n,o,q]	69[o,q]	55[n]	85	112[o,q,q]
Preventive Health Care, 2014[l]	Percentage of Children with Measles Immunization	86	98	96	93	94	97	93	93	91
	Percentage of Population Age 65 and Older with Influenza Immunization	55.4	50	72	69	26.9	49.7		74.5	67.9[s]

Overall Views of Healthcare System[c]							
Work Well, Minor Changes Needed	43%	41%	59%	31%	58%	44%	19%
Fundamental Changes Needed	46%	52%	33%	58%	37%	46%	53%
Needs to Be Completely Rebuilt	8%	6%	5%	85	3%	7%	23%

Reproduced from International Profiles of Health Care Systems (2017). Elias Mossialos and Ana Djordjevic London School of Economics and Political Science Robin Osborn and Dana Sarnak. The Commonwealth Fund. Retrieved from https://www.commonwealthfund.org/sites/default/files/documents/____media_files_publications_fund_report_2017_may_mossialos_intl_profiles_v5.pdf

(Unless noted otherwise): 2015 and 2016 Commonwealth Fund International Health Policy Surveys.

[a]Base: sought care after hours.

[b]Base: needed to see a specialist in past two years.

[c]Base: needed elective surgery in past two years.

[d]Access barrier because of cost defined as at least one of the following: did not fill/skipped prescription, did not visit doctor with medical problem, and/or did not get recommended care.

[e]Base: adults age 65 or older who are taking four or more prescription medications regularly.

[f]Coordination problem includes one or more of the following: test results/records not available at appointment or duplicate tests ordered; specialist lacked medical history or regular doctor not informed about specialist care; and received conflicting information from different doctors or healthcare professionals.

[g]Hospital discharge planning gap defined as: when discharged from the hospital, one did not receive written information about what to do when one returned home and symptoms to watch for; hospital did not make sure one had arrangements for follow-up care; someone did not discuss with one the purpose of taking each medication; and/or one did not know who to contact if one had a question about one's condition or treatment. Base: hospitalized overnight in past two years.

[h]Base: had ever been diagnosed with asthma or chronic lung disease, diabetes, heart disease, including heart attack, hypertension or high blood pressure.

[i]OECD Health Data 2015.

[j]2011.

[k]2012.

[l]Admissions resulting in a transfer are included.

[m]Marina Karanikolos, European Observatory on Health Systems and Policies 2017.

[n]Trends in mortality amenable to health care for selected countries. 2000—2014. World Health Organization mortality files (number of deaths by age group) and populations.

[o]List of amenable causes: Nolte and McKee 2004.

[p]Calculations by European Observatory on Health Systems and Policies 2016; amenable mortality causes based on Nolte and McKee 2004; mortality and population data from World Health Organization mortality files, released Sept. 2016.

[q]Age-specific rates standardized to European Standard Population 2013; data from 2014.

[r]OECD Health Data 2016.

[s]2013.

[t]Question asked on survey: "Which of the following statements comes closest to expressing your overall view of the healthcare system in your country?"

TABLE 13.4 Provider Organization and Payment in 19 Countries

	Provider ownership		Provider payment		Primary care role	
	Primary care	Hospitals	Primary care payment[a]	Hospital payment	Registration with GP required	Gatekeeping
Australia	Private	Public (~65% of beds), private (~35%)	~95% fee-for-service, ~5% incentive payments	Global budgets and case-based payment in public hospitals (includes physician costs); fee-for-service in private hospitals	No	Yes
Canada	Private	Public/private mix (proportions vary by region), mostly not-for-profit	Mostly fee-for-service (~45%–85%, depending on province), but some alternatives (e.g., capitation) for group practices	Mostly global budgets, case-based payment in some provinces (does not include physician costs)	Not generally, but yes for some capitation models	Yes, mainly through financial incentives varying across provinces (e.g., in most provinces, specialists receive lower fees for patients not referred)
China	Private/public mix (private village doctors and clinics; public township and community hospitals providing GP services)	Public (~55%)/private (~45%) mix (mainly public in rural areas, public and private in urban areas)	Fee-for-service for private providers, salaries and fee-for-service for GPs employed by hospitals	Mainly fee-for-service, with some pilot projects using case-based payments, capitation, or global budgets	Not generally, with exceptions in some areas	Not generally, with exceptions in some areas

England	Mainly private, limited number of NHS-owned practices with salaried physicians	Mostly public, some private	Mix capitation/fee-for-service/pay-for-performance; salary payments for a minority (the salaried GPs are employees of private group practices, not of the NHS)	Mainly case-based payments (60%) plus budgets for mental health, education, and research and training. All include physician costs, drug costs, etc.	Yes	Yes	Voluntary but incentivized: higher cost-sharing for visits and prescriptions without a referral from physician registered with GPs or specialist
France	Private	Mostly public (67% of capacity) some private for-profit (25%) and private not-for-profit	Mix fee-for-service/pay-for-performance/flat EUR40 [USD 48] bonus per year per patient with chronic disease and regional agreements for salaried GPs	Mainly case-based payments (includes physician costs in public hospitals but not in private) and non-activity-based grants for education, research, etc.	All patients aged over 18 years are requested to register with a referring physician	Yes	
Germany	Private	Public (~48% of beds), private nonprofit (~35%), private for-profit (~7%)	Fee-for-service	Case-based payment (includes physician costs)	No	Generally no, present in specific programs by sickness funds	

(continues)

TABLE 13.4 Provider Organization and Payment in 19 Countries

(continued)

	Provider ownership		Provider payment		Primary care role	
	Primary care	**Hospitals**	**Primary care payment**[a]	**Hospital payment**	**Registration with GP required**	**Gatekeeping**
India	Mainly public, some private especially in urban areas	Private non- and for-profit (~63% of beds) and public	Salary for staff at public providers, fee-for-service (paid out of pocket) for private providers	Global budgets for public hospitals	No	No
Israel	Nonprofit either salaried by health plan or health plan contractors	Public (~50%), private nonprofit (including health plans, ~45%), private for-profit (~5%)	Mainly capitation and some fee-for-service to private providers, salary if owned by health plan	Mainly per-diem and some case-based payments for inpatient care, fee-for-service for outpatient (all include physician cost)	Yes in the largest health plan (Clalit), no in the other three	Yes in two of the four health plans (including the largest, Clalit), no in the other two
Italy	Private	Mostly public (~80% of beds), some private (~20%)	Mix capitation (~70% of total), fee-for-service and limited P4P (~30%)	Subject to regional variation, mainly case-based payment (except hospitals owned by regional authorities) and global budgets (includes physician costs)	Yes	Yes

Japan	Mostly private	Mainly private nonprofit (~80% of beds), some public (~20%)	Most fee-for-service, some per-case daily or monthly payments	Case-based per diem payments and fee-for-service or fee-for-service only (includes physician costs)	No	No, but large hospitals and academic centers charge extra fees to patients not referred
Netherlands	Private	Mostly private, nonprofit	Mix capitation and fee-for-service for "core" activities (75% in total), some bundled payments and pay-for-performance negotiated with insurers	Mainly case-based payment (include physician costs)	No, but most patients register voluntarily	Yes
New Zealand	Private	Mostly public, some private	Mix capitation (~50% of total)/fee-for-service patient payments (~50%)	Global budgets (includes physician costs)	No	Yes
Norway	Mainly private (95% of general practitioners)	Almost all public, some private not-for-profit, some for-profit hospitals offering elective treatment only	GPs: capitation from municipal contracts (~35% of income), government-sponsored fee-for-service (~35%) and user-charges (~30%)	Somatic; global budgets (~50%) and case-based payment (~50%) (includes physician costs); psychiatric; 100% global budgets	No, but more than 95% of patients register voluntarily	Yes

(continues)

TABLE 13.4 Provider Organization and Payment in 19 Countries *(continued)*

	Provider ownership		Provider payment		Primary care role	
	Primary care	Hospitals	Primary care payment[a]	Hospital payment	Registration with GP required	Gatekeeping
Singapore	Almost all private, with some larger public clinics for lower-income population	Mainly public, 20%–30% private based on activity	Fee-for-service	For public hospitals, combination of global budgets and case-based payments	No	No, but public system requires referrals to provide services at subsidized prices
Sweden	Mixed, ~40% private, ~60% public	Almost all public, some private for-profit and not-for-profit	Mix capitation (~80% of total) and fee-for-service/limited pay-for-performance (~20% of total)	Global budgets (~66% of total) and case-based payment/limited pay-for-performance (includes physician costs)	Yes, in all counties except Stockholm	No
Switzerland	Private	Mostly public or publicly subsidized private, some private	Most fee-for-service, some capitation in managed care plans offered by insurers	Inpatient care: case-based payments for acute care, per-diem payments for psychiatric and rehabilitation care; subsidies from cantonal government	No, except in some managed care plans offered by insurers	No, except in some managed care plans with gatekeeping offered by insurers

Taiwan	98% clinics private	Mixed public (16% hospitals, 28% beds) and private not-for-profit (84% hospitals, 72% beds)	Fee-for-service predominant, some pay-for-performance, and capitation pilot under primary care global budget	Fee-for-service, diagnosis-related groups, case payment under hospital global budget	No	No
U.S.	Private	Mix of nonprofit (~70% of beds), public (~15%), and for-profit ~5%)	Most fee-for-service, some capitation with private plans, some incentive payments	Outpatient care: fee-for-service	No	In some insurance programs

Reproduced from International Profiles of Health Care Systems (2017). Elias Mossialos and Ana Djordjevic London School of Economics and Political Science Robin Osborn and Dana Sarnak. The Commonwealth Fund. Retrieved from https://www.commonwealthfund.org/sites/default/files/documents/___media_files_publications_fund_report_2017_may_mossialos_intl_profiles_v5.pdf

aAll bracketed figures in USD were converted from local currency using the purchasing power parity conversion rate for GDP in 2015 reported by the Organisation for Economic Co-operation and Development (2016).

their citizens having EHRs by 2009. While the U.K. has had mixed results, they initiated a massive effort in 2002 and have invested heavily in a national information technology network and automated patient records. As of 2005, during early forays into automating healthcare records and processes in their countries, expected expenditures and investment for each country's multiyear initiatives varied widely. The U.S. expected to spend a mere $125M or $0.43 per capita: this is incredibly telling as to the lack of understanding and intent of truly investing in this effort for a country the size and population of the U.S., since individual hospitals and health systems currently regularly spend hundreds of millions of dollars themselves implementing an EHR system. Australia planned for $97.9M or $4.93 per capita, Canada $1.0B or $31.85 per capita, Germany $1.8B or $21.20 per capita, Norway $57M or $11.43 per capita, and the U.K. $11.5B or $192.79 per capita (Frogner, Reinhardt, & Anderson, 2006). The bottom line is other countries started much earlier than the U.S. and outspent the U.S., per capita by orders of magnitude.

In order to compare HIS adoption and experiences between OECD countries and learn lessons from successful models that might be replicated by other countries, the OECD began efforts in 2007 to study e-health information technology and communications initiatives among OECD countries with the aim of identifying e-health strategy policy objectives, best practices, a framework for international criteria that could be compared between countries, and topics for international action and research agenda (Adler-Milstein, Ronchi, Cohen, Pannella Winn, & Jha, 2013). The study concluded that a lack of consistency and comparability between information technology and communications definitions, data, and statistics render illusive any conclusions on HIS use, adoption, or impact on patient care, as well

as identification of successful models from which to learn. This OECD study gave rise in 2010 to an effort to establish a framework of consistent definitions so that cogent and productive international comparisons between OECD countries could begin to learn from one another's progress and experience in HIS and communications to benefit patients and providers, and improve quality and cost performance. In 2010, an international benchmarking program among OECD countries was designed and initiated (Adler-Milstein et al., 2013). This study called for creating a benchmarking framework including consistent definitions for criteria, and conducted initial measures among OECD countries along four areas viewed as essential to a comprehensive health information technology and communications capability: provider-centric health records, patient-centric health records, health information exchange (HIE), and telehealth. Early results assessing the status of nationally accepted definitions for these four criteria showed agreement among these countries in definition of only one of the areas—provider-centric health records—and found neither consistency nor agreement among OECD countries for the other three definitions, patient-centric health records, health information exchange, and telehealth. This lack of measurable comparison between difference HIS models adopted results in inability to achieve learnings between countries on implementation and benefits of HIS so that valuable lessons learned are lost, hampering progress for all.

These countries rank as displayed in the following chart (Bradley, Gonzales, & Kaiser Family Foundation, 2017; Frogner et al., 2006) (**TABLE 13.5**).

As displayed in Table 13.1 above, health system structure, compensation for providers, and HIS adoption work together to drive care delivery behavior and patient access to health data. Methods used for providers to be paid for care influences their behavior, a lesson seen

TABLE 13.5 U.S. Compared to Other OECD Countries HIS, Outcomes, and Cost Statistics

Country	Health System Structure, % of GDP	EHR % Adoption IP/OP/HIE	HIS Highlights and Rankings* (for highest potential EHR Interoperability and HIS extra-regional functionality)	HIS Lowlights (Landi, 2018)	Health Outcomes/ Overall Health Care System Performance Rankings*	OECD Cost/ Capita (2017)
U.K.	9.6% GDP (David, 2015) National health system called National Health Service, includes seven regions.	While primary care is computerized, efforts to establish national EHR systems have eluded Great Britain to date, but initiatives still underway to connect primary care with other settings. Near 100% EHR adoption rate (2018). Allscripts top-rated EHR vendor.	All primary care settings automated. Readily available primary care, easily accessible, good service levels, emphasis on prevention and primary care. People have access and are welcomed into the system. They do not have to fight their way into the system for primary care, as in the U.S. A NHS number used as unique patient identifier (UPI). A Pervasive use of enterprise technology tools. Ranking: 13	Original goal to go paperless in primary care, urgent, and emergency by 2018 and all other settings by 2020 slipped to 2023. Not widely publicized, over a period of 20 years, billions spent in effort to implement a national EHR system, used an infrastructure vendor as general contractor. Failed several attempts using different commercial EHR vendors.	10/1	$4,246

(continues)

TABLE 13.5 U.S. Compared to Other OECD Countries HIS, Outcomes, and Cost Statistics

(continued)

Country	Health System Structure,% of GDP	EHR % Adoption IP/OP/HIE	HIS Highlights and Rankings* (for highest potential EHR Interoperability and HIS extra-regional functionality)	HIS Lowlights (Landi, 2018)	Health Outcomes/ Overall Health Care System Performance Rankings*	OECD Cost/ Capita (2017)
The Netherlands	10.1% GDP A Universal health insurance plan.	Near 100% EHR adoption rate (2018). ChipSoft top-rated EHR vendor.	All Dutch patients have unique identification number (burgerservicenummer). EHR systems in use at all hospitals. In 2011 Union of Providers for Health Care Communication (De Vereniging van Zorgaanbieders voor Zorgcommunicatie) data exchange established, uses IT infrastructure called AORTA. Pervasive use of enterprise technology tools. Ranking: 5	EHRs not standardized nationally nor interoperable between care areas. Information exchange underway but not complete. Patients must approve participation in data exchange. Patients request access to their health records from providers.	6/3	$5,386

| Canada | 10.4% GDP National healthcare system, 9 provinces | Gradual uptake of EHR systems province by province, supported by Canada Health Infoway. As of 2014, 42% of primary care providers had implemented EHR systems. Orion Health top-rated EHR vendor. Over 75% EHR system adoption rate (2018). | Provinces develop their own EHR systems and approaches. Health information technology adoption occurring across Canada gradually, province by province. Ranking: 10 | No national UPI. Limited interoperability, adoption slowed recently. 87% of primary care providers report patients not able to electronically access their health data. | 9/9 | $4,826 |

(continues)

TABLE 13.5 U.S. Compared to Other OECD Countries HIS, Outcomes, and Cost Statistics *(continued)*

Country	Health System Structure, % of GDP	EHR % Adoption IP/OP/HIE	HIS Highlights and Rankings* (for highest potential EHR Interoperability and HIS extra-regional functionality)	HIS Lowlights (Landi, 2018)	Health Outcomes/ Overall Health Care System Performance Rankings*	OECD Cost/ Capita (2017)
China	5.4% GDP	Limited functionality and interoperability of national EHR system. Neusoft top-rated EHR vendor. Playing role in global healthcare sector transformation as a digital health infrastructure producer. Gradual EHR adoption initiatives but lacking a major component of readiness.	Unique patient identifiers used, with EHR systems connecting to health insurance carriers for claims payment. Personally controlled UPIs enable data access and capture, part of national digital health strategy, with 4 million patients and 8,900 providers (2/3 in primary care) registered. Provides medication lists, prescription information, medical notes, referrals, and diagnostic imaging reports. Patient-supplied data includes allergies, adverse reactions, and advanced directives.	Lack of data and information standards, many types of EHRs. Interoperability lacking between EHRs and providers. Patients carry paper records from one healthcare setting to the next for information to be available among providers.		$762

Australia	9.1% GDP National health system, regional.	National eHealth strategy set by Australian Digital Health Agency (2016) (Glover). Cerner top-rated EHR vendor throughout Oceania. Near 100% EHR adoption rate (2018).	Pervasive use of enterprise technology tools. Ranking: 9		1/2	$4,543
New Zealand	9.0% GDP National health system.	In 2015, the Ministry of Health established the Digital Health Work Programme 2020, creating a single EHR system. Four regions promoting telehealth and capabilities to encourage citizens to participate in their health (Gauld). Cerner top-rated EHR vendor throughout Oceania. Near 100% EHR adoption rate (2018),	1/3 of primary care providers have EHR patient portals. Telehealth increasing. Systematized Nomenclature of Medicine—Clinical Terms (SNOMED CT) adopted as standard clinical terminology nomenclature for New Zealand. Pervasive use of enterprise technology tools. Ranking: 1	Interoperability between providers limited but on the rise.	7/4	$3,683

(continues)

TABLE 13.5 U.S. Compared to Other OECD Countries HIS, Outcomes, and Cost Statistics (continued)

Country	Health System Structure, % of GDP	EHR % Adoption IP/OP/HIE	HIS Highlights and Rankings* (for highest potential EHR Interoperability and HIS extra-regional functionality)	HIS Lowlights (Landi, 2018)	Health Outcomes/ Overall Health Care System Performance Rankings*	OECD Cost/ Capita (2017)
Germany	11.3% GDP	As of 2015 all SHI-insured have chip-enabled medical cards, containing mostly demographic and insurance coverage data. In 2015, eHealth Act was passed setting timelines for EHR implementation and infrastructure (Blümel, & Busse). Over 75% EHR system adoption rate (2018).	Akin to the MU program of the HITECH Act, part of the American Recovery and Reinvestment act of 2009 in the U.S., the eHealth Act includes penalties for non-participation and incentives for transmitting electronic medical reports (2016–2017), collecting and documenting emergency records (from 2018), and managing and reviewing basic insurance claims data online. Ranking: 6	The citizens of Germany became uncomfortable about privacy concerns surrounding the use of smart-cards for transmitting their personal information, and this initiative, which had enjoyed early momentum and success, faltered.	8/8	$5,728

France	11.5% GDP	Limited integrated EHR systems and network, totaling 0.8% of population and 731 hospitals (2016) (Durand-Zaleski). ChipSoft top-rated EHR vendor. Over 75% EHR system adoption rate (2018).	Unique patient and provider identifiers for primary care and hospitals settings. Interoperability achieved via chip-enabled patient health cards. National agency established to increase computerization and interoperability of EHR systems. Ranking: 15	Low penetration of automation and integration of existing EHR systems.	5/10	$4,902
Singapore		Plans for Construction and implementation of a National Electronic Health Record system is underway (Liu & Haseltine). Allscripts top-rated EHR vendor. Over 75% EHR system adoption rate (2018). Primary principles include: make the complex simple, value the importance of governance, address operational needs with discipline (Accenture).	This national system will give medical professionals, systems planners, researchers, and patients access to and eventually adding to their health data. Significant upgrade to healthcare infrastructures associated with high demand for HIS. Ranking: 4	System is under construction.		

(continues)

TABLE 13.5 U.S. Compared to Other OECD Countries HIS, Outcomes, and Cost Statistics   *(continued)*

Country	Health System Structure, % of GDP	EHR % Adoption IP/OP/HIE	HIS Highlights and Rankings* (for highest potential EHR Interoperability and HIS extra-regional functionality)	HIS Lowlights (Landi, 2018)	Health Outcomes/ Overall Health Care System Performance Rankings*	OECD Cost/ Capita (2017)
Taiwan		All hospitals and physician practices use EHRs (Cheng). Neusoft top-rated EHR vendor.	Taiwanese citizens carry a national health (NHI) card with current medical history (last 6 visits), diagnoses, prescribed medications, organ donation information, palliative care preferences, and other important health information. Providers report all care within 24 hours to National Health Insurance Administration (NHIA) for timely tracking of care and expenditures, public health data & infectious disease outbreaks, e.g., 2003 Severe Acute Respiratory Syndrome (SARS) outbreak. NHI card provides access to health data communication, spending only 1.07% of NHIA expenditures in 2014.	Lack of national infrastructure, resulting in lack of interoperability and low exchange of EHR data between hospitals and clinics.		

Country					
Sweden	10.9% GDP Universal healthcare insurance plan.	Extensive EHR use in hospitals and clinics (Glenngård). InterSystems top-rated EHR vendor.	Widespread e-prescribing and use of EHR systems in hospitals and provider offices. Ranking: 11	Systems used and capabilities, such as e-prescribing, vary between city councils. Patient access to EHR systems increasing but varies between locales.	2/6	$5,511
Norway	10.4% GDP Universal healthcare insurance plan.	National eHealth strategy initiated by National Directorate of Health in 2016 (Lindahl). Cerner top-rated EHR vendor throughout Oceania. InterSystems top-rated EHR vendor. Near 100% EHR adoption rate (2018)	Each citizen has UPI. Patient access project underway with access for 3.1 million residents to date. EHR systems used in all hospitals. National Health Network provides efficient and secure electronic exchange of patient information, secure messaging for practitioners. Pervasive use of enterprise technology tools. Ranking: 8	Lack of data standards hamper comprehensive quality improvement efforts. Primary care automated but fragmented.	3/4	$6,351
Japan	10.7% GDP Universal healthcare insurance plan.	Limited EHR networks and automation in health care nationally (Matsuda). Gradual EHR adoption initiatives but lacking a major component of readiness.	Unique patient identifier initiating 2018, using social security and tax ID number, called "My Number System" initiated in January 2016. Significant upgrade to healthcare infrastructures associated with high demand for HIS (Export. gov., 2018).	Projects underway for EHR systems, interoperability, and patient access to healthcare records.		$4,717

(continues)

TABLE 13.5 U.S. Compared to Other OECD Countries HIS, Outcomes, and Cost Statistics   *(continued)*

Country	Health System Structure, % of GDP	EHR % Adoption IP/OP/HIE	HIS Highlights and Rankings* (for highest potential EHR Interoperability and HIS extra-regional functionality)	HIS Lowlights (Landi, 2018)	Health Outcomes/ Overall Health Care System Performance Rankings*	OECD Cost/ Capita (2017)
Switzerland	12.3% GDP	2015 launched national EHR system: by 2017 patients and primary care providers opt in, hospitals and long-term care required by law to use this EHR system. Widespread adoption of EHRs in hospitals and clinical settings (Sturny). ChipSoft primary EHR vendor. Over 75% EHR adoption rate (2018).	eHealth Suisse administrative agency provides funding and coordination of EHR infrastructure and networks regionally and nationally and is a required health insurance subscription care including UPI. Ranking: 14	Varying levels of integration within hospital EHR systems. Primary care EHR system adoption only at its beginning.	4/6	$8,009

India	3.9% GDP	Ministry of Health and Family Welfare in 2015 initiated National Health Portal to provide information on diseases, health services, health programs, & insurance (Gupta & Bhatia). Allscripts top-rated EHR vendor. Gradual EHR adoption initiatives but lacking a major component of readiness.	National eHealth Authority setting standards and regulations to bring together multiple types of electronic systems in use across states, and public and private providers. Playing role in global healthcare sector transformation as a digital health infrastructure producer.	Disparity between states and regional systems, nascent effort to establish standards to enforce as states build EHRs and communications capabilities.	$238
Israel	7.4% GDP	Health plan EHRs link providers: hospitals, clinics, labs, pharmacies (Rosen & Waitzberg). Cerner top-rated EHR vendor.	Hospitals automated, not integrated with health plans. Ministry of Health project establishing data exchange to share data across health plans and providers. Citizen ID used as UPI. Significant upgrade to healthcare infrastructures associated with high demand for HIS. Ranking: 3	Patient rights to health records but limited electronic access. Secure messaging between patients and primary care providers expanding.	$2,834

(continues)

TABLE 13.5 U.S. Compared to Other OECD Countries HIS, Outcomes, and Cost Statistics *(continued)*

Country	Health System Structure, % of GDP	EHR % Adoption IP/OP/HIE	HIS Highlights and Rankings* (for highest potential EHR Interoperability and HIS extra-regional functionality)	HIS Lowlights (Landi, 2018)	Health Outcomes/ Overall Health Care System Performance Rankings*	OECD Cost/ Capita (2017)
Italy	8.9% GDP National health system delivered regionally	In 2002, New Health Information System (*Nuovo Sistema Informativo Sanitario*) initiated to create universal EHR (Donatini)	EHR initiative includes hospital, emergency, outpatient specialist, residential, and palliative care, and pharmacy data. Mattoni ("bricks") initiative initiated to create standardized data using common nomenclature and methodologies, encouraging national quality improvement initiatives and information exchange regionally and nationally. Significant upgrade to healthcare infrastructures associated with high demand for HIS.	EHR Initiative does not include primary care data. No national UPI. Some regional communication networks underway for sharing healthcare data among types of providers. Only partial e-prescribing, lagging original completion target of 2014.		$3,542

Denmark	10.2% GDP	National Agency for Health IT has implemented technology throughout Denmark's national health system. EHR systems are used in all hospitals, by region, using national standards for compatibility. EHR system usage my primary care providers ranked #1 (Vrangbaek).	Unique patient identifiers implemented nationally for citizens, each of whom has a medical information card with identifiers used in all health registries. Sundhed.dk national health data portal provides clinical resources for professionals and patient access to their data and information resources, and quality information for clinics, all using information technology to support care and access to information. Ranking: 2	DataFangst initiative (national database for quality assurance for primary care) abandoned in 2015 due to privacy concern of citizens.	$5,183
Hong Kong	Voluntary Health Insurance Scheme with public and private sectors in dual-track healthcare system (Hong Kong).	Opt-in and no-charge EHR system available to providers	Ranking: 7		
Finland	9.4% GDP (2015) Public and Private sectors of health system.	Near 100% EHR adoption, including EHR functionality, including image transfer, and telehealth capabilities (Zelmer et al., 2016)	Strong base for further development • EHR coverage 100%, 80% (private) • EHR information exchange 90% (public, hospital districts) • Electronical referrals and discharge letters 95% • Wide use of national solutions (ePrescription, eArchive, eAccess) Ranking: 12	Forerunners dilemma, aging infrastructure for early adopters, and low interoperability (eHealthweek, 2015)	EUR 3,803 (2015)

(continues)

TABLE 13.5 U.S. Compared to Other OECD Countries HIS, Outcomes, and Cost Statistics

Country	Health System Structure, % of GDP	EHR % Adoption IP/OP/HIE	HIS Highlights and Rankings* (for highest potential EHR interoperability and HIS extra-regional functionality)	HIS Lowlights (Landi, 2018)	Health Outcomes/Overall Health Care System Performance Rankings*	OECD Cost/Capita (2017)
U.S.	17.1% of GDP Combination of government programs such as Medicare and Medicaid, private insurance, self-pay, and Affordable Care Act (ACA).	Fewer than half of U.S. physicians used at least a basic EHR system in 2012 (The Commonwealth Fund; Health IT Dashboard, 2016). 2018 is over 90%	Stimulated by the 2009 American Recovery and Reinvestment Act, 94% of hospitals and physicians now use at least a "basic" EHR system and 75% of system (Health IT Dashboard, 2018)	Digital divide between "haves" and "have-nots"		$10,209
OECD overall (35 countries)	Osborn and Sarnak (2017)	Global spending on EHR systems will grow from $25.1 billion in 2017 to over $30.2 billion by 2020. Landi (2018)			11/11	$3,207/capita average across OECD
		*Includes 15 Countries (International Health Care System Profiles; Schneider, Sarnak, Squires, Shah, & Doty)	International Health Care System Profiles	*Includes 11 Countries (Schneider, Sarnak, Squires, Shah, & Doty)		(continued)

Data from The Commonwealth Fund (2018). What is the Status of Electronic Health Records. Retrieved from http://international.commonwealthfund.org/features/ehrs/; The Commonwealth Fund (2017). International Profiles of Health Care Systems. Retrieved from https://www.commonwealthfund.org/sites/default/files/documents/___media_files_publications_fund_report_2017_may_mossialos_intl_profiles_v5.pdf; Sawyer and Gonzales (2017). How does the quality of the U.S. healthcare system compare to other countries? Kaiser Family Foundation. Retrieved from https://www.healthsystemtracker.org/chart-collection/quality-u-s-healthcare-system-compare-countries/#item-start; Frogner, Reinhart, and Anderson (2006). Health Care Spending and Use of Information Technology in OECD Countries. The Commonwealth Fund. Retrieved from http://www.commonwealthfund.org/publications/in-the-literature/2006/may/health-care-spending-and-use-of-information-technology-in-oecd-countries.

over and over again. A provider's culture is the key supplier in an economic system driving health services in any country: behavior is a reflection of the monetary and societal expectations of their country. Systemic financial and cultural differences create different priorities and—fortunately or unfortunately—patient outcomes and experiences. In an example reflecting the impact and perhaps differences of culture in a country's health care, physicians in Canada recently signed a petition asking the government, which pays the doctors in a national health system organized by regions, to take their pay raise which had been recently added to their compensation and use it rather to increase nurses' pay and to increase patients' access to healthcare services. A fine gesture indeed, and we can each reflect on differences between a single payer health system as in Canada, versus the **"regulated free-market" system** of the U.S. in which physician compensation is typically an entrepreneurial venture, the foundation model, or being paid as employees.

Healthcare Information Management Systems Society and Electronic Medical Record Adoption Model: A System of Measurement of EHR Systems Adoption in Europe

As described in the Table 13.5, HIS adoption varies among OECD countries (Healthcare Information Management Systems Society [HIMSS] and Electronic Medical Record Adoption Model [EMRAM]—Europe). A measurement framework providing benchmarks for increasing levels of EHR adoption has been developed by HIMSS and widely accepted as an assessment tool of progress in the U.S. is also now adapted for use in Europe and Asia. The EHR adoption framework assesses functionality in eight defined categories as follows in Figure 13.5.

The **EMRAM EHR Adoption Framework** consists of eight levels (Levels 0–7) that reflect increased maturity of EHR functionality adoption by organizations leading to optimized capabilities to optimize patient care and support processes. **FIGURE 13.6** displays the participation as of 2015 around the globe in this program, including the U.S., Europe, and Asia.

Lessons to Learn from Emerging Countries

Emerging countries have much to accomplish to provide advanced medical services to urban settings as well as connect the unconnected to provide health-related information about the most basic human needs, such as clean water, vaccinations, and outbreaks of unrest and violence. We can all learn from ways to provide more with less from examples within these countries. **Consumer-oriented care**, driven by mobile health capabilities, integration of public health with primary health care, doing more with less, and skipping over earlier steps of traditional technologies to embrace digital and mobile health capabilities using ubiquitous infrastructure such as mobile phones versus client-server and other earlier technologies and applications within organizations gives a leg up to evolving nations in addressing the health needs of their populations (Glaser, 2016).

▶ Looking Forward Amidst Problems and Opportunity

In What Context are Our HIS Efforts Occurring?

Why do we study history? If we do not, we are doomed to repeat it. If not, we won't

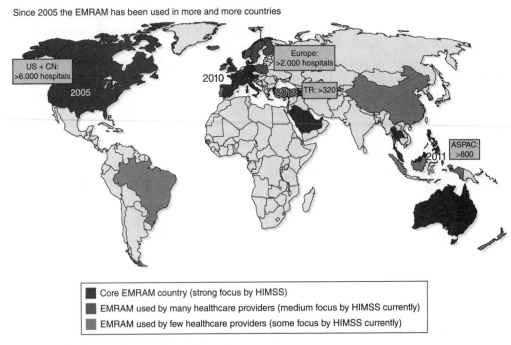

FIGURE 13.6 EMRAM evaluations across the globe.

understand where our goals have gone astray, and the forces that caused them to go astray. If we don't understand the "why" surrounding the issues and problem we are experiencing with HIS, these practices and unintended consequences will not only continue to haunt us, but their momentum will lead to greater issues and additional problems, confounding the problems and solutions. New generations of tech and HIS workers and managers will see the current context and its massive unintended consequences as normal. The "what" we do in HIS depends also on "how" HIS are accomplished. So, let's take a positive slant on this. The health professions exist to, "Above all, do no harm." As students of healthcare management and clinical professions, it is your job to understand how to improve where HIS falls short, and your role in leading and managing HIS in ways to improve the yield from HIS efforts.

The current system in which this work takes place is, in many cases, laden with some combination of some or all of the following issues:

- High costs.
- Poor outcomes.
- Growing incidence of chronic illness.
- Emphasis on a medical, acute, fee-for-service system, struggling to adapt to value-based care.
- Lack of access to care due to under-coverage as way to cut costs, which not only misses the point, but also exacerbates the problem (the chronically ill get sicker, increasing the illness burden to the society). The U.S. comes in last in prevention and primary care in comparison to other OECD countries.
- Differences between countries all striving to engage in a global economy give new meaning to the term "silos." HIS rooted

in the fee-for-service reimbursement system—must go through analogous changes to support value-based care.

- All nations face the need to pursue effective, value-based care, and all will depend on HIS and technology to accomplish this. Few are prepared for this task the way Denmark and The Netherlands are.

Ponder the Issues Facing Countries Internationally

Progress and the ability to successfully manage the health of populations and achieve value-based care will be done while squarely facing issues of health care today. These include:

- **HIS cost-effectiveness.** What's to gain for the effort expended in the U.S. and in other countries? In the U.S., health outcomes are last compared to all other OECD nations. Is this acceptable? Don't forget to factor into your cost-benefit equation the dissatisfaction of health providers, tragically punctuated by the terrible fact that in 2016, in the U.S., 465 physicians ended their lives. This relates to this discussion because statistically their number one dissatisfier is dealing with EHR systems and their impact on the practice of medicine. The shock of this evidence is reminiscent of when in 1999, the HMD published its report reporting evidence that due to medical errors, each year in U.S. hospitals 48,000–97,000 preventable deaths occur among patients who should have otherwise gone home (HMD, Kohn, Corrigan, & Donaldson, 2000). Professionals working in healthcare organizations, stunned by this evidence, had to face a difficult set of facts that could not be ignored, but challenged the very fabric of health care and the professionals who worked every day to do their best for patients and families.

Since the 1999 HMD report, evidence provided sadly reports that the number of preventable deaths occurring as the result of errors in care is 250,000–400,000+ each year in U.S. hospitals (James, 2012). As we begin our study of understanding HIS for the health professions, let us keep in mind this evidence, and ask ourselves: have we improved this situation as a result of deploying billions of dollars in HIS in U.S. hospitals? What about other countries? We must make sure that we are not implementing HIS technology only for technology's sake, but also to improve outcomes.

- **Restricted access to care.** In the U.S., healthcare cost control has been primarily focused on restriction of access to health care by restricting access to health insurance. The ACA has changed that for millions of citizens, however many insurance plans are so expensive they still represent a barrier to access to care, with high deductibles that are difficult for many people to afford. Additionally, regulatory efforts to improve the relationship of clinical outcomes to reimbursement incentives has been introduced through **value-based care initiatives**. These initiatives are designed to reward quality and cost-effectiveness with higher reimbursement rates for services with better outcomes (Davis, 2018; Jha, King, Patel, Furukawa, & Mostashari, 2013).

- **High prices**, pharmaceuticals, medical devices, and other supplies, have been identified as the primary reason for excessive costs in the U.S. healthcare system compared to other countries. Combined with the fee-for-service reimbursement system, this is a recipe for runaway costs, as is being experienced in the U.S. more than anywhere else in the world. Yes, excellent care services are available in the U.S., but we perform poorly on other essential outcomes measures, creating the value problem in U.S. health care. Further, access to insurance is typically limited to those who are privileged to have health insurance coverage. This coverage typically is accessed through an employment relationship, inclusion in a government-sponsored program such as Medicare, Medicaid/MediCal, **Children's Health Insurance Program (CHIP)**, or **safety net organizations**. Assuring quality of care while directly cutting costs is a difficult way to create value, and that is the transition U.S. health care finds itself in now. And until providers adapt their practices and processes to the reimbursement programs that reward improved quality and reduced cost outcomes, changing the **fee-for-service**, episodic approach to the structure of health care in the U.S. will be a challenge to their financial viability.

- **End-user experience problems** the EHR systems **User interface (UI)** and **User-experience (UX)** do far less than delight our clinical and business knowledge-workers—they are for the most part clunky and focus primarily on archaic data-entry methods, relegating society's highly valued knowledge-workers (MDs, RNs, therapists, and other clinicians) to the role of data-entry clerks, slaves to feeding the regulatory and financially based documentation demands of EHR systems with the data needed to calculate algorithms, capture data for performance metrics, report monthly statistics, and bill for chargeable codes. Too little is truly designed with clinicians' well-being and workflows in mind, using human-centered designed methods. Providers spend on average, two hours of documentation for every hour of patient face-time, half of which face-time is spent facing the computer,

each day tending to data entry tasks and upkeep of EHR systems and other computer-related tasks (Stanford White Paper, 2018). Many providers complain about the negative effect that EHR systems and other systems have had on their clinical practice and satisfaction with their professional experiences, and that these systems programmed by information technology professionals require physicians, nurses, and other health professionals to sequence and piece together workflows rather than enabling streamlined processes and creating frictionless use of systems in the delivery of care. Additionally, a common problem is that systems were programmed to recreate the same manual processes that were originally based on paper, automating those processes that were established according to an assembly line method versus using the power and opportunity of information technology and evolving infrastructure to streamline manual processes, collapsing handoffs to an integrated, knowledge-worker-focused way to delivering care and supporting providers and patients in the processes.

- **EHR vendors have grown** in their relevance to the future state of health organizations in the U.S., their influence has gone beyond the realm of support into that of control. As a consequence of opportunistic business models, vendors have ranged from convincing organizations to buy their products to convincing the government and others that health care is so unique that they are justified in being costlier to automate than technology products and solutions in other industries. Healthcare organizations are thus bearing the brunt of the very innovations they started on their, hoodwinked due to lack of savvy and education on the part of healthcare executives, the purchasers of these products, and the inability to listen to talent inside the organization, thinking that answers always have to come from outside the organization—consultants and vendors (Bresnick, 2017).

▶ Digital Health Around the Globe

The global healthcare environment will connect the many settings and data points involved in new healthcare eco-systems, supported with advancing cloud computing, availability of data from new sources widely distributed, such as sensors and mobile devices, and data networks. Capabilities for this global healthcare computing and care environment include distributed imaging systems and diagnostics, shared diagnostics services models, handheld devices and devices portals, clinical decision support networks, and provider solutions (Medical Device and Diagnosic Industry, 2013).

Global Trends Will Focus on Value-Based Care and Outcomes

As the mega-players, such as Google, Amazon, Apple, medical device companies, and others, get involved in health care in a big way, the opportunity to provide access to care and information supported by technology and HIS, is clear. Value-based and outcomes-based thinking are sweeping globally. We must also ask ourselves, in our rush to connect the unconnected, and digitally enable new forms of care from which much can come, how do we also do this in ways that preserve privacy, dignity, humanity, and rights of patients and consumers engaged in those solutions? These principles must be upheld beyond the walls of healthcare institutions and business associates, and extend to all forms of data used for health care for patients and consumers alike (Nicas, 2018).

Global Digital Health Applications

The use of networked devices connected to ubiquitous cellular and cloud-based infrastructure creates the ability to connect people living in areas without traditional infrastructure to information previously unavailable using traditional HIS methods. The balance between access to data versus IT security will be tested in ways that will also test our capabilities and resolve to deal with deep social and technical issues.

Changing Demographics

Aging of the population, coupled with chronic illness and the need to manage related risk factors *outside* of institutional settings, has led to a significant shift in the demographics served by health care. The world's population is still growing, but the growth in developed countries such as the U.S. and Japan is not due to increasing birth rates, but rather increased life expectancy achieved through the control of certain illnesses. In countries and regions where these diseases are not yet well controlled (such as Nigeria), mHealth can assist with the outreach to people living in areas lacking access to care and information. In other areas, such as Japan and Europe, the gradual transition to an older population is leading to concomitant needs for care of an elderly population and increased numbers of chronically ill persons. This set of factors has produced a demographic profile for these countries closer to that of the U.S. or other developed countries with lower death rates and gradually increasing life expectancy, resulting in greater need to care for people outside institutions (Riegelman, 2010).

🔍 *A GREATER POTENTIAL ROLE FOR DIGITAL HEALTH*

In Nigeria, for example, outreach to people living in outlying rural areas to communicate important health information and updates regarding disease outbreaks can help those populations avoid contagious disease or get access to precious vaccinations, thus aiding in the control of disease through the use of text messages and cell phones.

In another example, in Uganda, a **UNICEF**-sponsored program called mTrac helps health workers use simple texts sent on cell phones to track supplies of medicines and disease outbreaks electronically rather than using paper-based processes. In an area short on hospitals, but with good cell phone coverage and where vast numbers of the population has cell phones that can send and receive texts, this infrastructure is having a powerful effect on the ability of Ugandans to obtain information about where to access medicine and which places to avoid where a contagious disease outbreak has occurred. This information is shared with townspeople and public health workers to help keep track of what is going on regarding both medicine stock (and needs to reroute those supplies) and illnesses. A regional dashboard publishes this information along with a hotline from users of healthcare services so that corrections can be made (Luscombe, 2012). The mTrac technology initiative is relatively affordable and equips citizens with simple but important information that directly impacts their health. Additional funds have been used to train 8,000 more healthcare workers, and the same method can be used to track and report other problems, empowering citizens and health workers alike with information to help them protect their health. The possibilities of mHealth and its impact on communication of health information, ability to report disease outbreaks, and access medicine have had a transformative effect on this country and its predominantly rural, poor population

🔍 *CASE EXAMPLE: DIGITAL HEALTH APP GOES UNPROTECTED BY PROPER POLICY, POSING SECURITY RISKS*

In the U.K., in response to a report exposing an absence of policy around messaging apps in most NHS healthcare trusts and evidence of risky security practices in their use of mHealth messaging apps, the NHS published new guidelines found the majority of NHS trusts lacked a policy around in the healthcare setting—despite the security risks (Common Time Media Centre). The new guidelines cover instant messaging use and privacy policies for communicating patient data, which the report stated was being used by 97 percent of clinicians routinely to send patient data without security measures. This action was taken to address the lack of official policies around consumer messaging apps like Facebook Messenger and WhatsApp, establishing safety standards for app uses, requiring limiting use to only those apps that have appropriate encryption standards, end-user verification, and passcode protection (Davis, 2018).

Summary

In summary, global health is emerging for traditional healthcare participants and new players ushering in non-healthcare giants as well as innovators currently not yet detected broadly. No matter the technology used, health professionals must be involved in HIS development every step of the way to create the kinds of systems we need in today's challenging health and healthcare environment. Since each and every health profession now includes HIS in order to perform its work, clinical, business, and technology health professions now can only be done proficiently with HIS knowledge, ability, and activity. The U.S. health system has perhaps some of the greatest challenges to overcome compared to other countries, due to long-term reliance on the fee-for-service reimbursement methodology which is now transitioning to a value-based system. Countries internationally have endeavored to implement HIS support systems and infrastructures for their citizens, and none is without issues nor successes.

In the U.S., provider organization reliance on the HIS vendor marketplace as the source of solutions, and vendor influence within the government, among other factors, has complicated and increased the cost of automation of health care beyond what it costs in other industries. As health systems and providers transition their focus from acute care to population health management, emphasizing prevention, predictive analysis, and early intervention, chronic care management and care coordination now dominate the scene, while our structures, systems, reimbursement methods, and professionals are also transitioning from fee-for-service, acute, medical scenario to value-based reimbursement and care processes.

Basic administrative and clinical functions automating the majority of health activities and healthcare organizations are in place or underway in most nations, albeit using different types of systems, strategies, and financing mechanisms. The majority of healthcare organizations—as a result of the efforts of many professionals in the management, clinical, and technical ranks—have implemented core business systems in the areas of finance, human resources, supply chain management, and other administrative functions. Clinical functionality has been introduced into and is being used in the majority of healthcare organizations, similar to how EHR systems are now implemented in some form in U.S. hospitals, clinics, and provider practices. Given expectations from earlier efforts to automate health care, compared to the current HIS and their use, these issues listed above should be taken into consideration, and do form the basis of the content, comments and information covered in this text. This text is not written to simply teach students about the current state of HIS and how to sustain and manage those systems, staying in the current state of affairs. Rather, the goal of this text is, yes, to help students learn about HIS top to bottom, but to also understand what is wrong with and lacking in current HIS approaches, systems and their uses.

Health professionals around the world play a key role in understanding and knowing how to improve HIS uses, management, applications, and foci in order to improve clinical and cost outcomes across the board. As we enter the next wave of HIS activity, 60 years since the genesis of HIS, let us take stock of the good, bad, and ugly, so that healthcare outcomes improve. Patient experiences should resemble what they experience elsewhere in their lives as consumers, and the precious lives and careers of health professionals must be spent as wisely and productively as possible. Students of the health professions and the industry they are in would benefit greatly from studying the evolving progress and challenges of HIS into consideration. After all, these professionals are some of the most important knowledge-workers on the planet, enabling real progress to be achieved in health status of populations and the delivery of health services, while improving all healthcare workers' daily experience (Glaser, 2016).

Key Terms

Annual wellness visit and pre-work G0438 and G0439

Basic and comprehensive EHR systems

CCM behavioral healthcare management 20 minutes 99484

CCM initiation pre-work G0506

Children's Health Insurance Program (CHIP)

Chronic care management (CCM) 99490

complex CCM 60 minutes 99487

compulsory health insurance

Consumer-oriented care

CPT codes

digitally-enabled services

EMRAM EHR Adoption Framework

Fee-for-service

General care management services at rural health clinics G0511

Gross domestic product (GDP)

Health and Medicine Division (HMD) of the National Academies of Sciences, Engineering, and Medicine

HIS adoption

Institute for Health Care Improvement (IHI)

Life expectancy at birth

Mortality rates

National health service

National HIS network

Non-face-to-face

Non-governmental organizations (NGOs)

Organization for Economic Cooperation and Development (OECD)

Population health management programs

Primary care providers

Private health insurance

Regulated free-market system

Safety net organizations

Single payer model

Smart card

The Commonwealth Fund

transitional care management

transitional care management services 99495 and 99496

Triple Aims

UNICEF

USD per capita

User-experience (UX)

User interface (UI)

Value-based care initiatives

Voluntary health insurance

World Health Organization (WHO)

Discussion Questions

1. Why is it important to study HIS as used in countries around the world? What lessons and insights can be gained from this understanding of uses and issues with HIS in different ways in these countries?

2. What sources of research help us understand HIS uses in countries globally? What else, in your opinion, should these organizations be gathering data and reporting on regarding HIS use in countries globally?

3. In what ways do different countries' health system philosophies and structures influence their uses of and progress toward goals in HIS?

4. What countries stand out as being particularly strong in their uses of HIS? Which countries seem to be lagging? Why do you think these differences exist?

5. What relationship exists, if any, between healthcare expenditures per capita and HIS spending in various countries?

6. HIS has the potential to help health care be delivered more effectively, and to help improve health outcomes. In what ways are HIS being used in other countries to improve healthcare delivery and health outcomes that differ from the use of HIS in the U.S.?

7. Why does the U.S. lag in health outcomes while spending more per capita than any other country? What can be done to change this? What should be done as the highest priority to change this situation of poor performance in the U.S.?

8. In which health outcomes measures does the U.S. perform as well or better than other countries?

9. Do you think publicly or privately funded healthcare systems yield better results in the uses and adoption of HIS?

10. Which country does the best job overall in HIS, in your opinion, and what evidence supports that choice? Which country does the worst job over in HIS, in your opinion, and what evidence supports that choice?

11. Give one example of a country that spends lower on the per capita expenditures scale, but achieves better than average results for a health outcome measure for its population.

12. Why do countries such as The Netherlands, New Zealand, Norway, and Finland have 100 percent EHR system adoption rates? What have they done differently than other countries?

13. What does the HIMSS organization's EMRAM program do? Is this useful for the adoption of EHR systems? If so, in what ways?

14. What issues stand out as those faced by all countries as they strive to adoption HIS in meaningful ways to help their populations and the delivery of healthcare services?

15. What are potential strengths and drawbacks of the entry of global tech corporations such as Google, Amazon, and Microsoft into HIS for individual countries and internationally, among all countries? What might global HIS applications be, and how would those integrate with various national HIS strategies?

16. Give one example of an effective use of digital health in a developing country that could be extended to others.

17. What is the most surprising thing you learned from this chapter? What is the most disappointing thing you learned from this chapter?

References

Accenture. Singapore's Journey to Build a National Electronic Health Record System. Retrieved from https://www.accenture.com/no-en/~/media/Accenture/Conversion-Assets/LandingPage/Documents/1/Accenture-Singapore-Journey-to-Build-National-Electronic-Health-Record-System.pdf

Adler-Milstein, J., Ronchi, E., Cohen, G. R., Pannella Winn, L. A., & Jha, A. K. (2013). Benchmarking health IT among OECD countries: Better data for better policy. *Journal of the American Medical Informatics Association, 21*(1), 111–116. Retrieved from https://academic.oup.com/jamia/article/21/1/111/2909192

Anderson, G. F., Frogner, B. K., Johns, R. A., & Reinhardt, U. E. (2006, May). Health care spending and use of information technology in OECD countries. *Health Affairs, 25*(4), 819–831. Retrieved from http://content.healthaffairs.org/content/25/3/819.full

Anderson, G. F., Reinhardt, U. E., Hussey, P. S., & Petrosyan, V. (2003). It's the prices, stupid: Why the United States is so different from other countries. *Health Affairs, 22*(3). Retrieved from https://www.healthaffairs.org/doi/abs/10.1377/hlthaff.22.3.89

Bivens, J. (2018, October 18). *The unfinished business of health reform.* Retrieved from https://www.epi.org/publication/health-care-report/

Blümel, M., & Busse, R. The German health care system. Retrieved from https://international.commonwealthfund.org/countries/germany/

Bradley, S., Gonzales, S., & Kaiser Family Foundation. (2017, May 22). How does the quality of the U.S. healthcare system compare to other countries? Retrieved from https://www.healthsystemtracker.org/chart-collection/quality-u-s-healthcare-system-compare-countries/#item-start

Bresnick, J. (2017). 47-percent-of-it-pros-say-their -executives-are-big-data-illiterate. Retrieved from https://healthitanalytics.com/news/47-of-it-pros-say -their-executives-are-big-data-illiterate

Cheng, T.-M. The Taiwan health care system. Retrieved from https://international.commonwealthfund.org /countries/taiwan/

Claxton, G., Cox, C., Gonzales, S., Kamal, R., Levitt, L., & Kaiser Family Foundation. (2015). Measuring the quality of healthcare in the U.S. Retrieved from https:// www.healthsystemtracker.org/brief/measuring -the-quality-of-healthcare-in-the-u-s/?_sft _category=quality-of-care#item-start

Common Time Media Centre. NHS Trusts not discouraging WhatsApp and other consumer apps. Retrieved from https://www.commontime.com /expertise/press-releases/im-addendum

David, S. (2015). U.S. health care from a global perspective spending, use of services, prices, and health in 13 countries. Retrieved from http://www .Commonwealthfund.org/publications/issue-briefs /2015/oct/us-health-care-from-a-global -perspective

Davis, J. (2018). *UK NHS releases guidance on instant messaging apps in healthcare*. Retrieved from https://healthitsecurity.com/news/uk-nhs-releases -guidance-on-instant-messaging-apps-in-healthcare? eid=CXTEL000000307076

Donatini, A. The Italian health care system. Retrieved from https://international.commonwealthfund.org /countries/italy/

Durand-Zaleski, I. The French health care system. Retrieved from https://international.commonwealthfund .org/countries/france/

eHealthweek. (2015). National Finnish Ehealth and Esocial Strategy 2020, Riga, Lativa, 11–13 May 2015. Retrieved from https://www.eiseverywhere.com/file_uploads /de230237ea8487344065a4a5ef29f4c8_Sillanaukee _NationalFinnisheHealthandesocialStrategy2020.pdf

Etehad, M., & Kim, K. (2017). The US spends more on healthcare than other any other country—But not with better health outcomes. *The Los Angeles Times*. Retrieved from http://www.latimes.com/nation/la-na -healthcare-comparison-20170715-htmlstory.html

Export.gov. (2018). *Japan—Healthcare IT*. Retrieved from https://www.export.gov/article?id=Japan-health care-IT

Frogner, B., Reinhardt, U. E., & Anderson, G. (2006). Health care spending and use of information technology in OECD countries. *The Commonwealth Fund*. Retrieved from http://www.commonwealthfund.org /publications/in-the-literature/2006/may/health -care-spending-and-use-of-information-technology -in-oecd-countries

Gauld, R. The New Zealand health care system. Retrieved from https://international.commonwealthfund .org/countries/new_zealand/

Glaser, J. (2016). What emerging nations can teach us about health care. Retrieved from https://www .hhnmag.com/articles/7896-what-emerging-nations -can-teach-us-about-health-care

Glenngård, A. H. The Swedish health care system. Retrieved from https://international.commonwealthfund.org /countries/sweden/

Glover, L. The Australian health care system. Retrieved from https://international.commonwealthfund.org /countries/australia/

Gupta, I., & Bhatia, M. The Indian health care system. Retrieved from https://international .commonwealthfund.org/countries/india/

Health and Medicine Division of the National Academies of Sciences, Engineering, and Medicine. (1999). *To Err Is Human: Creating a safer health system*. Retrieved from http://www.nationalacademies.org/hmd/~/media /Files/Report%20Files/1999/To-Err-is-Human /To%20Err%20is%20Human%201999%20%20 report%20brief.ashx

Health and Medicine Division of the National Academies of Sciences, Engineering, and Medicine, Kohn, L. T., Corrigan, J., & Donaldson, M. S. (Eds.). (2000). *To Err Is Human: Building a safer health system*. Washington, DC: National Academy Press. Retrieved from https:// www.ncbi.nlm.nih.gov/pubmed/25077248

Health and Medicine Division of the National Academies of Sciences, Engineering, and Medicine. (2001). *Crossing the quality chasm: A new health system for the 21st century*. Retrieved from http://www .nationalacademies.org/hmd/~/media/Files /Report%20Files/2001/Crossing-the-Quality-Chasm /Quality%20Chasm%202001%20%20report%20brief .pdf

Health IT Dashboard. (2016). *Adoption of electronic health record systems among U.S. non-federal acute care hospitals: 2008–2015*. Retrieved from https:// dashboard.healthit.gov/evaluations/data-briefs/non -federal-acute-care-hospital-ehr-adoption -2008-2015.php#figure4

Health It dashboard. (2018). These data visualizations of key data and statistics provide quick access to the latest facts and figures about health IT. You can search all the quick stats below. Retrieved from https:// dashboard.healthit.gov/quickstats/quickstats.php

Hilstead, R., Bigelow, J., Bower, A., Girosi, F., Meili, R., Scoville, R., & Taylor, R. (2005). Can electronic medical record systems transform health care? Potential health benefits, savings, and costs. *Health Affairs*. Retrieved from https://www.healthaffairs.org /doi/10.1377/hlthaff.24.5.1103

HIMSS and EMRAM—Europe. Retrieved from https://www.himss.eu/healthcare-providers/emram

Hong Kong. Healthcare in Hong Kong. Retrieved from https://en.wikipedia.org/wiki/Healthcare_in_Hong_Kong

http://www.healthsystemtracker.org/wp-content/uploads/2015/09/Appendix-Measuring-the-quality-of-healthcare-in-the-U.S1.pdf

https://www.google.com/search?q=GDP+percent+spent+on+health+care+in+finland&oq=GDP+percent+spent+on+health+care+in+finland&aqs=chrome.69i57.16821j0j7&sourceid=chrome&ie=UTF-8

James, J. (2013). Patient engagement. *Health Affairs*. Retrieved from https://www.healthaffairs.org/do/10.1377/hpb20130214.898775/full/

Jha, A. K., Doolan, D., Grandt, D., Scott, T., & Bates, D. W. (2008, December). The use of health information technology in seven nations. *International Journal of Medical Informatics, 77*(12), 848–854.

Jha, A. K., King, J., Patel, V., Furukawa, M. F., & Mostashari, F. (2013). Office-based physicians are responding to incentives and assistance by adopting and using electronic health records. *Health Affairs, 32*(8), 1470–1477.

Kaiser Family Foundation. (2015). Primary Care providers' views of recent trends in health care delivery and payment. Retrieved from https://www.kff.org/health-reform/poll-finding/primary-care-providers-views-of-recent-trends-in-health-care-delivery-and-payment/?utm_campaign=KFF%3A+General&utm_source=hs_email&utm_medium=email&utm_content=21063887&_hsenc=p2ANqtz-_qLs9a6rgK5XfdGPJdYi7ZFnp2IKFvg8mo7yRuAo0vqBfIPcDOPR6zOTdloxjx9OxzBTHYzQsaNyC0V_WlK_y1NjzyEQ&_hsmi=21063887

Lindahl, A. K. The Norwegian health care system. Retrieved from https://international.commonwealthfund.org/countries/norway/

Landi, H. (2018). *Survey: Infrastructure, interoperability key barriers to global HIT development.* Retrieved from https://www.healthcare-informatics.com/news-item/ehr/survey-infrastructure-interoperability-key-barriers-global-hit-development

Liu, C., & Haseltine, W. The Singaporean health care system. Retrieved from https://international.commonwealthfund.org/countries/singapore/

Luscombe, B. (2012, August 27). Disease can't hide. *Time, 180*(9), 50–52.

Lyndon, J. (1846). *Thoreau's survey of Walden Pond in 1846.* Retrieved from https://www.walden.org/work/walden/

Martin, N., & Montagne, R. (2017). *Focus on infants during childbirth leaves U.S. moms in danger.* Retrieved from https://www.npr.org/2017/05/12/527806002/focus-on-infants-during-childbirth-leaves-u-s-moms-in-danger

Matsuda, R. The Japanese health care system. Retrieved from https://international.commonwealthfund.org/countries/japan

Medical Device and Diagnosic Industry. (2013). *Shaping a future-proof business strategy in the fast-moving medical equipment technology industry.* Retrieved from https://www.mddionline.com/global-healthcare-industry-year-2020

Nicas, J. (2018). The week in tech: Apple goes on the attack. *The New York Times.* Retrieved from https://www.nytimes.com/2018/10/26/technology/apple-time-cook-europe.html

OECD. (2018). *Health spending (indicator).* doi: 10.1787/8643de7e-en. Retrieved from https://data.oecd.org/healthres/health-spending.htm

Osborn, R., & Sarnak, D. (2017). London school of economics and political science. In E. Mossialos & A. Djordjevic (Eds.), International profiles of health care systems. New York, NY: The Commonwealth Fund. Retrieved from http://www.commonwealthfund.org/~/media/files/publications/fund-report/2017/may/mossialos_intl_profiles_v5.pdf?_ga=2.191316073.256625935.1520454166-1098622414.1508015335

Pearl, R. M. (2017). Mistreated. In *Why we think we're getting good health care—and Why we're usually wrong.* Retrieved from https://www.gsb.stanford.edu/faculty-research/books/mistreated-why-we-think-were-getting-good-health-care-why-were-usually-wrong

Peterson-Kaiser Health System Tracker. Retrieved from https://www.kff.org/peterson-kaiser-health-system-tracker/

Riegelman, R. (2010). *Public Health 101: Healthy people—healthy populations* (pp. 196–199). Sudbury, MA: Jones and Bartlett.

Rosen, B., & Waitzberg, R. The Israeli health care system. Retrieved from https://international.commonwealthfund.org/countries/israel/

Schneider, E. C., Sarnak, D. O., Squires, D., Shah, A., & Doty, M. M. (2017). Mirror, mirror: How the U.S. health care system compares internationally at a time of radical change. *The Commonwealth Fund*, July. Retrieved from https://www.commonwealthfund.org/publications/fund-reports/2017/jul/mirror-mirror-2017-international-comparison-reflects-flaws-and

Stanford White Paper. (2018, June). Stanford White Paper: Future of electronic health records. Retrieved from http://med.stanford.edu/ehr/whitepaper.html

Sturny, I. The swiss health care system. Retrieved from https://international.commonwealthfund.org/countries/switzerland/

Taylor, H., & Leitman, R. (2002). European physicians, especially in Sweden, Netherlands, and Denmark lead U.S. in use of electronic medical records. *Health Care News, 2*(18), Table 1. Retrieved from https://www.healthaffairs.org/doi/10.1377/hlthaff.25.3.819

The Commonwealth Fund. The U.S. health care system. Retrieved from https://international.commonwealthfund.org/countries/united_states/

The Skimm. (2018). Cigna and Canada docs want to shake up the healthcare industry. Retrieved from https://www.theskimm.com/2018/3/8/skimm-for-march-9th-4?jumpto=jumpto-6360209&type=emailurl&r=68f88cc1&utm_source=email&utm_medium=dsshare

U.S. Population Health Measures. (2015, September). Appendix: Measuring the quality of healthcare in the U.S. Retrieved from www.healthsystemtracker.org/wp-content/uploads/2015/09/Appendix-Measuring-the-quality-of-healthcare-in-the-U.S1.pdf

Versel, N. (2010). Germany halts smart card program for security review. *Fierce Mobile Healthcare*. Retrieved from http://www.fiercemobilehealthcare.com/story/germany-halts-smart-card-program-security-review/2010-01-26

Vrangbaek, K. The Danish health care system. Retrieved from https://international.commonwealthfund.org/countries/denmark/

Zelmer, J., Ronchi, E., Hyppönen, H., Lupiáñez-Villanueva, F., Codagnone, C., Nøhr, C., … Adler-Milstein, J. (2016). International health IT benchmarking: Learning from cross-country comparisons. Retrieved from https://academic.oup.com/jamia/article/24/2/371/2631498?rss=1

CHAPTER 14

Future HIS: Key Issues and Opportunities

"Technology doesn't solve humanity's problems. It was always naïve to think so. Technology is an enabler, but humanity has to deal with humanity's problems. I think we're both over-reliant on technology as a way to solve things and probably, at this moment, over-indexing on technology as a source of all problems, too."

Sundar Pichai, CEO, Google

LEARNING OBJECTIVES

By the end of this chapter, the student will be able to:

- Describe future Health Information Systems (HIS), including digital health capabilities, in relationship to population health management, patient experience, and value-based care.
- Explain the potential impact of increased and ubiquitous access to data, both positive and negative.
- Define key issues, including unintended consequences, that *must* be solved for HIS to improve and reach its potential.
- Identify issues associated with striking a balance between security of data and access and information.
- Describe the effects of HIS and technology on the future of research, policy, and public health.
- Describe the key attributes of an HIS culture of learning within an organization.

▶ Introduction

This chapter takes one last look at HIS and key issues that *must* be addressed for the future growth and success of quality-based care in the U.S. Amid the race to apply promising technologies to pressing priorities—population health management, value-based care, and improved experiences for patients and providers—the future is less about new core HIS and more about redesigning existing systems to better accommodate the value-based care. Today's key issues are those things that must not be swept under the rug, especially the serious shortcomings of those core systems, and how best to use them as the foundations for new technologies, such as digital health and artificial intelligence (AI). These new capabilities can be used to: adapt to the changing organizational models; engage with patients at the center and provide health care outside the four walls of institutions; anticipate, prevent, and more effectively treat the chronic illnesses rampaging our populations; keep the explosion of data tamed so that intelligence can be made of it; and assure security of personal health data of patients and the systems of our provider institutions.

The future of HIS is made more complex by the current context of the U.S. healthcare system, with its shifting priorities and regulatory changes complicating the use of HIS and adoption of new technology. This dynamic environment, paired with health care's unsustainable costs (of which technology plays a part) and the risk associated with layering new capabilities atop aging infrastructure, makes

for a challenge, indeed. This chapter covers future HIS, key issues associated with existing HIS, and opportunities for using new technologies to achieve a better, brighter future for health care and the health of our population.

▶ Understanding the Future of HIS

As we are all aware, our world is rapidly changing. We bank online, take Uber downtown, and connect with old friends via their Instagram stories. Health care is changing, too, albeit at the speed of health care. This pace is criticized by some as too slow, but for others it is too fast. In the words of Eric Topol in *The Creative Destruction of Medicine*, the gradual introduction of six major disruptive technologies over the past 40 years has gotten us to the point where revolutionary change is occurring in medicine and health care (**FIGURE 14.1**) (Topol, n.d.). These disruptive technologies include cell phones, smartphones, personal

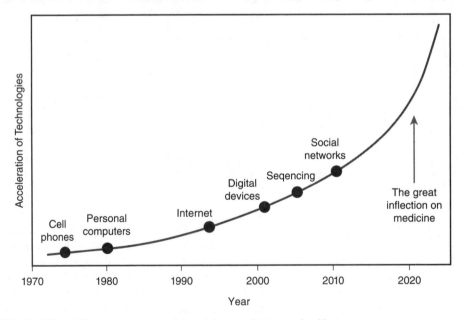

FIGURE 14.1 HIS transformative technologies and their application to health care.

Data from Eric Topol (2013). The Creative Destruction of Medicine: How the Digital Revolution Will Create Better Health Care. Perseus Books Group.

computers, the Internet, digital/mobile sensors and medical devices, AI, genomic sequencing, and social media or networks (dw2, 2012).

For the most part, health care is embracing these new technologies, and clinicians, patients, public health workers, researchers, and administrative workers are using them in an increasing variety of ways. This new **ubiquitous technology** plays a huge role in current transformation in the area of information ownership and access to care. Access to medical care has been constricted by gatekeepers of health insurance coverage. This barrier to care has been gradually erected due to a combination of factors, mostly revolving around accelerated costs of fee-for-service reimbursement method along with the need to maintain and increase profit margins for the insurance companies, pharmaceutical companies, electronic health record (EHR) vendors, suppliers, hospitals, and providers.

We have now entered a time in which the rules of this game are starting to change. We are seeing more equitable access to information (a large part of health care and public health) due to changing societal norms and the aforementioned ubiquitous technologies in the hands of most people today, used for myriad purposes of living and learning. What are these technical capabilities and combinations that have had such an enormous effect on the healthcare scene? This text has described many of these new technologies and how they might be used to address today's healthcare challenges including the transition to value-based care, population health management, and creating enhanced patient and provider experiences.

And in all these endeavors, it is best also to heed the cautions, even admonishments, of the Health and Medicine Division (HMD) of the National Academies of Sciences, Engineering, and Medicine report: *Health IT and Patient Safety: Building Safer Systems for Better Care* (2011). While written at a time focused largely on implementation of EHR systems, its lessons are generalizable to *all* HIS and new technology

implementation and adoption. This report summarizes and extrapolates existing evidence regarding the impact of HIS and technology on patient safety and recommends to Department of Health and Human Services (HHS) actions to take in conjunction with two key themes: using health IT to make patient care safer and continually improving the safety of health IT (HMD 2011). This report and its recommendations are consistent with the earlier HMD, formerly IOM, reports, *To Err is Human* and *Crossing the Quality Chasm*, and their admonitions to face down the medical errors crisis and maximize the safety of care via health IT. It shines a light on the unintended consequences of HIS and new technology adoption, issues which are discussed in several chapters of this text. Recent reports also identify that progress in addressing other hospital-acquired adverse events has been variable. In the past two decades since the HMD reports that focused on preventable errors in hospitals, additional areas of safety risk have been identified, such as diagnostic errors and in the use of health information technology. This is of particular concern for those reading this text: rates of preventable harm remain high, and HIS and technology are part of that safety risk equation. New approaches to address risk areas must be developed and prioritized when considering applications of new technologies. The data and analytical resources now available to use must be pointed at predicting potential errors by patient, preventing them from occurring, and routinely and continuously measuring safety performance (Bates & Singh, 2018).

Adapting to Ubiquitous Technologies and Data

"**Inflection point**." "Tipping point." "Convergence." "Innovation." These terms are commonly used today to indicate the excitement and hope that we are finally *there* in our ability to use new technologies in the modern healthcare and public health arenas, with empowered consumers as patients and people actively connected to clinicians, participating in the management of their health and medical care. Certainly, a great deal of data is floating around in provider organizations, institutions, and homes. In fact, we are awash with data residing in a staggering number of HIS (many of them still in "silos") in healthcare organizations, personal data stores and access capabilities via the Internet, mobile computing, medical devices, and sensors. We have reached the point where we struggle more with how to make organized sense of all these data than with how to create or gain access to the data, even though access to relevant information that meets the Five Rights of information remains a problem in many organizations and situations.

Over 40 years, healthcare organizations, physician practices, public health agencies, and individuals have hurried to automate, often within a singular domain. The end result has been the creation of isolated, disparate data and information silos, lacking perspective, failing at integration, and disregarding the need to coordinate and collaborate in the construction of those systems. This myopic approach to automation has resulted in huge amounts of computing power but very little ability to share those data outside the organizational—or even departmental—boundaries within which these systems were implemented, including a severely limited ability to share a patient's own data with that individual and his or her loved ones, and even greater limitations on the ability to do so securely.

Add to these the plethora of personalized data created from rapidly emerging mobile devices and sensors, increasingly linked together via the Internet of things (IoT) along with Internet-accessible health information from institutional EHR systems, imaging modalities, and other HIS, and one can readily see the exponential explosion in the volume of healthcare data. With this data, we have potentially generated levels of intelligence, specificity, and accessibility inversely proportional to the amount of data available. *Potentially* being the key word. Better

HIS planning, design, use, implementation, analytics, and integration into clinical and business workflows *must* be accomplished to make sense of all these systems and data. This accessibility to myriad sources is sometimes referred to as "Big Data," with an eye being cast toward vast opportunities for new markets, research, AI, improvements in the quality and cost of health care, and development of new knowledge based on intelligence gained from these enormous stores of data. One untoward aspect of the countless, disparate computing systems in health care is the disorganization, disconnectedness, and overall lack of cohesion of health data today (Mace, 2013). So, what does this mean for the future of HIS and technology in health care and public health? A lot!

The industry is implementing **data standards**, learning to think in terms of **Big Data**, and increasingly using flexible **cloud computing**. This new generation of analytics-oriented HIS allows for organizing dashboards, **business intelligence/clinical intelligence (BI/CI)** systems, and AI from a variety of data sources. In addition to BI/CI and AI, personal health intelligence is coming into play as part of the **quantified self** and digital health movements. As organizations and people become acclimated to ubiquitous technology and data, they are realizing that these digital resources are the future: the organizations that will thrive in the future will be those that best streamline their processes and adapt to these technologies. Cheaper and faster systems; better data, technologies, and devices; more powerful sensors, networks, security, and capacity; advancements in science and medicine such as genomics and nanotechnologies; optimized workflows; virtual care through telehealth and telemedicine; technology-enabled training and education; and personalized health information—these are real opportunities for organizations to innovate, improve, evolve, streamline, compete, and ultimately empower and attract people, professionals, customers, businesses, and success. This is now.

Eventually, those who do not adapt in such ways will be outmaneuvered by other businesses and providers and abandoned by empowered consumers who are experiencing better access and information in other walks of life. This adaptation has already happened in other industries and markets, which in turn is creating demand for those types of capabilities in health care, public health, and personal health. The days of information resting only with the privileged few with a degree or specialized access to the database or staff of analysts are rapidly becoming the past that, within a few decades, people will talk about incredulously or study in the "history" sections of their coursework.

The future goal of health information is *appropriate access to ubiquitous, personalized, specific information relevant to the situation, available to those who should have access to it, while honoring the privacy, security, and confidentiality of those whose information it is.* Included in this goal is access by patients to data stored in organizations' systems such as EHRs, for example, "open notes," a recent hot topic, where the trend is now to let patients see their physicians' notes in their EHR and allow patients to enter information into their own EHR. Patient-provided data has been a missing component of current EHR datasets, and this trend embodies the beginnings of true patient engagement. This supports getting critical, previously hard-to-ascertain data about lifestyle and behavioral influencers of patients and populations.

Additional innovations using technology in inpatient settings, such as location tracking, fall prevention, infection surveillance, and nurse communications advances, are helping solve long-standing safety and quality of care problems. Service improvement through the use of digital membership cards connected to software on a smartphone can allow for technology integration and consumer-friendly software applications to improve the patient experience. Forward-thinking organizations are using technology to implement service

improvements including wayfinding; digital (cell phone) insurance cards; taking co-payments online or by a staff member circulating through the admitting and registration areas with mobile credit card receiving capabilities (eliminating the need for patients to stand in lines, and reducing wait times); improving specialty scheduling delays; and other innovations that reduce mistakes, delays, frustrations, and inefficiencies. Through the use of technology, providers are able to place greater emphasis on patient involvement, education, and social media groups to help with chronic disease management. Predictive analytics can run against population data bases gathered through health information exchanges (HIEs) to anticipate those patients at greatest risk of advancing illness so that less intense, earlier interventions can stave off the worsening of a condition and keep patients' illnesses from worsening.

Implications for Healthcare Organizations and Professionals

The technology exists today to achieve these improvements and others, but organizations, providers, and schools of professional education must exert their will to change traditional organizational models and ways of delivering care and to create, innovate, and make proper use of new digital health and analytical capabilities. How long will it take to make these types of new models for enhanced care and services commonplace? This is difficult to predict. Certainly, the move toward value-based reimbursement to reward improved quality and cost outcomes is well underway. We have many of the software tools and technologies to make these things happen today, but adoption will take its own course and problems of inertia and ill-prepared infrastructures can be tough to overcome. Indeed, many of these technologies have been available for decades but have yet to make significant inroads in real-world settings. Many technologies and systems have been added in a piecemeal fashion over the years, resulting in silos of information and leaky, non-standard technology infrastructures. Thus, until markets and healthcare organizations change, the application of new technologies will trundle along in uneven fits and starts of adoption. As payment mechanisms now are beginning to acknowledge and reward the viability of clinical, business, and personal activities taking place using disruptive technologies such as mobile devices, smartphones, wireless sensors, and personal monitoring devices, the change will likely happen over a period of years, not decades. Many believe we are approaching the point of inflection in health care and public health—including this author, who has been devoted to this type of work for the past 30 years.

The caveat is that professionals who work in these healthcare organizations must be supported in this transition, while learning to work in new ways. This support should and will occur through new forms of training for the introduction of digital health to clinicians, as well as systems designed to create a better clinical experience for them and not burden them with loads of data entry formerly done by others. In this transition we must admit that organizations, regulations, and institutions are some of the slowest entities to change. Transforming the healthcare environment may ultimately rely on a generational change. However, it is being spurred on now by the government's recognition that current costs must be stemmed and the answer to today's epidemics of chronic, behavioral illnesses requires a different approach to care and to paying for that care: it is no longer volume of care but value that matters, rewarding better outcomes with better reimbursement. Clearly, realistic expectations must be cultivated when imagining this new vision for health care, public health, government reimbursement mechanisms, and interaction among professionals effectively using health and medical data around the world.

▶ Digital Health: Merging eHealth, mHealth, Social Media, Telemedicine, and Telehealth

New technologies and innovations in health care are emerging continuously. These technologies are often are used not individually, but rather in combinations to achieve new approaches to care. In this section, these innovations will be explored in the context of **digital health**: all of them with capabilities show great promise, as well as requirements for integrating them into the fabric of health care, including changing the ways we educate and train providers to prepare them for practice in the digital health age.

eHealth

eHealth comprises the technologies supporting an essential shift in methods, attitudes, and actions regarding health and wellness in our society today, summarized within an approach called digital health, and originally referred to as Health 2.0 (The Economist, 2012). As a nation and a world, we are striving to transform our expectations and the healthcare system(s) away from a focus on medicine and "sickness"—of course, necessary at appropriate times—and toward a focus on health. In this "wellness" mindset, people take active roles in managing and maintaining their own health. Health is the essence of what people care about and is ultimately what must be practically managed at the personal level due to its relationship to lifestyle and personal choices. It is also a key to how much medical care individuals eventually need when they reach the stage of vulnerability to chronic illness. More and more, people choose to digest information, including their own health data, interact with providers, and connect through new avenues of personalized technology. The World Health Organization (WHO) defines eHealth as the transfer of health resources and health care by electronic means, encompassing three main areas: (1) the delivery of health information, for health professionals and health consumers, through the Internet and telecommunications; (2) using the power of information technology (IT) and e-commerce to improve public health services, such as through the education and training of health workers; and (3) the use of e-commerce and e-business practices in health systems management (World Health Organization, n.d.). This wonderful definition encompasses the ultimate goal—a focus on health for people around the world, regardless of their ability to afford insurance or their geographical access to healthcare facilities. It also emphasizes the importance of (1) education, so that people can recognize the relationship between their daily lifestyle habits and their health, and (2) training, to use new electronic means to extend the healthcare workforce and help keep clinical professionals up to date on new information and skills.

eHealth encompasses a broad scope of electronic capabilities used for health and medicine. It includes organizationally based systems such as EHR systems and other HIS and technology, as well as collaboration spaces for researchers to share data and methods, **mHealth**, uses of mobile devices and social media for health purposes, **telemedicine**, and **telehealth**. "Digital health" is the more common term now used to capture mHealth, eHealth, telemedicine, and telehealth, with their synergistic uses and technologies.

Today's predominant health concerns—which, if left untended, may develop into illness—are rooted in lifestyle and everyday behaviors and must be addressed individual by individual, day by day, community by community, where and how we live. These lifestyle-borne diseases have reached crisis proportions, providing the tipping point for change health care and governmental institutions alike. This is where eHealth comes in: providing ubiquitous systems and infrastructure to connect clinicians with people, wherever they are, and when they are healthy as well as sick. One innovative way to adapt healthcare settings to be in closer proximity to where people live has been by placing contemporary but small storefronts in retail outlets and at employer sites where people can easily stop in and get non-urgent care, such as minute clinics in pharmacy outlets and department stores. HIS and technology provide the connectivity and necessary information support to make these sites small but viable and convenient healthcare settings. Both good health behaviors and access to good medicine are essential to health.

Future physicians will need medical training for eHealth technologies in their curricula. This should include ubiquitous technology's effects on the practice of medicine and the evolving role of physicians within it. Rather than being prepared in the traditional hierarchical role as the source of all medical knowledge and decision making, the role of physician will be more toward facilitating interpretation of digitally acquired diagnostic and predictive information. A role shift like this will look less like *telling* the patient what to do or what is going on, and more like *partnership* with the patient with the help of digital health technologies such as telemedicine, telehealth, miniaturized medical devices, portable diagnostics, 3-D printing, and other technologies being developed at a rapid pace (The Medical Futurist, 2018). Many colleges and universities that educate and train health and medical professionals now offer online coursework on emerging uses of technology, including training using **virtual reality** instruction and its adaptation to medical practice.

Progress in eHealth is advancing steadily, sometimes carefully through a maze of regulations needed to protect patient privacy. For instance, most medical and nursing schools are training their students to practice their disciplines using EHR systems. However, this process has been hampered by inflexible EHR systems and privacy regulations limiting their use by students (Pelletier, 2014). Barriers are being removed one by one when appropriate, such as overturned privacy legislation that had originally prohibited direct patient access to lab results (Conn, 2014). Now with patient portals as part of modern EHR systems, as incented by the Health Information Technology for Economic and Clinical Health (HITECH) Act of 2009 and Meaningful Use (MU) program, this type of change allows patients to play a more active role in their own healthcare decisions. These efforts are advocated for by patient groups, providers, laboratories, and EHR vendors.

🔍 CASE EXAMPLE: LIKE REALITY, BUT BETTER

Case Western Reserve University in Cleveland, Ohio, in collaboration with the Cleveland Clinic, is opening a health education lab using augmented reality rather than cadavers for instruction of anatomy for beginning students. Professors direct students through their anatomy lesson using augmented reality of human anatomy, which alleviates the common problems associated with a crowded lab using limited (and well-used) cadavers as the medium for this portion of their medical education. After their virtual training, which is overseen by a professor to make sure the learning is effectively taking place, the students spend two weeks in a traditional anatomy lab, bringing together their digital learning experience with the experience learning anatomy with a real human (**FIGURE 14.2**).

Innovation using augmented reality technologies has also been developed in Oslo, Sweden, at the Intervention Center for Oslo Hospital, where two-dimensional images coupled with images from MRIs and other radiological tests have been used to create augmented models of organs to help surgeons visualize what they will encounter in a complex surgery. This alternative to the two-dimensional images they would normally use before and during an operation can provide a 3D roadmap of what they will see when performing the procedure, and even help guide as it is being performed in the operating room (**FIGURE 14.3**).

Medical training must now prepare students for future practice by training them with new tools: augmented reality capabilities will increasingly provide 3D models from which to learn and

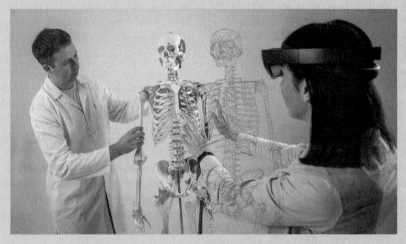

FIGURE 14.2 Medical education anatomy lab supported by augmented reality.
© Romaset/ Shutterstock.

practice. Other examples of ways that medical training adaptations to include opportunities for students to learn to about targeted therapies using technology including AI, such as using AI in tumor delineation, aiding surgeons with real-time information gained through mass spectrometry analysis of tumor markers, with the goal of conserving non-tumor tissue during tumor removal. Using mass spectrometry to analyze tumor markers, AI methodologies feed real-time information to surgeons resulting in tumor removal with maximum conservation of non-tumor tissue (Agar, 2018).

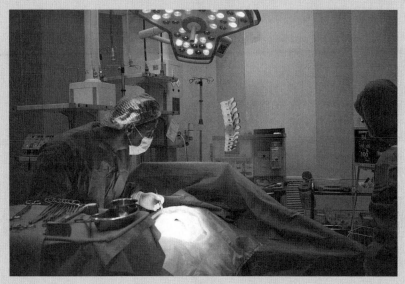

FIGURE 14.3 Surgeons visualize and explore augmented organ model before and during complex surgery.
© MONOPOLY919/ Shutterstock.

Issues of Access—the Digital Divide

New outreach portals are giving access to information or care in any and all circumstances and settings—urban, rural, local, remote, off-shore, insured, uninsured, rich, poor, and everything in between. However, a digital divide that was feared and anticipated has emerged: even with greater adoption and ubiquitous technologies, the "haves" and the "have nots" regarding health care persist. This chasm that exists between people as well as institutions and their ability to afford new IT systems will need to be addressed for eHealth to meet its promise and intended role in a new, connected healthcare system (Brino, 2014; Landi, 2017). While access to smartphones, desktop/laptop computers, broadband internet, or tablets in rural areas of the U.S. has been steadily increasing compared to urban and suburban areas, they still lag behind their urban and suburban counterparts, as portrayed in **FIGURE 14.4**.

It bears repeating that the usefulness of eHealth capabilities relies on the discipline of core HIS capabilities, including clinical integration and data stewardship, as represented in the HIS model. The ability to integrate clinically across organizational lines, and know exactly which data are being sent to whom with confidence in those data's integrity and security, does not get easier with Internet or mobile-based technologies. In many cases, it gets more complex. The fundamental principles of process design and data and systems

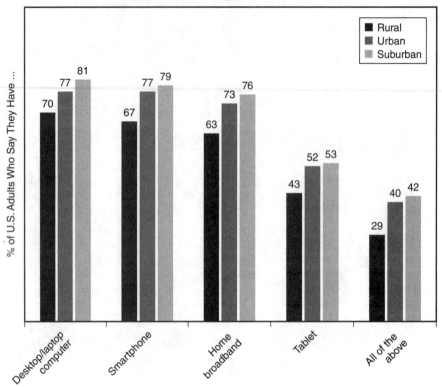

FIGURE 14.4 Digital access in rural, urban, and suburban areas of the U.S.

management remain absolutely critical. Poor data integrity means poor eHealth. This data integrity requirement extends to ensuring the protection of identifiable **personal health information (PHI)** according to standards set in the Health Insurance Portability and Accountability Act (HIPAA), no matter which medium is used to transmit those data.

mHealth

Also part of the overall set of digital health capabilities is **mHealth**, the use of mobile technologies for purposes of health care, public health, and health-related activities at the individual level. These activities can be clinical, educational, administrative, or research related: what matters is not the nature of the health activity, but rather the fact that it is enabled through the use of various mobile technologies. mHealth technologies include smartphones, mobile applications using tablets and smartphones, the Internet, **machine-to-machine (M2M)** wireless capabilities, personal computers, sensors and patient monitoring devices, social media, personalized health dashboards, and other applications connecting clinicians and patients or people in new, efficient ways, bypassing the need to be physically in each other's presence for caring or information sharing to take place. Mobile computing has removed physical barriers between individuals, individuals and organizations, individuals and information, and organizations and information. The new ways of interacting using mHealth are consistent with the new ways of communicating in other avenues of our lives. These methods—including social networking, business-to-consumer interactions, business-to-business interactions of commerce, and consumer-to-consumer connections—are taking off in health care, public health, and all matters health related. For example, in the U.S., the number of adults using mobile phones for health information increased from 232.2 million in 2012 to 258 million in 2015, with a projected 276.7 in 2020. Patient beliefs and physician preferences favor adoption of these new technologies to assist in health care in the same way that we are using new technologies in our daily lives (The Statistics Portal, n.d.). eHealth, mHealth, telehealth, and telemedicine technologies can be used for a multiplicity of increasingly advanced purposes, which in turn move along a continuum of uses (**FIGURES 14.5** and **14.6**).

Social Media and Digital Health

Social media, and online condition-related support groups can help people cope with health conditions. These online spaces feel private, but the security of the personal data being shared is debatable. The balancing act between access to personal data through non-secure social technology and the privacy of what is taking place in the healthcare workplace is being faced in healthcare organizations, public health entities, and homes alike. The fact that this is an evolving process is important: social media has advanced significantly, but security has not. Because these early experiences with social media occurred during less technology ubiquitous, pre- and early HIPAA days, the initial policies and practices were rooted in non-secure environments and, therefore, were less facile than requirements would dictate today. Today, social media use is embraced—and healthcare organizations are charged with preserving patient privacy, confidentiality, and security of PHI, while still using popular social functionality within secure networking

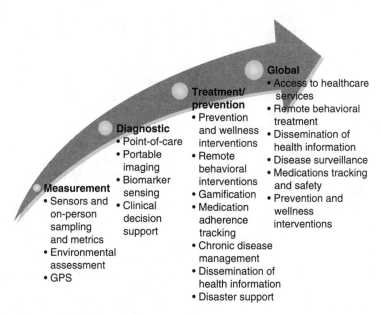

FIGURE 14.5 Continuum of mHealth tools from essentials.

Ubiquitous infrastructure in the form of mobile phones is now global, with more than 2 billion smartphones currently in use each day, and another 1 billion sold each year. In addition to calling and texting, among Americans alone, people access their mobile phones on average 50 times per day and spend on average 10 hours per day digitally connected, to conduct daily activities such as shopping for everything from clothes to groceries, ordering food, obtaining a ride, and reserving travel and entertainment.

Health care is behind the times in adopting modern mobile infrastructure and leading with patient experience. Legacy paper-based processes, regulations, and dominant vendors have left patients and providers weary and ready for digital disruption and convenience.

90% of health executives see digital ecosystems created through partnerships and effective use of platforms as the way forward.

More than 90% of patients believe they have the right to securely and easily access their health records, as well as share their medical history with whom they choose.

FIGURE 14.6 User mobile engagement and expectations.

Data from Docusign (2018). Reading the Signs: Three Patient and Provider Realities That Are Converging to Drive A Modern System of Agreement.

and other technology to create an interactive, engaged patient experience with informed providers. This balancing act requires understanding that the issues involved are partly technology related and partly human behavior and preference related.

How do healthcare organizations use social media? Organizational uses differ from consumer uses of social media, in that organizations focus on marketing and education, reviews, information gathering, and building support communities around specific diseases or processes such as cancer or diabetes. Additional areas of active use include patient education and human interest stories (Baum, 2013). Facebook, Twitter, LinkedIn, YouTube, Yelp, and other social media capabilities are being used across the U.S. by healthcare organizations and physician practices to communicate with patients and communities. Physicians, nurses, hospitals, and patient groups may engage one another through these social media platforms and are trusted contributors in the opinions of patients reading

the posts. Patients have many topics they like to discuss online, including support for a particular health-related cause; comments about health-related experiences; information sharing regarding particular health-related conditions; reviews of clinicians, treatments, payers, and hospitals; and sharing of images (Baum, 2013). Enhancing the patient experience for various groups such as young and healthy individuals, older populations, and persons with specific conditions such as cancer or multiple sclerosis, using self-help tools, monitors, and gadgets one can use at home, is a top priority for healthcare organizations.

Key policies and day-to-day practical decisions governing social media use by organizations include adherence to regulations and balancing HIPAA privacy/security adherence with access to and use of social media. Ultimately, social media comprise one more technology, and all technologies must follow overarching policies regarding protection of PHI and patients' rights to privacy, confidentiality, and security of data. Just because some information is available on a new platform (in this case, social media) does not mean it is acceptable to violate those guiding principles. The new technologies are simply additional means of transmitting and communicating information and making connections. Realistically, healthcare organizations should accept both the requirements of HIPAA and the reality of a world that embraces the use of social networking tools. As always, it is up to the human beings who use the technology to work and behave in ways that respect the privacy of patients who are, at that particular moment in their lives, vulnerable. Consequently, those who work in health care and public health must be held to a standard of appropriate behavior and concern for maintaining the privacy, confidentiality, and security of patients' information. Sharing PHI with anyone outside those parties involved in the care and administration of that care is not acceptable behavior, no matter how open a patient or employee prefers to be outside the workplace, either online or offline.

Additionally, when it comes to healthcare employees using social media outlets at their place of work, productivity can be a concern. Clearly, spending time on social media in ways that intrude on a person's work responsibilities is not something that can be left to random or individual attitudes or decisions. A quick email regarding a personal item that allows the employee to continue to attend to his or her duties is probably not a problem as long as it is used appropriately. Organizations are just what their name says: they are *organized*, which means that principles, values, policies, and rules provide structure to the workday. Everyone in the organization must adhere to acceptable norms in that environment. In some cases, organizations originally made the decision to block access to Internet sites other than those related to work. Once social media became ubiquitous, employees did not expect to use those sites at work because they expected that work computers would not be open to non-work-related sites. Gradually, however, these boundaries have

given way—but use of such technology still should not interfere with one's work. Much of this issue, therefore, has to do with expectations of the human beings involved. It is always preferable to educate employees regarding the principles that the organization stands for, and to make protection of patient information paramount. Within the bounds of that principle, behavior and policies can be implemented and responsible workers will maintain the desired balance. By establishing an environment of trust, empowerment, and informed responsibility, deviations from the norm can be seen in the context of a person's typical behavior, and judgments made taking those factors into considerations, based on technical, policy, and human factors.

Ultimately, employees of healthcare and public health organizations must understand that anything posted on Instagram, Facebook, Twitter, or social-media in any fashion is not private. Most of us know this already, having heard on the news or read online about physicians being reprimanded for comments made about cases on Facebook or other social media platforms. That is the bottom line.

Questions about how to handle the use of social media and networking are not unlike the questions that organizations pondered when HIPAA was implemented in the early 2000s. HIPAA, of course, has to do with the protection of PHI; ways to address the security of HIS technology that handles PHI, such as EHR systems; and the behavior of healthcare workers, clinicians, and business people who handle that kind of information all day, every day, so that the privacy and confidentiality of PHI are maintained. These are the same types of issues that arise with the introduction of evolving forms of social media into the mix of technologies available for use in healthcare organizations and throughout health and the population. When HIPAA was originally passed, HIS and technology mattered a lot to that process, meaning organizations had to build HIS to meet HIPAA-level security and technical standards. HIPAA compliance also must take into account the human beings who are handling and accessing the PHI. A major part of implementing HIPAA is education and training of the people involved, so that their decisions and choices as clinicians and business people working with PHI are made while understanding their responsibilities to protect the confidentiality and privacy of PHI. Education and training regarding why and how to protect and properly handle PHI in their daily work is as important as the technical work of the HIS professionals to ensure the security of computer systems and networks storing and translating the PHI.

Historically, before HIPAA was implemented, for instance, systems were accessible to those possessing a password to the system, so patient information was more easily accessed across a broader spectrum of roles, with fewer "need to know" qualifications than are in place today. It was a startling wake-up call to many who worked in health care to realize that they could no longer view PHI unless it was needed for them to do their jobs in caring for or conducting business necessary to the treatment or cure of the patient. Stiff reprimands are handed out if these rules are violated, including termination and, in many cases, penalties, sanctions, and legal action for breaches and blatant hacking and illegal sharing of private information. Social media outlets are largely the same: the technologies are built to be open. There is no way to tighten the security technically due to the nature of social media and networking and their basic purpose—namely, open sharing of comments, perspectives, questions, and other interactions between people. The key to protecting patient privacy, then, is to create secure, social media-type spaces, within the confined of the technology and secure infrastructure of a healthcare institution for patients to participate in sanctioned, secure chat groups, along with education and training of the people involved, so that they know how to regulate themselves and handle preservation of PHI privacy, confidentiality, and security in their

daily work and interactions using social media and other platforms. At the end of the day, whether we are talking about HIPAA or use of social media, the greatest risks for breaches of sensitive data are associated with the behaviors and choices of people, much more so than the security of systems.

▶ Emerging HIS Technologies and the Human–Machine Relationship

Emerging technologies are only as useful as their practical application and demonstration of value in achieving hoped for results in the form of benefits and creative goals designed into each pilot project or trial testing a new use of HIS. As HIS progresses into its new phases of eHealth, mHealth, telemedicine, and digital health, it is fueled by research, pilot projects, and intentions of improving health outcomes and health care. HIS research and grant projects focus on areas in information and decision support, clinical workflow improvement, care coordination, and understanding the impact of HIS on outcomes. Funding preferences for research currently favor the areas of medication management, outreach care for vulnerable populations, and practice-based research networks. Priority areas identified by the HMD include medication management, hypertension, diabetes, heart disease, case coordination, major depression, self-management/health literacy, cancer screening, frailty associated with old age, immunization, pregnancy and childbirth, and tobacco cessation treatment (Agency for Healthcare Research and Quality, n.d.). Such research projects reflect key concerns and represent major opportunities for improvement in health status and outcomes, especially in terms of ambulatory care. Insights will be gained and strides taken as a result of these research projects' findings that will steer evolving uses of HIS in new ways, with technologies being coupled with streamlined processes to achieve improved clinical and cost outcomes (Baum, 2013).

This pioneering work, which is moving outward beyond the existing edge of uses of HIS and technology, is a creative, arduous endeavor not for the faint of heart. But for those with the will to try and a creative spirit, many new applications continue to be developed in the hopes of being woven into a new fabric of healthcare and public health practices as we know them. Intrinsic to this journey is an evolving relationship between humans and the machines or technology they use. The progression circling around the evolving human–machine relationship piques the interests of those studying emerging technologies. As people adapt to new technologies, the focus of this evolution—historically fixated on using computers to replace humans doing work—changes as well. Currently, three main trends are visible in the innovative use of emerging technologies: (1) human work being augmented by technology, such as a healthcare professional conducting teletherapy sessions with patients suffering with mental illness, in an area where demand exceeds supply of mental health professionals such as psychologists and psychiatrists; (2) machines replacing the work of humans, such as a virtual assistant providing automated services to assist a person finding a needed health service in a new community or using genetic sequencing technology to determine the genetic makeup of cancer cells to enable precise determination of the medicine to used based on the specific abnormal genes and proteins; and (3) humans and machines working together, such as a mobile robot used by a surgeon while performing a surgical procedure or Bluetooth-enabled smart inhalers, helping the 94 percent of asthma patients who don't use inhalers as directed, and helping the 50 percent of asthma patients who are not well controlled by detecting inhaler use, reminding patients to use their medication, encouraging proper use of the

device, and gathering data about a patient's inhaler use that can help guide care (Holland, 2018). These increasingly refined interactions between people and computers will continue to be applied in ways that improve productivity, transform the customer or patient experience, and improve outcomes from clinical, cost, and competitive perspectives.

▶ Future Directions in Informatics, Data, and Analytics

Informatics

Considering the interface between clinicians and computers, opportunities for emerging technologies to be integrated into the workflows of clinicians and business professionals are limited only by our ingenuity, our technical prowess, and the boundaries of appropriate care in the essentially human-to-human interactions that compose health care and caring. Reactions—among clinicians and patients alike—to the presence of computers in the clinical exam room have been fierce and varied, with some complaining that this application takes the attention of the clinician away from the human interaction between healer and patient. Specific ways that technology might help clinicians and patients reestablish their human and therapeutic connections will be improvements to the often rudimentary, initial technology adoption that more often than not simply replicates the manual process on the computer.

In the future, enlightened implementation of technology will move health care away from burdensome technological procedures that currently relegate some of the most highly trained knowledge workers—namely, physicians, nurses, and other clinicians—to the role of data input clerks. Needed improvements and opportunities lie before us as we seek to refine the integration of technology with the work of these special professionals who devote their working lives to helping and healing others.

Data and Analytics

Greater data availability has proved to be a blessing and a curse. Covered in depth in Chapters 10 and 11, the volumes of data and the focus on those data will experience exponential growth in the future, surpassing current abilities to manage and make use of the data. Soon though, AI technologies be capable of sophisticated tasks such as being able to accurately interpret radiological images. This is thought to be able to eventually replace the current role of radiologists as we know it today, forcing that subspecialty to evolve. These types of capabilities are able to diagnose conditions based on training of algorithms through which large volumes of data have been pushed of patient and population images representing comparative norms. Analytics is maturing to accept voice inquiries, allowing more healthcare professionals to access complex databases—clearly a remarkable change from the difficulties experienced today in the quest to access and analyze large stores of data. Of course, this still requires the skills and knowledge of analysts who understand the analytical tools as well as data realities and composition of data stores, housing data that might be standardized within an institution, but have yet to standardized across organizations, except for the most frequent and basic common data elements required for programs such as MU or claims processing. All this takes time.

Data analytics skills are increasingly a desired skillset and a requisite for administrative and BI/CI decision making. Despite some healthcare workers finding any computer interface difficult to adapt to, the emerging generation of employees must arrive with better and more adaptable skills to successfully meet analytical needs and avoid data intimidation. Analytical capabilities will be the daily basis for roles-based performance, reporting, and communications for both business requirements and patient care.

Value-based care, population health management, personalized medicine, and new reimbursement approaches taken by payers, shifting risk to providers, all require timely and intelligent analytical capabilities to help healthcare organizations and providers navigate the transition from fee-to-service (volume based) to reimbursement plans that reward efficiency and improved outcomes (value based). One such program is Medicare Advantage, which shifts risk to providers, and pays physicians a fixed fee per patient. If the provider manages the care for the patient within that budget, they gain financially, and if they don't, they bear the loss (Galewitz, 2018). These new incentives provider a clear set of requirements for application of HIS and digital health technologies to enable effective, care management, population health management, value-based reimbursement programs.

▶ The Effect of New Technologies on Public Health

Digital Health's Potential for Improvements in Public Health

Clearly of high value and transformative in effect, digital health, including eHealth and mHealth, and improvements in UI/UX can vastly improve isolated individuals' and populations' ability to access health beneficial care, education, information, and professionals. This type of telecommunication and computer connection, whether on a provider-to-patient or provider-to-provider basis, increases efficiency in managing health and chronic illness—important elements as populations age and the prevalence of chronic disease increases.

Prevention Supersedes Cure

Amidst this technology revolution, and as a foundation for value-based care, there is some "getting back to basics." The idea of focusing on preventing disease (the wellness or health model) versus curing illness once it occurs (the sickness or medical model) is not a new one. If something can be prevented, that is a much better option than trying to fix it later. Whatever advancements are made using technology in health care should be grounded in principles that allow health care to be more efficient, more effective, more personalized, and preserving of time and space for caring and compassion. The caring relationship between care giver and care receiver can re-center, stripped of the layered-on administrative, pharmaceutical-based, insurance-driven healthcare processes. The very important work of capturing data and creating information with support from digital technologies—such as mobile devices, sensors, genomic sequencing, AI, and predictive analytics—can retreat into the background. For this reason, the focus of workflows and processes should be in support of the patient's interaction in new ways with their own data and with clinician and the patient. At present, we have wandered far afield of that central concept of the unique and intimate conversation between clinician and patient, due to the dominating focus on insurance processes and third-party domination of the clinical relationships and access to health care.

Reestablishing the essential connection between patients and their clinicians, supported by advanced data and analytical capabilities, along with the increased acceptance of risk by providers, will place insurance companies in a more balanced, proper position—no longer completely driving the access to care, but rather supporting it. The fundamental concept of insurance has always been to collect small amounts of money on a regular basis from many persons, pooling the risk as well as the money into a fund that can be dipped into when expenses occur for pool members who need medical and health care. The insurance tail has definitely been wagging the healthcare dog in this instance for quite some time—interestingly, within the same timeframe as the development of these new technologies. It has been 50 years since the beginning of managed care and the continual efforts of the government and payers to contain rapidly rising healthcare costs. Digital health, connected mobile devices, wearables, AI, and other technologies' abilities to help health and medical professionals connect with data, patients, and healthcare processes in new ways have the potential to be revolutionary change agents, to be sure, and if applied well, can help rebalance the respective roles of care and insurance coverage for that care. Using these technologies to improve access to and outcomes of health care gives new meaning to what it means to have "empowered" patients—those who are actively participating in managing their health care and maintaining their health.

▶ Alignment Between HIS and Population Health Management and Value-Based Care

Supporting Healthcare's Transition

We are now living the challenges and opportunities of health care. The future challenges of health care are upon us as we recognize we must achieve value—through improved cost and quality outcomes, through value-based care, by effectively managing the health of populations, and by addressing pressing public health issues including the opioid crisis, maternal and infant mortality. HIS and new technologies can help and are in fact essential in addressing all these things, requiring a concerted and coordinated effort across healthcare organizations, providers, the government, private payers, and public health efforts.

Moving Beyond Meaningful Use to Value-Based Care

Tracking the impact of HIS and technology to support population health management efforts and the overall cost of health care in the U.S. will be important for determining whether we are succeeding in improving the value of healthcare dollars spent. The ability to identify patients at most risk for advancing or deteriorating conditions and using connected technologies to help get them the care they need at home or in a skilled environment—before a crisis occurs and they end up in critical condition in a hospital or ED—is essential to value-based care and to controlling runaway costs and patient suffering. They don't want to go to the hospital if it can be avoided; they want to be cared for in their homes. The establishment of effective population health management programs, supported by needed HIS and technology can realistically address the highest cost categories more effectively (e.g., patients at the top 5 percent of risk, and certain periods of life such as the last three months of a patient's life, when we spend we spend over one-third of healthcare dollars per capita).

Kaiser Permanente and other integrated health providers that are able to assume and manage risk have proven this.

Additionally, political volatility, regulatory changes, growing social issues affecting health, amidst continuous technological evolution creates a complex web of considerations when planning for the use of new HIS and technologies. Leadership that stabilizes and focuses efforts at this time would be welcome, but that is not our reality in a toxic political environment and a healthcare system entrenched with those who continue to win with the status quo, and advocate for inertia and block dialogue about change (Nash, 2018).

But with the help of HIS-savvy healthcare professionals and innovative technologies available for real-world application, there is hope. We must press forward and remember that the goals of population health management and value-based care are applicable to the array of health conditions coming at us. Clearly, many healthcare leaders believe that bringing the care to patients rather than bringing patients to provider organizations is within our reach and it will happen. Forward thinking healthcare organizations are now building upon and moving beyond their focus on MU and overall performance metrics supporting efficiencies and effectiveness needed for population health management. Providers

🔍 CASE EXAMPLE: OPIOID RISK IDENTIFICATION

EHR vendors are adding capabilities to their systems to identify patients who may be at risk for opioid overuse. These capabilities work by helping support safe prescribing by providers at the point-of-care and integrating provider EHR systems with state Prescription Drug Monitoring Links (PDML), now available in 35 states. An EHR system vendor, Allscripts, recently added point-of-care access to this PDML database through their system The eCW EHR company has built a clinical decision support (CDS) into the EHR to estimates a patient's risk for opioid misuse, offering suggestions for alternatives opioids or opioid antagonists to prescribing providers (Monica, 2018a). This link saves what is estimated to be up to a seven-minute search of the mandatory databases by providers trying to access it directly during a patient visit, according to a study by researchers from Dartmouth-Hitchcock Medical Center published in the Journal of the American Medical Association Surgery Journal (Monica, 2018a; Stucke, Kelly, Mathis, Hill, & Richard, 2018).

are adapting what they put into place for MU and participating in the merit-based incentive payment system (MIPS) program, learning to use the levers it provides to successfully participate in value-based care and population health management. An imperative for providers, it either positively or negatively affects their reimbursement rates for Medicare patients, as a zero-sum program. For the 2017 baseline for qualification for providers, 93 percent of eligible clinicians in the MIPS track of the Quality Payment Program (QPP) received positive payment adjustments for their 2017 performance, while 5 percent of eligible clinicians' adjustments were negative; for those participating in the advanced alternative payment models (APM) track, 99,076 eligible clinicians reached the Qualifying APM Participant (QP) level. Special initiatives called the Small, Underserved, and Rural Support programs indicate recognized that this work is most challenging for small practices: these programs support eligible providers as is appropriate (Monica, 2018b).

As exciting as all the new technologies are, current status of progress along the EHR system "advanced" (vs. "basic") functionality front includes a recent study led by Julia Adler-Milstein. She and her colleagues examined the current state of progress along the lines of the goals of MU for adoption of basic versus advanced EHR system functionality, revealing widespread adoption of at least a basic EHR system but also the emergence of a digital divide in advanced EHR system uses in areas of performance measurement and patient engagement (Landi, 2017). These more advanced uses of EHR system functionality, in addition to basic capabilities, form the foundation for value-based care and population health management. In other words, organizations must have advanced EHR system functionality to: achieve cost-efficiencies needed for successfully navigating value-based care and reimbursement; engage patients in their own care; and successfully engage in population health management. This digital divide

in terms EHR functionality is a serious issue, since advanced capabilities are required for moving into the future. The organizations who are able to adopt the advanced functionality are a new version of the "haves" versus the "have nots." Those "haves" are typically larger health systems and the "have nots" are those with lesser resources, including small, rural, and safety net organizations. The performance management capabilities are necessary for organizations to improve their performance, and critical access organizations especially are not able to keep their adoption efforts sustained into the advanced EHR system capabilities category. Certainly this sounds the alarm that a U.S. health system, weakening in these critical access organizations, that serve high-risk and hard-to-reach populations, does not bode well for our collective ability to deal with the issues listed above that we face as a nation. Overall economic implications of this dynamic on the U.S. population are discussed later in this chapter. What is important to realize is this digital divide and the organizations affected by it are part of an overall picture related to excessive costs of health care that are borne by organizations and patients to their detriment, affecting them in ways beyond health and medical care.

In terms of current progress according to the goals of the HITECH Act, most hospitals now have adopted EHR systems, adopting at least "basic" system functionality, including the ability to document and manage individual patient care. This type of core EHR functionality has been widely adopted and a digital divide in "basic" system adoption has been largely avoided. It is in the advanced functionality of performance management and patient engagement that the digital divide has emerged, and this disadvantaged the critical access hospitals in their ability to continue to evolve and address the needs of their populations and their own ability to successful participate in value-based care processes.

Continued progress along the adoption curve of MU functionality and eHealth will reveal whether we have accomplished the desired improvements through the massive investments in technology made throughout the healthcare system. Eligible physicians, providers, and hospitals have increased their participation in MU programs and adoption of EHR systems, wearables, digital health capabilities, AI, and other emerging technologies. Tracking progress along this path of increasing innovation and adoption of integrated technologies will be important markers for future directions in HIS and new technologies, as EHR systems provide the foundation for successful population health management programs, leveraging the inflection in the application of new technologies. With the addition of large, traditionally non-healthcare companies to the mix, it will be a wide-open frontier for potential ways to engage patients and change health care from its traditional structures and affect public health in new ways. As healthcare talent enters to digital health world, it will be helpful to the initiatives of traditionally non-healthcare tech companies to blend the perspectives of high tech and health care. Recent additions to Google's healthcare initiative include Geisinger Health's CEO David Feinberg and former Cleveland Clinic CEO Toby Cosgrove, as Google organizes itself to enter and innovate in the healthcare space (Dietsche, 2018).

▶ Unintended Consequences

Significant statistics to monitor as we move ahead are those reflecting unintended consequences of HIS and adoption of new technologies. As exciting and urgent as advancements using digital health and analytics may be, these new technologies *must not* be layered atop current and legacy technologies to solve the problems they unintentionally have created. We must go to the core of these issues and address them. Where appropriate, we must swap out legacy

technologies that inherently, architecturally create problems. As more and improved literature is published from studies of the benefits and risks of HIS, insights will be gained into how we can ensure that the introduction of these new technologies does not hinder progress or introduce new forms of errors. Despite all the good intentions when implementing new technologies in health care, these technologies are disruptive and must be carefully managed and continually evaluated to ensure their effects are positive and not harmful.

Physician Dissatisfaction and Burnout

For example, the certainly unintended consequence of widespread physician dissatisfaction with their EHR systems and the effects on their practice of medicine was not anticipated with the HITECH Act nor with the good intentions of any organization implementing HIS. But this is the reality. And it must be solved, since EHR usage is important to the futures of healthcare organizations and provider practices. In a recent study, two-thirds of physicians responded that they are considering non-clinical career options, due to the administrative and regulatory burden of practicing medicine in today's environment—this represents an increase of 11 percent over the past three years (Landi, 2018) (**FIGURE 14.7**).

In another study, 89 percent of physician survey participants responded that practice of medicine has gotten worse due to the "business and regulation of healthcare (Landi, 2018)." According to Geneia's tool designed to measure national physician satisfaction, the physician misery index has is now 3.7 on a scale of 5 (5 being the most miserable) (Geneia, 2015). Loss of the zeal of physicians for the practice of medicine due to burdensome clerical work is something physicians are loath to tolerate and reflects a deep medical-social problem. This user interface and user experience problem, at

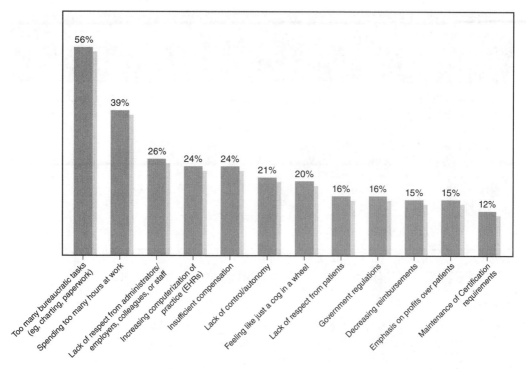

FIGURE 14.7 Top reasons for physician burnout.
Data from Medscape.

its root, has been created by paying inadequate attention to the perspective of the workflow and considerations of clinicians in the design and user interface of EHR systems, requiring burdensome data entry of regulatory and payer-driven documentation requirements. The rigidity and "data entry clerk" approaches to these processes also speaks to the age of the underlying architecture of most EHR systems, most importantly the big ones, such as Epic Systems, whose EHR systems now support over 60 percent of the hospital beds in the U.S. and equivalent proportions of ambulatory settings.

Surveillance: Outside the Protections of HIPAA

Buyer, be aware. Any device used or app downloaded includes the familiar terms of use, that one must click "yes" to be able to

use the device or app. In doing so, rights of data ownership are given away. This is happening daily with smartphones, Google Android devices, and Alexa, among many others (Phillips, Dowling, Shaffer, Hodas, & Volkova, 2017). This differs in the U.S. from the European Union (EU), which has recently adopted the General Data Protection Regulation (GDPR). Now, in the EU, the default is to not allow use of the data the company collects about an individual. The issue at the center of this debate is power over data. Americans, as contrasted people in Europe, have no control over data collected about them, except for children under 24. There are no rules: no government agency and no limits have ever been established for oversight. The EU says the U.S. approach is coercion under the EU law, a "take it or leave it" approach: "Give us your data or don't use our product." For example, the Google Android operating system requires users to give Google consent—"forced consent" in the

🔍 CASE EXAMPLE: WHY DOCTORS HATE THEIR COMPUTERS

In the words of Atul Gawande in *The New Yorker*, "Something's gone terribly wrong. Doctors are among the most technology-avid people in society; computerization has simplified tasks in many industries. Yet somehow we've reached a point where people in the medical profession actively, viscerally, volubly hate their computers." The story of an Epic implementation at Partners Health in the Boston area—12 hospitals and 70,000 employees, costing $1.6 billion—is sending a chilly wave through the industry, reinforcing numerous surveys and studies of physician dissatisfaction with the effects of the use of this system on their lives and practices of medicine. With two hours spent on the computer for every hour of face time with patients, and half the time in exam rooms with patients spent facing the computer, physicians are voicing feelings of being controlled by the computer rather than the computer aiding them in their work. The most overwhelming part of this story is that this exact system *supports well over half of the hospital beds in the U.S.*, and is, from a growing body of evidence, reducing the desire of those who we rely upon deeply, our physicians, to continue to do the work that we hold so precious. Something needs to be done (Gawande, 2018).

eyes of the EU law. In this case, the individual doesn't have the information or expertise to make a fair deal. In the U.S., the answer to the question, "Who owns the data?" is the company. In California, individual have access, but no ownership. How HIPAA affects this matters, but data collected for non-covered entities (e.g., weight loss apps, Facebook, Google and Apple devices) is out of HIPAA's scope. According to expert attorneys, companies in the U.S. have no intention of giving the same rights as the EU. This stark, interesting twist on data ownership connects with recent healthcare executives such as Geisinger Health's CEO David Feinberg and former Cleveland Clinic CEO Toby Cosgrove, who are leaving esteemed organizations healthcare organizations to join Google Health. For an example of how this lack of consumer protection is playing out in healthcare today: health insurers (payers) are gathering up data about individuals lifestyles and purchasing habits, and myriad other data from outside the healthcare system and protections of HIPAA, and using that data purchased from data brokers, to determine what your risk for healthcare costs will be and adjusting your rates accordingly (Allen, 2018). Trust that they

won't be giving discounts. (Think more along the lines of rate hikes.)

Overall Economic Effects of Health Care on the U.S. Population

HIS and technologies are a significant contributor to runaway healthcare costs, the economics of which are not only draining the finances of the hospitals, practices, and health systems that implement them, but they are an expensive part of a healthcare economic pricing construct that, along with pharma, payers, and other for-profit elements of the "business" of U.S. health care, is weakening the overall economic status of the vast majority of Americans by placing sustained downward pressure on wages and incomes. Healthcare spending is higher in the U.S. while quality is lower. And, this spending is not a result of overuse of services; rather, the cause is high prices for health services. Prices for pharmaceuticals, medical devices, insurance, and physician salaries are almost unvaryingly higher in the U.S. than in peer countries (Bivens, 2018). As a result, employees are facing

🔍 CASE EXAMPLE: EPIC'S FUTURE ROLE– INNOVATION OR LEGACY?

Created in 1979, the Epic Systems Company EHR was built using the Massachusetts General Hospital Utility Multi-Programming System (MUMPS) operating system, when systems and operating systems were extremely limited compared to the capacity of modern systems architectures. Also, underlying the original design of the system is allegiance to the billing process and administrative needs of organizations. Companies who built and still support EHR platforms centered on the business functions of healthcare companies have benefitted financially from their involvement in health care, and they lack the motivation to change the situation. Unfortunately, these widely implemented systems, through their UI/UX and workflow designs, are having a terrible effect on physicians' experiences and their motivations about the practice of medicine. This must be corrected for the sake of sustainable health for patients and populations. Epic can be a game-changer if they can technically and culturally change the underlying issues in their EHR, but it remains to be seen if the company can perceive reason to do so and act upon it.

🔍 CASE EXAMPLE: EHR SYSTEM SAFETY PROBLEMS IN PEDIATRIC SETTINGS

Recent studies have provided evidence that the use of EHR systems designed with adult patients in mind bear risks for pediatric patients, particularly around medications and dosage calculations built into the software. The assumption baked into HIS must not be that a child as simply a small adult. A team of researchers led by Raj Ratwani, Ph.D., reported that of 9,000 pediatric reports of issues identified, more than a third had an EHR usability issue that affected medication processes. In 609 of the 9,000 reports, or about 19 percent, the error "reached the patient (Reed, 2018)." Usability problems exist in EHR systems created by vendors not taking the unique needs of pediatric patients into mind, in this study resulting in 64 percent of errors identified associated with EHR-related problems, rather than a human error or technology glitch.

rising healthcare costs. The high cost of HIS products and services, particularly the large EHR systems such as Epic and Cerner, also contribute to this situation.

Additionally, the fee-for-service reimbursement system adds fuel to the cost of healthcare fire. While it bears repeating that population health management programs and value-based reimbursement will be helpful adjustments to this scenario, high prices, unless dealt with, will continue to create this downward pressure on wages and incomes of Americans, while making a very small percentage of

them very wealthy, including Judy Faulkner, CEO of Epic Systems and third on Forbes Richest "Self-Made" Women List (Spitzer, 2018), and co-founder and former CEO of Cerner Corporation, Neal Patterson, recently deceased. The expensive nature of Epic Systems EHR system, in particular, is common knowledge in health IT circles, validated in numerous news publications, such as Partners in Boston recently spending $1.2 billion implementing Epic's EHR system (McCluskey, 2015).

Thus far, the paucity of effective population health programs continues to allow this cost and high pricing situation in U.S. health-care act as an economic plague for Americans. As an example of how population health management can help, Kaiser has instituted a very effective system where physician salaries are on par with private pay docs across the board, but there is a much greater emphasis on prevention and the cost for Kaiser plans generally is more stable than other non-integrated delivery systems and health plans. Additional improvement is for the government to continue doing what Medicare has started with new codes for chronic care management and now many more programs/codes to encourage preventive care and care management that keeps patients healthy and out of the hospital for as long as possible. CMS has issued its own analysis showing that this approach works in reducing overall costs (Dickson, 2018). It is likely then only a matter of time before other commercial payers pick this up. In the meantime, the government has at least recently rattled its sword to go after the pharmaceutical industry money machine that charges more in the U.S. for the same drugs that sell for a fraction of the cost in other countries. We can hope that they have the will to do this, but many feel the "system" is so entrenched that changes like this are unlikely to happen until companies such as the pharmaceutical industry are paid based on outcomes as is common in the European Union (Nash, 2018). With its emphasis on digital health solutions and care management, Medicare Advantage and other **capitated plans** are headed in the right direction. The incentive model needs to be fixed to align all players in the same direction economically.

▶ Finding the Way Forward

For providers, investors, and vendors, the future of the HIS marketplace appears quite dynamic, as new products and services are being developed and innovated for HIS. Current federal investments and new standards are stimulating the development of many of these new products, as well as spurring the updating or retirement of old products that do not meet the new regulatory and industry requirements. For example, approximately 941 vendors provide more than 1,700 unique certified EHR system products in the U.S. It is anticipated those numbers will decrease in the next few years, as competitive processes weed out lower-quality products with lesser market shares while innovators introduce new ones.

Additional job opportunities have been emerged as a result of this growth in HIS, EHR systems, BI/CI, and other new technologies in health care and public health. Since HITECH was enacted, more than 50,000 HIS-related jobs have been created—and this number does not even count the jobs created in the new businesses developing the many new products described previously. Clearly, tracking the growth, maturation, and improvement of the products, jobs, and roles involved in the development and evolution of HIS will be an exciting adventure.

Social Determinants of Health and HIS

In the midst of considering the business implications of HIS and technology, a challenge includes evidence that medical care comprises a small percentage (only 10–30 percent) of determining health. Any new technology advancement in health care should take these other factors into consideration. Making medical care more effective is important, but health is a function of other things too, including genetics, social and behavioral factors, and individual behavior (**FIGURES 14.8** and **14.9**).

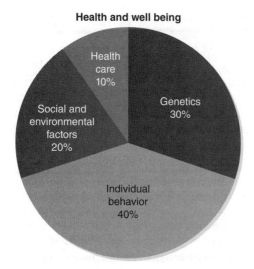

Health and well being

FIGURE 14.8 Proportional impact of factors on one's health.

Reproduced from Schroeder, SA (2007). We Can Do Better—Improving the Health of the American People. Kaiser Family Foundation. NEJM 357: 1221-8.

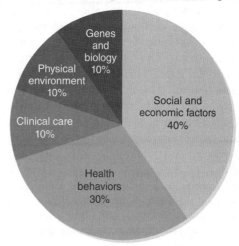

Factors influencing health and well-being

FIGURE 14.9 Factors determining health.

Data from MN Department of Health. Retrieved from http://www.health.state.mn.us/divs/opi/gov /chsadmin/intro.html

▶ Issues to Consider as the Future of HIS Unfolds

Finding the Balance: Security Versus Access to Health Information

With increased availability of HIS and access to data is the flip side of the accessibility coin—violation of privacy and security of PHI. The healthcare community is aggressively pursuing interoperability between systems in an effort to facilitate the exchange of data among a variety of organizations to care for individuals more efficiently, as well as to make widespread secondary use of data from those systems. In our rush to "connect the dots" between systems and organizations on behalf of interoperability, we are also challenged with numerous practical, technical,

and ethical issues. These issues center on finding the balance between access to data and systems and the intentions of "doing good"— with protection of the data and privacy of those whose lives are reflected in the data being a paramount concern. We are a long way from knowing exactly where the fulcrum of that balance should be centered—a balance that will be some right combination of technology and behavior. The Healthcare Information and Management Systems Society (HIMSS) is hoping to facilitate organizations achieving secure access through an initiative that measures stages of maturity of Infrastructure to support interoperability and data sharing across organizational boundaries.

Growing Data Management Needs with Healthcare Cyber-security Concerns

Evolution toward precision medicine, digital health, value-based care, and population health management is resulting in increased technology adoption and mounting pressures for interoperability, integration, and movement of data. The discipline of data management grows along with these ballooning data requirements. Concerns about security of healthcare data contained within systems or in motion and growing needs to exchange and have access to data for patient care improvements are often at odds. The balance between data security and data access have always been a priority, and continue so with interoperability, data exchange, and use of information for improved decision making comprising essential components of these initiatives and requirements. A recent survey of a variety of healthcare settings and organizational models, including provider practices and health systems, accountable care organizations (ACOs), federal agency providers, and skilled nursing facilities, as well as third parties such as pharmaceutical, payer, and technology vendors, indicate strong focus on the needs to keep sensitive data secure while requirements of the evolving healthcare marketplace demands the movement of data across organizational lines as well as increased uses of data to support clinical decision making and support improved value of care processes. **FIGURE 14.10** shows priorities of data managers responding to the survey, include PHI protection and HIPAA compliance, security, IT cost reductions, cloud computing, patient-care support, and sustainability as the near-term focal points.

Study findings identify the following findings for the majority of those participants and include (1) evolution of storage options and migration of processing environments to the cloud challenges data managers, as patient-care improvements simultaneously require increased movement of data; (2) delivery of high-quality care requires protecting sensitive data in motion; (3) security of healthcare data is essential to improving patient care outcomes by making pertinent and sensitive data available at the point-of-care; and (4) progress in health data management relies

on excellence in analytical tools applied to healthcare data.

While balancing near-term data management concerns, progress toward long-term goals must be achieved, including compliance with HIPAA data security requirements, data visibility, improvements in security, IT cost reductions, migration to a cloud environment, improved patient care service, and sustainability, as displayed in **FIGURES 14.11** and **14.12**.

All in all, in the rapidly changing healthcare environment, data management requirements increase with equal pressure for timely access to actionable data required at points-of-care, along with access to high-quality analytics. Patient care improvements rely on data integration and interoperability, and analytics to improve patient care, provider experience, and service excellence. Healthcare organizations will be devoting significant attention and resources to these elements of data management.

Cybersecurity in Health Care

In its current state, with few signs of improvement, cybersecurity in health care is very far from perfect. Anything connected to the internet is vulnerable and interoperability plus IoT and data from mobile devices leaves health care wide open, as many of those systems and devices were not developed with security in mind. Security priorities include (1) data privacy; (2) protection from hacking; and (3) an ultimate threat, power loss, or a grid collapse (Towards Data Science, n.d.).

These security problems cannot be ignored in the midst of innovation initiatives to meet HIS requirements of population health management, value-based care, and patient engagement, not to mention excitement about new digital health capabilities. Legacy systems using older technology are in healthcare organizations across the country, medical devices are being used that were designed without HIPAA-level security in mind, and IoT connections make HIPAA requirements to protect PHI infeasible. Whatever time and

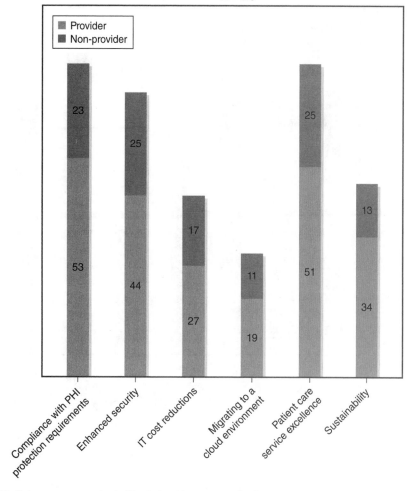

FIGURE 14.10 Data management priorities in healthcare organizations.

Data from Veritas Technologies LLC. (2018). How to Secure Sensitive Data While Supporting Improvements to Patient Care Delivery.

investment is required to achieve this goal, though, must happen if individuals' PHI is to remain secure and private. The next section describes cybersecurity in terms of the current state of health care. This most assuredly is an issue and area that deserves the highest priority, right along with the push to achieve data exchange and interoperability.

The U.S. healthcare system is a complex cacophony of HIS, technologies, devices, and access points struggling to reach some level of standardization but largely non-standardized. The introduction of the EHR systems providing the "home base" for much of this connectivity has occurred at a remarkably rapid pace, with the HITECH MU incentive program resulting in increased EHR adoption from approximately 9.4–96 percent of non-federal acute care hospitals over a period from 2008 to 2016 (ONC: EHR adoption rates on the rise, but barriers to interoperability remain).

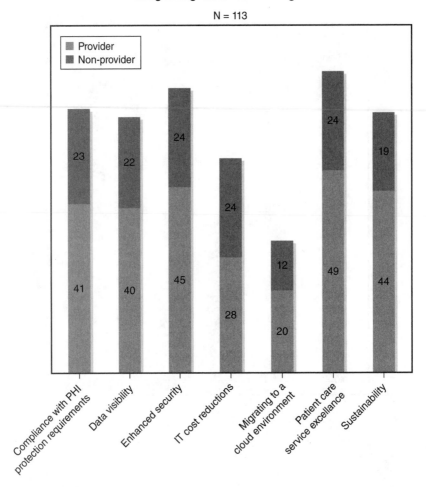

Long-term goals for data management

N = 113

FIGURE 14.11 Long-term data management priorities.

Data from Veritas Technologies LLC. (2018). How to Secure Sensitive Data While Supporting Improvements to Patient Care Delivery.

Use by type of facility varies within this statistic. According to the report, rates of adoption of at least a "basic" EHR system include:

■ Critical access hospitals increased from 20 percent in 2011 to 80 percent in 2015;
■ Rural hospitals increased from 22 percent in 2011 to 80 percent in 2015; and
■ Small hospitals increased from 22 percent in 2011 to 81 percent in 2015.

Significant variation in adoption of "basic" EHR systems by types of specialty

hospitals also was reported, referenced to as a digital divide between types of facilities:

■ Children's hospitals increased from 10 percent in 2008 to 55 percent in 2015;
■ General medicine hospitals increased from 12 percent in 2008 to 84 percent in 2015; and
■ Psychiatric hospitals increased from 7 percent in 2008 to 15 percent in 2015 (Advisory Board, 2016).

The Cybersecurity Act of 2015 established the Health Care Industry Cybersecurity

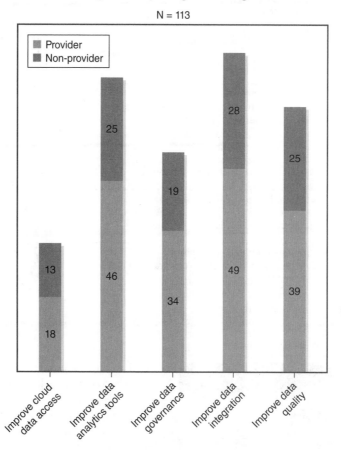

FIGURE 14.12 Data management strategies.

Data from Veritas Technologies LLC. (2018). How to Secure Sensitive Data While Supporting Improvements to Patient Care Delivery.

(HCIC) Task Force, which produced a Report on Improving HCIC, drawing on the help and hard work of a multidisciplinary group of subject matter experts in healthcare technology and security to assess and provide recommendations on the status of cybersecurity of health care in the U.S., in part due to the growing number of cyberattacks on healthcare facilities and technologies. Their recommendations and a few of their findings include the following (**FIGURE 14.13**).

The Task Force identified serious and pervasive vulnerabilities in healthcare information technologies and emphasized the need to address these in anticipation of the push toward interoperability that is a strong initiative in support of population health management, value-based care, and patient engagement. **FIGURE 14.14** identifies the elements of this situation, described as including: (1) insufficient numbers of available security subject matter experts working in healthcare institutions and throughout the healthcare ecosystem; (2) aging, legacy systems built upon older operating systems and lacking necessary security characteristics and capabilities; (3) data exchange and connectivity associated with MU requirements for interoperability preceding establishment of adequately secure infrastructure, networks, training and

Healthcare Cybersecurity is in Critical Condition

Severe lack of security talent
The majority of health delivery orgs lack full-time, qualified security personnel

Legacy equipment
Equipment is running on old, unsupported, and vulnerable operating systems.

Premature/over-connectivity
"Meaningful Use" requirements drove hyper-connectivity without secure design & implementation.

Vulnerabilities impact patient care
One security compromise shut down patient care at Hollywood Presbyterian and UK lospitals

Known vulnerabilities epidemic
One legacy, medical technology had over 1,400 vulnerabilities

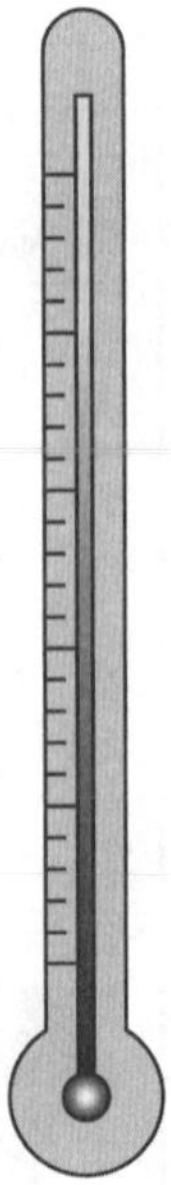

FIGURE 14.13 Cybersecurity risks in health care.

Reproduced from Health Care Industry Cybersecurity Task Force June 2017 Report On Improving Cybersecurity in the Health Care Industry. Retrieved from https://www.phe.gov/Preparedness/planning/CyberTF/Documents/report2017.pdf

Security and EHRs

By definition, EHR systems are intended to consolidate then distribute all data relevant to a patient's healthcare interaction with those involved in the care of that individual. The idea behind the EHR is to provide widespread, real-time access to all data relevant to the patient's care as that care is occurring—to providers, stakeholders, and the patient as well. Implied in this trusted patient-provider-data relationship is *security* of the data.

education, devices, and nodes on IoT capabilities; (4) occurrences of breaches taking advantage of these vulnerabilities that are impacting healthcare delivery, such as the recent security and ransoming incidents that resulted in shutting down Hollywood Presbyterian Hospital and hospitals in the U.K.; and (5) an epidemic of known vulnerabilities, giving the example of one medical technology with 1,400 vulnerabilities identified (Health Care Industry Cybersecurity Task Force, 2017).

With today's pressures to achieve interoperability, the situation is made worse; we are vigorously and, in the admonition of the report, prematurely attempting to connect things that are in this non-standard, non-open state, when the first wave of activity should be to standardize the items being connected to the degree possible, then apply additional technologies to do the connecting and interoperating. As it is, these additional layers are being applied to the highly variable types of systems and technologies largely as is, including medical devices developed without IoT-level security in mind, so that architecturally, we are adding points of vulnerability with each non-secure device added. This adds more variability yet again, exacerbating the problem.

The many points connecting within the healthcare ecosystem that must be taken into consideration in this security agenda are displayed in **FIGURE 14.15**: Healthcare Ecosystem,

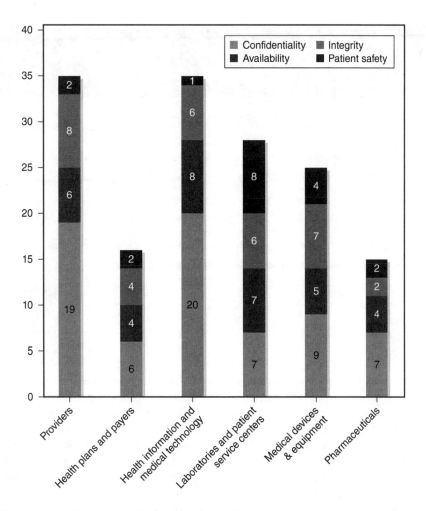

FIGURE 14.14   Security risks across the healthcare value chain.

including participants directly involved in care as well as vendors, health plans, public health services, and providers of supplies and materials involved in the healthcare supply chain.

In 2015, Congress established The HCIC Task Force with the charge to address cybersecurity issues in the healthcare industry as it works to secure and protect data and against incidents, intentional or unintentional. Healthcare data is vulnerable and valuable on dark markets. Healthcare cybersecurity is a key public health concern that needs immediate and aggressive attention. The Task Force identified six imperatives as part of its report:

1. Define and streamline leadership, governance, and expectations for HCIC.

2. Increase the security and resilience of medical devices and health IT.

3. Develop the healthcare workforce capacity necessary to prioritize and ensure cybersecurity awareness and technical capabilities.

🔍 *CASE EXAMPLE: ANOTHER GIANT ENTERS HEALTHCARE DELIVERY IN A NEW WAY*

Mega pharmacy chain CVS Health is on track to close on its acquisition of health insurer Aetna in fourth quarter of 2018 (Japsen, 2018). The potential of expanding urgent care service delivery (coupled with a payer relationship) into the more than 9,800 stores that already have space allocated to healthcare services is truly enormous: this makes health care closer and more convenient for many patients. A merger like this puts pressure on traditional urgent care settings, which differentiate themselves by having greater access to providers and services such as radiology and suturing. But with the Aetna group added to the core, the new CVS delivery channel competes with health systems, and leaves open the opportunity for new ways of delivering care, depending on how technology solutions are added to the mix.

The difference maker very well could be digital health. If secure, convenient, and patient-friendly technology also combines with physical access to healthcare clinics in neighborhoods around the country, the newly combined CVS and Aetna could introduce an entirely new level of disruptive presence in urgent care, the implications of which have not been experienced before. The deep pockets and standardization already in place at CVS present an ability to implement rapidly and broadly. Of course, details and plans must be worked out, but once those are, with Department of Justice approval to move forward, stay tuned: what is certain is that big changes are happening (Japsen, 2018).

4. Increase healthcare industry readiness through improved cybersecurity awareness and education.
5. Identify mechanisms to protect research and development efforts and intellectual property from attacks or exposure.
6. Improve information sharing of industry threats, weaknesses, and mitigations (Health Care Industry Cybersecurity Task Force, 2017).

▶ Issues Regarding Sharing Patient Data

Questions abound regarding exactly which information should be shared and under which circumstances. Certainly, common sense is an important guide here: if patients give permission and request their data be gathered from multiple institutions to aid in their care and prevent them from having to undergo repeated diagnostic tests or repeat answers to the same questions over and over again, *and* these data are presented only to those clinicians who need to see them, then that is appropriate use. Conversely, if those same data somehow become accessible without patients' understanding and permission to business ventures whose interests are more aligned with financial gain associated with the secondary use of data for commercial purposes, then we have crossed the line; those types of uses are inappropriate.

HIPAA is intended to prevent the latter circumstance from happening. Regulators are, in fact, levying stiff financial and organizational penalties for inappropriate uses of data and breaches of patient privacy and data security. HIPAA requires organizations to make earnest efforts to comply with this act's privacy and security requirements. Thus, if all organizations comply with the HIPAA requirements, all is well. Unfortunately, as diligently as organizations and individuals strive to thoroughly and properly implement HIPAA (and they are), mistakes are bound to happen and breaches occur. How many mistakes in this

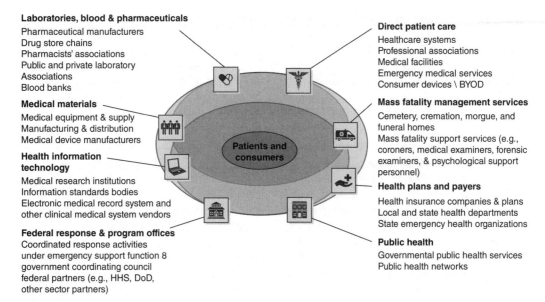

Laboratories, blood & pharmaceuticals
Pharmaceutical manufacturers
Drug store chains
Pharmacists' associations
Public and private laboratory
Associations
Blood banks

Medical materials
Medical equipment & supply
Manufacturing & distribution
Medical device manufacturers

Health information technology
Medical research institutions
Information standards bodies
Electronic medical record system and
other clinical medical system vendors

Federal response & program offices
Coordinated response activities
under emergency support function 8
government coordinating council
federal partners (e.g., HHS, DoD,
other sector partners)

Direct patient care
Healthcare systems
Professional associations
Medical facilities
Emergency medical services
Consumer devices \ BYOD

Mass fatality management services
Cemetery, cremation, morgue, and
funeral homes
Mass fatality support services (e.g.,
coroners, medical examiners, forensic
examiners, & psychological support
personnel)

Health plans and payers
Health insurance companies & plans
Local and state health departments
State emergency health organizations

Public health
Governmental public health services
Public health networks

Patients and consumers

FIGURE 14.15 Healthcare ecosystem.

area would be too many? Do penalties achieve the kind of impact they are intended to make? Would we avoid these problems if we stuck with paper records? Does it matter, or are we too far down this path to turn back?

The world has changed, and information and technology have become integral parts of how we live and work. It is not feasible to imagine that we can turn back, or de-install EHR systems from the many healthcare organizations that have implemented them. In fact, the government has, in effect, mandated their implementation by providing financial incentives and increased reimbursement for healthcare organizations and physician practices that implement these systems according to MU criteria. Ultimately, because the government pays for about half of all medical care in the U.S., the net effect is that those healthcare organizations and physician practices that implement EHR systems that have met MU criteria have a much better chance of remaining financially viable and surviving to care for patients into the future. Those that do not "earn" the enhanced levels of reimbursement for having

met MU criteria probably have a less rosy fate in store. So onward we must march through the swamps of expensive and difficult issues associated with implementing these systems and properly protecting the data they contain for the primary purposes of patient care and the secondary uses for research, policy, and public health (Donovan, 2018).

Another transformative development to consider when thinking about the use and sharing of data is genomic sequencing and the increasingly affordable availability of personal genomic data. How should genomic data be used? Shared? Stored? Does this type of data deserve protection or special treatment and if so, are currently certified EHR systems actually capable of providing this different level of treatment? Even if the systems are capable of making such distinctions, are organizations and the human beings who handle genomic data using those data in ways that are helpful to patients and properly packaging the data for secondary uses? Which policies, regulations, and practices accompany the creation, use, and availability of these powerfully informative data? Should healthcare organizations automatically make personal genomic data available to insurance companies? What are the ethical and moral considerations of payers in the use of these data and the coverage of the insured populations who pay premiums to those insurance companies for their medical and health care? These are just the beginning of a long list of questions dealing with a topic for which there are far more questions than answers. These issues concern not only the future, but also the present. The purpose of this section is not to try to answer all these questions or to stop interest or work in HIS and technology until all of these uncertainties have been resolved, but rather to get the reader thinking about them and to open up dialogue about what might be the best ways to proceed into a future characterized by genomic data's appropriate and specific use.

Stuck Between Two Worlds: Moving from Paper to Electronic Processes

Will we ever be paperless in health care? Do we want to be? For the past 40 years, healthcare organizations have been striving diligently to go electronic, under the assumption that when they do so, eventually paper will be eliminated. In fact, in many cases, once an EHR system is in place, the amount of paper produced and stored increases rather than decrease. This result comes as a surprise to many people, who think such an occurrence is counterintuitive. Paying close attention to forms policies, record storage practices, and moving the entire record to electronic is key to reducing this problem and must be part of the implementation process and objectives.

Research has shown that serious errors occur in dual media environments, i.e., a combination of electronic and paper, which is the case of many health providers. In this study, of 3,100 reports of EHR-related incidents, 85 percent were in mixed paper and EHR system environments, and 8 percent of those incidents created serious patient safety situations (LeGate, 2013). In truth, most EHRs are not a complete replacement for all paper processes in terms of the functionality they provide. Since most providers are using "basic" EHR system functionality, the combination of paper and electronic records and data is commonplace. The discipline of defining, redesigning, streamlining, simplifying, and standardizing processes and workflows is vital to digital health usability and viability. Letting go of traditional ways of doing work and automating and integrating the many paper forms used in healthcare organizations is a very difficult thing to do and is clearly one of the greatest struggles in HIS implementation. The relatively few "paperless" healthcare environments that exist in health care tend to be implementations that were built "from the ground up"—in other words, the systems implemented were part of a brand-new building or practice that opened from its first day of operation without paper. This is not the typical scenario for HIS implementations, of course. Most HIS implementations take place during the course and in the midst of an organization's normal operation and are rather painful transitions from all paper, and legacy systems, to new automated systems, resulting in a mixture of automated and paper workflows. It is only through an incredibly concerted effort to get rid of the paper, form by form, process by process, that the use of paper can be minimized and, in rare cases, eliminated. And, of course, any paper used in the care or accounting functions of a healthcare entity must be saved, typically forever. Many organizations invest in scanning old medical records into new EHR systems as a way to reduce paper charts significantly, although this process is very expensive and must be factored into the overall cost and effort associated with an EHR implementation project. Moreover, even if all the paper charts are gone, paper exists everywhere in organizations—in clinical and administrative offices, and nooks and crannies throughout.

The days of paperless healthcare environments, while closer, still lie in the future. Of course, paper records can be inappropriately accessed just as electronic data can, so the notion that only electronically processed and stored patient charts and financial accounts are subject to the risks associated with inappropriate access and breaches of PHI security, privacy, and confidentiality is false. Paper records also must be protected according to HIPAA standards and requirements.

▶ Future Impact of HIS and Technology on Research, Policy, and Public Health

Data emanate from numerous new electronic sources—from EHR systems going into healthcare organizations across the country, from other HIS, from mobile devices monitoring patient conditions such as diabetes and heart disease, and from sharing of data between many organizations through HIEs. Opportunities abound for obtaining HIPAA-compliant data from myriad sources for purposes of research, policy analysis, and public health purposes. As described in other chapters of this text, business and clinical informatics, access to Big Data, policy analysis, public health data surveillance, reporting, and health status insights are there for the taking. Certainly, the disciplined management and proper treatment of these data and the challenges associated with normalizing data from many disparate systems lie before us as obstacles to be overcome, but new integration technologies are on the near horizon to help solve these problems.

Healthcare professionals are applying many lessons from the mobile technologies, retail, and telecommunications industries as they enter the wide-open healthcare data analytics frontier, and their exciting new solutions will create vast opportunities and wonderful "sandboxes" for researchers, policy analysts, and public health professionals alike. For example, predictive analytics accessing Big Data can improve quality of care immeasurably by sweeping through combinations of data stores to find and address serious and difficult to identify issues such as managing sepsis (a life-threatening blood infection that strikes quickly) before it gets out of control. Sepsis is both deadly and quick in its action: patients who get antibiotics more than six hours after the infection starts have only a 40 percent chance of survival. In fact, sepsis causes more deaths each year than prostate cancer, breast cancer, and HIV/AIDS combined. By informing clinicians in real time about this condition and enabling them to intervene early in the disease course, HIS and technology could ensure that ineffective treatments that will not work can be changed in time to save the patient.

As seen in this example, Big Data enables clinicians to explore large data sets and identify difficult to find problems and solutions. They can adopt a population health management perspective and gather intelligence regarding how their healthcare organization is performing with targeted conditions, based on real-time analysis driven by intelligent algorithms data and their own reality, not general assumptions or national statistics. From there, clinicians can make changes in real time, can compare their performance to that of peers within their organization, and can benchmark their outcomes against those in other populations. The timeliness of these analytical data queries surpasses that of the traditional retrospective data reporting and analytics, through which trends may be spotted, but only when it is too late to do anything other than identify flawed processes so as to prevent the same problems from occurring again. The possibilities are tremendous in this unfolding arena of near real-time analytics and connecting multiple disparate data sources to find clear areas for improving clinical outcomes and cost performance.

From Public Health to Personalized Medicine

The HIS innovations described in this chapter are needed tools to achieve population health, improve public health, and make personalized medicine a reality. Personalized medicine occurs when providers, with the aid of diagnostic and genetic tests, identify specific biological characteristics that help specify which medical treatments and procedures will work best for a patient. Working in concert, providers and patients agree on targeted treatment and prevention plans using the diagnostic information along with the patient's other data and preferences. Implementation of personalized medicine entails an implementation progression including many of the digital health capabilities described in this chapter, as well as strategies involving patients, education and awareness, secure infrastructure, value-based care processes and reimbursement, and access to care for these types of services and initiatives (**FIGURE 14.16**).

▶ HIS Learning Culture

Creating a culture of collaboration in the organization means finding the balance between collaboration and control, access and security, discipline in managing information and systems and freedom in insight, information, knowledge, and transparently reporting and studying errors or near errors that occur, so that root causes and solutions can be determined and addressed. Important in establishing an open, trusting, and responsible culture is the development of guiding principles. Those expressions of an organization's closest held ideals, priorities, and desired behaviors that should be deferred to not just when things are going well, but especially when they are not. Guiding principles express emotional content as well as decision making guidance. When a group of people with different viewpoints come together to make a decision, their ability to hold steady and listen to one another so that various viewpoints are considered sincerely, is one important use of guiding principles (Oliver & Jacobs, 2007).

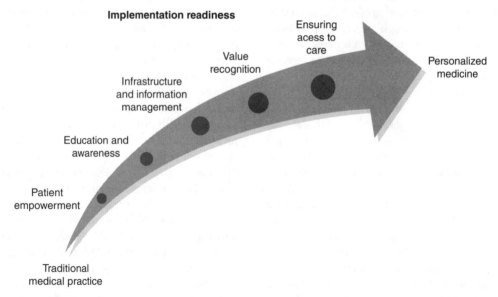

FIGURE 14.16 Progression of strategies by area of need for the transition from traditional medical practice to personalized medicine.

Data from Pritchard, D., et al. (2016). Strategies for integrating personalized medicine into healthcare practice. Future Medicine Personalized Medicine.

It is important to point out that this chapter is intended to point out the importance of developing, encouraging, and protecting a culture of learning for the organization launching out on the forever journey of HIS Strategic Planning and the impact that HIS can enable on patient care, providers, and an organization and very nature and capabilities.

Summary

"When people say, 'Wow, there's a lot of challenges,' I always say, 'There's no better time to be alive.'"

Sundar Pichai, Gelles (2018)

Summarizing the future of HIS and technology is a mighty task, but if we follow along with the themes of this text, we can track the types of changes in technologies and advancement of opportunities to improve health status, clinical outcomes, cost performance, and the outlook for our future in health care.

The predominant change in HIS and technology going into the future is based on the fact that it is now ubiquitous: IT infrastructure is present in all aspects of our lives in an increasing number of forms, such as mobile devices, sensors, cell and smartphones, Internet access, Big Data analytics, personalized data, and other forms of technology and data. More than ever, as technologies allow for vast data sharing possibilities, sound data management practices and the discipline of data stewardship become essential. Personalized care, therapies, and preventive strategies are all made feasible by the pervasive availability of data, both organizationally and personally. eHealth, mHealth, social media, telemedicine, and telehealth offer new opportunities in health care and public health, capitalizing on technological advancements in other avenues of our lives. The growth of HIS provides opportunities for eHealth and mHealth to be productively used in the informatics, research, policy, and public health spheres as represented in the HIS model.

Emerging technologies are beginning to undergo pilot testing in health care and public health, and the outlook is already promising although inflated. With their ability to improve healthcare services and access to health care and information, these technologies invite patients to get engaged in the management of their health. They provide opportunity for citizens around the world to get access to health data and be active participants in their health. The human–machine relationship will become ever more important in such a world, and creative solutions to improving human–machine, machine–machine, and human–human connections must accompany this evolution. The Hype Cycle for emerging technologies highlights a select few among thousands of new tools, all in different stages of development and adoption, and it remains to be seen which ones will stick.

Informatics is evolving in sync with the application of new technologies, resulting in new options and better-informed practices of medicine, nursing, other clinical and business disciplines, and public health. Data and analytics are evolving owing to the explosion in data volumes and greater accessibility to such data as a result of widespread adoption of EHR systems and other HIS; such data and analytics have the potential to both inform and revolutionize clinical care, healthcare and population health management, and public health opportunities.

The government's role in health care in the U.S. is tracking along with progress in the areas of EHR systems and their adoption, incentives for HIS and technology advancements, and goals of the Affordable Care Act. The government's role in HIS and EHR system adoption through HITECH, HIPAA compliance, and public health measures will play an influential part in the continued progress, innovation, and participation in these arenas.

Innovators and entrepreneurs who develop new HIS and technology products are also making key contributions to the progress and evolution in health care. New applications of technologies developed in other industries such as telecommunications are finding exciting places in improving the delivery of health care and the availability of data for analytics and public health advancements in the U.S.

The blue sky of inflection of healthcare and emerging technologies is not without clouds: issues of unintended consequences and ethical considerations, if not outright dilemmas, arise with new uses of HIS and technology. In this age of systems interoperability and data exchange, finding the balance between access to systems and data versus protecting the security of PHI is a continual struggle that must be debated and attended to diligently. This challenge involves not only ensuring the security of systems, but also educating and training the human beings who handle those data and access those systems so their behaviors and choices will protect the privacy of the data. Sharing patient data safely should be part of every healthcare organization's overall data management strategy and responsibilities, whether those data exist on paper or on a hard drive.

Realistically, the idea of a future without paper remains far from reality. How long will it take us to get there? Will some organizations be able to afford the sustained effort to get there? Is this truly the ultimate goal? Diligence in streamlining and simplifying workflows and processes as part of HIS implementations can help organizations gradually eliminate the need to print and maintain partial paper portions of the record alongside EHR systems, thereby improving efficiency and realizing the gains of electronic systems throughout healthcare organizations and public health (and saving many trees in the process).

Finally, health professionals must be involved in HIS development every step of the way to create the kinds of systems we need in today's challenging health and healthcare environment. Also, each and every health profession now includes HIS in order to perform its work, and their training and education must include the newly emerging technical aspects of their profession. So clinical, business, and technology health professions now can only be done proficiently with HIS knowledge, ability, and activity. The U.S. health system has perhaps some of the greatest challenges to overcome compared to other countries, due to its reliance on the fee-for-service reimbursement methodology now attempting to evolve to a value-based system, where providers are taking up more of the risk associated with cost and quality outcomes and successful management of populations. U.S. reliance on the vendor marketplace as the source of solutions complicates and increases to cost of automation of health care. Added to this challenge is the fact that acute care can no longer be the primary focus of hospitals and health systems. Value-based care, prevention, wellness, chronic care management, and care coordination now dominate the scene, while our structures, systems, and professionals previously set for localized, acute, medical, sickness-based scenarios. Our system of care must change enabled by the technology to support care across the continuum, with secure interoperability, digital health capabilities, patient engagement, and new modalities of care that meet the patients where they live and carry about their daily activities.

Our health depends on it.

Key Terms

Big Data	Capitated plans	Digital health
Business intelligence/clinical intelligence (BI/CI)	Cloud computing	eHealth
	Data standards	Inflection point

Machine-to-machine
(M2M)
mHealth

Personal health information
(PHI)
Quantified self
Telehealth

Telemedicine
Ubiquitous
technology
Virtual reality

Discussion Questions

1. Does "ubiquitous availability" of HIS technologies systems mean?
2. Place yourself in an imaginary future time—say, 5 or 10 years from now—and describe health care, the use of emerging technologies, research, and public health scenarios. What are potential improvements in each of those scenarios and what are potential problems?
3. Which new technologies will likely have an impact on health care and public health? Consider mobile devices, expanding Internet access, Big Data and analytics, smart/mobile phones, and wireless technologies.
4. eHealth, mHealth, social media, and telemedicine are overlapping but useful labels for capabilities slightly unique from one another. Discuss the scope and impact of each, and challenges in their use in health care and public health.
5. If you were the administrator of a community hospital, would you support the use of social media? Why or why not? What about if you were the chief legal counsel? The vice president of marketing?

6. Use the HIS model to describe ways in what HIS and management support mHealth.
7. Emerging technologies and human–machine relationships go hand in hand. In what ways do improvements in human–machine relationships help the advancement and application of emerging technologies to health care and public health?
8. Where do new technologies used in health care fall today on the Hype Cycle? Which do you think have the most promise?
9. Do you expect the U.S. federal government to keep its money and hand in efforts to advance HIS, especially EHR systems? What are its reasons for stimulating the adoption of EHR systems? Will those reasons persist into the future? Is there a relationship between the government's interest in EHR systems and interoperability of systems and its interest in public health?
10. Describe the most concerning of the issues and ethical considerations described in this chapter. Which of these issues seem solvable, and which do not?

References

Advisory Board. (2016, June 2). Fewer hospitals are integrating EHR data. Retrieved from ly-briefing/2016/06/02/ehr-adoption-rates-rising-barriers-to-interoperability

Agar, N. (2018, May 17). WMIF, First Look. Retrieved from https://www.youtube.com/watch?v=A0KSo3DfV5Q

Agency for Healthcare Research and Quality. (n.d.). Health information technology ambulatory safety and quality. Retrieved from http://healthit.ahrq.gov/sites/default/files/docs/page/findings-and-lessons-from-the-improving-quality-through-clinician-use-of-health-it.pdf

Allen, M. (2018, July 17). Health insurers are vacuuming up details about you—And it could raise your rates. Retrieved from https://www.propublica.org/article/health-insurers-are-vacuuming-up-details-about-you-and-it-could-raise-your-rates

Bates, D. W., & Singh, H. (2018). Two decades since To Err Is Human: An assessment of progress and emerging priorities in patient safety. *Health Affairs.* Retrieved from https://www.healthaffairs.org/doi /abs/10.1377/hlthaff.2018.0738?utm_source =Newsletter&utm_medium=email&utm_content =Health+Affairs++November+Issue%3A+Patient +Safety%3B+What+the+Midterms+Mean+For +Health+Care%3B+The+Medicaid+Wave%3B +Hatch+Amendment&utm_campaign=HASU +%28Copy%29

Baum, S. (2013, July 20). Wow of the week: A detailed breakdown of how hospitals are using social media. Retrieved from http://medcitynews.com/2013/07/wow -of-the-week-a-detailed-breakdown-of-how -hospitals-are-using-social-media/#ixzz2dhgapI7Z

Bivens, J. (2018, October 10). *The unfinished business of health reform—Reining in market power to restrain costs without sacrificing quality or access.* Retrieved from https://www.epi.org/publication/health-care-report/

Brino, A. (2014). RCM trends reveal haves and have-nots. *HealthcareITNews.* Retrieved from https:// www.healthcareitnews.com/news/rcm-trends -reveal-haves-have-nots

Conn, J. (2014, February 3). HHS issues rule granting patients direct access to lab test results. Retrieved from http://www.modernhealthcare.com/article/20140203 /NEWS/302039958?AllowView=VDl3UXk1TzdDdm VCbkJiYkY0M3hlMEdwakVVZEQrND0=&utm _source=link-20140203-NEWS-302039958&utm _medium=email&utm_campaign=hits&utm _name=top#

Dickson, V. (2018). Chronic care management program showing signs of saving money, improving care. Retrieved from https://www.modernhealthcare.com /article/20180220/NEWS/180229988

Dietsche, E. (2018). Google taps Geisinger CEO to oversee health efforts. Retrieved from https://medcitynews .com/2018/11/google-geisinger-ceo/?utm _campaign=MCN%20Daily%20Top%20Stories&utm _source=hs_email&utm_medium=email&utm _content=67393963&_hsenc=p2ANqtz --jPU5_Ot4WcB8LRWS5b2gZh03znzyG 2tAzIFNV4NBPrqgKtPV7_Zup IqeNXFbr3yYcBd06DT48HkRKqh40 7HqSvLmZQQ&_hsmi=67393963

dw2. (2012). Smartphone technology, super-convergence, and the great inflection of medicine. Retrieved from http://dw2blog.com/2012/03/25/smartphone -technology-super-convergence-and-the-great -inflection-of-medicine/

Feeley, D. (2017, November 28). The triple aim or the quadruple aim? Four points to help set your strategy. Retrieved from http://www.ihi.org/communities /blogs/the-triple-aim-or-the-quadruple-aim-four -points-to-help-set-your-strategy

Galewitz, P. (2018). Some Florida medicare advantage plans shift their financial risk to doctors. *Kaiser Health News.* Retrieved from https://www.miamiherald.com /latest-news/article219445380.html

Gartner. (2013, August 19). *Gartner's 2013 Hype Cycle for Emerging Technologies Maps Out Evolving Relationship between Humans and Machines.* Stamford, CT. Retrieved from http://www.gartner.com/newsroom /id/2575515

Gawande, A. (2018). Why doctors hate their computers. *The New Yorker.* Retrieved from https://www .newyorker.com/magazine/2018/11/12/why-doctors -hate-their-computers

Gelles, D. (2018). Sundar Pichai of Google: Technology doesn't solve humanity's problems. *The New York Times.* Retrieved from https://www.nytimes.com/2018/11/08 /business/sundar-pichai-google-corner-office .html?emc=edit_ca_20181109&nl=california-today& nlid=5142229720181109&te=1

Geneia. (2015). *Geneia survey finds physicians believe quality patient time may be gone—Invites physicians to compete in the joy of medicine challenge.* Retrieved from https:// www.geneia.com/news-events/press-releases/2015 /march/geneia-survey-finds-physicians-believe -quality-patient-time-may-be-gone

Health and Medicine Division of the National Academies of Sciences, Engineering, and Medicine. (2011). *Health IT and patient safety: Building safer systems for better care.* Retrieved from www.nationalacademies .org/hmd/Reports/2011/Health_IT_and _Patient_Safety_Building_Safer_Systems_For_Better _Care.aspx

Health Care Industry Cybersecurity Task Force. (2017). *Report on improving cybersecurity in the health care industry.* Retrieved from https://www.phe .gov/Preparedness/planning/CyberTF/Documents /report2017.pdf

Holland, K. (2018). *6 Tech innovations that will shape healthcare in 2018.* Retrieved from https://www .healthline.com/health-news/tech-innovations -healthcare-2018#4

Japsen, B. (2018, November 5). The pharmacy chain could be a threat to hospitals and health systems by entering into the urgent care market. *HealthLeaders.* Retrieved from https://www.healthleadersmedia.com/strategy /if-cvs-bets-big-urgent-care-hospitals-should-worry

Johnson, T. (2017, December 8). *Strategic planning in the healthcare industry.* Retrieved from https://www .balancedscorecard.org/BSC-Basics/Blog /ArtMID/2701/ArticleID/1119/Strategic -Planning-in-the-Healthcare-Industry

Landi, H. (2017). *Study: In use of advanced EHR functions, digital divide is emerging.* Retrieved from https:// www.healthcare-informatics.com/news-item/ehr /study-use-advanced-ehr-functions-digital-divide -emerging

Landi, H. (2018). *Study shows rise in physician burnout, female doctors report higher levels of dissatisfaction.* Retrieved from https://www.healthcare-informatics.com/news-item/ehr/study-shows-rise-physician-burnout-female-doctors-report-higher-levels-dissatisfaction

Mace, S. (2013, August 3). Disconnected health data "beyond absurd," says innovator and patient. *HealthLeaders Media.* Retrieved from http://www.healthleadersmedia.com/page-3/TEC-294920/Disconnected-Health-Data-Beyond-Absurd-Says-Innovator-and-Patient

McCluskey, P. D. (2015). Partners' $1.2b patient data system seen as key to future. Retrieved from https://www.bostonglobe.com/business/2015/05/31/partners-launches-billion-electronic-health-records-system/oo4nJJW2rQyfWUWQlvydkK/story.html

Monica, K. (2018a). eClinicalWorks launches new EHR-integrated opioid risk tool. Retrieved from https://ehrintelligence.com/news/eclinicalworks-launches-new-ehr-integrated-opioid-risk-tool?eid=CXTEL000000104554

Monica, K. (2018b). 93% of MIPS eligible clinicians earned federal incentives in 2017. Retrieved from https://ehrintelligence.com/news/93-of-mips-eligible-clinicians-earned-federal-incentives-in-2017?eid=CXTEL000000104554&elqCampaignId=7443&elqTrackId=0cd01e1b4b31454c86cdb821168aedfa&elq=5576b79665194335ba3ca1d101596e4d&elqaid=7866&elqat=1&elqCampaignId=7443

Nash, D. (2018, October 26). Our broken healthcare system: How scared should we be? *MedPage Today.* Retrieved from https://www.medpagetoday.com/columns/focusonpolicy/75947

Pelletier, S. G. (2014, January). Bridging the gap: Integrating electronic health records into medical education. *AAMC Reporter.*

Phillips, L., Dowling, C., Shaffer, K., Hodas, N., & Volkova, S. (2017). *Using social media to predict the future: A systematic literature review.* Retrieved from https://arxiv.org/pdf/1706.06134.pdf

Reed, T. (2018). Study: It's still too easy to make mistakes in pediatric electronic health records. Retrieved from https://www.fiercehealthcare.com/hospitals-health-systems/study-it-s-still-too-easy-to-make-mistakes-pediatric-electronic-health?mkt_tok=eyJpIjoiTm1OalkyVXhNVGN3

WVdVeCIsInQiOiJiYjhSMFFEb2gxXC9TZU9HRUF2dStqaFREWmVPY005MFF2a3dvYTJTT2w2dlBtd1JYQ1VxcmgzaW5uMHh6dWQWQ5N3laeVpqZ1jZLZ2UxWWFzMjNMM11PZGZKZE56SGlDcmpTcU5GGXC9KRmpkUpknkNENIVGhlaU42UmNWa11BbGtEUEdkIn0%3D&mrkid=751246

Spitzer, J. (2018, July 12). Epic founder Judy Faulkner comes in 3rd on Forbes' richest women list. Retrieved from https://www.beckershospitalreview.com/healthcare-information-technology/epic-founder-judy-faulkner-comes-in-3rd-on-forbes-richest-women-list.html

Steciw, A. (n.d.). What is telemedicine, and how does it affect health IT? Retrieved from http://searchhealthit.techtarget.com/healthitexchange/healthitpulse/what-is-telemedicine-and-how-does-it-affect-health-it/

Stucke, R. S., Kelly, J. L., Mathis, K. A., Hill, M. V., & Richard, J. B. (2018, August 22). Association of the use of a mandatory prescription drug monitoring program with prescribing practices for patients undergoing elective surgery. *JAMA Surgery.* Retrieved from https://jamanetwork.com/journals/jamasurgery/article-abstract/2696623

The Economist. (2012, May 3). The quantified self: Counting every movement. *The Economist, Technology Quarterly: Q12012.* Retrieved from http://www.economist.com/node/21548493

The Medical Futurist. (2018). How to prepare the future generation of physicians. Retrieved from https://medicalfuturist.com/how-to-prepare-the-future-generation-of-physicians

The Statistics Portal. (n.d.). Number of smartphone users in the United States from 2010 to 2022 (in millions)*. Retrieved from https://www.statista.com/statistics/201182/forecast-of-smartphone-users-in-the-us/

Topol, E. (n.d.). *The creative destruction of medicine: How the digital revolution will create better health care.* New York, NY: Basic Books.

Towards Data Science. (n.d.). IoT + machine learning is going to change the world. Retrieved from https://towardsdatascience.com/iot-machine-learning-is-going-to-change-the-world-7c4e0cd7ac32

World Health Organization. (n.d.). *Trade, foreign policy, diplomacy and health: E-health.* Retrieved from http://www.who.int/trade/glossary/story021/en/

Glossary

Accountable Care Organizations (ACOs) A group of physicians, hospitals, and other healthcare providers who come together voluntarily, as part of cooperative frameworks to deliver care in the most effective and low-cost settings in conjunction with the Affordable Care Act and other government-sponsored initiatives, and to give coordinated high-quality care to patients. ACOs coordinate care from primary to acute care, depending on the needs of the patient.

Activation Applying a new software system to do the real work of an organization or putting the system into production.

Active directory (AD) Servers that maintain lists of users, computers, and printers, along with any associated passwords and security settings. A misconfigured or inaccessible AD server can cause users and computers to have access, connectivity, and password issues.

Adoption To adopt disruptive health information systems (HIS) and technology means that organizations adapt to automated work processes—a huge change from the paper-based processes and workflows that typically take much longer with even the most conservative of estimates, and through adoption the providers and the healthcare industry change the ways that clinical care is provided and the work of health care is done.

Adoption curve A theory to explain the adoption of disruptive technology as described by Rogers in 1962 in his landmark book, *Diffusion of Innovations*.

Advisory groups End-user groups that play a critical part in designing HIS plans and projects by providing information to developers and implementation teams. These multidisciplinary advisory groups also serve as steering committees throughout the HIS life cycle.

Affordable Care Act Legislation passed by Congress and signed into law by President Barack Obama in 2010, including a "Patient's Bill of Rights."

Agency for Healthcare Research and Quality (AHRQ) One of 12 agencies within the U.S. Department of Health and Human Services. Its mission is to improve the quality, safety, efficiency, and effectiveness of health care for Americans. AHRQ sponsors, conducts, and disseminates research to aid in informed decision making and improve the quality of healthcare services. Formerly known as the Agency for Health Care Policy and Research.

Aggregation The act of combining data points, such as the diagnoses and lab results of patients, with other points of data for the purpose of analysis. Aggregated data enhance healthcare providers' information and knowledge through tracking, reporting, and predicting health status, treatment outcomes, cost ratios and financial performance, and a myriad of other useful analyses.

Alleviating Clerical Work Computerization of clinical tasks transfers tasks from paper forms and manual processes with the aim of relieving health professionals of many mundane manual tasks, while improving efficiencies and documentation for reimbursement and analytics purposes. However, evidence is building that providers are frustrated and that many physicians and patients feel the benefits of electronic health record (EHR) systems are overshadowed by the detractors.

Alliance for Nursing Informatics (ANI) Supported by both American Medical Informatics Association (AMIA) and Health Information Management Systems Society (HIMSS), ANI is a professional group that represents more than 2000 nurses and brings together 18 independent nursing informatics groups.

All-in-one (AIO) computers Integrate the computer case and system components into the monitor so that the entire computer is contained all-in-one unit (except for the keyboard and mouse), which is typically a 24- to 27-inch LCD plasma screen, often needed in clinical areas with space constraints, such as in operating room (OR) or emergency room (ER).

Alternative Payment Models (APMs) Provide a method whereby Medicare may compensate higher rates to healthcare providers for their Medicare beneficiaries. Most providers who participate in APMs will also be subject to MIPS, but will receive favorable scoring with compatible higher reimbursement rates.

Ambulatory care systems CIS applications that assist caregivers in performing consultations, treatments, or interventions in an outpatient setting, such as a medical clinic. These have needs similar to those served by inpatient clinical and business applications, but slightly different priorities. Two important areas of emphasis in ambulatory care settings are financial and administrative systems—which include billing, eligibility determinations and authorizations, claims processing, general financial, human resources, and materials management applications—and clinical systems—which support scheduling, appointment reminders, EHRs and personal health records (PHRs), transcription, prescription management, disease management, and patient communications.

American College of Medical Practice Executives (ACMPE) A membership association for professional administrators and leaders of medical group practices.

American Health Information Management Association (AHIMA) A health information management professional association with more than 67,000 members that administers accreditation for Registered Health Information Administrators (AHIAs) and certification for coders and health information technicians (Registered Health Information Technicians (RHITs).

American Medical Informatics Association (AMIA) An association of leading informaticists: clinicians, scientists, researchers, educators, students, and other informatics professionals who rely on data to connect people, information, and technology. This organization holds conferences at which members present findings from studies and reports on informatics development and use of systems to enhance their disciplines.

American Recovery and Reinvestment Act (ARRA, 2009) Commonly referred to as the Stimulus Act. This act's Title IV set Health Information Technology for Economic and Clinical Health Act (HITECH) into place. This act (1) created a strategic plan for a nationwide interoperable health information system, a plan that must be updated annually; and (2) called for a leadership structure consisting of two committees to advise the Office of the National Coordinator, a Health Information Policy Committee, and a Health Information Standards Committee.

Analytics The process of inspecting and evaluating aggregated data, looking for patterns and statistics to gain insights that help improve processes, creating information leading to new knowledge that improve efficiency and effectiveness of health care and public health.

Ancillary clinical support processes The wide range of healthcare services, such as laboratory testing, radiology, pharmacy, etc., provided to support the work of healthcare institutions and providers. These services can be classified into three categories: diagnostic, therapeutic, and custodial.

Annual wellness visit and pre-work G0438 and G0439 Annual wellness visits involve the completion of questionnaires by Medicare patients for either new or established patients as the code does not differentiate. The initial AWV, G0438, is performed on patients who have been enrolled with Medicare for more than 1 year. A patient is eligible for her/his subsequent AWV, G0439, one year after her/his initial visit.

Antivirus Software designed to identify and destroy computer viruses or other malware.

Appliances Servers that are fully supported and managed by a vendor (usually installed with a proprietary operating system and software) are called appliances. They are typically self-contained, requiring only a network connection; are easy and fast to deploy; and can be a preferred method for delivering a server application, as healthcare organizations or customers do not have to address all the complications and delays involved in setting up the server themselves.

Artificial intelligence (AI) A way of making a computer, a computer-controlled robot, or a software program perform analyses, "learn" patterns, and predict in similar manner to ways intelligent humans think.

Automation The use of technology to optimize productivity in the workflows, processes, production of goods, and delivery of services.

Backbone networks (BNs) A part of computer network that interconnects various network components, providing a path for the exchange of information between different LANs or subnetworks. A backbone can tie together diverse networks in the same building, in different buildings in a campus environment, or over wide areas.

Bar-code scanners Used to automate the input of patient and medical information and supplies, including patient ID from bar-coded wristbands or ID tags, and medication administration that uses pharmacy bar-coded labels. Bar-code scanners are manufactured in wired or wireless configurations, with the wireless modality being both more popular and more expensive.

Basic EHR system An EHR system that has functionality on at least one clinical unit that includes patient demographics, physician notes, nursing assessments, patient problem lists, laboratory and radiology reports, and diagnostic test results, as well as computerized ordering for medications.

Big Data A recently coined term to describe how the types and amounts of data or information are becoming incredibly large. Understanding data/information's relevance to the world and to specific industries will increasingly become an imperative to optimize performance.

Biomedical informatics Informatics as applied to health care; an interdisciplinary field that studies uses of biomedical data, information, and knowledge for scientific study, clinical care, analytics, and decision making. Both art and science, it is aimed at improving and transforming health and clinical care, organizations, processes, and research capabilities through the use of HIS and technology.

Blade server technology Represents an advance in increasing server density and reducing server costs. Blade servers are stored in a compact enclosure called a blade chassis, which has a reduced size and uses less energy. These types of servers boast higher availabilities achieved by sharing common components, such as network, storage, cabling, and power infrastructure. Three-to-four times more blade servers can fit in the same cabinet space as rack-mounted servers.

Blockchain Middleware that is, a distributed, immutable ledger for transactions and data, with applications anticipated in everything from supply chain to patient identity. The hope is that blockchain, or distributed ledger, or "the blockchain" depending on one's vernacular can be transformative in solving some of health care's most persistent problems: identity, data integrity, patient control over their own data.

Branch circuit monitoring system (BCMS) Allows to fully utilize power infrastructure and manage capacity as data center grows and changes. Whether you are retrofitting an existing facility, or planning for growth or new construction, BCM system can help reduce energy costs, track power usage, and prevent downtime.

Bring-your-own-device (BYOD) Method requiring organizational information technology policies and standards to implement in organizations, in which increasing numbers of end users seek to use their personal smart phones and/or tablets for both personal and work use.

Business continuity plan (BCP) A plan to help ensure that business processes can continue during a time of emergency or disaster during which computer systems and/or networks are down. Such emergencies or disasters might include a fire or any other case where HIS systems and thus clinical care and administrative functions are not able to occur as they would under normal conditions.

Business intelligence (BI) The practice of pulling together or aggregating data from a variety of systems and sources into meaningful and useful information to support decision making and insights for business purposes.

Campus networks A proprietary local area network (LAN) or a set of interconnected LANs serving a healthcare organization, corporation, government agency, university, or similar organization. In this context, a typical **campus** encompasses a set of buildings in close proximity.

Canned A predefined report from an HIS menu that end users can access regularly. An example would be an accounts receivable report that has been designed with the same information and is updated for use over a repetitive, determined interval (e.g., daily, weekly, monthly).

Capital budget Includes a summary of all costs needed to carry out projects and cost estimate detailing start-up and intermittent capital expenditures.

Capitated plans A healthcare plan that allows payment of a flat fee for each patient it covers. Under a capitated contract, a commerncial payer, HMO, or managed care organization pays a fixed amount of money for its members to the healthcare provider.

CCM 99490 Medicare began reimbursing for chronic care management (CCM) services using CPT Code 99490. This service is for Medicare patients with multiple chronic conditions and is non-face-to-face care, often enabled by a digital health platform and call center capability.

Care management Connects patients with providers in ways that personalize the interaction based on the preferences and conditions and/or diagnoses of the patient. Key characteristics include a digital health platform connected to patients, their family, and caregivers, integrated with provider EHR systems and patient medical devices. A healthy care management platform makes way for regular patient interaction with remote providers who provide medical advice based on a personalized care plan as well as behavioral, nutritional, and preventive support.

CCM behavioral healthcare management 20 minutes 99484 A CPT code that involves at least 20 minutes of *non-face-to-face* care management time directed by a practitioner, per calendar month for any behavioral health or psychiatric condition being treated by the primary care practitioner, including substance use disorders, that, in the clinical judgment of the practitioner, warrants BHI services.

CCM initiation pre-work G0506 The G0506 code is a CPT code that includes comprehensive assessment and care planning for patients requiring chronic care management services. It is particularly appropriate when the CCM initiating visit is a less complex visit (such as a level 2 or 3 evaluation and management (E/M) visit). G0506 can be billed along with higher level E/M visits if the practitioner's effort and time exceeded the usual effort described in the initial visit E/M code. G0506 can also be billed when the initiating E/M visit addresses problems unrelated to Chronic Care Management and the CCM-related work is not included in the initial visit code.

Centers for Disease Control and Prevention Provides online resources for dependable health information.

Centers for Medicare & Medicaid Services (CMS) A federal agency that administers Medicare, Medicaid, and the State Children's Health Insurance Program; a lead agency in implementing health care and healthcare reform in the United States under HITECH, ACA, and HIPAA standards and regulations.

Central data repositories (CDRs) A location that serves to store large amounts of information, provides a replication of data from the source systems, organizes the data for extraction for analytics, and may provide an environment for disaster recovery. Also called a data warehouse.

Central processing unit (CPU) The hardware within a computer that carries out the instructions of a computer program and operating system.

Certified Professional in Healthcare Information and Management Systems (CPHIMS) A professional certification program for healthcare information and management systems professionals, administered by HIMSS.

Change management An approach to transitioning employees, departments, and entire organizations toward a future state. In HIS, this refers to helping people transition to the new HIS system, workflows, and processes.

Change Management Board (CMB) A committee that makes decisions regarding whether proposed changes to a software project should be implemented. The CMB is constituted of the organization's project stakeholders or their representatives, and information technology leadership.

Chief information officer (CIO) The chief executive in charge of HIS and information technology at a healthcare organization.

Chief medical informatics officer (CMIO) A physician appointed to the HIS department or team who represents the perspective, leadership, processes, workflows, and needs of physicians to shape the HIS architecture and systems, during planning, implementations, and on-going support phases of HIS.

Chief Nursing Officer (CNO) or Chief Nursing Informatics Officer (CNIO) Sometimes called chief nursing executive or chief nursing informatics executive. An organizational role that is instrumental in working with the HIS department or team and who represents the perspectives, leadership, processes, workflows, and needs of nursing professionals so as to shape the HIS architecture, workflows, processes, data, and implementations.

Children's Health Insurance Program (CHIP) A program administered by the U.S. federal government agency CMS that provides matching funds to states to provide health insurance to families with children. The program was designed to cover uninsured children in families with incomes that are modest but too high to qualify for Medicaid/MediCal. Also known as State Children's Health Insurance Program (SCHIP).

Circuit The pathway by which electronic signals, data packets, or messages between servers and/or clients travel. Copper wire, fiber-optic cable, and wireless transmissions are three of the most common circuit types deployed today; switches, routers, and gateways are devices used to enable circuits to transmit information.

Client In terms of data structure, the computer, such as a PC, tablet, or laptop, that a user uses to access the server and tap into data.

Clinical data A more complex set of data, as compared to demographic data, including lab results, previous or ongoing conditions, and so on.

Clinical decision support Focuses on using knowledge management to get clinical advice based on multiple factors of patient-related data. CDS enables integrated workflows, provides assistance at the time of care, and offers care plan recommendations. And it also provides clinicians, staff, patients, or other individuals with knowledge and person-specific information, intelligently filtered or presented at appropriate times, to enhance health and health care.

Clinical information system (CIS) A computerized system that supports clinical diagnosis, treatment planning, and medical outcomes evaluations. It keeps health history, prescriptions, doctor's notes and dictation, and all other information together electronically, and replaces the paper charts of the past. Department-specific CIS systems include laboratory information systems, pharmacy information systems, radiology information systems, medical imaging systems, long-term care systems, and others.

Clinical intelligence (CI) Much like business intelligence, the practice of pulling together or aggregating data into meaningful and useful information for clinical purposes.

Cloud computing Shared pools of configurable computer system resources and higher-level services that can be rapidly provisioned with minimal management effort, often over the Internet. Cloud computing relies on sharing of resources to achieve coherence and economies of scale, similar to a public utility.

Cloud storage A cloud computing model in which data is stored on remote servers accessed from the internet, or "cloud." It is maintained, operated, and managed by a cloud storage service provider on storage servers that are built on virtualization techniques.

Commercial off-the-shelf Software that is widely commercially available, sold in large quantities, and not necessarily modified for the user or organization.

Common business-oriented language (COBOL) Developed in 1959, based on previous programming language design work by Grace Hopper, commonly referred to as "the (grand)mother of COBOL." Primarily used in business, finance, and administrative systems for companies and governments, COBOL is imperative, procedural, and since 2002, object-oriented. It is estimated that 70-80 percent of all business transactions worldwide are written in COBOL today.

Communication Key to sincere, passionate participation of all parties, bringing to bear the needed interaction and dialogue to foster collaboration, and eventually acceptance of change associated with the introduction of new HIS systems that enable new ways of doing work.

The Commonwealth Fund A private U.S. foundation whose stated purpose is to "promote a high performing healthcare system that achieves better access, improved quality, and greater efficiency, particularly for society's most vulnerable and the elderly."

COBOL (See common business-oriented language)

Comparative effectiveness research (CER) Research with the goal of providing the best possible synthesis of existing research results to clinicians so that these findings may be put into use. CER is based on "comparative effectiveness"—the comparative effectiveness of various treatments, processes, and approaches to care reflects the benefits of one method relative to another method, not relative to some absolute metric. CER studies are mostly based on current evidence and metrics, with the understanding that additional evidence and metrics will emerge over time.

Complex CCM 60 minutes 99487 As of 2017, CPT 99487 is reimbursed by Medicare to account for extended care coordination time spent with especially complex patients. This code reimburses for the first 60 minutes of non-face-to-face care coordination by clinical staff.

Comprehensive EHR system An EHR system that includes basic functionality plus 14 other clinical functionalities and is used throughout the entire hospital, clinic, practice, or health system. The functionalities include patient demographics, physician notes, nursing assessments, problem lists, medication lists, discharge summaries, advance directives, lab reports, radiology tests, medications, consultation requests, nursing orders, clinical guidelines, clinical reminders, drug allergy results, drug–drug interactions, drug–lab interactions, drug dosing support, and many ways to view images, results, and more.

Compulsory health insurance Health insurance under an obligatory public scheme, set by regulations and enforced by law. Payment for such insurance amounts to a tax. The obligation may be placed on employers to pay contributions on behalf of employees. Contributions may be income-related and progressive. Compulsory health insurance is usually administered by public bodies.

Computer room air handlers (CRAHs) An energy efficient, reliable, low maintenance, and cost-effective cooling solution for data centers. CRAHs draw in the hot air, and then cold water traveling through large pipes absorbs the heat. Subsequently, roof or wall condensers release the heat outside the data center, and large, heavy-duty water chillers cool and recirculate the water. As a contingency, in case commercial or utility water sources become unavailable, many data centers have wells that can hold tens of thousands of gallons of water.

Computerized physician order entry (CPOE) Also called computerized physician order entry. The process in which a physician electronically enters orders or instructions into an EHR system for a patient's care, rather than the orders or instructions being transcribed by a ward clerk or other ancillary personnel from the clinician's hand-written order.

This relays information directly from the source (e.g., a physician or nurse practitioner) to the pharmacy or laboratory or other destination to which the order for a test or therapy is directed. CPOE is intended to reduce medical errors by avoiding errors of transcription, and allowing the ordering physician or provider to directly verify the correctness of the order at the point of entry, thus reducing the frequency of needing to catch errors elsewhere in the process path.

Consumer-oriented care Refers to third-tier health insurance plans that allow members to use health savings accounts, Health Reimbursement Accounts, or similar medical payment products to pay routine healthcare expenses directly, but a high-deductible health plan protects them from catastrophic medical expenses. High-deductible policies cost less, but the user pays medical claims using a prefunded spending account, often with a special debit card provided by a bank or insurance plan.

Containers Emerging service platforms, such as Kubernetes clusters running Docker, encapsulating applications in containers with their own operating environment that use SDN to map network addresses to individual workloads.

Continuous power source (CPS) A type of flywheel-driven utility power feed for data centers used as backup power. The flywheel is driven by high-speed turbines. Robust and environmentally friendly, CPS systems are more expensive and slower to assume the primary load than UPS systems.

Contractual guidelines Terms and conditions negotiated as part of agreements with vendors of software, hardware, and services to help prevent the organization from spending the allocated funds without the project being completed and provide incentives and establish accountabilities for the vendor to hold up their end of the bargain.

Control Objectives for Information and Related Technology (COBIT) An information technology governance framework developed in the 1990s by the IT Governance Institute. COBIT is useful for HIS governance, oversight, and process audit, and includes requirements for the control and security of sensitive data.

Coordination problem includes one or more of the following: test results/records not available at appointment or duplicate tests ordered;

specialist lacked medical history or regular doctor not informed about specialist care and received conflicting information from different doctors or healthcare professionals.

CPT codes The United States' standard for how medical professionals document and report medical, surgical, radiology, laboratory, anesthesiology, and evaluation and management services. All healthcare providers, payers, accreditation organizations, and facilities use Current Procedural Terminology (CPT) codes.

Creating New Knowledge The learning organization creates and manages information in ways that enable it to learn from experiences through data analysis and evidence, creating information and data-driven processes. The needs of patients evolve over time, and healthcare organizations must continuously adapt to these changing needs. The ability to be data driven and put new knowledge into practice relies on an organizational culture that embraces this adaptation and thirst for new knowledge, as well as implementing it into clinical and administrative processes and enabling value-based care.

Crossing the Quality Chasm A report published in 2001 by the Health and Medicine Division (then called the Institute of Medicine) of the National Academies of Sciences, Engineering, and Medicine (the National Academies) that provides analysis of underlying causes in response to solid evidence of alarming quality problems in the United States and makes suggestions for improvement including Six Aims for quality of care.

Cryptocurrencies Digital asset designed to work as a medium of exchange that uses strong cryptography to secure financial transactions, control the creation of additional units, and verify the transfer of assets.

Current Procedural Terminology (CPT) A set code maintained by the American Medical Association that describes medical, surgical, and diagnostic services. CPT codes are designed to communicate uniform information about medical services and procedures for administrative, financial, accreditation, reimbursement, and analytical purposes.

Current state An organization's current use of technology, systems, data, workflow, and key processes. It includes interviews and documentation of systems' and processes' strengths, weaknesses, opportunities, and failures (threats).

Current systems review The process of documenting all existing systems in the organization as the baseline for creating an HIS and technology migration plan to take the organization from its current state to its desired future state of automation.

Customer resource management (CRM) The use of technology to organize and manage an organization's interactions with current and future customers. In health care, CRMs intersect with sales, marketing, customer care, technical support, and billing.

Dashboard Graphically presented, often-used, distilled data sets made available in a central presentation interface or location to provide users with easy access.

Data Facts and statistics collected together for reference or analysis, the analysis and aggregation of which leads to the creation of information. In health care, data may be general (e.g., gender, age) or clinical (e.g., diagnosis, test result, prescription, allergies).

Database An organized collection of data, generally stored and accessed electronically from a computer system. Where databases are more complex, they are often developed using formal design and modeling techniques.

Data center management systems (DCMSs) Hardware and software systems that allow data center personnel to design and proactively manage these and additional data center technologies; they can help reduce unplanned system downtime caused by poor planning or a lack of standardized and documented processes and procedures. A DCMS may include power protection and distribution management, air-conditioning and environmental controls, intelligent cable management, cabinet space management, server and network device remote access, and asset management and tracking.

Data centers The facilities where HIS are located; they are vital to the successful implementation and ongoing support of providing healthcare applications. Data centers can be remotely hosted, commercially owned co-hosted data centers, or maintained on site.

Data delivery and translation The art of taking critical information from a database and bringing it to the correct personnel in a format that they understand and can readily apply to their work.

Data democratization The ability for information in a digital format to be accessible to the common end user. The goal of data democratization is to allow non-specialists to be able to gather and analyze data without requiring outside help.

Data dictionary A directory or database that contains definitions and descriptions of the data elements in the systems of an organization; also referred to as a type of metadata ("data about data").

Data mining The act of extracting information from a data set for use in data analytics.

Data model A map or visual representation showing how data are organized according to key aspects of the organization, including processes and relationships between the various data elements. In healthcare organizations, these key aspects would include patients, providers, employees, financial data, and suppliers, among others. A data model is helpful in the systems engineering and programming processes to illustrate data layout.

Data ownership The determination of data rights and responsibilities: whether the patient, provider, HIS vendor, or the healthcare organization owns the data collected through the HIS. It is advantageous for the healthcare organization to own its data—a point that should be addressed in the original vendor contract. Within the organization, the CIO is responsible for providing leadership for data strategy, management, and stewardship.

Data security The need for data in general and each discrete data element to be secure in terms of its access and use. In health care, very specific legal requirements and regulations govern the creation, storage, access, and use of data.

Data sharing Making data available for more than one person to access and use. This sharing process can be for an individual's purpose or it may be for a team or organization. Both technical considerations and security issues arise in regard to the sharing of data.

Data sources In health care, HIS capture many different types of data from many different sources. These include clinical, personal, transactional, payer, third party, regulatory, external evaluation organizations, government, and other sources.

Data standards Facilitate the secure sharing of data between clinicians through system interoperability.

Data structures The methods and formats used to organize data in a computer, often described in terms of records, files, and arrays.

Data visualization A general term that describes any effort to help people understand the significance of data by placing it in a visual context. Patterns, trends, and correlations that might go undetected in text-based data can be exposed and recognized easier with data visualization software.

Database servers Servers that maintain a healthcare organization's database instances; they are frequently clustered or configured with multiple servers to support large database sizes and perform tasks such as data analysis, storage, data manipulation, archiving, and other non-user specific tasks.

Decision rights Accountability of establishing the guideposts needed to boost forward progress and appropriate performance in the use of IT and the decision mechanisms encompassed throughout the organization needed to weigh in and oversee the many decisions that must be made throughout an HIS and technology project.

Decision support systems (DSS) A computer-based analytics information system that supports flexible clinical and organizational decision making activities, typically using data from many source systems.

Deep learning (DL) DL assists in health care's quest to leverage data for the purpose of analytics and innovation of care. It is a way that machine learning employs brain simulation, creating artificial neural networks that learn and become deeper with multiple layers by being fed with data and training algorithms, making them sharper and easier to use and improving machine learning and steps toward real AI. A key aspect of deep learning is that these layers of features are not designed by human engineers but they are learned from data using a general-purpose, computer-driven, learning procedure.

Dematerializing information Information that is distributed electronically, because it no longer has ties to a physical piece of paper in a specific location.

Diagnosis-related groups (DRGs) A system to classify diagnoses treated and hospital cases into one of originally 467 groups. Groups are based on similarities in resource consumption rather than any clinical relationship between the diagnoses, to be used as the basis for Medicare reimbursement for hospitals. This system of classification was developed as a collaborative project by Robert B. Fetter of the Yale School of Management and John D. Thompson of the Yale School of Public Health.

Digital health The convergence of digital technologies with health, health care, living, and society to enhance the efficiency of healthcare delivery and make medicines more personalized and precise.

Digital signage Uses server technology and IP networks to electronically display information, such as organizational training or news, advertising, or other healthcare-related messages, using liquid crystal displays (LCDs) or plasma displays that are placed in various public or internal locations within hospitals and work areas. Digital wayfinding uses digital signage technology, but adds touchscreen technology to allow users to interact with the LCD-presented information.

Disaster recovery (DR) The process of preparing for and getting data and systems back after they are lost, disabled, or damaged in a system failure.

Disaster recovery plan (DRP) A documented process or set of procedures to recover and protect a business infrastructure in the event of a disaster. Such a plan, ordinarily documented in written form, specifies procedures an organization is to follow in the event of a disaster and involves the establishment of off-site redundant systems at various levels of readiness that can be activated if disaster disables the core HIS of an organization.

Distributed antennae system A network of antenna nodes separated by distance and connected to a common source for the purpose of providing wireless service within a geographic area or structure.

Domain Name System (DNS) Servers that enable users and servers to contact websites and other servers by maintaining a directory listing of server and website names. It is important for organizations to ensure that their DNS servers are properly configured, and if an update or modification is required, thorough testing must be performed.

Donabedian's Health Care Quality Framework A landmark piece of work in the healthcare quality arena; it offers a complementary framework with which to examine HIS. Developed by Avedis Donabedian, a health services researcher at the University of Michigan, this conceptual model describes healthcare quality according to structure, process, and outcomes, and was originally published in 1966.

Dynamic Host Configuration Protocol (DHCP) Servers that assign a unique address to each computer on the network. A misconfigured or inaccessible DHCP server can cause both servers and end users' computers to receive duplicate or incorrect addresses, making them unable to function.

eHealth As defined by the World Health Organization, the transfer of health resources and health care by electronic means, encompassing three main areas: (1) delivery of health information, for health professionals and health consumers, through the Internet and telecommunications; (2) use of the power of IT and e-commerce to improve public health services, such as through the education and training of health workers; and (3) use of e-commerce and e-business practices in health systems management.

Electronic data interchange (EDI) The transfer of specifically structured information from one machine to another, without human interaction. The information is formatted to communicate specifically with the originator and the recipient, and the machines may vary. Rules and standards for EDI between providers/healthcare organizations and payers (insurance companies or intermediaries) are established by HIPAA.

Electronic document management A major part of the transition from paper to electronic records; a system that involves scanning paper documents and using technology to convert the image to editable text.

Electronic health record (EHR) A collection of health information accessed, stored, and processed electronically, about individual patients or populations, the goal of which is to replace paper records in healthcare provider organizations. This digital format is theoretically capable of being shared across different healthcare settings, "following" patients wherever they might seek care. EHR systems span multiple care settings, track and store a patient's information over a longitudinal time horizon, and contain functionality that assists in activities associated with maintaining a person's health, as well as information and functionality pertaining to episodes of that person's illnesses and medical treatments.

Electronic Medical Record Adoption Model (EMRAM) EMRAM was developed over a decade ago by HIMSS as part of their analytics division, with the intention of assisting hospitals and outpatient healthcare organizations to measure and track their progress toward more robust EHR systems. This model consists of eight gradually increasing levels of electronic medical record (EMR) functionality, beginning with Level 0 (an EHR system without the three main ancillary systems installed, e.g., laboratory, radiology, and pharmacy information systems) to Level 7 (complete EMR, including governance, analytics, external Health Information Exchange (HIE), Disaster Recovery, Privacy, Security, and other capabilities).

Electronic tracking board systems Support the real-time tracking of critical information pertinent to the flow of care for individual patients. Tracking board systems consist of room-sized LCD or plasma computer monitors connected to an EHR or another clinical application. They are often used in emergency departments of hospitals.

Emergency power off (EPO) A control mechanism, formally known as a "disconnecting means." Once this button is pressed, all electricity to the data center is shut off.

EMR-as-a-service (EaaS) A subscription-based electronic medical record (EMR) model which can be utilized for storing, sharing, provisioning, and cleansing medical records. Qualified entities can be the customer, including hospitals, pharmacies, and the patients.

Encryption-in-transit An important control that ensures the security of all data traffic containing confidential or ePHI information, such as network traffic, web activity, email messaging, file transfers, text messaging, and instant messaging.

End users Individuals who use the products after they have been fully developed and marketed.

Enterprise resource planning (ERP) system A cross-divisional, organization-wide system that supports core business functions of an organization in the arenas of finance, human resources, and supply chain management. ERP applications should be tied to a common database. ERPs facilitate integration of administrative and business information, and accessibility to that information by those who need it to perform their jobs in those areas. Enterprise-wide ERP systems facilitate business-related information flow throughout an organization.

Enterprise systems Help organizations move forward in a coordinated, comprehensive fashion, across departmental lines and business units.

Enterprise-monitoring Servers which are used to monitor servers, applications, storage, and network services. Such servers can send alerts or resolve failed services, thereby greatly increasing system uptime.

Executive information systems (EIS) An early term describing a type of analytics system that facilitates and supports senior executive information needs. Providing easy access to internal and external information relevant to organizational goals it also was a predecessor to decision support systems and business intelligence/clinical intelligence systems.

Extraction, transformation, and load (ETL) A process that extracts data from outside sources, transforms those data to fit operational specifications, and then loads the results to the end destination (such as a central data repository).

Extranets A private network that uses Internet Protocol technology and the public telecommunication system to securely interact with or share information or operations with suppliers, vendors, partners, customers, or other businesses.

Fast Healthcare Interoperability Resources (FHIR) A standard describing data formats and elements, web standards, and an application programming interface for exchanging healthcare information electronically. The standards framework was created by the Health Level Seven (HL-7) International Healthcare Standards organization.

Fee-for-service The model where payers such as insurance companies or government agencies like the Veterans Affairs (VA) and CMS reimburse care providers per service provided. This older model has led to the early and current HIS systems used in the United States being built to support fee-for-service billing processes. The transition away from fee-for-service care, toward value-based care, is slow in part because reimbursement for procedures and services is a more straightforward task than is billing for successful health outcomes, as required for value-based reimbursement.

Fiber Channel over Ethernet (FCoE) A storage protocol that enables fiber channel communications to run directly over Ethernet. FCoE makes it possible to move fiber channel traffic across existing high-speed Ethernet infrastructure and converges storage and IP protocols onto a single cable transport and interface.

Firewall A network security system that monitors and controls incoming and outgoing network traffic based on predetermined security rules. A firewall typically establishes a barrier between a trusted internal network and untrusted external network, such as the Internet.

Five Rights of Clinical Decision Support A principle to guide and support clinical decisions: right information, to the right person, in the right format, via the right medium or channel, at the right time or point in the workflow.

Five Rights of Health Information Management A principle to guide and support HIS decisions, much like the Five Rights of Clinical Decision Support: right time, right route, right person, right data, right use.

Five-year cost estimate One of the most informative and revealing exercises in the overall work of HIS planning. It includes not just software license fees, often discussed throughout the organization as the "cost" of a new system, but also software support fees, hardware and devices plus their maintenance, implementation and training costs, staffing expenses, and a thorough list of all start-up and one-time capital costs and operating expenses with annual increases for inflation and wages, for all identifiable components of the project. This is one of the most eye-opening tasks of HIS planning, and one that must not be skipped.

Future state An organization's vision of where it wants to be in 5–10 years. To begin HIS planning, an organization must know its current state and then develop a vision and HIS architecture for its desired future state. The HIS plan becomes an organized migration path between the two, moving the organization from current to future states.

Gap analysis Ensures that the technology areas are acceptable and ready to support HIS implementations, it is common for organizations to complete a technology assessment or gap analysis well before the HIS implementation begins. Areas in need of improvement that are found in the assessment (i.e., "gaps") can then be addressed or remediated, allowing the HIS deployment to proceed without being hampered by technology issues.

General care management services at rural health clinics G0511 A CPT code for a Medicare program for Federally Qualified Health Centers and Rural Health Centers that reimburse providers when specified service requirements are met.

Generally Accepted Accounting Principles (GAAP) A common set of accepted accounting principles, standards, and procedures that companies and their accountants must follow when they operate finance functions or departments and compile financial statements. GAAP improves the clarity and consistency for the communication of financial information.

Genomic sequencing Easy and increasingly accessible, personal genetic sequence technology now can be used for innovative healthcare applications and medical treatments, such as precision in determining cancer therapies based on the genetic sequence matched with the analysis and literature on cancer therapies to determine the best course of action.

Governance The process of thoughtful, organized, balanced decision making for projects and arbitration of issues that arise during the processes of change, which is essential to HIS success.

Gross domestic product (GDP) A monetary measure of the market value of all the final goods and services produced in a period of time, often annually or quarterly. Nominal GDP estimates are commonly used to determine the economic performance of a whole country or region and to make international comparisons.

Guiding principles Statements about the things the group agrees on at a principles and high level of thinking—statements that the group goes back to as it struggles with decisions, priorities, habits, inertia, or methods, which it will, often. They remind the group of what they agree on, what they seek to do on a higher level, and help the group get past the tight spots as it navigates priorities and decisions, in spite of the self-interest of individuals or departments or functions that have "owned" certain work or functions in the past.

Hard disk drives (HDDs) An electromechanical data storage device that uses magnetic storage to store and retrieve digital information using one or more rigid rapidly rotating disks (platters) coated with magnetic material. The platters are paired with magnetic heads, usually arranged on a moving actuator arm, which read and write data to the platter surfaces.

Hardware The physical machines that use software to perform their functions. Hardware in an HIS architecture includes computers, servers, tablets, printers, devices, and more.

Health Alert Network (HAN) A program under the Centers for Disease Control and Prevention designed to ensure that communities have rapid and timely access to emergent health information on a 24/7 basis. Most state-based HAN systems have access to 90 percent of the communities they represent.

Health and Medicine Division (HMD) of the National Academies of Sciences, Engineering, and Medicine HMD (formerly the Institute of Medicine) is the collective scientific national academy of the United States. The name is used interchangeably in two senses: (1) as an umbrella term for its three quasi-independent honorific member organizations (the National Academy of Sciences (NAS), the National Academy of Engineering (NAE), and the National Academy of Medicine (NAM)) and (2) as the brand for studies and reports issued by the operating arm of the three academies, the National Research Council (NRC).

Health Informatics Enhancing the use of those systems to improve how work is done and deriving meaning from data.

Health information exchanges (HIEs) Communication of healthcare information electronically across organizations within a locale, region, community, state, or nation. The goals of HIE are to improve access to and retrieval of clinical data or other information relevant to a patient's care, to reduce waste, and to provide better and more timely care. HIE is also useful to public health authorities in identifying events or conditions for which they are monitoring and conducting surveillance on behalf of the public's health (e.g., infections such as tuberculosis), or those associated with potential bioterrorism (e.g., smallpox or anthrax).

Health Information Management (HIM) A health information and coding department within a healthcare organization.

Health Information Management Model Provides a visual representation of the overall scope of health information system (HIS) and the gradual layers that build on one another to create a comprehensive HIS arena.

Health Information Management Systems Society (HIMSS) A not-for-profit professional organization dedicated to promoting a better understanding of healthcare information and management systems.

Health Information Systems (HIS) The information technology that supports healthcare functions. It includes all computer systems (including hardware, software, operating systems, and end-user devices connecting people to the systems), networks (the electronic connectivity between systems, people, and organizations), processes, and workflows embedded in those systems, and the data those systems create and capture through the use of software.

Health Information Technology (HIT) See *Health information system (HIS)*.

Health Information Technology for Economic and Clinical Health (HITECH) Act Part of the $787 billion American Recovery and Reinvestment Act (ARRA) stimulus package, this legislation requires the U.S. government to lead the development of standards that allow for nationwide electronic exchange and use of health information to improve quality and coordination of care. It (1) created a strategic plan for a nationwide interoperable health information system, a plan that must be updated annually; (2) allocated $36 billion in incentives and programs supporting the implementation of EHR systems; and (3) called for a leadership structure consisting of two committees to advise the coordinator, a Health Information Policy Committee and a Health Information Standards Committee.

Health Information Trust Alliance (HITRUST) A privately held company located in the United States that, in collaboration with health care, technology, and information security leaders, has established a Common Security Framework (CSF) that can be used by all organizations that create, access, store, or exchange sensitive and/or regulated data. The CSF includes a prescriptive set of controls that seek to harmonize the requirements of multiple regulations and standards.

Health Insurance Portability and Accountability Act (HIPAA) Federal legislation aimed at improving the U.S. health system's efficiency and effectiveness by introducing standards governing the use and communication of healthcare information, originally targeting the objective of facilitating movement of people and their information from one insurance plan to another when they changed employment. The HIPAA regulations set standards for electronic data interchange. The HIPAA Privacy Rule protects the privacy of individually identifiable health information; the HIPAA Security Rule sets national standards for the security of electronic protected health information; the HIPAA Breach Notification Rule requires covered entities and business associates (of healthcare providers) to provide notification following a breach of unsecured protected health information; and the confidentiality provisions of the Patient Safety Rule protect identifiable information being used to analyze patient safety events and improve patient safety.

Health Level 7 International (HL7) A set of international standards for transfer of clinical and administrative data between software applications used by various healthcare providers. These standards focus on the application layer, which is "layer 7" in the OSI model.

Health services research Research that examines access to health care, care costs, and care outcomes. The main goals of health services research are to identify the most effective ways to organize, manage, finance, and deliver high-quality care; to reduce medical errors; and to improve patient safety.

Heating, ventilating, and air-conditioning (HVAC) systems Comprising the heating, air-conditioning, and ventilation systems in a residential or commercial building. A building's HVAC system encompasses components such as ductwork and air handlers which are essential to system performance. HVAC systems utilize water to absorb excess heat.

HIS adoption To adopt health information systems (HIS) and technology means that organizations adapt to automated work processes a huge change from the paper-based processes and workflows that typically take much longer than anticipated with even the most conservative of estimates, and through adoption the providers and the healthcare industry change the ways that clinical care is provided and the work of health care is done.

HIS architecture The comprehensive, structured collection of HIS systems and infrastructure within an organization.

HIS Business Plan Provides the structure to conceptualize and document a balanced HIS application software portfolio based on the purpose, clinical and business activities, and information requirements of your organization. Using the framework, it is straightforward to organize and design an application portfolio for any type of healthcare organization. This framework provides a non-technical, visual tool to help with education and communication about HIS and the planning process for any healthcare organization. The output of this framework tool is a basic, simple, but thorough conceptualization of the operational and management needs of your organization and how HIS and applications should be architected and prioritized to support those needs.

HIS design Connects the content and framework of systems to the workflow of the organization's knowledge workers.

HIS development Includes user and system/workflow planning, design, building or programming the system, testing, documentation, deployment, and maintenance according to the steps in process called System Develop Life Cycle.

HIS fundamentals Ideas, methods, practices, and principles that are so basic to HIS and that more advanced, elegant, and complex HIS initiatives and capabilities cannot be imagined or discussed, let alone achieved, without complete agreement on these basic building blocks from the onset.

HIS governance The leadership and organizational structures, policies, and decision making processes that make sure the organization's HIS and technology plans and projects sustain and extend the organization's strategies and objectives, are conducted fairly, and make the best use of the organization's resources. Governance is conducted throughout the organization, from the highest levels of decision making at the board of directors, down through executive and mid-level management, and to multidisciplinary advisory committees selecting and implementing systems and representing end users.

HIS management Proper HIS management includes the day-to-day oversight, controls, and quality assurance of systems planning, people, process, and technology, 365 days per year, 24 hours per day. Managing HIS involves the techniques and activities deployed to achieve HIS goals and objectives in a healthcare organization. These HIS management methods include generally accepted methods and standards for planning, implementing, supporting, and managing core HIS.

HIS model Provides a visual representation of the overall scope of HIS and the gradual layers that build upon one another to create a comprehensive HIS arena.

HIS planning The art and management rigor of taking the time to create and architect a plan for an HIS system and its implementation that will support the overall HIS Strategy and organization's progress to its "future state," where the organization wants to be in the next 5–10 years.

HIS Planning Framework Provides a conceptual structure needed to conduct HIS planning discussions that include all key stakeholders, not just information technology (IT) or consultants and vendors driving the HIS agenda.

HIS Strategic Plan Includes strategic HIS initiatives, projects, business plans, and capital and operating budgets, all the way to individual assignments. The Strategic HIS Plan moves the organization toward its desired future state.

HIS strategic planning The business plan that aligns the future state of a healthcare organization to its market and external environment, and adapts the organization to the complex changing needs of the population it services and the providers who work within it.

HIS strategy The art and methods of aligning an HIS plan with an organization's mission, values, strategies, and goals.

HIS systems and management Building the foundation consisting of HIS that support healthcare activities and the competent management of those systems, so they support and feed the other layers of the model.

Home health HIS applications Customized to meet the unique requirements found in the home health environment. This functionality includes monitoring patients for specific conditions, developing treatment plans, identifying measures that can be taken and communicated to the home health site, and communicating with caregivers in homes between visits using mobile technology.

Hospital discharge planning gap When discharged from the hospital, the patient did not receive written information about what to do when he/she returned home and symptoms to watch for; hospital did not make sure he/she had arrangements for follow-up care; someone did not discuss with the patient the purpose of taking each medication and/or the patient did not know who to contact if he/she had a question about his/her condition or treatment.

Human-centered design A design and management framework that develops solutions to problems by involving the human perspective in all steps of the problem-solving process. Practitioners understand the value of a longitudinal record of care, since care is safer this way since the provider knows what medications the patient is on and other relevant history, as well as the benefit of establishing a relationship with their patients through the means comfortable for those patients.

Hype cycle A visual representation of the life cycle stages a technology goes through from conception to maturity and widespread adoption. Many of the technologies on this curve will be meaningful parts of the future in health care and public health; others will not. Of the technologies analyzed, five categories or trends are identified: democratized AI, digitalized ecosystems, do-it-yourself biohacking, transparently immersive experiences, and ubiquitous infrastructure.

Hyper converged infrastructure (HCI) A software-defined IT infrastructure that virtualizes all of the elements of conventional "hardware-defined" systems. HCI includes, at a minimum, virtualized computing, a virtualized SAN, and virtualized networking. HCI typically runs on commercial off-the-shelf servers.

Hypertext Transfer Protocol (HTTP) An application protocol for distributed, collaborative, and hypermedia information systems.

Hypervisor or virtual machine monitor (VMM) A piece of computer software, firmware, or hardware that creates and runs virtual machines (VMs).

Identity and access management (IAM) Servers that automate and streamline the management of user, computer, and application accounts and passwords; their use can significantly reduce the number of help desk or IT staff needed for these tasks.

Immuno-Oncology The study and development of treatments that take advantage of the body's immune system to fight cancer. A digital health relationship to this type of initiative may include genomic sequencing and advanced computer processing and analytics to identify and match candidate therapies and patients.

Implement/implementation The act of setting in place (installing) and activating (initiating and putting into production) the use by trained end users of the infrastructure, hardware, and software laid out in the organization's HIS plan.

Implementation planning The process of HIS requirements definition, systems selection, elements of contract negotiation, system specification, documentation of the setting in which the system will be implemented, and development of a step-by-step, milestone-driven implementation plan.

Implementing HIS The set of activities that result in a software system going from a business plan to a fully utilized HIS, usually replacing a previously used legacy system or paper process that has limited functionality and capabilities.

Individually identifiable health information (IIHI) As defined and protected by HIPAA, information that can be connected to a patient individually. Common identifiers include name, address, Social Security number, date of birth, or ZIP code.

Inflection point In math, the point on a curve at which the curve changes curvature or direction; used in the worlds of history, technology, and business to describe a significant point or moment of change.

Informaticist A person practicing the science of informatics, applying the use of information and information systems to a specific discipline such as medicine, nursing, analytics, and other areas of expertise in health care.

Informatics The use of information systems and technology to redesign, improve, and recreate the ways disciplines such as the practice of medicine, nursing, medical imaging, and public health do their work.

Information technology governance (ITG) Structured and formal processes designed to mitigate the risk of failure and increase user satisfaction ratings once HIS are implemented. ITG can be divided into two additional areas. IT demand governance (ITDG) is a decision making and oversight process by which healthcare organizations effectively evaluate, select, prioritize, and fund their HIS investment—in other words, decide what IT should be working on. IT supply-side governance (ITSG) focuses on making sure the IT organization operates in an efficient and organized fashion—essentially, who in IT should be doing what IT is doing.

Information Technology Infrastructure Library (ITIL) The most commonly adopted ITG framework in use in healthcare organizations today, ITIL was first developed in the early 1990s by the British government. Its fundamental objective is to describe an integrated set of seven process-oriented best practices for managing IT services.

Infrastructure The "electronic highway" that carries data, images, voice, and information traffic between the myriad users of the health information systems and technology. It includes data centers, computers, computer networks, database management devices, and software systems. There is nothing more important than a reliable, robust network infrastructure as the foundation of an organization's HIS and technology plan.

Infrastructure servers Provide core services that support server system functionality and that need to be implemented properly if a healthcare organization expects to rely on its business and clinical applications.

Infrastructure-as-a-service (IaaS) A cloud computing service from vendors that provides virtual machines, servers, storage, network, and other infrastructure-type computing components.

Instant messaging or chat Used often in healthcare environments as the real-time communication needs of clinicians and IT personnel expand. It allows users to send messages or files to each other. In a healthcare setting, a secured instant messaging application is required to avoid issues with electronic protected health information (ePHI) or other sensitive information traveling over unsecured networks, such as the Internet. Instant messaging has the additional benefit of giving others notice of an individual's presence or status, such as whether he or she is online, offline, busy, or in a meeting.

Institute for Health Care Improvement (IHI) An independent not-for-profit organization based in Boston, MA. IHI mobilizes teams, organizations, and nations to envision and achieve a better health, quality of care, and healthcare future.

Institute of Electrical and Electronics Engineers (IEEE) technologies A professional association with its corporate office in New York City and its operations center in Piscataway, New Jersey. It was formed in 1963 from the amalgamation of the American Institute of Electrical Engineers and the Institute of Radio Engineers.

Integration A system in which two or more products work closely together to combine different functionalities into one product. Integrated data are maintained in one location; this supports clear, high-quality solutions.

Intelligent optical character recognition (OCR) The mechanical or electronic conversion of images of typed, handwritten, or printed text into machine-encoded text, whether from a scanned document, a photo of a document, a scene photo (e.g., the text on signs and billboards in a landscape photo), or from subtitle text superimposed on an image (e.g., from a television broadcast).

Interfaces A system in which where two or more separate software products communicate under limited capacity. Data are maintained in multiple locations and therefore require much more administration.

International Electrotechnical Commission (IEC) An internationally recognized standards-setting organization. ISO/IEC 38500 is an ITG framework that describes six guiding principles for the effective, efficient, and acceptable use of IT: responsibility, strategy, acquisition, performance, conformance, and human behavior.

International Organization for Standardization (ISO) An internationally recognized standards-setting organization. ISO/IEC 38500 is an ITG framework that describes six guiding principles for the effective, efficient, and acceptable use of IT: responsibility, strategy, acquisition, performance, conformance, and human behavior.

International Statistical Classification of Diseases and Related Health Problems (ICD) The standard tool for codifying diagnoses and conditions for epidemiology, health management, and clinical purposes. ICD-10 was endorsed by the Forty-Third World Health Assembly in May 1990 and promptly adopted internationally, but implemented in the United States only recently.

Internet of things (IoT) The collective network of computer-embedded devices, appliances, vehicles, and other connection points that contain sensors, software, computing electronics, and connectivity to perceive, connect, and exchange data, used across all industries.

Internet Small Computer Systems Interfaces (iSCSI) an Internet Protocol (IP)-based storage networking standard for linking data storage facilities. iSCSI provides block-level access to storage devices by carrying SCSI commands over a TCP/IP network. It is used to facilitate data transfers over intranets and to manage storage over long distances. It can be used to transmit data over local area networks (LANs), wide area networks (WANs), or the Internet and can enable location-independent data storage and retrieval.

Interoperability The ability of different information technology systems and software applications to communicate, exchange data, and use the information that has been exchanged.

Intranets A computer network that uses Internet Protocol technology to share data, information, operational systems, or computing services within an organization.

Intrusion detection systems (IDSs) An intelligent monitoring and analysis system that detects irregular or inappropriate data traffic occurring on the corporate network; it generates alerts to network and system administrators describing the offending system or device.

IT demand governance (ITDG) A decision making and oversight process by which healthcare organizations effectively evaluate, select, prioritize, and fund their HIS investment—in other words, decide what IT should be working on.

IT service delivery Process area that is important for the proper implementation and support of HIS applications. This area defines the services; describes the roles and responsibilities of those who pay for services (i.e., the customers), those who use the services (i.e., the users), and those who provide the services (i.e., the service providers); and defines the service quality, availability, and timeliness expectations.

IT service support An important managerial process area that encompasses the support processes needed to ensure acceptable service to users of HIS. Often, this includes a service or help desk as well as performance metrics.

IT supply-side governance (ITSG) Ensures that the IT organization operates in an efficient and organized fashion. Essentially, it defines HIS priorities, and guidance regarding who in IT should be doing what.

The Joint Commission Formerly the Joint Commission for Accreditation of Health Care Organizations. Founded in 1951, this independent, not-for-profit organization accredits and certifies more than 20,000 healthcare organizations and programs in the United States. Joint Commission accreditation and certification indicates an organization's commitment to meeting certain quality and performance standards, through a survey process that measures and reports on that organization's adherence to the standards, and identification of areas of noncompliance that must be corrected to maintain accreditation.

Key performance indicators (KPIs) A type of performance measurement used by an organization to evaluate its success.

Keyboard, video, and mouse over Internet Protocol (KVMoIP) devices Centralized systems that give system administrators keyboard, monitor, and mouse access over the network, eliminating the requirement and additional cost to provide these peripheral devices for each server.

Knowledge worker An employee or worker whose main value is his or her knowledge in specific areas of expertise; a person who "thinks for a living." In health care, this label applies to anyone making patient care, diagnostic, business, or strategic decisions. Knowledge workers are the targets of many information technology and HIS initiatives; these systems create a workplace or platform that supports the integration of data and information and functions to support the work and decisions of the knowledge workers.

Laboratory Information System (LIS) A CIS application that supports chemistry, pathology, blood bank, instrumentation, calculations, calibrations, and results management areas within clinical settings. Core functions of a LIS include test requisition processing, scheduling and cataloging specimen collection, and test processing; delivering results of completed tests that have been verified and recorded, and results directly reported into patient records; identifying abnormal results and alerts; providing statistical reports for laboratory management and patient summary reports; performing quality control and charge capture functions; and supporting laboratory operations management.

Legacy systems In computing, a legacy system is an existing or timeworn method, technology, computer system, or application program, "of, relating to, or being a previous or outdated computer system," yet still in use. Often referencing a system as "legacy" means that it paved the way for the standards or advancement that would follow it.

Life expectancy at birth How long, on average, a newborn can expect to live, if current death rates do not change. It is one of the most frequently used health status indicators.

Local area networks (LANs) A type of network made of groups of devices located within the same geographic area, such as one or more floors within a building, or multiple buildings in close proximity to each other. LANs are the primary networks used by desktops, servers, and network and other devices to communicate when they are in close proximity with each other.

Logical Observation Identifiers Names and Codes (LOINC) A database and universal standard for identifying and codifying clinical observations, including laboratory tests, clinical measurements and physician reports. It was developed in 1994 at the Regenstrief Institute, a U.S.-based not-for-profit organization in an initiative led by Dr. Clem McDonald, who also pioneered the first ambulatory electronic medical record. LOINC and meets the demand for a common terminology and electronic database for clinical care and management. It is publicly available at no cost.

Long-term care (LTC) systems CIS applications designed to aid in the delivery of care for patients who are older than age 65 or who have a chronic or disabling condition that needs constant supervision. LTC facilities can provide nursing home care, home health care, and personal or adult day care for individuals. LTC systems include clinical, financial, and administrative management functionality that is designed to address the unique requirements of the LTC environment.

Machine learning A branch of AI that uses data analytics of data obtained through processes, to automate models that improve as they are increasingly fueled with data. It is based on the idea that computers can learn from data through the identification of increasingly precise patterns and then base decisions on those learnings.

Machine-to-machine   (M2M) When   two machines "talk" to each other without a human intercepting or feeding that information to a second machine; for example, a sensor on a patient feeding medical data to a physician's computer through cloud computing.

Malware Malicious software; a class of dangerous, destructive software programs that include viruses and spyware. Designed to disrupt productivity, damage organizations, gather information illegally, or gain access to restricted computer systems.

Managing change The earthy reality of what happens when new HIS are brought into the organization, from ideas expressed in the HIS strategic plan all the way to changes in clinician or administrative workflow.

Managing vendors One of the most important areas to become proficient in when managing and implementing new HIS, since organizations rely heavily on external companies (vendors) whose business model is to produce, deliver, and support HIS software, hardware, and services.

Master patient/person index (MPI) A unique identifier, numbering methodology, and database that is used across departments and entities within a health system or health information data exchange by assigning each individual a unique identifier. It connects each patient's/person's information from disparate systems that each use different identification schemes.

Meaningful Use (MU) Also called Meaningful Use criteria. The set of standards and criteria defined by HITECH and used by the CMS (including Medicare and Medicaid programs) that governs the qualification of vendor software products for participation in the Meaningful Use incentive programs by providers and healthcare organizations using those EHR software products. Eligible providers and hospitals can earn incentive payments and avoid financial penalties later in the program by meeting specific criteria. The goal of Meaningful Use is to promote the spread of adoption of EHRs and thereby improve efficiency and quality of health care.

Medicaid (called MediCal in California) A U.S. government insurance program for persons of all ages whose income and resources are insufficient to pay for health care. This income-based program is jointly funded by the state and federal governments and managed by the states.

Medical administration records (MARs) The functionality within an EHR system used by nurses and other clinicians to plan, record, track, and report a patient's medications, dosages, and timing; it serves as a legal record of the drugs administered to a patient at a facility by a healthcare professional. Sometimes referred to as drug charts or eMARs.

Medical devices Devices that are used, worn, or implanted in patients to provide biometric feedback and regulation, such as pace makers and blood pressure monitors. New data sources in the form of mobile, wearable, and implantable medical devices as well as numerous consumer, commercial devices capable of monitoring personal physiological parameters are now available to the mainstream for many conditions as well as personal health monitoring. This can be a source of needed data for medical care, preventive, and population health efforts. These types of precise and reliable devices include smart medical devices and wearables that monitor, for example, cardiac function and blood sugar levels and give immediate early warnings of changes and problems for these patients.

Medical Group Management Association (MGMA) Professional organization of medical practice managers.

Medical homes A team-based healthcare delivery model led by a healthcare provider to provide comprehensive and continuous medical care to patients with a goal to obtain maximal health outcomes.

Medical imaging systems (MISs) CIS applications that provide clinical support processes. MISs support image management, image processing, enhancement, visualization, access, and storage.

Medicare A national social insurance program, administered by the U.S. federal government agency CMS since 1965, that guarantees access to health insurance for Americans aged 65 and older and younger people with disabilities. Medicare provides recipients with a defined medical benefit.

Medicare Access and CHIP Reauthorization Act (MACRA) A U.S. statute that changes the payment system for doctors who treat Medicare patients to gradually include quality of patient outcomes as well as cost of care. It revises the Balanced Budget Act of 1997 and was the largest scale change to the American healthcare system following the Affordable Care Act ("ObamaCare") in 2010.

Medication administration record (MAR) The report that serves as a legal record of the pharmaceuticals administered to a patient at a facility by a healthcare professional. The MAR is a part of a patient's permanent record on their medical chart and/or EHR.

Merit-Based Incentive Payment System (MIPS) The program that determines Medicare payment adjustments. Using a composite performance score, eligible clinicians (ECs) may receive a payment bonus, a payment penalty, or no payment adjustment.

Metadata Data about data.

Metropolitan area networks (MANs) A large computer network which extends to a city or to a large university campus is termed as MAN. The purpose of MAN is to provide the link to the Internet in the long run. A MAN usually incorporates a number of LANs to form a network. This large network MANs backbone comprises an optical fiber set-up.

mHealth Mobile health; the use of mobile technologies for purposes of health care, public health, and health-related activities at the individual level. mHealth technologies include smartphones, mobile applications using tablets, Internet, machine-to-machine wireless capabilities, sensors and patient monitoring devices, and more.

Middleware Software that connects software applications to the data and technology supporting the application. As a transaction layer, it enables communication and data management for multiple or distributed software applications.

Milestone payment structure A payment structure agreed upon by the healthcare organization (the customer paying for software and hardware) and the vendor (the provider and seller of software and hardware products). A milestone-based plan differs in important ways from a payment plan based on dates or the passage of time; the former is advantageous for the organization because it incents the vendor to achieve defined progress steps, or milestones, in the implementation of new HIS software and hardware. Milestone payments should be defined in the vendor contract.

Mission Strategies defined and developed for reflecting the organization's core purpose and reason for existing.

Mobile application management (MAM) Gives organizations control over mobile application delivery and app store management, blacklist/whitelist functionality, application tracking, and application security. In addition, it provides a framework for managing a healthcare organization's internal customized mobile applications.

Mobile computers Used in healthcare settings include workstations on wheels (WOWs), laptops, tablets, and smartphones. WOWs, which are also referred to as computers-on-wheels (COWs) or mobile workstations, are mobile carts that integrate with client computers and peripherals. They can function as either a mobile system or, by locking the wheels at the base of the cart, a stationary system.

Mobile computing strategy It considers the following: (1) what the mobile platform will be; (2) whether enterprise directory integration will be needed; (3) which devices and native applications will be supported; and (4) which telecommunications management capabilities and restrictions will be applied.

Mobile content management (MCM) Provides encryption for files and attachments, content expiration, screen capture controls, and online/offline access to secure content. Some MCM products have advanced functionality that restricts data from being physically stored on a mobile device, yet provides full access and functionality to the content.

Mobile device management (MDM) Encompasses managing mobility at the mobile device level, with secure e-mail, calendaring, contacts, web browsing, and application store management being standard areas that are typically covered. Enrollment and automatic profile/application capabilities; remote administration; screen passcode settings, remote wipe for lost or stolen devices, and encryption at rest and in transit; secure web browser capability; persistent push e-mail delivery; and compliance/auditing, asset, device, location, and network tracking are additional features that are found in MDM products.

Mortality rate A measure of the number of deaths in a particular population, scaled to the size of that population, per unit of time.

National Academy of Medicine (NAM) Part of the National Academies of Science, Engineering, and Medicine, National Academy of Medicine provides national and international advice on issues relating to health, medicine, health policy, and biomedical science. It aims to provide unbiased, evidence-based, and authoritative information and advice concerning health and science policy to policy-makers, professionals, leaders in every sector of society, and the public at large.

National Health Service (NHS) A comprehensive healthcare service in the United Kingdom, under government administration, established by the National Health Service Act of 1946 and subsequent legislation. Virtually, the entire population is covered, and health services are free except for certain minor charges.

National Health System Strategic Plan Provides direction for the management and development of all aspects of the health system over the next 10 years.

National HIS network Connects desktops, devices, and servers to existing host systems, while reducing network infrastructure complexity and costs.

National Provider Identifier (NPI) A unique 10-digit number required by HIPAA for all healthcare providers to be used in all transactions by healthcare organizations. Providers include both individual (doctors, nurses, dentists) and organizational (hospitals, health systems, clinics, skilled nursing/long-term care facilities, home health, and other) healthcare providers.

Natural Language Processing (NLP) The ability of a computer program to understand human language as it is spoken. NLP is a component of artificial intelligence (AI).

Network In HIS, as in all other computerized industries, computers that are linked exchange data using connections. These connections form a network via linkages, which are enabled through fiberoptics, cables, wires, routers, switches, Wi-Fi, and other technologies, to facilitate communications and resource sharing among a wide variety of users.

Network functions virtualization (NFV) NFV simplifies data infrastructure by leveraging inexpensive hardware and allowing workloads to be migrated to customer data centers.

Network infrastructure initiative This foundational capability is a key component of Phase I of the HIS plan. This is the upgrade or rebuild of the infrastructure necessary to provide the strong foundation and "electronic highway" for the data and connectivity required as part of the new portfolio of application software systems to be implemented.

Network infrastructure project An HIS planning project to lay the foundation, or implement the technology, capabilities, and network monitoring and management systems comprising the "information highway" for new HIS systems and processes. This project includes necessary hardware and software for establishing an entire network and communications between all end users accessing systems and data. The project also includes resources that enable network connectivity, communication, operations, and management of an enterprise network.

Network Interface Card (NIC) A hardware component in each computer that enables that computer to physically connect to the network and transfer data over a network cable. Network cables connect the NIC to a wall jack or directly to a network switch using a copper or fiber-optic cable.

Networking A digital telecommunications network which allows nodes within the network to share resources. In computer networks, computing devices exchange data with each other using connections between nodes. These data links are established over cable media such as wires or optic cables, or wireless media such as WiFi.

Next-Generation (NG) Address the traffic inspection and application awareness drawbacks of stateful inspection firewalls and are now replacing those traditional firewalls. Two of the most important features of NG firewalls are deep network packet inspection and application awareness. Deep packet inspection examines the network packet payload for anomalies and known malware, while application awareness is a feature that enables NG firewalls to better identify and manage web application traffic.

Non-face-to-face, digitally-enabled care Patients manage their health by wearing digital tools, such as wearables and apps. Patients have firm beliefs about who should access their data. Consumers are leading the way by accessing EHRs and using digital tools through applications and portals and defined for specific use cases and patient preferences.

Non-governmental organizations (NGOs) Usually not-for-profit and sometimes international organizations independent of governments and international governmental organizations (though often funded by governments) that are active in humanitarian, educational, health care, public policy, social, human rights, environmental, and other areas to affect changes according to their objectives.

Normalization The process of organizing data to minimize anomalies, redundancies, and dependencies. Normalization isolates data so that additions, deletions, and modifications of a field can be made in just one table and then propagated through the rest of the database.

Nursing informatics The use of computers to support and enhance nursing workflow, documentation, management, analytics, and care processes as well as the use of information for analysis of quality and effectiveness properties of clinical care.

Office of the National Coordinator for Health Information Technology (ONC) An agency created by HITECH. A staff division of the Office of the Secretary, within the U.S. Department of Health and Human Services (HHS), the ONC is primarily focused on coordinating nationwide efforts to implement and use health information technology.

Ongoing maintenance This includes operational upkeep of HIS including on-going training, software releases, fixing programs and equipment that break, answering end-user questions, updates and upgrades to the system software, hardware, and access points, and providing these services on a measured timely basis usually through a help system.

Open systems interconnection model (OSI) Developed in 1984, a model of the process of sending data to a receiving device (data transfer). The OSI model has seven layers: physical, data link, network, transport, session, presentation, and application.

Operating budget A detailed projection of the company's revenues and expenses and HIS operating expenses and inputs for the current or upcoming fiscal year. These budgets record the expected cash flows as well as account for all day-to-day operational expenses necessary to support and maintain HIS systems and activities.

The Organisation for Economic Co-operation and Development An intergovernmental economic organization with 36 member countries, founded in 1961 to stimulate economic progress and world trade.

Outcomes research Research that studies the end results of medical care—the effect of the healthcare process on the health and well-being of patients and populations. Conducted by agencies, research universities, healthcare providers, and others, outcomes research evaluates the results of the healthcare process in the real-life world of the healthcare provider organization, public health, and individual health status.

Outpatient systems CIS and business applications designed to assist in the delivery of care for patients who are hospitalized for less than 24 hours. These ambulatory care systems include practice management systems for clinical administration and CIS applications that assist caregivers in performing consultations, treatments, or interventions in an outpatient setting, such as a medical clinic. Examples of the types of procedures that are performed in this environment include minor surgical and medical procedures, dental services, dermatology services, and diagnostic procedures such as blood tests and X-rays.

Patient accounting An administrative application that manages billing and accounts receivable and is typically interfaced or integrated into a health provider EHR application.

Patient flow Represents the movement of patients through healthcare processes and healthcare facilities. It involves the medical care, physical resources, data communication, and internal systems needed to get patients from the point of admission to the point of discharge while maintaining quality and patient/provider satisfaction.

Pay for performance In contrast to the fee-for-service payment model, a payment model that rewards healthcare providers for meeting certain performance measures for quality and efficiency. Providers are paid based upon preestablished targets for delivery of healthcare services.

Peak volumes In terms of HIS and technology, the volume of highest usage or traffic that the system will experience. An HIS system must be built to easily accommodate current and future peak volumes.

Personal health records (PHRs) A health record maintained by the patient/person that contains data relevant to only that patient's care/person's health. In contrast, an EMR or EHR is maintained by the healthcare organization and, respectively, includes a comprehensive record of clinical data for the patient cared for at that institution or practice, or longitudinally across geographies and time.

Pharmacy information system (PIS) A complex CIS application that is tightly integrated with clinical care, particularly with nursing personnel and workflows. Because medication errors are always a concern with pharmacy systems, integration is a high priority to ensure the proper delivery of care.

Phishing email Scam email designed to lead users to make their computers vulnerable to malware, often through tricks and links in the email.

Picture archiving and communication system (PACS) A system that manages image storage, local and remote retrievals, and distribution and presentation of PACS image files.

Picture archiving and communication systems (PACSs) CIS applications that provide clinical support processes. PACS applications manage image storage, local and remote retrievals, and distribution and presentation of PACS files. Recent advances with PACS applications have added features such as improved turnaround time for results, elimination of film loss, support for teleradiology, and reduction of physical space requirements for storage.

Pixels These are each discrete data element as well as the brand, age, and location of the equipment, who ordered, and who "read" the image. A patient's electronic or written prescription is one data element with myriad sub-data elements including the clinician's order, drug's manufacturer, age, production batch, dosage, supply chain history, and other relevant information.

Platform-as-a-service (PaaS) A cloud computing service from vendors that provides operating system, database, web server, development level, and other platform-type computing components.

Policies The organization's rules of engagement, that is, how it oversees all activities and sets rules that everyone follows.

Policy analysis Analysis that produces reports and recommendations for policy makers at local, state, and national governmental levels.

Population health management An approach to health that aims at improving the health of an entire population, a covered population that a health system or other healthcare organization serves, or a community.

Population health management programs Improve the health outcomes of a group by monitoring and identifying individual patients within that group. Typically, these programs use a business intelligence tool to aggregate data and provide a comprehensive clinical picture of each patient.

Power-over-Ethernet (POE) Describes any of several standard or ad hoc systems which pass electric power along with data on twisted pair Ethernet cabling. This allows a single cable to provide both data connection and electric power to devices such as wireless access points, IP cameras, and VoIP phones.

Practice management system Software that deals with the day-to-day operations of a medical or clinical practice, including appointment scheduling, maintaining lists of insurance payers, performing billing tasks, and generating reports.

Predictive analytics Algorithms based on more and more data being fed through them, then pinpointing the type of analysis to provide actionable information so that performance and outcomes can be improved.

Primary care providers A physician who provides both the first contact for a person with an undiagnosed health concern as well as continuing care of varied medical conditions, not limited by cause, organ system, or diagnosis. The term is primarily used in the United States.

Primary uses of data The transactions of the systems that support activities of professionals and organizations as work is conducted (e.g., patient care delivery, care management, patient care support processes, clinical care and therapies, financial and other administrative processes, and patient self-management and engagement).

Private clouds Proprietary networks and data centers that supply secure, hosted services for use within a particular organization; these are increasingly popular among healthcare organizations.

Private health insurance Health care and medicine provided by entities other than the government.

Processes End-to-end methods of healthcare providers and organizations, patients, and public health professionals.

Product life-cycle support A stipulation in the vendor contract that includes licensing and updates for software for a set period (typically 10–20 years). It obligates the vendor to "care" for an HIS system with regular updates, bug fixes, and enhancements.

Program management Functions or "offices" coordinate the myriad of projects that organizations take on, involving different areas, multiple stakeholders, and varying characteristics.

Project management The discipline of planning, organizing, documenting, securing, managing, leading, and controlling resources to achieve specific goals. A project is a temporary endeavor with a defined beginning and end.

Project management office (PMO) The role of a PMO is to ensure the policies, coordination, planning, integration, management tools, techniques, compliance, and communication to multiple projects on behalf of the organization and the benefits it is seeking from the investment of time, energy, consistency, methodology, and resources in projects.

Project Management Professional (PMP) A certification offered through the Project Management Institute.

Project managers (PMs) Responsible for developing project plans as part of the project planning process, including careful definition of HIS project scope, timetable, and resource requirements. It is always important to include stakeholders in the definition process and build their roles into the project plan. PM responsibilities include allocating

work tasks, setting expectations for project roles, tracking tasks and accountabilities, addressing issues, communicating effectively to management and stakeholders, and controlling project activities according to milestones set collaboratively.

Protected/Personal health information (PHI) Demographic information, medical history, test and laboratory results, insurance information, and other data that are identifiable to a particular person or patient, and that are collected by a healthcare professional or organization to identify an individual and deliver appropriate care. Healthcare organizations are forbidden by HIPAA to access or use PHI in any ways other than those needed in the direct care and business processes surrounding that care on behalf of the person or patient, without specific written permission from that person.

Public clouds A type of computing in which a service provider makes resources available to the public via the Internet. Resources vary by provider but may include storage capabilities, applications, or virtual machines. Public clouds such as Amazon Web Services, sell services to anyone on the Internet, typically consumers.

Public health The health of the community at large. Public health careers and research focus on improving the health of communities through education, research, and promotion of health lifestyle choices, as well as protecting the safety of the public through surveillance for disease outbreaks and measurement of health status of a population. The agenda of public health emphasizes the social determinants of health as well as disease processes.

Public Health Institute Promotes health, well-being, and quality of life for people across the nation and around the world.

Public health organizations Entities that exist to monitor, protect, and improve the public's health. Among other roles, they serve as a "safety net" by providing health care for patients who are uninsured or underinsured (e.g., through public health county hospitals and community clinics).

Quality management system A type of HIS that combines data from several different systems (such as EHR, laboratory, and patient accounting systems) and gives the healthcare organization a platform for developing and tracking desired quality metrics by which it will measure and report its performance regarding quality of care.

Quality Payment Programs (QPPs) MACRA replaced the Sustainable Growth Rate (SGR) program, and its fee-for-service reimbursement model, with a new two-track value-based reimbursement system called the Quality Payment Program (QPP). This program is the latest in a series of steps the Centers for Medicare and Medicaid Services (CMS) has taken to incentivize high quality of care over service volume. The QPP improves Medicare by helping eligible clinicians focus on care quality and making patients healthier.

Quantified self A movement to incorporate technology into daily life, tracking measurable wellness activities, outputs, and states through self-monitoring and sensor devices. Outputs monitored include steps taken, blood pressure, oxygen levels, sleep patterns, exercise performance, and myriad other functions. A helpful component of digital health and personalized medicine. Also called body hacking, life-logging, and self-tracking.

Radio frequency identification (RFID) Uses electromagnetic fields to automatically identify and track tags attached to objects. The tags contain electronically stored information. Passive tags collect energy from a nearby RFID reader's interrogating radio waves.

Radiology information systems (RISs) CIS applications that provide clinical support processes. RISs provide functionality that manages test requisitions, schedules procedures, manages test results, identifies charges, and delivers patient test and department management reports. In addition, radiology systems are capable of performing image enhancements, computed tomography (CT) scans, ultrasound imaging, angiography, magnetic resonance imaging (MRI) scans, nuclear medicine functions, radiation therapy, computerized patient-specific treatment planning programs, and surgery.

Random access memory (RAM) A form of computer data storage that stores data and machine code currently being used. A random-access memory device allows data items to be read or written in almost the same amount of time irrespective of the physical location of data inside the memory.

Recovery point objective (RPO) Refers to the total time (in minutes, hours, or days) for which data might be lost.

Recovery time objective (RTO) Refers to the total time (in minutes, hours, or days) during which a server or service can remain unavailable before it is restored to full functionality.

Redundancy One of the simplest concepts that should be implemented at all levels of systems design, HIS construction, and disaster recovery planning. Where possible, having two instances of server, storage, or network system components—such as CPUs, HDDs, NICs, storage host bus adaptor (HBA) cards, system controllers, and cabling—will enable the hardware system to support the HIS and remain operational should a failure occur that is restricted to any one of the components.

Redundant array of independent drives (RAID) A method of storing duplicate data on two or more hard drives. It is used for data backup, fault tolerance, to improve throughput, increase storage functions, and to enhance performance.

Regional health information organization (RHIO) Typically, a not-for-profit health information exchange or collaboration of providers coming together to share data for the purpose of improving care within that region. Providers may include regionally related hospitals and hospital systems, clinics, physician practices, emergency responders such as paramedics, tumor registries, imaging centers, and community clinics.

Registered Health Information Administrator (RHIA) Accreditation provided by the AHIMA for health information professionals, including baccalaureate education from an accredited university or college and successful accreditation testing.

Registered Health Information Technicians (RHITs) Certification provided by the AHIMA for coders and medical records technicians, including a 2-year training and education from an accredited program.

Regulated free-market system A system in which the prices for goods and services are determined by the open market and by consumers. In a free market, the laws and forces of supply and demand are free from any intervention by a government, or by other authority. A regulated free market is subject to working within the regulatory compliance of governmental laws and oversight.

Regulatory compliance A section in the vendor contract stating that the vendor guarantees that the system complies with and will be made to continue to comply with all federal and applicable state laws and regulations, including HIPAA, HITECH and Meaningful Use criteria, the ARRA, and the Affordable Care Act (ACA).

Remote hosting A computing method by which a computer server remains separate from the organization using the system, from which data and information are accessed via a private or public network. This approach is intended to free the organization from tasks required for day-to-day system management, and the management services are often paid for on a monthly basis.

Request for Information (RFI) A precursor to a Request for Proposal.

Request for Proposal (RFP) A request issued to vendors by organizations to define information and system requirements and initiate the bidding process for HIS and technology systems.

Research, Policy, and Public Health Eventually improving the health of populations through evidence-based change driven by well-informed research, policy, and public health.

Revenue Cycle Management (RCM) The process that manages charge capture, claims processing, payment/reimbursement, and revenue generation.

Roles Roles in HIS cover the gamut and include responsibilities in planning, governance, management, design, development, activation/implementation, and ongoing maintenance of HIS products and services.

Role-based access control (RBAC) A method of restricting network access based on the roles of individual users within an enterprise. RBAC lets employees have access rights only to the information they need to do their jobs and prevents them from accessing information that does not pertain to them.

Roles-based use An updated and more practical view of systems, which assumes that every employee needs access to data, not just executives. This approach modifies data delivery with regard to the person's position, duties, and personal preference.

Rural Assistance Center Provides health services-related information for rural America.

Safety net organizations Provide health services to uninsured and low-income people, increasingly are looking for ways to coordinate services among providers to improve access to and quality of care and to reduce costs.

Secondary uses of data The use of data by organizations outside of the original healthcare provider, such as public health groups, policy makers, and research institutions. These third parties use data for the purposes of education, regulation, research, public health, homeland security, and public policy support. Secondary uses of data can reveal ways to improve healthcare processes, health outcomes, population health status, and overall effectiveness in health care.

Secure Socket Layer (SSL) the standard security technology for establishing an encrypted link between a web server and a browser. This link ensures that all data passed between the web server and browsers remain private and integral.

Security information event management (SIEM) A critical technology designed to automate and intelligently analyze system logs for anomalies and inappropriate activity.

Server A host computer at the center of a computer network that stores data or software and is accessed by clients (the input/output computers that users use). While a server resides at one end of a communication circuit, a client is the input/output hardware device at the user's end of a communication circuit or computer system.

Service level agreements (SLAs) An agreement between a service provider and its customer, wherein service provider performance is tracked and measured for adherence. For example, in a typical healthcare environment, HIS outages can be categorized with critical, high, medium, or low SLAs regarding how much time can transpire before the system must return to an operational state.

Single payer model National health systems in which providers, hospital systems, and the payer are all part of the same unified health system, such as in the United Kingdom. These health systems tend to be better positioned to set up standardized HIS and infrastructure, and thus opportunity for effective population health management programs.

Single sign-on (SSO) A type of log-in system for opening up a secure session with roles-based access to numerous applications by computer system end users (e.g., healthcare organization employees). The user has to remember only a single log-in and password, and the SSO system will automatically log the user into various other applications. SSO is designed to save clinician and administrator time.

Six Aims of Crossing the Quality Chasm Six areas to strive for in terms of patient care as listed in the Institute of Medicine's 2001 report, *Crossing the Quality Chasm*: safe, effective, patient centered, timely, efficient, and equitable.

Six S's of Sources of Public Health Data Data sources that inform public health; they include single case or small series, statistics, surveys and sampling, self-reporting, sentinel monitoring, and syndromic surveillance.

Smart card Using technical standards adopted in other industries to improve the security and privacy of patient information, these provide the secure card carrier for portable medical records, reduce healthcare fraud, support new processes for portable medical records, provide secure access to emergency medical information, enable compliance with government initiatives and mandates, and provide the platform to implement other applications as needed by the healthcare organization.

Social media Online condition-related support groups can help people cope with health conditions. These online spaces feel private, but the security of the personal data being shared is debatable. The balancing act between access to personal data through non-secure social technology and the privacy of what is taking place in the healthcare workplace is being faced in healthcare organizations, public health entities, and homes alike.

Software A unified set of computer programs designed to support related functions and work of end users; any set of machine-readable instructions that a computer uses to perform specific operations. In health care, common software functions include the types of software represented in the HIS planning framework—namely, patient and provider support, institutional processes, and clinical and management reporting and analytics.

Software/systems development life cycle (SDLC) A methodology designed to ensure that end-state solutions meet user requirements in support of the healthcare organization's strategic goals and objectives. SDLC steps include conceptual planning, planning and requirements definition, design, development and testing, implementation, operations and maintenance, and disposition.

Software-as-a-service (SaaS) A cloud computing service from vendors that provides applications and services, such as CRM, email, communications, enterprise web content management, and other software programs.

Software-defined networking An approach to cloud computing that facilitates network management and enables programmatically efficient network configuration in order to improve network performance and monitoring.

Source data The origin of data elements and information found in computer systems and electronic media, which is often interfaced from source systems, or input by users or other means.

Spyware Malware that is designed to collect information about a user or from a computer system without the user's knowledge or consent.

Standardization Industry (in theory, at least) agrees to a set of standards. Health Level Seven International (HL7) is one of the largest and most influential organizations "dedicated to providing a comprehensive framework and related standards for the exchange, integration, sharing, and retrieval of electronic health information that supports clinical practice and the management, delivery and evaluation of health services."

Steering committee A committee internal to the organization, often with cross-departmental representation, with a primary focus on guiding strategic decisions concerning future realization of the organization's investment projects, such as HIS and technology.

Stewardship Making sure the definition of each data element is accurate and consistent in its use by those interacting with it, taking responsibility for making sure it is managed according to the goals of the organization, and taking care of it by regularly checking on consistency, accuracy, accessibility, and safety of data. Data stewardship accompanies an overall data management program, inserting into the fabric of the organization the necessary leadership and education as part of the organization's data resources.

Storage area networks (SANs) A dedicated back-end computer system designed to efficiently and cost-effectively store and transfer a healthcare organization's server data.

Strategic Initiatives Prongs of an HIS strategy and plan that can be broken down into phases. A good HIS strategy has three to five strategic initiatives in operation at any given time, with an equal number in the pipeline.

Strategic Plan Phases Include the following three phases: (1) foundational infrastructure, (2) basic core HIS systems, and (3) advanced HIS capabilities.

Strategic Plan Stages Include the following stages: (1) planning, (2) system development/ selection, (3) implementation/production, and (4) ongoing support and evaluation of the new system capability.

Strategies At the uppermost levels of an organization's agenda are directional statements or overarching aims directly tied to mission and vision; the large-scale ways that the organization will be able to successfully move itself forward toward its purpose.

Strengths, Weaknesses, Opportunities, and Threats (SWOT) analysis A useful tool in HIS planning and determining future and current states.

Subject matter experts (SMEs) A professional who brings departmental or functional expertise to bear in the project planning and implementation processes.

Sub-second response time A measure referring to the amount of time that passes between the user entering a process on a computer (such as conducting a search, filling in a field, or pressing the Enter key) and the machine/system responding to that action; a gauge of capacity and responsiveness of a server's or system's configuration.

Supply chain management (SCM) A system that manages delivery of services to clients. In health care, this is healthcare services to patients.

System design The process of architecting the HIS system. System design is done in concert with overall process redesign, including interfaces required for sharing data between those systems feeding and those receiving data.

System selection The process for making decisions about which new software systems to bring into the organization. Methodologies for system selection include project description and requirements definition, budgetary requirements (both capital and operating expenditures over five years), documentation of how this new system will fit into the overall HIS portfolio of applications, justification of the new system (an analysis of why a new system is proposed vs. not using something that already exists in the organization's HIS portfolio), draft implementation plan and timetable, staffing and other resource requirements, technical underpinnings and specifications of the new system, interface and integration requirements, data management plans, reporting requirements and key performance indicators produced through the use of the new system, system selection decision timing and process, key contract guidelines and performance criteria for the winning vendor, and other components, all documented in a comprehensive HIS business plan.

Systematized Nomenclature of Medicine— Clinical Terms A systematic, computer-based collection of medical terms that allow a consistent way to index, store, retrieve, and aggregate medical data across specialties and sites of care.

Tap 'n go technology Provides significant benefits to healthcare organizations that are deploying VDI desktops. It enables users to quickly log in and out of computers with just the "tap" of their ID badge. When moving from computer to computer, the user's desktop session is transferred seamlessly based on the proximity of the ID badge to a workstation, bringing it over to the next computer exactly as it was left in the previous computer. If an application was opened on one computer, the same application remains open when the user moves to the next computer.

Technical standards Ensure common protocols for transmitting data along the various steps between layers.

Telecommunications Defined as the electrical transmission of data among systems, whether through analog, digital, or wireless media. Data transmissions can occur across a variety of media types, such as copper wires, coaxial cable, fiber, or airwaves. Both large and small healthcare organizations today utilize these data transmission types and mediums. Data communication networks consist of three basic hardware components: servers, clients, and circuits.

Telehealth The remote delivery of health-related information from one site to another via electronic communications to improve a person's health awareness and access to health-related information.

Telemedicine The remote delivery of clinical services using technology.

The United Nations International Children's Emergency Fund (UNICEF) Created by the United Nations General Assembly on December 11, 1946, to provide emergency food and healthcare to children in countries that had been devastated by World War II.

Thick Data This type of data is by nature more subjective, visceral, and intuitive. The term refers to the murkiness or difficulty in measurement of data sets (e.g., how the patient feels about his progress in physical therapy). Quality measures will involve anthropological and ethnographical intelligence. For example, if a post-surgical orthopedic knee patient complies with all range of motion allowances, yet extreme pain persists, we will not have accomplished a quality outcome. The patient's perceptions and motivations will come into play. Intuitively, the industry will need even more subjective and patient-supplied data to satiate Thick Data's appetite.

Thin-client computers Small machines that rely on a server to perform and store all data processing and can be likened to client dumb terminals from the mainframe era.

To Err Is Human An HMD report that provides solid evidence of alarming quality problems and makes suggestions for improvement. It describes high levels of avoidable medical errors in U.S. hospitals that result in as many as 98,000 patients dying every year—patients who should have been discharged from the hospital successfully.

Transitional care management Services codes 99495 and 99496 are Current Procedural Terminology (CPT) codes in effect since January 1, 2013. These codes are used for patients discharged from an inpatient setting to the patient's community setting (e.g., home, assisted living).

Transmission Control Protocol/Internet Protocol (TCP/IP) model Also known as the Internet model. This model illustrates the process of sending data to a receiving device (data transfer). The TCP/IP model has three layers: application group, internetwork group, and hardware group.

Triple Aims The Triple Aim is a framework developed by the Institute for Healthcare Improvement that describes an approach to optimizing health system performance. The Triples Aim includes: (1) improved outcomes, (2) better patient care, and (3) lower costs. Hospitals and health systems have adopted it as framework for major provisions of the Patient Protection and Affordable Care Act.

Trojan A hacking malware that appears to perform a desirable function yet, after it gains access to a system, causes system harm or steals unauthorized data. Often appears as an email attachment.

Ubiquitous availability Always accessible, at any place or time. In terms of HIS and technology, this term refers to how increasingly more people and organizations have and use various technologies and hardware, such as mobile phones.

Ubiquitous technology Computing is made to appear anytime and everywhere. In contrast to desktop computing, ubiquitous computing can occur using any device, in any location, and in any format.

UNICEF (United Nations International Children's Emergency Fund) The United Nations International Children's Emergency Fund was created December 11, 1946 by the United Nations General Assembly, to provide emergency food and health care to children in countries devastated during World War II.

Unified Communications (UC) Technology that involves the integration of real-time communication services, such as instant messaging and presence, VoIP and VoWLAN, video conferencing, and web conferencing.

Unified computing systems (UCS) A next-generation data center platform that increases server density, performance, availability, management, and efficiency beyond blade server technology by uniting multiple blade server chassis, networks, and storage infrastructures into a single cohesive system.

Uninterruptable power supply (UPS) A type of battery-supported utility power feed for data centers used as backup power. While less expensive than CPS systems, UPS systems are not "green" and require more regular maintenance and replacement.

USD per capita Measures the average income earned per inhabitant in a given area (city, region, country, etc.) in a specified year. It is calculated by dividing the area's total income by its total population.

User experiences (UXs) The attitudes, emotions, and satisfaction experienced by the end-user in interacting with a computer product, in the context of usability, access, and pleasure of individual interactions as well as the broader relationship with the product. UX design takes all elements of the interaction of the user so that they are easy, relevant, efficient, and pleasant.

User interfaces (UIs) The visual and physical environment in which humans interact with machines or computers, including the design of that interaction and its sequencing, the devices involved, and a variety of mechanisms such as keyboards, mouse, screens, voice-activation, visual elements such as menus, icons, and buttons, and devices such as pens.

Users Include professionals, business people, and analysts who rely on HIS systems, reporting capabilities, and connectivity to perform the work of the organization. Users drive workflow, processes, and data creation and capture as a byproduct of their use of HIS systems.

Value realization Involves the following four areas: strategic alignment, architectural excellence and balance, realization of intended system benefits, and HIS services delivery.

Value-based care Provides proactive, comprehensive medical, and behavioral care managed in such a way to enhance the overall outcomes and wellness for the patient.

Value-based care initiatives Designed to reward quality and cost-effectiveness with higher reimbursement rates for services with better outcomes.

Values Understanding the ways the organization wants to behave, the philosophies it wants to support, its guiding principles, and the ways it wants to do its work.

Velocity, Volume, and Variety (Three V) The usefulness, amount, and variety of data, all of which are increasing.

Very early smoke detection apparatus (VESDA) Systems monitor for smoke particles and sound alerts when they are detected. VESDA is a very early warning aspirating smoke detection solution.

Virtual desktop infrastructure (VDI) A desktop-centric service that hosts user desktop (PC) environments on remote servers, which are accessed over a network remotely. For users, this means they can access their desktop from any location, without being tied to a single client device.

Virtual machines (VMs) A software computer that, like a physical computer, runs an operating system and applications. VMs comprise a set of specification and configuration files and is backed by the physical resources of a host. They run on servers running Windows, Linux, and Solaris operating systems, and on logical partition arrays (LPARs) in UNIX-based servers.

Virtual private network (VPN) Extends a private network across a public network and enables users to send and receive data across shared or public networks as if their computing devices were directly connected to the private network.

Virtual reality An interactive computer-generated experience taking place within a simulated environment. It incorporates mainly auditory and visual feedback.

Virtual tape libraries (VTLs) Backup systems that use disk-based arrays to emulate tape libraries. With these systems, the storage medium can be switched from tapes to disks while continuing to use the existing tape backup software. VTLs lack the advanced features of disk-based backup systems.

Virtualization A technology advance that has significantly reduced the amount of server infrastructure needed to support today's healthcare environments. This feature takes advantage of a server's unused processing power by creating multiple virtual server instances, which typically increases server density by a factor of 10–15.

Virus A malware computer program that attempts to spread throughout application software programs, workstations, servers, and entire networks by replicating itself and replacing other files.

Vision Outlining a long-term and evolving view of the organization's place in that environment or market in the future.

Voice over Internet Protocol (VoIP) A family of technologies that enables Internet Protocol networks to be used for voice applications such as telephony, messaging, and collaboration.

Voice over wireless local area network (VoW-LAN) A technology that is designed to integrate mobile devices using the Wireless local area network (WLAN). This is particularly useful as more clinical applications are developed for use with smartphones, tablets, and portable computers.

Voice technology Machine or program to receive and interpret dictation or to understand and carry out spoken commands.

Voluntary health insurance The decision to join and the payment of a premium is voluntary. Together with out-of-pocket payments, its premiums are considered a private revenue source. In higher-income countries, it tends to be complementary or supplementary to publicly funded benefits.

Wearable technologies Smart electronic devices (electronic device with micro-controllers) that can be incorporated into clothing or worn on the body as implants or accessories.

Web conferencing used frequently in healthcare organizations because of its simplicity, convenience, and low cost. It enables users at multiple locations to hold audio meetings and share desktop computer applications or applications from their mobile devices over the IP network. Given the never-ending quest to reduce costs, web conferencing is being widely embraced as a solution that enables organizations to reduce employee travel requirements while increasing collaboration between all stakeholders. Web conferencing solutions can be cloud based or deployed using an on-premises architecture.

Wide area network (WAN) A network built from groups of devices located in diverse geographic areas. WANs connect backbone networks and metropolitan area networks; they can connect devices that are located around the world.

Wide area networks (WANs) A telecommunications network or computer network that extends over a large geographical distance/place. Wide area networks are often established with leased telecommunication circuits.

Wireless local area networks (WLANs) A local area network that uses high-frequency radio signals to transmit and receive data over distances of a few hundred feet.

Wireless wide area networks (WWANs) A wide area network that provides service to large geographic areas through separate areas of coverage, referred to as cells. Cell phones, smartphones, tablets, and hot spots are mobile devices commonly used to connect to WWANs.

Workflow Sequence of common tasks of healthcare providers and organizations, patients, and public health professionals, supported by technology and used to guide HIS design.

Workflow redesign The process of mapping out current workflows and analyzing how the organization gets work done (the current state). It also helps planning for the future by mapping out how EHRs will create new workflow patterns to improve the organization's efficiency and healthcare quality (the future state). During the workflow redesign process, all aspects of the organization need to be looked at from an electronic point of view.

World Health Organization (WHO) A specialized agency of the United Nations that is concerned with international public health. It was established on April 7, 1948 and is headquartered in Geneva, Switzerland. The WHO is a member of the United Nations Development. WHO's primary role is to direct international health within the United Nations' system and to lead partners in global health responses.

Worms Malware that replicates itself in a system; worms are "stand-alone" programs and do not need to attach themselves to another file to spread.

Zero-client computers Similar to thin-client computers but offer the additional advantage of having no local hard drive or operating system to secure or maintain. They are well suited to furthering desktop virtualization and integrating with WOWs due to their light weight, small form factor, and ease of management.

Index

Note: Page numbers followed by *f*, *t*, *b*, and *e* indicate figures, tables, boxes, and exhibits respectively.